FOM-Edition Research

FOM University of Applied Sciences, in close cooperation with recognized European universities, offers extra-occupational doctoral programs to very good master's graduates. This series of publications provides the framework for making excellent dissertations from these doctoral programs accessible to the interested professional public. Thus, the series makes it possible for the empirical results, innovative concepts and well-founded analyses from the field of economics to be widely recognized and to enrich the scientific discourse.
Apart from this series, FOM University of Applied Sciences founded a scientific publication series, the FOM-Edition, which is specifically dedicated to the publication projects of its lecturers. The FOM-Edition is divided into the following sections: textbooks, case study books, specialist books, and an international subseries.

More information about this series at http://www.springer.com/series/16193

Nils Eikelmann

Value Based Performance Measures

Theoretical Evaluation and Empirical Analysis of their Application and Value Relevance on a European Level

With a Foreword by Prof. Dr. Roland Wolf

Springer Gabler

FOM Hochschule

Nils Eikelmann
ISF – Institute for Strategic Finance
FOM – University of Applied Science for
Economics and Management
Essen, Germany

Dissertation, Universidad Católica San Antonio de Murcia (UCAM), 2018

ISSN 2524-7026 ISSN 2524-7034 (electronic)
FOM-Edition Research
ISBN 978-3-658-31428-6 ISBN 978-3-658-31429-3 (eBook)
https://doi.org/10.1007/978-3-658-31429-3

This Springer Gabler imprint is published by the registered company Springer Fachmedien Wiesbaden GmbH part of Springer Nature.
The registered company address is: Abraham-Lincoln-Str. 46, 65189 Wiesbaden, Germany

Foreword

The performance of companies has always been the focus of business analysis. In addition to profit as the traditional measure of a company's success, other absolute and, in particular, relative indicators are also used and evaluated. The assessment of companies in the field of classic annual financial statement analysis has a long tradition and has been accompanied for years by various empirical studies on the significance and meaningfulness of selected key figures. Analyses of the capital market relevance of possible ratios for describing or forecasting the development of the share price of listed companies are described more or less regularly in the literature.

Since the beginning of the 1990s, key figures based on the concept of shareholder value have also been used for corporate management purposes and are also published more or less intensively by listed companies. However, the companies apply differently designed value concepts and are therefore not directly comparable with each other for the assessment or even measurement of performance. A standardized approach based on the data published in annual reports would make it possible to compare companies worldwide.

And this is precisely where the work starts, examining in detail the annual reports of the companies in the Stoxx Europe 600 to determine whether and to what extent value concepts are applied. Then, in addition to selected traditional indicators such as EPS, PER, ROE, ROI and ROS, value-oriented indicators such as ROCE-Spread and Value Added are determined on the basis of a standardised approach. Finally, comprehensive statistical analyses for the years 2012 - 2016 are used to examine the indicators for their suitability to explain the development of shareholder value. The result of the detailed analysis of major companies in Europe shows that the traditional ratios can explain a good 70% of the development of share prices. However, the value-oriented indicator Value Added is significantly better and therefore superior to the traditional indicators and is able to explain the development of shareholder value measured in terms of share price performance at almost 80%.

The study thus provides for the first time a cross-national analysis of the value management of listed companies in Europe compared to the previously mainly nationally oriented studies. The theoretical basis for measuring the performance of companies as well as of previous relevant studies is presented in detail and in an accomplished manner, and a standardized approach for determining value added is presented. With this standardized approach, this work can also be seen in the tradition of the research on value-oriented capital market analysis at the isf Institute for Strategic Finance of FOM, to assess the performance of companies worldwide using standardized key figures such as Value Added, Value Rate and Price-Value-Ratio, thus increasing capital market efficiency through valuable information for the financial community.

Prof. Dr. Roland Wolf

Preface by the Editors

The FOM University of Applied Sciences (FOM), understands its dual study programs in the field of economic sciences – i.e. the combination of working experience or professional training with graduating higher education – as complementary to the German academic landscape. Offering target group specific and appealing study conditions, FOM creates opportunities for employees for personal development and simultaneously facilitates companies' attempts to qualify their employees according to the demands that result from demographic development and increased qualification requirements.

Since 2010, FOM, in close cooperation with recognized European universities, offers extra-occupational doctoral programs to very good master's graduates. These doctoral programs significantly take into account the specific needs of working doctoral candidates: The clearly structured process schedule enables the doctoral candidates to plan their dissertation in detail. In addition, the dates for research seminars, presentation weeks as well as doctoral workshops are communicated far in advance in order to enable the doctoral candidates to coordinate their professional and private annual planning with their dissertation project. The programs offer doctoral students from across Europe the opportunity to graduate extra-occupational within a network of intensive interaction between universities and supervising professors. By joining various cultures transnationally, they, therefore, strengthen the European guiding principle. As the highest academic degree, the doctorate enjoys an important role on the job market. It indicates a high level of scientific competence, may increase career prospects, and opens up job opportunities at management level.

This series of publications provides the framework for making excellent dissertations from these doctoral programs accessible to the interested professional public by means of a recognized academic publishing house. Thus, the series makes it possible for the empirical results, innovative concepts and well-founded analyses to be widely recognized and to enrich the scientific discourse.

Dr. Nils Eikelmann wrote his dissertation at UCAM Universidad Católica San Antonio de Murcia (UCAM, Spain). The thesis deals on a theoretical basis with the framework conditions for applying value based performance measures and analyses selected value concepts. Furthermore, it contains an empirical study which analyses annual reports of European companies with the purpose to investigate the application of value based performance measures in practice, the calculation of a standardized value-based performance measure and a value relevance study in order to compare the value relevance of a value based performance measure with the value relevance of traditional key figures. We warmly congratulate Dr. Eikelmann on his outstanding PhD thesis.

Our sincere gratitude goes to Prof. Dr. Ángel Meseguer Martínez (UCAM) and Prof. Dr. Roland Wolf (FOM) who were responsible for supervising this dissertation. Additional gratitude goes to Prof. Dr. Nicolás Gonzálvez Gallego (UCAM) and Prof. Dr. Sonja Harms (FOM) who reviewed this dissertation.

With this series of publications, we hope to add a new facet to the often lively and fruitful dialogue between universities and professional practice, and to inspire more graduates to pursue an extra-occupational doctoral program.

Essen

Prof. Dr. Burghard Hermeier
President

Prof. Dr. Thomas Heupel
Vice President Research

Acknowledgement

I write this dissertation after my admission to the doctoral program of the FOM Hochschule für Oekonomie & Management and Universidad Católica San Antonio de Murcia while simultaneously being employed at innogy SE in Essen. This dissertation has been handed in at the university in Murcia in the middle of 2018.

Many people contributed to make this doctoral thesis a valuable and successful experience.

First of all, I would like to thank and I am full in debt to my two advising professors. Prof. Dr. Roland Wolf inspired me to write this dissertation, supported me throughout the whole time and successfully retained my motivation at a high level during the whole participation in the doctoral program. Prof. Dr. Ángel Mesegeuer Martínez continually improved this dissertation substantially with his insightful feedback.

I want to show my gratitude to the FOM Hochschule für Oekonomie & Management and the Universidad Católica San Antonio de Murcia which enabled me to write this dissertation. In particular, I would like to thank Dr. Alexander Zureck, Professor Mercedes Carmona Martínez and Professor Gonzalo Wandosell Fernández de Bobadilla.

For the valuable support of my employer, innogy SE, by flexible working hours and the possibility to give me a time off, I would like to thank Christian Fenger and Wolfgang Miserre representatively.

Furthermore, many thanks to my colleagues of the doctoral program who have always been available for discussions, in particular Sebastian Kuhlmann and Julia Winteroth.

In addition to the already named persons I would like to thank my friends, particularly Carlo, Jan, Julia, Nora, Patrizia, Sebastian and Viktoria for their patience and understanding during the time of dissertation as well as their insightful feedback.

Last but not least, I would like to thank my girlfriend Pia, the love of my life, for her support. Especially I would like to thank my parents, Claudia and Rolf Eikelmann, for their valuable and great support during my whole education. Without them this work would not have been possible.

Nils Eikelmann

Table of Contents

List of Illustrations

List of Tables

List of Formulas

List of Abbreviations

APV	Adjusted Present Value
CAPM	Capital Asset Pricing Model
CDS	Credit Default Swap
CFROI	Cash Flow Return on Investment
DAX	German Stock Index
EBIT	Earnings before interest and taxes
EBITDA	Earnings before interest, taxes, depreciation and amortisation
EPS	Earnings per Share
EVA	Economic Value Added
EU	European Union
FCF	Free Cash Flow
FIFO	First in first out
FTE	Flow to Equity
GCF	Gross Cash Flow
GIB	Gross Investment Base
HDAX	Stock index consisting of DAX, MDAX and SDAX companies
IASB	International Accounting Standards Board
IFRS	International Financial Reporting Standards
IIRC	International Integrated Reporting Council
LIFO	Last in first out
MDAX	Mid Cap DAX
MSCI	Morgan Stanley Capital International
MVA	Market Value Added
NOA	Net Operating Assets
NOPAT	Net Operating Profit after taxes
NOPLAT	Net Operating Profit less adjusted taxes
PAAinE	Pro-Active Accounting Activities in Europe
PER	Price Earnings Ratio
REVA	Refined Economic Value Added
ROCE	Return on Capital Employed
ROI	Return on Investment
ROIC	Return on Invested Capital
RONA	Return on Net Assets
SDAX	Small cap DAX
S&P	Standard & Poor's
SVA	Shareholder Value Added
TCF	Total Cash Flow
TecDAX	Technology DAX
VBM	Value Based Management
VIF	Variance Influence Factor
WACC	Weighted Average Cost of Capital

List of Symbols

α	Manager's share in company's equity capital
$ASS_{i,t}$	Total assets of company i at the end of period t
bv_t	Book value of equity capital in period t
$BVE_{i,t}$	Book value of equity capital of company i at the end of period t
$CFROI$	Cash Flow Return on Investment
$COUNTRY_{i,t}$	Country in which company i is located in period t
CVA	Cash Value Added
D_t	Transfer payments from company to shareholders (including dividends)
DC	Market value of debt capital
$DIV_{i,t}$	Dividend payment of company i in the period t
$\tilde{\varepsilon}$	Standard normal distributed disturbance term
e_{jt}	Random disturbance term
$E_t\ (D_{t+i})$	Expected future dividends
$EBIT$	Earnings before interest and taxes
EBT	Earnigns before taxes
EC	Market value of equity capital
$EPS_{i,t}$	Earnings per Share of company i at the end of period t
EVA	Economic Value Added
F	Market Value of manager's expenditures on private consumption
FCF	Free Cash Flow
FTE	Flow to Equity
GCF	Gross Cash Flow
GIB	Gross Investment Base
i	Risk adjusted interest rate
i_{DC}	Interests paid for debt capital
$Industry_{i,t}$	Industry of company i in period t
$LEV_{i,t}$	Leverage ratio of company i at the end of period t
MV_{DC}	Market value of debt capital
MVA	Market Value Added
NDA	Non depreciable assets
$NOA_{i,t}$	Net operating assets of company t at the end of period t
$NOPAT$	Net Operating Profit After Taxes
oa_t	Operating assets at date t
ox_t^a	Operating earnings for period t
$P_{i,t}$	Market value of company I at the end of period t
P_t	Present value of expected future dividends / Value of equity capital respectively of a share at time t
p_{t+T}	Present Value of a payment in period t + T
$PER_{i,t}$	Price-Earnings-Ratio of company i at the end of period t
r	Risk-adjusted discount rate / Stewart's r

$r_{j,t+1}$	Expected return of security j at the end of period t
r_{DC}	Cost of debt capital
r_{EC}	Cost of equity capital
r_f	Risk free interest rate
$R_f^{-\tau}$	Risk free interest rate increased by factor one
r_m	Return of market portfolio
R_n	Terminal Value
$RISK_{i,t}$	Risk allocated to company i in period t
$ROE_{i,t}$	Return on Equity of company i at the end of period t
$ROI_{i,t}$	Return on Investment of company i at the end of period t
$ROS_{i,t}$	Return on Sales of company i at the end of period t
s	Tax rate of company
S_0	Purchase price of sold equity capital
S_i	Market value of manager's remaining equity capital
$\Delta SALES_{i,t}$	Change in sales of company i in period t
ß	Beta factor
TC	Market value of total capital
TCF	Total Cash Flow
TV	Terminal Value
V	Market Value of Company
V_t	Book value of equity capital at time t
v_t	Information variable / other information than abnormal earnings
$VA_{i,t}$	Value added of company i at the end of period t
W	Manager's wealth
$WACC$	Weighted average cost of capital
x_t^a	Residual income of period t
x_t	Profit
$x_{j,t+1}$	Excess return
x_t^a	Residual earnings in period t
$\tilde{x}^a$	Estimated residual earnings in future periods
y_t	Book value of equity capital in period t
Φ_t	Set of available information at the end of period t

1 Introduction

1.1 Problem Description

Today, the majority of managers lead companies on the basis of the Shareholder Value approach and pursues Value Based Management.[1] Also annual business reports of large European companies contain commitments to the Shareholder Value approach. For example, Anheuser-Busch InBev describes its strategic goals as follows: "A long-term strategic mind set motivates us to continually seek – and seize upon – opportunities for future growth and shareholder value creation."[2] Telefónica outlines its focus on Shareholder Value creation in the following way: "This intensification of investment is consistent with our commitment to continuous improvement of financial flexibility as well as an attractive payment to our shareholders."[3] By pursuing the Shareholder Value approach, companies have to generate an adequate rate of return for their shareholders.[4] Otherwise investors will withdraw their capital.[5]

Challenging framework conditions exacerbate this goal attainment. A crucial factor is capital procurement. Due to globalisation and the continuing expansion of activities in several countries, worldwide capital demand is rising.[6] Domestic capital markets are no longer sufficient to satisfy the capital demand of companies. As a consequence, they have to acquire capital on foreign markets.[7]

Beside globalisation of capital markets, the importance and influence of institutional and foreign investors rose in the last decade.[8] For example, in Germany 62 % of shareholders in the DAX are institutional investors.[9] These increased investor activities lead to higher expectations concerning the performance of companies.[10]

---

1 Cf. Bezemer, P.-J., Zajac, E. J., Naumovska, I., et al. (2014), pp. 1-2; Firk, S., Wolff, M. (2018), p. 52; Loderer, C., Roth, L., Waelchli, U., et al. (2010), p. 5; Lopatta, K., Kaspereit, T. (2014), p. 475; Rieg, R. (2015), p. 193.

2 Quotation taken from: Anheuser-Busch InBev (2013), p. 3.

3 Quotation taken from: Telefonica (2013), p. 42.

4 Cf. Losbichler, H. (2012), pp. 266-267; Rappaport, A. (1986), pp. 55-56.

5 Cf. Moir, L., Kennerley, M., Ferguson, D. (2007), p. 388.

6 Cf. Didier, T., Schmukler, S. L. (2013), p. 112; Dillerup, R., Stoi, R. (2016), p. 193; Lattwein, J. (2002), p. 113; Reichmann, T. (2011), p. 636; Riedl, J. B. (2000), p. 107; cf. contradictory Bris, A., Koskinen, Y., Nilsson, M. (2014) outlines that cost of capital decreases in the timespan after the introduction of the Euro (investigation period 1991-2006) for companies in the euro zone, pp. 554-556.

7 Cf. Bris, A., Koskinen, Y., Nilsson, M. (2014), p. 554-555; the authors explain that due to the introduction of the currency Euro companies have easier access to foreign capital markets in the euro zone; Hanauer, M., Kaserer, C., Rapp, M. S. (2013), p. 469; Meyer, M. (2005), p. 1; Weber, J., Schäffer, U. (1999), p. 226.

8 Cf. Horváth, P., Gleich, R., Voggenreiter, D. (2012), p. 279; Mallin, C. (2012), pp. 179-181; Schmolke, K. U. (2007), p. 702; Yeh, T.-m. (2014) p. 312.

9 Cf. Schneider, U. (2012), p. 519-520.

10 Cf. Athanassakos, G. (2007), p. 1397.

N. Eikelmann, *Value Based Performance Measures*, FOM-Edition Research,
https://doi.org/10.1007/978-3-658-31429-3_1

The financial crisis between 2007 and 2009 also has effects on capital procurement.[11] Gearing is more difficult for two reasons. Firstly, banks do not deal in credit in the same way as they did before the crisis.[12] Secondly, as a reaction to turbulence within several banks and state interventions during the financial crisis the Basel Committee on Banking Supervision adapted the set of regulations, now called Basel III.[13] In comparison to Basel II, banks have to meet higher requirements concerning the common equity capital ratio, implement a capital conservation buffer and reach liquidity key figures like the liquidity coverage ratio and the net stable funding ratio.[14] The more restrictive loan origination[15] fosters the importance of capital markets.[16]

After the financial crisis the common European currency is pressurized in the European sovereign debt crisis. Whole states like Greece, Portugal, Spain or Ireland have heavy financial problems.[17] Banks and capital markets in these countries are very vulnerable. This leads to a shortage in liquidity which in turn exacerbates the challenge of capital procurement for companies.[18] The European Central Bank reacts to both crises among other things with a period of low interest rates in order to reduce the effects of the crisis on European economies and to foster bank lending to companies.[19] On the basis of low interest rates, the asset class of shares is again a focus of investor's interests. The alternatives to shares are rare.[20] Nonetheless, the current period of low interest rates does not ease the situation concerning the capital procurement as companies compete globally for capital.[21]

Against the backdrop of increasing competition for capital and a more restrictive debt capital allocation, the challenge for companies is to ensure a constant supply of capital at appropriate prices.[22]

---

11 Cf. Elyasiani, E., Mester, L. J., Pagano, M. S. (2014), p. 62; Kahle, K. M., Stulz, R. M. (2013), pp. 282-283; the authors review different theories which deal with the shortage of capital supply during the financial crisis; the first year of crisis is 2007 (p. 281); the last year of the crisis is 2009 (p. 282).

12 Cf. Garcia-Appendini, E., Montoriol-Garriga, J. (2013), p. 273; Hristov, N., Hülsewig, O., Wollmershäuser, T. (2012), pp. 569-570; Krol, F. (2009), pp. 94-95.

13 Cf. King, M. R. (2013); pp. 4144-4145; Rossignolo, A. F., Fethi, M. D., Shaban, M. (2013), p. 1323.

14 Cf. Cabral, R. (2013), p. 110-112.

15 Cf. Allen, B., Chan, K. K., Milne, A., et al. (2012), pp. 163-166; Hofmann, J., Schmolz, S. (2014), p. 35; contradictory Dietrich, Hess and Wanzenried do not see a negative influence on bank performance due to the new net stable funding ratio, cf. Dietrich, A., Hess, K., Wanzenried, G. (2014), p. 14.

16 Cf. Coenenberg, A. G., Salfeld, R. (2007), p. 37; Spremann, K., Gantenbein, P. (2005), p. 23.

17 Cf. Eichler, S., Hielscher, K. (2012), pp. 552-553; Moro, B. (2014), pp. S9-S10; the development of the CDS spread of Greek bonds clarifies the extent of the financial problems, cf. Grammatikos, T., Vermeulen, R. (2012), pp. 521-522.

18 Cf. Kousenidis, D. V., Ladas, A. C., Negakis, C. I. (2013), pp. 351-352.

19 Cf. Cour-Thimann, P., Winkler, B. (2012), p. 772; Eichler, S., Hielscher, K. (2012), pp. 554-555, 564; Fiordelisi, F., Galloppo, G., Ricci, O. (2014), pp. 49-50.

20 Cf. Schier, S. (03.12.2014), p. 26; Sommer, U. (15.12.2014), p 1.

21 Cf. Krol, F. (2009), p. 94; Weber, J., Bramsemann, U., Heineke, C., et al. (2017); Zwirner describes that the total capital costs of companies do not change despite the low interest rates as the cost for equity capital have risen, cf. for details Zwirner, C. (2014), pp. 381-386.

22 Cf. Baetge, J., Kümmel, J. (2003), p. 48; Dobbs, R., Kim, A., Lund, S. (2011), pp. 82-93.

Beside the trend on the capital markets, managers have to be aware of the development in financial reporting. Between investors and management principal agent relationships exist which are caused by the separation of ownership and control.[23] Financial Reporting has the objective to reduce these information asymmetries.[24]

As mentioned, the importance of institutional and foreign investors is growing. These investors have more comprehensive information needs which companies have to satisfy.[25] Equity capital providers become the primary target group of the reporting of companies.[26]

The IFRS react to this development. The management approach obliges companies to report internal information to the public, for instance via the segment reporting.[27] Nevertheless, communication through annual reports is problematic. The IFRS-accounting is among other things criticised for its orientation towards the past[28] and its intensified application of Fair Value accounting.[29] For investors it is more difficult to analyse the annual reports because the quantitative extent of these reports has increased enormously.[30] Hence, the IFRS annual accounts cannot completely satisfy the information needs of investors.[31]

Several companies publish so-called pro-forma key figures in their annual reports, e.g. EBIT or EBITDA.[32] The IASB does not regulate these key figures. Managers decide on the way of calculation autonomously.[33] For investors this is a problem as managers can influence these key figures easily according to their interests and disguise the real performance of the companies.[34]

As a consequence, the question arises in which way companies should communicate their increase in Shareholder Value. This question is important to answer.[35] A comprehensive external reporting reduces cost of capital[36] and helps companies to persist and to differentiate in the competition of capital.[37] Furthermore, investors are intensively claiming information about a company's activities and its effects on Shareholder Value.[38]

A solution is the extension of legally fixed reporting standards. This development is called Value Reporting.[39] With the additional information of Value Reporting investors are able to evaluate a company on more comprehensive data.[40] Value based key figures

23 Cf. Gong, J. J. (2011), p. 4.
24 Cf. Peters, S. (2009), pp. 260-261.
25 Cf. Gronwald, T., Nasev, J. (2013), p. 52; Pape, U. (2010), pp. 179-180.
26 Cf. Velte, P., Stiglbauer, M., Sepetauz, K. (2011), p. 124.
27 Cf. Königsgruber, R., Palan, S. (2013), p. 7.
28 Cf. Wellner, K.-U. (2001), p. 42.
29 Cf. Kühnberger, M. (2014), p. 429; cf. for further details Kühnberger, M. (2014), the author contrasts advantages and disadvantages of Fair Value accounting (pp. 434-442).
30 Cf. Christensen, B. E., Glover, S. M., Wood, D. A. (2012), pp. 133-134.
31 Cf. for a comprehensive critique of IFRS: Frings, G. W., Frings, M. C., Mastilak, C. (2012a), pp. 17-21.
32 Cf. Bassen, A., Frank, R., Madsen, O., et al. (2012), p. 360.
33 Cf. Reimsbach, D. (2014), p. 482.
34 Cf. Doyle, J. T., Jennings, J. N., Soliman, M. T. (2013), pp. 41-42.
35 Cf. Macharzina, K., Wolf, J. (2012), pp. 232-233.
36 Cf. Britzelmaier, B. (2013b), p. 189.
37 Cf. Hilpisch, Y. (2005), p. 205.
38 Cf. Laier, R. (2011), p. 1.
39 Cf. Britzelmaier, B. (2013b), pp. 189-193.
40 Cf. Schierenbeck, H., Wöhle, C. B. (2012), p. 769.

like EVA, CFROI or SVA are one part of Value Reporting.[41] They are a way to show investors at one glance the company's performance by indicating an increase or decrease of Shareholder Value at the end of the period.[42]

Academic literature mentions several advantages of value based key figures and theoretical concepts.[43] The problem is that companies adapt these developed theoretical concepts to their practical needs.[44] Investors cannot compare economic developments of different companies as even key figures with the same name can be calculated in many different ways.[45]

Furthermore, a high number of value based key figures exist out of which companies can choose.[46] It is a difficult choice for managers of a company which performance measures they should implement, in order to steer the organisation best.[47]

Considering described developments on capital markets and in reporting, the current state of research is as follows: Despite the long period of investigation of key figures and their determination of significance, authors do not agree on a common superior key figure. On the contrary: Investigations draw different conclusions.[48] This discussion about the best key figures is referred to as Metric War in academic literature.[49] Despite many analyses, there is no consensus as to whether value based performance measures are superior to traditional key figures.[50] Due to its high popularity several analyses deal with the EVA and its significance. The analysis of other value based performance measures does not have the same scope.[51] The number of articles which compare the value relevance of value based performance measures and traditional ones is limited.[52] Unanswered is the question which effects the application of value concepts have on Shareholder Value development of a company in contrast to companies which do not use value concepts.[53] Closely related to this question is the issue in which dimension value based key figures

41 Cf. Chari, L. (2009), pp.46-47.
42 Cf. Hoffjan, A., Schroll, S. (2010), p. 410.
43 Cf. Weber, J., Schäffer, U. (2016), p. 183-184; ; frequently flaws of traditional key figures are mentioned in this context, cf. exemplary Horster, J., Knauer, T. (2012), pp. 119-121.
44 Cf. Hahn, G. J., Burger, A., Kuhn, H. (2011), p. 310; Schäffer, U., Lewerenz, U. (2011), p. 298.
45 Cf. Jacque, L. L., Vaaler, P. M. (2001), p. 817; the authors illustrate that more than 160 kinds of conversion exist which can be used to calculate the EVA.
46 Cf. Meyer, M. (2005), p. 62.
47 Cf. Ittner, C. D., Larcker, D. F. (1998), p. 205.
48 Cf. exemplary for two contrary position about a value based performance measure: Bacidore, J. M., Boquist, J. A., Milbourn, T. T., et al. (1997) and Ferguson, R., Leistikow, D. (1998); cf. also the empirical study of Barton, J., Hansen, T. B., Pownall, G. (2010) who analyse the value relevance of key figures across 46 countries and cannot determine a common superior key figure.
49 Cf. Myers, R. (1996).
50 Cf. Elgharbawy, A., Abdel-Kader, M. (2013), p. 104; El-Sayed Ebaid, I. (2011), pp. 70-71; Schultze, W., List, T., Schabert, B., et al. (2018), p. 514; cf. for a comprehensive overview over several investigations Ittner, C. D., Larcker, D. F. (2001), pp. 358-362 and Schremper, R., Pälchen Oliver (2001), pp. 543-546.
51 Cf. Ittner, C. D., Larcker, D. F. (2001), p. 361; cf. for an overview of empirical studies with analysing value relevance of EVA: Gundel, T. (2012), pp. 158-160.
52 Cf. Schremper, R., Pälchen Oliver (2001), p. 543.
53 Cf. Knauer, T., Silge, L., Sommer, F. (2018); Rapp, M. S., Schellong, D., Schmidt, M., et al. (2011), p. 172.

support investors in their decisions.[54] To sum up: Value relevance research is a research field in which research questions are not completely and comprehensively answered[55] despite a large number of publications and empirical research.[56]

Beside the analysis of value relevance of value based performance measures, academic literature examines which kinds of value concepts are used by companies.[57] In Germany, many DAX companies use value based key figures.[58] Further need for research is seen in an intensive comparison of applied value concepts.[59] An investigation about the implementation of value concepts across a large population of companies is also necessary.[60] Many of the empirical studies focus on single countries.[61] Cross-national investigations about the application of value based performance measures are rare.[62] Many studies concerning Value Based Management (VBM) focus on Anglo-American companies.[63]

In the context of value based performance measures and the Shareholder Value approach the remuneration of management is a further topic. The way in which the performance of management is influenced, in the sense of shareholders if the remuneration is linked to a value based key figure, should also be investigated.[64]

1.2 Objectives

This dissertation has three objectives. The first objective is to examine the application of value based key figures on a European level. Many articles in academic literature deal with the question which key figures German companies use. Investigating the implementation of value concepts on a European level is a much broader perspective in order to assess the application of value based measures.[65]

Within the context of application of value based key figures, it is essential to describe the framework conditions in which companies use them: The dominance of the Shareholder Value approach,[66] conflicts of interests between managers and investors due to the separation of ownership and control,[67] and the competition for capital.[68] The illustration of the framework conditions should stress the necessity of Value Reporting for companies in today's business environment. Furthermore, it is necessary to evaluate the most popular

---

54 Cf. Laier, R. (2011), p. 289.
55 Cf. Barth, M. E. (2000), p. 26.
56 Cf. Kothari, S. P. (2001), p. 106.
57 Cf. exemplary for investigations about the application of value concepts in the DAX: Aders, C., Herbertinger, M., Schaffer, C., et al. (2003) and Quick, R. (2012).
58 Cf. Borm, M., Britzelmaier, B., Kraus, P., et al. (2012), p. 27.
59 Cf. Arbeitskreis Internes Rechnungswesen der Schmalenbach-Gesellschaft (2010), p. 798.
60 Cf. Burkert, M., Lueg, R. (2013), p. 33.
61 Cf. exemplarily the studies of Aders, C., Herbertinger, M., Schaffer, C., et al. (2003), Laier, R. (2011), Malmi, S., Ikäheimo, S. (2003), Ruhwedel, F., Schultze, W. (2002).
62 Cf. for cross-national studies Firk, S., Schrapp, S., Wolff, M. (2016), Horváth, P., Minning, F. (2001).
63 Cf. Rapp, M. S., Schellong, D., Schmidt, M., et al. (2011), p. 174.
64 Cf. Schäffer, U., Botta, J. (2011), p. 316.
65 Cf. Burkert, M., Lueg, R. (2013), p.33.
66 Cf. Bezemer, P.-J., Zajac, E. J., Naumovska, I., et al. (2014), pp. 1-2.
67 Cf. Gong, J. J. (2011), p. 4.
68 Cf. Macharzina, K., Wolf, J. (2012), pp. 232-233.

value based key figures on the basis of uniform criteria in order to clarify strengths and weaknesses of each single value concept.

The second objective is to calculate a uniform value based performance measure so that it is possible to compare the performance of selected companies during the investigation period. So far, this is not possible because companies adapt the key figures to their individual needs or do not publish them in the annual report.[69]

The third objective is to conduct a value relevance analysis in which the value relevance of the previously calculated value based performance measure is compared with value relevance of selected traditional key figures.

This dissertation reduces some of the listed research gaps. Investigating the implementation of value concepts on a European level corresponds to the demand concerning the missing investigations of value based key figures within a large population of companies.[70] In addition, the focus is on European companies, not Anglo-American ones.[71] Underlining the necessity of Value Reporting in combination with describing the current situation at capital markets helps investors get a better understanding of the effects of Value Reporting on a theoretical basis.[72] This dissertation delivers new insights to the discussion about the value relevance of value based and traditional key figures in the context of the Metric War as it investigates the value relevance in an unique economic situation in Europe.[73]

Beyond named research gaps, academic researchers are identifying a gap between academic research and practice. This means that results from academic research, in this case management accounting research, are not communicated properly to practitioners even though they are relevant for them. Therefore, research should also deliver insights or solutions for practice. By investigating the named issues, this dissertation aims to contribute to the reduction of the gap between research and practice.[74]

1.3 Structure of Work

This dissertation is divided in five chapters. The first chapter summarises the problem description, the relevance of the topic and presents the objectives of this work.

The second chapter illustrates the conditions under which companies apply value based performance measures. In the first part the concepts of VBM and the Shareholder Value approach are presented. Due to the high importance of cost of capital in these two concepts the calculation of cost of equity capital on the basis of the Capital Asset Pricing Model (CAPM) is presented.

After introducing principles on which companies act in today's business world, the relationships between managers and shareholders will be described on basis of the Principal Agent theory. For this purpose the application of the Principal Agent theory in this work is justified and the basic structure of Principal Agent relationships and kinds of

69 Cf. Schäffer, U., Lewerenz, U. (2011), p. 298.
70 Cf. Burkert, M., Lueg, R. (2013), p. 33.
71 Cf. Rapp, M. S., Schellong, D., Schmidt, M., et al. (2011), p. 174.
72 Cf. Laier, R. (2011), p. 289.
73 Cf. Ittner, C. D., Larcker, D. F. (2001), pp. 358-362; Schremper, R., Pälchen Oliver (2001), pp. 543-546.
74 Cf. extensively Nicolai, A., Seidl, D. (2010), p. 1257; Tucker, B., Parker, L. (2014).

information symmetries are presented. Following on from the work of Meckling and Jensen, the importance of key figures as a tool for reducing information asymmetries will be explained. Beside the relationship between manager and investor it is also important to analyse the effect of information asymmetries on cost of capital which is done in the following part. The part concludes with a critical discussion of the Principal Agent theory and its assumptions.

After analysing the relationship of managers and shareholders, the relevance of information for the formation of stock prices will be investigated. For this purpose the efficient market model and empirical studies are presented. This part is followed by a presentation of the composition of the group of shareholders and an analysis of their information needs.

In the context of the Principal Agent theory and efficient market model the role of accounting of companies will be assessed. Afterwards, the core principles of IFRS are introduced, followed by a critical assessment of the accounting standard from the investors' point of view. The last part of the chapter deals with the Value Reporting as a supplement of legal reporting and classifies the disclosure of value based performance measures into the reporting of companies.

The third chapter focuses on value based performance measures and their characteristics. In order to make differences clear between value based performance measures and traditional ones, the first part of the chapter focuses on the commonly used traditional key figures Price Earnings Ratio (PER), Earnings per Share (EPS), Return on Equity (ROE), Return on Sales (ROS) and Return on Investment (ROI).

The second part of the chapter introduces value based performance measures with the help of a general systematisation and listing their advantages in comparison to traditional key figures. This part ends with an introduction of the criteria for assessment of the selected value concepts.

The third part of the chapter starts with an explanation of the concept of residual income which is the justification for applying value based performance measures. In total the third and fourth parts introduce and assess the value based performance measures ROCE Spread, Value Added, EVA, CFROI, CVA, DCF and MVA on a theoretical basis. For every key figure the calculation and its specific characteristic are presented and in a second step each key figure is assessed on the previous defined evaluation criteria.

The fifth and last part of the third chapter outlines the current status of research with regard to the application of value based performance measures and with regard to value relevance analysis of value based performance measures. Before presenting empirical studies which deal with value relevance analysis, the common research approaches and classification of capital market studies are discussed.

The fourth chapter contains the empirical study and consists of four parts. The first part identifies open questions in scientific literature and derives objectives and hypotheses for the study on the basis of the previously presented status of research. Then the applied methodology for each part of the study is explained. For the value relevance analysis this includes the question which model should be used, what is the theoretical basis for the regression equation, which variables are part of the model and which statistical method is applied. Finally, the data base is specified and described.

The second part shows the results of the empirical study while in the third part the results are interpreted. Finally, the last part of the chapter points out the limitations of this study.

The last chapter of this dissertation summarises the insights gained and shows avenues for future research.

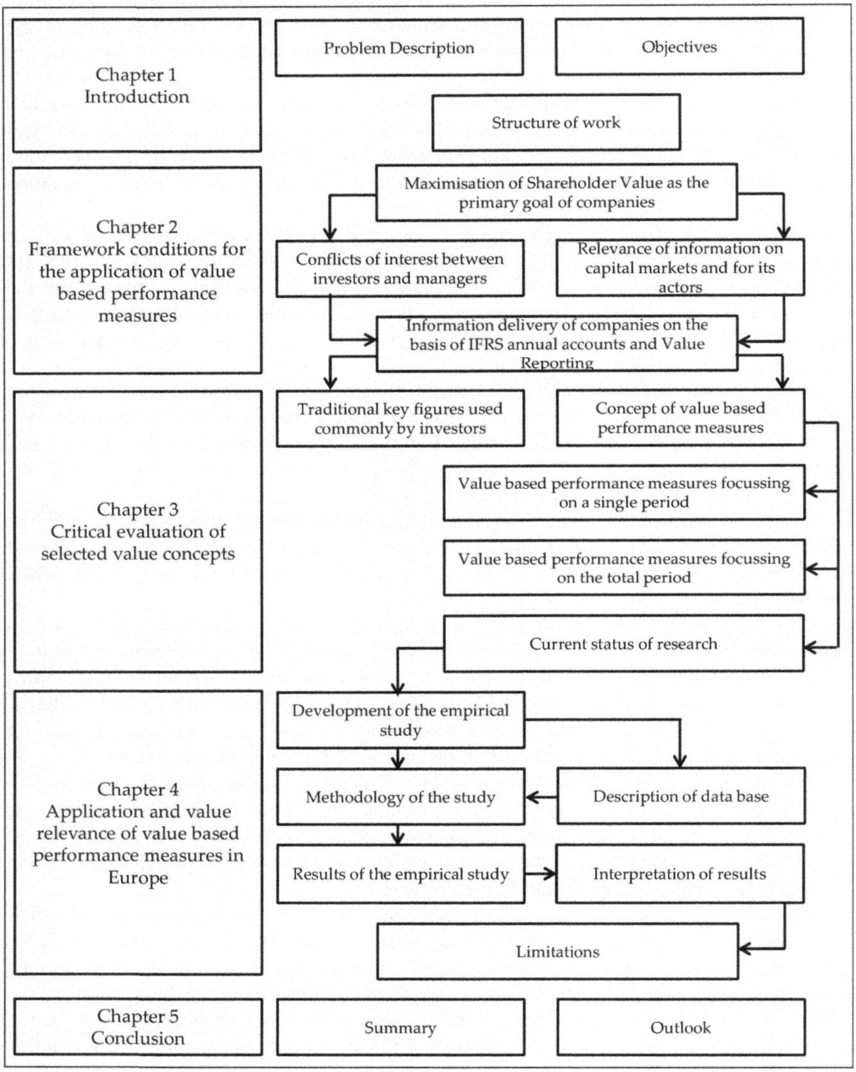

Source: Own illustration

Illustration 1: Structure of work

2 Framework Conditions for the Application of Value Based Performance Measures

2.1 Maximisation of Shareholder Value as Primary Goal of Companies

2.1.1 Necessity of Value Based Management for Companies in Today's Business EEnvironment

2.1.1.1 Development of Value Based Management

Value Based Management (VBM) is a wide spread management philosophy.[75] It can be seen as the fourth stage of Strategic Management[76] or as the fourth stage in managerial accounting.[77] Famous authors who characterise the ideas behind this philosophy are e.g. Fruhan,[78] Rappaport,[79] Copeland[80], Stern and Stewart[81] as well as Lewis.[82]

For the purpose of this work, VBM summarises the diverse management approaches which focus on the augmentation of company value. The Shareholder Value approach is one example of VBM. The difference between the two terms is the definition of their objectives. The Shareholder Value approach strives to increase the return of equity capital providers, whereas VBM in general wants to increase the value of the company.[83]

Even if the Shareholder Value approach is only a part of VBM, the popularity of Rappaport's approach initiated the development of VBM. The economic circumstances fostered the spread of VBM. During the 1980ies many hostile takeovers, undertaken by so-called Corporate Raiders, took place in the United States. Companies tried to protect themselves by identifying and closing gaps between market and book value by increasing the market value of the company. In many companies the objectives of shareholders and managers were diverse and led to bad financial results.[84] At the beginning of 1990ies, American consulting companies, mainly Stern Stewart & Co. and Holt Planning Associates (later Boston Consulting Group), fostered the implementation of the theoretical

75 Cf. Britzelmaier, B. (2013b), p. 15; Velthuis, L. J., Wesner, P. (2005), pp. 1-2.

76 Cf. For detailed description of phases of Strategic Management Palli, M. C. (2004), pp. 31-43.

77 Cf. for detailed description of four phases of managerial accounting Ittner, C. D., Larcker, D. F. (2001), pp. 351-352.

78 Cf. Fruhan, W. (1979).

79 Cf. Rappaport, A. (1986).

80 Cf. Copeland, T. E., Koller, T., Murrin, J. (1991).

81 Cf. Stewart, G. B. (1999).

82 Cf. Lewis, T. G., Lehmann, S. (1992); Lewis, T. G., Stelter, D. M., Casata, T., et al. (1995).

83 Cf. for a detailed differentiation between the terms VBM and shareholder value Riedl, J. B. (2000), pp. 85-86; Stiefl, J., Westerholt, K. von (2008), pp. 4-6; cf. contradictory Velthuis, L. J., Wesner, P. (2005), pp. 1-2 who describe VBM as the practical conversion of the Shareholder Value approach; cf. for an overview of the status of research of VBM Lueg, R., Schäffer, U. (2010).

84 Cf. Stiefl, J., Westerholt, K. von (2008), pp. 8-10.

N. Eikelmann, *Value Based Performance Measures*, FOM-Edition Research,
https://doi.org/10.1007/978-3-658-31429-3_2

concepts within the companies.[85] During the New Economy phase at the end of 1990ies VBM finally established as a main guideline for management decisions.[86]

Over time and until today, the economic circumstances prescribe the necessity of VBM for companies:[87]

- Separation of ownership and control: Several companies are not managed directly by their owners. In these cases managers and owners need a common objective in order to steer the company in the sense of its owners.[88]
- Shortcomings of traditional key figures[89] and reinforced application of Cash Flow based measures for evaluating performance of companies.[90]
- Financial analysts evaluate the performance of a company on the basis of selected key figures and give a buying, selling or holding advice.[91]
- Growing importance of institutional investors.[92]
- Globalisation of capital markets.[93]
- Increased capital procurement via international capital markets.[94]
- Application of own shares for mergers and acquisition activities.[95]
- Threat of a hostile takeover.[96]

2.1.1.2 Elements and Objectives of Value Based Management

The main objective of VBM is to increase the company's value in the long-term.[97] This leads to the necessity of continuous control of Shareholder Value development.[98] Besides this primary objective, VBM also supports management by determining if products and activities are delivering a contribution to the company's value or by making investment decisions. Company owners are enabled by VBM to assess the performance of managers. Last but not least, VBM aligns the interests of managers and owners. By focusing on increasing the company value, they have one common objective.[99] Shortly, VBM is a management strategy or approach which strives to reduce conflicts between shareholders and owners, to influence managers to make decisions under consideration of its effects on

85 Cf. Baum, H.-G., Coenenberg, A. G., Günther, T. (2013), p. 310.
86 Cf. Coenenberg, A. G., Salfeld, R. (2007), pp. 9-7.
87 Cf. for an overview of economic framework conditions Dillerup, R., Stoi, R. (2016), pp. 193-194; Pape, U. (2010), p. 9.
88 Cf. Imberger, K. (2003), p. 25.
89 Cf. for detailed remarks about shortcomings of traditional key figures Knorren, N. (1998), pp. 10-16.
90 Cf. Imberger, K. (2003), pp. 18-19.
91 Cf. Friedrich, N. (2007), pp. 39-40.
92 Cf. Stührenberg, L., Streich, D., Henke Jörg (2003), p. 1.
93 Cf. Fiss, P. C., Zajac, E. J. (2004), pp. 501; Pape, U. (2010), p. 9.
94 Cf. Bris, A., Koskinen, Y., Nilsson, M. (2014), pp. 554-555.
95 Cf. Coenenberg, A. G., Salfeld, R. (2007), pp. 8-9.
96 Cf., Blyth, M. L., Friskey, E. A., Rappaport, A. (1986), p. 48.
97 Cf. Kraus, P. (2011), pp. 8-9; Stiefl, J., Westerholt, K. von (2008), p. 5; cf. also the empirical study of Ryan, H. E., Trahan, E. A. (2007) which comes to the conclusion that VBM improves economic performance.
98 Cf. Dillerup, R., Stoi, R. (2016), pp. 196-197.
99 Cf. Hilpisch, Y. (2005), pp. 131-133.

the company value and finally leads to an increase of the value of the company.[100] It is undoubtedly the Controlling department that is especially responsible for monitoring goal attainment in the sense of VBM and provides management with information. In this context key figures seem to be a convenient instrument.[101]

Four features characterise VBM: Future-oriented, risk-oriented, Cash Flow-oriented and a clear focus on company value.[102] The focus on future is not surprising as the main objective of VBM is to ensure the long-term existence of a company. For this purpose decisions have to be evaluated against their consequences on the long-term company value. It is decisive how the company will perform in future.[103]

The second characteristic, risk-oriented, describes the attitude of equity capital providers. From their point of view, a company is an investment with a certain risk factor. For this risk factor the company has to deliver an adequate rate of return. The higher the risk, the higher the required rate of return.[104] If the expected rate of return is not delivered, equity capital providers will withdraw their capital. Costs of equity capital are nothing other than opportunity costs.[105] By considering the required rate of return, the hurdle rate for companies raises as the costs for equity capital are not included in the profit disclosed in the profit and loss statement.[106] In order to fulfil the required returns by investors, companies at least have to reach a level of profit which covers the total cost of capital. The illustration below contrasts the assessment of success on the basis of balance sheet profits and from VBM's perspective.[107]

The third characteristic of VBM is the focus on Cash Flow based measures.[108] The principles of dynamic investment theory are transferred to the valuation of a company. This means that Cash Flows of a company are mathematically discounted in order to derive the value of the company. Changes in company value are often measured in key figures based on Cash Flows.[109]

The forth characteristic of VBM, clear focus on company value, refers to the main objective. If a company strives to increase its value, every decision has to be checked against this target. This applies also for every concept which is categorised as VBM.[110]

The characteristics of VBM show a combination of insights of capital market and investment theory.[111] Elements of investment theory are transferred to corporate evaluation. The company is an investment object which generates Cash Flows. Following on from these Cash Flows, a present value can be calculated. Hereby the distribution over

---

100 Cf. Losbichler, H. (2012), p. 266; Ryan, H. E., Trahan, E. A. (2007), p. 113.
101 Cf. Ossadnik, W., Barklage, D. (2003). pp. 1286-1287.
102 Cf. Krol, F. (2009), pp. 61-66; cf. for similar characteristics Ebeling, C. (2007), pp. 3-4; Tappe, R. (2009), pp. 68-71.
103 Cf. Aders, C., Herbertinger, M., Wiedemann, F. (2003), pp. 356-358.
104 Cf. Horváth, P. (2011), pp. 443-445.
105 Cf. Reim, J. (2015), p. 554.
106 Cf. Behringer, S. (2014), p. 101.
107 Cf. Auer, M. (2007), pp. 302-303; Wolf, R. (2014), pp. 7-9; Wuntsch, M. v., Bach, S. (2012), p. 21.
108 Cf. Ebeling, C. (2007), p.3.
109 Cf. Tappe, R. (2009), pp. 70-71.
110 Cf. Weber, J., Bramsemann, U., Heineke, C., et al. (2017), pp. 17-19.
111 Cf. Britzelmaier, B. (2013a), p. 208.

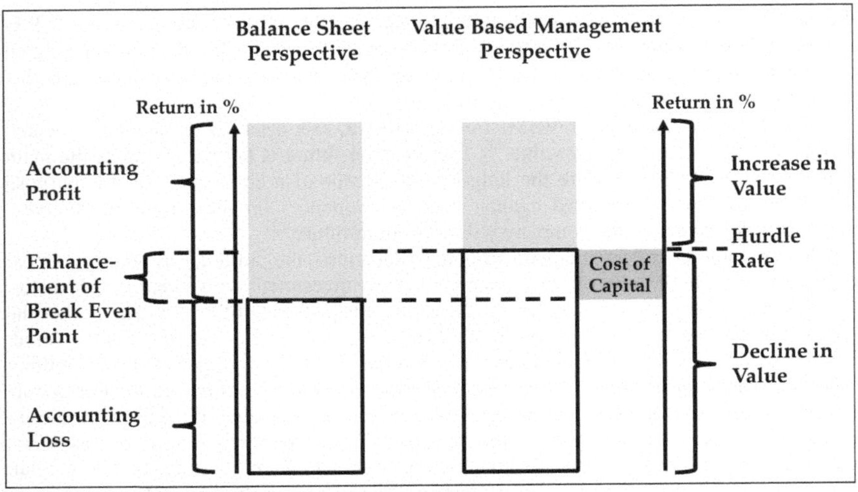

In the style of: Behringer, S. (2014), p. 101; Kraus (2011), p. 7

Illustration 2: Comparison of hurdle rates from a balance sheet perspective and VBM perspective

time and level of Cash Flows as well as the inherent risk for these Cash Flows are considered.[112] Insights from capital market theory are used by calculating the cost of equity capital. Regularly the CAPM is used for this purpose.[113] In total, VBM is not an invention of a completely new management approach, but a useful combination of established theories.[114]

VBM does not only consist of financial or controlling aspects.[115] Apart from value based performance measures, which are a method to determine value creation in the sense of VBM, further topics and areas can be assigned to VBM. For example, development and assessment of corporate strategies, the structure of management compensation dependent on a company's performance or the appropriate communication to the capital market.[116] Due to its various aspects it is difficult and costly to implement VBM successfully in a company. Companies have often underestimated these efforts.[117]

Many aspects of VBM are summarised and categorised in the VBM accounting framework which divides the process of VBM in six steps.[118] The first step is to choose appropriate organisational objectives. This step also refers to the application of value

112 Cf. Schönherr, M. (2016), pp. 59-60.

113 Cf. Dinstuhl, V. (2003), p. 24.

114 Cf. Baum, H.-G., Coenenberg, A. G., Günther, T. (2013), p. 310.

115 Cf. Haspeslagh, P., Noda, T., Boulos, F. (2001), p. 68; Hirsch, B. (2006), p. 271.

116 Cf. Coenenberg, A. G., Salfeld, R. (2007), pp. 10-13; Hirsch, B. (2006), p. 271.

117 Cf. Haspeslagh, P., Noda, T., Boulos, F. (2001), pp. 66-67.

118 Cf. for a comprehensive description and an overview of many aspects of VBM Ittner, C. D., Larcker, D. F. (2001).

based performance measures because they play an important role in aligning internal objectives with an increase of company value.

The second step is to develop a strategy and to select an organisational design which fits to the defined objectives in the first step.[119] Examples for a developed strategy are cost leadership strategy or innovation strategy on which a company can focus. Organisational design refers to the structure of a company, like decentralisation or allocation of decision rights to managers.[120]

The third step comprises the identification of value drivers. These are factors which lead to an increase of company value.[121] Exemplary methods for identifying cost drivers are activity-based costing, strategic cost management or Balanced Scorecard.[122]

In the fourth step the company develops action plans, selects performance measures and sets targets which are associated with the value drivers identified in step three.

The fifth step is to evaluate the performance of the company and its managers. In order to take current results and development into account, it is necessary that a company continuously reassesses the organisational objectives, strategies, organisational design, value drivers and control system. So, this process is iterative and starts again at step one.[123]

The VBM accounting framework stresses the important role of appropriate performance measures and designed control systems in the context of VBM. Key figures are involved in step one with setting the organisational objectives and in step four and five within the decision for the relevant key figures and observing them.[124] The application of key figures in the context of VBM is essential because they are an important tool for managers to make decisions which increase the company value and communicate achieved successes to external shareholders and stakeholders.[125]

2.1.2 Shareholder Value Approach as one Characteristic Form of Value Based Management

2.1.2.1 Shareholder Value Network

Shareholder Value and VBM are closely connected. A clear commitment to Shareholder Value is part of a successful VBM implementation.[126] In the context of this dissertation the Shareholder Value approach is of importance because it is the theoretical justification for the proclaimed superiority of value based performance measures against traditional ones.[127]

---

119 Cf. Ittner, C. D., Larcker, D. F. (2001), p. 353.
120 Cf. Ittner, C. D., Larcker, D. F. (2001), pp. 362-364.
121 Cf. Ittner, C. D., Larcker, D. F. (2001), p. 368.
122 Cf. Ittner, C. D., Larcker, D. F. (2001), pp. 368-371.
123 Cf. Ittner, C. D., Larcker, D. F. (2001), p. 353.
124 Cf. Ittner, C. D., Larcker, D. F. (2001), pp. 353, 358-362.
125 Cf. Holler, A. (2009), pp. 1-2.
126 Cf. Haspeslagh, P., Noda, T., Boulos, F. (2001), p. 67.
127 Cf. Palli, M. C. (2004), pp. 224-225.

The Shareholder Value approach mainly bases on Alfred Rappaport's book "Creating Shareholder Value" in which he describes the essentials of this management approach.[128] Shareholder Value describes the market value of equity capital of a company or in other words: It is the difference between market value of total capital of a company and the market value of its debt capital.[129] Companies following the Shareholder Value approach have one common goal: Increase Shareholder Value and thereby increase the assets of company owners.[130]

The calculation of Shareholder Value is based on the discount of future Cash Flows. The calculation is separated into two phases. In a detailed forecast period Cash Flows are calculated and discounted by the cost of capital. The costs of capital are the required rates of return a company has to generate at a minimum in order to satisfy its investors.[131] The second phase is the period after the forecast period. It is assumed that the company exists infinitely. Therefore, a so called Terminal Value is calculated which summarises all Cash Flows that will be generated after the forecast period until infinity.[132]

The coherence between the single valuation components and the Shareholder Value is illustrated with the help of the Shareholder Value Network. Management makes decisions which influence the value drivers. The value drivers in turn have an effect on the valuation components from which the Shareholder Value is finally derived.[133]

As illustration three demonstrates the network is divided into four levels. On the first level Rappaport defines three areas on which management decisions must concentrate to increase Shareholder Value. Operating decisions comprise all tasks in the areas purchasing, producing and selling. This also includes cross-departmental functions like Human Resources.[134] Examples are choice of products or pricing policy.[135] Investment decisions have an influence on the composition of a company's asset in the categories non-current and current assets. Examples for concrete actions are the purchase of a new production machinery or the replenishment of inventories.[136] Decisions in the area of financing influence the capital structure.[137]

On the second level of the network seven value drivers are listed. The value drivers are variables which managers of a firm can influence with their decisions. Operating decisions influence sales growth, operating profit margin and income tax rates, whereas working capital and fixed capital are affected by investment decisions. The management

128 Cf. Rappaport, A. (1986); cf. also further publications of Rappaport: Blyth, M. L., Friskey, E. A., Rappaport, A. (1986); Rappaport, A. (1983); Rappaport, A. (1987); Rappaport, A. (2006); cf. For an extensive illustration of development of Shareholder Value approach Heilbron, J., Verheul, J., Quak, S. (2014).

129 Cf. Körnert, J., Wolf, C. (2007), p. 133.

130 Cf. Kraus, K., Strömsten, T. (2012), p. 188; Lorson, P. (1999), p. 1329.

131 Cf. Moir, L., Kennerley, M., Ferguson, D. (2007), p. 389; Paul, J. (2014), pp. 149-153.

132 Cf. Lorson, P. (1999), p. 1333; Paul, J. (2014), pp, 149-153.

133 Cf. Faltz, F. (1999), p. 19; Skrzipek, M. (2005), pp. 18-19.

134 Cf. Meyer, C. A. (2007), pp. 140-141.

135 Cf. Rappaport, A. (1986), p. 76.

136 Cf. Metze, T. (2010), p. 46.

137 Cf. Meyer, C. A. (2007), pp. 140-141.

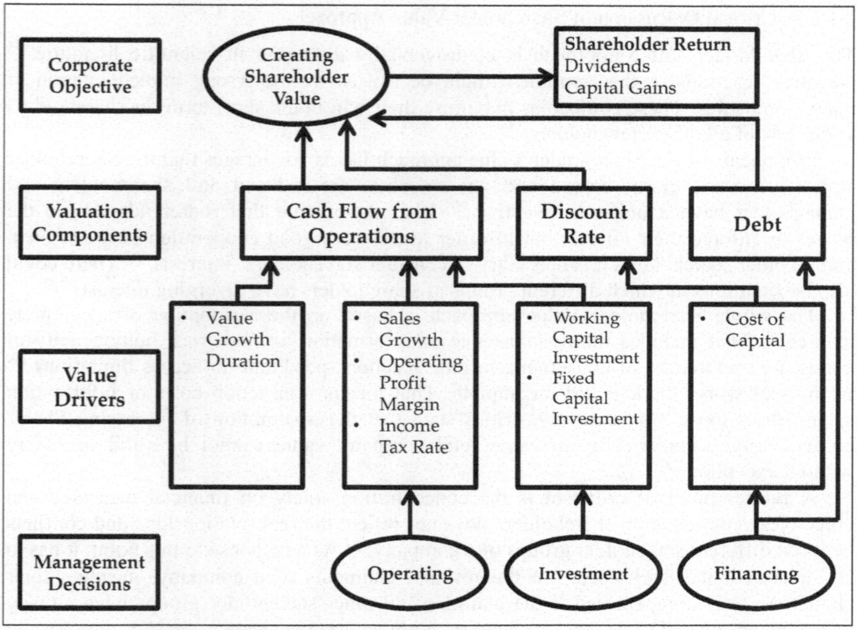

Adapted from: Rappaport, A. (1986), p. 76
Illustration 3: Shareholder Value Network

increases or decreases costs of capital with financing decisions.[138] Value growth duration describes the time in which an investment delivers a return above the cost of capital.[139]

On the third level the valuation components Cash Flow, discount rate and debt capital are listed. Increasing Cash Flows will increase the Shareholder Value. A reduction of discount rate respectively of its capital costs is a second possibility for companies to increase Shareholder Value.[140] Cash Flow and discount rate are both necessary for determining company value. Then debt capital is deducted in order to receive Shareholder Value.[141]

The corporate objective of creating Shareholder Value is finally at the top of the network. Shareholders receive returns in two ways: Share prices increase and shareholders are able to sell their investment with a profit, if their purchase price is below the actual price or the company pays a dividend.[142] All liquid funds which a company cannot invest in projects with an adequate rate of return should be distributed to shareholders.[143]

138 Cf. Wall, F., Greiling, D. (2011), pp. 97-98.
139 Cf. Faltz, F. (1999), p. 19; Wall, F., Greiling, D. (2011), pp. 97-98.
140 Cf. Tischer, S., Hildebrandt, L. (2014), p. 1008-1009.
141 Cf. Meyer, C. A. (2007), p. 139.
142 Cf. Rappaport, A. (1987), p. 59.
143 Cf. Rappaport, A. (2006), p. 72.

2.1.2.2 Critical Discussion of Shareholder Value Approach

The Shareholder Value approach is controversially discussed in scientific literature.[144] Negative reactions to this approach might be caused by the wrong implementation in many companies. These companies maximise their win in the short-term for shareholders at the cost of all other stakeholders.[145]

Proponents of the Shareholder Value approach list as advantages that the Shareholder Value increases, moral hazard and agency costs are reduced and shareholders and management have a uniform objective.[146] It might be true that shareholders have the power to enforce their interest but in order to ensure a good cooperation between them and all other stakeholders it is necessary to consider stakeholders' interests.[147] There could also be situations in which different groups of shareholders have diverging interests.[148]

The whole Shareholder Value approach is based on the assumption of a complete market.[149] That includes the nonexistence of information asymmetries, homogeneity of goods, no preferences of consumers, infinite reaction speed and no access limitations.[150] In the real world markets are incomplete. That means transaction costs or information asymmetries exist. Consequently, critics state that the assumption of increasing Shareholder Value automatically increases total company value cannot be valid in reality without exceptions.[151]

A further point of criticism is the concentration solely on financial measures and objectives. The focus on shareholders does not reflect the real relationships and conflicts between different stakeholder groups of a company.[152] As a response to this point, it has to be stressed that shareholders are the residual claimants of a company, meaning their claims are only compensated if the claims of all other stakeholder groups have already been compensated. This higher risk requires a higher compensation.[153]

Connected with the above mentioned issues a question can be raised concerning how many objectives a company should have. In the case of the Shareholder Value approach there is only one single objective. Independent from the objective itself, it is advantageous that a company and its managers have only one objective to fulfil because managers can fully concentrate on reaching this goal. Trade-offs are avoided.[154]

A further advantage is the fact that it is easier for shareholders to control the management as the goal of Shareholder Value enhancement can be controlled by shareholders independently.[155]

In practice, the Shareholder Value approach leads to a lot of discussion, especially in Germany. Managers can use this approach as justification for dismissal of employees.[156]

144 Cf. Raynor, M. E. (2009) who contrasts arguments for and against Shareholder Value.
145 Cf. Zinkann, R. (2010), pp. 92-94.
146 Cf. Elgharbawy, A., Abdel-Kader, M. (2013), p. 104.
147 Cf. Franke, G., Hax, H. (2009), pp. 2-3.
148 Cf. Fiss, P. C., Zajac, E. J. (2004), pp. 501-502.
149 Cf. Ballwieser, W. (2009), pp. 94-95.
150 Cf. Fischbach, R., Wollenberg, K. (2007), p. 275.
151 Cf. Loderer, C., Roth, L., Waelchli, U., et al. (2010), pp. 7-8.
152 Cf. Ballwieser, W. (2009), p. 95.
153 Cf. Keay, A., Adamopoulou, R. (2012), pp. 7 -8; Rappaport, A. (1987), p. 59; Stier, C. (2017), p. 54.
154 Cf. Jensen, M. C. (2002), pp. 237-238; Stier, C. (2017), pp. 55-56.
155 Cf. Keay, A., Adamopoulou, R. (2012), p. 8.

An empirical study shows that this proclaimed coherence is doubtful. It investigates the coherence between Shareholder Value creation and job creation. In the sample the companies which create Shareholder Value also create jobs. In contrast, those companies which are not able to overcome the hurdle rate of costs of capital have to reduce the number of employees.[157]

A point of criticism is also the short-term time horizon associated with the Shareholder Value approach, although neither Rappaport nor other representatives of VBM claim short-term oriented thinking. Decisive is the development of Shareholder Value in the long-term.[158]

Despite arguments for and against Shareholder Value it is fact that worldwide most companies follow this approach today.[159] As an alternative to Shareholder Value approach the Stakeholder Approach has been developed.[160] Events like the financial crisis in 2008 and 2009 as well as global challenges like climate change foster the popularity of the Stakeholder approach.[161]

In contrast to the Shareholder Value approach, managers do not focus only on one group, the shareholders, but also consider needs of other groups,[162] e.g. employees, suppliers, customers, government or communities.[163] These groups also have an interest in the continuing existence of the company and therefore have claims against it. By focusing also on other groups, the Stakeholder approach tries to overcome one point of criticism of the Shareholder Value approach.[164]

Some empirical studies confirm that financial performance increases if managers follow the Stakeholder approach.[165] Critics however state that managers face the difficulty balancing the partly contradicting interests of different stakeholder groups.[166] Therefore, the concept is difficult to operationalise and there are several trade-offs between the groups.[167] Furthermore, critics mention the contentual haziness of the concept. In scientific literature authors often mix or do not differentiate between the different aspects of stakeholder management.[168]

---

156 Cf. Ballwieser, W. (2009), p. 95.

157 Cf. Bughin, J., Copeland, T. E. (1997), pp. 162-164; cf. for similar argumentation Losbichler, H. (2012), p. 268.

158 Cf. Losbichler, H. (2012), p. 269; Paul, J. (2014), p. 165.

159 Cf. Bezemer, P.-J., Zajac, E. J., Naumovska, I., et al. (2014), pp. 1-2; Kraus, K., Strömsten, T. (2012), p. 188.

160 Cf. basically for more information about Stakeholder approach Donaldson, T., Preston, L. E. (1995); Freeman, R. E. (2010); Poeschl, H. (2013), pp. 127-151; Skrzipek, M. (2005), pp. 47-78.

161 Cf. Wall, F., Greiling, D. (2011), p. 92.

162 Cf. Mayr, S. (2010), p. 54; Poeschl, H. (2013), pp. 127-129.

163 Cf. Donaldson, T., Preston, L. E. (1995), p. 69.

164 Cf. Mayr, S. (2010), p. 54.

165 Cf. Tantalo, C., Priem, R. L. (2016), pp. 315-316.

166 Cf. Tantalo, C., Priem, R. L. (2016), pp. 314-315.

167 Cf. Ballwieser, W. (2009), p. 95.

168 Cf. Donaldson, T., Preston, L. E. (1995), p. 66; Stoney, C., Winstanley, D. (2001), pp. 605-607; cf. for an extensive explanation for perspectives of stakeholder management Donaldson, T., Preston, L. E. (1995), pp. 69-71; Mayr, S. (2010), pp. 57-60.

2.1.3 Calculation of Cost of Capital as a Crucial Part of Value Based Management and Shareholder Value Approach

2.1.3.1 Calculation of Cost of Equity Capital with the CAPM and Calculation of Cost of Debt Capital

A decisive factor for VBM as well as for the Shareholder Value approach is the cost of capital.[169] Companies have to reach a certain profit threshold which covers all costs including the total cost of capital.[170] In the context of the Shareholder Value approach cost of capital are the discount factor used for discounting the Cash Flows. So, companies strive to lower cost of capital in order to increase ceteris paribus Shareholder Value.[171]

For value based performance measures, the cost of capital has a fundamental importance. They are the connecting element between the part of the key figure, which is calculated on the basis of accounting and the objective of the company to increase its Shareholder Value.[172]

A wide spread measure for cost of capital is the Weighted Average Cost of Capital (WACC).[173] Prerequisites for the calculation of WACC are the determination of cost of equity and debt capital which are weighted with the equity and debt ratio.[174] The debt and equity ratio are calculated on basis of market values.[175] Formula one shows the calculation of WACC.

$$WACC = r_{EC} \times \frac{EC}{TC} + r_{DC} \times \frac{DC}{TC} \times (1 - s)$$

Source: Formula taken from Perridon, L., Steiner, M., Rathgeber, A. (2016), p. 245

Formula 1: Calculation of WACC including tax shield

with

r_{EC} = cost of equity capital

r_{DC} = cost of debt capital

EC = market value of equity capital

DC = market value of debt capital

TC = market value of total capital

s = Tax rate of company

It is important to differentiate if the WACC is calculated including taxes or without taxes. Costs for debt capital reduce the company's tax burden, therefore the costs of debt capital are reduced by the tax rate.[176] This effect is named tax shield. In the above mentioned formula the tax shield is expressed by the term (1-s).[177]

---

169 Cf. Dillerup, R., Stoi, R. (2016), p. 205.

170 Cf. Auer, M. (2007), pp. 302-303; Wuntsch, M. v., Bach, S. (2012), p. 21.

171 Cf. Tischer, S., Hildebrandt, L. (2014), pp. 1008-1009.

172 Cf. Weißenberger, B. E. (2003), p. 243.

173 Cf. Tischer, S., Hildebrandt, L. (2014), p. 1008.

174 Cf. Schneider, N. C. (2007), p. 41; Tinz, O. (2010), p. 59.

175 Cf. Becker, H. P. (2016), p. 92.

176 Cf. Becker, H. P. (2016), p. 92.

177 Cf. Hachmeister, D. (2009), p. 69; Reinke, J. (2010), pp. 129-130.

The WACC approach suffers under the circularity problem. The WACC can only be calculated, if market values of equity and debt capital are known for determining equity and debt ratios. But these values in turn depend on the weighted average cost of capital.[178] Two ways exist, in order to avoid this problem. Firstly, a company can assume a target capital structure or secondly conduct an iterative calculation of total value of capital and WACC.[179]

A direct observable measure for cost of equity capital does not exist so that estimation models have to be used.[180] The CAPM, the most common model for this purpose, measures the cost of equity capital with the help of three components: Risk free rate, market's risk premium and beta factor.[181] The CAPM is based on Markowitz portfolio theory[182] and on the following assumptions:[183]

- Investors are risk averse.
- Investors assess shares on the basis of the insights of the portfolio theory. This means that each share is evaluated on its expected value and its standard deviation of return.
- The expectations of all investors are homogenous. Consequently, they allocate the same expected values and standard deviations to each share.
- The investment period is one period.
- The capital market is complete, that means transaction costs and taxes do not exist, all participants have equal access to the capital market, all investment possibilities are randomly separable and no information asymmetries exist.
- Investors can invest in a risk free asset.
- All shares are tradable and infinitely divisible.

Under these assumptions investors face two kinds of risk: Systematic and unsystematic risk. Systematic risk describes risks which have influence on all shares. The unsystematic risk comprises share specific risks which can be eliminated by diversification.[184] Examples of systematic risks are changes of interest rates or inflation or other issues influencing the general economic situation of companies.[185]

It is assumed that the portfolios of all investors consist of a mixture of risk free and risky investments. Concerning the risky investments, investors identify efficient portfolios. Efficient portfolios guarantee an investor at a given volatility or risk the highest

178 Cf. Becker, H. P. (2016), p. 94; Reinke, J. (2010), pp. 130-131; Tinz, O. (2010), p. 60.

179 Cf. Drukarczyk, J., Schüler, A. (2016), pp. 101-102; Hoffmann, W. (2011), p. 120; Schacht, U., Fackler, M. (2009), pp. 217-218; Tinz, O. (2010), p. 60.

180 Cf. Botosan, C. A. (2006), p. 32.

181 Cf. Auer, M. (2007), p. 302; Botosan, C. A. (2006), p. 32. The CAPM was developed by Lintner, J. (1965), Mossin, J. (1966) and Sharpe, W. F. (1964). Cf. for an overview of further developments of CAPM Shih, Y.-C., Chen, S.-S., Lee, C.-F., et al. (2014). Cf. for a short overview of further methods for cost of equity capital calculation Dillerup, R., Stoi, R. (2016), pp. 205-206.

182 Cf. Seifert, U. (2006), p. 47, cf. extensively for basics of portfolio theory Markowitz, H. (1952).

183 Cf. for a list of these assumptions exemplarily Seifert, U. (2006), pp. 48-49, Weber, G. (2006), p. 70; Weber, S. (2008), p. 20; p. 29.

184 Cf. Seifert, U. (2006), pp. 49-50; Weber, G. (2006), pp. 66-67.

185 Cf. Dillerup, R., Stoi, R. (2016), p. 207; Lütkeschürmer, G. (2012), p. 35.

possible return.[186] Volatility / risk and expected return are the only criteria used by investors for their investment decisions. They will only choose a share with higher volatility if the return is adequately higher.[187]

Considering additionally the possibility of risk free investments, the straight line in illustration four, also named Capital Market Line, shows efficient investment possibilities for every degree of risk. As the Capital Market Line is a straight line, it can be concluded that with a higher risk taken by the investor the return increases proportionally. The tangent point of Capital Market Line and efficient curve of risky portfolios is the only efficient portfolio for risky investments because it delivers the highest profit for a given risk. All other risky portfolios are located below that point meaning that they have a lower return.[188]

In order to determine its own portfolio, an investor chooses a mixture of market portfolio and risk free investment according to their individual risk attitude. A cautious investor chooses a portfolio with 0 % volatility and receives in this example a return of 2.5 %. Moving on the capital market line to the right implies a riskier investment but also a chance to receive higher profit. Portfolios which are not on the Capital Market Line are not efficient because another portfolio exists which has the same risk but offers an investor a higher return. For a full risky investment an investor chooses to invest all its funding in the market portfolio.[189]

According to the assumptions of the CAPM all investors have homogenous expectations. Therefore, all investors construct the same market portfolio. The market portfolio is the only efficient portfolio for risky investments. Thus, investors always combine the risk free investment with a certain degree of the market portfolio.[190]

With reference to the market portfolio the CAPM enables users to calculate individual cost of equity capital. The beta factor connects the specific investment with the market portfolio by capturing the volatility of the investment object in comparison to the overall market risk.[191] In other words: It values the risk of the considered share in relation to the market risk.[192] It has to be considered that the beta factor only comprises the systematic risk. Thus, the CAPM does not consider the unsystematic risk in the cost of equity capital calculation and does not refund investors for taking unsystematic risk.[193]

For interpreting the beta factor, three thresholds are important: A beta factor of "one" means that the risk of the share exactly corresponds to the risk of the market. A value higher than "one" implies that the share fluctuates stronger than the market. A value below "one" and higher than "zero" stands for a lower volatility than the market portfolio. A value of "zero" means that the investment has no risk.[194]

186 Cf. Berk, J. B., DeMarzo, P. M. (2011), p. 388.
187 Cf. Schacht, U., Fackler, M. (2009), p. 212.
188 Cf. Berk, J. B., DeMarzo, P. M. (2011), pp. 395-398.
189 Cf. Berk, J. B., DeMarzo, P. M. (2011), pp. 397-399; Seifert, U. (2006), p. 49; Weber, G. (2006), pp. 70-71.
190 Cf. Berk, J. B., DeMarzo, P. M. (2011), p. 406, Laux, H., Schabel, M. M. (2009), pp. 175-176; Weber, S. (2008), pp. 17-20.
191 Cf. Berk, J. B., DeMarzo, P. M. (2011), p. 408; Hachmeister, D. (2009), p. 70.
192 Cf. Hoffmann, W. (2011), p. 121.
193 Cf. Reinke, J. (2010), pp. 132-133; Seifert, U. (2006), p. 51, Weber, S. (2008), p. 23.
194 Cf. Hoffmann, W. (2011), p. 121, Reinke, J. (2010), p. 135.

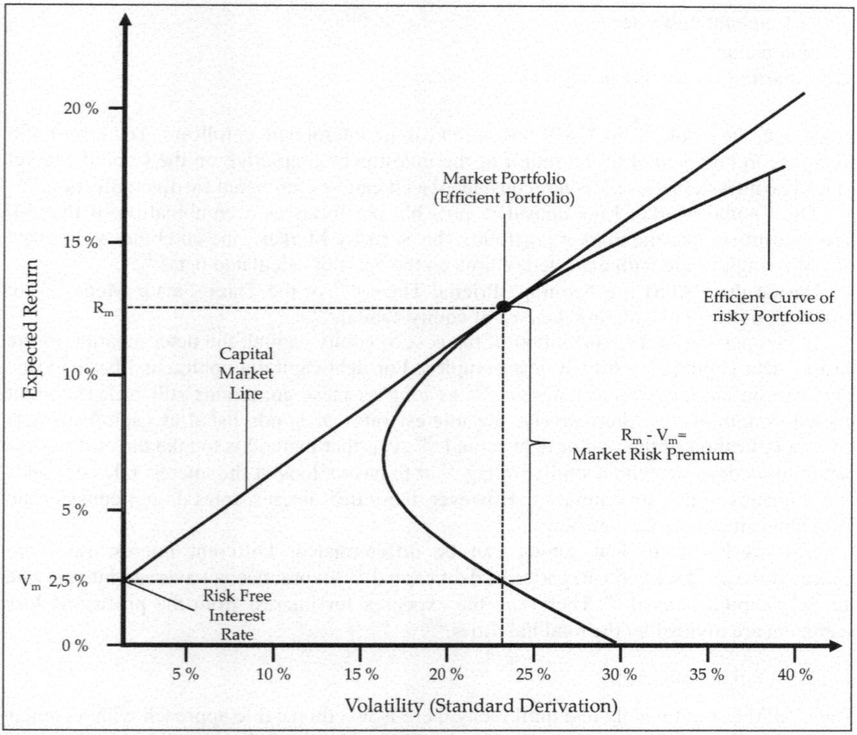

Source: In the style of: Berk, J., deMarzo, P. (2011), p. 407

Illustration 4: Capital Market Line and Market Risk Premium

Formula two shows the calculation of the cost of equity capital according to the CAPM. The difference between the return of the market portfolio and the risk free interest rate is named as the market risk premium.[195] The cost of equity capital is the expected market risk premium reduced by the risk free interest rate and multiplied by the beta factor which expresses the company's individual risk.[196]

$$r_{EC} = r_f + \beta \times (r_m - r_f)$$

Source: Formula taken from: Brealey, R. A., Myers, S. C., Allen, F. (2011), p. 245

Formula 2: Formula of Capital Asset Pricing Model

with

r_{EC} = cost of equity capital / expected stock return

195 Cf. Fama, E. F., French, K. R. (2002), p. 637.

196 Cf. Becker, H. P. (2016), p. 93.

r_f = risk free interest rate
β = beta factor
r_m = return of the market portfolio

In the end, the result of the CAPM equation can be interpreted as follows: The return of a share has to correspond to the return of the investment alternative on the Capital Market Line. The unsystematic risk is not considered as it can be eliminated by diversification.[197]

The Capital Market Line considers possible portfolios as a combination of the risk free investment and the market portfolio. The Security Market Line combines volatility / risk of a single share with expected returns on the basis of calculated betas.[198]

Beside the CAPM the Arbitrage Pricing Theory[199] or the Three Factor Model[200] are further options for calculating the cost of equity capital.[201]

In comparison to the calculation of the cost of equity capital, the determination of the cost of debt capital is relatively less complex. For debt capital a contractual basis exists. This can be the basis for calculations[202] as long as these conditions still reflect current market conditions.[203] Alternatively, the interest rates of bonds listed at capital markets give an indication of the cost of debt capital.[204] A further method is to take the cost of debt capital of companies with a similar rating[205] or to have a look at the interest rates of bonds of companies of the same industry. However, these debt interest rates do not consider the individual situation of a company.[206]

Various kinds of debt capital can be differentiated. Different interest rates are allocated to the identified categories of debt capital.[207] In practice, an average interest rate for debt capital is used.[208] Therefore, the expenses for interest from the profit and loss statement are divided by the total liabilities.[209]

2.1.3.2 Critique of CAPM

The CAPM is used widely and until today there is no comparable approach with a similar acceptance.[210] Nevertheless, scientific literature has identified flaws in CAPM which can

197 Cf. Berk, J. B., DeMarzo, P. M. (2011), p. 408.
198 Cf. Berk, J. B., DeMarzo, P. M. (2011), p. 410, Spremann, K. (2008), p. 287; Weber, S. (2008), pp. 22-23.
199 Cf. basically for Arbitrage Pricing Theory Ross, S. A. (1976).
200 Cf. basically for the Three Factor Model Fama, E. F., French, K. R. (1992); Fama, E. F., French, K. R. (1993).
201 Cf. Brealey, R. A., Myers, S. C., Allen, F. (2011), pp. 227-231 for an overview of Arbitrage Pricing Theory and Three Factor Model.
202 Cf. Dillerup, R., Stoi, R. (2016), p. 205; Riedl, J. B. (2000), p. 199; Schneider, N. C. (2007), pp. 41-42.
203 Cf. Baetge, J., Niemeyer, K., Kümmel, J., et al. (2015), p. 363.
204 Cf. Reinke, J. (2010), pp. 138-139; Schacht, U., Fackler, M. (2009), p. 216.
205 Cf. Nowak, K. (2003), p. 87; Schacht, U., Fackler, M. (2009), p. 216.
206 Cf. Ernst, D., Schneider, S., Thielen, B. (2010), pp. 74-75; Riedl, J. B. (2000), pp. 200-201.
207 Cf. Ernst, D., Schneider, S., Thielen, B. (2010), p. 75.
208 Cf. Becker, H. P. (2016), p. 92; Schneider, N. C. (2007), p. 42.
209 Cf. Hoffmann, W. (2011), p. 120, Kraus, P. (2011), pp. 21-22.
210 Cf. Kraus, P. (2011), p. 21; Kreyer, F. (2009), p. 27; Schneider, N. C. (2007), p. 43.

be roughly divided into two areas. On the one hand the assumptions and on the other, the theoretical constructs of market portfolio and risk free interest rate are criticised.[211]

Many of the critique of CAPM refer to the assumptions which do not correspond to reality. Market participants do not have homogenous expectations and market frictions like taxes exist.[212] The assumption of the CAPM that it refers to one period is a further deviation from realistic investment periods. However, CAPM is used for discounting Cash Flows of several periods which clearly contradicts the theoretical assumptions on which the CAPM is based.[213]

But apart from the assumptions the calculation offers discretion. It is an open question which measure should be used in practice for determining the riskless interest rate.[214] The risk free interest rate is a theoretical measure which does not exist in reality. Therefore, a substitute has to be found. Regularly the interest rates of long-term government bonds are used.[215] A problem is that the risk free investment alternative and the company actually must have the same time period for defining an adequate interest rate. Typically DCF calculation assumes an indefinite time period whereas government bonds have a limited time period.[216]

Also problematic is the collocation of the market portfolio which comprises in theory all possible investment possibilities. In practice, substitutes like the index to which a share belongs are taken.[217] A further problem is that the market risk premium bases on an average of past returns. The market risk premium fluctuates by changing the considered time interval so that it is difficult to derive from the theoretical model of CAPM a market risk premium in practice[218] and the return of market portfolio depends on the selected stock index. Also the values of beta factors depend on the superordinate market index so that beta factors can change by changing the market index.[219]

The cost of equity capital calculation bases on historical beta factors. It is assumed that conditions of the past remain unchanged for the future.[220] Furthermore, the calculation of beta factors requires that a company is listed at a stock exchange.[221] In practice, the calculation of beta factors for companies which are not listed at a stock market is conducted on the basis of comparable companies which are listed on stock markets.[222]

The CAPM is a single factor model. This means that the market risk, expressed by the beta factor, is the only factor which expresses the return of a share.[223] It is probable that beta does not consider all risk factors existing in the market.[224]

---

211 Cf. Brown, P., Walter, T. (2013), p. 44; Cai, C. X., Clacher, I., Keasey, K. (2013), pp. 51-52.
212 Cf. Düsterloh von, E. (2003), p. 126; Lütkeschürmer, G. (2012), p. 41.
213 Cf. Rausch, B. (2008), p. 44.
214 Cf. Sharpe, W. F. (1970), p. 420; cf. extensively for determing the risk free rate Baetge, J., Niemeyer, K., Kümmel, J., et al. (2015), pp. 376-384.
215 Cf. Düsterloh von, E. (2003), p. 124; Lütkeschürmer, G. (2012), p. 28; Seifert, U. (2006), p. 47.
216 Cf. Baetge, J., Niemeyer, K., Kümmel, J., et al. (2015), pp. 376-377.
217 Cf. Auer, M. (2007), p. 302; Brown, P., Walter, T. (2013), p. 46; Seifert, U. (2006), p. 52.
218 Cf. Drukarczyk, J., Schüler, A. (2016), p. 252; Hachmeister, D. (2009), p. 70.
219 Cf. Botosan, C. A. (2006), p. 32; Lütkeschürmer, G. (2012), p. 42.
220 Cf. Auer, M. (2007), p. 302-303.
221 Cf. Hoffmann, W. (2011), p. 121.
222 Cf. Schacht, U., Fackler, M. (2009), p. 215.
223 Cf. Seifert, U. (2006), p. 47, Spremann, K. (2008), p. 297; Weber, S. (2008), p. 23.
224 Cf. Cooper, S. (2006), p. 41.

Despite its flaws the CAPM is used widely also due to a lack of alternatives,[225] but it should be noted that by using the CAPM flaws are taken into account. The CAPM is based on unrealistic assumptions and government bonds and indexes used are substitutes for the theoretical risk free investment possibility and the market portfolio.[226]

2.2 Conflicts of Interest Between Investors and Managers

2.2.1 Classification of Principal Agent Theory and Justification of its Application

The previous chapters outline that companies act on the principles of VBM today. Therefore, the majority of companies adapt the Shareholder Value approach as one characteristic form of VBM.[227] One advantage of the Shareholder Value approach is the ability of shareholders to control managers because the increase of Shareholder Value is the common objective. This chapter has a closer look at the relationship between shareholders, respectively investors on the one side and managers on the other.[228]

The theoretical framework for analysing this relationship is the Principal Agent Theory.[229] In general, it is widely used to explain various issues in economics.[230] The Principal Agent Theory belongs to the field of New Institutional Economics which consists of the theory of economic contracts, the Property Rights Theory and the Transaction Cost Theory.[231] The Principal Agent Theory is one part of the theory of economic contracts, besides the theory of implicit contracts and the theory of relational contracts.[232]

Examples for principal-agent relationships are the relation between doctor and patient, creditor and debtor, employer and employee. One person can be principal as well as agent in different situations like the supervisory board. Towards the board of director it is principal but towards the shareholders it is the agent.[233]

On the basis of the scientific literature the Principal Agent Theory consists of two streams: The principal-agent theory and the positivist agency theory. The principal-agent theory tries to explain principal agent problems mathematically and the positivist agency

225 Cf. Lütkeschürmer, G. (2012), p. 43; Schneider, D. (2001), p. 2513.

226 Cf. Weiß, M. (2006), p. 32; cf. for an overview of typical practical application of CAPM: Matschke, M. J., Brösel, G. (2013), p. 704.

227 Cf. Bezemer, P.-J., Zajac, E. J., Naumovska, I., et al. (2014), pp. 1-2; Kraus, K., Strömsten, T. (2012), p. 188.

228 Cf. Keay, A., Adamopoulou, R. (2012), p. 8.

229 Important publications in the context of Principal Agent Theory are: Akerlof, G. A. (1970), Fama, E. F. (1980); Fama, E. F., Jensen, M. C. (1983a); Fama, E. F., Jensen, M. C. (1983b); Grossman, S. J., Hart, O. D. (1983); Holmstrom, B. (1979); Jensen, M. C. (1983); Jensen, M. C., Meckling, W. H. (1976); Ross, S. A. (1973); Shavell, S. (1979).

230 Cf. Jost, P.-J. (2001), pp. 32-34 for a general overview of areas of application for Principal Agent Theory.

231 Cf. Blum, U., Dudley, L., Leibbrand, F., et al. (2005), p. 45.

232 Cf. for an overview of the three parts of economic contract theory Richter, R., Furubotn, E. G. (2003), pp. 173-185.

233 Cf. Picot, A., Dietl, H., Franck, E., et al. (2012), pp. 89-90.

theory prefers explanations based on empirical insights.[234] The overarching objective of the theory is to find out in what way contracts have to be concluded to be efficient.[235]

There are four reasons why the Principal Agent Theory is used for explaining the relationship of managers and shareholders. Firstly, this theory is well suited for all cases when property and corporate management are divided. This applies to many companies.[236] Secondly, within the scientific literature there is a connection between Shareholder Value approach and the Principal Agent Theory. The application of Shareholder Value approach and some advantages are partly justified with insights of the Principal Agent Theory.[237] Thirdly, the underlying assumptions of the Principal Agent Theory depict the reality better than theories based on neoclassic assumptions.[238] Fourthly, the Principal Agent Theory concentrates on the relationship between individuals or homogenous groups of individuals. In order to evaluate the purpose of value based key figures and their communication to capital market participants, it is vital to characterise and analyse the relationship of the two parties investors / owners and managers. Therefore, the Principal Agent Theory seems well suited.[239]

2.2.2 *Structure of Principal Agent Relationships*

The Principal Agent Theory always considers two subjects: Principal and agent. The principal delegates a task to the agent who will accomplish it. By delegating a task to an agent, the principal hinges its welfare on the agent's action.[240] The conditions of cooperation are summarised in a contract between both parties.[241] Despite the contract principal as well as agent try to maximise their personal utility.[242] Thus, it is very probable that the agent does not always act under consideration of principal's interest. The agent can make decisions which do not maximise the principal's welfare but his own.[243]

It is obvious that conflicts of interests between both parties exist. The principal aims to maximise its utility by increasing the work effort of the agent and by minimising the remuneration. In contrast, the agent maximises its utility by reducing its work effort and by maximising his own remuneration.[244] The Principal Agent Theory tries to give advice as to how contracts, laws and rules of cooperation have to be concluded in order to reduce these conflicts of interests between principal and agent and to ensure the best possible result of cooperation.[245]

---

234 Cf. Jensen, M. C. (1983), p. 334; Mueller, F. (2011), pp. 90-92; Richter, R., Furubotn, E. G. (2003), p. 176.
235 Cf. Käfer, T. M. (2006), p. 62.
236 Cf. Paulitschek, P. (2009), pp. 21-22.
237 Cf. Elgharbawy, A., Abdel-Kader, M. (2013), p. 104; Klein, J. (2008), pp. 28-32; Ryan, H. E., Trahan, E. A. (2007), pp. 111-112.
238 Cf. Blum, U., Dudley, L., Leibbrand, F., et al. (2005), pp. 43-44; cf. for a distinction of New Institutional Economics from the neoclassical model Söllner, A. (2008), pp. 32-37.
239 Cf. Richter, R., Furubotn, E. G. (2003), pp. 177-180.
240 Cf. Ross, S. A. (1973), p. 134; Urban, M. P. (2015), pp. 15-16; Wendt, S. (2011), p. 30.
241 Cf. Alparslan, A. (2006), p. 13.
242 Cf. Kleinschmidt, M. (2007), p. 44; Ross, S. A. (1973), p. 134.
243 Cf. Busse, D. (2012), p. 91; Elschen, R. (1991), p. 1004.
244 Cf. Jost, P.-J. (2001), pp. 16-17.
245 Cf. Janocha, M. (2014), p. 57.

Generally, the Institutional Economics base on different assumptions in contrast to the neoclassical market model.[246] The Principal Agent Theory implies asymmetric information between principal and agent. The consequence is that gaining information has a certain price which has to be paid.[247] The consequence for the principal is that he cannot evaluate completely if the task's fulfilment depends on exogenous influences or on the agent's work effort.[248] Contracts which are concluded between principal and agent are basically complete contracts. This means that the contracts cover all possible scenarios and problems. In case of breach of contract both parties can assert their claims in court. Renegotiations are not possible and necessary.[249] Both, principal and agent, act under the premise of bounded rationality[250] and behave opportunistically.[251] They can differ in their risk attitude. In general, the principal is risk neutral and the agent risk averse.[252] Due to different risk attitudes principal and agent can decide for different actions.[253]

New Institutional Economics and neoclassic theory have partly the same assumptions. Both are based on the assumption of methodological individualism. This means that the behaviour of societies or groups is always based on and is influenced by, the behaviour of individuals. Furthermore, both assume that individuals try to maximise their utility.[254] In the light of Principal Agent Theory also companies are an organisation which consists of several contracts between all involved individuals.[255] Therefore, the objective of analysis is always the single principal-agent relationship.[256]

Due to information asymmetries agency costs appear. They can be separated into three parts:[257] Monitoring expenditures by the principal, bonding expenditures by the agent and residual loss.[258] Monitoring expenditures of the principal comprises all costs which the principal must expend in order to control the agent's action.[259] Bonding expenditures describes the costs the agent expends in order to convince the principal of its quality and to gain his trust.[260] Despite monitoring and agent's bonding a loss of welfare remains due to information asymmetry. This is the residual loss.[261]

246 Cf. Heim, F.-B. (2015), p. 59.
247 Cf. Eisenhardt, K. M. (1989), p. 59; Richter, R., Furubotn, E. G. (2003), pp. 237-239.
248 Cf. Scholz, A. (2008), p. 19.
249 Cf. Richter, R., Furubotn, E. G. (2003), pp. 237-239.
250 Cf. Richter, R., Furubotn, E. G. (2003), pp. 237-239; Urban, M. P. (2015), p. 18.
251 Cf. Müller, M. (2006), p. 83.
252 Cf. Käfer, T. M. (2006), pp. 62-63; Mueller, F. (2011), p. 92.
253 Cf. Eisenhardt, K. M. (1989), p. 58.
254 Cf. Söllner, A. (2008), pp. 35-36.
255 Cf. Jensen, M. C. (1983), p. 327; Jensen, M. C., Meckling, W. H. (1976), p. 310.
256 Cf. Jensen, M. C. (1983), p. 327.
257 Cf. Jensen, M. C., Meckling, W. H. (1976), p. 308, who originally made this division of agency costs.
258 Cf. Schenk, U. (2003), p. 75: Spremann, K. (1989), p. 22.
259 Cf. Kleinschmidt, M. (2007), p. 45; Richartz, J. (2009), p. 72.
260 Cf. Schachtner, D. (2002), p. 38; Scholz, A. (2008), p. 64.
261 Cf. Schachtner, D. (2002), p. 38; Scholz, A. (2008), p. 64.

2.2.3 Kinds of Information Asymmetries and Resulting Information Problems

2.2.3.1 Hidden Characteristics and Adverse Selection

On the basis of the structure of principal-agent relationships principals have the difficulty to choose the best possible agent for a task. Therefore, principals need to know the agent's attributes before offering and concluding a contract. But due to information asymmetries only the agent itself knows exactly his attributes before contract closing.[262] The principal can completely evaluate the agent's characteristic only after contract closing. This kind of information asymmetry is Hidden Characteristics.[263]

By offering an average contract to agents and without the possibility to differentiate between good and bad agents, it is possible that bad agents imitate characteristics and attributes of good agents and delude the principal.[264] In reverse, good agents do not consider the average offer of the principal because the incentives to accept it are too low.[265] Then the principal chooses a bad agent he actually would not have chosen.[266] Consequently, the information asymmetry concerning the agent's characteristic can lead to selection of bad agents. This agency problem is named adverse selection.[267]

Possible solutions in order to avoid respectively reducing the agency problem of adverse selection are signalling, screening and self-selection.[268] Signalling means that the agent demonstrates the principal that he has the necessary characteristics and attributes to complete the principal's task to his satisfaction.[269] Sending signals causes costs for the agent. For good agents the costs of a reliable signal are lower than the resulting advantages. For bad agents the costs of a reliable signal exceed their advantages, so they are not willing to produce such a signal. If these requirements are not fulfilled, signals would not make any sense because every agent can produce them.[270] Signals enable and facilitate principals the selection of appropriate agents.[271]

In case of screening the principal tries to collect as much information about the agent's characteristics as possible.[272] Self-Selection implies that the principal offers different kind of contracts to an agent. On the basis of the agent's selection he is able to assess the agent's quality.[273]

262 Cf. Deckow, F. (2006), p. 26; Schneider, K. (2011), p. 73.

263 Cf. Klein, J. (2008), p. 30; in scientific literature the terms for information asymmetries and agency problems are not defined in a uniform way (cf. Alparslan, A. (2006), p. 20; Berger, S. (2012), p. 113; cf. for different definitions exemplary Arrow, K. J. (1986), p. 1184; Jost, P.-J. (2001), p. 25; Picot, A., Dietl, H., Franck, E., et al. (2012), p. 95; Spremann, K. (1990), pp. 564-572. Within the scope of this dissertation the definition of information asymmetries according to Jost, P.-J. (2001) is applied.

264 Cf. Derenthal, K. (2009), p. 56; Piehler, M. (2007), p. 13.

265 Cf. Grimpe, C. (2005), p. 135.

266 Cf. Dahlhaus, C. (2009), p. 83.

267 Cf. Hehn, M. (2011), p. 71; Pleier, N. (2008), p. 104; cf. Akerlof, G. A. (1970) for an example of adverse selection.

268 Cf. Piehler, M. (2007), p.13-14; Schenk, U. (2003), pp. 69-70.

269 Cf. Picot, A., Dietl, H., Franck, E., et al. (2012), p. 96.

270 Cf. Mankiw, N. G., Taylor, M. P. (2012), p. 577, Wendt, S. (2011), pp. 29-30.

271 Cf. Ostrowski, O. (2007), pp. 87-88.

272 Cf. Piehler, M. (2007), p. 13.

273 Cf. Spremann, K. (1989), p. 30; Grichnik, D. (2000), p. 198.

2.2.3.2 Hidden Action and Hidden Information

After contract closing two kinds of information asymmetry can occur: Hidden Action and Hidden Information.[274] Hidden Action describes the information asymmetry that the principal cannot completely control and monitor the agent's action after the contract closing.[275] The consequence is that the principal cannot associate the agent's work effort and the work result because external factors can influence the result.[276]

Hidden Information defines information asymmetries when it is possible for the principal to control and monitor the agent's action but he is not able to evaluate it.[277] Hidden Information emerges if the principal has only a limited knowledge about the necessary actions for task fulfilment.[278]

Due to these information asymmetries the agent can act opportunistically despite the contract. The resulting agency problem is Moral Hazard.[279] Examples for Moral Hazard are the usage of enterprise resources for private purposes ("consumption on the job"), reduced work effort ("shirking")[280] or the enlargement of the company despite negative rates of returns ("empire building").[281]

Possible solutions for the agency problem of Moral Hazard are incentive systems,[282] information systems[283] and monitoring.[284] The principal initiates monitoring activities. Besides controlling the result, he is able to make additional observations during the agent's task execution.[285] He introduces systems which enable him to monitor the agent's action and behaviour.[286] Nevertheless, the principal cannot completely monitor the agent because this would be too costly for him.[287]

Apart from monitoring the agent, the principal can reduce information asymmetries by implementing information systems. These systems enable him to assess the influence of external factors on the agent's work result. Then he assesses the agent's work effort.[288] Every kind of information monitored contributes to a better contract between principal and agent.[289]

Further possibilities to reduce Moral Hazard are incentives or sanctions which can be tied only to the result. A connection between incentives / sanctions and the agent's behaviour is not possible due to Hidden Action as information asymmetries. Incentive systems lead to an alignment of principal's and agent's interest.[290] If the agent is restricted

274 Cf. Baumann, S. (2008), p. 86.
275 Cf. Hehn, M. (2011), p. 71.
276 Cf. Elschen, R. (1991), p. 1005; Jost, P.-J. (2001), pp. 25-27.
277 Cf. Hehn, M. (2011), p. 71; Scheer, L. (2008), p. 80.
278 Cf. Derenthal, K. (2009), pp. 56-57; Scheer, L. (2008), p.80.
279 Cf. Baumann, S. (2008), p. 86; Wendt, S. (2011), p. 32.
280 Cf. Bültel, N. (2011), p. 104; Greiling, D. (2009), p. 348.
281 Cf. Endres, K. (2007), pp. 58-59.
282 Cf. Endres, K. (2007), pp. 58-59.
283 Cf. Alparslan, A. (2006), p. 34.
284 Cf. Endres, K. (2007), pp. 85-86.
285 Cf. Arrow, K. J. (1986), p. 1190; Paulitschek, P. (2009), pp. 38-39.
286 Cf. Greiling, D. (2009), p. 348.
287 Cf. Holmstrom, B. (1979), p. 74.
288 Cf. Alparslan, A. (2006), p. 34.
289 Cf. Grossman, S. J., Hart, O. D. (1983), pp. 42-43; Holmstrom, B. (1979), p. 89.
290 Cf. Wendt, S. (2011), p. 34.

in his action by contract, these measures are summarised with the term bonding activeties.[291]

2.2.4 Relationship Between Investors and Managers on the Basis of the Principal Agent Theory

2.2.4.1 The Model of Jensen and Meckling

Under the heading of Principal Agent Theory many theories and models are summarized. The model of Jensen and Meckling has been selected as it illustrates the problems of separation of ownership and control demonstratively.[292] Concerning the behaviour of managers, Jensen and Meckling show the consequences if ownership and control of a company are separated.[293]

The most important model assumptions are: All tax-rates are zero, outside equity shares are non-voting shares, no other financial instruments apart from shares are available and that there is a single manager for the company with a fixed wage.[294]

Assuming that a manager owns the complete equity capital of a company, he takes decisions which will maximise his utility. He can receive utility in two different ways for his work effort. Either he earns pecuniary returns or he gets non-pecuniary returns e.g. in form of better furniture for his office or the respect of his employees. A trade-off between these two utility functions exists. If the manager increases the consumption of non-pecuniary returns, the pecuniary returns will decrease and vice versa. The manager chooses the combination of both utility functions that offers him the highest possible utility.[295]

In a first step the manager starts to sell 5 % of his equity capital to outside shareholders. His behaviour concerning utility maximisation is now changing as he only has to bear a part of the costs of his non-pecuniary benefits.[296] As he strives to maximise his utility he has to adapt the combination of utility functions by consuming more non-pecuniary benefits and less pecuniary ones.[297] This behaviour has the advantage for the manager that he can reduce his work effort for the company due to the fact that the incentive in form of pecuniary benefits has decreased simultaneously with his sold equity capital.[298]

291 Cf. Piehler, M. (2007), p. 14.

292 Cf. Alparslan, A. (2006), p. 4 who also focuses on selected models of Principal Agent Theory in order to illustrate resulting problems; cf. Kräkel, M. (2015), pp. 271-283 who gives an overview of further models which illustrate the problem between managers and shareholders.

293 The following explanations and examples base on the model of Jensen and Meckling, cf Jensen, M. C., Meckling, W. H. (1976). Beside the agency problems between shareholders and managers the Agency Theory deals also with agency problems of debt capital which are not further considered in the context of this dissertation, cf. Ewert, R. (1989), pp. 285-289; Jensen, M. C., Meckling, W. H. (1976), pp. 333-343.

294 Cf. for detailed list of model assumption Jensen, M. C., Meckling, W. H. (1976), p. 314.

295 Cf. Jensen, M. C., Meckling, W. H. (1976), p. 312; Lazar, C. (2007), p. 41.

296 Cf. Hermanns, J. (2006), p. 43.

297 Cf. Jensen, M. C., Meckling, W. H. (1976), p. 312.

298 Cf. Hermanns, J. (2006), p. 44.

The trade-off between company value and private consumption is illustrated graphically in illustration five. The ordinate measures the market value of the company and the abscissa measures the expenditure of the manager on non-pecuniary benefits. The line from point V on the ordinate to point F on the abscissa represents the manager's utility possibilities, similar to a budget restriction. Point $\bar{V}$ symbolizes the point at which he completely concentrates his work effort on the increase of market value of the company, thus on increasing its pecuniary benefits. Consequently, the highest company value is reached at this point. Moving along the line to point $\bar{F}$ implies that he gives up parts of pecuniary benefits in favour of non-pecuniary benefits. Arriving at point $\bar{F}$ means a total concentration of manager's utility on non-pecuniary benefits. The slope of the line is -1. One currency unit which the manager uses for non-pecuniary benefits reduces the market value of the company by one currency unit. The manager's tendency is represented by the utility curves U_1, U_2 etc. The point at which the manager reaches, under given conditions, maximum utility is where indifference curve U_2 is tangent to line $\overline{VF}$. V^* is the market value of the company, F^* the costs of consumed non-pecuniary benefits. This implies that a potential buyer is willing to pay price V^* for the company, presumed that the new owner can force the old owner and manager to retain its current consumption F^* of non-pecuniary benefits.[299]

In a second step the old owner sells a share of its equity capital, $1 - \alpha$. The manager's share is α. On condition that consumption of F^* remains constant the new owner pays a price in the amount of $(1 - \alpha) \times V^*$. Of course the assumption that the new owner can force the old owner and manager to limit its consumption of non-pecuniary benefits is not realistic. The consequence of the reduction of shares in equity capital for the manager is that he no longer has to pay one currency unit per consumed unit of non-pecuniary benefit, but only $\alpha \times 1$ currency unit. The line $\overline{VF}$ shifts to V_1F_1. This line has a slope of $-\alpha$. The line V_1F_1 also has an intersection point with line $\overline{VF}$ in point D because the manager still has the consumption possibility he had as the only owner before. But the manager wants to maximize his utility, so he chooses point A. He increases its consumption of non-pecuniary benefits at the expense of the company value which falls to point V_0. The difference between V^* and V_0 represents the cost of the additional consumption of the manager.[300]

Provided that market participants act on rational expectations, a buyer is not willing to pay $(1 - \alpha) \times V^*$ for the equity capital of the company. He is aware of the fact that the manager increases his consumption of non-pecuniary benefits while selling shares of equity capital. So, he includes this fact in his price calculation.[301]

299 Cf. Jensen, M. C., Meckling, W. H. (1976), pp. 315-317; Lazar, C. (2007), pp. 40-41.
300 Cf. Jensen, M. C., Meckling, W. H. (1976), pp. 317-318.
301 Cf. Jensen, M. C., Meckling, W. H. (1976), p. 318.

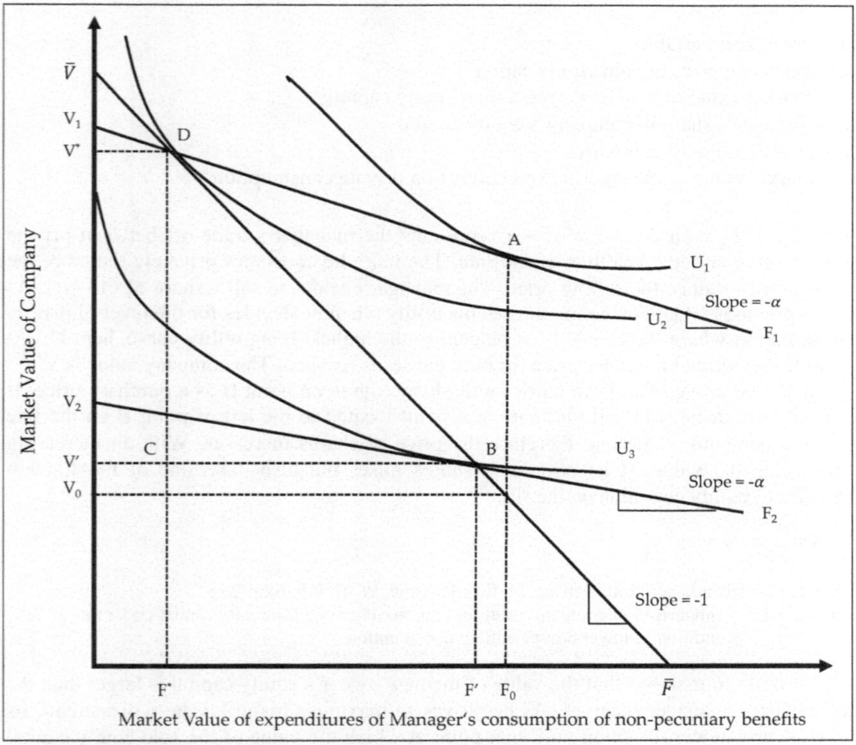

Source: Adapted from: Jensen, M. C., Meckling, W. H. (1976), p. 316

Illustration 5: Development of market value of company and manager's expenditures for private consumption

The wealth of the manager consists of two parts: The first part is the payment he receives from the new buyer for his sold share of equity capital (S_0). The second part is the value of his remaining equity capital (S_i). This value can also be expressed as a function of its fractional ownership (α) and the level of consumption of non-pecuniary benefits (F).[302]

$$W = S_0 + S_i = S_0 + \alpha \times V(F, \propto)$$

Source: Formula adapted from: Jensen, M. C., Meckling, W. H. (1976), p. 318

Formula 3: Composition of manager's wealth

302 Cf. Jensen, M. C., Meckling, W. H. (1976), p. 318.

with
W = manager's wealth
S_0 = purchase price of sold equity capital
S_i = market value of manager's remaining equity capital
α = manager's share in company's equity capital
V = market value of company
F = market value of manager's expenditures on private consumption

The line V_2F_2 with the slope of $-\alpha$ represents the manager's trade-off between private consumption and his wealth after the sale. The more he consumes privately the more the investor will reduce the selling price. The manager decides to sell a share of $(1-\alpha)$. As in the previous situations he maximises his utility when he decides for the level of private consumption where the line V_2F_2 is tangent to the highest lying utility curve, here U_3. At point B the optimal purchase price for both parties is reached. The company value is V'.[303]

It can be proved that both parties will always agree on point B as a purchase price. If the manager decides to sell his share at a point located to the left of point B on the line $\overline{VF}$, the company value and therefore the price of shares increases. With an increasing firm value the value of its remaining shares raises but also the value of the fraction $(1-\alpha)$ of equity capital is on the rise.[304]

$$(1-\ \alpha) \times V' > S_0$$

Source: Formula adapted from: Jensen, M. C., Meckling, W. H. (1976), p. 318
Formula 4: Comparison of company value and purchasing price for equity capital under the condition of lower non-pecuniary consumption

Formula four shows that the value of the new owner's equity capital is larger than the payment the manager receives. As he strives to maximise his utility he will increase its level of private consumption until that point at which the value of the sold equity capital equals its received payment.[305]

If the manager decides to sell his share at a point located to the right of point B on the line $\overline{VF}$, the company value decreases due to the increased consumption of non-pecuniary benefits. The new owner has paid too much for its shares.[306]

$$(1-\ \alpha) \times V(F,\alpha) < S_0 = (1-\ \alpha) \times\ V'$$

Source: Formula adapted from: Jensen, M. C., Meckling, W. H. (1976), p. 318
Formula 5: Comparison of company value and purchasing price for equity capital under the condition of higher non-pecuniary consumption

Both parties will only accept the purchase price S_0, if it represents the current value of the company $(1-\ \alpha) \times\ V'$.

303 Cf. Jensen, M. C., Meckling, W. H. (1976), p. 318.
304 Cf. Jensen, M. C., Meckling, W. H. (1976), pp. 318.
305 Cf. Jensen, M. C., Meckling, W. H. (1976), p. 318.
306 Cf. Jensen, M. C., Meckling, W. H. (1976), p. 318.

Referring to formula three the manager's wealth after the sale of equity capital corresponds to the reduced market value of the company.[307]

$$W = S_0 + \alpha \times V' = (1 - \alpha) \times V' + \alpha \times V' = V'$$

Source: Formula adapted from: Jensen, M. C., Meckling, W. H. (1976), p. 319
Formula 6: Manager's wealth after sale of equity capital

Considering this fact means simultaneously that the reduction of company value does only impact the manager. His wealth is reduced by the difference between V^* and V'. These costs are agency costs in the form of a residual loss. The loss concerning the company value is partly compensated by the increase of private consumption from F* to F'. The triangle, limited by the points D, B and C, represents the loss in welfare due to agency costs for the manager.[308]

The explanations of Jensen and Meckling prove the existence of agency conflicts and agency costs in companies where ownership and management are separated.[309]

The structure of separated ownership and control is a feature of publicly-listed companies which are in the focus of this dissertation. Therefore, it is assumed in the following that agency conflicts between management and shareholders respectively potential investors exist.[310] These insights of agency theory are confirmed by empirical studies.[311]

Of course there are also agency conflicts between management and other stakeholders. But in contrast to equity capital providers these stakeholder claims are based on contracts and are therefore better protected. Equity capital providers only have residual claims after the satisfaction of the claims of all other stakeholder groups.[312]

2.2.4.2 Accounting and Reporting of Key Figures as Important Tools for Reducing Information Asymmetries

Jensen and Meckling demonstrate that the insights of the Principal Agent Theory can be transferred to the relationship between shareholders and management.[313] Shareholders take the role of principal and managers the role of agents.[314] Shareholders are not able to observe in detail if managers make appropriate decisions.[315] In addition, the ownership structure of large cooperations is regularly widespread and investors have investments in

307 Cf. Jensen, M. C., Meckling, W. H. (1976), pp. 318-319.
308 Cf. Jensen, M. C., Meckling, W. H. (1976), p. 319; Lazar, C. (2007), pp. 42-44.
309 Cf. for similar conclusion Kräkel, M. (2015), p. 279; Paulitschek, P. (2009), p. 48.
310 Cf. Geiersbach, K. (2011), p. 30; Teall, J. L. (2007), p. 7.
311 Cf. for a short overview of empirical studies, Thomsen, S., Pedersen, T. (2000), p. 689.
312 Cf. Borowicz, F. (2006), pp. 6-7.
313 Cf. Franco-Santos, M., Lucianetti, L., Bourne, M. (2012), pp. 97-98 for a short overview of articles dealing with Principal Agent Theory in the context of performance measurement systems.
314 Cf. Elschen, R. (1991), pp. 1010-1011; Fama, E. F., Jensen, M. C. (1983a), pp. 331-332; Pfeiffer, G. M., Shields, T. W. (2015), pp. 779-780; Wang, C. (1997), pp. 72-73; Bernheim, D., Whinston, M. D. (1986), p. 924 classify the relationship between shareholder and management as a typical principal agent relationship and not as a case of common agency.
315 Cf. Arrow, K. J. (1986), pp. 1184-1185.

several firms so that their focus and attention is dispersed.[316] Thus, it is probable that managers as risk-averse agents do not always act in the interest of shareholders.[317]

The interest of shareholders is that the value of their investment increases, thus they strive for an increase of Shareholder Value. The managers on the other side are not shareholders of the company or only have a small amount of shares. As illustrated with the help of Jensen's and Meckling's model managers have other possibilities to maximise their utility.[318] Examples are name recognition, higher prestige, reduced work effort or higher income.[319]

This conflict of interests cannot completely be solved by concluding contracts because not every action of the agent is observable and there exists several alternative actions for each issue. The relationship between manager and shareholder is based on implicit contracts.[320]

The information asymmetries and the behaviour of managers also depend on the structure of ownership. In many companies the ownership is dispersed so that many people own small amounts of shares. In these cases it is difficult to control managers' behaviour. But in some companies large shareholders exist who have the possibility to control the management more strictly and limit agency problems.[321]

The existing information asymmetries between shareholders and managers lead to agency problems. While making investment decisions, information asymmetries, i.e. investors do not exactly know the company's current performance, need to be considered.[322] Investors assume an average quality of company's performance before the concrete investment process. The adverse selection can induce good performing companies to leave the market. But good companies and investors have the possibility to reduce information asymmetries in the form of Hidden Characteristics with the help of signalling, self-selection and screening.[323] Capital providers have, before an investment decision, the problem that managers of a company distort the economic performance in order to negotiate better conditions.[324]

Signalling can comprise that a company achieves certain values of selected key figures.[325] But independently if a key figure conveys good or bad news, managers have an incentive to release them as early as possible to investors. The release of key figure's forecasts shows investors that a manager is aware of changes in a company's environment and can adapt the company to the new circumstances.[326] Also the structure of corporate finance,[327] the usage of disclosure options and the application of certain valuation methods

316 Cf. Fama, E. F. (1980), p. 293, 295.
317 Cf. Ewert, R. (1989), pp. 284-285; Shavell, S. (1979), p. 66.
318 Cf. Picot, A., Dietl, H., Franck, E., et al. (2012), pp. 330-333; Skrzipek, M. (2005), pp. 13-14.
319 Cf. Picot, A., Dietl, H., Franck, E., et al. (2012), p. 331.
320 Cf. Torabian, F. (2010), p. 40.
321 Cf. Brealey, R. A., Myers, S. C., Allen, F. (2011), pp. 902-903.
322 Cf. Breuer, W. (2013), pp. 157-158.
323 Cf. Bizenberger, R. (2008), pp. 101-102.
324 Cf. Torabian, F. (2010), pp. 40-41.
325 Cf. Breuer, W. (2013), pp. 165-166.
326 Cf. Truemann, B. (1986), pp. 53-55, 70-71.
327 Cf. Breuer, W. (2013), pp. 165-166.

in accounting can have signalling effect for investors.[328] In this context it is important that the company builds up a kind of trust with investors in order to demonstrate that the signals are reliable.[329] Self-Selection means in this case that the company offers various possibilities of investment.[330] Screening implies that the investor starts to collect necessary information which he needs for the investment decision on his own.[331]

After investing in a company, the investor faces the information asymmetries of Hidden Information as well as Hidden Action[332] and the resulting agency problem of Moral Hazard.[333] Hidden Information means that the shareholders are not able to evaluate the management's decision.[334] Hidden Action in this context means: The shareholders see the result of board of directors' decisions but they cannot evaluate completely if the higher profit bases e.g. on the new company strategy or if other factors influence the result.[335] On the basis of the theoretical analysis above two possible solutions exist for this problem: Monitoring and incentive systems.[336]

The company's accounting plays an important role in this context as it is the primary instrument for monitoring the managers' activities.[337] Complete control is not possible as not all kinds of information are disclosed within the framework of the company's reporting activities. Nevertheless, the annual reports are an important instrument of control. For shareholders the balance sheet profit is important as it is the basis for dividend payments and therefore an important part of their return.[338] Furthermore, capital providers use the public information of a company, in order to estimate the future development of a company.[339]

The legal accounting rules make an individual negotiation between principal and agent redundant. From the principal's point of view this is positive because a certain amount of information he receives from the agent is legally fixed. Nevertheless, the agent still has some scope of discretion.[340] In order to control if accounting standards are fulfilled, companies are regularly audited which can also be assessed as a kind of monitoring.[341]

Further measures companies may adopt to inform shareholders and investors about the company's performance are summarised under the topic of Investor Relations. With the help of Investor Relations companies can reduce their cost of capital and ceteris paribus increase the Shareholder Value. The investors reduce the cost for their capital because more information about the company is available and this reduces their investment risk.

---

328 Cf. Scott, W. R. (2012), pp. 475-476; Wagenhofer, A., Ewert, R. (2015), p. 334; cf. for a detailed description of a signalling model in accounting Wagenhofer, A., Ewert, R. (2015), pp. 323-334.
329 Cf. Breuer, W. (2013), pp. 165-166.
330 Cf. Bizenberger, R. (2008), p. 102.
331 Cf. Bizenberger, R. (2008), p. 102.
332 Cf. Huchzermeier, M. (2006), pp. 22-23.
333 Cf. Arrow, K. J. (1986), p. 1184.
334 Cf. Arrow, K. J. (1986), pp. 1184-1185.
335 Cf. Grossman, S. J., Hart, O. D. (1983), p. 10; Picot, A., Dietl, H., Franck, E., et al. (2012), p. 93.
336 Cf. Torabian, F. (2010), pp. 39-43.
337 Cf. Schaier, S. (2008), pp. 127-128.
338 Cf. Müller, M. (2006), pp. 88-89.
339 Cf. Gjesdal, F. (1981), pp. 208-209; Torabian, F. (2010), pp. 37-38.
340 Cf. Schenk, U. (2003), pp. 92-93; Torabian, F. (2010), pp. 43-44.
341 Cf. Beekes, W., Brown, P., Zhan, W., et al. (2016), p. 266.

Beside fiscal objectives Investor Relations measures have the objective to create trust between investors and company.[342]

Part of Investor Relations is the disclosure of additional information, e.g. the voluntary disclosure of key figures. Investors interpret this as a trustworthy signal.[343] But they have to consider that managers also can control the publication of key figures. It is likely that companies tend to publish good news earlier and withhold negative developments[344] or even manipulate key figures.[345] For example, a company discloses Cash Flow forecasts if there is a large increase in its Cash Flows and when earnings develop negatively.[346]

Key figures cannot only be used in the context of external accounting and for communication with capital providers but also for internal control systems. In this context the supervisory board monitors the board of directors with the help of internal control systems which contain selected key figures. These activities are monitoring activities and reduce the manager's Moral Hazard.[347]

Managers take the role of the agent relative to shareholders. Company-internal they are principals and control the subordinated managers.[348] In this context they are also confronted with agency problems. For control and monitoring purposes they regularly use an internal control system, too. It is important that internal control key figures correspond to the development of external key figures which are important for shareholders. Otherwise the company will not reach external return objectives.[349]

In order to decrease the agent's discretionary scope of action within the context of information transmission, the integration of external and internal accounting is preferred. If shareholders and management have the same information available, information asymmetries between both parties are reduced. The management has to show on the basis of which key figures the company is steered and controlled.[350]

In addition to external accounting and internal control system, managers of large corporations, which are listed at the stock market, experience the use of another kind of monitoring: The company's current stock price. The development of the stock price induces managers to act in the interest of shareholders.[351]

Furthermore, monitoring conflicts of interest between shareholders and managers are reduced with the help of incentive systems. The remuneration of the manager is connected with the company's profit.[352] Due to Hidden Information it is only possible to evaluate the

342 Cf. Grüning, M. (2011a), p. 51; Healy, P. M., Palepu, K. G. (2001), pp. 429-430; Kirchhoff, K. R. (2009), pp. 36-41; cf. for an overview of studies concerning the coherence between disclosure levels and cost of capital Fields, T. D., Lys, T. Z., Vincent, L. (2001), pp. 277-278. Results of empirical studies are mixed about this coherence.

343 Cf. Wasley, C. E., Wu, J. S. (2006), p. 392.

344 Cf. Scott, W. R. (2012), p. 466.

345 Cf. Jensen, M. C., Murphy, K. J. (1990), p. 246.

346 Cf. Wasley, C. E., Wu, J. S. (2006), pp. 390-391.

347 Cf. Picot, A., Dietl, H., Franck, E., et al. (2012), p. 98.

348 Cf. Ostrowski, O. (2007), pp. 88-90.

349 Cf. Müller, M. (2006), pp. 89-92.

350 Cf. Kahle, H. (2003), pp. 774-776; Schaier, S. (2007), pp. 121-123; Schaier, S. (2008), pp. 125-128; Schenk, U. (2003), pp. 231-232; Wohlgemuth, F. (2007), pp. 92-96.

351 Cf. Fama, E. F., Jensen, M. C. (1983b), p. 313.

352 Cf. Lambert, R. A., Larcker, D. F., Weigelt, K. (1993), p. 441; Wang, C. (1997), pp. 72-73.

manager on the basis of the result and not to evaluate its behaviour. In scientific literature there are several articles which deal with the question how to measure the company's success. In this context key figures play an important role as they are regularly the basis of assessment.[353] For an alignment of interests between agent and principal value based key figures like EVA seem well suited as they consider cost of capital in their calculation.[354] In practice, only a few firms use value based key figures for evaluating the manager's performance.[355]

Institutional investors often take a monitoring role concerning the level of salaries of management. In companies in which an institutional investor is one of the five largest investors payments to management are more aligned to performance of managers.[356] Owners with large shares have the power to force managers to increase the Shareholder Value.[357] Institutional investors additionally engage in monitoring activities in order to gain further information about the company's performance.[358]

By using appropriate key figures, shareholders can reduce the monitoring expenditures as they can evaluate the performance of management and company with the help of these key figures. Premises are that the agent has an incentive to act on the basis of a key figure, is able to influence the key figure, it cannot be manipulated by the management, is understandable and can be calculated with an acceptable effort. [359]

Control and incentives systems are complementary parts. The control system detects agent's misconduct and the incentive system has the effect that the agent acts according to the principal's interest. With the help of the control system the key figures on which the agent's remuneration is based can be determined. So, both systems refer partly to the same key figures.[360]

In total, the principal has to consider that the installation of control or incentive systems causes additional costs. The principal contrasts these costs with the reduction of agency costs and tries to find an optimum of control and monitoring and discretionary of the agent.[361]

Principals have the possibility to delegate monitoring tasks to financial intermediaries. These intermediaries undertake the monitoring of agents substitutional for agents.[362]

In general, the Principal Agent Theory leads to the conclusion that it is beneficial for a company to reduce existing information asymmetries to investors and shareholders.[363]

---

353 Cf. Jensen, M. C., Murphy, K. J. (1990), pp. 248-249; Picot, A., Dietl, H., Franck, E., et al. (2012), pp. 97-98; Wellner, K.-U. (2001), pp. 202-203.

354 Cf. Dekker, H. C., Groot, T., Schoute, M., et al. (2012), pp. 1234-1235; Gladen, W. (2014), pp. 225-230.

355 Cf. Dekker, H. C., Groot, T., Schoute, M., et al. (2012), p. 1215; Bouwens, J., Lent, L. von (2007), p. 681-683; Stark, A. W., Thomas, H. M. (1998), p. 446.

356 Cf. Janakiraman, S., Radhakrishnan, S., Tsang, A. (2010), pp. 673-676; cf. Almazan, A., Hartzell, J., Starks, L. T. (2005) and Hartzell, J., Starks, L. T. (2003), who detect similar effects of institutional ownership on management salaries.

357 Cf. Cornett, M. M., Marcus, A. J., Saunders, A., et al. (2007), p. 1792; Thomsen, S., Pedersen, T. (2000), pp. 691-692.

358 Cf. Chen, X., Harford, J., Li, K. (2007), pp. 303-304.

359 Cf. Siefke, M. (1999), pp. 51-54.

360 Cf. Dahlhaus, C. (2009), pp. 92-93.

361 Cf. Dahlhaus, C. (2009), p. 92.

362 Cf. Bizenberger, R. (2008), pp. 103-105; Healy, P. M., Palepu, K. G. (2001), pp. 407-410.

363 Cf. Leven, F.-J. (1998), pp. 46-47.

Two components play an important role in this context: Legally fixed accounting[364] and key figures. They take a decisive part as they are a solution to reduce agency problems before and after contract closing. They are used in the context of monitoring[365] and are also part of incentive and control systems.[366] These tools help to control the opportunistic behaviour of agents. Table 1 contains a summary of the insights gained on the basis of the Principal Agent Theory.[367]

Table 1: Kind of information asymmetries between investors and managers, resulting agency problems and possible solutions[368]

Point of Principal Agent Relationship	**Before contract closing**	**After contract closing, before action decision**	**After contract closing, after action decision**
Type of Information Asymmetry	Hidden Characteristic	Hidden Information	Hidden Action
Reasons for Information Asymmetry	Investors cannot exactly and completely evaluate the performance of a company	Investors are not able to evaluate the quality of manager's decisions	Investors see the result of manager's decisions but they do not know the work effort of managers and the influence of external factors
Agency Problems	Adverse Selection	Moral Hazard	
Solutions	**Signalling** Publication of additional information, company achieves values of selected key figures	**Monitoring** Accounting is the primary instrument of investors, often additional information is available due to Investor Relations, monitoring of key figures and stock price development by investors	
	Self-Selection Company offers various investment alternatives	**Incentive Systems** Remuneration of manager is connected with key figures which reflect the investors' interests	
	Screening Investors collect necessary information for investment decision on their own	**Control Systems** Supervisory Board controls the manager's performance with the help of key figures, Managers themselves control the performance of subordinate mangers with key figures	
	Trust		
	Reputation		

In the style of: Dahlhaus, C. (2009), p.82; Klein, J. (2008), p. 30; Torabian, F. (2010), p. 43

364 Cf. Gjesdal, F. (1981), pp. 208-211; Schenk, U. (2003), p. 92; Scott, W. R. (2012), pp. 124-127; Skrzipek, M. (2005), p. 13.

365 Cf. Breuer, W. (2013), pp. 165-166; Labbé, M., Schädlich, F. (2008), pp. 329-331;Schenk, U. (2003), p. 92.

366 Cf. Picot, A., Dietl, H., Franck, E., et al. (2012), p. 98; Reichelstein, S. (2000), pp. 243-245; Wellner, K.-U. (2001), pp. 202-203.

367 Cf. Eisenhardt, K. M. (1989), pp. 64-65.

368 In some publications the Hidden Intention as information asymmetry and the Hold Up as resulting agency problems are additionally considered, cf. exemplary Picot, A., Dietl, H., Franck, E., et al. (2012), p. 93-95. In this dissertation this aspect is not further considered.

Of course, key figures in the context of control and incentive systems are not the only option to discipline managers. In total, their discretionary scope of action is limited by e.g. board of directors, the shareholders' meeting, the competition on goods market, their reputation on the labour market, the control of annual accounts by an auditor and the threat of a company take-over.[369]

2.2.5 *Effects of Information Asymmetries on Cost of Capital*

Between investors and managers information asymmetries exist.[370] The processing of information at capital markets and the information asymmetries probably have an influence on the capital costs which are an important part of VBM.[371] The presented theoretical approaches investigate the coherence between information asymmetry and cost of capital.[372]

The cost of equity capital consists of two components: The riskless interest rate and the firm-specific risk premium. The publishing of information influences the firm-specific risk premium. Releasing more public information through annual reports or other sources of information helps investors to estimate future cash flows more precisely and with a lower uncertainty.[373] Thus, it is assumed that cost of capital decreases with more relevant public information.[374]

The model of Merton[375] assumes that information asymmetries exist on the level of investors and not on the level of single securities.[376] Consequently, there are no information asymmetries between investors and companies.[377] One investor is not able to get information about every investment possibility, only about a subset of them. The subsets about which the investors are informed differ from investor to investor. Investors consider only shares in their portfolio about which they are fully informed and have invested the set-up costs.[378]

In the model the market capitalisation of a firm depends on the number of fully informed investors. The more investors a company has, the higher is its market capitalisation. The contrary relationship is valid for cost of capital.[379] Merton concludes that a company can increase its investor base and simultaneously decrease its cost of capital

369 Cf. Kräkel, M. (2015), pp. 287-332.
370 Cf. chapter 2.2.4.1 for the theoretic prove of existing information asymmetries between management and shareholders.
371 Cf. Easley, D., O'Hara, M. (2004), pp. 1553-1557.
372 Within scientific literature the approaches are divided into three categories: Spread approach, liquidity orientated approach and estimation risk oriented approach, cf. exemplarily Lammert, J. (2010), pp. 18-27.
373 Cf. Christensen, P. O., de la Rosa, L. E., Feltham, G. E. (2010), pp. 817-818; Dumontier, P., Raffournier, B. (2002), p. 119.
374 Cf. Christensen, P. O., de la Rosa, L. E., Feltham, G. E. (2010), pp. 817-818. More literature sources.
375 Cf. extensively Merton, R. C. (1987).
376 Cf. Labhart, P. (1999), pp. 72-74.
377 Cf. Lammert, J. (2010), p. 26.
378 Cf. Merton, R. C. (1987), p. 488.
379 Cf. Merton, R. C. (1987), p. 500.

with reporting which is also able to attract the attention of investors who have not yet invested the fixed set up costs for the receiver.[380]

In the context of Merton's model reporting takes an important role because with the help of reporting a company can send out signals to investors in order to increase their awareness of the company and to convince them to invest the set-up costs.[381]

The theoretical work stream of the liquidity approaches analyse the effect of information on capital market liquidity.[382] All models consider three parties which are involved in a transaction: A market maker, investors who are well informed and investors who trade out of liquidity reasons.[383] The market maker offers a price for which he buys the shares, the bid price and a price at which he sells shares, the ask price. After each conducted transaction the market maker adapts both prices.[384] The market maker does not know in advance if its counterparty has insider information available and trades on the basis of it or if the trading partner wants to make the deal out of liquidity reasons. By setting a spread, the market maker avoids making losses in transaction with a better informed party.[385]

The relationship between bid-ask spread and cost of capital is as follows: The higher the spread, the higher the cost of capital respectively the expected rate of return.[386] In order to decrease the cost of capital, the bid-ask spread has to be reduced. Companies can reduce the difference between bid and ask prices by a higher amount of available information.[387] Disclosure of information increases the liquidity of a share.[388] The spread declines with an increasing liquidity.[389] An increased liquidity of a security is an incentive for buying for traders who may need liquidity in the future.[390] Furthermore, a higher liquidity leads to reduced transaction costs which in turn lead to decreased cost of capital.[391] The models belonging to the liquidity approaches draw mainly two conclusions: Increased liquidity leads to reduced cost of capital[392] and reducing information asymmetry leads to reduced cost of capital.[393]

380 Cf. Merton, R. C. (1987), pp. 500-501.
381 Cf. for transferring the results from Merton's model to reporting Banzhaf, J. (2006), pp. 179-180; Fischer, A. (2003), pp. 58-59; Labhart, P. (1999), pp. 80-82.
382 The following publications can be classified to the liquidity approaches: Amihud, Y., Mendelson, H. (1986); Baiman, S., Verrecchia, R. E. (1996); Copeland, T. E., Galai, D. (1983); Diamond, D. W., Verrecchia, R. E. (1991); Glosten, L. R., Milgrom, P. (1985); Lambert, R. A., Leuz, C., Verrecchia, R. E. (2011); Lambert, R. A., Verrecchia, R. E. (2015); Leuz, C., Verrecchia, R. E. (2000); cf. for an overview of publications of liquidity approach Fischer, A. (2003), p. 55; Lammert, J. (2010), p. 21.
383 Cf. Fischer, A. (2003), pp. 51-53.
384 Cf. Glosten, L. R., Milgrom, P. (1985), p. 76.
385 Cf. Glosten, L. R., Milgrom, P. (1985), p. 72.
386 Cf. Amihud, Y., Mendelson, H. (1986), pp. 229-230.
387 Cf. Glosten, L. R., Milgrom, P. (1985), p. 74.
388 Cf. Diamond, D. W., Verrecchia, R. E. (1991), pp. 1325-1326.
389 Cf. Copeland, T. E., Galai, D. (1983), p. 1468; Glosten, L. R., Milgrom, P. (1985), pp. 97-98.
390 Cf. Baiman, S., Verrecchia, R. E. (1996), p. 17.
391 Cf. Amihud, Y., Mendelson, H. (1986), pp. 230-231, 246-247.
392 Cf. Diamond, D. W., Verrecchia, R. E. (1991), pp. 1325-1326; Lambert, R. A., Verrecchia, R. E. (2015), p. 440.
393 Cf. Diamond, D. W., Verrecchia, R. E. (1991), p. 1325.

The estimation risk approach forms the third group of theoretical approaches for explaining the coherence between information asymmetries and cost of capital.[394]

The CAPM of Sharpe, Lindner and Mossin does not consider the parameter uncertainty.[395] It assumes that a security's return and payoff distribution are certain and true but in reality it depends on the quality of information investors receive.[396] The models of the estimation risk approach assume that for every security a different amount of information is available. The results differ from CAPM's result without any parameter uncertainty.[397] Estimation risk describes the risk of the covariance structure of returns under the condition of incomplete information. The risk decreases if more information is available on a security.[398] The parameter uncertainty is not the same for every security because a different number of observations for each security is available on which the estimation is based.[399] Estimation risk is non-diversifiable.[400]

An insight of the models is that securities to which investors have a lot of information available have smaller betas in comparison to a CAPM without estimation risk. Investors demand higher returns for security with low information because they are riskier.[401] The level of estimation risk also influences the stock prices. Securities with high information have higher prices than under the condition of complete information and securities with low information have lower prices.[402]

The models show coherence between information asymmetries and cost of capital. Independent of which approach is chosen, the correlation between information asymmetries and cost of capital is the same. The less information asymmetries are observable, the lower the cost of capital. This coherence supports one of the objectives of application of value based performance measures.[403]

Despite the assumed coherences the presented models are based on special premises and assumptions which have a direct influence on the models' result.[404] Empirical studies can partly confirm the theoretical assumptions[405] but a comprehensive position in the

394 The following publications can be classified to the estimation risk approaches: Barry, C. B., Brown, S. J. (1985); Coles, J. L., Loewenstein, U. (1988); Coles, J. L., Loewenstein, U., Suay, J. (1995); Handa, P., Linn, S. C. (1993); cf. for an overview of publications of estimation risk approach Fischer, A. (2003), p. 57; Lammert, J. (2010), p. 25.

395 Cf. Coles, J. L., Loewenstein, U. (1988), p 279.

396 Cf. Botosan, C. A. (2006), p. 33.

397 Cf. Barry, C. B., Brown, S. J. (1985), p. 408.

398 Cf. Handa, P., Linn, S. C. (1993), p. 89.

399 Cf. Coles, J. L., Loewenstein, U. (1988), p. 298.

400 Cf. Botosan, C. A. (2006), p. 33.

401 Cf. Barry, C. B., Brown, S. J. (1985), p. 412.

402 Cf. Handa, P., Linn, S. C. (1993), p. 82.

403 Cf. for transferring the results from liquidity and estimation risk approach to reporting: Banzhaf, J. (2006), pp. 182-183; Fischer, A. (2003), pp. 51-59; Wenzel, J. (2005), pp. 119-121; apart from the presented studies also the model of Hughes, Liu and Liu proves a coherence between information asymmetry and cost of capital, cf. extensively Hughes, J. S., Liu, J. (2007).

404 Cf. Fischer, A. (2003), p. 59; Lammert, J. (2010), pp. 27-28.

405 Cf. exemplarily the studies of Botosan, C. A. (2006); Clinch, G. (2013); Easley, D., Hvidkjaer, S., O'Hara, M. (2002); Easley, D., O'Hara, M. (2004); Healy, P. M., Hutton, A. P., Palepu, K. G. (1999); Lambert, R. A., Leuz, C., Verrecchia, R. E. (2007); Leuz, C., Verrecchia, R. E. (2000); Schultze, W., List, T., Schabert, B., et al. (2018) which supports the negative coherence between information asymmetries and cost of capital.

scientific literature cannot be detected.[406] However, the majority of theoretical models and empirical studies support a negative coherence between cost of capital and level of disclosure. Therefore, one of the central objectives of Value Reporting can be confirmed.[407]

2.2.6 Critiques of Principal Agent Theory

Principal Agent Theory has proponents and critics. This chapter tries to concisely contrast the most important arguments of the two groups.

The assumptions and premises of a neoclassical model do not consider the complex conditions in reality,[408] so Principal Agent Theory consists of assumptions beyond neoclassical theory, for example the existence of transaction costs, information asymmetries or incentive problems. On the basis of these assumptions it is possible to deal with problems which are not part of neoclassical models.[409] Many empirical studies confirm the theoretical insights of agency theory.[410] The insights scientists gain from the theory concerning the effects of information systems, the influence of different risk attitudes and design of appropriate incentives are very fruitful.[411]

Despite the fact that Principal Agent Theory is widely used in economics, there are also some points that are seen critically in scientific literature. The transfer from theory to practice is a common problem. In general, the conclusions and suggestions made on the basis of Principal Agent Theory are very complex. Examples are the incentive systems for managers. In practice, managers still have a large discretionary scope. This is the case because the cost of specifying every complex relation and the resulting consequences in the contract between manager and company are too high. So, despite the insights of Principal Agent Theory, the attempt is made to keep contracts as simple as possible.[412]

Monitoring in the sense of the theory means that the results on which the agent is evaluated are assessed in a neutral and objective way. In the real world this is not necessarily the case. An example is the judgments of students by their professors which are also not completely neutral.[413]

A further limitation is that penalties in the context of Principal Agent Theory are often seen as monetary penalties. But in reality there is a much broader scope how to sanction agents for misbehaviour like dismissal.[414]

The utility maximization of individuals is doubtful as individuals in reality often show other kinds of behaviour like altruism.[415] The costs of an agent are his working effort and

406 Cf. exemplarily the studies of Botosan, C. A. (1997); Christensen, P. O., de la Rosa, L. E., Feltham, G. E. (2010) which come to divergent results in comparison to previous named studies.

407 Cf. Botosan, C. A. (2006), p. 31, 39; Leuz, C., Wysocki, P. D. (2016), pp. 548-550.

408 Cf. Bizenberger, R. (2008), pp. 99-100.

409 Cf. Schenk, U. (2003), pp. 59-60; Söllner, A. (2008), pp. 32-37.

410 Cf. Eisenhardt, K. M. (1989) for an overview and a short evaluation of empirical studies in the context of Principal Agent Theory, pp. 65-70.

411 Cf. Eisenhardt, K. M. (1989), p. 57, 72.

412 Cf. Arrow, K. J. (1986), pp. 1192-1193; Jensen, M. C., Murphy, K. J. (1990), p. 227; Richter, R., Furubotn, E. G. (2003), pp. 238-239.

413 Cf. Arrow, K. J. (1986), pp. 1193-1994.

414 Cf. Arrow, K. J. (1986), p. 1194.

415 Cf. Siefke, M. (1999), p. 52.

that he suffers under his work. This assumption does not necessarily fit to reality as many managers enjoy working in a responsible position.[416]

Many models of Principal Agent Theory illustrate the effects on the basis of the analysis of one period. In reality the cooperation between principal and agent endures regularly more than only one period.[417]

2.3 Relevance of Information on Capital Markets and for its Actors

2.3.1 Price Formation on Capital Markets Depending on the Level of Information

2.3.1.1 Efficient Market Model and Levels of Market Efficiency

The Principal Agent Theory describes the relationship between managers and investors in companies in which ownership and control are separated. Therefore, it is a theoretical justification for accounting and also the publication of key figures. Its application is not limited to capital market orientated companies. Nonetheless, it has a special relevance for these companies. Regularly these companies have a high degree of separation between ownership and control. Investors have limited opportunities of influence in such a setting so that the reduction of information asymmetries is especially important.

The focus of this chapter is on the processing of information through capital markets as the relationship between company and capital markets is the second relevant relationship in which information plays a crucial role.[418] A decisive question is to what extent capital markets are capable of processing information and to reflect available information in prices.[419] So, besides the Principal Agent Theory the neoclassical finance theory is the theoretical basis for explaining the necessity of value based performance measures.[420]

Companies act on capital markets in order to find capital providers and satisfy their demand for capital.[421] The stock market has mainly three service functions which it fulfils for investors: To inform them about supply and demand, to allocate supply and demand, in order to find a market price at which the market is cleared and finally to close the transactions at the current price.[422]

The prices of shares depend on the supply and demand of investors.[423] The stock price is based on the assumptions and estimations of prospect profits and Cash Flows of a company and also inherent risks connected with them.[424] Capital market participants estimate the future payment flows on the basis of information disclosed and process information which they have received through other information channels. Therefore, it can be concluded that information plays an important role in the context of price

416 Cf. Klein, J. (2008), p. 32; Janocha, M. (2014), p. 59; Siefke, M. (1999), p. 52.
417 Cf. Fama, E. F. (1980), p. 304; Holmstrom, B. (1979), pp. 89-90; Paulitschek, P. (2009), p. 71.
418 Cf. Wassermann, H. (2011), pp. 72-75.
419 Cf. Weber, J., Bramsemann, U., Heineke, C., et al. (2017), pp. 116-117.
420 Cf. Riedl, J. B. (2000), p. 93 who also chooses these both theories for justifying the existence of VBM.
421 Cf. Lindemann, J. (2004), p. 9; Pape, U. (2015), pp. 11-12.
422 Cf. Pape, U. (2015), pp. 11-12; Spremann, K., Gantenbein, P. (2005), p. 35.
423 Cf. Laux, H. (2006b), p. 117; Ruf, M. (2014), p. 21.
424 Cf. McLemore, P., Woodward, G., Zwirlein, T. (2015), pp. 76-77; Wagenhofer, A., Ewert, R. (2015), p. 92.

formation on capital markets.[425] On new disclosed information investors revise their expectations and a new share price is formed.[426]

The Dividend Discount Model summarises these thoughts and assumes a constant dividend until infinity as the basis for today's appropriate stock price.[427]

$$P_t = \sum_{n=1}^{\infty} \frac{E_t\ (D_{t+n})}{(1+r)^n}$$

Source: Formula adapted from: Lee, C. M. (2001), p. 235
Formula 7: Dividend Discount Model

with
P_t = present value of expected future dividends
$E_t\ (D_{t+n})$ = expected future dividend
r = risk-adjusted discount rate

The term $E_t\ (D_{t+n})$ denotes the sum of expected future dividends in period t+n. Dividends are estimated on the basis of information available in period t. r is the risk-adjusted discount rate for the dividends. The current stock price is the present value of expected future dividends.[428]

According to the random-walk hypothesis stock prices do not follow a certain pattern. This means that changes in stock prices are independent from each other. Otherwise, it would be possible for investors to use past stock prices for prediction of future stock prices and to earn a profit on the basis of this analysis.[429] Stock prices react to new information in efficient markets. Positive information leads to an increase of stock prices and negative ones to a decrease. Because new information appears randomly, the price changes are also random.[430] As a result of several empirical studies, the statements of the random-walk hypothesis are partly falsified.[431] Nevertheless, the random-walk hypothesis can be used to describe the price formation process in an efficient market and how prices adapt if new information is available.[432]

The price formation process depends on the level of information efficiency of the capital market.[433] In an efficient market stock prices comprise all information available und adjust prices accordingly to this information. Conditions for this model are that there are no transaction costs, all information is available free of charge and all market

425 Cf. Jähnchen, S. (2009), pp. 20-21; Pfaff, D., Bärtl, O. (1998), pp. 758-759.
426 Cf. Wagenhofer, A., Ewert, R. (2015), p. 117.
427 Cf. Hielscher, U. (1999), pp. 15-18, Schreiner, A. (2007), pp. 23-24.
428 Cf. Lee, C. M. (2001), pp. 235-236.
429 Cf. Brealey, R. A., Myers, S. C., Allen, F. (2011), pp. 342-345; Elton, E. J., Gruber, M. J., Brown, M. J., et al. (2011), pp. 399-400.
430 Cf. Malkiel, B. G. (2005), pp. 1-2; Sharpe, W. F., Alexander, G. J., Bailey, J. V. (1999), p. 95.
431 Cf. for acceptance of random walk hypothesis Hasan, M. S. (2004); Payne, J. E., Sahu, A. P. (2004); for mixed results Girmes, D. H., Benjamin, A. E. (1975); Mills, T. C., Jordanov, J. V. (2003); for a rejection of random walk hypothesis Poshakwale, S. (2002); Tabak, B. M. (2003); Taylor, S. J. (1982).
432 Cf. Hielscher, U. (1999), pp. 84-88, Schmidt-Tank, S. (2005), pp. 18-19.
433 Cf. Laux, H. (2006b), p. 117.

participants interpret the information in the same way. In reality these conditions are fulfilled unlikely.[434] If a capital market is information efficient, it can fulfil its allocation function and distribute the capital to its optimal utilisation.[435]

The general equation for price formation is the following:

$$E(p_{j,t+1}|\Phi_t) = [1 + E(r_{j,t+1}|\Phi_t)]p_{jt}$$

Source: Formula adapted from: Fama, E. F. (1970), p. 384
Formula 8: Price formation on capital markets

with
$p_{j,t}$ = price of security j at time t
Φ_t = set of available information at the end of period t
$r_{j,t+1}$ = expected return of security j at the end of period t

Where $E(p_{j,t+1}|\Phi_t)$ describes the expected return of security j based on the set of available information Φ_t at the end of the period. $p_{j,t}$ denotes the price of security j at time t and $p_{j,t+1}$ is the price of security j at time t+1. $r_{j,t+1}$ summarises the expected return of the security at the end of the period. The equation shows that the expected price of security depends on the expected return which in turn is depending on the set of information available.[436] The data which is included in the set of information, Φ_t, depends on the specific form of market efficiency.[437]

Investors have the possibility to earn excess returns which are above the expected return.

$$x_{j,t+1} = p_{j,t+1} - E(p_{j,t+1}|\Phi_t)$$

Source: Formula adapted from: Fama, E. F. (1970), p. 385
Formula 9: Excess return

with
$x_{j,t+1}$ = excess return

The excess return, $x_{j,t+1}$, is the difference between the actual price and the expected return which was estimated at the beginning of the period.[438]

In a complete efficient market the price reflects all information available, so the following equation must be valid:[439]

434 Cf. Fama, E. F. (1970), pp. 387-388; Laux, H., Schabel, M. M. (2009), p. 156.
435 Cf. Vollmer, R. (2008), p. 42.
436 Cf. Fama, E. F. (1970), p. 384.
437 Cf. Sharpe, W. F., Alexander, G. J., Bailey, J. V. (1999), pp. 94-95.
438 Cf. Fama, E. F. (1970), pp. 384-385.
439 Cf. Brown, S. J. (2011), p. 80; Fama, E. F. (1970), p. 385.

$$E(x_{j,t+1}|\Phi_t) = 0$$

Source: Formula adapted from: Fama, E. F. (1970), p. 385
Formula 10: Excess return in completely efficient markets

In an efficient market excess returns do not exist because the complete set of information available is included in security prices.[440] Referring to the Dividend Discount Model above, it follows that all investors estimate identical future Cash Flows and dividend streams for a share. Thus, the stock price is an optimal measure for fundamental value of the stock.[441]

In empirical research capital markets are divided into one of three categories according to their processing of information within the price formation process.[442] Weak capital markets only consider historical prices in their price formation.[443] The technical share analysis tries to predict prospective share prices by analysing and identifying patterns in past share prices.[444] At capital markets with weak information efficiency it is senseless because the information is already included in current stock prices, so that an investor has no chance to generate an excess return.[445]

Capital markets in the semi-strong form refer to all public available information, e.g. announcements of company's earning.[446] Fundamental share analyses do not help investors to generate excess returns.[447] All publicly available information is already contained in share prices so that no investor has an incentive to search for and analyse information.[448]

Capital markets in the strong form include all information in stock prices.[449] The consequence is that despite the fact only some groups have monopolistic access to information, the market is available to process them with an indefinite speed. In the end no private information exists anymore.[450] The incentive for collecting and analysing information is gone for market participants as such information is publicly available immediately.[451] The strong form does not exist in reality. It can be viewed as a benchmark

440 Cf. Abergel, F., Politi, M. (2013), p. 13; Sharpe, W. F., Alexander, G. J., Bailey, J. V. (1999), p. 95.
441 Cf. Hawawini, G., Viallet, C. (2011), pp. 311-312; Konté, M. A. (2010), p. 19.
442 The division into three categories bases on Fama, cf. for a detailed description Fama, E. F. (1970) and Fama, E. F. (1991). Cf. for comments and critics Grossman, S. J. (1976); Grossman, S. J., Stiglitz, J. E. (1980); Le Roy, S. F. (1976); Schwartz, R. A. (1970); Sharpe, W. F. (1970). In the framework of his second article Fama labels the three categories according to the methods for examining level of market efficiency. The categories in the order of increasing information efficiency are also named as tests for return predictability, event studies and tests for private information, cf. for more details Fama, E. F. (1991).
443 Cf. Fama, E. F. (1970), pp. 383, 414-415.
444 Cf. Eidel, U. (1999), p. 12; Neely, C. J., Weller, P. A., Ulrich, J. M. (2009), p. 467.
445 Cf. Malkiel, B. G. (1991), pp. 211-212; Vollmer, R. (2008), p. 50.
446 Cf. Fama, E. F. (1970), pp. 383, 414-415.
447 Cf. Eidel, U. (1999), p. 12; Vollmer, R. (2008), p. 50.
448 Cf. Möller, H. P., Hüfner, B. (2001), p. 1281.
449 Cf. Fama, E. F. (1970), pp. 383, 414-415.
450 Cf. Kugler, P. L. (2006), pp. 10-11.
451 Cf. Eidel, U. (1999), pp. 12-13; Salzer, E. (2004), pp. 67-68.

and the highest form of market efficiency.[452] A higher level of information efficiency includes a lower level of information efficiency.[453]

It is important to note that the level of market efficiency cannot directly be tested. In order to compare the theoretical price with the actual price, an asset pricing model is necessary for calculating the theoretical price.[454]

2.3.1.2 Critique of Efficient Market Model

The concept of information efficiency is partly criticised in the scientific literature. The critique concentrates especially on the assumptions of the model. Fama defined as a necessary condition that capital market participants homogenously interpret available information. Without this assumption information can be interpreted in different ways and this leads to diverging expectations about prospective stock price developments. Stock prices are not able to adapt immediately to new information because not all capital market participants interpret them in the same way.[455]

The assumption of complete efficiency of capital markets has the consequence that investors have no incentive to collect, process and evaluate information because the market prices immediately contain all information available.[456] Uninformed and informed traders are able to make profits at the same level but uninformed traders only observe the market price. If information is not free of charge, it is necessary that informed traders can hide their collected information and earn a higher return than non-informed traders.[457]

Traders can only hide their information when stock prices do not fully reflect all available information and the price system is less informative for uninformed individuals. But if information is costly and the prices reflect all information available, markets break down. All traders who so far have collected information stop this activity. It is a necessary condition when information is costly, that the market must have some noise in order to create a return for information collectors.[458] The described situation is also named as the information paradox meaning that information efficiency of market and collecting of information through capital market participants exclude each other.[459]

The no-trade theorem stresses the rationality of investors. If they have different levels of information, better informed traders try to take advantage of their knowledge. But, in order to realise this, they need a trading partner. Complete rational investors who have a lower level of information conclude in this situation that such a transaction would be unfavourable. Consequently, better informed investors do not have the possibility to realize an excess return despite their higher level of information. Due to no realized trades

452 Cf. Fama, E. F. (1970), p. 414.
453 Cf. Sharpe, W. F., Alexander, G. J., Bailey, J. V. (1999), pp. 93-94.
454 Cf. Fama, E. F. (1991), pp. 1575-1576.; Henschke, S. (2009), pp. 28-29; Reifschneider, C. (2007), p. 15. In scientific literature this problem is named as joint hypothesis problem.
455 Cf. Vollmer, R. (2008), pp. 55-56.
456 Cf. Grossman, S. J. (1976), pp. 581-582.
457 Cf. Grossman, S. J. (1976), pp. 573-574.
458 Cf. Grossman, S. J., Stiglitz, J. E. (1980), pp. 393-395, 404-405.
459 Cf. Brunnermeier, M. K. (2001), pp. 26-27; Hens, T., Rieger, M. O. (2016), p. 279; Schredelseker, K. (2001), pp. 136-137.

markets will collapse.[460] The no-trade scenario is considered as an extreme situation which underlies strict assumptions.[461]

Nevertheless, the assumptions that all individuals act rationally does not correspond with reality. The so-called noise traders do not act on the basis of rational behaviour, but more on the basis of feeling and opinions.[462] For example, they follow the advices of brokers or financial gurus believing to receive information about future development of stock prices.[463] Although they ensure that the market is liquid, their expectations indeed influence the stock prices. The more noise traders act on the market, the more worthwhile is the collection of information because stock prices are more distorted.[464] Examples for irrational behaviour of investors are the acting on past data,[465] aversion for losses[466] or the framing effect which describes that the same information in another context is perceived differently.[467] The research field of behavioural finance deals with irrational behaviour and social factors and how both influence stock price formation on capital markets.[468] The existence of noise trading is an explanation for the high amount of trading on stock markets because individuals react differently to information available and have different levels of information.[469]

The resulting question is if rational investors can compensate the effects of noise traders on stock prices. Under the condition that the actions of irrational investors are not correlated, their action will offset each other. Consequently, prices are determined by rational investors.[470]

Even if the actions of irrational investors do not offset each other, rational investors have the possibility of arbitrage.[471] Arbitrage describes the process of earning a profit by identifying and using different prices for the same asset.[472] Due to arbitrage the stock prices converge to the price which reflects all information available.[473] In reality the possibilities of arbitrage are limited because prices do not immediately converge to fundamental value. It may take quite a long time.[474] Investors have to bear holding costs. Furthermore, transaction costs and costs for gathering necessary information exist.[475]

460 Cf. Brunnermeier, M. K. (2001), pp. 36-37; Krebs, D. M. (1988), p. 118; Milgrom, P., Stokey, N. (1982), pp. 17-24; Ross, S. A. (2005), pp. 42-43.
461 Cf. Krebs, D. M. (1988), p. 118.
462 Cf. Black, F. (1986), pp. 529-533.
463 Cf. Shleifer, A., Summers, L. H. (1990), pp. 23-24.
464 Cf. Black, F. (1986), pp. 529-533.
465 Cf. Shleifer, A., Summers, L. H. (1990), p. 24.
466 Cf. Altman, M. (2010), p. 203; Kahneman, D., Tversky, A. (1979), pp. 272-273.
467 Cf. Altman, M. (2010), p. 203; Tversky, A., Kahneman, D. (1992), p. 298. Altman, M. (2010), also gives an introduction to underlying Prospect Theory.
468 Cf. basically for an introduction to behavioural finance: Baker, H. K., Nofsinger, J. R. (2010); Elton, E. J., Gruber, M. J., Brown, M. J., et al. (2011), pp. 438-454; Shleifer, A. (2000).
469 Cf. Lee, C. M. (2001), p. 244.
470 Cf. Rau, R. (2010), p. 335; Rubinstein, M. (2001), pp. 19-20.
471 Cf. Kugler, P. L. (2006), pp. 18-19.
472 Cf. Laux, H., Schabel, M. M. (2009), p. 159; Sharpe, W. F., Alexander, G. J., Bailey, J. V. (1999), p. 284.
473 Cf. Lee, C. M. (2001), pp. 235-236; Shleifer, A. (2000), pp. 3-4.
474 Cf. Shleifer, A. (2000), pp. 14-15.
475 Cf. Dyckman, T. R., Morse, D. (1986), p. 44; Konté, M. A. (2010), p. p. 20; Lee, C. M. (2001), pp. 245-246.

Sometimes it could also be a problem that perfect substitutes for a security do not exist, so investors can only use imperfect substitutes which make arbitrage risky.[476] Therefore, it can be stated that capital markets are nearly free of arbitrage. Only at short notice is arbitrage possible.[477] Market prices are a combination on the basis of trading activities of noise traders and rational investors who try to find possibilities for arbitrage but have to consider the costs that are associated with arbitrage.[478]

The insight so far is that the scientific literature does not deliver a generally accepted theory about price formation on capital markets. The no-trade theorem, the information paradox, the existence of noise-trader and social factors that can influence the stock prices are set against the efficient market hypothesis. Therefore, the next chapter takes a look at the insights gained from empirical studies about the level of information efficiency on capital markets.[479]

2.3.1.3 Empirical Insights on the Information Efficiency of Capital Markets

Most studies confirm the weak form of information efficiency on capital markets.[480] These studies statistically test, if past returns explain future returns. The majority of these studies does not find a statistical relevant correlation, so that markets are at least efficient in the weak form.[481] It should not go unmentioned that some studies find evidence that past returns can explain future returns but only under special circumstances.[482]

It is especially interesting to investigate if markets are semi-strong efficient because the use of insider information is strictly limited by law in many countries. Investors and capital market intermediaries are limited to the use of public information.[483] Commonly event studies are used in order to assess if a market is efficient in the semi-strong form. A study defines an event, e.g. publication of an unexpected profit. With the help of a pricing model an expected return is computed and compared with the actual return. Abnormal returns on the day of publication indicate that the market is efficient in the semi-strong form. But if it is possible for investors to yield abnormal returns days after the announcement, the market is not able to incorporate the new information immediately in its price formation.[484] The empirical results about semi-strong efficient markets are ambivalent.[485]

---

476 Cf. Shleifer, A. (2000), pp. 13-14.

477 Cf. Spremann, K., Gantenbein, P. (2005), p. 42.

478 Cf. Lee, C. M. (2001), p. 246.

479 Cf. Vollmer, R. (2008), pp. 61-62.

480 Cf. Eidel, U. (1999), p. 13; Fabozzi, F. J. (2015), p. 593; Rau, R. (2010), p. 336; Wichels, D. (2002), p. 56.

481 Cf. exemplarily Bessembinder, H., Chan, K. (1998); Fama, E. F., Blume, M. E. (1966); Fama, E. F., MacBeth, J. D. (1973); Jensen, M. C., Benington, G. A. (1970).

482 Cf. exemplarily Brock, W., Lakonishok, J., LeBaron, B. (1992); Lo, A. W., Mamaysky, H., Wang, J. (2000); Sullivan, R., Timmermann, A., White, H. (1999).

483 Cf. Dyckman, T. R., Morse, D. (1986), pp. 6-7; Sharpe, W. F., Alexander, G. J., Bailey, J. V. (1999), p. 93.

484 Cf. Elton, E. J., Gruber, M. J., Brown, M. J., et al. (2011), pp. 416-419; Mondello, E. (2015), pp. 30-31.

485 Cf. Eidel, U. (1999), pp. 13-15; Elton, E. J., Gruber, M. J., Brown, M. J., et al. (2011), p. 427; Fabozzi, F. J. (2015), p. 593; Sharpe, W. F., Alexander, G. J., Bailey, J. V. (1999), p. 103; cf. exemplarily for studies supporting the efficient market hypothesis in the semi-strong form Busse, J. A., Green, T. C. (2002); Fama, E. F., Lawrence, F., Jensen, M. C., et al. (1969); Landsman, W. R., Maydew, E. L. (2002).

Although capital markets in developed countries are efficient in the semi-strong form, empirical studies reveal market anomalies. The anomalies can be classified into three different categories: Time based or seasonal anomalies, anomalies which refer to attributes of companies and further anomalies.[486] Two well-known examples for seasonal anomalies are the January and Monday effect. The January effect describes the phenomenon that especially small firms have more abnormal returns in January than during the rest of the year.[487] The Monday effect refers to empirical studies which show that on Mondays returns are worse than the rest of the week.[488] An example for anomalies referring to the structure of a company is the so-called size effect. Empirical studies prove that investors can access returns by investing in small firms in terms of market capitalization.[489] A further anomaly is that firms with high book-to-market-equity ratio, that means they have a low market capitalisation and a high equity book value, earn higher returns than predicted by the CAPM.[490] The post earnings announcement drift describes the lagged reactions of stock prices to the announcement of unexpected earnings.[491] Empirical studies prove that abnormal returns exist for months after announcement of earnings. The sign of abnormal returns corresponds to the sign of the unexpected earnings.[492] The post earnings announcement drift is an indication that the market does not react instantly and does not process information completely in the sense of market efficiency in the semi-strong form.[493]

Combining theoretical and empirical insights, it can be summarised that stock prices are not as efficient as assumed in theory. The capital market anomalies as well as the existence of noise traders indicate that stock prices do not completely reflect all information available. Nevertheless, they are a proxy for the fundamental value of a company.[494] Neither theoretical literature nor empirical studies can give a clear answer about the exact level of information efficiency of capital markets.[495] It can be assumed that markets are at least efficient in the weak form and mostly also in the semi-strong form but not continuously due to market anomalies which occur from time to time.[496] The existence of bubbles, like the dot.com bubble at the end of 1990s, could be a sign that markets are not efficient.[497] The existence of anomalies like the January effect are not a

486 Cf. Mondello, E. (2015), pp. 31-33, cf. extensively for an overview of empirical studies for market efficiency and detected market anomalies Elton, E. J., Gruber, M. J., Brown, M. J., et al. (2011), pp. 400-427; Rau, R. (2010), pp. 335-340; Vollmer, R. (2008), pp. 63-92.

487 Cf. Fama, E. F. (1991), pp. 1586-1587; Gultekin, M. N., Gultekin, N. B. (1983); Kato, K., Schallheim, J. S. (1985); Keim, D. B. (1989); Reinganum, M. R. (1983).

488 Cf. French, K. R. (1980); Gibbons, M. R., Hess, P. (1981); Lawrence, H. (1986).

489 Cf. Banz, R. W. (1981); Keim, D. B. (1983); Reinganum, M. R. (1981).

490 Cf. Chan, L. K. C., Hamao, Y., Lakonishok, J. (1991); Fama, E. F., French, K. R. (1992); Rosenberg, B., Reid, K., Lanstein, R. (1985).

491 Cf. Rau, R. (2010), pp. 338-339; cf. exemplarily for empirical investigations Bernard, V. L., Thomas, J. K. (1989); Foster, G., Olsen, C., Shevlin, T. (1984); Liu, W., Strong, N. (2003).

492 Cf. Bernard, V. L., Thomas, J. K. (1989); Bernard, V. L., Thomas, J. K. (1990); Foster, G., Olsen, C., Shevlin, T. (1984).

493 Cf. Bernard, V. L., Thomas, J. K. (1989), pp. 32-34; Bernard, V. L., Thomas, J. K. (1990), pp. 307-308.

494 Cf. Lee, C. M. (2001), p. 237; Reifschneider, C. (2007), pp. 18-20.

495 Cf. Vollmer, R. (2008), p. 92-94.

496 Cf. Wichels, D. (2002), p. 57; Theis, J. C. (2014), pp. 37-38.

497 Cf. Malkiel, B. G. (2005), p. 2.

reason per se to refuse the efficient market hypothesis because the absolute level of the abnormal returns is in average very low. Furthermore, the seasonal anomalies depend largely on investor trading patterns.[498]

Beyond the debate how markets process information, the assumption that stock markets are able to set prices rationally is not refused by most empirical studies.[499] That means, stock markets are able to react rationally to changes in earnings or dividends but they do not react to events which are not relevant from an economic point of view.[500]

A supporting fact for the efficiency of captital markets is that only partly professional investors or investment funds are able to beat the market and earn excess returns.[501] These insights so far indicate that accounting and information which is based on accounting data has its right to exist because it can improve the price formation process on capital markets.[502] With reference to the information paradox a certain level of inefficiency is necessary in order to give investors an incentive for information research. For further discussions it is assumed that capital markets are nearly efficient in the semi-strong form.[503] This means that capital markets consider mostly all publicly available information. Based on the insights of Behavioural Finance as well as from empirical studies which detect market anomalies, it can be concluded that market value does not always reflect the fundamental value of a company.[504]

Despite the focus of this chapter on the processing of information of capital markets, it should be mentioned that of course not only the information of a company influences the share prices. Furthermore, other factors like conjuncture, level of interest rates, liquidity of shares, current structure of ownership and psychological factors like personal preferences or mood at capital markets influence prices. However, these factors cannot be influenced by the company.[505]

2.3.2 Crucial Actors on Capital Markets and their Information Needs

2.3.2.1 Classification of Actors on Capital Markets

The previous chapter states that it is worthwhile for companies to communicate information to the capital market as stock prices regularly react to this information under the premise of nearly semi-strong information efficiency. As a next step, it is necessary to look at the actors on capital markets which are the receivers of the disclosed information and to point out their information needs. The presented actors receive information about the value based performance measures.

498 Cf. Fama, E. F. (1991), pp. 1586-1587.

499 Cf. exemplarily for empirical investigation Marsh, T. A., Merton, R. C. (1986); cf. for contradictory empirical results Le Roy, S. F., Porter, R. D. (1981).

500 Cf. Marsh, T. A., Merton, R. C. (1986), p. 483.

501 Cf. Malkiel, B. G. (2005), pp. 2-9; cf. extensively for an empirical investigation Malkiel, B. G. (1995); Schmidt-Tank, S. (2005), p. 20.

502 Cf. Möller, H. P., Hüfner, B. (2001), p. 1286; Reifschneider, C. (2007), pp. 27-29; Wichels, D. (2002), p. 57; Theis, J. C. (2014), pp. 37-38.

503 Cf. Torabian, F. (2010), p. 45; Wenzel, J. (2005), p. 97.

504 Cf. Theis, J. C. (2014), pp. 24-25.

505 Cf. Banzhaf, J. (2006), pp. 135-137.

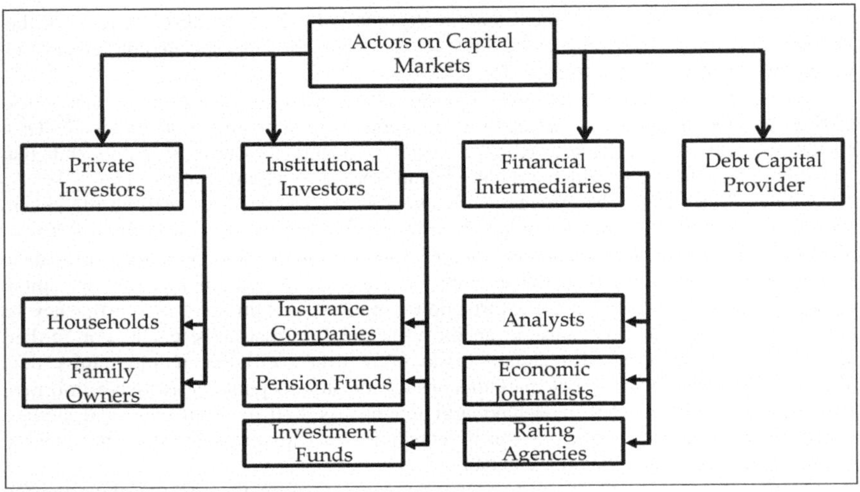

In the style of: Ruf, M. (2014), p. 104
Illustration 6: Actors on Capital Markets[506]

On capital markets actors can be roughly divided into four groups: Private investors, institutional investors, financial intermediaries and debt capital providers.[507] Illustration six gives an overview of the classification.

Private investors are individual persons who invest their own money.[508] The group of private investors is the largest group by absolute numbers. Each private investor possesses only low financial resources in comparison to family owners, financial intermediaries or institutional investors. As this group is homogenous, it is difficult and expensive for companies to communicate with them.[509] Nevertheless, it is worthwhile to attempt such communication as the financial resources are enormous in total.[510] Private investors play an important role because they hold many shares of Western European companies. Beside households a further important investor group are families which control firms. In several cases family owned companies are not listed at the stock market.[511]

In comparison to institutional investors private investors decide on little available information. Due to the Internet the discrepancy between these two investor groups is

506 Cf. for possible capital market participants also American Institute of Certified Public Accountants (AICPA) (1994), pp. 8-9; Thomsen, S., Pedersen, T. (2000), p. 692.

507 Cf. extensively for a description of actors on capital markets Fabozzi, F. J. (2015), pp. 63-106; the categorization of capital market participants bases on the classification of Ernst, E., Gassen, J., Pellens, B. (2009), pp. 26-27; Kirchhoff, K. R., Piwinger, M. (2014), pp. 1086-1088; Wassermann, H. (2011), pp. 46-55.

508 Cf. Ruf, M. (2014), pp. 105-106.

509 Cf. Gantzhorn, A. (2016), p. 140.

510 Cf. Kirchhoff, K. R., Piwinger, M. (2014), p. 1086.

511 Cf. Faccio, M., Lang, L. H. P. (2002), pp. 366-367.

reduced.[512] Private investors have on average the lowest level of expertise.[513] Nevertheless, there are also private investors who have a broad knowledge base.[514] Due to their limited time and knowledge to evaluate companies and their stock comprehensively, private investors often use the services offered by financial intermediaries.[515]

A further sub group of private investors beside households are family owners whose primary interest is to ensure the survival of the firm.[516] This is in contrast to the main objectives of institutional investors whose objectives are Shareholder Value maximisation and liquidity.[517] Family ownership is often linked with a long-term commitment of the family to the company as they take simultaneously the roles of owners and managers.[518] Often family companies have a risk-averse attitude as the family's wealth may be invested in the company.[519]

Institutional investors are juristic persons and invest on behalf of their clients.[520] In contrast to the private investor group institutional investors are focused on financial performance.[521] They are professional investors and have a high level of expertise.[522] In contrast to private investors they are a very small group in numbers but have access to huge financial resources.[523] Their importance has risen throughout recent decades.[524] Typical institutional investors are insurance companies, pension funds or investment funds.[525] Also sovereign Wealth Funds belong to this group. These are investment funds which are owned by states. They manage funds from state sources of income. Examples are Norway's Government Pension Fund or Saudi Arabia's SAMA Foreign Holdings.[526]

The group of institutional investors can be roughly divided into two subgroups: On the one hand independent investors, like mutual funds and on the other hand so-called grey institutions like bank trusts or insurance companies which have a connection / business relationship with the company in which they invest. Thus, independent institutional investors monitor firm's activities and also influence the management. Grey institutions cannot act in the same way as they might negatively impact the business relationship with these companies.[527]

---

512 Cf. Ruf, M. (2014), pp. 105-106.
513 Cf. Gantzhorn, A. (2016), p. 140.
514 Cf. Wassermann, H. (2011), p. 54.
515 Cf. Huchzermeier, M. (2006), p. 73; Zülch, H., Benary, C.-E., Hottmann, J. (2016), pp. 1509-1515.
516 Cf. Fiss, P. C., Zajac, E. J. (2004), p. 508.
517 Cf. Thomsen, S., Pedersen, T. (2000), p. 693.
518 Cf. Thomsen, S., Pedersen, T. (2000), p. 693.
519 Cf. Pedersen, T., Thomsen, S. (2003), p. 34.
520 Cf. Ruf, M. (2014), pp. 106-107.
521 Cf. Pedersen, T., Thomsen, S. (2003), p. 35; Thomsen, S., Pedersen, T. (2000), p. 694.
522 Cf. Huchzermeier, M. (2006), p. 78; Shu, T. (2013), p. 696.
523 Cf. Kirchhoff, K. R., Piwinger, M. (2014), p. 1087; Köhler, K. (2015), p. 128.
524 Cf. Chen, X., Harford, J., Li, K. (2007), p. 280; Davis, G. F. (2008), pp. 11-21; Ferreira, M. A., Matos, P. (2008), p. 499; Johnson, R. A., Schnatterly, K., Johnson, S. G., et al. (2010), pp. 1590-1591; Kirchhoff, K. R., Piwinger, M. (2014), p. 1087; cf. extensively for a description of the development of the influence of institutional investors in the USA Davis, G. F. (2008).
525 Cf. Bassen, A. (2002), pp. 14-16; Fabozzi, F. J. (2015), pp. 66-71; Zülch, H., Benary, C.-E., Hottmann, J. (2016), pp. 1509-1515.
526 Cf. Fabozzi, F. J. (2015), pp. 73-75.
527 Cf. Ferreira, M. A., Matos, P. (2008), pp. 500-501.

Independent institutional investors try to maximise the Shareholder Value. It is not a surprise that several empirical studies confirm that their presence increases firm value and performance.[528] The consequent orientation to the Shareholder Value approach is based on their clients' expectations of constant profits. The pressure to succeed leads to regular changes in their portfolio in contrast to private investors.[529] The profit demands of their clients lead to comprehensive research before final investment decisions. Due to large financial resources and influence this investor group is at the centre of the Investor Relations activities of a company.[530] Although Institutional Investors are considered as one group within the context of this dissertation, the objectives and interests are not homogenous within this group. Concerning information needs this group is quite homogenous and definable in contrast to the other groups.[531]

After the financial crisis the financial community and the public expect that institutional investors monitor carefully the managers of companies in which they invest. This development increases the importance of their research and consequently the importance of their information needs for companies.[532]

Financial intermediaries are not directly active on the capital market but they play an important role as they analyse the company's performance and economic development on capital markets and communicate it to investors.[533] Examples for financial intermediaries are analysts, economic journalists or rating agencies.[534] Especially for investors with low expertise this group is important. Financial intermediaries often influence the investment decisions of private investors.[535] So, financial intermediaries have an opinion-forming function for private investors.[536]

Financial analysts have the task to collect and analyse information about a firm, develop a forecast about their future earnings and give other capital market participants a recommendation to buy, hold or sell the company's shares.[537] They are specialised in certain industries and concentrate on a few companies in order to get detailed knowledge about these companies.[538] Due to their contact with managers, their know-how and experience they have advantages in analysing information in comparison to investors.[539] In a semi-efficient capital market the task of analysts would be senseless as the stock price already includes all available information. In reality the information distribution of analysts increases the information efficiency of capital markets.[540] The Internet enables

528 Cf. Cornett, M. M., Marcus, A. J., Saunders, A., et al. (2007), p. 1772-1773; Ferreira, M. A., Matos, P. (2008), pp. 500-501, Hartzell, J., Sun, L., Titman, S. (2014), pp. 66-68.

529 Cf. Huchzermeier, M. (2006), pp. 77-78.

530 Cf. Ruf, M. (2014), pp. 106-107; cf. Ruf, M. (2014) p. 105 for a comparison of attributes of private and institutional investors.

531 Cf. Fochler, R. (2000), pp. 323-325.

532 Cf. Callen, J. L., Fang, X. (2013); pp. 3047-3048; Mallin, C. (2012), p. 177.

533 Cf. Franco, G. de, Hope, O.-K., Vyas, D., et al. (2015), p. 76.

534 Cf. Ruf, M. (2014), p. 104.

535 Cf. Kirchhoff, K. R., Piwinger, M. (2014), p. 1087.

536 Cf. Achleitner, A.-K., Bassen, A., Pietzsch, L., et al. (2002), p. 29; Huchzermeier, M. (2006), p. 73.

537 Cf. Erkilet, G., Kholmy, K. (2016), pp. 38-39; Healy, P. M., Palepu, K. G. (2001), p. 416; Kahlenberg, M. (2009), p. 492.

538 Cf. Huchzermeier, M. (2006), p. 75.

539 Cf. Wichels, D. (2002), pp. 28-29.

540 Cf. Wichels, D. (2002), pp. 29-30.

investors access to information. Due to the huge amount of available information analysts remain still necessary.[541] It is important from an investor's point of view that analysts conduct their information analysis independently. Analysts face a trade-off between the competition for clients and their reputation. In order to avoid this conflict of interest, many institutional investors engage their own analysts.[542] Nevertheless, there is a risk that the forecasts of financial analysts can be biased.[543]

Economic journalists publish their articles in newspapers, specialised economic journals or via the Internet. Through these communication channels their assessments are circulated widely. Especially private investors are interested in their reports.[544] Journalists often reinforce the assessment of analysts by processing them in their publications. Hereby, the analyst's assessment is spread to more recipients. The information process is reciprocal between analysts and journalists as analysts take information out of publications for their work.[545]

Rating agencies are a further group which does not actively act on capital markets. Their task is to evaluate the creditworthiness of companies.[546] The three largest rating agencies are Moody's Investors Service, Standard & Poor's Ratings Group and Fitch Ratings.[547] Considering the insights of Principal Agent Theory, information asymmetries are reduced because the rating is made public. For companies a good rating is essential. Investment funds often invest only in companies which have a certain level of rating.[548]

Two points of criticism arise concerning the role of rating agencies: Firstly, the influence of the issuer on ratings. Companies instruct as well as pay rating agencies. There may be conflicts of interests and the rating loses objectivity.[549] Secondly, capital market participants might overestimate the ratings. This can lead to the situation that investors do not conduct their own analysis.[550]

The function of credit rating agencies is also evaluated critically due to past events. For example, the agencies gave Enron or WorldCom a high rating just a few days before their insolvency.[551] Their role during the subprime mortgage crisis also gives rise to doubts about their market function.[552]

Debt capital providers[553] have a contractually fixed claim and receive their interest payments independently from the economic performance of the company. Therefore it is in their interest that the company remains able to compensate the interest payments.[554]

541 Cf. Wichels, D. (2002), p. 30.
542 Cf. Wichels, D. (2002), p. 35.
543 Cf. Dechow, P., Ge, W., Schrand, C. (2010), pp. 389-390.
544 Cf. Huchzermeier, M. (2006), pp. 75-76.
545 Cf. Ruf, M. (2014), pp. 109-110.
546 Cf. Nye, R. P. (2014), p. 4.
547 Cf. Nye, R. P. (2014), p. 4.
548 Cf. Fabozzi, F. J. (2015), pp. 91-95.
549 Cf. Bühren, C., Pleßner, M. (2015), pp. 324-325.
550 Cf. Fabozzi, F. J. (2015), pp. 95-97.
551 Cf. Fabozzi, F. J. (2015), pp. 95-97.
552 Cf. Baghai, R. P., Servaes, H., Tamayo, A. (2014), pp. 1961-1962; Lugo, S., Croce, A., Faff, R. (2015), p. 1703.
553 Debt capital providers are also capital market actors when they purchase bonds on capital markets. From an economic perspective they are investors, from a legal perspective they are creditors, cf. Böcking, H.-J. (1998), p. 21.
554 Cf. Bieg, H., Kußmaul, H., Waschbusch, G. (2016), p. 148; Metten, M. (2010), pp. 17-18.

Due to this interest they also have information needs concerning a company's performance. But in contrast to equity capital providers, their focus is on liquidity and past performance rather than increase of Shareholder Value and prospective development.[555]

The presented illustration of capital market actors is simplified. A further actor, not considered, is the government of a country which can also heavily influence capital market events. Governments regulate financial markets, among other things, by setting disclosure rules for companies which force them to give certain information to their investors. They can also take the role of a financial intermediary by providing loans or liquidity to industries which are in a critical economic situation or influence their monetary policy via the central bank.[556]

The government as owner does not prioritise Shareholder Value maximisation as a primary goal, rather political goals like low output prices or employment are more important.[557] For purposes of this dissertation, a concentration on the named four groups of actors is sufficient as these groups are the main receivers of a company's Investor Relation activities and therefore also the receivers of communicated value based performance measures.[558]

2.3.2.2 Information Needs of Actors

2.3.2.2.1 Insights from empirical studies

After identifying relevant actors on capital markets in the previous chapter, this chapter points out their information needs based on empirical studies.[559] In order to understand information needs, it is helpful to clarify the objective of collecting information of all investor groups: To estimate the prospective economic development optimally. Financial intermediaries as well as institutional investors base their investment decisions on quantitative models for which they need data about future profits or Cash Flows. The more and better information they have, the better their estimates. It is in a company's interest to deliver its actual and potential investors the information they need.[560] Table 2 gives an overview of the empirical studies taken and the main sources of information for different investor groups.

To summarise: All empirical studies show that the information contained in annual reports still plays an important role for all groups of investors.[561] This shows the fact that investment decisions of institutional investors are also influenced by the level of disclosure standards in a country. Primarily firm characteristics like size or the investment opportunities determine their purchase decision, but a decisive country-specific effect is the level of disclosure standards. Institutional investors prefer investing in countries which have high disclosure standards.[562]

555 Cf. Bastini, K. (2015), pp. 60-62; Fiss, P. C., Zajac, E. J. (2004), p. 506.
556 Cf. Fabozzi, F. J. (2015), pp. 78-91.
557 Cf. Pedersen, T., Thomsen, S. (2003), p. 37; Thomsen, S., Pedersen, T. (2000), p. 693.
558 Cf. Köhler, K. (2015), pp. 193-194.
559 Cf. for an overview of used Investor Relation instruments for satisfying information needs of groups at capital market Fochler, R. (2000), p. 331.
560 Cf. Vater, H., Meckel, M., Hoffmann, C., et al. (2008), p. 2605.
561 Cf. Dyckman, T. R., Morse, D. (1986), p. 8.
562 Cf. Ferreira, M. A., Matos, P. (2008), pp. 500, 506-510, 523.

Table 2: Overview of empirical studies analysing the information sources of different investor groups

Authors	Year of Publication	Capital market participants analysed	Insights concerning information sources used
Barker, R. G.[563]	1999	American analysts and fund managers	– High relevance of accounting information which is a reliable source of information.
Achleitner, A.-K., Bassen, A., Pietzsch, L. et al.[564]	2002	Analysts	– Personal conversations with managers – Analysis of data of financial statements disclosed. – Key figures are used to analyse financial performance. – Qualitative information like corporate strategy or quality of management is also used.
Hodge, F. D.[565]	2003	American investors	– Annual business reports are an important part of information processed.
Glaum, M., Friedrich, N.[566]	2006	Analysts of telecommunication industry	– Direct contact with company representatives – Analysis of financial statements
Hodge, F. D., Pronk, M.[567]	2006	Mixed survey group	– Internet is an important information channel. – Professional investors analyse financial statements. – Non-professional investors focus more on management's analysis and comments.
PwC[568]	2007	Analysts	– Accounting data is primarily used for calculating Cash Flows for valuation models.
PAAinE[569]	2009	Analysts and professional investors	– High relevance of information contained in annual business reports. – Balance sheet and financial statements are the most relevant parts. – Important instruments for analysing are key figures.

563 Cf. Barker, R. G. (1999).
564 Cf. Achleitner, A.-K., Bassen, A., Pietzsch, L., et al. (2002).
565 Cf. Hodge, F. D. (2003).
566 Cf. Glaum, M., Friedrich, N. (2006).
567 Cf. Hodge, F., Pronk, M. (2006).
568 Cf. PwC (2007), https://www.pwc.com/gx/en/ifrs-reporting/pdf/measuringassetssurvey.pdf.
569 Cf. Pro-Active Accounting Activities in Europe (PAAinE) (2009).

Authors	**Year of Publication**	**Capital market participants analysed**	**Insights concerning information sources used**
Ernst, E., Gassen, J., Pellens, B.[570]	2009	Private Investors	– High importance of press information like newspapers or economic magazines. – 44 % use the annual business report for investment decisions whereas balance sheet and income statement are most important parts. – 32 % use the quarterly reports. – 40 % consult banks or brokers.
Ernst, E., Gassen, J., Pellens, B.	2009	Institutional Investors	– Direct contact to management – High importance of quarterly and annual business reports. – Important parts are balance sheet, income statement and appendix.
Gassen, J., Schwedler, K.[571]	2010	European financial analysts and fund managers	– Accounting data is primary source of information. – Insider information is also relevant. – Most important parts of reports are income statement and balance sheet.
Pellens, B., Schmidt, A.[572]	2014	Private investors	– High importance of newspapers or magazines as well as quarterly and annual reports. – Balance sheet and income statement have the highest relevance.
Pellens, B., Schmidt, A.	2014	Institutional Investors	– Direct contact to management – Quarterly and annual reports which have the highest reliability of all information sources used.
Brown, L. D., Call, A. C., Clement, M. B.[573]	2015	Analysts	– Direct contact to management – Accounting information is a reliable source of information.

Nevertheless, institutional investors or analysts do not use only accounting information for important decisions.[574] Besides accounting there are further information sources.[575] Also information about the whole economy or the industry are necessary which have influence on stock prices and are therefore relevant for investors.[576]

570 Cf. Ernst, E., Gassen, J., Pellens, B. (2009).
571 Cf. Gassen, J., Schwedler, K. (2010).
572 Cf. Pellens, B., Schmidt, A. (2014).
573 Cf. Brown, L. D., Call, A. C., Clement, M. B., et al. (2015), pp. 3-4.
574 Cf. Lee, C. M. (2001), p. 248.
575 Cf. Dyckman, T. R., Morse, D. (1986), p. 86.
576 Cf. Vollmer, R. (2008), p. 110.

One important source of information is the direct contact with management.[577] It can be assumed that institutional investors gain insider information from direct conversations with management.[578] On the basis of insider information it is possible to anticipate performance development and avoid possible losses by selling shares.[579] As institutional investors or analysts do research on a large scale, they profit from economies of scale.[580]

The detailed valuation models and the high influence of institutional investors differentiate the needs of information from this capital market actor group in comparison to the needs of private investors. The information needs of institutional investors are very comprehensive. They expect detailed information about both the present and future performance of a company.[581]

To sum up: The main information source for institutional investors is direct contact with management. But also the data delivered by financial statements and public disclosure is used intensively. Private and individual investors concentrate on filtered and processed information, like articles in the press or recommendations of analysts. Nevertheless, for individual investors the use of financial statements has a relatively high importance[582] as well as for rating agencies and debt capital providers.[583]

2.3.2.2.2 Importance of Key Figures within Information Research of Investors

The importance of key figures can be derived from the importance of annual financial statements proven by the presented empirical studies.[584] The key figures summarise the information contained in balance sheet and profit and loss statement.[585] Furthermore, the fundamental analysis, regularly used by intermediaries and institutional investors, proves the regular use and importance of key figures.[586]

The fundamental analysis can be divided into four steps. Firstly, an investor does a strategic analysis in order to get information about the company's business environment. Secondly, an information analysis of accounting information is conducted. Thirdly, prospective payoffs are calculated on the basis of information collected and converted in a fourth step into a valuation model, e.g. a DCF model.[587] For a further quantitative analysis of the economic situation key figures can be used. Beside quantitative factors the funda-

577 Cf. Achleitner, A.-K., Bassen, A., Pietzsch, L., et al. (2002), pp. 35-36; Bassen, A. (2002), pp. 134-135; Gassen, J., Schwedler, K. (2010), pp. 499-503.

578 Cf. Wassermann, H. (2011), pp. 56-57.

579 Cf. Ke, B., Huddart, S., Petroni, K. (2003), p. 317. The authors come to the conclusion that insiders anticipate earnings trends up to 2 years.

580 Cf. Johnson, R. A., Schnatterly, K., Johnson, S. G., et al. (2010), pp. 1593-1594.

581 Cf. Kirchhoff, K. R., Piwinger, M. (2014), p. 1087.

582 Cf. Zülch, H., Benary, C.-E., Hottmann, J. (2016), pp. 1509-1515.

583 Cf. Buschmeier, A. (2011), pp. 150-151; Khakad, F. (2009), pp. 19-20.

584 Cf. exemplarily the studies of Pro-Active Accounting Activities in Europe (PAAinE) (2009), p. 8 and Achleitner, A.-K., Bassen, A., Pietzsch, L., et al. (2002), pp. 36-37.

585 Cf. Hienerth, C. (2010), pp. 37-38; Palupski, R. (2002), p. 141.

586 Cf. Gassen, J., Schwedler, K. (2010), pp. 499-500; Wolf, R., Hoffmann, H. (2017), p. 380.

587 Cf. Demirakos, E. G., Strong, N., Walker, M. (2004), p. 223; Erkilet, G., Kholmy, K. (2016), pp. 39-40.

mental analysis considers qualitative attributes of a company, like management quality or market position. The final objective is to receive a final market value of a company.[588]

In developed countries analysts use primarily the fundamental analysis in order to reach an investment decision.[589] At Athena's stock market listed companies, mutual funds and other investment companies also name the fundamental analysis as the most important tool for investment decisions.[590] Common key figures used are first accounting based key figures like price-earnings-ratio, earnings per share, NOPAT and return on equity. Secondly, discounted Cash flow measures are used and thirdly value based performance measures like the EVA.[591] Further empirical studies also prove the application of key figures by professional investors and analysts.[592]

Investors and analysts calculate key figures for analysis of company's performance or as a basis for deeper investigations.[593] In the context of purchase initiation investors also have a look at key figures in order to evaluate if a purchase of a share is worthwhile.[594]

Rating agencies base their assessment of companies partly on key figures calculated on the basis of financial accounting data. This fact underlines the importance of key figures for this group.[595] Debt capital providers also use key figures before giving loans or to control the financial performance of a company during the redemption of the credit.[596]

In the study of PAAinE respondents are asked for areas of improvement regarding annual reports. In third place of the ranking of what users like to have is that trends in growth and profitability are clearly shown in the annual report.[597] A possible solution is key figures which summarise data and show trends.[598]

In contrast, the disclosure of key figures does not meet the primary information needs of private investors as many of them do not have the knowledge to interpret them. Rather they are interested in the interpretation of disclosed key figures. This task is fulfilled by the group of financial intermediaries.[599]

588 Cf. Banzhaf, J. (2006), pp. 132-133, cf. for a graphic illustration of single steps of fundamental analysis Banzhaf, J. (2006), p. 133.
589 Cf. Maditinos, D. I., Sevic, Z., Theriou, N. G. (2007), p. 34.
590 Cf. Maditinos, D. I., Sevic, Z., Theriou, N. G. (2007), p. 37.
591 Cf. Maditinos, D. I., Sevic, Z., Theriou, N. G. (2007), p. 42.
592 Cf. Achleitner, A.-K., Bassen, A., Pietzsch, L., et al. (2002); Pro-Active Accounting Activities in Europe (PAAinE) (2009); PwC (2007), https://www.pwc.com/gx/en/ifrs-reporting/pdf/measuringassetssurvey.pdf.
593 Cf. Bastini, K. (2015), pp. 46-47.
594 Cf. Spremann, K., Gantenbein, P. (2005), p. 17.
595 Cf. Buschmeier, A. (2011), pp. 150-151; Wappenschmidt, C. (2009), p. 99.
596 Cf. Khakad, F. (2009), pp. 19-20; Theis, J. C. (2014), p. 67.
597 Cf. Pro-Active Accounting Activities in Europe (PAAinE) (2009), p. 6.
598 Cf. Hienerth, C. (2010), pp. 37-38; Palupski, R. (2002), p. 141.
599 Cf. Huchzermeier, M. (2006), p. 79.

2.4 Information Delivery of Companies on the Basis of IFRS Annual Accounts and Value Reporting

2.4.1 Role of Accounting in the Context of Principal Agent Theory, Theory of Efficient Capital Markets and Information Needs of Investors

The insights of the Principal Agent Theory as part of new institutional economics and the theory of efficient markets as part of neoclassic show that it is necessary for companies to report about their performance and activities to capital market actors.[600] Due to the market efficiency in the nearly semi-strong form the reporting of companies directly influences the price formation on capital markets as reporting transforms insider information into public information. As a valuation tool investors mainly use the fundamental analysis which directly gathers data from the published information. So companies also influence with their disclosure behaviour the precision of investors' fundamental analysis. Also the role of financial intermediaries has become clear. They support the information processing on capital markets and process information on behalf of other capital market participants. Their analysis mainly bases on accounting information. All market participants who delegate the research task to analysts establish a kind of indirect demand for reporting information. So, reporting and accounting information influences the stock price of a company on capital markets. The annual reports are one of the most important information sources for investors.[601]

With the help of accounting the information received earlier by other information sources are confirmed reliably for capital market participants. Thus, the disclosure of financial information has a confirmatory role. This information allows third parties to check if information about company's performance reported earlier by management is reliable and true.[602]

It also reduces the gap between well-informed investors on the basis of private information and the rest of investors. By reducing this information gap, public disclosure increases the efficiency of capital markets.[603] Furthermore, accounting influences the assessment of management's performance because information about a company's performance is sent to market participants in order to reduce existing information asymmetries.[604]

So far, two objectives have been attributed to financial reporting: On the one hand its information role, that investors use financial reporting as a main source for investment decisions (ex-ante or valuation role of accounting information). On the other hand it has a stewardship role. Company's stakeholders have the information available to control management's actions (ex-post or stewardship role of accounting information). The second role has been explained with the help of the Principal Agent Theory.[605]

600 Cf. Wenzel, J. (2005), pp. 91-107.

601 Cf. Erkilet, G., Kholmy, K. (2016), p. 38.

602 Cf. Wagenhofer, A., Ewert, R. (2015), p. 130; cf. for an empirical analysis of the confirmation hypothesis Ball, R., Jayaraman, S., Shivakumar, L. (2012).

603 Cf. Zhang, G. (2001), p. 366.

604 Cf. for similar argumentation and conclusions in this paragraph Labhart, P. (1999), pp. 60-67.

605 Cf. Beyer, A., Cohen, D. A., Lys, T. Z., et al. (2010), p. 296; Brüggemann, U., Hitz, J.-M., Selhorn, T. (2013), pp. 8-9.

Accounting standards have the main purpose to reduce existing information asymmetries between owners and managers. With the help of accounting standards it is avoided that every owner has to negotiate individually with the company and agree on the content of information supply.[606] Also for the company reduced information asymmetries have positive effects as a reduction in information asymmetry leads to a decreased uncertainty on investors' side what results in reduced cost of capital for companies.[607]

Key figures play an important role in this context as the analysis of information needs of capital market participants and the discussion in the context of the Principal Agent Theory reveals.[608]

The importance of accounting can also be proved by theory and empirical studies but also with the help of several financial crises in the last decades, e.g. the Asian financial crisis in 1997, the Enron scandal and the financial crisis in 2008.[609] The reaction to these crises is commonly a tightening of regulation. As a reaction to the Enron and WorldCom scandal, the Sarbanes-Oxley Act in 2002 which strengthens the role of auditors and prescribes companies to reveal weaknesses of their internal control system in the annual report was introduced.[610]

Now this chapter analyses on the one hand the legally prescribed reporting obligations of companies and on the other hand the scientific discussion about voluntary reporting and its advantages.[611]

2.4.2 IFRS as Rules for Disclosing Financal Statements

The obligation of companies to publicly disclose can be divided into four areas with the help of the criteria publication frequency and basis of decision-making. The criterion of publication frequency divides publication into regular publications and publication which occurs only if certain events happen. Parts of the regular publication are the quarterly and annual reports of companies on the basis of the IFRS. The basis of decision-making roughly indicates for which decisions stakeholders take which information source. The systematisation of publication is illustrated in figure 7.[612]

In the European Union all companies whose securities are admitted to trading on a regulated market in one member state have to prepare their consolidated financial statements on the basis of IFRS for fiscal years beginning on or after 1st January 2005.[613] The decision that companies have to applicate IFRS rules only on group accounts level is a comprise because so far accounting data has been used for several purposes in the different EU member states beside information like taxation or pay out restrictions.[614]

606 Cf. Brown, P. (2011), pp. 270-271; Gantzhorn, A. (2016), pp. 114-115; Theis, J. C. (2014), pp. 24-28.

607 Cf. Erkilet, G., Kholmy, K. (2016), p. 41.

608 Cf. Trautwein, A. (2007), p. 26; Wenzel, J. (2005), pp. 91 – 107 who also justifies the reporting activities of companies on the basis of neoclassic and new institutional economic theories.

609 Cf. Leuz, C., Wysocki, P. D. (2016), p. 526.

610 Cf. Leuz, C., Wysocki, P. D. (2016), p. 563.

611 Cf. Pellens, B. (2001), p. 1742.

612 Cf. Ruhnke, K., Simons, D. (2012), pp. 44-45.

613 Cf. Daske, H., Gebhardt, G. (2006), p. 463, Erkilet, G., Kholmy, K. (2016), p. 35.

614 Cf. Brüggemann, U., Hitz, J.-M., Selhorn, T. (2013), p. 10.

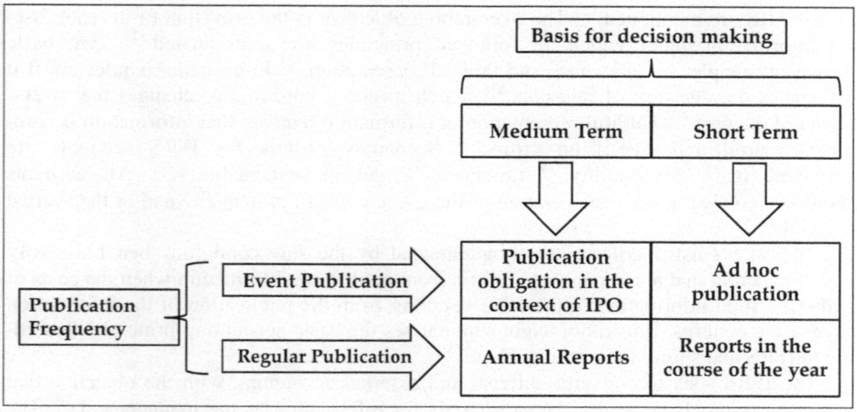

Source: In the style of: Ruhnke, K., Simons, D. (2012), p. 45
Illustration 7: Systematisation of companys' publication[615]

The adoption of IFRS has increased substantially around the world in recent years.[616] More than 120 countries have adopted IFRS accounting rules,[617] amongst others the 27 member countries of the EU.[618] Since 2008 the New York Stock Exchange offers listed companies the possibility to publish their financial reports under IFRS instead of US GAAP.[619] Many other countries have started convergence projects in order to align their rules with IFRS.[620]

An annual financial statement consists of a statement of financial position, statement of comprehensive income (which is further divided into separate income statement and other comprehensive income), notes, statements of cash flows and statement of changes in equity. For companies listed at a stock market, a segment reporting and the calculation of earnings per share are obligatory parts. The financial review by management or management report is not a mandatory element according to IFRS but for example for German companies it is mandatory because the German local GAAP stipulates it.[621]

IFRS are created for equity and debt capital providers and consider their information needs primarily.[622] IFRS contain a framework in which all basic principles for accounting

615 Cf. for a similiar classification of publication Gantzhorn, A. (2016), pp. 14-15.
616 Cf. Daske, H., Gebhardt, G. (2006), pp. 463-464; Daske, H., Hail, L., Leuz, C., et al. (2013), p. 496; George, E. T. de, Li, X., Shivakumar, L. (2016), p. 899.
617 Cf. Erkilet, G., Kholmy, K. (2016), p. 33.
618 Cf. Byard, D., Li, Y., Yu, Y. (2011), p. 70.
619 Cf. Erkilet, G., Kholmy, K. (2016), p. 35.
620 Cf. Ball, R. (2006), p. 9.
621 Cf. Hippel, B. (2011), pp. 3, 13; Müller, S. (2007), pp. 33-36; Ruhnke, K., Simons, D. (2012), p. 47; for an overview of parts of IFRS financial statements Pellens, B., Fülbier, R. U., Gassen, J., et al. (2017), pp. 177-244; Ruhnke, K., Simons, D. (2012), pp. 45-48.
622 Cf. IFRS Foundation (2016), Conceptual Framework QB2-QB3, QB10; Lüdenbach, N., Hoffmann, W.-D., Freiberg, J. (2015), § 1, Marginal Number 5.

under IFRS are mentioned.[623] The overarching objective is the provision of decision useful information under which all followed principles are subordinated.[624] Two basic primary principles are relevance and faithful presentation.[625] Information is relevant, if it influences the decision of investors,[626] which means it confirms or changes the assessments of the past.[627] Faithful presentation of information requires that information is complete, neutral and free from errors.[628] Secondary criteria for IFRS accounts are comparability,[629] verifiability,[630] timeliness[631] and understandability.[632] All accounts should be created under consideration of the going concern principle[633] and of the accrual principle.[634]

The so far listed criteria are complemented by the side condition "benefits justify costs" meaning that a company can refrain from publishing information when the costs of gathering such information or the costs resulting from the publication of the information exceed the benefits. Illustration eight summarises the basic accounting principles according to IFRS and shows their relationship.[635]

The IFRS seek to converge internal and external accounting with the objective that external persons have nearly the same basis for information as the management.[636] The management approach[637] is explicitly shown in the segment reporting which should base on the internal organisational and reporting structure but is not limited to segment reporting.[638] It is used in every case when internal data is used for compiling the data for accounting.[639] Examples are the support of controlling for identifying cash generating units for impairment tests or the calculation of indirect costs for capitalising self-produced assets.[640]

623 Cf. IFRS Foundation (2016), Conceptual Framework, cf. for an overview of the most important accounting principles Pellens, B., Fülbier, R. U., Gassen, J., et al. (2017), pp. 95-126.
624 Cf. IFRS Foundation (2016), Conceptual Framework QB2, IAS 1.9; Lüdenbach, N., Hoffmann, W.-D., Freiberg, J. (2015), § 1, Marginal Number 16.
625 Cf. IFRS Foundation (2016), Conceptual Framework QC17; Lüdenbach, N., Hoffmann, W.-D., Freiberg, J. (2015), § 1, Marginal Number 17; Pricewaterhouse Coopers (PWC) (2017), 1.27.
626 Cf. IFRS Foundation (2016), Conceptual Framework QC6.
627 Cf. IFRS Foundation (2016), Conceptual Framework QC7; Pricewaterhouse Coopers (PWC) (2017), 1.64.
628 Cf. IFRS Foundation (2016), Conceptual Framework QC12.
629 Cf. IFRS Foundation (2016), Conceptual Framework QC20-QC25.
630 Cf. IFRS Foundation (2016), Conceptual Framework QC26-QC28.
631 Cf. IFRS Foundation (2016), Conceptual Framework QC29.
632 Cf. IFRS Foundation (2016), Conceptual Framework QC30-QC32; Pricewaterhouse Coopers (PWC) (2017), 1.28; cf. for an overview of the three criteria Ernst & Young (2018), pp. 50-51.
633 Cf. IFRS Foundation (2016), Conceptual Framework 4.1, IAS 1.25.
634 Cf. IFRS Foundation (2016), IAS 1.27.
635 Cf. IFRS Foundation (2016), QC35-QC39.
636 Cf. Pellens, B., Fülbier, R. U., Gassen, J., et al. (2017), p. 1022.
637 Cf. for information about the management approach Wagenhofer, A. (2006), p. 4; Weißenberger, B. E. (2007), pp. 167-226.
638 Cf. Pellens, B., Fülbier, R. U., Gassen, J., et al. (2017), p. 1022.
639 Cf. Wagenhofer, A. (2006), p. 4; Weißenberger, B. E. (2007), p. 169.
640 Cf. IAS 36 for impairment tests and IAS 16 / 38 for capitalizing tangibles and intangible assets, cf. Weißenberger, B. E. (2007) for an overview of accounting standards with management approach elements p. 179.

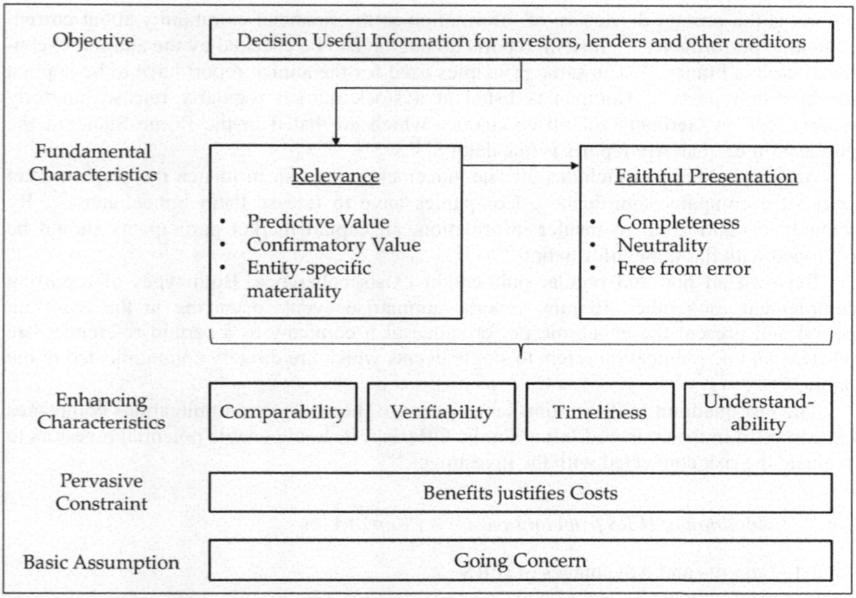

Source: In the style of: Ernst & Young (2018), p. 46; Pellens, B., Fülbier, R. U., Gassen, J. et al. (2017), p. 111

Illustration 8: Accounting Principles of IFRS

In respect of key figures the management approach is of high importance. Managers decide for key figures which support them in increasing the Shareholder Value of a company. So, this information is relevant for investors and supports them in their investment decisions.[641]

The presented principles of IFRS and the management approach demonstrate that the IFRS accounts want to enable the readers to estimate the future cash flows of a company.[642] This corresponds to the information needs of most investors and is an explanation as to why annual accounts are often used as a reliable source of information.[643]

The category reports in the course of the year, shown in illustration seven, summarises all reports which are published between two annual reports.[644] Interim reports mainly have two functions: Firstly, they should ensure the allocation efficiency of the capital market. Secondly, they are an additional instrument of performance control and reduce information asymmetry between management and shareholders.[645] The main purpose of these

641 Cf. Weißenberger, B. E. (2007), p. 170.

642 Cf. IFRS Foundation (2016), Conceptual Framework QB3; Pellens, B., Fülbier, R. U., Gassen, J., et al. (2017), pp. 100-101.

643 Cf. chapter 2.3.2.2.

644 Cf. Gibson, C. H. (2013), p. 341, cf. for an overview of studies which deal with the value relevance of interim reports Dumontier, P., Raffournier, B. (2002), pp. 121-123.

645 Cf. Coenenberg, A. G., Federspieler, C. (1999), p. 169.

reports is the prompt disclosure of information to the financial community about current economic performance.[646] Interim reports do not have to be checked by the auditor, exceptional case is France.[647] The same principles used for the annual report have to be applied for interim reports.[648] Companies listed at a stock market regularly release quarterly reports, e.g. in Germany for all companies which are listed in the Prime Standard the publication of quarterly reports is mandatory.[649]

Ad hoc publication includes all announcements that can influence the stock market price of a company significantly. Companies have to release them immediately.[650] By immediate publication of insider information, all capital market participants should be equipped with the same information.[651]

Between ad hoc and regular publication exists coherence. Both types of reporting complement each other. Regular reports summarise events occurring in the reporting period and present the economic performance of a company to a certain reference date whereas ad hoc publication refers to single events which are directly communicated to the public.[652]

The last quadrant in illustration seven refers to the information obligations companies have to fulfil in the course of Initial Public Offering. It should enable potential investors to evaluate the risk connected with the investment.[653]

2.4.3 Evaluation of IFRS from an Investor's Point of View

2.4.3.1 Benefits and Advantages of IFRS

Following the overview of basic accounting principles of IFRS, this chapter evaluates the advantages and disadvantages resulting from IFRS application especially relating to the situation in the EU.[654] Firstly, the advantages and benefits are presented followed by the disadvantages and costs out of IFRS application. In this context particularly the flaws of IFRS reporting from an investor's point of view should be considered.[655]

Due to the dispersion of Shareholder Value approach and globalisation the importance of global capital procurement increases. Therefore, it is important for companies to

646 Cf. Haenelt, T. (2009), p. 26; cf. also the empirical study of Landsman, W. R., Maydew, E. L. (2002) who analyse that the informativeness of interim reports has increased over time.

647 Cf. Coenenberg, A. G., Federspieler, C. (1999), pp. 170-172.

648 Cf. Gibson, C. H. (2013), p. 341, Haenelt, T. (2009), p. 18.

649 Cf. Prätsch, J., Schikorra, U., Ludwig, E. (2012), pp. 77-78; Zantow, R., Dinauer, J. (2011), p. 91. The German stock market is divided into General and Prime Standard. Companies listed at the General Standard can apply the legal rules for interim reports. Companies in the Prime Standard have more comprehensive publication obligations.

650 Cf. Hauser, S. E. (2003), p. 119; Wittich, G. (2001), pp. 15-17; Zimmermann, J., Werner, J. R., Hitz, J.-M. (2011), p. 30.

651 Cf. Gros, M. (2010), p. 61; Hauser, S. E. (2003), p. 119.

652 Cf. Fülbier, R. U. (1998), p. 277; Griewel, E. (2006), p. 194.

653 Cf. Pellens, B. (2001), p. 1748; Ruhnke, K., Simons, D. (2012), p. 70.

654 Cf. extensively of an overview of studies dealing with advantages and disadvantages of IFRS adoption: George, E. T. de, Li, X., Shivakumar, L. (2016).

655 Cf. also for critics about IFRS exemplarily Frings, G. W., Frings, M. C., Mastilak, C. (2012a) and contradictory comment Renwick, C. (2012) and authors' response Frings, G. W., Frings, M. C., Mastilak, C. (2012b).

disclose their financial statements in a globally acknowledged accounting standard like IFRS.[656] Companies listed on international stock exchanges have a basic incentive to provide foreign investors with accounting standards they are familiar with because this facilitates capital procurement from these investors and enables companies to communicate with investors worldwide.[657] Investors would also have the possibility to exert pressure on companies to follow the IFRS rules. Otherwise, they require higher rates of return or withdraw their capital.[658]

The increased application of IFRS strengthens comparability and transparency resulting in better functioning capital markets.[659] For example, analysts do not have to make such a high number of adjustments to the financial statements of companies which are located in different countries.[660] IFRS facilitate the consolidation of foreign subsidiaries in group accounts.[661] For capital market participants the cost of processing information across different countries reduces what has direct effects on the information efficiency of capital markets. Reducing national differences in financial reporting should lead to an increase in cross-border capital flows and investments.[662] Furthermore, costs for companies and investors reduce in total as a single set of accounting standards can be used transnationally.[663] An example for increased cross-border investment is the fact that American investment funds increase their shares in companies applying IFRS. In general, it can be stated that IFRS facilitate the investment activities of international investment funds because financial statements are more comparable for them.[664]

IFRS group accounts are a reliable source of information because auditors have to check and sign for the correspondence of financial reporting with IFRS.[665] Using the same standards empowers auditors to enforce these rules more intensively.[666] One further important factor for ensuring reporting quality is effective enforcement of IFRS rules which ensures that rules have to be used consequently by companies.[667]

Proponents of IFRS state that in general IFRS are more capital market orientated and provide the recipients of financial reports with more information in comparison to the most local GAAPs.[668] A further advantage is that IFRS contain less discretion for

656 Cf. Cuijpers, R., Buijink, W. (2005), p. 489.
657 Cf. Cuijpers, R., Buijink, W. (2005), p. 495.
658 Cf. Damant, D. (2006), p. 30.
659 Cf. Ball, R. (2006), p. 7; Brüggemann, U., Hitz, J.-M., Selhorn, T. (2013), , p. 2; Chen, C., Young, D., Zhuang, Z. (2013), pp. 881-884; Pellens, B., Tomaszewski, C. (1999), p. 201.
660 Cf. Ball, R. (2006), p. 11.
661 Cf. Pellens, B., Tomaszewski, C. (1999), p. 201.
662 Cf. Ball, R. (2006), p. 11; Daske, H., Hail, L., Leuz, C., et al. (2008), p. 1092; Erkilet, G., Kholmy, K. (2016), p. 37.
663 Cf. Leuz, C., Wysocki, P. D. (2016), p. 584.
664 Cf. Brown, P. (2011), pp. 273-274.
665 Cf. Dechow, P., Ge, W., Schrand, C. (2010), p. 368; Gantzhorn, A. (2016), pp. 116-118; Healy, P. M., Palepu, K. G. (2001), p. 779; Kausar, A., Shroff, N., White, H. (2016), p. 157.
666 Cf. Ball, R. (2006), p. 7.
667 Cf. Brown, P. (2011), pp. 279-280; Horton, J., Serafeim, G., Serafeim, I. (2013), p. 388; cf. the empirical study of Christensen, H. B., Hail, L., Leuz, C. (2016) who shows difference in liquidity effects between different EU-countries in implementing two EU directives on security regulation.
668 Cf. Daske, H., Hail, L., Leuz, C., et al. (2008), pp. 1091-1092; Daske, H., Hail, L., Leuz, C., et al. (2013), p. 502; Erkilet, G., Kholmy, K. (2016), p. 37; Horton, J., Serafeim, G., Serafeim, I.

companies and earnings management than most local GAAPs.[669] The introduction of IFRS offers companies located in countries with a local GAAP of low quality a possibility to increase the quality of their disclose by using the IFRS.[670]

The IFRS often prescribe Fair Values[671] as a primary measure for recognition on balance sheet.[672] Fair Value Accounting transfers more timely information into the financial statements because Fair Values cannot be influenced by managers. They are observable measures on an independent market.[673] In a survey of investors they clearly prefer the Fair Value concept of IFRS. But their preference is limited to Fair Values directly derived from the market figures. Fair Values which are based on the model to market approach are assessed as less useful for decision-making.[674] The application of Fair Values is not uncontroversial but in many cases the alternative – the historical cost approach – is a worse solution.[675]

The quality of IFRS can be measured with the help of the quality of financial analysts' forecasts. Empirical studies generally approve a better quality of analysts' forecasts, so it can be concluded that information delivery due to IFRS adaption has been improved.[676] Financial analysts are a group which especially benefits from IFRS. They are able to compare financial statements of companies located in different countries better than before IFRS introduction.[677] Of course, comparability is limited to the extent at which national accounting practices can be retained under IFRS.[678]

Byard et al. document that analysts' information environment improves due to the introduction of IFRS but only within countries with strong enforcement mechanisms and local GAAPs that differ significantly from IFRS.[679]

Despite remaining national accounting practices and individual firm incentives the variability of ratios has declined after the introduction of IFRS in Europe indicating that accounting standards across countries have converged due to IFRS application.[680] In

(2013), p. 390; cf. also the empirical study of Barth, M. E., Landsman, W. R., Lang, M. H. (2008) who proves a higher accounting quality for voluntary IFRS adopters.

669 Cf. Daske, H., Hail, L., Leuz, C., et al. (2008), pp. 1091-1092.

670 Cf. Cuijpers, R., Buijink, W. (2005), p. 496.

671 According to IFRS the Fair Value is defined as "the price that would be received to sell an asset or paid to transfer a liability in an orderly transaction between market participants at measurement date" (quote taken from: IFRS 13.9).

672 Cf. for an extensive discussion about the pros and cons of Fair Value Accounting Kühnberger, M. (2014); Laux, C., Leuz, C. (2009).

673 Cf. Ball, R. (2006), pp. 12-13; Kühnberger, M. (2014), p. 434.

674 Cf. CFA Institute Centre for Financial Market Integrity (2007), p. 18; Gassen, J., Schwedler, K. (2010), pp. 504-506; cf. also the empirical study of Barth, M. E., Landsman, W. R., Young, D., et al. (2014) for a prove of value relevance of fair values measures for investors of financial companies.

675 Cf. Laux, C., Leuz, C. (2009), p. 827.

676 Cf. Chalmers, K., Clinch, G., Godfrey, J. M., et al. (2012), pp. 704-707; Erkilet, G., Kholmy, K. (2016), pp. 50-60; Horton, J., Serafeim, G., Serafeim, I. (2013), pp. 400-401; cf. for an overview and summary of several empirical studies; Healy, P. M., Palepu, K. G. (2001), pp. 417-418.

677 Cf. Brown, P. (2011), pp. 273-274, cf. the empirical studies of Horton, Karamanou, Chalmers.

678 Cf. Brown, P. (2011), p. 275.

679 Cf. Byard, D., Li, Y., Yu, Y. (2011), p. 84.

680 Cf. the empirical study of Jones, S., Finley, A. (2011).

relation to the value relevance of accounting, empirical results are mixed.[681] In the empirical study of Daske and Gebhardt experts rating of financial statements are analysed for IFRS accounts. The authors take scores from yearly best annual reports contests in Germany, Austria and Switzerland and modify them for their analysis.[682] For their sample the ratings of experts has improved. Thus, this is a sign that accounting quality has increased since IFRS introduction.[683] An interesting finding is that also the transparency of financial statements of mandatory adopters increases and not only those of voluntary adopters.[684]

From the Principal Agent Theory point of view reporting is a kind of monitoring and therefore ensures that the management acts in the sense of shareholders.[685] Several empirical studies conclude that better reporting increases the efficiency of the investment process.[686] Thus, IFRS reduce agency costs. The relationship between companies and capital lenders experience a higher degree of efficiency due to increased transparency.[687]

Due to reduced information asymmetries and reduced adverse selection problems disclosure also increases market liquidity. Empirical literature confirms this coherence.[688]

It is assumed in scientific literature that a high quality accounting and reporting reduces cost of equity and debt capital.[689] Theoretical and empirical studies also indicate a negative coherence between disclosure and cost of capital. In comparison to the effects on liquidity, the results are mixed because the effects are often limited to a subgroup of firms within empirical studies.[690]

Within their empirical analysis Daske et al. detect that cost of capital decreases in the context of IFRS introduction. This means that capital market participants lower their required rate of return due to more transparency and information available.[691] Furthermore, they prove with their empirical study the importance of enforcement as they show that liquidity and cost of capital effects are significantly higher in countries with a strong enforcement mechanism.[692]

Christensen et al. ascribe the positive effects of IFRS to the change of enforcement mechanism and not to the quality of accounting standards. The positive effect on liquidity is limited to five countries in the EU which simultaneously had changes in their enforcement mechanisms.[693]

681 Cf. for an overview of empirical studies Brown, P. (2011), pp. 276-277.
682 Cf. Daske, H., Gebhardt, G. (2006), pp. 467-471.
683 Cf. Daske, H., Gebhardt, G. (2006), pp. 473-486.
684 Cf. Daske, H., Gebhardt, G. (2006), p. 488.
685 Cf. Leuz, C., Wysocki, P. D. (2016), p. 550.
686 Cf. exemplarily Badertscher, B., Shroff, N., White, H. D. (2013), Chen et al., Goodman et al., cf. for an overview Leuz, C., Wysocki, P. D. (2016), p. 551.
687 Cf. Ball, R. (2006), pp. 11-12.
688 Cf. Leuz, C., Wysocki, P. D. (2016), pp. 546-548 for an overview of the current state of research.
689 Cf. Dechow, P., Ge, W., Schrand, C. (2010), p. 384; Wagenhofer, A., Ewert, R. (2015), p. 131.
690 Cf. Leuz, C., Wysocki, P. D. (2016), pp. 548-550 for an overview of the current status of research.
691 Cf. Daske, H., Hail, L., Leuz, C., et al. (2008), pp. 1112-1115; cf. also for similar results the empirical study of Karamanou, I., Nishiotis, G. P. (2009).
692 Cf. Daske, H., Hail, L., Leuz, C., et al. (2008), p. 1120.
693 Cf. Christensen, H. B., Hail, L., Leuz, C. (2013), pp. 148-150.

Aharony et al. prove that the value relevance of goodwill, research and development expenditures and asset revaluation has improved after the IFRS introduction.[694] Florou and Kosi determine a negative coherence for the cost of debt capital after IFRS application.[695] Contrary to this, the study of Cuijpers and Buijink cannot confirm this negative coherence between cost of capital and transparency.[696] Furthermore, a significant reduction of information asymmetries cannot be proven.[697] Elbakry et al. conclude that key figures under IFRS are more informative than key figures based on local German or UK GAAP.[698] Thus, empirical evidence on positive effects of IFRS introduction is mixed.[699]

2.4.3.2 Costs and Flaws of IFRS Reporting

After analysing benefits and advantages for companies and investors due to IFRS application in the EU, this chapter now lists potential costs and disadvantages.

One of the named advantages is that IFRS increase reporting quality. This is questionable because IFRS offer the management a lot of discretion. Many standards are based on private information and require judgement.[700] It is difficult for external persons to detect this implicit right of choices.[701] Managers can use this discretion to hide true economic performance or to avoid covenant violations.[702] It is also probable that auditors and managers interpret this discretion offered by IFRS in a different way from country to country.[703] These facts limit the comparability of economic performance of different companies.[704]

It is a decisive question what the concrete influence of accounting standards on reporting quality really is. Application of accounting standards always involves a lot of private information and offers companies a lot of discretion. The way firms use this discretion depends on factors like a countries' legal system, market forces, ownership structure, compensation or financing agreements as well as the current situation of the

694 Cf. Aharony, J., Barniv, R., Falk, H. (2010), pp. 551-564, cf. also the study of Jermakowicz, E. K., Prather-Kinsey, J., Wulf, I. (2007) who have similar results for the value relevance of earnings and the book value of equity. Devalle, A., Onali, E., Magarini, R. (2010) demonstrate different effects on value relevance for earnings and book values of equity.

695 Cf. Florou, A., Kosi, U. (2015), pp. 1409-1410.

696 Cf. Cuijpers, R., Buijink, W. (2005), pp. 508-513.

697 Cf. Cuijpers, R., Buijink, W. (2005), pp. 518-519.

698 Cf. Elbakry, A. E., Nwachukwu, J. C., Abdou, H. A., et al. (2017), p. 11.

699 Cf. exemplarily the studies of Bhat, G., Callen, J. L., Segal, D. (2014) who find no improvement of credit risk informativeness under IFRS, while Wu, J. S., Zhang, I. X. (2014) find evidence for a higher informativeness under IFRS, given a strong enforcement mechanism in a country.

700 Cf. Burgstahler, D. C., Hail, L., Leuz, C. (2006), p. 984; Daske, H., Hail, L., Leuz, C., et al. (2013), pp. 500-501; cf. for a basic overview of various discretions Coenenberg, A. G., Haller, A., Schultze, W. (2014), pp. 1010-1011.

701 Cf. Küting, K., Weber, C.-P. (2015), pp. 39-42.

702 Cf. Burgstahler, D. C., Hail, L., Leuz, C. (2006), p. 986.

703 Cf. Ball, R. (2006), p. 22.

704 Cf. Frings, G. W., Frings, M. C., Mastilak, C. (2012a), pp. 18-19; Küting, K., Weber, C.-P. (2015), pp. 23-24.

company itself.[705] This argument questions the increased comparability and transparency in the context of IFRS introduction because companies have the possibility to influence reported information in a way that they do not become more informative. This argument still holds in countries with strong enforcement because enforcement only ensures that reported information corresponds to IFRS and does not change reporting incentives or reduce discretion offered by IFRS.[706] Following the argumentation structure of the incentive view, it becomes clear that due to local different incentives in the EU the differences in accounting do not suddenly disappear despite uniform accounting standards.[707]

Burgstahler, Hail and Leuz detect in their empirical study that capital markets improve the informativeness of earnings by offering companies incentives to report in a more transparent way. The intensity of earnings management also depends on the strength of the legal system and enforcement of accounting rules.[708] Accounting rules within the European Union can differ across countries. For example, the United Kingdom is often assessed as an economy which fosters transparency whereas Germany or Italy are regularly evaluated as insider economies.[709]

Ball et al. documented that IFRS adoption per se does not lead to a higher quality in accounting. Also enforcement and companies' reporting incentives play an important role in this study.[710]

Kothari et al. demonstrate that managers often withhold bad news but inform investors quickly about good news. The authors assume career incentives for managers for this behaviour. The immediate publication of bad news can for example be triggered by litigation risk.[711] The presented incentive view is at least partly confirmed by the fact that despite IFRS introduction country-specific reporting patterns still can be detected.[712]

The incentive view[713] goes back to the work of Watts and Zimmerman and the Positive Accounting Theory which both say that the way how managers use discretion offered by accounting standards is influenced by the given incentives. The Positive Accounting Theory can be seen as a theoretical construct and explanation why managers conduct earnings management and influence numbers in profit and loss statements and on balance sheets.[714]

The Positive Accounting Theory[715] considers the accounting choice of managers as a result of the economic consequences connected with the accounting choice. It refers to

---

705 Cf. Ball, R., Robin, A., Wu, J. S. (2003), 235-238; Brüggemann, U., Hitz, J.-M., Selhorn, T. (2013), pp. 10-11; Daske, H., Hail, L., Leuz, C., et al. (2008), pp. 1092-1093; Leuz, C., Wysocki, P. D. (2016), pp. 583-584.

706 Cf. Daske, H., Hail, L., Leuz, C., et al. (2008), pp. 1092-1093.

707 Cf. Brown, P. (2011), p. 271.

708 Cf. Burgstahler, D. C., Hail, L., Leuz, C. (2006), p. 985.

709 Cf. Burgstahler, D. C., Hail, L., Leuz, C. (2006), p. 989.

710 Cf. Ball, R., Robin, A., Wu, J. S. (2003), for further empirical studies confirming the incentive view cf. exemplarily Ball, R., Kothari, S. P., Robin, A. (2000); Ball, R., Shivakumar, L. (2005); Burgstahler, D. C., Hail, L., Leuz, C. (2006); Jeanjean, T., Stolowy, H. (2008).

711 Cf. Kothari, S. P., Shu, S., Wysocki, P. D. (2009), pp. 241-242.

712 Cf. Leuz, C., Wysocki, P. D. (2016), p. 587.

713 Cf. for an overview of empirical studies Leuz, C., Wysocki, P. D. (2016), pp. 583-584.

714 Cf. Healy, P. M., Palepu, K. G. (2001), pp. 419-420; Kothari, S. P. (2001), p. 111; Leuz, C., Wysocki, P. D. (2016), pp. 583-584.

715 Cf. basically for Positive Accounting Theory Watts, R. L., Zimmerman, J. L. (1978); Watts, R. L., Zimmerman, J. L. (1979); Watts, R. L., Zimmerman, J. L. (1986).

elements of the Principal Agent Theory. Managers act as agents, recipients of annual reports as principals.[716] Both parties agree on a set of accounting choices. Auditors control the adherence of these rules. Managers as agents act opportunistically and try to maximise their wealth.[717] They make their accounting choices in dependence of existing control mechanism by principals.[718] On the basis of these assumptions the theory has developed three hypotheses.

- Firstly, managers prefer accounting choices which increase their compensation if their compensations depend on accounting numbers (bonus hypothesis).[719] They try to shift reported earnings from future periods to the present period.[720]
- Secondly, managers make their accounting choices to fulfil debt covenants. Thus, the higher the leverage ratio, the more likely managers try to increase company's income in current periods in order to fulfil debt covenants (debt/equity hypothesis).[721]
- Thirdly, especially large firms try to avoid political pressure by reducing profits as politicians assess large profits as a sign of a monopoly (political cost hypothesis).[722]

In total, the statement of Positive Accounting Theory is that accounting does not illustrate the real economic situation but to adapt it to the objectives of agents or principals.[723] Despite empirical studies which confirm the hypothesis[724] the Positive Accounting Theory is also criticized in the scientific literature for its research methods and methodologies as well as for science issues.[725]

The effects of Positive Accounting Theory are limited because the market seems to be able at least to a certain degree to determine the reporting quality.[726] From the Principal Agent Theory's point of view IFRS should be a signal of high-quality. Implementation of accounting standards happens on different levels, therefore for agents with low quality this signal is easy to imitate. It has become more difficult for companies to differentiate by using IFRS.[727] In order to create a trustworthy signal, a worldwide effective enforcement mechanism of IFRS rules would be needed.[728] However, in an empirical study the authors

716 Cf. Collin, S.-O. Y., Tagesson, T., Andersson, A., et al. (2009), pp. 145-146; Falkman, P., Tagesson, T. (2008), p. 273.

717 Cf. Collin, S.-O. Y., Tagesson, T., Andersson, A., et al. (2009), pp. 145-146; Watts, R. L., Zimmerman, J. L. (1990), pp. 134-137.

718 Cf. Falkman, P., Tagesson, T. (2008), p. 273; Tietz-Weber, S. (2006), p. 52.

719 Cf. Milne, M. J. (2002), pp. 372-373; Watts, R. L., Zimmerman, J. L. (1990), pp. 138-139.

720 Cf. Holthausen, R. W., Leftwich, R. W. (1983), p. 84; Watts, R. L., Zimmerman, J. L. (1986), p. 208.

721 Cf. Holthausen, R. W., Leftwich, R. W. (1983), p. 86; Milne, M. J. (2002), pp. 372-373; Watts, R. L., Zimmerman, J. L. (1986), pp. 210-220; Watts, R. L., Zimmerman, J. L. (1990), p. 139.

722 Cf. Holthausen, R. W., Leftwich, R. W. (1983), p. 85; Milne, M. J. (2002), pp. 372-373; Watts, R. L., Zimmerman, J. L. (1986), p. 354; Watts, R. L., Zimmerman, J. L. (1990), p. 139.

723 Cf. Heiden, M. (2006), p. 167.

724 Cf. for an overview of empirical studies Fields, T. D., Lys, T. Z., Vincent, L. (2001), pp. 265-275; Watts, R. L., Zimmerman, J. L. (1986), pp. 244-268, cf. exemplarily for empirical studies Bowen, R. M., Noreen, E. W. (1981); Holthausen, R. W. (1981).

725 Cf. for an overview of critical comments Boland, L. A., Gordon, I. M. (1992); Watts, R. L., Zimmerman, J. L. (1990), pp. 140-149.

726 Cf. Daske, H., Hail, L., Leuz, C., et al. (2013), pp. 533-535.

727 Cf. Ball, R. (2006), pp. 22-23.

728 Cf. Ball, R. (2006), p. 24.

analyse that the market is able to differentiate between companies which adopt IFRS only from the name but do not change their reporting behaviour and companies which adopt IFRS in order to change their reporting behaviour and increase transparency.[729] Indeed so-called serious adopters of IFRS experience a decline in the cost of capital.[730] Thus, the market is able to differentiate up to a certain degree between the reporting qualities of companies.[731]

A further problem that diminishes the benefit of comparability is that the implementation of IFRS does not have the same quality in every country. Some countries have a developed accounting and auditing profession whilst others are less robust.[732] On these factors it also depends how the IFRS rules are controlled. An example is the impairment rules. It is not probable that auditors in all countries will go with the same degree of accuracy and thoroughness through a company's asset.[733] The different level of implementation of IFRS within different countries could increase processing costs because differences are not at the highest level of accounting standards visible, they are hidden at deeper levels.[734]

Also the increased application of Fair Value does not have only positive effects. Fair Values make financial reporting more volatile.[735] A financial crisis could heavily influence the values, market prices could be distorted by noises and it is a premise that liquid markets are available which is not always the case.[736] If markets are not available, the IFRS prescribe a market to model approach which gives companies a lot of discretion.[737]

One named advantage is that IFRS are more capital market related than most local GAAPs. This results also in a higher complexity of those accounting standards. Methods, definitions and accounting rules are in average more complex in comparison to local GAAPs.[738]

It is problematic that IFRS try to satisfy the information needs of various groups. Therefore, standard setters make compromises. This leads to the situation that the illustration of company's performance does not perfectly fit to the decision a single investor has to make in a certain situation.[739]

As mentioned in previous chapters, investors try to estimate prospective Cash Flows of a company in order to determine if an investment is worthwhile.[740] A general flaw of the IFRS is that they are mainly orientated towards the past. Therefore, it is questionable how far they fulfil their aim to support investors' decisions.[741] For evaluating the future development, the orientation towards the past is less useful because much information is

---

729 Cf. Daske, H., Hail, L., Leuz, C., et al. (2013), pp. 495-500.
730 Cf. Daske, H., Hail, L., Leuz, C., et al. (2013), pp. 517-525.
731 Cf. Daske, H., Hail, L., Leuz, C., et al. (2013), pp. 533-535.
732 Cf. Ball, R. (2006), pp. 15-16.
733 Cf. Ball, R. (2006), p. 17.
734 Cf. Ball, R. (2006), p. 22.
735 Cf. Kühnberger, M. (2014), p. 430.
736 Cf. Ball, R. (2006), pp. 12-13; Laux, C., Leuz, C. (2009), pp. 831-832.
737 Cf. Ball, R. (2006), p. 13; Laux, C., Leuz, C. (2009), p. 828.
738 Cf. Erkilet, G., Kholmy, K. (2016), p. 37.
739 Cf. Dechow, P., Ge, W., Schrand, C. (2010), p. 348.
740 Cf. Oberdörster, T. (2009), pp. 17-18; Steinhauer, L. (2007), p. 31.
741 Cf. Koelen, P. (2009), pp. 41-42.

obsolete at the time of disclosure.[742] Additionally, several scandals in the past reduce investors' trust in the accounting in general.[743]

Although this chapter summarises costs and benefits of IFRS accounting and presented the results of selected empirical studies, one has to be aware that in total a quantitative cost benefit analysis is difficult to conduct. Empirical studies have a limited data base of companies for examining regulatory effects. That means, companies are not randomly selected for statistical analysis and often an unaffected control group does not exist. Consequently, it is difficult to identify externalities and spill over effects which all companies of a sample are influenced by.[744] A further flaw of empirical studies is that there is a bias towards large companies due to data availability and that the positive effects of IFRS are overestimated.[745] Also for examining possible benefits out of IFRS introduction, it is difficult for scientists to separate the effects connected with IFRS introduction from simultaneously occurring effects like other institutional or market changes.[746] Therefore, caution is appropriate in the interpretation of the results of these studies and allocating all benefits and costs solely to IFRS.[747]

To sum up the insights from IFRS evaluation: Many empirical studies prove that benefits at capital markets and macroeconomic benefits exist. Studies show that stock market liquidity increases or bid-ask spread decreases due to IFRS adoption. At capital markets IFRS adoption increases the information of earnings or the quality of information for analysts. On a macroeconomic level IFRS lead to an increase of investment.[748] However, on the level of financial reporting it is still unclear if financial statements have become more transparent and comparable due to IFRS adoption.[749]

In total the results are contradictory because increased transparency could not be documented but positive financial capital market and macroeconomic effects exist.[750]

Despite differences remaining between countries using IFRS all market participants benefit from uniform accounting standards as they ensure that all capital market participants speak the same financial language in a world in which markets are globalised.[751]

The benefits and costs summarised so far can similarly be found in a survey of German investors concerning the IFRS introduction in Germany. The most important benefits the managers expect are higher comparability, transparency and a better combination of internal and external reporting. Expected disadvantages are an increased volatility of earnings, the complex nature of IFRS and high costs for implementing IFRS.[752] The analysis of IFRS reporting and information needs of investors shows that

742 Cf. Wehrheim, M., Schmitz, T. (2009), p. 154.

743 Cf. Funk, W., Rossmanith, J. (2008), p. 286; Weber, R. J. (2011), p. 1.

744 Cf. Christensen, H. B., Hail, L., Leuz, C. (2013), pp. 147-148; Leuz, C., Wysocki, P. D. (2016), pp. 532-535.

745 Cf. Brüggemann, U., Hitz, J.-M., Selhorn, T. (2013), p. 20.

746 Cf. Christensen, H. B., Hail, L., Leuz, C. (2013), p. 148; Leuz, C., Wysocki, P. D. (2016), p. 585.

747 Cf. Leuz, C., Wysocki, P. D. (2016), pp. 587-589.

748 Cf. Brüggemann, U., Hitz, J.-M., Selhorn, T. (2013), pp. 16-17.

749 Cf. Brüggemann, U., Hitz, J.-M., Selhorn, T. (2013), p. 22.

750 Cf. Brüggemann, U., Hitz, J.-M., Selhorn, T. (2013), p. 29.

751 Cf. Brown, P. (2011), p. 280.

752 Cf. Jermakowicz, E. K., Prather-Kinsey, J., Wulf, I. (2007), p. 175.

Table 3: Benefits / Advantages and costs / disadvantages of IFRS[753]

Benefits / Advantages	**Costs / Disadvantages**
– Worldwide known accounting standards which facilitate global capital procurement.	
– Increased comparability and transparency of financial reports and therefore more efficient capital markets.	– Reporting quality is not solely influenced by accounting standards but also by the incentives for management (Incentive view). – Due to different incentives and a different level of implementation of IFRS comparability and transparency of financial reports are limited despite uniform accounting standards. – Managers make accounting choices dependent on the economic consequences and not solely with the motivation to inform financial community (Positive Accounting Theory). – The solely signal of application of IFRS is not trustworthy because bad agents can imitate that easily.
– Reliable source of information due to control through auditors.	– IFRS offers a company's management a lot of discretion. Implicit rights of choice are difficult to detect for external persons.
– Application of Fair Value measures.	– Application of Fair Value measures.
– In general higher capital market relevance than local GAAPs.	– Higher complexity in comparison to most local GAAPs.
– Increased accounting quality documented by more precise forecasts of financial analysts and higher rating of annual reports.	– IFRS try to satisfy information needs of various groups so that illustration of performance does not always fit to single investor's needs.
– Reduced information asymmetries which result in higher market liquidity and lower cost of capital.	– Much information contained refers to past events and is less useful for estimation of fundamental value.

IFRS reporting does not cover all of the information needs and has some disadvantages which investors try to compensate by using other sources of information. Due to this perception Value Reporting develops.[754]

753 Cf. for bibliographical references the footnotes in chapter 2.4.3.
754 Cf. Laier, R. (2011), p. 146.

2.4.4 *Value Reporting as a Supplement of IFRS Reporting*

2.4.4.1 Definition and Objectives of Value Reporting

Due to the described flaws and dissatisfaction with legal reporting and the remaining information asymmetries between shareholders and management many companies extend the reporting and voluntarily provide further information to the public.[755] But this dissatisfaction is not the only cause for the development of Value Reporting. In accordance with the rise of VBM and especially the Shareholder Value approach the current reporting practices are also assessed with a focus on shareholders' interest.[756] Further reasons for the development of Value Reporting are the increased importance of global capital markets for capital procurement[757] and the increased information needs of investors. With a more comprehensive reporting companies want to support fundamental and performance analysis of investors.[758] In this context the role of institutional investors and financial intermediaries, which have comprehensive information needs, has to be highlighted.[759]

Value Reporting is addressed to the whole financial community, including equity and debt capital providers as well as information intermediaries.[760] Reporting is insofar a challenge for companies as they have to fulfil the divergent information needs of these groups. Private investors in average do not need such detailed information as institutional investors.[761]

In the context of Value Reporting many terms occur. For a clear definition of Value Reporting, it is necessary to differentiate it from Investor Relations, Business Reporting and Financial Accounting.[762] Investor Relations comprises the whole communication activities of a company towards capital markets.[763] Examples for Investor Relation activities range from press briefings on annual results, newsletter for private investors to road shows or the shareholders' meeting.[764] Business Reporting refers to the whole financial reporting and is divided into Financial Accounting and Value Reporting. So, Business Reporting refers to both elements of reporting: The obligatory and voluntary elements.[765]

755 Cf. Laier, R. (2011), p. 146.
756 Cf. Achleitner, A.-K., Bassen, A., Pietzsch, L., et al. (2002), p. 33; Fischer, T. M., Becker, S., Wenzel, J. (2001), p. 2001.
757 Cf. Ruhwedel, F., Schultze, W. (2002), p. 602.
758 Cf. Serfing, K. (2008), p. 184.
759 Cf. Chen, X., Harford, J., Li, K. (2007), p. 280; Johnson, R. A., Schnatterly, K., Johnson, S. G., et al. (2010), pp. 1590-1591.
760 Cf. Fochler, R. (2000), pp. 322-323; cf. for a detailed description of these groups and their information needs chapter 2.3.2.2.
761 Cf. Weber, J., Bramsemann, U., Heineke, C., et al. (2017), pp. 247-249; cf. also the analysis of information needs of investors in chapter 2.3.2.2.
762 Cf. Peemöller, V. H., Hofmann, S. (2005), p. 213; within scientific literature there do not exist a uniform definition of the listed terms.
763 Cf. Steinhauer, L. (2007), p. 3.
764 Cf. Piwinger, M. (2009), p. 19.
765 Cf. Grüning, M. (2011b), pp. 6-7; Ruhwedel, F., Schultze, W. (2002), p. 608. Within the Anglo-American literature the term Business Reporting is more a synonym for Value Reporting. Cf. for a definition American Institute of Certified Public Accountants (AICPA) (1994), p. 2.

Financial Accounting refers to the legally prescribed reporting of companies. In the EU this refers to all parts of the IFRS annual accounts.[766]

Value Reporting provides recipients of company reports with information about the current and prospective performance of a company[767] in financial and non-financial, quantitative and qualitative form.[768] Therefore, it is necessary that the legal reporting is extended[769] and complemented with further information.[770] Value Reporting has two aims: Reduce the gap between current stock price and intrinsic value of the company[771] and reduce existing information asymmetries between the financial community and the company.[772]

On the basis of Value Reporting the financial community can improve their fundamental analysis and the estimation of the risk-return profile of the company.[773] Due to its importance and influence parts of scientific literature consider Value Reporting as a value driver in Rappaport's Shareholder Value network.[774]

Value Reporting contains information which a company discloses mainly on a voluntary basis. Nevertheless, there may be intersections between Financial Accounting and Value Reporting, e.g. the segment report or the description of potential risks and chances in the management report.[775] In parts of scientific literature Value Reporting is strictly limited to voluntary parts of reporting. The problem is that the content and extent of Value Reporting is constantly changing due to adaptions to legally prescribed reporting. Thus, in this dissertation Value Reporting refers to all elements of reporting which enable recipients to better estimate the current and prospective economic performance of a company.[776]

The development from financial accounting to business reporting was initiated in the USA by the publication of the American Institute of Certified Public Accountants (ACIPA). The report was named after the chairman of the responsible committee, Jenkins Report.[777] This report is the starting point for the development from Financial Accounting to Business Reporting in the following years. It states that users need a lot of information for determining company value. The report recommends to improve segment reporting as

---

766 Cf. Griewel, E. (2006), p. 77; Grüning, M. (2011b), pp. 6-7, cf. chapter 2.4.2 for more information about IFRS reporting.

767 Cf. Fischer, T. M., Wenzel, J., Kühn, C. (2001), p. 1209.

768 Cf. Böcking, H.-J. (1998), p. 44; Fischer, T. M., Wenzel, J. (2002), p. 327.

769 Cf. Arbeitskreis Externe Unternehmensrechnung der Schmalenbach-Gesellschaft (2002), p. 2337; Günther, T. (2004), p. 35.

770 Cf. Freidank, C.-C., Weber, S. C. (2009), p. 312.

771 Cf. Wenzel, J. (2005), pp. 109-113.

772 Cf. Heumann, R. (2005), p. 5; Labhart, P., Volkart, R. (2009), pp. 205-206; Schultze, W., List, T., Schabert, B., et al. (2018), pp. 512-513.

773 Cf. Baetge, J., Kümmel, J. (2003), pp. 52-53; Fischer, T. M., Zirkler, B. (2008), p. 589.

774 Cf. Achleitner, A.-K., Bassen, A., Pietzsch, L., et al. (2002), p. 34; Labhart, P., Volkart, R. (2009), p. 208; cf. extensively for the Shareholder Value approach chapter 2.1.2.

775 Cf. Heumann, R. (2005), pp. 12-13.

776 Cf. for similar definition of Value Reporting Arbeitskreis Externe Unternehmensrechnung der Schmalenbach-Gesellschaft (2002), p. 2337; Grüning, M. (2011b), pp. 5-7; Heumann, R. (2005), pp. 12-13; Labhart, P. (1999), pp. 29-31; Ruhwedel, F., Schultze, W. (2002), pp. 608-609.

777 Cf. Wohlgemuth, F. (2007), p. 16 and cf. for the full report American Institute of Certified Public Accountants (AICPA) (1994); cf. for a critical assessment of the report Seidel, L. J. (1995).

this helps investors to identify risk and opportunities better[778] or to give users forward-looking information.[779] It also stresses that a company's reporting should not be limited to pure financial data. Non-financial information also helps users to determine the prospective Cash Flows of a company.[780]

The first aim of Value Reporting is to reduce existing information asymmetries between capital market participants and the company.[781] Information asymmetries cause adverse selection and moral hazard agency problems. Value Reporting can therefore be considered as a kind of signalling. Companies try to illustrate their economic potential.[782] The reduction of information asymmetry leads to reduced capital costs.[783] As investors get more information, they can better estimate Cash Flows and will therefore reduce their claims.[784]

The second aim is to reduce the gap between the intrinsic value and stock price.[785] The intrinsic value is the value of the company which is based on all available information. Thus, it is the company value on a strong efficient market.[786] In general, the management has access to all information and is aware of the intrinsic value. External investors do not have such a comprehensive basis of assessment and come to divergent values.[787] The cause for different assessments is that capital markets are nearly efficient in the semi-strong form. This is the reason why Value Reporting is necessary. In a capital market which is efficient in the strong form Value Reporting would be senseless.[788]

With the help of VBM a company increases the inner value.[789] In a second step management has to ensure that the increased inner value is transformed into an adapted stock price. The adequate instrument in this case is Value Reporting.[790] An overvaluation exists if the stock price is above the intrinsic value and an undervaluation if the stock price is below the intrinsic value. In both scenarios it is necessary that the stock price and intrinsic value approximate each other. It might be surprising that Value Reporting also has the function to avoid overestimation by the market.[791] An overestimation can be an incentive for management to initiate cost cuts in order to hold the high stock price. These

778 Cf. American Institute of Certified Public Accountants (AICPA) (1994), p. 20.
779 Cf. American Institute of Certified Public Accountants (AICPA) (1994), p. 22.
780 Cf. American Institute of Certified Public Accountants (AICPA) (1994), pp. 25-28.
781 Cf. Bej, T. (2015), p. 109; Cheung, Y.-L., Jiang, P., Tan, W. (2010), p. 262; Pellens, B., Hillebrandt, F., Tomaszewski, C. (2000), p. 178.
782 Cf. Baetge, J., Solmecke, H. (2006), p. 18; Schultze, W., List, T., Schabert, B., et al. (2018), pp. 512-513.
783 Cf. Bej, T. (2015), p. 109; Labhart, P., Volkart, R. (2009), p. 208; cf. also chapter 2.2.5.
784 Cf. Elliot, R. K., Jacobson, P. D. (1994), p. 81; Fischer, T. M., Klöpfer, E. (2006), p. 4.
785 Cf. Griewel, E. (2006), p. 78.
786 Cf. Wohlgemuth, F. (2007), p. 16.
787 Cf. Banzhaf, J. (2006), pp. 141-143.
788 Cf. Aders, C., Herbertinger, M., Wiedemann, F. (2003), p. 357; Labhart, P., Volkart, R. (2009), pp. 205-206, cf. for a detailed description and analysis concerning the information efficiency of capital markets chapter 2.3.1.
789 Cf. Kraus, P. (2011), pp. 8-9; cf. extensively for details about Value Based Management chapter 2.1.1.
790 Cf. Bej, T. (2015), p. 109; Günther, T., Beyer, D. (2001), pp. 1623-1624; cf. the empirical study of Cheung, Y.-L., Jiang, P., Tan, W. (2010) who proves that Chinese companies are rewarded by the market for comprehensive reporting.
791 Cf. Ruhwedel, F., Schultze, W. (2002), p. 606.

short-term cost cuts can cause damage to the company in the long-term. An example is the reduction of machine maintenance intervals.[792]

An ideal-typical situation for a company is given if the stock price fluctuates slightly around the inner value.[793] An exclusion of all volatility is not possible due to the several factors by which the stock price is influenced beyond a company's control and due to the psychological behaviour of individuals.[794]

2.4.4.2 Reduction of Communication Gaps by Value Reporting

Value Reporting has to reduce five communication gaps which might occur in the context of capital market communication. The illustration below gives an overview of possible communication gaps.[795]

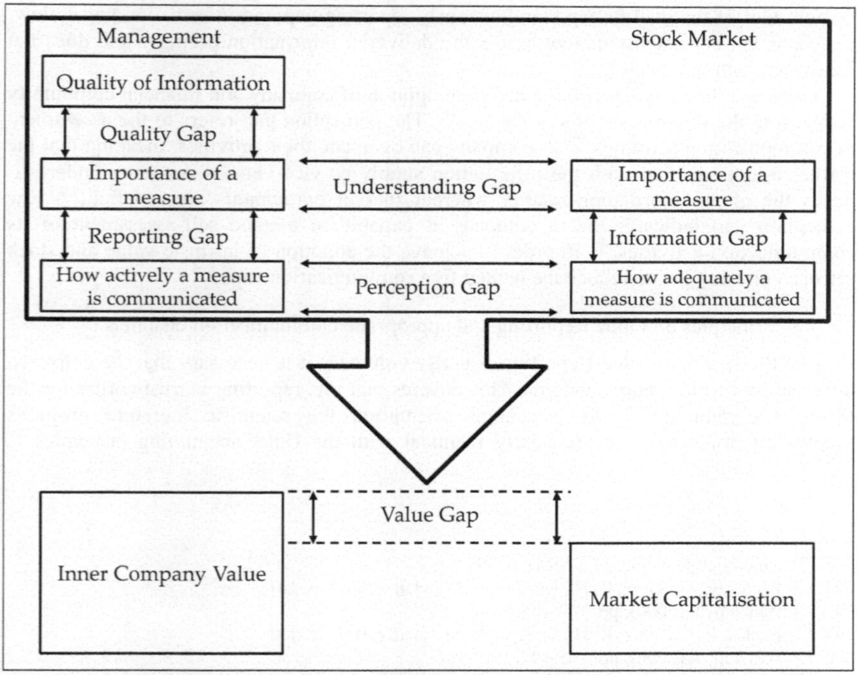

In the style of: Banzhaf, J. (2006), p. 145, Mikolajek-Gocejna, M. (2014), p. 100
Illustration 9: Communication gaps in the context of Value Reporting

792 Cf. Koller, T., Goedhart, M., Wessels, D. (2010), p. 525.
793 Cf. Aders, C., Herbertinger, M., Wiedemann, F. (2003), pp. 357-358.
794 Cf. Günther, T., Beyer, D. (2001), p. 1624; Laier, R. (2011), p. 154.
795 Cf. basically for communication gaps Eccles, R. G., Herz, R. H., Keegan, E. M., et al. (2001), pp. 130-142.

An information gap exists if a company reports about a key figure, but does not deliver sufficient information or low quality information about it. It is also possible that a company does not deliver any kind of information.[796]

If a company informs the financial community about a key figure but is not able to explain which importance this key figure has for steering the company, reporting gaps occur.[797] Consequently, information receivers cannot assess the information properly. In case that an information gap as well as a reporting gap exist, a company does not communicate decisive information to the financial community.[798]

A quality gap describes the problem that a company has an indicator system which is not able to measure key figures of the necessary quality and at a level of quality demanded by investors.[799] Consequently, a company gives unreliable key figures to the market. This problem often emerges in the context of non-financial key figures like customer satisfaction. Out of the quality gap simultaneously reporting gap and information gap follow. The financial community cannot assess the delivered information properly and does not receive enough information.[800]

Understanding gap describes a different opinion of company and financial community concerning the importance of key figures.[801] The perception gap refers to the assessment of communication activities.[802] A company can overstate their activities, meaning that the market is not satisfied with the information supply or vice versa a company underestimates the given information quality whereas market participants are satisfied. A low perception gap indicates that a company is capable of a good self-assessment of its communication activities.[803] In order to achieve the adoption of intrinsic value and stock price, a company has to reduce the named five communication gaps.[804]

2.4.4.3 Principles of Value Reporting and appropriate communication channels

Despite the fact that Value Reporting is partly voluntary it is necessary that the delivered information fulfil certain standards. This ensures that this reporting is trustworthy for the financial community.[805] As a general orientation the scientific literature proposes accounting principles that are nearly identical with the IFRS accounting principles.[806]

796 Cf. Mikołajek-Gocejna, M. (2014), p. 99.
797 Cf. Eccles, R. G., Herz, R. H., Keegan, E. M., et al. (2001), p. 131.
798 Cf. Banzhaf, J. (2006), pp. 144-145.
799 Cf. Eccles, R. G., Herz, R. H., Keegan, E. M., et al. (2001), p. 131.
800 Cf. Banzhaf, J. (2006), pp. 145-146.
801 Cf. Mikołajek-Gocejna, M. (2014), p. 100.
802 Cf. Mikołajek-Gocejna, M. (2014), p. 100.
803 Cf. Banzhaf, J. (2006), pp. 146-147.
804 Cf. Banzhaf, J. (2006), p. 147.
805 Cf. Baetge, J., Solmecke, H. (2006), p. 18; Baetge, J., Kümmel, J. (2003), pp. 55-56.
806 Cf. Arbeitskreis Externe Unternehmensrechnung der Schmalenbach-Gesellschaft (2002) who lists up clarity, comparability, balanced illustration of chances and risks, structure of reporting according to single segments; cf. Banzhaf, J. (2006), pp. 147-155, who names decision usefulness, comparability, value relevance and reliability as principles; cf. extensively for a derivation of accounting principles for Value Reporting Heumann, R. (2005), pp. 53-87; cf. Pellens, B., Hillebrandt, F., Tomaszewski, C. (2000), p. 182.

Value Reporting should consider the accounting principles of completeness, materiality, continuity, comparability, comprehensibility, future orientation and reliability.[807]

An exception is the prudence principle. It should not be applied to Value Reporting. This would have the consequence that companies have to stress the risks and not the existing chances in their outlook for future development. Rather risks and chances should be presented in a balanced way.[808]

An additional accounting principle for Value Reporting is value relevance of information. This implies that information facilitates or specifies the fundamental analysis of investors.[809]

The management approach is of special importance. Information on which base management acts are especially qualified for reducing information asymmetries between management and investors.[810] This also applies to the internal control system of a company which can be presented with its most important key figure in the context of Value Reporting.[811]

In order to increase credibility of Value Reporting and underline that the voluntary reporting corresponds to the IFRS framework, all information should be checked by the auditor.[812] This also increases investor's trust in forward-looking information about the development of the company described by management because there is a positive coherence between the chosen level of independent audit and the market reaction to management's forecasts.[813]

Value Reporting is not bound to a special medium but the most important platform is the annual business report of a company.[814] The advantage is that many relevant investors and potential investors analyse the business report and that the Value Reporting contents are subject to auditor's approval. This leads to an increased credibility of information.[815] The management commentary section is suitable for extending the company's reporting with the elements of Value Reporting.[816]

In addition the Internet is important as new information can be communicated immediately,[817] globally and at low costs to the financial community.[818] But despite the advantages of the Internet the annual report still remains one of the most important communication channels with shareholders and a possibility for companies for self-presentation.[819]

807 Cf. Pellens, B., Hillebrandt, F., Tomaszewski, C. (2000), p. 182.

808 Cf. Baetge, J., Solmecke, H. (2006), p. 21.

809 Cf. Banzhaf, J. (2006), pp. 152-153.

810 Cf. Arbeitskreis Externe Unternehmensrechnung der Schmalenbach-Gesellschaft (2002), p. 2339.

811 Cf. Baetge, J., Solmecke, H. (2006), p. 23.

812 Cf. Arbeitskreis Externe Unternehmensrechnung der Schmalenbach-Gesellschaft (2002), p. 2340; Paetzmann, K. (2012), pp. 265-266.

813 Cf. Ball, R., Jayaraman, S., Shivakumar, L. (2012), pp. 136-140, 163-164.

814 Cf. Pellens, B., Hillebrandt, F., Tomaszewski, C. (2000), p. 180.

815 Cf. Wenzel, J. (2005), pp. 242-243.

816 Cf. Fischer, T. M., Zirkler, B. (2008), pp. 588-589; cf. Picard, N., Behncke, N., Hoffmann, T. (2014) for a summary of the important rules for management summary, pp. 945-946.

817 Cf. Fischer, T. M., Klöpfer, E. (2006), p. 10; Pellens, B., Hillebrandt, F., Tomaszewski, C. (2000), p. 180.

818 Cf. Labhart, P., Volkart, R. (2001), p. 135.

819 Cf. Fiss, P. C., Zajac, E. J. (2004), p. 505.

At the beginning of the century the Value Reporting of the German DAX companies is improvable because much information contained in the annual business reports are not part of the reporting via the Internet.[820] Further possibilities to present content of Value Reporting are conferences with analysts,[821] the shareholders' meeting, road shows or press releases.[822]

In general, companies listed on capital markets voluntarily give more information to the public.[823] The publication behaviour of companies is influenced by the capital market on which they are listed because the market authority has certain requirements for publication. Therefore, companies are forced to reveal certain information as a requirement for listing on an index.[824]

Apart from the listed objectives and connected advantages the publication of information and in addition voluntary information can also have some disadvantages for companies. The collection and preparation of information causes additional costs. Direct costs are higher expenditures for creating, auditing[825] and the disclosure of an annual business report. Furthermore, indirect costs occur. They describe the costs due to publication of competition-relevant information and costs for losing an advantage in competition.[826] Of course, there are areas which are very sensible like detailed results from competitor and market analysis, information about prospective strategy and the internal management control system including information about segment-specific costs of capital.[827] Especially concerning the disclosure of prospective information, companies bear the risk of possible court proceedings.[828] It is especially important for companies not to overload its actual and potential investors with information. All relevant information should be presented in a summarised and compact manner.[829]

Nevertheless, it can be assumed that a company's management is able to estimate the risk and costs of additional reporting properly in order to avoid large disadvantages for their company.[830]

2.4.4.4 Elements of Value Reporting

In the previous chapter accounting principles for Value Reporting are mentioned in order to show the main principles on which reporting is based. This chapter goes into more

820 Cf. Fischer, T. M., Becker, S., Wenzel, J. (2001), p. 2007; cf. for more details the empirical study of Fischer, T. M., Becker, S., Wenzel, J. (2001).

821 Cf. Pellens, B., Hillebrandt, F., Tomaszewski, C. (2000), p. 202.

822 Cf. Beck, R. (2003), p 40; Laier, R. (2011), p. 162.

823 Cf. Dumontier, P., Raffournier, B. (2002), p. 144.

824 Cf. Dumontier, P., Raffournier, B. (2002), p. 144.

825 Cf. Filzen, J. J., Peterson, K. (2015), p. 1572 who prove a direct coherence between financial statements complexity and the level of auditor fees: the higher the complexity the higher the fees for auditors.

826 Cf. Healy, P. M., Hutton, A. P., Palepu, K. G. (1999), p. 488; Henselmann, K. (2005), p. 297; Leuz, C., Wysocki, P. D. (2016), pp. 551-552; Steinhauer, L. (2007), p. 99.

827 Cf. Henselmann, K. (2005), pp. 300-301; cf. extensively Henselmann, K. (2005) for a critical review of disclosure of additional information in the context of Value Reporting.

828 Cf. Leuz, C., Wysocki, P. D. (2016), pp. 552-553; Steinhauer, L. (2007), p. 99; cf. contradictorily Müller, M. (1998), p. 135.

829 Cf. Ruf, M. (2014), p. 109.

830 Cf. Labhart, P., Volkart, R. (2009), p. 211.

detail and presents concepts which cluster the information desired in the context of Value Reporting. All classification of Value Reporting contents are theoretical constructs so that in practice companies should adapt the reporting contents to the needs of their industry and their own situation.[831]

Table four contains examples for possible classification of Value Reporting contents. In total, the named information elements are very similar.[832]

Table 4: Possible classifications of Value Reporting elements[833]

Author (Year)	Categories of Value Reporting
Müller, M. (1998)	– Total Return Reporting – Value Added Reporting – Strategic Advantage Reporting
Labhart, P. (1999)[834]	– Financial Perspective – Management Perspective – Customer Perspective – Process Perspective – Development Perspective
Pellens, B., Hillebrandt, F., Tomaszweski, C. (2000)[835]	– Shareholder Return Reporting – Corporate Return Reporting – Detailed Financial and per Share Reporting – Value Tools Reporting – Future Objectives Reporting
Arbeitskreis Externe Unternehmensrechnung der Schamlenbach-Gesellsechaft (2002)[836]	– Capital Market oriented data – Market Valuation – Chance-Risk Profile – Information about not disclosed assets on balance sheet – Information about strategy and performance

In this dissertation the structuring of Value Reporting according to Müller is used. He divides the reporting in three separate areas Total Return Reporting, Value Added Reporting and Strategic Advantage Reporting. Possible elements in these three areas are illustrated in illustration 10.[837]

831 Cf. Achleitner, A.-K., Bassen, A., Pietzsch, L., et al. (2002), p. 34.
832 Cf. Steinhauer, L. (2007), pp. 104-105; cf. for a presentation and description of selected classification patterns of Value Reporting contents Morich, S. (2007), pp. 270-282.
833 Cf. for an extensive overview Fischer, T. M., Klöpfer, E. (2006), p. 7.
834 Cf. extensively Labhart, P. (1999), pp. 263-271.
835 Cf. extensively Pellens, B., Hillebrandt, F., Tomaszewski, C. (2000), pp. 181-186.
836 Cf. extensively Arbeitskreis Externe Unternehmensrechnung der Schmalenbach-Gesellschaft (2002), pp. 2338-2339.
837 Cf. extensively Müller, M. (1998).

Value Reporting

Total Return Reporting	Value Added Reporting	Strategic Advantage Reporting
Objective Generated profits from investors' point of view	Objective Realized value added to Shareholder Value	Objective Current and prospective factors of success
Content • Development of stock prices • Development of dividends • Volatility of stock price • Virtual portfolio • Comparison of stock price development with index and competitors	Content • Internal control system • Top key figures used • Illustration of key figures development over time • Incentive system for management • Calculation of cost of capital	Content • Strategic objectives • Information about the industry • Projection about company's development • Intellectual capital resources: employees, research & development, supplier structure etc.
Timeframe • Past • Present	Timeframe • Past • Present • Future	Timeframe • Present • Future

In the style of: Müller, M. (1998), p. 125; Zirkler, B., Nobach, K. (2008), p. 379
Illustration 10: Elements of Value Reporting[838]

Total Return Reporting deals with the profit investors achieve with their investments in a company at the capital market.[839] Referring to the Shareholder Value Network and the principles of VBM, it is important for investors to receive an adequate return on their investment by dividend payments or increases in share prices.[840] That is the reason why a company should include this information in its Value Reporting.[841] Within this section a company reports about development of stock prices, dividends, rating and risk of the investment.[842]

By presenting the past development of stock prices and dividends, the company facilitates the evaluation by recipients of the report of past performance.[843] Commentary concerning the volatility of the share price is also helpful. The company can comment high breaks.[844] A further proposal is to present a virtual portfolio in which dividends are

838 Further information concerning Value Reporting contents taken from Fischer, T. M., Wenzel, J. (2002), p. 329.
839 Cf. Morich, S. (2007), p. 629.
840 Cf. Horváth, P. (2011), pp. 443-445.
841 Cf. Müller, M. (1998), p. 129.
842 Cf. Fischer, T. M., Wenzel, J. (2002), p. 327.
843 Cf. Wenzel, J. (2005), pp. 219-222.
844 Cf. Fischer, T. M., Klöpfer, E. (2006), p. 9.

invested in purchasing further shares and the performance of the company in comparison to the underlying index or to comparable companies in the same industry.[845]

The detailed performance explanation should not be limited to the past. In the context of Value Reporting investors are especially interested in prospective developments, so a company can state target values for certain key figures.[846] The IFRS already oblige companies to compute the key figure EPS.[847] For satisfying the special information needs of debt capital providers, a company can provide readers with rating information.[848]

Total Return Reporting mostly summarises information which is already available via other information sources. The collection of this information is a kind of service function from the company.[849] But the commentary and explanation of developments in stock price are particularly important for private investors.[850] Besides this, the first section has the purpose to demonstrate the created Shareholder Value to the financial community.[851]

The second part of Value Reporting, Value Added Reporting, has the objective to show the financial community the realised value added to Shareholder Value in a period.[852] In this context it is useful to present and explain the company's internal control system and top key figures.[853] Value based performance measures are well suited in this context as they are able to show the value generated in the sense of the Shareholder Value approach.[854] In practice, many companies do not show a value based performance measure but instead a pro forma key figure like EBIT or EBITDA.[855] Independent of which kind of key figure a company uses it is necessary to show and explain its calculation.[856] In the light of the fact that companies often conduct individual adaptations to value based performance measures or other key figures, the explanation of the calculation is important for investors by assessing the values of key figures.[857] As already mentioned in the context of the first section, it is desirable for the financial community if a company states target values for the presented key figures so that the Value Added Reporting is not limited to a retrospective.[858] Furthermore, a variance analysis could be helpful for readers of financial reports.[859] With the help of internal steering systems external persons are able to control the performance of the company in the last period and have an estimate about the

845 Cf. Pellens, B., Hillebrandt, F., Tomaszewski, C. (2000), pp. 182-183.
846 Cf. Fischer, T. M., Zirkler, B. (2008), pp. 591-593.
847 Cf. Zirkler, B., Nobach, K. (2008), p. 381; cf. IAS 33.
848 Cf. Zirkler, B., Nobach, K. (2008), p. 381.
849 Cf. Müller, M. (1998), p. 127; Pellens, B., Hillebrandt, F., Tomaszewski, C. (2000), p. 182.
850 Cf. chapter 2.3.2.2. Private and individual investors concentrate on filtered and processed information. Thus the Total Return Reporting corresponds to this information need.
851 Cf. Müller, M. (1998), p. 131.
852 Cf. Fischer, T. M., Zirkler, B. (2008), pp. 589-590.
853 Cf. Fischer, T. M., Klöpfer, E. (2006), p. 8.
854 Cf. Labhart, P. (1999), pp. 266-267; Pellens, B., Hillebrandt, F., Tomaszewski, C. (2000), pp. 184-185.
855 Cf. Wenzel, J. (2005), pp. 215-216.
856 Cf. Fischer, T. M., Klöpfer, E. (2006), p. 8.
857 Cf. Baetge, J., Solmecke, H. (2006), p. 24; Müller, M. (1998), p. 132.
858 Cf. Heumann, R. (2005), p. 137; Pellens, B., Hillebrandt, F., Tomaszewski, C. (2000), p. 186.
859 Cf. Baetge, J., Solmecke, H. (2006), p. 24.

performance in the coming periods.[860] A comparison of performance between companies based on internal control systems is not possible because many different concepts exist and within one concept various ways of calculation are possible.[861]

Closely connected with the internal control system and the top key figure are incentive systems for management. Value Added Reporting is the place in which a company provides readers with the detailed design of the incentive system.[862]

Capital costs are an important value in the context of VBM. Also for value based performance measures like EVA or CVA the disclosure of capital costs and a detailed calculation increase the reader's understanding.[863] Therefore, companies need to split up the calculation and also give information about costs of equity capital and debt capital.[864] For calculation of costs of equity capital the CAPM is used in most cases. The single calculation components, riskless rate of interest, beta factor, market risk premium, have to be explained in this context.[865]

The Strategic Advantage Reporting puts the emphasis on the prospective development of the company and its Shareholder Value creation in future.[866] In the context of the fundamental analysis and the used calculation methods, like DCF approaches, investors use the information given in this section in order to estimate prospective Cash Flows. So, this part reduces the uncertainty inherent in projections.[867]

One purpose of this part is to illustrate the chances and risks the company faces in the future.[868] For investors it is important to know the risks. Consequently, risk reporting is a main part of Strategic Advantage Reporting.[869] In Germany companies are obliged by local German GAAP to explain their risks and chances in the management's report section of the annual business report.[870] Whereas the first two parts of Value Reporting focus on financial information, this part gives insight into many non-financial areas.[871]

Müller divides Strategic Advantage Reporting into three sub-areas: Objectives, company environment and strategies and measures. At first, a company explains its objectives in terms of market share, turnover and profit growth for the future. In a second step information about the industry in which the company acts and its competitors are given. At last, the company explains with which strategies and measures it plans to fulfil its objectives.[872] This division shows that for the financial community it is decisive which

860 Cf. Heumann, R. (2005), p. 137, Paetzmann, K. (2012), pp. 135-136, 265.
861 Cf. Kley, K.-L. (2003), p. 843.
862 Cf. Pellens, B., Hillebrandt, F., Tomaszewski, C. (2000), p. 185.
863 Cf. Bej, T. (2015), p. 112; Fischer, T. M., Klöpfer, E. (2006), p. 8; Fischer, T. M., Zirkler, B. (2008), p. 590.
864 Cf. Morich, S. (2007), p. 277.
865 Cf. Fischer, T. M., Zirkler, B. (2008), pp. 590-591.
866 Cf. Fischer, T. M., Wenzel, J. (2002), p. 327.
867 Cf. Fischer, T. M., Wenzel, J. (2002), p. 327; Müller, M. (1998), p. 135.
868 Cf. Wenzel, J. (2005), pp. 222-223.
869 Cf. Fischer, T. M., Klöpfer, E. (2006), p. 10.
870 Cf. Fischer, T. M., Zirkler, B. (2008), pp. 582-583.
871 Cf. Wenzel, J. (2005), pp. 223-227.
872 Cf. Morich, S. (2007), p. 272: Müller, M. (1998), pp. 137-138; cf. for an overview of examples for possible Strategic Advantage Reporting contents Fischer, T. M., Klöpfer, E. (2006), p. 11.

intellectual capital resources a company has in order to conduct planned strategies and measures. Possible information can concern employer satisfaction, structure of suppliers, processing time in production etc.[873]

Strategic Advantage Reporting can also avoid sells of shares by investors. If the current development of the stock prices does not correspond to the expectations of investors, they might consider selling their shares. Strategic Advantage Reporting shows the positive factors that will lead to an increase in the share price in the long-term and reinforce the investor in its purchase decision.[874]

A survey among users reveals that the reporting efforts of companies in the context of Strategic Advantage Reporting could be improved. Investors like to have more information about prospective financial development as well as a clear illustration of trends in growth and profitability.[875]

By providing the financial community with forecasts in the financial statements, a company's management could prove its forecast ability. Investors can derive from the quality of forecasts management's forecast ability in reference to investment projects. Beside satisfying information needs a company can demonstrate its ability to estimate the success of investment projects.[876]

2.4.4.5 Integrated Report as Latest Development of Value Reporting

The latest development concerning the voluntary reporting behaviour is the integrated report which is a summary of a company's strategy, its performance and its prospects. Readers should extract from the report how a company creates value in the short, medium and long term.[877] The focus of this report is with which resources a company wants to create value for its shareholders and stakeholders in the future.[878] The aim of integrated reporting is to provide primarily investors and further stakeholders with a short and compact collocation of the information they needed and to ensure an efficient allocation of capital.[879]

Therefore, the IIRC identifies six value drivers which influence the potential of a company to create value: Financial capital, manufactured capital, intellectual capital, human capital, social and relationship capital as well as natural capital.[880] Similar to the IFRS the integrated report underlies some guiding principles, e.g. connectivity of

873 Cf. Morich, S. (2007), p. 272; Zirkler, B., Nobach, K. (2008), p. 383.

874 Cf. Müller, M. (1998), p. 128.

875 Cf. Pro-Active Accounting Activities in Europe (PAAinE) (2009), p. 6.

876 Cf. Goodman, T. H., Neamtiu, M., Shroff, N., et al. (2014), p. 334.

877 Cf. International Integrated Reporting Council (IIRC) (2013), http://integratedreporting.org/resource/international-ir-framework/, p. 7; cf. for an overview of empirical studies which deals with integrated reporting Velte, P., Stawinoga, M. (2016); cf. for an overview of the basic principles of Integrated Reporting Picard, N., Behncke, N., Hoffmann, T. (2014).

878 Cf. International Integrated Reporting Council (IIRC) (2013), http://integratedreporting.org/resource/international-ir-framework/, pp. 2, 4.

879 Cf. International Integrated Reporting Council (IIRC) (2013), http://integratedreporting.org/resource/international-ir-framework/, p. 4; Velte, P., Stawinoga, M. (2016).

880 Cf. International Integrated Reporting Council (IIRC) (2013), http://integratedreporting.org/resource/international-ir-framework/, pp. 11-12.

information, future orientation or conciseness.[881] Integrated reporting can be seen as a reaction on the financial crisis in 2007 / 2008. Companies should demonstrate that they create Shareholder Value on a long-term basis, not on a short term one.[882]

One part of the integrated report deals with the illustration of company's performance. Therefore, key figures are an appropriate means because the development of value drivers can relatively easily and concisely be explained with the help of key figures.[883] The reporting framework stresses that presented key figures should be consistent with key figures the company used internally and that quantitative information should be accompanied by an explanation of calculation methods and explanations for derivation from target values.[884] These guidelines are very similar to the management approach the IFRS follows. It also corresponds to the principles and contents of Value Reporting[885]

Empirical studies show that mainly larger companies tend to implement integrated reporting. But so far the reporting quality is low and reporting methods differ strongly between companies.[886]

To sum up: The integrated reporting is a summary of the most important elements of the comprehensive annual report of a company, e.g. it contains information from financial, corporate social responsibility, corporate governance and compensation reports.[887] It is also a reaction on the increasing complexity of financial statements and the changing reporting circumstances like the growing importance of intangible assets and environmental and social issues.[888] It helps companies to combine financial and non-financial information and increase the shareholders' understanding of the company's value chain.[889] The principles of Value Reporting are still valid. The report has a clear future orientation to support investors in the context of their capital allocation decisions.[890] The integrated reports also consider the information needs of investors against the backdrop of Shareholder Value approach.[891]

The second chapter illustrates what the framework conditions for the application of value based performance measures are. Companies act on the basis of principles of VBM and Shareholder Value approach resulting in the objective to generate a profit above their cost of capital. The Prinicpal Agent Theory reveals that key figures as part of the reporting

881 Cf. International Integrated Reporting Council (IIRC) (2013), http://integratedreporting.org/resource/international-ir-framework/, pp. 16-23.
882 Cf. Maniora, J. (2015); Velte, P., Stawinoga, M. (2016).
883 Cf. Wulf, I., Niemöller, J., Rentzsch, N. (2014), p. 150.
884 Cf. International Integrated Reporting Council (IIRC) (2013), http://integratedreporting.org/resource/international-ir-framework/, pp. 30-31.
885 Cf. Wulf, I., Niemöller, J., Rentzsch, N. (2014), p. 152.
886 Cf. Velte, P., Stawinoga, M. (2016).
887 Cf. Velte, P., Stawinoga, M. (2016).
888 Cf. Velte, P., Stawinoga, M. (2016); Wulf, I., Niemöller, J., Rentzsch, N. (2014), pp. 158-159.
889 Cf. Lee, K.-W., Yeo, G. H.-H. (2016), p. 1222; Picard, N., Behncke, N., Hoffmann, T. (2014), pp. 947-948.
890 Cf. Picard, N., Behncke, N., Hoffmann, T. (2014), p. 950; Wulf, I., Niemöller, J., Rentzsch, N. (2014), pp. 154-155.
891 Cf. Wulf, I., Niemöller, J., Rentzsch, N. (2014), pp. 148-149.

can reduce information asymmetries between managers and investors[892] by illustrating the companies' performances.[893] Nearly semi-efficient capital markets use accounting as one important source of information for price formation. Key figures are an important element of companies' reporting[894] and an important tool for investors to summarize accounting data and analyse the performance of a company.[895] In the context of Value Reporting companies have incentives to voluntarily give more information to the capital market, – among other things the disclosure of value based performance measures, – in order to stabilise the stock price close to the inner value.

892 Cf. chapter 2.2.4.2 about Principal Agent Theory and key figures.
893 Cf. Fischer, T. M., Zirkler, B. (2008), pp. 589-590.
894 Cf. chapter 2.4.4 about Value Reporting and Integrated Reporting.
895 Cf. chapter 2.3.2.2 about the information research of investors.

3 Critical Evaluation of Selected Value Concepts

3.1 Traditional Key Figures Used Commonly by Investors

3.1.1 Systematisation of Traditional Key Figures

After analysing the framework condition for the application of key figures, this chapter focuses on the presentation and assessment of value based performance measures.

In the context of this dissertation performance measures are defined as "metrics used to quantify the efficiency and/or effectiveness of an action." A performance measurement system is a set of several metrics.[896] Key figures are numbers that summarise and describe precisely a selected issue.[897] Despite the focus on value based performance measures companies should use a variety of financial and non-financial measures as companies with a variety in their performance management system are more successful on the stock market.[898]

Key figures have two functions: Information and control function.[899] They inform the addressee about an issue so that he is able to build an opinion or the key figure is a kind of indicator for an expected development.[900] Due to the aggregation of information they enable the handling of a mass of data and also the comparison of companies and their performance.[901] They are often used by investors for analysing the annual or quarterly accounts of companies in order to increase transparency and reveal issues that are only difficult to detect without them.[902] The main purpose of key figures is to summarise information and reveal cause-effect relationships.[903]

From a company's perspective key figures enable an organisation to demonstrate how successful the planned strategy is transferred into financial results. Key figures have a high importance because they are easy to interpret.[904] Companies invest in performance measurement systems because they help them to consequently monitor their objective of delivering Shareholder Value.[905] But simply installing such a system is not sufficient. A part to Shareholder Value creation can only be reached if design and development are fitting to the company,[906] e.g. it is crucial that the key figures correspond to the company's

896 Definition quoted from: Neely, A., Gregory, M., Platts, K. (1995), pp. 80-81.
897 Cf. Barth, T., Barth, D. (2008), p. 136.
898 Cf. Ittner, C. D., Larcker, D. F., Randall, T. (2003), pp. 716, 727-728; Schmeisser, W., Clausen, L. (2009), pp. 74-75.
899 Cf. Horzella, A. (2010), p.91.
900 Cf. Siepermann, M. (2008), pp. 150-151.
901 Cf. Hauschildt, J. (1996), p. 3.
902 Cf. Baetge, J., Kirsch, H.-J., Thiele, S. (2004), p. 35.
903 Cf. Weissmann, F. (2005), p. 70.
904 Cf. Melnyk, S. A., Bititci, U., Platts, K., et al. (2014), p. 173.
905 Cf. Franco-Santos, M., Lucianetti, L., Bourne, M. (2012), p. 79.
906 Cf. Franco-Santos, M., Lucianetti, L., Bourne, M. (2012), pp. 96-97.

N. Eikelmann, *Value Based Performance Measures*, FOM-Edition Research,
https://doi.org/10.1007/978-3-658-31429-3_3

environment and strategy in order to properly report the company's current situation.[907] A balanced key figure system consists of financial as well as non-financial key figures.[908]

In their control function key figures support managers in decision making, e.g. a certain threshold has to be exceeded, in order to conduct an investment project or there exist predefined values of key figures single departments within a company have to fulfil.[909] Outgoing from the two functions of key figures, they support decisions by managers due to their information function and steer their behaviour as they set thresholds for making investments.[910]

Traditional key figures can be clustered according to statistical aspects.[911] Absolute numbers contain single numbers like cash balance, sums like balance sheet total and differences like the profit taken from the profit and loss statement.[912] Ratios are divided into the groups relation ratios, classification ratios and index ratios.[913] Relation ratios are key figures which consist of two logical related numbers which are then mathematically connected, e.g. return on equity. Classification ratios describe the share of one part in relation to total parts, e.g. equity ratio. Index ratios connect the same key figures which differ in time, e.g. a price index or actual turnover compared to planned turnover.[914] Examples for traditional key figures are return on equity, return on total capital, return on sales, return on assets or return on investment.[915]

Beside the publication of necessary and prescribed earning numbers according to IFRS, companies tend to reveal additional key figures which are adjusted or modified. Two incentives exist for managers to reveal voluntarily additional key figures, also named as pro forma key figures. Firstly, managers want to influence the assessment of their company by analysts in a positive way by eliminating certain expenses and fulfilling performance targets defined by analysts. This behaviour is named as opportunistic non-GAAP earnings disclosure. The second motive is that managers want to demonstrate what the true long-run economic performance of a company is and to eliminate transitory items from earnings. This enables investors and analysts to better estimate the future performance. Concerning the two incentives, it is difficult for persons outside the company to differentiate between the two motives of managers and thus to evaluate the quality of the key figures.[916]

Due to these circumstances a uniform definition of key figures and their calculation would be preferable from an investor's point of view. This claim is congruent to one principle of Value Reporting, namely comparability. For financial key figures an

907 Cf. Ittner, C. D., Larcker, D. F., Randall, T. (2003), p. 715; Melnyk, S. A., Bititci, U., Platts, K., et al. (2014), p. 174.

908 Cf. Fiedler, R., Gräf, J. (2012), pp. 335-336.

909 Cf. Barth, T., Barth, D. (2008), p. 136; Ewert, R., Wagenhofer, A. (2014), p. 513.

910 Cf. Coenenberg, A. G., Schultze, W. (2002), p. 612.

911 Cf. Barth, T., Barth, D. (2008), p. 137; Behringer, S. (2014), pp. 89-90; Brühl, R. (2016), pp. 425-427; key figures can be grouped according to several other aspects, e.g. operating functions (procurement, sales), data sources (accounting, cost accounting), temporal structure (key figures measuring the status quo at a certain point in time or key figures that refer to a period).

912 Cf. Barth, T., Barth, D. (2008), p. 137; Homburg, C. (2017), p. 1232.

913 Cf. Baetge, J., Kirsch, H.-J., Thiele, S. (2004), pp. 147-149; Groll, K.-H. (2000), pp. 9-12.

914 Cf. Homburg, C. (2017), p. 1232; Ohliger, T. (2016), p. 102; Weissmann, F. (2005), p. 72.

915 Cf. Schmeisser, W., Clausen, L. (2009), p. 86; Schneider, N. C. (2007), p. 45.

916 Cf. Beyer, A., Cohen, D. A., Lys, T. Z., et al. (2010), pp. 321-323.

intercompany comparability can be ensured by explaining single components of a key figure and the premises for their calculation.[917]

3.1.2 Price Earnings Ratio and Earnings per Share

The PER is one of the most popular key figures used by investors and analysts.[918] Many investors rely on accounting or accounting key figures by coming to an investment decision.[919] Therefore, before introducing value based performance measures selected common traditional key figures are presented and analysed. The PER and EPS are widely used key figures in order to evaluate the performance of a company, especially in America and Great Britain. This is the reason for the selection within the framework of this dissertation.[920]

The PER shows the assessment of a company on the stock market as a multiple of its profit.[921] The higher the PER, the longer the time until a company has earned the stock price through its annual earnings.[922] If an investor would buy shares of a company this key figure reveals after how many years the investment has amortised. The premise is that the earnings remain constant over these time period.[923] PER is a reciprocal return key figure because the denominator contains the earning figure.[924]

The PER is calculated as follows:

$$PER = \frac{Market\ price\ per\ share}{Earnings\ per\ Share}$$

Source: Formula adapted from: Garrison, R. H., Noreen, E. W., Brewer, P. C. (2012), p. 687
Formula 11: Calculation of PER

Basically, a PER above "one" indicates an overvaluation and a PER below "one" an undervaluation.[925] If two companies do not differentiate in their share price and their return on equity, investors prefer the company with the lower PER.[926]

As PER includes the stock price, the key figure summarises the risk and future growth possibilities expected by the shareholders and market participants.[927] This is the reason why it is possible to calculate the PER also with the expected earnings of the next period.[928]

917 Cf. Baetge, J., Solmecke, H. (2006), pp. 20-21.
918 Cf. Hasler, P. T. (2011), p. 305.
919 Cf. Elshandidy, T. (2014), p. 177.
920 Cf. Günther, T. (1997), p. 50; Wagenhofer, A. (2013), p. 253.
921 Cf. Busse, F.-J. (2003), p. 212; Groll, K.-H. (2000), p. 70.
922 Cf. Gräfer, H., Gerenkamp, T. (2016), p. 140.
923 Cf. Schmidlin, N. (2013), p. 112.
924 Cf. Baetge, J., Kirsch, H.-J., Thiele, S. (2004), p. 459.
925 Cf. Coenenberg, A. G., Haller, A., Schultze, W. (2014), p. 1158; Penman, S. H. (2013), p. 80.
926 Cf. Coenenberg, A. G., Haller, A., Schultze, W. (2014), p. 1158; Perridon, L., Steiner, M., Rathgeber, A. (2016), p. 249.
927 Cf. Wisniewski, T. P., Lightfoot, G., Lilley, S. (2012), p. 110.
928 Cf. Schmidlin, N. (2013), p. 112.

As the stock price is constantly changing, the PER also fluctuates.[929] This key figure can be used to assess the current stock price of a company. A sector average of the PER is needed which then can be multiplied with a company's earnings in order to receive an adequate PER. This value can be compared with the actual PER.[930] In some cases its difficult to use PER as a measure for comparison. Take successful and highly priced companies, e.g. Amazon. Their PER is not comparable with competitors.[931]

As a rule of thumb, investors assume that the PER should not exceed the profit growth rate.[932] Companies with high earnings growth rates have a high PER because the prospective earnings are included in the share price. Companies with low earnings growth rates show a low PER because the outlook reveals that the earnings are not growing so fast. The stock price reacts accordingly.[933] The PER is influenced by several factors like earnings growth rate, market position, capital structure, risk and management quality.[934]

Advantages of this key figure are that it is easy to calculate, it is well-known on an international level and the market evaluation of a company can be compared with the help of PER of a peer group.[935]

A key disadvantage is that the key figure is only usable for companies which generate profits. If a company reveals a loss, the key figure is useless.[936] A further disadvantage is that the stock price is influenced by many factors which partly can only be influenced in the long-term.[937] The EPS figure as part of PER calculation is a book value which can be manipulated by utilising accounting rules.[938]

The EPS is an important key figure for stocks evaluation at capital markets[939] and one of the most used key figures in the US.[940] IFRS prescribe companies to calculate basic and diluted EPS[941] in order to compare the performance of companies in a better way.[942]

Basic EPS is calculated as the division of profit or loss attributable to ordinary equity holders and the weighted average number of ordinary shares outstanding during the period.[943]

Diluted earnings per share consider earnings effects through interest payments due to convertible or option bonds.[944] The nominator is increased by dividends and interests recognised in the period and all other changes that would result from a conversion of all potentially convertible shares. The weighted number of shares in the denominator has to

929 Cf. Perridon, L., Steiner, M., Rathgeber, A. (2016), p. 249.
930 Cf. Küting, K., Weber, C.-P. (2015), p. 333.
931 Cf. Brealey, R. A., Myers, S. C., Allen, F. (2011), p. 105.
932 Cf. Groll, K.-H. (2000), p. 71.
933 Cf. Garrison, R. H., Noreen, E. W., Brewer, P. C. (2012); p. 687; Schmidlin, N. (2013), p. 113.
934 Cf. Schmidlin, N. (2013), pp. 114-116.
935 Cf. Heese, V. (2011), p. 66.
936 Cf. Heese, V. (2011), p. 67; Hasler, P. T. (2011), p. 307.
937 Cf. Schmidlin, N. (2013), pp. 114-116.
938 Cf. Hasler, P. T. (2011), p. 329.
939 Cf. Lüdenbach, N., Hoffmann, W.-D., Freiberg, J. (2015), § 35, marginal number 1.
940 Cf. Laier, R. (2011), p. 58.
941 Cf. IFRS Foundation (2016), IAS 33.66.
942 Cf. IFRS Foundation (2016), IAS 33.1.
943 Cf. IFRS Foundation (2016), IAS 33.10.
944 Cf. Baetge, J., Kirsch, H.-J., Thiele, S. (2004), p. 456.

be increased by the potential number of outstanding additional shares if all shares would have been converted.[945]

The general way of calculation for this key figure is:

$$EPS = \frac{Earnings}{Weighted\ average\ number\ of\ shares\ outstanding}$$

Source: Formula adopted from: Krause, H.-U., Arora, D. (2010), p. 43
Formula 12: Calculation of EPS

A high value of EPS shows investors that a share might be attractive because the company is able to generate a high profit. The contrary is valid for low EPS key figures.[946]

EPS is a convenient key figure to compare the performance of a single company over time. Nevertheless, it has to be considered that this key figure does not deliver information about the level of profitability. If two companies differ significantly in their share prices, the company with the higher share price has delivered a poorer profitability.[947]

Despite the named purpose of EPS and the fact that value relevance research indicates that earnings per share delivers useful information to investors,[948] this key figure is criticised within scientific literature. EPS alone can be a misleading key figure. Due to a lower EPS key figure a company does not necessarily deliver a poorer performance than a comparable company. The number of shares influences the result heavily. As a complementary key figure, the Return on Equity should come into consideration.[949] Beyond the leeway for manipulation due to the number of shares, the key figure can distort the true performance due to a different structure of the equity capital. EPS key figure considers only the capital stock and not capital contained in reserves.[950] Furthermore, the earnings number in the nominator can be influenced with accounting policy. Insofar, it is questionable if EPS key figures are really a good basis for comparing companies.[951] In total, the key figure is not convenient for a profitability analysis. The earnings are not only based on the basic capital but on the total equity capital.[952] This key figure is part of the key figure Price Earnings Ratio (PER).[953]

3.1.3 Return on Equity and Return on Sales

ROE shows the return a company generates on equity capital and thus reveals how efficient the company is in using the available equity capital.[954] The ROE is calculated as follows:

945 Cf. IFRS Foundation (2016), IAS 33.32.
946 Cf. Loose, T. (2009), p. 20; Wagenhofer, A. (2013), p. 253.
947 Cf. Krause, H.-U., Arora, D. (2010), pp. 43-44.
948 Cf. exemplarily the empirical study of Balsam, S., Lipka, R. (1998).
949 Cf. Coenenberg, A. G., Haller, A., Schultze, W. (2014), pp. 1155 – 1157.
950 Cf. Baetge, J., Kirsch, H.-J., Thiele, S. (2004), pp. 454-455.
951 Cf. Lüdenbach, N., Hoffmann, W.-D., Freiberg, J. (2015), § 35, marginal number 3.
952 Cf. Brösel, G. (2014); pp. 213-215; Küting, K., Weber, C.-P. (2015), pp. 308-309.
953 Cf. Krause, H.-U., Arora, D. (2010), p. 44.
954 Cf. Heusinger von Waldegge, S. (2009), p. 194; Steger, J. (2014), p. 47.

$$ROE = \frac{EBT}{Equity\ Capital}$$

Source: Formula adapted from: Steger, J. (2014), p. 48
Formula 13: Calculation of ROE

It is obvious that against the background of the Shareholder Value approach and VBM this key figure is important because companies try to maximise the ROE under consideration of the leverage effect.[955] Companies should generate a ROE which is above the average long term interest rate for investments at the capital market. Otherwise, investors would stop their investments because alternative investments with a higher return exist.[956]

For calculating the denominator, an average value of equity capital can be used in order to compare a dynamic figure in the nominator and a static figure in the denominator.[957]

Formula thirteen shows the calculation of ROE before taxes. This key figure enables a comparison of different company performances across different countries because the influence of national tax laws is eliminated.[958] However, the ROE is influenced by the capital structure. So a better basis for comparisons between companies independent from their capital structure is the key figure ROA.[959] A further disadvantage of ROE is that this key figure is not only influenced by economic performance of a company but also by its accounting policy. Both parts of this key figure base on the companies accounting and can be influenced by a company.[960]

ROS describes the margin of a company, so what profit is generated with each euro of turnover.[961] It indicates how profitable a company generates profit out of his sales.[962] The price structure on the markets on which the company offers its products and services as wells as its cost structure influences the level of ROS.[963]

$$ROS = \frac{EBIT}{Sales}$$

Source: Formula adapted from: Küting, K., Weber, C.-P. (2015), p. 330
Formula 14: Calculation of ROS

The formula above shows the ROS before tax and interest rates. This definition enables a better comparison between companies as the capital structure does not influence the key figure.[964] The level of ROS depends strongly on industries. A comparison over time

955 Cf. Gräfer, H., Gerenkamp, T. (2016), p. 61; cf. for an explanation of the leverage effect Zantow, R., Dinauer, J. (2011), pp. 523-524.
956 Cf. Brecht, U. (2012), p. 206.
957 Cf. Coenenberg, A. G., Haller, A., Schultze, W. (2014), p. 1153.
958 Cf. Coenenberg, A. G., Haller, A., Schultze, W. (2014), p. 1153.
959 Cf. Lummert, S., Schumacher, M. (2009), p. 74; Steger, J. (2014), p. 48.
960 Cf. Becker, H. P. (2016), p. 10; Koch, J. (2005), p. 59; Pape, U. (2015), p. 275.
961 Cf. Brecht, U. (2012), p. 181.
962 Cf. Wöltje, J. (2013), p. 502.
963 Cf. Pape, U. (2015), p. 275.
964 Cf. Krause, H.-U., Arora, D. (2010), p. 38.

between companies of the same industries is more meaningful.[965] An increasing ROS and constant sale prices indicate better productivity, a decreasing ROS provides evidence that the cost structure of a company is not as efficient as before.[966]

3.1.4 *Return on Investment*

The ROI is the top key figure of the well-known DuPont performance measurement system. The key figures ROS and capital turnover are subsequent key figures.[967] The performance measurement system enables the user to have a look at the profitability structure via the ROS and at the asset structure via the capital turnover. Both key figures are further subdivided so that all influencing factors can be analysed.[968]

The ROI is calculated as following:

$$ROI = ROS \times Capital\ turnover$$

Source: Formula adapted from: Stephan, J. (2006), p. 21
Formula 15: Calculation of ROI[969]

The ROI shows the relation between invested capital and resulting earnings. It corresponds to the return on capital.[970] A sole analysis of the ROI does not deliver many fruitful insights for investors,[971] so that the DuPont performance measurement system in total should be used to analyse profitability and development of turnovers.[972] The division of the return on assets formula into ROS and capital turnover enables managers to better understand in what way they can influence this key figure.[973] As the ROI measures the profitability, the basic rule is that the higher the ROI the better for a company.[974]

In practice, the ROI is used to control the performance of the past period and to identify room for improvements with the help of the total performance measurement system. It can also be applied in the context of planning and calculated prospective profitability.[975] ROI can be used to assess the success of a single business unit or of the whole company.[976]

The obvious advantage of the ROI is its easy calculation and the possible quick comparison of different alternatives.[977] Further advantages of the ROI system are that also

965 Cf. Krause, H.-U., Arora, D. (2010), p. 38; Preißler, P. R. (2008), p. 34.
966 Cf. Laier, R. (2011), p. 56.
967 Cf. Preißler, P. R. (2008), p. 49; Prätsch, J., Schikorra, U., Ludwig, E. (2012), pp. 282-283.
968 Cf. Preißler, P. R. (2008), pp. 50-51; Steger, J. (2014), p. 128.
969 Cf. for an overview of the complete DuPont performance measurement system Stephan, J. (2006), p. 21.
970 Cf. Hauerdinger, M., Probst, H.-J. (2006), p. 189.
971 Cf. Baetge, J., Kirsch, H.-J., Thiele, S. (2004), p. 503.
972 Cf. extensively for analysis with the help of DuPont measurement system Baetge, J., Kirsch, H.-J., Thiele, S. (2004), pp. 503-517.
973 Cf. Garrison, R. H., Noreen, E. W., Brewer, P. C. (2012), p. 476.
974 Cf. Prätsch, J., Schikorra, U., Ludwig, E. (2012), p. 282.
975 Cf. Prätsch, J., Schikorra, U., Ludwig, E. (2012), p. 282; Stephan, J. (2006), pp. 20-21.
976 Cf. Neely, A., Gregory, M., Platts, K. (1995), p. 89; Perridon, L., Steiner, M., Rathgeber, A. (2016), p. 672.
977 Cf. Mohnen, A. (2002), p. 52.

external persons can calculate it. It is an established tool for analysing the profitability of a company and enables the user to identify weak spots.[978] The ROI is independent from the capital structure of the analysed company. On the one hand, this is an advantage because the ROI cannot be manipulated by the leverage effect. On the other hand, the ROI does not consider the financing risk inherent with a high leverage ratio.[979]

A large influence on the resulting ROI is the amount of depreciation. It influences the nominator as well as the denominator. Therefore, it is difficult to compare different business segments with divergent depreciation structures. The influence of deprecation has a further negative effect. Companies with highly depreciated assets have ceteris paribus a higher ROI.[980] This effect leads to higher ROI for companies which postpone necessary investments which may negatively impact long term economic performance.[981] An argument against this point is that basically all companies are in a steady state in which reinvestments and depreciation correspond to each other so that distortions do not occur.[982] A way to avoid this problem would be to calculate the ROI with historical costs so that no depreciation is included.[983]

The disadvantage of ROI is that the ROI alone has no explanatory power. Only in combination with other key figures can fruitful insights be derived. In comparison with other performance measurement systems, like the Balanced Scorecard, the ROI system focuses on profitability and only includes financial key figures.[984] Further disadvantages mentioned within the scientific literature are that costs of capital are not considered[985] and the application of ROI leads to short-term decisions by managers because they want to increase the ROI at the expense of the long-term success of the company.[986] The ROI also does not consider the distribution of earnings over time and is limited to one period.[987]

3.2 Concept of Value Based Key Figures

3.2.1 Systematisation of Value Based Key Figures

The development of value based performance measures begins with the Shareholder Value approach, the spread of VBM, the importance of financial markets, the spread of IFRS and development of Value Reporting. These developments make it necessary for companies to assess their performance under the conditions of the Shareholder Value approach.[988] Value based performance measures have the objective to align managers'

978 Cf. Ossadnik, W. (2009), p. 265; Steger, J. (2014), p. 130.
979 Cf. Lorson, P. (2004), pp. 81-82.
980 Cf. Plaschke, F. J. (2003), pp. 140-141; Mohnen, A. (2002), pp. 55-56.
981 Cf. Groll, K.-H. (2003), p. 23.
982 Cf. Plaschke, F. J. (2003), p. 141.
983 Cf. Perridon, L., Steiner, M., Rathgeber, A. (2016), p. 673.
984 Cf. Garrison, R. H., Noreen, E. W., Brewer, P. C. (2012), p. 479; Steger, J. (2014), p. 130.
985 Cf. Bromwich, M., Walker, M. (1998), p. 397.
986 Cf. Garrison, R. H., Noreen, E. W., Brewer, P. C. (2012), p. 479; Neely, A., Gregory, M., Platts, K. (1995), p. 89.
987 Cf. Mohnen, A. (2002), pp. 52-53.
988 Cf. Coenenberg, A. G., Fischer, T. M., Günther, T. (2012), pp. 837-838; Steinhauer, L. (2007), p. 288; cf. extensively chapters 2.1.1 and 2.1.2 about VBM and Shareholder approach for an illustration of developments which make it necessary to use value based performance measures.

objectives with the Shareholder Value approach.[989] Companies have to select appropriate investment projects which deliver an adequate rate of return. They have to control their performance and to communicate created value to the capital market.[990] Traditional key figures are no longer sufficient to satisfy the information needs of managers and investors.[991]

With value based performance measures managers and investors have a tool which shows the creation of value in the sense of the Shareholder Value approach.[992] Within the context of Value Reporting value based performance measures are a convenient way of communicating the performance.[993] Also value based performance measures have information and control function.[994] Thus, they are a way of ensuring internal orientation according to the principles of VBM and a kind of external proof for achieved performance objectives.[995]

Value based performance measures are defined as key figures which capture the development or value added to the Shareholder Value of a company. Therefore, they consider the cost of equity capital in their calculation.[996] In other words: All value based performance measures are based on the concept of residual income. This implies that a company has to earn more than its costs of its invested capital.[997] Examples for value based performance measures are Economic Value Added (EVA), Cash Flow Return on Investment (CFROI) or Cash Value Added (CVA).[998]

As the Shareholder Value approach focuses on the market value of equity capital, the question could arise why value based performance measures are needed instead of directly referring to market values. This would be possible if complete capital markets exist. Actually, this is not the case so that values based on market measures could be influenced by several other factors than firm performance or could be distorted due to wrong expectations of market participants.[999] Instead, book values are not influenced by expectations of the market participants or the general mood on capital markets and can therefore be better used than market values for evaluating the performance of a company.[1000]

Within scientific literature a systematisation of value based performance measures is regularly made on the basis of two criteria: Data basis for calculation and type of key figure.[1001] Data basis refers to the basis of calculation that means is the key figure based

989 Cf. Brück, C., Ludwig, J., Schwering, A. (2018), pp. 386-387; Holler, A. (2009), p. 28.
990 Cf. Günther, T., Beyer, D. (2001), p. 1623.
991 Cf. Ossadnik, W. (2009), p. 325.
992 Cf. Fiss, P. C., Zajac, E. J. (2004), p. 514; Günther, T. (2002), p. 97; Hoffjan, A., Schroll, S. (2010), p. 410; Knauer, T., Silge, L., Sommer, F. (2018).
993 Cf. Töpfer, A., Duchmann, C. (2006), p. 39.
994 Cf. Ewert, R., Wagenhofer, A. (2000), p. 4.
995 Cf. Knauer, T., Silge, L., Sommer, F. (2018); Ossadnik, W. (2009), p. 326; Baetge, J., Kümmel, J. (2003), p. 56.
996 Cf. Ewert, R., Wagenhofer, A. (2014), p. 516.
997 Cf. Biddle, G. C., Bowen, R. M., Wallace, J. S. (1999), p. 70.
998 Cf. Karrer, M. (2006), p. 159; Weber, J. (2009), p. 297.
999 Cf. Wollscheid, D. (2013), pp. 27-30; extensively chapter 2.3.1.1 about the levels of information asymmetries on capital markets.
1000 Cf. Wollscheid, D. (2013), pp. 27-30.
1001 Cf. Ewert, R., Wagenhofer, A. (2014), pp. 516-517; Töpfer, A., Duchmann, C. (2006), pp. 30-31; cf. for a more detailed systematization Schumann, J. (2008), p. 99.

on a Cash Flow figure or an earnings figure. The criterion type of key figure differentiates if the value based performance measure is an absolute or a relative number.[1002]

For the systematisation in the context of this work a third criterion should be included: Time horizon. Value based performance measures could be further differentiated between key figures which measure the performance of one single period and performance measures which refer to the total period. The latter ones are often used to determine the value of a company in the context of corporate valuation.[1003] Despite the Shareholder Value approach focuses on long term performance many value based performance measures focus on one period. This can be seen as an operationalisation of VBM.[1004]

The performance measures focussing on a single period are often used as ex post performance measures, thus in order to analyse and assess the performance of a company in the past periods.[1005] The key figures including several periods in their analysis are used as ex ante key figures in order to determine the possible performance of a company in the next periods.[1006]

In illustration 11 ROCE Spread and RONA Spread are mentioned as value based performance measures. In order to avoid misunderstandings: ROCE and RONA when taken by themselves are not value based performance measures. If the cost of equity capital is deducted from ROCE and RONA, the resulting difference is a value based performance measure in the sense of this dissertation. Therefore, the ROCE and RONA spread which both include the cost of capital in their calculation refer to the difference of ROCE / RONA and cost of capital and not solely to the key figure itself.[1007]

Type of key figure	Absolute Key Figure		Relative Key Figure	
Time Horizon→	Single Period	Total Period	Single Period	Total Period
Data Basis ↓				
Cash Flow	CVA SVA	DCF	CFROI SVR	
Earning	EVA EP Value Added	MVA	ROCE Spread RONA Spread	

In the style of: Dillerup, R., Stoi, R. (2016), p. 204; Langguth, H. (2008), p. 138; Ossadnik, W. (2009), p. 329; Steger, J. (2014), p. 154; Stüker, D. (2008), p. 105; Töpfer, A., Duchmann, C. (2006), p. 31

Illustration 11: Systematisation of value based performance measures

1002 Cf. Karrer, M. (2006), p. 159.

1003 Cf. Heier, K., Karsten, E., Müller-Wenzel, C., et al. (2015), p. 8; Hoffjan, A., Schroll, S. (2010), p. 411; Schumann, J. (2008), pp. 97-99; Steger, J. (2014), p. 153; Zell, M. (2008), p. 152.

1004 Cf. Hoffjan, A., Schroll, S. (2010), p. 410.

1005 Cf. Coenenberg, A. G., Mattner, G. R., Schultze, W. (2003), p. 2; Lachnit, L., Müller, S. (2012), pp. 255-256.

1006 Cf. Lachnit, L., Müller, S. (2012), pp. 255-256.

1007 Cf. Heusinger von Waldegge, S. (2009), pp. 72-73; Langguth, H. (2008), pp. 177-178.

3.2.2 Advantages of Value Based Key Figures and Flaws of Traditional Key Figures

The development of value based performance measures was mostly initiated by the dissatisfaction of managers with traditional performance measures in the period between 1990 and 2000. The scientific literature contains points of criticism concerning traditional key figures which value based performance measures should overcome.[1008] The application of value based key figures should focus a company on Shareholder Value creation.[1009]

During the dissemination phase of VBM many studies attest traditional key figures a low correlation to the development on capital markets.[1010] Consulting companies which develop concepts for value based performance measures show in their studies that the new developed key figures have a higher correlation to the share price development.[1011] These results are controversially discussed within the scientific literature. Other studies come to reverse results and ascribe traditional key figures a higher coefficient of determination.[1012]

The traditional key figures like return on equity or return on sales are criticised within the scientific literature because they do not adequately consider the alignment of the company to the equity capital providers interests'.[1013] In order to consider these interests, cost of equity capital providers should be included within the calculation. Consequently, one point of criticism of traditional key figures is that they do not include these costs in their calculation.[1014] Their results are too positive from the perspective of an equity capital investor.[1015] Value based performance measures can include cost of equity capital, e.g. by using the CAPM.[1016]

A further point of criticism is the missing consideration of risk. Investors claim a higher return for riskier investments. The costs of capital which are included in the calculation of value based performance measures do reflect these risks because they increase with riskier investments.[1017] Traditional key figures also do not deal with the capital structure of a company which also leads to risk for the investor, e.g. through a high leverage.[1018]

Traditional performance measures are influenced by external accounting rules.[1019] This is problematic as the basis for their calculation can be distorted due to explicit or implicit rights of choice within accounting rules. Consequently, the computed key figures do not reflect the true performance.[1020] Examples are different methods of depreciations which influence traditional key figures and the performance evaluation of a company.[1021]

1008 Cf. Ittner, C. D., Larcker, D. F. (1998), pp. 205-206; cf. exemplarily Holler, A. (2009), pp. 29-30; Rappaport, A. (1986), pp. 19-49.
1009 Cf. Ittner, C. D., Larcker, D. F. (2001), p. 358.
1010 Cf. Günther, T. (1997), pp. 50-54; Lattwein, J. (2002), p. 112.
1011 Cf. exemplarily the studies of Lewis, T. G., Stelter, D. M. (1993) and O'Byrne, S. F. (1997).
1012 Cf. exemplarily the studies of Biddle, G. C., Bowen, R. M., Wallace, J. S. (1997) and Chen, S., Dodd, J. L. (2001) and Landsman, W. R., Shapiro, A. C. (1995).
1013 Cf. Kremer, P. (2008), pp. 64-65.
1014 Cf. Biddle, G. C., Bowen, R. M., Wallace, J. S. (1999), p. 70; Karrer, M. (2006), pp. 151-152.
1015 Cf. Knorren, N. (1998), pp. 11-12; Riedl, J. B. (2000), pp. 113-116.
1016 Cf. Behringer, S. (2014), pp. 101-102.
1017 Cf. Günther, T. (1997), p. 55; Schmeisser, W., Rönsch, M., Zilch, I. (2009), p. 2.
1018 Cf. Günther, T. (2002), p. 90.
1019 Cf. Ittner, C. D., Larcker, D. F. (1998), p. 209.
1020 Cf. Günther, T. (1997), pp. 54-55.
1021 Cf. Stephan, J. (2006), pp. 33-35.

In the opinion of the critics accounting data is only in a limited way convenient for controlling purposes.[1022]

Many traditional key figures like return on equity or return on capital measure the historical performance. Reason for this is the basis of the data of these key figures which is used for calculation. The data base results from disclosed accounting which refers also to past periods.[1023] Against the background of VBM and the Shareholder Value approach, the measurement of historical performance is not relevant as future earnings and Cash Flows are decisive for a company's success. The effects of today's investment in the future are not considered within the calculation scheme of these key figures.[1024] Furthermore, the focus on the current period can set incorrect incentives for managers who try to increase short-term earnings to the detriment of long-term success.[1025]

Traditional key figures also do not consider the present value of money.[1026] An investment project over several years may deliver negative economic performance in the first years but a positive performance in the latter years of the project. In total, the project increases the Shareholder Value of a company. So, a total assessment of a project or also a company is only possible if prospective developments are considered. Besides this, the timing of Cash inflows and outflows can determine if a present value is positive or negative and the project should be conducted.[1027]

Closely connected with the flaw of ignoring the present value of money and accounting figures as a basis for data is the disadvantage of focusing on the performance of a single period. From a shareholder's perspective it is not sufficient. Several following periods have to be included in the calculation of the key figure.[1028]

To sum up: Traditional key figures are criticised for the following points:[1029]

- Low correlation between traditional key figures and development at capital markets
- No consideration of cost of equity capital
- No consideration of risk
- Scope for manipulation of key figures due to accounting as data basis for calculation
- Description of historical performance
- No consideration of present value of money
- Focus on the performance of a single period

Some points of criticism should be relativised according to the purpose for which a key figure is used. If a key figure is used for controlling, the past performance is relevant and a consideration of future developments not necessary. The extent of criticism within parts of scientific literature is exaggerated and should be assessed with caution. Nevertheless,

1022 Cf. Pape, U. (2010), p. 31.
1023 Cf. Hauschildt, J. (1996), pp. 1-2; Junginger, M. (2005), p. 56.
1024 Cf. Zell, M. (2008), p. 151.
1025 Cf. Knorren, N. (1998), pp. 12-13.
1026 Cf. Banzhaf, J. (2006), p. 99; Stephan, J. (2006), p. 35.
1027 Cf. Beck, R. (2003), pp. 18-19; Stephan, J. (2006), p. 35.
1028 Cf. Knorren, N. (1998), pp. 12-13; Riedl, J. B. (2000), pp. 111-112.
1029 Cf. for an overview of flaws of traditional key figures: Beck, R. (2003), p. 6; Günther, T. (2002), p. 89; Junginger, M. (2005), p. 56; Kremer, P. (2008), p. 65; Pape, U. (2010), p. 32; Riedl, J. B. (2000), pp. 110-121; Schmeisser, W., Clausen, L. (2009), pp. 87-88; Schmeisser, W., Rönsch, M., Zilch, I. (2009), pp. 2-3.

this discussion reveals that companies should complement their traditional key figures with value based ones.[1030]

3.2.3 *Evaluation Criteria for Value Based Performance Measures*

The evaluation criteria for value based performance measures are derived from the identified point of criticism from traditional key figures. The named disadvantages should be all or at least partly solved with the application of value based performance measures. In the following the evaluation criteria are presented.[1031]

1. Goal congruence with Shareholder Value approach

A key figure has to create the right incentives for managers. That means that an increase in a key figure reflects an increase in the Shareholder Value of company. Especially concerning key figures focusing on one period, this could be problematic as investments generate negative Cash Flows at the beginning but are in total still worthwhile for the company and should be conducted.[1032] Ideally a key figure has the same sign in any period during the investment project as the expected present value at the beginning of the project.[1033]

For the purpose of evaluation of value based performance measures, this criterion does not come directly into consideration. The other criteria selected like risk consideration and present value of money are more verifiable. If they are fulfilled, sufficient goal congruence between a company's objective and manager's behaviour is achieved.[1034]

A possible way to operationalise this criterion is to define resulting values from the Discounted Cash Flow method as equal to Shareholder Value. This would lead to a comparison of every selected key figure with the DCF approach. Then the DCF approach itself could not be assessed.[1035] In the following assessment this criterion is considered indirectly with the criteria present value of money, future orientation and considering risk.

2. Resistance against manipulation

Managers can influence performance measures in two ways: Firstly, through their working effort so that the performance of the company improves and the key figures change accordingly. Secondly, they manipulate them. By manipulating key figures, managers harm a company twice. On the one hand, the true economic performance decreases because management is concentrated on disguising true performance and on the other hand, the remuneration is higher than justified if key figures determine a part of managements' salaries.[1036] If a manager's success is assessed on the basis of a key figure, the manager has a strong incentive to manipulate the result in order to increase its

1030 Cf. Günther, T. (1997), p. 59; Weber, J., Schäffer, U. (2016), p. 184.
1031 Cf. Knorren, N. (1998), pp. 16-17; Zell, M. (2008), p. 152.
1032 Cf. Coenenberg, A. G., Schultze, W. (2002), pp. 612-614.
1033 Cf. Mohnen, A., Bareket, M. (2007), p. 2.
1034 Cf. Schultze, W., Hirsch, C. (2005), pp. 22-23.
1035 Cf. Weber, J., Bramsemann, U., Heineke, C., et al. (2017), p. 72.
1036 Cf. Pfaff, D., Stefani, U. (2003), pp. 65-68.

payment. It is in the company's interest to select a key figure that is resistant to manipulation and reflects the true performance of the managers and its department.[1037]

Closely connected to this criterion is the criterion of future orientation. Prospective developments cannot be calculated in a completely objective way because certain assumptions have to be made for their calculation.[1038] Therefore, it is useful if a company establishes rules for key figure calculation which are as distinct as possible, in order to limit the range for manipulation.[1039]

In general, key figures based on Cash Flows are assessed as less prone to manipulation because they are not influenced as much as earnings by discretion in accounting, e.g. by different methods of deprecation. In the context of the following analysis this criterion is assessed by the data basis for calculation of a key figure.[1040]

3. Data basis for calculation

Due to the accounting principles and the main purpose of IFRS accounting, information delivery, the IFRS data can be assessed as relevant.[1041] Furthermore, accounting data are easily available for company internal and company external persons.[1042] Concerning its resistance against manipulation, the IFRS offers a lot of indirect rights of choice which are difficult to compare across companies.[1043] Therefore, key figures based on book values can be influenced by utilising accounting rules and in the end the resulting value of the key figure can be manipulated.[1044]

A further problem in using accounting data is that the data has already become obsolete at the time of publication. This problem concerns external persons outside the company which do not have access to internal data.[1045]

4. Present value of money

This implies that the key figure reflects financial consequences of a project decision directly in the period of decision. This immediate reflection is only possible for key figures which include present values because most projects start with negative Cash Flows at the beginning so that key figures without considering present value show negative effects.

Normally, present values are calculated on the basis of Cash Flows. Preinreich and Lücke show that under certain conditions present values can be computed with earnings and come to the same result. Some value based performance measures base on earnings instead of Cash Flows. For using key figures, it is important that a change in a key figure corresponds to a change in the present value of the company's Cash Flows.[1046] Assump-

1037 Cf. Kremer, P. (2008), pp. 88-89; Laux, H. (2006a), pp. 91-92.
1038 Cf. Kremer, P. (2008), pp. 88-89; Laux, H. (2006a), p. 91.
1039 Cf. Schultze, W., Hirsch, C. (2005), p. 25.
1040 Cf. Beck, R. (2003), pp. 13-14; Schmeisser, W., Rönsch, M., Zilch, I. (2009), p. 2.
1041 Cf. Kremer, P. (2008), pp. 115-116; cf. also chapter 2.4.3 and the analysis of advantages and disadvantages of IFRS.
1042 Cf. Fiedler, R., Gräf, J. (2012), p. 339.
1043 Cf. Kremer, P. (2008), pp. 116-117.
1044 Cf. Freidank, C.-C., Reibis, C. (2008), p. 293.
1045 Cf. Schmeisser, W., Clausen, L. (2009), p. 73.
1046 Cf. Herbertinger, M. (2002), pp. 36-37; Laux, H. (2006a), p. 89.

tions for the validity of the Lücke theorem are the clean surplus accounting and congruence principle. The IFRS rules violate these principles with e.g. the assessment of financial assets held for sale or the revaluation method for assets.[1047]

A disadvantage for key figures with present value is that it might induce managers to initiate projects with positive present values but there are insufficient incentives to complete these projects successfully because the positive effect has already been considered in the key figure.[1048] A clear advantage is that managers do not cancel prospect projects due to their negative effects at the beginning and thus increase the long-term success of the company.[1049]

5. Future orientation

As the main goal of investors is to predict prospective future Cash Flows and earnings, a key figure should have forward looking elements and not focus on solely historical performance.[1050] This can be done by estimating possible investments and resulting Cash Flows out of these projects.[1051] A point of critique is often that key figures foster short-term actions of managers that damage the long-term economic performance of a company. By considering both time horizons, this point of critique becomes obsolete.[1052]

The imminent danger in using value based performance measures which refer to one period is that projects are excluded due to a negative value in a single period. In total the project might be positive, so that it would be economically rational to conduct it.[1053]

6. Considering risk

Investors demand a higher return for a riskier investment. Key figures can include the risk by discounting earnings / Cash Flows with a risk adjusted interest rate. These discount rates are regularly the cost of capital.[1054] The risk is determined by the operations of a company and its capital structure.[1055] In bigger companies it makes sense to calculate cost of equity capital according to business segments because these segments differ in their risk and therefore have different hurdle rates which they have to fulfil.[1056]

7. Simplicity

An important factor of successful VBM adopters is that the majority of employees can explain and understand the composition of the value based metric.[1057] Therefore, it is a crucial factor to keep the value based performance measure as simple as possible in order to ensure a company-wide understanding.[1058] Managers have to know which factors

1047 Cf. Kremer, P. (2008), pp. 113-114.
1048 Cf. Kremer, P. (2008), pp. 87-88.
1049 Cf. Kremer, P. (2008), p. 88.
1050 Cf. Ittner, C. D., Larcker, D. F., Randall, T. (2003), p. 717.
1051 Cf. Günther, T. (2002), p. 90.
1052 Cf. Neely, A., Gregory, M., Platts, K. (1995), p. 99.
1053 Cf. Weißenberger, B. E. (2003), p. 261.
1054 Cf. Beck, R. (2003), p. 18; Günther, T. (2002), p. 90.
1055 Cf. Rappaport, A. (1986), pp. 21-23.
1056 Cf. Malmström, B. (2006), p. 641.
1057 Cf. Haspeslagh, P., Noda, T., Boulos, F. (2001), p. 68; Kremer, P. (2008), p. 82.
1058 Cf. Haspeslagh, P., Noda, T., Boulos, F. (2001), p. 70.

influence the value of the key figure.[1059] Also part of this criterion is the circumstance that users of a key figure know in advance of an action the resulting effect on the key figure. In other words: It must be transparent in what way the key figure reacts.[1060]

Connected with simplicity is the cost-benefit relationship of a performance measure. It means how costly the measurement of performance is. Especially for small and medium sized enterprises, this question is important as their resources are limited. Ideally, the key figure should be easily to calculate and to be applied within the company.[1061]

8. Correlation with capital market development

A further criterion which is not assessed in the course of the following analysis is the correlation of single key figures to the capital market development. As empirical studies present divergent results and no uniform conclusions, the assessment of this aspect does not help to differentiate the key figures and their abilities from each other.[1062]

In order to give an overview, the following enumeration summarises all evaluation criteria.[1063] The first evaluation criterion "including cost of capital" has not been explicitly mentioned in this chapter as it is part of the definition of value based performance measure.[1064]

- Including cost of capital
- Data basis for calculation (availability and quality of data)
- Present value of money
- Future orientation
- Considering risk
- Simplicity

The selection of the later presented value based performance measures has been conducted on the basis of their relevance in theory and practice.[1065] It also has to be noted that a lot of variations of the same value based performance measures exist. Consequently, no uniform definition within the scientific literature is available.[1066] This leads to the problem that companies are relatively free in the calculation of value based key

---

1059 Cf. Schultze, W., Hirsch, C. (2005), p. 26.

1060 Cf. Kremer, P. (2008), p. 82; Schultze, W., Hirsch, C. (2005), pp. 23-25.

1061 Cf. Neely, A., Gregory, M., Platts, K. (1995), p. 84.

1062 Cf. exemplarily the empirical studies of Biddle, G. C., Bowen, R. M., Wallace, J. S. (1997) and Siebrecht, F., Heidorn, T., Klein, H.-D. (2001).

1063 Cf. exemplarily for similar criteria for assessing traditional key figures and value based performance measures Fiedler, R., Gräf, J. (2012), p. 339; Herbertinger, M. (2002), pp. 36-41; Horster, J., Knauer, T. (2012), p. 119; Groll, K.-H. (2000), pp. 22-27; Knorren, N. (1998), pp. 16-18; Schultze, W., Hirsch, C. (2005), pp. 15-33; Schumann, J. (2008), pp. 102-112; Stührenberg, L., Streich, D., Henke Jörg (2003), p. 64; Zell, M. (2008), p. 152.

1064 Cf. Ewert, R., Wagenhofer, A. (2014), p. 516.

1065 Cf. Fiedler, R., Gräf, J. (2012), p. 338 name EVA and CVA as most frequently applied key figures; Freidank, C.-C., Reibis, C. (2008), p. 293 lists EVA and CFROI as the most famous key figures; Heusinger von Waldegge, S. (2009), pp. 72-73 lists EVA, EP, ERIC, CVA and CFROI as well-known concepts of value based performance measurement; Junginger, M. (2005), p. 61 names DCF, EVA and CFROI; Schumann, J. (2008), p. 101, who lists among others EVA, ERIC, CVA and SVA as important value based performance measures.

1066 Cf. Freidank, C.-C., Reibis, C. (2008), p. 293; Günther, T. (2002), p. 92.

figures.[1067] Non uniform defined key figures limit the comparability of performance between different companies in the end so that it is difficult for investors to assess which company performs best.[1068]

Concluding to this chapter, it should be mentioned in advance that the following illustration and assessment of value based performance measures aims to show what divergent approaches the value concepts pursue and stress the resulting advantages and disadvantages than to find a superior concept out of the selected key figures. On the basis of the presented criteria this is problematic because apart from a theoretical discussion these criteria are difficult to operationalise.

Take as an example the criterion of resistance against manipulation. Key figures which include future periods in their calculation do not fulfil this requirement in the same manner as key figures which concentrate on past periods. The estimation of prospective developments always offers more possibilities for manipulation than the drawing on published performance data.

A further complicating factor is that the scientific literature has no uniform positions concerning many criteria.[1069] There will be no key figure which fulfils all criteria listed. For a company it is important to select an appropriate key figure for a specific purpose and to be aware of the advantages and disadvantages. A company will use a mixture of traditional and value based performance measures.[1070] Beside the right mixture of key figures for companies it is also decisive to connect the messages of single key figure with each other. In this way the analysis of key figures delivers an overall image of the company's performance.[1071]

3.3 Value Based Performance Measures Focussing on a Single Period

3.3.1 Concept of Residual Income (Preinreich-Lücke Theorem)

Many value based performance measures like EVA, CFROI or Economic Profit base on the concept of residual income.[1072] The Preinreich-Lücke[1073] theorem describes that a present value could be calculated with Cash Flows as well as with earnings and expenses. In both cases the result is identical.[1074] This theorem is the justification for the application of periodic value based performance measures which are based on earnings. Present values are identical to those ones calculated on the basis of Cash Flows.[1075]

1067 Cf. Freidank, C.-C., Reibis, C. (2008), p. 293.
1068 Cf. Hauschildt, J. (1996), pp. 8-9.
1069 Cf. Schumann, J. (2008), pp. 105-108.
1070 Cf. Hesselmann, C. (2006), p. 75; Schultze, W., Hirsch, C. (2005), pp. 28-30.
1071 Cf. Hauschildt, J. (1996), pp. 5-7.
1072 Cf. Coenenberg, A. G., Schultze, W. (2002), p. 606; Coenenberg, A. G., Schultze, W. (2003), pp. 119-120; Lindemann, J. (2004), p. 85.
1073 In Germany Lücke proved that present values on the basis of Cash Flows and present values on the basis of earnings and expenditures correspond to each other. Within the Anglo-American scientific literature this prove was conducted by Preinreich and Edwards / Bell. Cf. for more details Edwards, E. O., Bell, P. W. (1961); Lücke, W. (1955); Preinreich, G. (1938).
1074 Cf. Bromwich, M., Walker, M. (1998), pp. 394-396; Coenenberg, A. G., Mattner, G. R., Schultze, W. (2003), p. 7; Ewert, R., Wagenhofer, A. (2000), p. 10.
1075 Cf. Kahle, H. (2003), p. 776; Pfaff, D., Stefani, U. (2003), p. 58; Stüker, D. (2008), p. 110.

In order to receive identical results, certain conditions have to be fulfilled.

- Clean Surplus Accounting / Clean Surplus Accounting Relation: This term summarises that all transactions a company conducts are recognised in the profit and loss statement apart from increase or decrease of equity capital.[1076] This means that dividend payments do not affect the profit and loss statement. They reduce the book value of equity capital.[1077]
- Congruent Principle: The sum of cash in and out flows and the sum of expenditures and earnings has to be equal over the whole life time of the company (total period).[1078]
- Interest rate used for calculation: The interest rates used for calculation of cost of capital and present value calculation have to be identical.[1079]

If these assumptions hold, the present value on the basis of Cash Flows equals the present value on the basis of expenditures and profits.[1080] This has the consequence that for making an investment decision it is irrelevant if the decision is made on the basis of Cash Flows or accounting figures.[1081]

Of course the theorem can be transferred to the calculation of company value.[1082] Starting point is the Dividend Discount Model which can be modified so that the company value is expressed by the residual income.[1083]

$$P_t = \sum_{T=1}^{n} E_t\,(D_{t+T}) \times p_{t+T} + R_n \times p_{t+n}$$

Source: Formula taken from: Lindemann, J. (2004), p. 83
Formula 16: Dividend Discount Model with Terminal Value

with
P_t = Value of equity capital respectively of a share at time t
D_t = Transfer payments from company to shareholders (including dividends)
$p_{t+T} = \frac{1}{(1+i_{t+1}) \times (1+i_{t+2}) \times \ldots \times (1+i_{t+T})}$ = Present value of a payment in period t+T
i = risk adjusted interest rate
R_n = Terminal Value

1076 Cf. Lehmann, G. (2012), p. 56; Schultze, W., Hirsch, C. (2005), p. 51.
1077 Cf. Biddle, G. C., Bowen, R. M., Wallace, J. S. (1999), pp. 70-71; Ohlson, J. A. (1995), p. 662.
1078 Cf. Ewert, R., Wagenhofer, A. (2000), p. 10; O'Hanlon, J., Peasell, K. (2002), pp. 230-231; Schultze, W., Hirsch, C. (2005), p. 51.
1079 Cf. Pfaff, D., Stefani, U. (2003), p. 59.
1080 Cf. for a simple example which illustrates the Preinreich-Lücke Theorem Coenenberg, A. G., Fischer, T. M., Günther, T. (2012), pp. 844-845.
1081 Cf. Schultze, W., Hirsch, C. (2005), p. 53.
1082 Cf. Lehmann, G. (2012), p. 56; Schultze, W., Hirsch, C. (2005), p. 52.
1083 Cf. for the all further illustrated calculation steps Lindemann, J. (2004), pp. 85-89 from which formula 16 – 24 are adapted. For the derivation of the residual income formula cf. additionally exemplarily the following sources: Biddle, G. C., Bowen, R. M., Wallace, J. S. (1999), pp. 70-71; Ewert, R., Wagenhofer, A. (2000), pp. 10-15. Even if the used formula might slightly differ the procedure of deriving the residual income valuation formula is the same.

Residual income is defined as the difference between accounting profit and the cost of capital which a company has used to generate this profit.[1084] The calculation of cost of capital is conducted on the basis of capital to the beginning of the period.[1085]

$$x_t^a = x_t - i_t \times V_{t-1} = (ROE_t - i_t) \times V_{t-1}$$

Source: Formula taken from: Lindemann, J. (2004), p. 86
Formula 17: Definition of residual income

with
x_t^a = residual income of period t
V_t = Book value of equity capital at time t
x_t = profit
ROE_t = Return on equity of period t
i = risk adjusted interest rate

In order to transfer the Dividend Discount Model in a form that only contains book values, it is necessary to describe dividends with the help of accounting terms. The change of equity capital from one period to another corresponds to the difference of profit and transferred payments to shareholders.

$$V_t - V_{t-1} = x_t - D_t$$

Source: Formula taken from: Lindemann, J. (2004), p. 86
Formula 18: Explanation of Dividends through accounting figures I

In the following, this equation can be converted so that the dividends are the profit of a period minus the difference of the change in equity capital.

$$D_t = x_t - (V_t - V_{t-1})$$

Source: Formula taken from: Lindemann, J. (2004), p. 86
Formula 19: Explanation of Dividends through accounting figures II

Formula seventeen has to be converted so that it expresses the profit x_t. That yields

$$x_t = x_t^a + i_t \times V_{t-1}$$

Source: Formula taken from: Lindemann, J. (2004), p. 86
Formula 20: Converted residual income formula

The term of formula twenty can be inserted in formula nineteen. Thus, dividends are expressed by the following term:

1084 Cf. O'Hanlon, J., Peasell, K. (2002), p. 231; Pfaff, D., Stefani, U. (2003), pp. 53-54; Weißenberger, B. E. (2009), p. 44.
1085 Cf. Bromwich, M., Walker, M. (1998), p. 394-395; Weißenberger, B. E. (2009), p. 44.

$$D_t = x_t^a + i_t \times V_{t-1} - (V_t - V_{t-1})$$

$$= D_t = x_t^a - V_t + V_{t-1} + i_t \times V_{t-1}$$

$$= D_t = x_t^a - V_t + V_{t-1} \times (1 + i_t)$$

Source: Formula taken from: Lindemann, J. (2004), p. 88
Formula 21: Converted dividend formula

This term can be inserted in formula sixteen of the Dividend Discount Model.

$$P_t = \sum_{T=1}^{n} [x_{t+T}^a - V_{t+T} + V_{t+T-1} \times (1 + i_{t+T})] \times p_{t+T} + R_n \times p_{t+n}$$

$$= \sum_{T=1}^{n} x_{t+T}^a \times p_{t+T} - \sum_{T=1}^{n} V_{t+T} \times p_{t+T} + \sum_{T=0}^{n-1} V_{t+T} \times p_{t+T} + R_n \times p_{t+n}$$

$$= \sum_{T=1}^{n} x_{t+T}^a \times p_{t+T} - V_{t+n} \times p_{t+n} + V_t \times p_t + R_n \times p_{t+n}$$

Source: Formula taken from: Lindemann, J. (2004), p. 88
Formula 22: Combination of residual income and Dividend Discount Model

The Preinreich-Lücke theorem assumes that the total period is considered. This means mathematically that the limit has to be calculated.
$\lim_{n\to\infty}[\sum_{T=1}^{n} x_{t+T}^a \times p_{t+T} - V_{t+n} \times p_{t+n} + V_t \times p_t + R_n \times p_{t+n}]$

$$= V_t + \sum_{T=1}^{\infty} x_{t+T}^a \times p_{t+T}$$

Source: Formula taken from: Lindemann, J. (2004), p. 88
Formula 23: Calculation of limit for combined formula of Dividend Discount Model and residual income

It is assumed that the terms $V_{t+n} \times p_{t+n} \to 0$ and $R_n \times p_{t+n} \to 0$. The result is the residual income formula which shows that the company value can be expressed by equity capital and present values of residual values.[1086]

$$P_t = V_t + \sum_{T=1}^{\infty} E_t(x_{t+T}^a) \times p_{t+T}$$

Source: Formula taken from: Lindemann, J. (2004), p. 89
Formula 24: Residual income valuation formula

1086 Cf. also for the Residual Income Valuation formula Stüker, D. (2008), p. 111.

As explained at the beginning, the validity of the Preinreich-Lücke Theorem depends on certain assumptions. In practice, the existence of these assumptions can partly be doubted. Within the IFRS accounting the Clean Surplus assumption is breached e.g. by the revaluation of assets according to IAS 16.[1087] But advantages of residual income models in contrast to Cash Flow models are that they clearly express the coherence between return and cost of capital for its users and that they can better explain entity values on capital markets.[1088]

3.3.2 Result-Based Key Figures

3.3.2.1 ROCE Spread and Value Added

3.3.2.1.1 Calculation

According to the systematisation of value based performance measures the ROCE spread is a relative key figure which bases on earning figures.[1089] It shows the average return on the capital invested in a company.[1090] In other words: It reveals the company's profitability per Euro of invested capital.[1091] The ROCE is a modified return on capital key figure.[1092] As ROCE is a measure for profitability, it is the management's aim to increase ROCE.[1093] For operating purposes it is a method to split up the ROCE calculation to its single components, in order to better understand which measures have which effect on the ROCE. This procedure is named value driver tree.[1094] Formula 25 shows the calculation of the ROCE which is calculated by the division of EBIT and Capital Employed.[1095]

$$ROCE = \frac{EBIT}{\emptyset\ Capital\ Employed}$$

Source: Formula adapted from: Quick, R. (2012), p. 245
Formula 25: Calculation of ROCE[1096]

The EBIT has the aim to illustrate the company's profitability without consideration of capital structure and tax burdens. Thus, EBIT is a pre-tax key figure[1097] which shows a

1087 Cf. Ewert, R., Wagenhofer, A. (2000), pp. 20-21; Funk, W., Fredrich, I. (2011), p. 462; Kahle, H. (2003), pp. 779-780; Weißenberger, B. E. (2009), p. 44; cf. also for criticism of the Preinreich-Lücke Theorem Schneider, D. (2001), p. 2510.

1088 Cf. Coenenberg, A. G., Schultze, W. (2002), p. 607; Schumann, J. (2005), p. 22; for an extensive discussion of advantages and disadvantages of residual income models in contrast to Cash Flow models Coenenberg, A. G., Schultze, W. (2002), pp. 606-610.

1089 Cf. Bode, D., Wiens, H. (2015), p. 24; Töpfer, A., Duchmann, C. (2006), p. 31.

1090 Cf. Hauer, G., Ultsch, M. (2010), p. 90; Quick, R. (2012), p. 245.

1091 Cf. Behringer, S. (2014), p. 94.

1092 Cf. Behringer, S. (2014), p. 94; Kajüter, P. (2007a), p. 444.

1093 Cf. Rutherford, B. A. (2002), p. 74.

1094 Cf. Bode, D., Wiens, H. (2015), pp. 35-36 for an example of such a value driver tree.

1095 Cf. Karrer, M. (2006), p. 159.

1096 The ROCE can also be calculated as an after-tax key figure: NOPAT / Capital Employed. Consequently an after tax has to be used for calculating the ROCE spread, cf. Poeschl, H. (2013), pp. 107-108.

1097 Cf. Krause, H.-U., Arora, D. (2010), pp. 16-17.

kind of operating result.[1098] It is often used for internal performance analysis as many external influence factors are eliminated.[1099]

Instead of the EBIT it is also possible to use EBITA which excludes amortisations on Goodwill. Using another earning number in the nominator, the denominator has to be adapted and the amortisations of Goodwill in total have to be added to the Capital Employed. Especially for assessment of performance of single business segments within a company, the EBITA is convenient because the managers of the segments cannot influence the Goodwill.[1100] By applying EBIT or EBITA, the ROCE calculation typically does not consider the financial results. It focuses instead on the operating result and assets necessary for operation.[1101]

A further effect of using EBIT or EBITA is that these are earning numbers before interests so that debt capital and equity capital providers are equally considered.[1102]

Capital Employed contains all assets necessary for conducting the business of a company.[1103] It reflects the sum of capital which the company has over a longer time-horizon available and for which it has to generate an adequate rate of return. Basically, it consists of equity capital and interest bearing parts of debt capital.[1104]

It has to be mentioned that a uniform pattern of calculation for the Capital Employed does not exist.[1105] It can be calculated via the asset side or the liability side of the balance sheet. Illustration 12 shows both ways of calculation which lead to identical results.

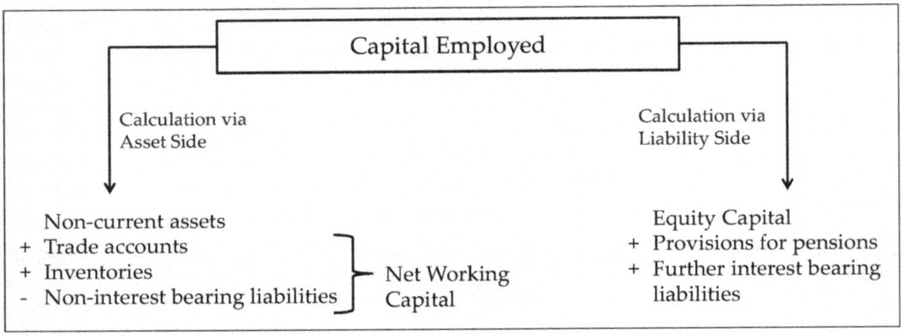

Source: Own illustration[1106]
Illustration 12: Calculation of Capital Employed

1098 Cf. Bode, D., Wiens, H. (2015), p. 29.
1099 Cf. Langguth, H. (2008), p. 177; Gräfer, H., Gerenkamp, T. (2016), p. 149.
1100 Cf. Kajüter, P. (2007a), p. 445.
1101 Cf. Laier, R. (2011), p. 51; Töpfer, A., Duchmann, C. (2006), p. 31.
1102 Cf. Behringer, S. (2014), p. 94.
1103 Cf. Bausch, A., Buske, A., Hagemeier, W. (2011), p. 364; Quick, R. (2012), p. 245.
1104 Cf. Laier, R. (2011), p. 52; Pape, U. (2015), p. 277.
1105 Cf. Kajüter, P. (2007a), p. 444; Schmidlin, N. (2013), p. 47.
1106 Calculation of Capital Employed via asset side based on Werner, H. (2013), p. 326; calculation of Capital Employed via liability side based on Wöltje, J. (2011), p. 221.

On the asset side the noncurrent assets and the Net Working Capital are added.[1107] Net Working Capital is the sum of inventories and accounts receivable minus interest free liabilities, like trade payables and customer deposits and advances.[1108] On the liability side Capital Employed is calculated as the sum of equity capital, provisions for pensions and all further interest bearing liabilities like liabilities to banks or bonds.[1109] Regularly, the calculation scheme for the liability side is applied because less data has to be collected.[1110] The user can calculate an average value over the analysed period or for reasons of simplification the value at the end of the period can be applied.[1111]

Non-interest bearing debt capital is not considered in the calculation of Capital Employed as it is capital which the company can use nearly free of charge and it is not required to create an return on this capital.[1112] This is the reason why e.g. accounts payable[1113] and all other liabilities that are available interest-free for the company are deducted.[1114] Short term provisions, customer prepayments, trade payables and accrued and deferred items are the typical balance sheet items which are deducted from the balance sheet total.[1115] It is assumed that the interest free components are calculated in the price the companies pay to its suppliers and are already considered in the profit and loss statement.[1116] Nominator and denominator have to correspond to each other. The profit and loss statement does not contain interest rates for interest-free liabilities, consequently this capital should not be included in the denominator.[1117] In some manner also for this capital costs of capital occur but in another form, like discounts due to an earlier payment.[1118]

The key figures ROCE and RONA correspond to each other. The difference is the calculation of the denominator. For the ROCE calculation the liability side of the balance sheet is used, for the RONA calculation the operating assets are derived from values of the asset side of the balance sheet.[1119] Also the ROIC is a key figure which is similar to the ROCE. It is calculated by dividing NOPLAT and Invested Capital.[1120] Invested Capital is defined as sum of working capital and non-current assets.[1121]

1107 Cf. Werner, H. (2013), p. 326.
1108 Cf. Wöltje, J. (2013), p. 410.
1109 Cf. Wöltje, J. (2011), p. 221.
1110 Cf. Beck, R. (2003), p. 114; Bode, D., Wiens, H. (2015), pp. 31-32.
1111 Cf. Ewert, R., Wagenhofer, A. (2000), p. 27.
1112 Cf. Biddle, G. C., Bowen, R. M., Wallace, J. S. (1999), p. 70; Pape, U. (2015), p. 277.
1113 Cf. Schmidlin, N. (2013), p. 47.
1114 Cf. Behringer, S. (2014), p. 94.
1115 Cf. Gladen, W. (2014), p. 69; Krause, H.-U., Arora, D. (2010), p. 49.
1116 Cf. Bode, D., Wiens, H. (2015), p. 32.
1117 Cf. Ewert, R., Wagenhofer, A. (2000), p. 27.
1118 Cf. Kajüter, P. (2007a), p. 444.
1119 Cf. Gladen, W. (2014), pp. 68-69; Gräfer, H., Gerenkamp, T. (2016), pp. 148-149; Prätsch, J., Schikorra, U., Ludwig, E. (2012), p. 302; Wohlgemuth, F. (2007), pp. 205-206.
1120 Cf. Koller, T., Goedhart, M., Wessels, D. (2010), p. 40.
1121 Cf. Krause, H.-U., Arora, D. (2010), p. 48.

ROCE is often combined with the cost of capital in order to analyse if a company is successful in satisfying the required rate of return from all capital providers.[1122] A comparison with the cost of capital is possible as the ROCE contains only the capital for which a company pays interest rates.[1123] The ROCE spread means that the WACC is deducted from ROCE.[1124] The calculation is as following:

$$ROCE\ Spread = ROCE - WACC$$

Source: Formula adapted from: Poeschl, H. (2013), p. 108
Formula 26: Calculation of ROCE Spread

Often the ROCE is calculated as a pre-tax key figure. It is important to note that consistently the cost of capital before tax has to be applied for calculating the ROCE spread.[1125]

If the ROCE exceeds the WACC, a company has jumped over the hurdle rate and is successful in creating Shareholder Value.[1126] If WACC and ROCE equal each other, a company is at least successful in covering the required rate of return. If the WACC is higher than the ROCE, the company destroys Shareholder Value because it cannot satisfy the profitability demands of investors.[1127]

There are three possibilities to increase the ROCE spread: The company is successful in increasing the ROCE through increased turnovers with constant returns. So, the company has profitable growth. The second possibility is to lower the cost of capital, e.g. by substituting equity capital by cheaper debt capital.[1128] The third possibility is to increase profitability. The company has a higher profit but with the same capital employed.[1129]

The ROCE spread is computed as the difference between ROCE and the cost of capital.[1130] It is a relative value based performance measure. Multiplying the ROCE spread by the Capital Employed yields the Value Added as an absolute number.[1131]

$$Value\ Added = (ROCE - WACC) \times Capital\ Employed$$

Source: Formula adapted from: Alter, R. (2013), p. 74
Formula 27: Calculation of Value Added

1122 Cf. Bausch, A., Buske, A., Hagemeier, W. (2011), p. 365; Laier, R. (2011), p. 51.
1123 Cf. Brühl, R. (2016), p. 439.
1124 Cf. Middelmann, U. (2001), p. 503; Poeschl, H. (2013), p. 108.
1125 Cf. Middelmann, U. (2001), p. 501; Pape, U. (2015), pp. 277-278.
1126 Cf. Hauer, G., Ultsch, M. (2010), p. 91; Kajüter, P. (2007b), pp. 34-35; Poeschl, H. (2013), p. 108.
1127 Cf. Alter, R. (2013), pp. 71-72; Wahlen, J. M., Baginski, S. P., Bradshaw, M. T. (2015), p. 263.
1128 Cf. Beck, R. (2003), pp. 116-117; Dillerup, R., Stoi, R. (2016), pp. 198-200; Groll, K.-H. (2000), p. 74.
1129 Cf. Dillerup, R., Stoi, R. (2016), pp. 198-200.
1130 Cf. Nowak, K. (2003), pp. 152-153.
1131 Cf. Alter, R. (2013), p. 74; Berlien, O., Kirsten, A. S., Oelert, J., et al. (2006), p. 598; Kajüter, P. (2007b), p. 34; Prätsch, J., Schikorra, U., Ludwig, E. (2012), pp. 301-302.

3.3.2.1.2 Evaluation

Today, ROCE as a key figure is popular due to its easy calculation.[1132] It is widely used for performance comparisons of single segments within one company or for comparisons between competitors over a period of time.[1133] Especially for comparisons of performance among firms in an international context the ROCE is a convenient key figure[1134] because the ROCE is independent from national tax laws and capital structure.[1135]

The ROCE can be used in many situations for performance evaluation.[1136] It can be best applied to assess short-term performance.[1137] The advantage of ROCE, ROCE spread and Value Added is that due to its calculation for one period they are directly observable and do not include a forecast of an unsecure development of the company.[1138]

Beside the listed advantages the ROCE and the two derived key figures ROCE Spread and Value Added are criticized in the scientific literature. The critique also refers to the key figures EBIT and Capital Employed which are part of the ROCE calculation.

The application of pro forma key figures like EBIT or EBITDA is criticised. There is no uniform standard way of calculation for these key figures so that companies are free in calculating and changing it.[1139] As EBIT key figures ignore important expenses and profit parts, namely interest and taxes, these key figures do not illustrate the profitability completely.[1140]

The EBIT / EBITA key figures can contain extraordinary result components. They are not eliminated during the calculation and may distort EBIT of one period.[1141]

A huge advantage is that due to ignoring capital structure and tax payments the EBIT key figure is well suited for comparisons of companies, also across countries.[1142] Also for investors or analysts the EBIT can easily be calculated on the basis of the annual or quarterly accounts.[1143]

A critique is referring to the calculation of Capital Employed. There is no uniform and widely accepted definition so that the comparability of this key figure is limited.[1144]

The calculation of Capital Employed offers potential for earnings management. It is calculated on the basis of book values which can be influenced with accounting policy.[1145] The EBIT key figures also base on book values and can be influenced through accounting policy.[1146]

Beyond a manipulation of book values, the key figure can be distorted by assignment of balance sheet items to the single components of calculation. If a company can

1132 Cf. Watson, D., Head, A. (2010), p. 164.
1133 Cf. Laier, R. (2011), pp. 51-52; Watson, D., Head, A. (2010), p. 164.
1134 Cf. Krause, H.-U., Arora, D. (2010), p. 51; Wöltje, J. (2011), p. 221.
1135 Cf. Wöltje, J. (2016a), p. 439.
1136 Cf. Bausch, A., Buske, A., Hagemeier, W. (2011), p. 368.
1137 Cf. Lumby, S., Jones, C. (2003), p. 43.
1138 Cf. Knorren, N. (1998), p. 205.
1139 Cf. Brösel, G. (2014), p. 187; Weißenberger, B. E. (2006), pp. 62-63.
1140 Cf. Gladen, W. (2014), p. 65.
1141 Cf. Bode, D., Wiens, H. (2015), p. 29.
1142 Cf. Krause, H.-U., Arora, D. (2010), p. 17; Pape, U. (2015), p. 271.
1143 Cf. Weißenberger, B. E. (2003), p. 127.
1144 Cf. Karrer, M. (2006), p. 159.
1145 Cf. Dahlhaus, C. (2009), p. 179.
1146 Cf. Bode, D., Wiens, H. (2015), p. 29.

substitute bank credits with a capital form which is deducted in the context of the Capital Employed calculation, the ROCE improves without a real increase in the company's profitability.[1147]

Moving from the single components of ROCE calculation to the whole figure, a first problem is that no uniform calculation method for ROCE has been established in practice due to the different ways of calculation for EBIT and Capital Employed. Companies are able to adapt the calculation of the key figures to their needs and for investors it is difficult to compare key figures even if they are all labelled as ROCE.[1148]

A further disadvantage according to the scientific literature is that the calculation draws on book values. Therefore, the calculation is relatively simple. The resulting flaw is the leeway for manipulation through accounting policy.[1149]

A further problem that results from the application of book values is the influence of depreciation on the results. The amount of depreciations influences the result and gives an advantage to companies which have completely depreciated assets.[1150]

The influence of book values becomes clearer when comparing the definition and extent of assets and liabilities of IFRS and local German GAAP. Calculating ROCE on the basis of these two different accounting standards leads to different values due to the divergent definitions of assets and liabilities.[1151]

Some criticisms refer to the fact that ROCE is a relative key figure. ROCE alone can lead to mismanagement because it is not evident from ROCE or ROCE spread which absolute number of profit lies behind this relative key figure. It does not reveal the financial size. Thus, ROCE should be complemented with further key figures, preferably absolute numbers.[1152]

The ROCE also has some weak points for which traditional key figures are criticised. It focuses on the performance of one period and does not consider the time value of money.[1153] As the ROCE is a key figure which measures the performance of one period, the accompanying disadvantage of misleading short term incentives is inherent in this key figure.[1154] Furthermore, it is a key figure based on book values and focuses on the performance of past periods.[1155]

The ROCE itself does not consider cost of capital, capital structure or risk. Only in the combination with the WACC and by calculating the ROCE spread or Value Added these components are included in the calculation.[1156] The costs of capital are the hurdle rate for investment decisions.[1157]

1147 Cf. Gladen, W. (2014), pp. 71-72.
1148 Cf. Lumby, S., Jones, C. (2003), p. 43.
1149 Cf. Kajüter, P. (2007a), p. 446.
1150 Cf. Laier, R. (2011), p. 52.
1151 Cf. Weißenberger, B. E. (2007), p. 388.
1152 Cf. Alter, R. (2013), p. 72; Lumby, S., Jones, C. (2003), p. 43.
1153 Cf. Lumby, S., Jones, C. (2003), p. 43; Stührenberg, L., Streich, D., Henke Jörg (2003), p. 31; Watson, D., Head, A. (2010), p. 164.
1154 Cf. Kajüter, P. (2007a), p. 445.
1155 Cf. Hasler, P. T. (2011), p. 461; Stührenberg, L., Streich, D., Henke Jörg (2003), p. 64.
1156 Cf. Herbertinger, M. (2002), p. 109.
1157 Cf. Lattwein, J. (2002), p. 133.

Table 5: Evaluation of ROCE and ROCE Spread

Evaluation Criteria	**ROCE**	**ROCE Spread / Value Added**
Including of cost of capital	–	+
Data basis for calculation (Availability of data)	+ (bases on book values of annual accounts)	+ (bases partly on book values of annual accounts)
Data basis for calculation (Quality of data)	0 (Book values)	0 (Book values)
Present value of Money	–	–
Future Orientation	–	–
Considering risk	–	+ (included within calculation of WACC)
Simplicity	+	+

Source: In style of: Fiedler, R., Gräf, J. (2012), p. 339

Despite a clear communication that cost of capital is the hurdle rate for projects managers might reject projects with a profit above that hurdle rate. The reason for this behaviour is that the additional project has a profit below the current ROCE. An execution of this project leads to a decrease of ROCE in total. This is often not in the manager's interest. His salary only increases if the ROCE rises.[1158] However, a project which has a return above the cost of capital is worthwhile to conduct for a company although the ROCE decreases.[1159]

The ROCE spread is a comparison of book values used for ROCE calculation and market values included in the WACC. A comparison and mixture of those two kinds of measures of value is not appropriate and meaningful according to some critics. A comparison should be done on the basis of book values or market values solely. Table five gives an overview of the evaluation of ROCE and ROCE Spread.[1160]

It is important to notice that a single key figure like ROCE Spread or Value Added does not contain total value added or destroyed in a period. An investment project lasting several years might deliver negative economic performance in the first years but a positive one in latter years. In total, the project increases the Shareholder Value of a company. So, a total assessment of a project or also a company is only possible if prospective developments are considered. This is valid for all value based performance measures focussing on a single period.[1161] This means that Value Added does not exactly reflect the increase in Shareholder Value of a period. It reflects the generated surplus by current investments. The increase in Shareholder Value could be calculated with the sum of

1158 Cf. Alter, R. (2013), p. 74; Rutherford, B. A. (2002), p. 75.
1159 Cf. Coenenberg, A. G., Mattner, G. R., Schultze, W. (2003), pp. 14-16.
1160 Cf. Kajüter, P. (2007a), p. 445.
1161 Cf. Ewert, R., Wagenhofer, A. (2000), pp. 15-16; Stüker, D. (2008), pp. 115-117; Weißenberger, B. E. (2009), pp. 44-45.

discounted Value Added of all periods at the beginning of the investment.[1162] Although a negative Value Added occurs partly, an investment could be worthwhile in total.[1163]

3.3.2.2 Economic Value Added

3.3.2.2.1 Calculation

The concept of EVA was developed by the US consulting firm Stern Stewart. It gained a lot of attention and has become part of the control system of many companies.[1164] Sometimes it has been adopted under different names, e.g. Thyssen Krupp Value Added[1165] or Geschäftswertbeitrag at Siemens AG.[1166] In general, the EVA is applied for internal control purposes on a periodical basis.[1167] The field of application for EVA is not limited to internal control systems. It can also be used as a measure for compensation.[1168]

According to the systematisation of value based performance measures, EVA is an absolute key figure based on earnings which focuses on the performance of a single period.[1169] The EVA is based on the concept of residual income.[1170] The EVA considers every investment as worthwhile when it exceeds the cost of capital and thus increases the market value of a company.[1171] A positive EVA signals a profit above the cost of capital.[1172] An EVA which amounts to zero signals that the company is able to cover the required rate of return but without an increase of Shareholder Value in that period.[1173] A negative EVA indicates that the company is not successful in satisfying the demanded return on capital.[1174]

There are three possibilities to increase the EVA: Increase of NOPAT while keeping invested capital constant, a decrease of capital invested while keeping NOPAT constant or a reduction of cost of capital while keeping NOPAT and capital invested constant.[1175] Companies can improve EVA by fostering investments in projects with a return above the

1162 Cf. Coenenberg, A. G., Schultze, W. (2002), p. 613; Schultze, W., Weiler, A. (2007), p. 136.

1163 Cf. Coenenberg, A. G., Schultze, W. (2002), p. 613; Coenenberg, A. G., Mattner, G. R., Schultze, W. (2003), pp. 16-17.

1164 Cf. Biddle, G. C., Bowen, R. M., Wallace, J. S. (1999), p. 71; Böcking, H.-J., Nowak, K. (1999), p. 281; Chiwamit, P., Modell, S., Yang, C. L. (2014), p. 145; the EVA concept mainly base on the book „The Quest for Value.“

1165 Cf. Loose, T. (2009), p. 31.

1166 Cf. extensively Camphausen, B. (2013), pp. 176-179.

1167 Cf. Eilenberger, G., Ernst, D., Toebe, M. (2013), p. 232.

1168 Cf. Böcking, H.-J., Nowak, K. (1999), pp. 281-282.

1169 Cf. Langguth, H. (2008), p. 138; Mensch, G. (2008), p. 274.

1170 Cf. Böcking, H.-J., Nowak, K. (1999), p. 282; Eilenberger, G., Ernst, D., Toebe, M. (2013), p. 233; cf. chapter 3.3.1.

1171 Cf. Böcking, H.-J., Nowak, K. (1999), p. 282.

1172 Cf. Heier, K., Karsten, E., Müller-Wenzel, C., et al. (2015), p. 12; Varnholt, N. T., Lebefromm, U., Hoberg, P. (2012), p. 444.

1173 Cf. Schneider, N. C. (2007), p. 49.

1174 Cf. Varnholt, N. T., Lebefromm, U., Hoberg, P. (2012), p. 444.

1175 Cf. Heier, K., Karsten, E., Müller-Wenzel, C., et al. (2015), p. 15.

cost of capital and by cancelling projects which do not deliver a return above the cost of capital.[1176]

The calculation of EVA consists of three components: The profit figure, named as NOPAT, a figure that measures a company's investment base, named as Net Operating Assets (NOA) and the cost of capital.[1177] The three components reflect the three decision fields of management: NOPAT reflects the operating decisions of management, NOA reflects the investment and disinvestment decisions and cost of capital the financial decisions.[1178]

NOPAT is a measure for the result of the operating activities of a company.[1179] It includes tax expenses in its calculation. Financing components, like interest rates for debt capital, are not considered.[1180] NOPAT shows the income if the company would completely own equity capital and does not have any debt capital.[1181] It includes expenses for depreciation and amortisation.[1182] But apart from these two kinds of expenditures, it is very similar to Cash Flow measures as all of its other components have a direct effect on cash.[1183] In contrast to the previous presented performance measures ROCE spread and Value Added, the EVA is an after tax value based performance measure.[1184]

It is necessary that the cost of capital used for EVA calculation has to be calculated taking tax effects into consideration. Cost of capital has to correspond to the profit figure NOPAT. The tax shield is included in the cost of capital calculation.[1185]

The costs for debt capital are also considered in the context of the cost of capital calculation because the NOPAT is calculated under the assumption of a company completely financed with equity capital.[1186]

The third component of EVA calculation, NOA, is defined as the sum of capital needed for operating the company deducted by interest free capital[1187] and non-operating assets, e.g. like assets under construction or shares classified as current assets.[1188] Operating assets which are not included in the balance sheet have to be added.[1189] An asset is necessary for operating if it is needed for ensuring operational readiness or if it serves

1176 Cf. Camphausen, B. (2013), p. 171; Stewart, G. B. (1999), pp. 118-119; cf. for an extensive illustration of possible measures to increase EVA Stiefl, J., Westerholt, K. von (2008), pp. 89-174.

1177 Cf. Böcking, H.-J., Nowak, K. (1999), pp. 282-283; Laux, H. (2006a), p. 158.

1178 Cf. Mensch, G. (2008), p. 274.

1179 Cf. Brühl, R. (2016), p. 445; Zirkler, B. (2002), p. 99.

1180 Cf. Böcking, H.-J., Nowak, K. (1999), p. 283; Heier, K., Karsten, E., Müller-Wenzel, C., et al. (2015), pp. 13-14.

1181 Cf. Junginger, M. (2005), p. 68; Rickards, R. C. (2009), p. 31.

1182 Cf. Nguyen, T., Romeike, F. (2013), p. 503.

1183 Cf. Baetge, J., Kirsch, H.-J., Thiele, S. (2004), p. 470; Schmeisser, W. (2010), p. 30.

1184 Cf. Heier, K., Karsten, E., Müller-Wenzel, C., et al. (2015), pp. 13-14.

1185 Cf. Böcking, H.-J., Nowak, K. (1999), p. 284; Graumann, M. (2014), p. 824; cf. for further details about cost of capital calculation chapter 2.1.3.

1186 Cf. Böcking, H.-J., Nowak, K. (1999), p. 283; Heier, K., Karsten, E., Müller-Wenzel, C., et al. (2015), pp. 13-14.

1187 Cf. Mensch, G. (2008), p. 275.

1188 Cf. Böcking, H.-J., Nowak, K. (1999), p. 284; Graumann, M. (2014), p. 826.

1189 Cf. Wellner, K.-U. (2001), p. 86.

Table 6: Calculation of NOA and NOPAT[1190]

Net Operating Assets	**NOPAT**
Current Assets	Net Income
– Short-term liabilities	+ Taxes
= Working Capital	= Net Income before taxes
+ Non-current assets	+ Interest expenses (1-tax rate)
= Net assets	= Earnings before interest and taxes
+ / – Adjustments	+ / – Adjustments
	= Net Operating Profit before Taxes
	– Taxes (adjusted)
= Net Operating Assets	= Net Operating Profit after Taxes

Source: In reference to: Kraus, P. (2011), p. 24

for selling goods and services.[1191] The NOA is relatively similar to the Capital Employed calculation[1192] because it does not contain any capital which is free of interests.[1193] Table six gives an overview about the calculation scheme of NOPAT and NOA.

The EVA can be calculated with the help of two formulas: Capital charge formula and value spread formula.[1194]

$$EVA = NOPAT - (NOA \times WACC)$$

Source: Formula adapted from: Stewart, G. B. (1999), p. 137
Formula 28: Calculation of EVA (Capital Charge formula)

The Capital Charge formula demonstrates that the NOPAT has to cover the total cost of capital and a positive EVA can only be achieved if NOPAT is higher than the product of Invested Capital and WACC.[1195]

$$EVA = (r - WACC) \times NOA$$

Source: Formula adapted from: Stewart, G. B. (1999), p. 137
Formula 29: Calculation of EVA (Value Spread formula)

The return measure in the value spread formula is named as Stewart's R.[1196] It is comparable to the ROCE because it captures the return on capital without considering the method of financing.[1197] It is the result of the division of NOPAT and NOA.[1198]

1190 Cf. for a further calculation scheme Baetge, J., Kirsch, H.-J., Thiele, S. (2004), p. 471; Siebrecht, F., Heidorn, T., Klein, H.-D. (2001), p. 561.
1191 Cf. Gundel, T. (2012), p. 44.
1192 Cf. Schmeisser, W., Rönsch, M., Zilch, I. (2009), p. 29.
1193 Cf. Zirkler, B. (2002), p. 100.
1194 Cf. Böcking, H.-J., Nowak, K. (1999), p. 283.
1195 Cf. Schneck, O. (2006), p. 61.
1196 Cf. Dahlhaus, C. (2009), p. 186.

The Value Spread formula directly indicates through the term $(r - WACC)$ if a company is successful in creating Shareholder Value.[1199] The NOA gives an indication about the size of the company.[1200]

In order to illustrate which components influence NOPAT, NOA and cost of capital, value driver trees are used in practice.[1201]

For analysing how the EVA develops over the course of time the so called Delta EVA is convenient. It is the difference between the EVA of the current and the previous period.[1202]

3.3.2.2.2 Conversions

From the perspective of Stern & Stewart the balance sheet is not an appropriate source of data for calculating a performance measure. Therefore, EVA calculation includes four stages of adjustments of balance sheet data. These adjustments are named conversions. Their purpose is to modify balance sheet numbers into economically expressive numbers from a shareholder's point of view.[1203] The conversions are used for a transition from an accounting model to an economic model.[1204] In addition, effects of accounting policy on EVA should be limited.[1205]

Four types of conversions are defined: Operating, Funding, Shareholder and Tax Conversions.[1206] In total, 164 possible conversions exist.[1207] On average, companies apply between ten and fifteen conversions.[1208] Consequently, a uniform method of calculation for EVA does not exist because each company individually selects the convenient conversions.[1209] It is important that conversions which are applied for correcting NOPAT correspond to the conversions applied for NOA. Otherwise, the calculation of EVA is misleading.[1210]

Operating conversions deal with the question of numbers included in NOPAT or NOA which are necessary for operating the company. Non-operating components and extraordinary issues are eliminated.[1211] Examples are buildings which are leased to third parties

1197 Cf. Stewart, G. B. (1999), p. 86.
1198 Cf. Junginger, M. (2005), p. 68.
1199 Cf. Dreher, M. (2010), pp. 368-369.
1200 Cf. Gundel, T. (2012), p. 17.
1201 Cf. exemplarily for a value driver tree of EVA Fiedler, R., Gräf, J. (2012), p. 340; Graumann, M. (2014), p. 829; Günther, T. (2002), p. 95; Stiefl, J., Westerholt, K. von (2008), p. 96.
1202 Cf. Kajüter, P. (2007a), p. 448; Mohnen, A. (2002), pp. 203-205.
1203 Cf. Böcking, H.-J., Nowak, K. (1999), p. 285.
1204 Cf. Stephan, J. (2006), p. 81; cf. for an overview of the most important conversions Biddle, G. C., Bowen, R. M., Wallace, J. S. (1999), p. 72; Laux, H. (2006a), p. 160; cf. for a detailed description of conversions Gundel, T. (2012), pp. 43-139.
1205 Cf. Hachmeister, D. (2003), p. 99.
1206 Cf. Dahlhaus, C. (2009), p. 187.
1207 Cf. Dahlhaus, C. (2009), p. 187; Hamilton, J., Rahman, S., Lee, A. C. (2009), p. 270; Stephan, J. (2006), p. 81; Zirkler, B. (2002), p. 99.
1208 Cf. Dahlhaus, C. (2009), p. 187; Eidel, U. (1999), p. 73; Hamilton, J., Rahman, S., Lee, A. C. (2009), p. 271; Weißenberger, B. E. (2009), p. 47.
1209 Cf. Dahlhaus, C. (2009), pp. 187-188.
1210 Cf. Mensch, G. (2008), p. 282.
1211 Cf. Heier, K., Karsten, E., Müller-Wenzel, C., et al. (2015), p. 13; Zirkler, B. (2002), p. 99.

or production halls which are not used anymore. These assets do not show a direct coherence to the production process of the company.[1212] Furthermore, all assets listed under the position Asset under Construction are deducted and are not part of NOA. As long as these assets are under construction, they do not deliver a contribution to the operating result of the company.[1213] The NOPAT is reduced by financial income and financial costs components because these profits and costs have not a direct coherence to the operating activities of the company.[1214]

Funding conversions have the objective to determine the true financing of a company.[1215] In the context of funding conversions mostly leasing and rented assets are analysed. Leased and rented assets are capitalised and added to the NOA. Correspondingly, the expenses for these assets in the profit and loss statements are deducted and not part of NOPAT.[1216] Similar to the calculation of Capital Employed all debt capital which is free of interest rates is deducted.[1217]

Tax conversions adapt the tax burden due to the included conversions in the EVA calculation.[1218] As the assumption is that the company is completely financed by equity capital, the tax expenditures have to be adapted.[1219] The tax paid for non-operating expenditures and profits has to be corrected.[1220] The tax shield is included in the cost of capital calculation. So far included tax saving effects due to interest rates for debt capital have to be reversed.[1221] The deferred tax assets on balance sheet are corrected for NOA calculation because tax expenses are limited to tax which have a direct effect on Cash Flow.[1222] Deferred tax assets are prospective accounts respectively liabilities and do not have a coherence to the performance of a company in the current period.[1223] An effect of tax conversions is that in international companies local tax advantages or disadvantages due to national tax laws are not included in the calculation of NOPAT and NOA.[1224]

Shareholder conversions assess assets from the shareholder's perspective. If an asset has a higher value than documented on the balance sheet, the difference is added for EVA calculation.[1225] Within this context the term Equity Equivalents is often used. This term named the economic assessment of the company's asset from a shareholder's perspective and the capitalisation of expenditures which are not capitalised on balance sheet.[1226] With the help of capitalisation of expenditures which are not capitalised according to IFRS the EVA concept gives managers an incentive to not postpone important investments.[1227]

1212 Cf. Zirkler, B. (2002), p. 100.
1213 Cf. Kremer, P. (2008), p. 123.
1214 Cf. Baetge, J., Kirsch, H.-J., Thiele, S. (2004), pp. 465-466.
1215 Cf. Hostettler, S. (2002), p. 100; Zirkler, B. (2002), p. 101.
1216 Cf. Laux, H. (2006a), p. 159; Schmeisser, W. (2010), p. 29.
1217 Cf. Kremer, P. (2008), p. 122; Zirkler, B. (2002), p. 101.
1218 Cf. Heier, K., Karsten, E., Müller-Wenzel, C., et al. (2015), p. 13.
1219 Cf. Weißenberger, B. E. (2007), p. 267; Zirkler, B. (2002), p. 101.
1220 Cf. Baetge, J., Kirsch, H.-J., Thiele, S. (2004), p. 467.
1221 Cf. Coenenberg, A. G., Fischer, T. M., Günther, T. (2012), p. 849; Hesselmann, C. (2006), p. 82; Schmeisser, W. (2010), p. 29.
1222 Cf. Baetge, J., Kirsch, H.-J., Thiele, S. (2004), p. 467; Weißenberger, B. E. (2007), p. 268.
1223 Cf. Hostettler, S. (2002), p. 222.
1224 Cf. Zirkler, B. (2002), p. 102.
1225 Cf. Heier, K., Karsten, E., Müller-Wenzel, C., et al. (2015), p. 13.
1226 Cf. Stewart, G. B. (1999), p. 91.
1227 Cf. Hahn, D., Hintze, M. (2006), p. 94.

An example for Equity Equivalents is the LIFO reserve.[1228] If price for stock materials are rising continually, the LIFO method has the effect that the inventory values are understated because they are assessed with older, lower prices. By calculating inventory values with the help of the FIFO method and subtracting FIFO value from LIFO value, this difference is capitalised for NOA calculation. The FIFO method is assessed as a better approximation of market value for inventories.[1229]

Another example is the capitalisation of expenditures for research and development. Similar to these expenditures also costs for employee education or costs for marketing efforts can be seen as an investment in the future. These expenditures are capitalised in the year in which they occur and then depreciated over the time period of the useful life of the underlying products.[1230] The adaptions influence both: NOPAT because expenditures have to be deducted and NOA because assets have to be added.[1231]

The IFRS rules make some conversions redundant and consider already some proposal of Stern & Stewart. The capitalisation of certain development expenditures is already mandatory.[1232] The conversion concerning leased assets is as of 2019 redundant with the application of IFRS 16.[1233] Also the capitalisation of LIFO reserve is obsolete because IAS 2 does not allow this method.[1234]

Depending on the number of conducted conversions, four stages of EVA could be differentiated: The EVA without any modifications of balance sheet data is named Basic EVA. The Disclosed EVA contains 12 standard conversions. The Tailored EVA is the third stage and is a kind of EVA which contains selected number of conversions individually taken for a company and its situation. The True EVA contains all possible modifications and is the most accurate form of the EVA.[1235] However, due to the high number of conversions it is more a theoretical optimum and has little relevance in practice.[1236]

Managers have to answer the question of how many conversions are really necessary in order to receive an adequate EVA. A limitation of conversions reduces the effort of EVA calculation and can also deliver a good illustration of the economic performance. However, too few conversions do not deliver a good economic assessment of the company's situation because the key figure is influenced by accounting rules.[1237]

1228 Cf. for several examples of Equity Equivalents Stewart, G. B. (1999), pp. 112-117.
1229 Cf. Laux, H. (2006a), p. 159; Stewart, G. B. (1999), pp. 113-114.
1230 Cf. Fackler, M., Wimschulte, J. (2009), pp. 327-328; Gundel, T. (2012), pp. 95-97; Laux, H. (2006a), pp. 160-161.
1231 Cf. Baetge, J., Kirsch, H.-J., Thiele, S. (2004), p. 469; Gundel, T. (2012), p. 97.
1232 Cf. Hahn, D., Hintze, M. (2006), p. 95; cf.
1233 Cf. IFRS Foundation (2016), IFRS 16.
1234 Cf. IFRS Foundation (2016), IAS 2.
1235 Cf. Böcking, H.-J., Nowak, K. (1999), p. 285; Fackler, M., Wimschulte, J. (2009), pp. 323-324; Stephan, J. (2006), p. 81.
1236 Cf. Zirkler, B. (2002), pp. 99-100.
1237 Cf. Schneck, O. (2006), p. 62.

3.3.2.2.3 Evaluation

The EVA concept is easily communicable and understandable.[1238] It is relatively easyily applicable for companies and can be used for assessing single projects.[1239] But the scope of application is broader. The key figure can be used not only for measuring performance of single investment projects but also for evaluating segments or a whole company.[1240] In practice, it is a problem that the EVA is mostly implemented only on the highest measurement level of a company. Single segments or strategic business units are not assessed on the basis of EVA.[1241]

EVA is based on numbers of accounting. The effort for collecting the basic data is therefore relatively low.[1242] The conversions enable companies to adapt the EVA to their specific needs and create a company-individual performance measure.[1243]

EVA is a value based performance measure. Thus, one of its advantages is that it includes the cost of capital in its calculation.[1244] Due to consideration of cost of capital the EVA also considers the risk which is connected with a specific investment.[1245]

The Shareholder conversions enable a company to consider not capitalised but important operating assets in their performance calculation. Furthermore, the capitalisation of these assets or selected expenditures reflects more the shareholder assessment of a company than the accounting perspective.[1246] By capitalising important investments which are not capitalised according to IFRS rules managers have an incentive to conduct these investments if necessary because the EVA is in the year of the investment not reduced by the full amount of investment. Instead, the resulting depreciation expenditures reduce the EVA over time.[1247]

Some of the listed advantages can be discussed controversially and be assessed as disadvantages. The calculation on book values is a good example. The possibility of manipulation due to accounting policy which influences book values is immanent.[1248] The NOPAT includes expenses for amortisation and depreciation and can be influenced separately by accounting policy in this area.[1249]

So, in its basic version the EVA suffers from the same problem as ROCE Spread and Value Added because these key figures are also based on accounting data. Only the True EVA partially overcomes the disadvantages but the effort for its calculation is exceptionally higher.[1250]

Here is the next conflict for the company: The more conversions are applied, the more complex the EVA calculation becomes. This can be a problem due to decreasing

1238 Cf. Heier, K., Karsten, E., Müller-Wenzel, C., et al. (2015), p. 15; Junginger, M. (2005), p. 69; Zirkler, B. (2002), p. 98.
1239 Cf. Hahn, D., Hintze, M. (2006), p. 97.
1240 Cf. Heese, V. (2011), p. 134.
1241 Cf. Hostettler, S. (2003), p. 117.
1242 Cf. Groll, K.-H. (2003), p. 63; Laier, R. (2011), p. 120.
1243 Cf. Heier, K., Karsten, E., Müller-Wenzel, C., et al. (2015), pp. 15-16.
1244 Cf. Groll, K.-H. (2003), pp. 64-65.
1245 Cf. Mensch, G. (2008), p. 282; Wöltje, J. (2011), p. 221.
1246 Cf. Graumann, M. (2014), p. 829.
1247 Cf. Hahn, D., Hintze, M. (2006), p. 97.
1248 Cf. Heier, K., Karsten, E., Müller-Wenzel, C., et al. (2015), p. 16; Mensch, G. (2008), p. 285.
1249 Cf. Baetge, J., Kirsch, H.-J., Thiele, S. (2004), p. 470.
1250 Cf. Böcking, H.-J., Nowak, K. (1999), p. 288.

comprehensibility of the concept.[1251] The costs for implementation increase with number of conversions, too.[1252] In practice, companies tend to implement too many conversions which lead to the described problem.[1253]

The capitalising of research and development expenditures does not offer managers an incentive to postpone these investments anymore and to save costs in this area. This is important because it is decisive for the prospective development of a company.[1254] However, it offers managers some discretion because it is possible for them to classify expenditures as research and development expenditures which are not really belonging to this category. Then these expenditures are not decreasing EVA in this period.[1255]

The EVA is based on book values including expenses for amortization and depreciation. Companies with assets with book values of zero which are still used for production have an advantage because these assets are not included in the NOA. Companies with relatively new assets reveal under the same circumstances a lower EVA. Also for temporal performance comparisons of one company this can be problematic because the performance of a company can remain the same but only due to lower book values of its assets the EVA improves. ROCE spread and Value Added suffer from the same problem.[1256]

The increasing EVA due to lower book values can lead to the circumstance that managers focus on the wrong objectives. At the beginning, the EVA concept supports managers to identify invested capital which does not deliver its contribution to an increase of Shareholder Value or operating process which can be improved. But EVA incentivises managers to reduce invested capital as much as possible. In the long run, this harms the company because necessary investments have not been made. So, managers have to be aware not to stress the objective of reducing NOA too extensively.[1257]

The individual calculation due to the selection of convenient conversions is an advantage for companies using this concept but a clear disadvantage for all investors because EVAs between different companies are not comparable.[1258] Also when only analysing the EVA of one company, it is difficult for analysts to assess what conversions have been selected by management if no further information is given in the annual report.[1259] The comparability of EVA is per se limited because it is an absolute key figure and influenced by the size of a company.[1260]

In practice, companies commonly select a few conversions in order to limit the effort for calculating EVA. This has the consequence that the book values are not completely transformed into the values according to the economic model which better reflects the assessment of shareholders.[1261]

1251 Cf. Hostettler, S. (2003), pp. 119-120; Zirkler, B. (2002), p. 99.
1252 Cf. Hamilton, J., Rahman, S., Lee, A. C. (2009), p. 285.
1253 Cf. Hostettler, S. (2003), p. 117.
1254 Cf. Mensch, G. (2008), p. 282.
1255 Cf. Mensch, G. (2008), p. 282.
1256 Cf. Groll, K.-H. (2003), pp. 65-67; Schumann, J. (2008), pp. 125-126.
1257 Cf. Ittner, C. D., Larcker, D. F. (1998), p. 214; Stiefl, J., Westerholt, K. von (2008), p. 168.
1258 Cf. Gundel, T. (2012), p. 22; Heier, K., Karsten, E., Müller-Wenzel, C., et al. (2015), p. 16; Rickards, R. C. (2009), p. 157.
1259 Cf. Baetge, J., Kirsch, H.-J., Thiele, S. (2004), p. 474; Gräfer, H., Gerenkamp, T. (2016), p. 149.
1260 Cf. Mensch, G. (2008), p. 275; Stewart, G. B. (1999), p. 167.
1261 Cf. Groll, K.-H. (2003), p. 63.

A further point of criticism is the sole consideration of financial issues and ignoring qualitative factors like employee or customer satisfaction. However, this could be transferred to every presented value based performance measure.[1262] But the EVA concept raises the claim to itself to be able to completely steer a company.[1263] It is often recommended that this performance measure be integrated into an existing Balanced Scorecard system.[1264]

In total, the EVA suffers under many problems which are already mentioned in the context of ROCE Spread and Value Added. Also the EVA does not indicate the change of Shareholder Value of one period. It only indicates and gives to a degree to extent to which the enterprise value has changed.[1265]

The EVA focuses on one period. Managers can postpone costs into the next period and thus disburden the EVA of the current period. For single investment projects an incomplete picture is given by the EVA. This is a problem that all measures have which concentrate on performance measurement of one period.[1266] Consequently, EVA neither consider prospective developments[1267] nor the present value of money.[1268] Therefore, EVA can be used best for the assessment of the performance for a single period in the past. Table seven summarizes the most important results of the key figure evaluation.[1269]

Table 7: Evaluation of EVA

Evaluation Criteria	**EVA**
Including of cost of capital	+
Data basis for calculation (Availability of data)	+ (bases on book values of annual accounts)
Data basis for calculation (Quality of data)	0 / + (Book values but with many conversions quality of data increases)
Present value of Money	–
Future Orientation	–
Considering risk	+ (included within calculation of WACC)
Simplicity	0 / – (depends on number of applied conversions)

Source: In style of: Fiedler, R., Gräf, J. (2012), p. 339

1262 Cf. Böcking, H.-J., Nowak, K. (1999), p. 288; Nowak, K. (2003), p. 158.
1263 Cf. Böcking, H.-J., Nowak, K. (1999), p. 288.
1264 Cf. Laier, R. (2011), p. 126; Zirkler, B. (2002), p. 103.
1265 Cf. Dreher, M. (2010), p. 369; Kahle, H. (2003), p. 777; cf. chapter 3.3.2.1.1 for an extensive explanation of this problem.
1266 Cf. Schumann, J. (2008), p. 125; Stephan, J. (2006), p. 82; Stiefl, J., Westerholt, K. von (2008), p. 167.
1267 Cf. Dreher, M. (2010), p. 371.
1268 Cf. Stührenberg, L., Streich, D., Henke Jörg (2003), p. 60.
1269 Cf. Kley, K.-L. (2003), p. 840; Schmeisser, W., Rönsch, M., Zilch, I. (2009), p. 25.

To sum up: The EVA is a tool for controlling the performance of a single period and it is not well suited for the purposes of performance comparison between different companies due to the high number of possible conversions.[1270]

3.3.3 Cash Flow Based Key Ffigures

3.3.3.1 Cash Flow Return on Investment

3.3.3.1.1 Calculation of Dynamic Cash Flow Return on Investment

Similar to the EVA, the CFROI has been developed by a consulting company, namely Holt Planning Associates. This company was later acquired by the Boston Consulting Group (BCG).[1271] The objective of BCG is to provide companies with a key figure which enables them to check the resource allocation within the company and to provide managers with a figure which enables them to check if the company is successful in creating value for shareholders.[1272]

Two ways of calculating CFROI exist: The dynamic and the static method.[1273] The CFROI transfers the method of internal rate of return from a single investment project to a whole company.[1274] In general, the interal rate of return is the interest rate at which the present value of an investment equals zero.[1275] The mathematical method to calculate the interest rate is iteration.[1276]

The calculation of CFROI consists of four parts: Gross Investment Base (GIB), Gross Cash Flow (GCF), average useful life of assets and net value of non-depreciable assets.[1277] Knowing the parts of the calculation, the CFROI can be defined as follows: It is the interest rate at which the GIB corresponds to the sum of GCFs and non-depreciable assets.[1278] This means that the CFROI is the interest rate at which the present value of an investment is zero.[1279] Therefore, the CFROI can be interpreted as the average return on the capital invested in the company.[1280] The noticeable difference to the previous presented performance measures is that the CFROI transfers book values to Cash Flows.[1281] The following formula shows the calculation for the dynamic CFROI.

$$CFROI = -GIB + GCF \times \left(\frac{(1 + CFROI)^n - 1}{(1 + CFROI)^n \times CFROI} \right) + \frac{NDA}{(1 + CFROI)^n} = 0$$

Source: Taken from: Britzelmaier, B. (2013), p. 224
Formula 30: Calculation of dynamic CFROI

1270 Cf. Laier, R. (2011), p. 124.
1271 Cf. Lorenz, M. (2009), p. 16; Schaefer, C. (2004), p. 50.
1272 Cf. Schaefer, C. (2004), p. 50.
1273 Cf. Preißner, A. (2010), p. 384; Sawczyn, A. (2011), p. 71.
1274 Cf. Obermeier, T., Gasper, R. (2008), p. 178.
1275 Cf. Götze, U. (2008), p. 96; Peters, H. (2009), p. 122; cf. extensively for the internal rate of return method: Götze, U. (2008), pp. 96-107.
1276 Cf. Gräfer, H., Gerenkamp, T. (2016), p. 147; Langguth, H. (2008), p. 172.
1277 Cf. Hoffjan, A., Schroll, S. (2010), p. 417; Schaefer, C. (2004), p. 51.
1278 Cf. Krol, F. (2009), p. 74; Obermeier, T., Gasper, R. (2008), p. 178.
1279 Cf. Poeschl, H. (2013), p. 112.
1280 Cf. Lewis, T. G., Stelter, D. M., Casata, T., et al. (1995), p. 44; Krol, F. (2009), p. 74.
1281 Cf. Hahn, D., Hintze, M. (2006), p. 98.

The capital of a company is divided into two parts: The GIB and the non-depreciable assets.[1282] The GIB is the investment payment at the beginning.[1283] By calculating CFROI it is assumed that all investments projects are restarted. Therefore, historical costs are used.[1284] GIB contains the assets which a company uses to create the GCFs every year.[1285] The GIB is derived from the sum of assets. As a first step cumulative depreciations are added because the GIB is based on historical costs. Secondly, historical costs of assets are adapted according to inflation so that they reflect fair values. In a third step expenses for rents or leases are added because according to the CFROI approach these expenditures are a kind of debt capital and have to be considered within the GIB. As a next step in the calculation debt capital, is free of interest, is deducted. At last, the goodwill is deducted.[1286] The objective of adapting the prices in accordance with inflation rates is not to calculate replacement costs but to show the amount of value of assets the company possesses on the basis of today's prices.[1287]

At the end of the useful life the non-depreciable assets are a kind of return the company receives from selling these assets. The resulting profit is added to the Cash Flows resulting from the GIB.[1288] In other words: The net value of non-depreciable assets is assessed as a payment for the company at the end of the investment project.[1289] The liquidity due to the assumed sale of non-depreciable assets has to be discounted in order to include this payment into the CFROI calculation.[1290]

In most cases companies simply base the calculation of GIB and non-depreciable assets on balance sheet values. Nevertheless, it is possible to include expenditures for research, for education of employees or costs for entering new markets in the GIB.[1291] These components are not commonly part of CFROI calculation.[1292]

Examples for assets which are depreciated are tangible and intangible assets, expenditures for leasing or capitalised expenditures for research.[1293] Examples for assets which are considered as non-depreciable are current assets, financial assets and property.[1294]

The GCF is the amount of money which the company has available for investments, for pay-outs to shareholders and payment of interest rates to debt capital providers.[1295] The GCF is an after tax profit measure. It is regularly calculated indirectly. That means that values from the profit and loss statement are used for calculation. Starting point is the

1282 Cf. Groll, K.-H. (2003), p. 74; Obermeier, T., Gasper, R. (2008), p. 179.
1283 Cf. Bieg, H., Kußmaul, H. (2011), p. 336; Brecht, U. (2012), p. 202; Schaefer, C. (2004), p. 51.
1284 Cf. Herbertinger, M. (2002), p. 161.
1285 Cf. Brecht, U. (2012), p. 200.
1286 Cf. Bieg, H., Kußmaul, H. (2011), p. 334; Graumann, M. (2014), p. 819; Lewis, T. G., Stelter, D. M., Casata, T., et al. (1995), pp. 40-43; Poeschl, H. (2013), pp. 112-113; Wöltje, J. (2011), pp. 226-227.
1287 Cf. Günther, T. (1997), p. 216.
1288 Cf. Bieg, H., Kußmaul, H. (2011), p. 336; Brecht, U. (2012), p. 202.
1289 Cf. Coenenberg, A. G., Mattner, G. R., Schultze, W. (2003), p. 11; Schaefer, C. (2004), pp. 56-57.
1290 Cf. Hoffjan, A., Schroll, S. (2010), p. 418.
1291 Cf. Schaefer, C. (2004), p. 52.
1292 Cf. Herbertinger, M. (2002), p. 162; Lewis, T. G., Stelter, D. M., Casata, T., et al. (1995), p. 59.
1293 Cf. Obermeier, T., Gasper, R. (2008), p. 179.
1294 Cf. Obermeier, T., Gasper, R. (2008), p. 179.
1295 Cf. Weißenberger, B. E. (2007), p. 284.

Table 8: Calculation of Gross Investment Base and Gross Cash Flow

Gross Investment Base	**Gross Cash Flow**
Balance Sheet Total	Profit after taxes
+ cumulative depreciations on tangible and fixed assets	+ Depreciations on tangible fixed assets
+ Adaption due to inflation	+ Debt interest rates (including expenditures for rents and leases)
+ Capitalised expenses for rented or leased assets	
– Goodwill	
– Interest-free debt capital including provisions	
= Gross Investment Base	= Gross Cash Flow

Source: In reference to: Graumann, M. (2014), p. 820; Lewis, T. G., Stelter, D. M., Casata, T. et al. (1995), p. 41

profit of companies after taxes. Then interest expenses, depreciation and expenses for leased or rented assets are added.[1296] Extraordinary expenses or profits are eliminated.[1297] Variations in the level of provisions or inventories which are also typically included in Cash Flow calculations are not part of GCF calculation. The reason for this is that it is not the primary aim of GCF to capture all movements in liquidity but to reflect the profit an investor can expect out of his investment in a business.[1298] The CFROI approach assumes that the computed GCF remains constant over the whole useful life.[1299] Table 8 summarises the calculation of GIB and GCF.

The last component of the CFROI calculation is the average useful life of assets. It is the time period for which the GCFs are expected to be generated. As the GIB consists of many different assets the useful life is an average value. It is computed with the following formula:[1300]

$$Useful\ life = \frac{book\ value\ of\ depreciable\ assets}{expenses\ for\ annual\ depreciation}$$

Source: Taken from: Graumann, M. (2014), p. 820
Formula 31: Calculation of useful life

This formula assumes that all assets are depreciated according to a straight-line method.[1301] If a company uses another method of depreciation distortions occur.[1302]

1296 Cf. Bieg, H., Kußmaul, H. (2011), p. 335; Obermeier, T., Gasper, R. (2008), p. 180.
1297 Cf. Hahn, D., Hintze, M. (2006), p. 98; Herbertinger, M. (2002), p. 163.
1298 Cf. Behringer, S. (2014), p. 107; Lewis, T. G., Stelter, D. M., Casata, T., et al. (1995), pp. 61-62; Groll, K.-H. (2003), p. 79; cf. contradictory Plaschke, F. J. (2003), p. 143, who considers long term provisions in the calculation of GCF.
1299 Cf. Stührenberg, L., Streich, D., Henke Jörg (2003), p. 43.
1300 Cf. Günther, T. (1997), p. 217.
1301 Cf. Obermeier, T., Gasper, R. (2008), p. 180.
1302 Cf. Langguth, H. (2008), p. 168.

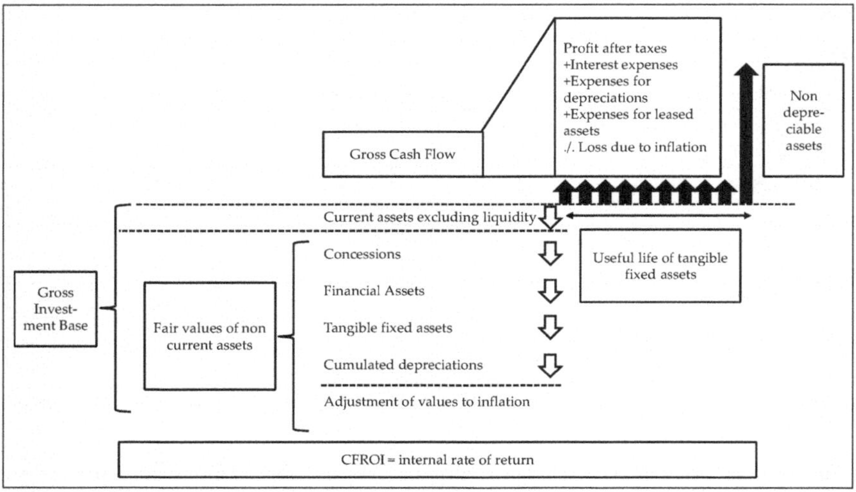

Source: Taken from: Bieg, H., Kußmaul, H. (2011), p. 336; Lewis, T. G., Stelter, D. M.; Casata, T. et al. (1995), p. 45

Illustration 13: Calculation of dynamic CFROI

The CFROI alone does not lead to a conclusion concerning the success or failure of a company in one period. The costs of capital, the WACC, are the adequate standard of comparison.[1303] If the CFROI is above the WACC the company has created Shareholder Value, if the CFROI is below the WACC Shareholder Value has been destroyed.[1304] As the CFROI measures the performance after tax deduction, it is important to compare the key figure with a WACC after taxes.[1305] The illustration 13 summarises the method of calculation of the dynamic CFROI with all presented components.

The CFROI calculation of BCG rejects the CAPM approach for calculating the cost of equity capital. Instead, costs of capital are calculated on the basis of a market portfolio and not for every company individually.[1306] However, within the scientific literature the common WACC approach is often suggested.[1307] The difference between CFROI and WACC is named CFROI spread.[1308]

3.3.3.1.2 Calculation of Static Cash Flow Return on Investment

Due to the complexity inherent with the calculation, BCG develops a second way of calculating CFROI. The components GIB and GCF remain the same. The new component

1303 Cf. Bieg, H., Kußmaul, H. (2011), p. 337.

1304 Cf. Brecht, U. (2012), p. 202; Hasler, P. T. (2011), pp. 276-277; Krol, F. (2009), p. 74.

1305 Cf. Kajüter, P. (2007a), p. 451.

1306 Cf. Eidel, U. (1999), pp. 64-65; Graumann, M. (2014), p. 821.

1307 Cf. exemplarily Britzelmaier, B. (2013a), p. 225; Stiefl, J., Westerholt, K. von (2008), p. 57; Weißenberger, B. E. (2007), p. 285.

1308 Cf. Junginger, M. (2005), p. 69.

is the so-called sinking fund depreciation.[1309] The static CFROI is computed according to the following formula:

$$CFROI = \frac{GCF - sinking\ fund\ depreciation}{GIB}$$

Source: Taken from: Lehmann, G. (2012), p. 64
Formula 32: Calculation of static CFROI

It is problematic that investments in the nominator are not included. The CFROI concepts assume that all assets can be used until the end of the calculated useful life and no replacements are necessary. Thus, the Cash Flow alone tends to illustrate the company's performance to positive. This is the reason why sinking fund depreciations have to be subtracted.[1310]

It is the amount of money which the company has to invest every year at the given interest rate. At the end of the useful life of the assets the invested amount corresponds to the costs of the assets contained in the GIB.[1311]

The sum of economic depreciations reflects the amount of money necessary for a replacement purchase of all assets.[1312] This is a theoretical part of the CFROI concept. It is not necessary in reality that a company invests free cash in investments.[1313] Regularly, the economic depreciation is below the depreciation based on accounting values due to the investment of capital at the given interest rate and due to the fact that the calculated useful life is above the useful life used on balance sheet.[1314]

The static and the dynamic approach differ in their results. The dynamic approach assumes that free available cash is invested at the calculated interest rate, the CFROI. The static approach implies that these cash means are invested at an interest rate which corresponds to the WACC. So, the dynamic method leads to higher results if the CFROI is higher than the WACC.[1315]

3.3.3.2 Cash Value Added

The CVA is a performance measure in absolute numbers which is based on the concept of CFROI. It captures the surplus of Cash Flows over the cost of capital.[1316] The CVA is a key figure which measures the performance of a single period.[1317] It can be computed for a whole company or for single segments within a company.[1318] The CVA is comparable to the EVA because both key figures capture a company's excess over the cost of capital.[1319]

1309 Cf. Plaschke, F. J. (2003), p. 145; Poeschl, H. (2013), pp. 113-114.
1310 Cf. Ewert, R., Wagenhofer, A. (2014), p. 524; Weißenberger, B. E. (2009), p. 49.
1311 Cf. Poeschl, H. (2013), pp. 113-114; Wöltje, J. (2011), p. 227.
1312 Cf. Groll, K.-H. (2003), p. 88; Hoffjan, A., Schroll, S. (2010), p. 418.
1313 Cf. Groll, K.-H. (2003), p. 90.
1314 Cf. Plaschke, F. J. (2003), p. 145.
1315 Cf. Stiefl, J., Westerholt, K. von (2008), pp. 54-55; Weber, J., Bramsemann, U., Heineke, C., et al. (2017), pp. 76-77.
1316 Cf. Langguth, H. (2008), pp. 173-174; Wöltje, J. (2011), p. 228.
1317 Cf. Steger, J. (2014), p. 158; Weißenberger, B. E. (2009), p. 49.
1318 Cf. Wöltje, J. (2011), p. 228.
1319 Cf. Britzelmaier, B. (2013b), p. 165.

The CVA can be calculated with the Value Spread formula or the Capital Charge formula.[1320] According to the Value Spread formula the CVA is defined as the surplus of CFROI over the cost of capital multiplied by the GIB. It shows the hurdle rate for a company.[1321]

$$CVA = (CFROI - WACC) \times GIB$$

Source: Taken from: Hachmeister, D. (2003), p. 99
Formula 33: Calculation of CVA with Value Spread formula

The Capital Charge formula deducts from the GCF the sinking fund depreciations and the cost of capital.[1322] The GCF has to cover the sinking fund depreciation as well as the cost of capital.[1323]

$$CVA = GCF - sinking\ fund\ depreciation - (WACC \times GIB)$$

Source: Taken from: Weißenberger, B. E. (2009), p. 49
Formula 34: Calculation of CVA with Capital Charge formula

Similar to previous presented key figures a company is successful in creating Shareholder Value if the CVA is higher than zero. Values below zero indicate that Shareholder Value is destroyed.[1324] Analogous to the EVA concept, the CVA signals if Shareholder Value increases or decreases but it does not express the exact extent of value added or value destroyed.[1325]

In order to calculate the change of the value created between two periods, the CVAs of these two periods have to be subtracted. This results is the Delta CVA which is comparable to the Delta EVA.[1326]

On the basis of the CVA also a value based performance measure for the total period can be derived which states the Shareholder Value. The prospective CVAs have to be discounted with the cost of capital and then added up. The invested capital has to be added to this sum and the cost of debt capital subtracted.[1327]

3.3.3.3 Evaluation of Cash Flow Return on Investment and Cash Value Added

The evaluation of CFROI and CVA is summarised within one chapter because the CVA calculation is strongly based upon CFROI calculation. Both key figures have common advantages and disadvantages.[1328] The CFROI approach is based on historical costs. This is an advantage because the age of assets does not influence the calculation.[1329] Thus, the CFROI overcomes one of the flaws of EVA and Value Added. By calculating these key

1320 Cf. Steger, J. (2014), p. 158.
1321 Cf. Hachmeister, D. (2003), p. 99; Karrer, M. (2006), p. 161.
1322 Cf. Weißenberger, B. E. (2009), p. 49.
1323 Cf. Weißenberger, B. E. (2007), p. 284.
1324 Cf. Langguth, H. (2008), p. 174; Steger, J. (2014), p. 159.
1325 Cf. Langguth, H. (2008), p. 174.
1326 Cf. Kajüter, P. (2007a), p. 452; Schmeisser, W. (2010), p. 36.
1327 Cf. Hoffjan, A., Schroll, S. (2010), pp. 419-420.
1328 Cf. Stiefl, J., Westerholt, K. von (2008), pp. 56-57.
1329 Cf. Preißner, A. (2010), p. 384; Wöltje, J. (2016a), p. 447.

figures, companies with depreciated assets achieve a better key figure than companies with non-depreciated assets. With the help of CFROI it is possible to compare companies or segments with different age structures of assets.[1330]

One advantage of CFROI is that typical distortions of key figures which are based on book values are avoided due to the calculation of Cash Flows.[1331] This means that distortions due to financing decisions or effects of different depreciation methods are eliminated.[1332] As also depreciations are not considered, the CFROI is appropriate within industries in which the depreciation does not reflect the real devaluation of assets.[1333] In some parts of the scientific literature it is mentioned that despite implication of Cash Flows the CFROI depends on a certain degree on book values because book values are used to calculate the GCF through the indirect method.[1334]

The CFROI considers the inflation and thus current costs for assets.[1335] However, the technique regularly used for considering inflation does not really reflect the real price development of single assets because one inflation rate is used for adapting the prices of all tangible and intangible fixed assets.[1336]

The CFROI is regularly based on the annual report of the last fiscal year. Consequently, it is a key figure which analyses past performance.[1337] The consideration of inflation adapts the price level of assets but does not change the fact that the calculation bases on historical values.[1338]

It is important to note that the CFROI is a key figure which measures the performance of one single period despite the application of the method of internal rate of return.[1339] A future orientation is not included within the concept.[1340] The approach does not offer managers incentives to assess the long term effects of an investment.[1341] Due to the fact that prospective developments are not included within the calculation[1342] it is simply assumed that the calculated GCFs remain constant over the useful life.[1343] This assumption does not correspond to reality.[1344] The assumption of constant prospective GCF is problematic. The CFROI assumes a fix pattern of the future, in order to assess the current performance.[1345] If the Cash Flow is in one period high due to short-term measures, this suggests an obvious increase of Shareholder Value.[1346]

1330 Cf. Lewis, T. G., Stelter, D. M., Casata, T., et al. (1995), pp. 49-51; Groll, K.-H. (2003), p. 94; Wöltje, J. (2011), pp. 224-225.
1331 Cf. Bieg, H., Kußmaul, H. (2011), p. 338; Hahn, D., Hintze, M. (2006), p. 102.
1332 Cf. Wöltje, J. (2011), p. 224.
1333 Cf. Hasler, P. T. (2011), p. 275.
1334 Cf. Krol, F. (2009), p. 75; Stührenberg, L., Streich, D., Henke Jörg (2003), p. 49.
1335 Cf. Bieg, H., Kußmaul, H. (2011), p. 338.
1336 Cf. Bieg, H., Kußmaul, H. (2011), p. 339; Groll, K.-H. (2003), p. 77.
1337 Cf. Bieg, H., Kußmaul, H. (2011), p. 339.
1338 Cf. Schaefer, C. (2004), pp. 58-59.
1339 Cf. Groll, K.-H. (2003), p. 73.
1340 Cf. Eidel, U. (1999), pp. 331-332.
1341 Cf. Dahlhaus, C. (2009), p. 184.
1342 Cf. Hahn, D., Hintze, M. (2006), p. 102.
1343 Cf. Graumann, M. (2014), p. 822; Preißner, A. (2010), p. 384.
1344 Cf. Bieg, H., Kußmaul, H. (2011), p. 339.
1345 Cf. Herbertinger, M. (2002), p. 165.
1346 Cf. Hachmeister, D. (1997), p. 572.

In addition to the missing future orientation, the CFROI itself does not consider cost of capital and no risk connected with the investment.[1347]

Further points of criticism are the simplified calculation of useful life and the strong dependence of GIB on accounting rules so that regularly non capitalised expenditures are not considered within GIB.[1348] Especially the calculation of useful life can lead to problems if companies use different methods of depreciation.[1349] Also the exclusion of goodwill from GIB calculation is critically discussed because segments with a high Goodwill can more easily reach a higher CFROI.[1350]

In this context, it has to be stated that the CFROI is difficult to calculate for external persons, especially concerning the division of the GIB into depreciable and non-depreciable part and the estimation of the historical cost of all assets.[1351] For an internal analysis enough data should be available. External persons only can make assumptions concerning the calculation of useful life and the applied methods of depreciations.[1352]

A critical point is the complexity of the CFROI model in comparison to Value Added or EVA. It is more difficult to communicate success based on this model. In addition, the calculation is relatively complex[1353] and time consuming.[1354] Consequently, some authors criticise the complexity which makes it nearly impossible for managers to understand this measure and act accordingly.[1355] This point of criticism applies for both methods because also the second method bases on several assumptions even if it might be easier to calculate the CFROI.[1356] The CVA is also a key figure which is not easily explained to shareholders because CFROI is a relevant component for calculating this key figure.[1357]

Comparisons of the quality of dynamic CFROI reveals that between the real internal rate of return and the CFROI differences exist. Only in the case that the Cash Flows remain constant and the growth rate equals the internal rate of return, the CFROI equals the given internal rate of return. Assuming an increasing Cash Flow profile of projects, the following distortions occur. If the growth rate of investments is above the real internal rate of return, the CFROI is lower than the rate of return. This means it underestimates the real return. In the situation that growth rates of investments are below the internal rate of return or negative, the CFROI overestimates the return. The reverse statements apply for projects with a decreasing Cash Flow profile. If the growth rate is above the internal rate of return, the CFROI overestimates the return of these projects. If the growth rate is below the internal rate of return, the CFROI shows a too low return.[1358]

1347 Cf. Herbertinger, M. (2002), p. 170.

1348 Cf. Hahn, D., Hintze, M. (2006), p. 102.

1349 Cf. Günther, T. (1997), p. 310; Obermeier, T., Gasper, R. (2008), p. 180; Schaefer, C. (2004), p. 56.

1350 Cf. Herbertinger, M. (2002), pp. 165-166.

1351 Cf. Gräfer, H., Gerenkamp, T. (2016), p. 148; Groll, K.-H. (2003), p. 95.

1352 Cf. Plaschke, F. J. (2003), pp. 148-149.

1353 Cf. Krol, F. (2009), p. 75.

1354 Cf. Kajüter, P. (2007a), p. 452.

1355 Cf. Ittner, C. D., Larcker, D. F. (1998), p. 214; Hauer, G., Ultsch, M. (2010).

1356 Cf. Groll, K.-H. (2003), p. 94.

1357 Cf. Fiedler, R., Gräf, J. (2012), p. 339.

1358 Cf. Burger, A., Ulbrich, P., Ahlemeyer, N. (2010), pp. 571-572; Dahlhaus, C. (2009), p. 182; Hachmeister, D. (1997), pp. 566-568.

Table 9: Evaluation of CFROI and CVA

Evaluation Criteria	**CFROI**	**CVA**
Including of cost of capital	–	+
Data basis for calculation (Availability of data)	+ / – (bases on book values of annual accounts and further internal data for calculation of inflation and useful life; data is only easily available for internal analysis)	+ / – (bases on book values of annual accounts and further internal data for calculation of inflation and useful life; data is only easily available for internal analysis)
Data basis for calculation (Quality of data)	+ (Cash Flow basis)	+ (Cash Flow basis)
Present value of Money	–	–
Future Orientation	–	–
Considering risk	–	+ (included within calculation of WACC)
Simplicity	–	–

Source: In style of: Fiedler, R., Gräf, J. (2012), p. 339

But also the new way of calculation and the concept of economic depreciation are criticised. The depreciation has the effect that under-performing companies have a higher return than they should have. The reason for this is that the level of cost of capital influences the level of CFROI. This is problematic as the CFROI should only reflect the economic performance of the company. The higher the cost of capital, the lower is the economic depreciation and the higher the CFROI.[1359] Table 9 summarizes the evaluation of CFROI and CVA.

Similar to ROCE the CFROI as a relative measure may set incorrect incentives because the CFROI increases only if a new investment has a profit rate above the current CFROI. But an investment is worthwhile if it has a return rate above the cost of capital.[1360] This disadvantage is inherent in relative key figures. The CVA as an absolute key figure does not have this disadvantage.[1361]

1359 Cf. Groll, K.-H. (2003), pp. 91-92.
1360 Cf. Ewert, R., Wagenhofer, A. (2014), p. 526; Plaschke, F. J. (2003), p. 154.
1361 Cf. Weber, J., Bramsemann, U., Heineke, C., et al. (2017), pp. 61-62.

3.4 Value Based Performance Measures Focussing on the Total Period

3.4.1 Discounted Cash Flow

3.4.1.1 Calculation

According to the classification of value based performance measures a differentiation between key figures focussing on one period and key figures analysing the performance of the total period exists. In this chapter and the following one the key figures Discounted Cash Flow (DCF) and Market Value Added (MVA) are presented as examples for value based performance measures which refer to the total period.[1362]

The DCF method is based on the Shareholder Value approach of Rappaport. The corporate value is determined by future Cash Flows which illustrate the development of the company.[1363] It is the standard approach for corporate valuation[1364] and also in Germany it is the most common method for this purpose.[1365] There are several variations of the DCF approach which differentiate according to the kind of Cash Flow or the cost of capital.[1366]

Despite several variations the procedure is identical. Forecasted Cash Flows of prospective periods are discounted with an appropriate cost of capital interest rate.[1367] A company has to decide on a calculation method, forecast the Cash Flows, calculate the cost of capital and calculate the value of the total capital or the value of equity capital.[1368]

The DCF approaches can be divided into equity and entity approach. The entity approach computes the total corporate value which means the value of equity and debt capital. For receiving solely the market value of equity capital, the value of debt capital has to be subtracted from the entity value.[1369] In contrast, the equity method directly calculates the value of equity capital.[1370] All approaches lead theoretically to identical results if the same conditions and interest rates are assumed[1371] but this alignment of the different approaches is difficult in practice. That results in the fact that different approaches leads to different results at first sight. The illustration 14 gives an overview of the DCF approaches and methods.[1372]

1362 Cf. chapter 3.2.1 for an overview of the systematisation of value based performance measures.

1363 Cf. Dillerup, R., Stoi, R. (2016), p. 225.

1364 Cf. Kreyer, F. (2009), p. 23; Schacht, U., Fackler, M. (2009), p. 207; Schmeisser, W., Spree, J. (2008), p. 132; cf. for an overview of further methods for corporate valuation: Ernst, D., Schneider, S., Thielen, B. (2010), pp. 1-11.

1365 Cf. Busse, F.-J. (2003), p. 192; Lorenz, M. (2009), p. 13.

1366 Cf. Hölscher, R. (2010), p. 195; cf. for an overview of DCF approaches Baetge, J., Niemeyer, K., Kümmel, J., et al. (2015), pp. 353-508; Ballwieser, W., Hachmeister, D. (2016), pp. 137-202; Drukarczyk, J., Schüler, A. (2016), pp. 81-107; cf. for an illustration of the coherence between the different Cash Flows Nowak, K. (2003), p. 47.

1367 Cf. Dück-Rath, M. (2005), pp. 37-39; Ernst, D., Schneider, S., Thielen, B. (2010), pp. 8-9; Timmreck, C. (2006), p. 22.

1368 Cf. Schacht, U., Fackler, M. (2009), p. 208.

1369 Cf. Henschke, S. (2009), p. 11; Hölscher, R. (2010), p. 195.

1370 Cf. Busse, F.-J. (2003), p. 193; Hölscher, R. (2010), p. 198.

1371 Cf. Heusinger von Waldegge, S. (2009), pp. 75-76; Kreyer, F. (2009), p. 24.

1372 Cf. Matschke, M. J., Brösel, G. (2013), p. 732.

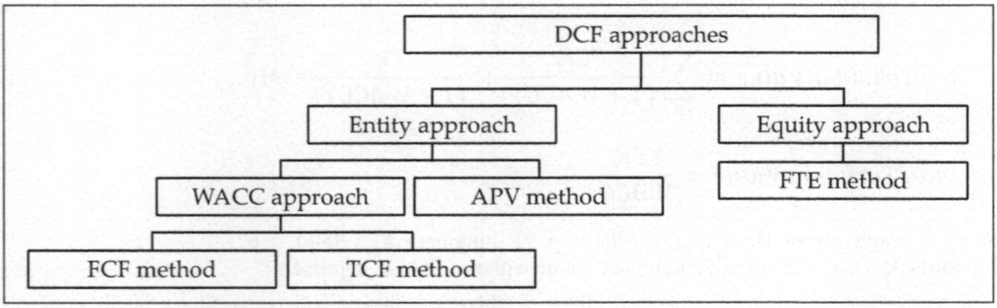

Source: Taken from: Matschke, M. J., Brösel, G. (2013), p. 699
Illustration 14: Overview of DCF approaches

The entity methods are the WACC and APV approach. The WACC approach contains the FCF and the TCF method.[1373] A common feature is that these approaches compute the corporate value in two steps: Firstly, the value of the total capital is calculated and in a second step the value of debt capital is deducted. Result is the Shareholder Value.[1374] The applied Cash Flows all consider the liquidity which is available for equity and debt capital providers.[1375]

The WACC approach calculates the value of a company by discounting FCF with the WACC.[1376] The FCF is defined as the Cash Flow which represents the financial surplus of the company after subtracting the costs of all worthwhile investment projects.[1377] The investment projects are necessary for a company to stay competitive and at least maintain its position within the competition.[1378] The FCF shows the amount of liquidity which can be transferred to equity and debt capital providers.[1379]

The debt interest rates reduce the tax payments of a company, so this advantage has to be considered within the calculation.[1380] The WACC approach considers that in the discount rate.[1381] Consequently, the FCF has to be reduced by the interest rate which results from tax saving effects. Otherwise, this effect would be considered twice.[1382]

Additionally, the FCF is independent from the capital structure of a company.[1383] It reflects a company completely financed with equity capital.[1384]

1373 Cf. Baetge, J., Niemeyer, K., Kümmel, J., et al. (2015), p. 360; Schmeisser, W., Spree, J. (2008), p. 134.
1374 Cf. Obermeier, T., Gasper, R. (2008), p. 162; Schmeisser, W., Spree, J. (2008), p. 141.
1375 Cf. Kreyer, F. (2009), p. 25; Schmeisser, W., Spree, J. (2008), p. 141.
1376 Cf. Schmeisser, W., Spree, J. (2008), p. 142.
1377 Cf. Obermeier, T., Gasper, R. (2008), p. 159; Schmeisser, W., Spree, J. (2008), p. 137.
1378 Cf. Kruschwitz, L., Löffler, A. (2006), p. 3.
1379 Cf. Obermeier, T., Gasper, R. (2008), p. 159; Schmeisser, W., Spree, J. (2008), p. 137; Stier, C. (2017), p. 60.
1380 Cf. Nowak, K. (2003), p. 27.
1381 Cf. Hölscher, R. (2010), p. 196.
1382 Cf. Schacht, U., Fackler, M. (2009), p. 210.
1383 Cf. Schacht, U., Fackler, M. (2009), p. 211; Wuntsch, M. v., Bach, S. (2012), p. 65.
1384 Cf. Ballwieser, W., Hachmeister, D. (2016), p. 139; Schmeisser, W., Spree, J. (2008), p. 143.

$$Shareholder\ Value = \sum_{t=1}^{T} \frac{FCF_t}{(1 + WACC)^t} + \frac{TV}{(1 + WACC)^n} - MV_{DC}$$

$$with\ Terminal\ Value = \frac{FCF_n}{WACC}$$

Source: Adapted from: Becker, H. P. (2016), p. 93; Junginger, M. (2005), p. 67
Formula 35: Calculation of Shareholder Value with the WACC approach

with
FCF_t = Free Cashs Flow of period t
TV = Terminal Value
MV_{DC} = Market Value of debt capital
$WACC$ = Weighted average cost of capital with tax shield

The TCF method is very similar to the FCF method. The only difference is the consideration of the tax shield within Cash Flow calculation instead of including it in the discounting rate. Thus, the TCF approach uses costs of capital which do not include the tax shield.[1385] The TCF represents the cash which is available for equity and debt capital providers after deducting all tax payments and adding the tax shield.[1386] The disadvantage is that a subsequent determination concerning the capital structure is not possible because this decision has to be made in the context of Cash Flow calculation.[1387]

$$Shareholder\ Value = \sum_{t=1}^{T} \frac{TCF_t}{(1 + WACC)^t} + \frac{TV}{(1 + WACC)^n} - MV_{DC}$$

Source: Adapted from: Schmundt, W. (2008), p. 22
Formula 36: Calculation of Shareholder Value with TCF approach

with
TCF_t = Total Cash Flow
$WACC$ = Weighted average cost of capital without tax shield

The APV method also uses the FCF but discounts them in a first step with the cost of equity capital. The result is the enterprise value of a company without debts. Then the value is adjusted by the present value of tax shield. At last, the market value of debt capital is subtracted.[1388] The tax shield increases the company value because a company could save tax payments by substituting equity capital by debt capital.[1389] The APV approach is helpful for determining the enterprise value if the leverage ratio of a company

1385 Cf. Schacht, U., Fackler, M. (2009), pp. 223-224; Schmeisser, W., Spree, J. (2008), pp. 144-145.
1386 Cf. Drukarczyk, J., Schüler, A. (2016), p. 102; Nowak, K. (2003), pp. 32-33.
1387 Cf. Schmundt, W. (2008), p. 22.
1388 Cf. Henschke, S. (2009), p. 13; Schmeisser, W., Spree, J. (2008), p. 146.
1389 Cf. Nowak, K. (2003), pp. 33-34; Wuntsch, M. v., Bach, S. (2012), pp. 70-71.

is not constant over time. The WACC approach is more convenient if the ratio is constant.[1390]

$$Shareholder\ Value = \sum_{t=1}^{T} \frac{FCF_t}{(1 + r_{EC})^t} + \sum_{t=1}^{T} \frac{s \times i_{DC} \times DC}{(1 + i_{DC})^t} +$$

$$\frac{TV}{(1 + r_{EC})^n} - MV_{DC}$$

Source: Adapted from: Schmundt, W. (2008), p. 23
Formula 37: Calculation of Shareholder Value with APV approach

with
s = tax rate of the company
i_{DC} = interest rate for debt capital
DC = Market value of debt capital
r_{EC} = cost of equity capital

The equity approach directly computes the Shareholder Value. As the calculation methodology is different to the entity approaches, a different Cash Flow has to be applied: The Flow to Equity (FTE). It captures the financial surplus after interest expenses for debt capital, so it measures the amount of liquidity is left for equity capital providers.[1391] The calculation scheme of FTE requires that the costs for debt capital are exactly planned in advance.[1392] The discount rate is not the WACC but solely the cost of equity capital.[1393]

$$Shareholder\ Value = \sum_{t=1}^{T} \frac{FTE_t}{(1 + r_{EC})^t} + \frac{TV}{(1 + r_{EC})^n}$$

Source: Taken from: Burger, A., Ulbrich, P., Ahlemeyer, N. (2010), p. 196
Formula 38: Calculation of Shareholder Value with the Equity approach

Table 10 gives an overview of the calculation scheme of the different kind of Cash Flows used in the context of the DCF approaches and shows the coherence between them.

As it is not affordable to compute a Cash Flow for every single period only the following immediate periods are planned in a detailed way.[1394] In general, the detailed planning phase is limited from three up to approximately ten years.[1395] The prediction of Cash Flows is based on forecasted balance sheets and profit and loss statements from

1390 Cf. Henschke, S. (2009), p. 13.
1391 Cf. Baetge, J., Niemeyer, K., Kümmel, J., et al. (2015), pp. 366-367; Wuntsch, M. v., Bach, S. (2012), p. 68.
1392 Cf. Schmundt, W. (2008), p. 13.
1393 Cf. Becker, H. P. (2016), p. 95; Schmeisser, W., Spree, J. (2008), p. 138.
1394 Cf. Düsterloh von, E. (2003), p. 135; Wuntsch, M. v., Bach, S. (2012), pp. 63-64.
1395 Cf. Heusinger von Waldegge, S. (2009), p. 77; Schacht, U., Fackler, M. (2009), p. 207.

Table 10: Calculation and coherence between different kinds of Cash Flows[1396]

Free Cash Flow / Total Cash Flow / Flow to Equity
EBIT
+ Provisions
= Gross Cash Flow before Taxes
– Corporate income taxes under the assumption of no leverage
– Expenses for investments
= Free Cash Flow (FCF)
+ Tax shield
= Total Cash Flow (TCF)
– Interest payments for debt capital
+ Rising of new credit
– Amortisation of credit
= Flow to Equity (FTE)

Source: Adapted from: Ballwieser, W., Hachmeister, D. (2016), p. 138; Kruschwitz, L., Löffler, A. (2006), p. 2; Matschke, M. J.; Brösel, G. (2013), p. 712

which the Cash Flows are derived.[1397] The forecast itself additionally is based on an analysis of the past development of the company[1398] and analysis of growth potential and competitive position in the future.[1399] This includes the position of the company within its industry, a consideration of the strength and weaknesses and an analysis of the competitors.[1400]

After the detailed planning phase it can be assumed that the company is liquidated or still exists. In the first case the revenues from selling the remaining assets have to be discounted.[1401]

Regularly it is assumed that the activities of the company continue indefinitely. The last Cash Flow of the detailed planning phase is seen as the Cash Flow for all further years.[1402] Factors that should be included in the Terminal Value calculation are the forecasted economic development of the whole industry and the competitive position of the company.[1403] Often the Cash Flow used for Terminal Value calculation is normalised. This means that the investments correspond to depreciation expenditures so that the

1396 These kinds of Cash Flows are not defined uniformly within scientific literature, cf. for a comparison of different definitions Matschke, M. J., Brösel, G. (2013), pp. 710-711; Stier, C. (2017), p. 62.

1397 Cf. Dillerup, R., Stoi, R. (2016), p. 227; Drukarczyk, J., Schüler, A. (2016), p. 125.

1398 Cf. Nowak, K. (2003), pp. 49-50.

1399 Cf. Wuntsch, M. v., Bach, S. (2012), p. 62; cf. extensively for the forecast of Cash Flows Diedrich, R., Dierkes, S. (2015), pp. 160-237.

1400 Cf. Diedrich, R., Dierkes, S. (2015), p. 184.

1401 Cf. Dillerup, R., Stoi, R. (2016), p. 226; Schacht, U., Fackler, M. (2009), p. 220.

1402 Cf. Drukarczyk, J., Schüler, A. (2016), p. 127; Hölscher, R. (2010), p. 193.

1403 Cf. Busse, F.-J. (2003), p. 219.

company is able to continue its activities but does not grow anymore.[1404] The Terminal Value represents the company's steady state.[1405] It is computed with the help of the mathematical construct of perpetuity.[1406]

For determining the cost of equity capital, the CAPM model is used.[1407] The debt interest rates are aligned to long term interest rates of government bonds.[1408] Both values are then used for WACC calculation.[1409]

3.4.1.2 Evaluation

The DCF methods are often used for corporate evaluation. One pragmatic reason is that they are appropriate for nearly all kinds of companies independent from their size.[1410] A further reason for the wide application is often stated within scientific literature: Cash Flows are less influenced by management's accounting policy and are assessed as a more reliable figure.[1411]

Unfortunately, DCF methods cannot be used for companies which generate mostly negative Cash Flows. A negative present value does not deliver helpful insights.[1412] Also their application for fast growing young companies is problematic because these companies need all of their financial liquidity for investments and have no free Cash Flows available which can be transferred to debt or equity capital providers.[1413]

Due to discounting of Cash Flows the present value of money is considered. The discounting factor is the cost of capital which ensures a consideration of risk within the DCF approach.[1414] Furthermore, the prospective development of the company and its growth opportunities are considered. The DCF approach is not limited to one single period.[1415]

The forecast of Cash Flows relies on several assumptions which do not have to be fulfilled in the future as assumed. So, a degree of uncertainty is inherent in the context of forecasting.[1416] Furthermore, the forecast of Cash Flows is very complex and elaborate.[1417] On the other hand, the manager is forced to intensively deal with the company's further development and its economic environment. This reduces forecast errors in contrast to approaches which are less elaborate like the multiplicator method.[1418] A disadvantage is that the Cash Flows are forecasted on the basis of one fixed strategy. Possible action alternatives which might exist in the future are not included in the Cash Flow forecast.[1419]

1404 Cf. Schacht, U., Fackler, M. (2009), p. 219.
1405 Cf. Schacht, U., Fackler, M. (2009), p. 219.
1406 Cf. Heusinger von Waldegge, S. (2009), p. 77; Obermeier, T., Gasper, R. (2008), p. 162.
1407 Cf. Hölscher, R. (2010), p. 193; Timmreck, C. (2006), p. 23.
1408 Cf. Busse, F.-J. (2003), p. 222.
1409 Cf. for an extensive description of the CAPM model and WACC calculation chapter 2.1.3.
1410 Cf. Hasler, P. T. (2011), p. 241.
1411 Cf. Hasler, P. T. (2011), p. 241; Riedl, J. B. (2000), p. 231.
1412 Cf. Heusinger von Waldegge, S. (2009), p. 84.
1413 Cf. Lukas, A. (2004), p. 110.
1414 Cf. Dillerup, R., Stoi, R. (2016), p. 228.
1415 Cf. Dillerup, R., Stoi, R. (2016), p. 228.
1416 Cf. Lukas, A. (2004), p. 109; Wuntsch, M. v., Bach, S. (2012), p. 62.
1417 Cf. Heusinger von Waldegge, S. (2009), p. 86; Riedl, J. B. (2000), p. 232.
1418 Cf. Hasler, P. T. (2011), p. 242; Modello, E. (2015), p. 310.
1419 Cf. Dück-Rath, M. (2005), pp. 114-115.

However, the influence of the detailed calculated Cash Flows is in contrast relatively low.[1420] In contrast, the share of the terminal value at the total enterprise value is very large so that the assumptions for this calculation are especially important.[1421] Derivations can lead to large differences in the resulting enterprise value.[1422] The number of periods for which detailed Cash Flows are calculated and the Terminal Value have further effects on the corporate value. The reason is that the assumptions between both phases differ and lead to different Cash Flows.[1423]

Also the assumptions underlying the forecast have a strong influence on the resulting value because both phases are based on certain assumptions which determine the development of Cash Flows.[1424] One of these assumptions is the going concern assumption which might not be realistic but is chosen for pragmatic reasons. A justification for a certain lifetime is de facto not possible and respectively difficult to determine.[1425]

In the context of DCF approaches the CAPM is often criticised due to its unrealistic assumptions. The discount rate is a main influence factor for determining the enterprise value. Nevertheless, the critique of CAPM is valid for all value based performance measures that use this model.[1426]

The focus on Cash Flows of single firms can lead to non-consideration of important connections of these firms to other firms which are necessary for economic success.[1427] For external persons DCF calculations are difficult to conduct or to comprehend because they have no access to such a comprehensive database like the managers of a company.[1428]

In order to distinguish the Discounted Cash Flow from the value based performance introduced before, it is not assessed as appropriate for the periodical management control of a company.[1429] It is rather more convenient for assessing the effects of a change in the company's strategy or an analysis of the future development. So its different attributes lead to a different purpose of this value based performance measure and for value based performance measure which determines the performance of the total period.[1430] Instead, the purpose of value based performance measures focussing on a single period is the ex post performance measurement and the assessment of the performance of management. The table below summarises the evaluation and gives an overview of the fulfilment of the defined criteria.[1431]

1420 Cf. Heusinger von Waldegge, S. (2009), p. 80.

1421 Cf. Düsterloh von, E. (2003), pp. 140-141; Kreyer, F. (2009), p. 33; Nowak, K. (2003), p. 83; Wuntsch, M. v., Bach, S. (2012), p. 62.

1422 Cf. Hasler, P. T. (2011), p. 244; Modello, E. (2015), p. 311.

1423 Cf. Ernst, D., Schneider, S., Thielen, B. (2010), pp. 84-87.

1424 Cf. Heusinger von Waldegge, S. (2009), p. 83.

1425 Cf. Diedrich, R., Dierkes, S. (2015), pp. 226-227; Kreyer, F. (2009), p. 31; Kruschwitz, L., Löffler, A. (2006), pp. 6-7.

1426 Cf. Matschke, M. J., Brösel, G. (2013), p. 727; cf. for an overview of the CAPM and its flaws Düsterloh von, E. (2003), pp. 124-127 and chapter 2.1.3.

1427 Cf. Matschke, M. J., Brösel, G. (2013), pp. 733-734.

1428 Cf. Junginger, M. (2005), p. 67.

1429 Cf. Fiedler, R., Gräf, J. (2012), p. 339.

1430 Cf. Lattwein, J. (2002), p. 142.

1431 Cf. Coenenberg, A. G., Mattner, G. R., Schultze, W. (2003), p. 2; Lachnit, L., Müller, S. (2012), pp. 255-256.

Table 11: Evaluation of Discounted Cash Flow approaches

Evaluation Criterion	Discounted Cash Flow Methods
Including of cost of capital	+
Data basis for calculation (Availability of data)	+ (bases on book values of past annual accounts and forecasts)
Data basis for calculation (Quality of data)	+ (Cash Flows)
Present value of Money	+
Future Orientation	+
Considering risk	+ (included within calculation of WACC)
Simplicity	– (depends on effort invested for forecasts of EVA of future periods)

Source: In style of: Fiedler, R., Gräf, J. (2012), p. 339

It can be stated that the DCF approaches fulfil nearly all evaluation criteria. However these positive effects are at the expense of a simple calculation.

3.4.2 Market Value Added

3.4.2.1 Calculation

The EVA concept can also be used for calculating the Shareholder Value or the corporate value of the company.[1432] The MVA is a total key figure which refers to the total period.[1433] Two kinds of calculation for MVA exist: The ex-ante and the ex post calculation.[1434]

From a market's point of view the MVA measures the difference between the market value and the book value of a company.[1435] A positive MVA indicates that a company is able to constantly generate a profit which is above its cost of capital, a negative one the contrary.[1436]

From a company's point of view the MVA is defined as the present value of the EVAs of prospective periods[1437] plus the NOA at time of assessment.[1438] Analogous to the DCF approach, the EVAs are discounted with the cost of capital.[1439]

Only if the expectations of capital market participants and the managers of a company totally correspond to each other, the external and internal way of calculation of MVA or

1432 Cf. Schmeisser, W., Rönsch, M., Zilch, I. (2009), p. 30.
1433 Cf. Schmeisser, W. (2010), p. 31; Stewart, G. B. (1999), p. 153.
1434 Cf. Gundel, T. (2012), pp. 40-42.
1435 Cf. Böcking, H.-J., Nowak, K. (1999), p. 288.
1436 Cf. Fackler, M., Wimschulte, J. (2009), p. 333.
1437 Cf. Camphausen, B. (2013), p. 171; Eilenberger, G., Ernst, D., Toebe, M. (2013), pp. 232-233.
1438 Cf. Dahlhaus, C. (2009), p. 188; Schmeisser, W., Rönsch, M., Zilch, I. (2009), p. 31.
1439 Cf. Camphausen, B. (2013), p. 171.

the ex-ante and ex post calculation will lead to identical results. Otherwise, the calculations lead to divergent results because each party is assuming other EVAs.[1440] The ex-ante calculation can be used to value stocks.[1441]

$$MVA = \sum_{t=1}^{n} \frac{EVA}{(1 + WACC)^t}$$

Source: Taken from: Langguth, H. (2008), p. 163
Formula 39: Ex ante calculation of MVA

From the market's point of view the MVA is the difference of market value of the company and the invested capital, NOA. Market value is defined as the sum of equity and debt capital. The market value of equity capital corresponds to the market capitalisation.[1442] The debt capital is often assessed on the basis of its book values.[1443] In this context the MVA is a kind of operational Goodwill because it is the additional value on the company's asset. The second method of MVA calculation is an ex post calculation so it is not suitable for forecasts.[1444]

$$MVA = Market\ value\ of\ capital - Invested\ Capital\ (NOA)$$

Source: Taken from: Fiordelisi, F., Molyneux, P. (2006), p. 60
Formula 40: Ex post calculation of MVA

The illustration below shows the two ways of calculation for MVA.

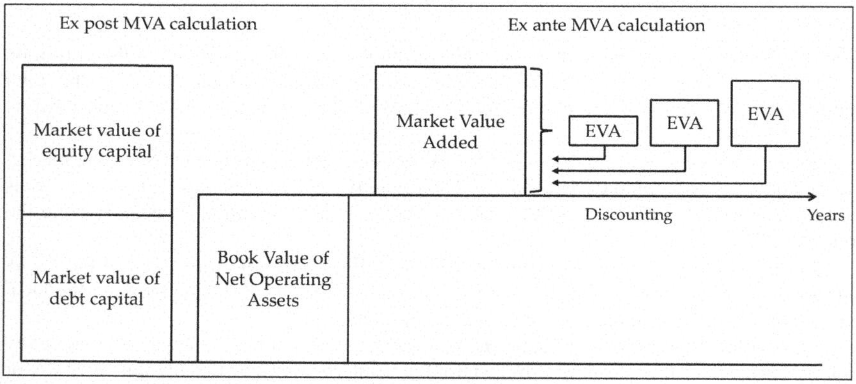

Source: In the style of: Britzelmaier, B. (2013), p. 145; Holler, A. (2009), p. 69
Illustration 15: Ex ante and ex post calculation of MVA

1440 Cf. Bausch, A., Buske, A., Hagemeier, W. (2011), p. 376.
1441 Cf. Holler, A. (2009), p. 69.
1442 Cf. Hahn, D., Hintze, M. (2006), p. 95; Holler, A. (2009), p. 68.
1443 Cf. Fackler, M., Wimschulte, J. (2009), p. 333; Hahn, D., Hintze, M. (2006), p. 95.
1444 Cf. Langguth, H. (2008), p. 164.

The objective of the company is to increase the MVA as high as possible.[1445] The MVA approach establishes a connection between the EVA and MVA approach and by this way a connection between EVA and corporate evaluation.[1446]

The NOA and NOPAT of future periods are computed on the basis of planned balance sheet and profit and loss statement values. Out of these two figures the future MVAs can be calculated.[1447] A detailed planning of future values is not necessary for every period but only for those EVAs which fall into the planning phase.[1448] The detailed planning period regularly covers a time period of 3 up to 5 years.[1449] The remaining EVAs are calculated with the mathematical construct of perpetuity. Often the EVA of the last planning period is assumed as constant and is the basis for the calculation of perpetuity.[1450]

With the help of variance analysis managers can use the MVA to identify the causes for a deviation between planned and actual values.[1451]

3.4.2.2 Evaluation

The connection between EVA and MVA facilitates internal communication and creates synergy effects between accounting and controlling because both key figures base on the same theoretical concept.[1452]

As illustrated in the context of the criteria for evaluation of performance measures, the consideration of several periods is important. The MVA fulfils this criterion because EVAs of several periods are included in this calculation.[1453] By this way, the MVA also considers the growth opportunities of a company in the future.[1454]

DCF and MVA approach both refer to several periods and have the objective to determine the value of a company. However, both approaches only lead to identical results under certain conditions. These conditions are the assumptions of the Preinreich-Lücke theorem.[1455]

The MVA calculated ex ante strongly depends on the planning premises and underlying assumptions which are used to estimate the EVAs of future periods.[1456]

In the context of corporate valuation it is problematic that the MVA is based on book values because this leads to distortions due to accounting policy.[1457] The quality of MVA strongly depends on the conversions conducted for calculating the capital figure NOA or the profit measure NOPAT.[1458] But despite the conversions distortions cannot be

1445 Cf. Fiordelisi, F., Molyneux, P. (2006), p. 61; Hahn, D., Hintze, M. (2006), p. 96; Stewart, G. B. (1999), p. 153.
1446 Cf. Junginger, M. (2005), p. 68; Stewart, G. B. (1999), p. 153.
1447 Cf. Stephan, J. (2006), p. 83; Zirkler, B. (2002), p. 103.
1448 Cf. Zirkler, B. (2002), p. 103.
1449 Cf. Fackler, M., Wimschulte, J. (2009), p. 332.
1450 Cf. Zirkler, B. (2002), p. 103.
1451 Cf. Zirkler, B. (2002), p. 103.
1452 Cf. Coenenberg, A. G., Salfeld, R. (2007), p. 265; Richter, F., Honold, D. (2000), p. 267.
1453 Cf. Stephan, J. (2006), p. 82.
1454 Cf. Ramezani, C. A., Soenen, L., Jung, A. (2002), p. 57.
1455 Cf. Nguyen, T., Romeike, F. (2013), p. 504; Stephan, J. (2006), pp. 83-88.
1456 Cf. Laier, R. (2011), p. 130, Schabel, M. M. (2004), p. 90.
1457 Cf. Coenenberg, A. G., Salfeld, R. (2007), p. 265.
1458 Cf. Böcking, H.-J., Nowak, K. (1999), p. 288; Fackler, M., Wimschulte, J. (2009), p. 332.

Table 12: Evaluation of MVA

Evaluation Criterion	MVA ex-ante	MVA ex post
Including of cost of capital	+	+
Data basis for calculation (Availability of data)	+ (bases on book values of past annual accounts and forecasts)	+ (bases on book values of annual accounts and market values)
Data basis for calculation (Quality of data)	0 (Book values)	– (Book and market values)
Present value of Money	+	+
Future Orientation	+	+
Considering risk	+ (included within calculation of WACC)	+ (included within calculation of WACC)
Simplicity	0 / – (depends on effort invested for forecasting EVA of future periods)	– (depends on calculation of invested capital which is difficult to compute for external persons)

Source: In style of: Fiedler, R., Gräf, J. (2012), p. 339

completely eliminated.[1459] A further problem resulting from using book values is that only companies with the same accounting standards can be compared.[1460]

Further influencing factors are variations on the stock market which limit the comparability of MVAs calculated at different points in time. This point of criticism only applies to the ex post MVA calculation because the stock prices are used to assess the market value of equity capital.[1461]

The reason why MVA is used only for determining company values and not for operational decisions or controlling management activities is that it can only be calculated for companies listed on stock markets. Beyond that fact it can only be calculated on the company level and not the level of single business units and consequently, it does not support managers in decision making.[1462]

Similar to the DCF approaches the MVA fulfills nearly all evaluation criteria. But also for key figures of this type a simple calculation is not possible.

1459 Cf. Nguyen, T., Romeike, F. (2013), pp. 504-505.
1460 Cf. Schabel, M. M. (2004), p. 90.
1461 Cf. Laier, R. (2011), p. 130; Ramezani, C. A., Soenen, L., Jung, A. (2002), p. 57.
1462 Cf. Fiordelisi, F., Molyneux, P. (2006), p. 61.

3.5 Overview of the Current State of Research

3.5.1 Application of Value Based Performance Measures in Europe

After analysing and assessing selected concepts of value based performance measures, this part of the chapter presents an overview of selected empirical studies. Before going into detail, it has to be mentioned that due to a huge diversity in samples and research methods it is difficult to simply transfer results to similar contexts or even generalise them.[1463]

This first part of the chapter deals with selected empirical studies which analyse the application of value based performance measures in practice. This comprises mainly two questions: Which companies give information about value based performance measures in their annual report and which kind of key figures do they use?[1464]

The analysis of empirical studies reveals three different research methods in order to get more information about the application of value based performance measures in practice. The first method is to send questionnaires to responsible managers,[1465] the second one is to conduct interviews[1466] and the third one is to analyse annual reports.[1467]

Horváth and Minning developed a questionnaire and determined the importance and extent of Value Based Management in Germany, Great Britain, France and Italy. This study is one of a few which analyses the disclosure behaviour on a cross-national level. The data base consists of two groups: The largest companies of a country, measured by market capitalisation and companies which are listed at the new markets and companies which have nearly completed their IPO.[1468]

One part of the questionnaire deals with the implemented key figures. The analysis of German companies reveals that within the group of the large companies as well as in the group of the new market companies the DCF method is widespread. Approximately half of the companies implement it. But the EVA method, which many of large companies apply, is only used in one company of the second group. The CFROI is implemented by approximately 30 % of the large companies and by approximately 15 % of companies of the new market group.[1469]

Also in the other countries the majority of companies use the EVA: 54 % of Italian companies, 43 % in France, 34 % in Germany and 14 % in Great Britain. A further insight is that regularly larger companies and continental European companies apply value based key figures. The EVA concept is more widespread than the CFROI concept. In all

1463 Cf. Ittner, C. D., Larcker, D. F. (2001), p. 357.

1464 Cf. exemplarily for extensive description of value based performance measure application in single companies Borchers, S. (2006); Haeger, B. (2006); Middelmann, U. (2001).

1465 Cf. exemplarily the empirical studies of Aders, C., Herbertinger, M., Schaffer, C., et al. (2003); Athanassakos, G. (2007); Horváth, P., Minning, F. (2001); Ryan, H. E., Trahan, E. A. (1999).

1466 Cf. exemplarily the empirical studies of Malmi, S., Ikäheimo, S. (2003); Weber, J. (2009).

1467 Cf. exemplarily the studies of Firk, S., Schrapp, S., Wolff, M. (2016); Gitt, N., Völl, W., Kettenring, T. (2013); Rapp, M. S., Schellong, D., Schmidt, M., et al. (2011); Schultze, W., Steeger, L., Schabert, B. (2009).

1468 Cf. Horváth, P., Minning, F. (2001), p. 274.

1469 Cf. Horváth, P., Minning, F. (2001), pp. 274-277.

countries many companies use the DCF method which can be seen as supplementary to the other concepts.[1470]

Malmi and Ikäheimo conducted interviews with managers of six selected Finish companies. Based on their interviews they want to examine the usage of Value Based Management and illustrate the differences between the selected companies.[1471] The interviewed companies nearly all use value based performance measures. But they implement them on different levels. Half of the companies calculate the performance measure at a group and divisional level, but not at the level of business units or below. Two companies also defined the performance measure at a business level. The application of value based performance measures does not lead to an abolishment of traditional key figures like ROI, net sales or net profit. They rather complement the already existing key figures. Some companies combine financial measures with non-financial ones. Finally, the authors conclude that introducing Value Based Management does not solve the problem of selecting and using different key figures.[1472]

Concerning target setting, some companies of the sample use traditional performance measures rather than value based ones. This is surprising insofar as they state that they introduce Value Based Management in their company. Other companies use EVA for target setting and combine it with other performance measures.[1473] In four of six companies the authors note a higher importance of the cost of capital which influences the operative decisions of these companies.[1474]

The reasons for introducing Value Based Management is mainly an increasing international competition and pressure from financial markets. Furthermore, the authors suppose that also the organisational power of responsible managers and the independence of divisions determine the adoption and the intensity of adoption of Value Based Management. But none of the six companies adopt Value Based Management in such an extent as it is described in scientific literature.[1475]

Schäffer and Lewerenz detect in the context of their empirical study that companies adapt the theoretical concepts to their needs. This means that companies simplify the method of calculation or develop value concepts and name them individually. Often the complexity of calculation is reduced so strongly that only the core concept remains, namely the profit after the deduction of capital costs.[1476] This insight corresponds to the results of the empirical study of Malmi and Ikäheimo which also detects that companies simplify the theoretical concepts of value based performance measures.[1477]

Rapp et al. takes as a sample 178 German companies from the stock indices DAX, MDAX, SDAX and TecDAX. The time period investigated is 2002-2008.[1478] The data source of the authors is the annual reports of the companies.[1479] Over the time period the number of companies which use value based performance measures increase. In 2002 26

1470 Cf. Horváth, P., Minning, F. (2001), pp. 277-281.
1471 Cf. Malmi, S., Ikäheimo, S. (2003), pp. 240-241.
1472 Cf. Malmi, S., Ikäheimo, S. (2003), p. 242.
1473 Cf. Malmi, S., Ikäheimo, S. (2003), p. 243.
1474 Cf. Malmi, S., Ikäheimo, S. (2003), p. 246.
1475 Cf. Malmi, S., Ikäheimo, S. (2003), pp. 248-250.
1476 Cf. Schäffer, U., Lewerenz, U. (2011), p. 298.
1477 Cf. Malmi, S., Ikäheimo, S. (2003), pp. 248-250.
1478 Cf. Rapp, M. S., Schellong, D., Schmidt, M., et al. (2011), pp. 176-177.
1479 Cf. Rapp, M. S., Schellong, D., Schmidt, M., et al. (2011), p. 178.

% of the sample firms published such a key figure in their annual report. In 2008 this share increases to 42 %. In 2008 87 % of all DAX companies publish a value based performance measure, while only 17 % of all TecDAX companies do so.[1480]

In line with further empirical studies the authors detect that companies with value based performance measures are larger than companies without these measures.[1481] Furthermore, companies with value based management systems have lower growth rates, are more diversified, have a higher leverage and a less concentrated ownership structure in comparison to non-adopters.[1482]

In contrast to other presented studies, the empirical study of Burkert and Lueg not only focuses on whether or not a company uses value based key figures. They investigate the influence of the CEO's and CFO's business-related education and tenure on the implementation and sophistication of Value Based Management.[1483] The managers' education describes their ability and willingness to understand accounting and financial data as well as their ability to structure, process and evaluate information. Tenure is the duration of their employment.[1484] The sample comprises of 52 companies listed in the German HDAX. The researchers do not rely solely on annual reports, they also conduct interviews with responsible managers in the companies.[1485]

The results show that the CEO's educational background does not correlate with Value Based Management sophistication. In contrast, the CFO's educational background has an influence on the sophistication. Concerning the tenure, the results are similar. A short tenure of a CFO has a positive correlation to the application of Value Based Management. But if a CFO has a profound education, the effect of a short tenure can be compensated. This also means that CFOs with a long tenure can foster the usage of Value Based Management if they have the necessary educational background. Also the perceived environmental uncertainty influences the application of Value Based Management. Environmental uncertainty means that there are no predictable changes in the external environment. They lead to a low reliability of Value Based Management because it is a management practice based on accounting figures which are predicted for a long period of time. The empirical study confirms that a high environmental uncertainty decreases the sophistication of Value Based Management.[1486]

Even if this study does not directly investigate value concepts of companies, it reveals company internal factors affecting the application of Value Based Management and therewith the application of value based performance measures.[1487]

Table thirteen illustrates publications which deal with the application of value based performance measures and summarises the most important insights.

1480 Cf. Rapp, M. S., Schellong, D., Schmidt, M., et al. (2011), pp. 180-181.
1481 Cf. confirmatory Gitt, N., Völl, W., Kettenring, T. (2013); Ryan, H. E., Trahan, E. A. (1999).
1482 Cf. Rapp, M. S., Schellong, D., Schmidt, M., et al. (2011), pp. 181-182.
1483 Cf. Burkert, M., Lueg, R. (2013), pp. 3-4.
1484 Cf. Burkert, M., Lueg, R. (2013), pp. 6-8.
1485 Cf. Burkert, M., Lueg, R. (2013), pp. 9-10.
1486 Cf. Burkert, M., Lueg, R. (2013), p. 12-17.
1487 Cf. Burkert, M., Lueg, R. (2013), p. 18.

Table 13: Overview of empirical studies dealing with the application of value based performance measures

Authors	**Year of Publication**	**Period investigated and Method**	**Results / Insights**
Ryan, H. E.; Trahan, E. A.	1999	Questionnaire based survey; first dispatch in November 1996; US-companies	– DCF is the most widespread method – Different performance measures are often combined. – Key figures are regularly implemented on a corporate level. – Application of VBM depends on size and profit margin of a company.
Horváth, P.; Minning, F.	2001	Questionnaire based survey; Companies in Great Britain, France, Italy and Germany, first dispatch: Not specified	– The DCF approaches and EVA approach are the mostly applied. – The EVA concept is more frequently used than the CFROI concept. – Value based performance measures are predominantly used by large and continental European companies.
Peixoto, S.	2002	Questionnaire base survey; Companies in Portugal; first dispatch: At the end of 1999	– Out of 32 surveyed companies 26 uses a DCF approach, 22 the CFROI concept, 28 apply the ROIC and 11 the EVA concept. – DCF, CFROI and EVA are mainly used for long-term planning and investment decisions. – The majority of companies implemented the key figures only on corporate level.
Ruhwedel, F.; Schultze, W.	2002	Analysis of business reports; Companies of the German DAX100 at 31.12.2000	– 47 % of DAX companies disclose the EVA or a similar key figure, 47 % compare the ROCE with capital costs and 12 % uses the CVA. – Clear differences exist concerning the publication behaviour between DAX and MDAX companies.
Aders, C.; Herbertinger, M.; Schaffer, C.; Wiedemann, F.	2003	Questionnaire based survey and analysis of business reports; German DAX100 at the 30.12.2002	– EVA and Value Added concepts are the most applied value based performance measures. – Companies conduct less adaption of result or profit figure than suggested in literature. – In most cases companies implementted value based performance measures only on a corporate level.

Authors	**Year of Publication**	**Period investigated and Method**	**Results / Insights**
Malmi, T.; Ikäheimo, S.	2003	Interview based survey with managers of six Finnish companies, point of time: Not specified	– Value based performance measures are mainly implemented on group and divisional level of companies, but not on lower levels. – Value based performance measures supplement traditional key figures and do not replace them. – Main reasons for introducing VBM are pressure from financial markets and increasing international competition. – None of the companies implemented VBM to the extent suggested in literature.
Fischer, T. M.; Rödl, K.	2005	Analysis of annual reports of the DAX companies of the year 2000	– 60 % of DAX companies give information about a value based performance measure. – Relative and absolute key figures on the basis of earnings dominate. – Cash Flow based key figures are only applied rarely. – Calculation is often not comprehensible and not standardised.
Athanassakos, G.	2007	Questionnaire based survey; 39 Canadian companies; first dispatch: March 2000	– ROIC and DCF are the most widespread methods – Only 24 % of EVA users are satisfied with this method. – Large companies, companies in low-risk and low-growth industries and companies with young and high educated top-managers tend to implement VBM methods.
Schultze, W.; Steeger, L.; Schabert, B.	2009	Analysis of business reports of the 100 largest companies in Germany; time span: 2000 – 2005	– Large differences between the application of VBM between DAX and Non-DAX companies. – Cash Flow based performance measures are only used by a minority of companies. – Companies prefer key figures which are based on EVA or Value Added concepts.

Authors	**Year of Publication**	**Period investigated and Method**	**Results / Insights**
Weber, J.	2009	Interviews with 26 head of controlling of DAX companies; point of time: March 2005 – September 2006	– Over 90 % of interviewed companies use value based performance measures. – Differences concerning the kind and the number of value based key figures. – Managers state that the complexity of value based performance measures exacerbates their application. – Majority of managers assess VBM critically.
Arbeitskreis Internes Rechnungswesen	2010	Analysis of VBM systems of BASF, RWE, VW and Bosch	– Figures for calculating the capital base are derived from the IFRS balance sheet. – All four companies determine nearly the same interest-free capital components which are deducted from the capital base. – Inconsistencies in the procedure concerning the calculation of key figures before tax or after tax.
Günther, T.; Gonschorek, T.	2011	Questionnaire based survey; 307 medium-sized German companies, first dispatch: Not specified	– VBM has a high importance for the companies, but – Value based performance measures are only in 38 % of companies of the sample applied.
Laier, R.	2011	Analysis of annual reports of DAX companies for fiscal year 2008	– 50 % of DAX companies report intensively about VBM. – The Value Reporting of the remaining 50 % is in need of improvement. – 20 of 30 companies published a value based performance measure.
Schäffer,U.; Lewerenz, U.	2011	Analysis and comparison of annual reports of DAX companies in 2004 and 2009	– In 2004 17 of 30 companies use value based performance measures. – In 2009 16 of 30 companies use value based performance measures. – Majority uses key figures which base on EVA or Value Added concepts. – Companies adopt the calculation of key figures to their individual needs.

Authors	Year of Publication	Period investigated and Method	Results / Insights
Rapp, M. S.; Schellong, D.; Schmidt, M.; Wolff, M.	2011	178 German companies form the stock indices DAX, MDAX, SDAX and TecDAX in the time span 2002 - 2008	– In 2002 26 % of companies disclose value based performance measures in their annual report. – In 2008 the share increases to 42 %. – 87 % of all DAX companies publish a value based performance measure, but only 17 % of TecDAX companies.
Quick, R.	2012	Analysis of annual reports of DAX, MDAX, TecDAX and SDAX companies, time span: 2006-2008	– Nearly all DAX companies publish a value based performance measure. – The share of such companies is decreasing from the DAX to MDAX, SDAX and TecDAX. – Publication of key figure depends on different factors: The share index, the extent of turnover, the size, the liquidity situation and the leverage ratio.
Burkert, M.; Lueg, M.	2013	Analysis of annual reports and interviews with 52 managers of companies in the German HDAX	– CFO's educational background and tenure influence the sophistication of VBM. The larger both factors, the higher the probability of applying VBM instruments and methods. – In contrast high environmental uncertainty decreases the sophistication of VBM.
Gitt, N.; Völl, W.; Kettenring, T.	2013	Analysis of annual reports of 110 DAX, MDAX and TecDAX companies; time span: 2007 - 2010	– 2007: 38 % disclose a value based performance measure. – 2010: 46 % disclose such a key figure. – Reason for increase is the financial crisis. – Larger companies and companies in capital-intensive industries use more often value based performance measures. – Most widespread key figures base on EVA or Value Added concepts. – Only three companies use the CVA or CFROI concept.

Authors	Year of Publication	Period investigated and Method	Results / Insights
Firk, S.; Schrapp, S.; Wolff, M.	2016	Analysis of annual reports of MSCI Europe and S&P 500 companies; time span: 2005 - 2010	– Highest application rate of value based performance measures in Germany. – Implementation rates vary between countries throughout Europe. – Slightly decreasing implementation rates during the time span of investigation.
Firk, S.; Schrapp, S.; Wolff, M.	2018	Analysis of a sample of European companies on the basis of the STOXX Europe Total Market Index; time span: 2005-2014	– Capital-intense and diversified companies benefit stronger than other companies from implementing VBM systems. – Instiutional investors positively influence the adoption of VBM.

Source: Own table

On the basis of the selected articles the main insights for the application of value based performance measures are summarised in the following:

- More companies use value based concepts and publish them in their annual reports today in comparison to the beginning of the century.[1488]
- The majority of companies use the EVA, DCF or Value Added.[1489]
- Cash Flow based concepts are only applied by a small number of companies.[1490]
- Many companies adapt the theoretical concepts to their needs or simplify them.[1491]
- In tendency, larger companies use more probable a value based performance measure.[1492]
- Also the characteristics of top management, especially the CFO, influence, if a company uses value based management methods.[1493]
- Mainly value based performance measures are implemented only on a corporate level and not on a segment level.[1494]
- The number of studies which analyse the disclosure behaviour on a cross-national basis is rare.[1495]

1488 Cf. Gitt, N., Völl, W., Kettenring, T. (2013), pp. 101-102; Rapp, M. S., Schellong, D., Schmidt, M., et al. (2011), pp. 180-181.

1489 Cf. Ryan, H. E., Trahan, E. A. (1999), pp. 48-51; Horváth, P., Minning, F. (2001), pp. 274-281; Schäffer, U., Lewerenz, U. (2011), pp. 297-298.

1490 Cf. Gitt, N., Völl, W., Kettenring, T. (2013), pp. 103-106; Ruhwedel, F., Schultze, W. (2002), p. 621.

1491 Cf. Aders, C., Herbertinger, M., Schaffer, C., et al. (2003), p. 721; Schäffer, U., Lewerenz, U. (2011), pp. 298.

1492 Cf. Athanassakos, G. (2007), pp. 1405-1410; Gitt, N., Völl, W., Kettenring, T. (2013), pp. 102-103; Horváth, P., Minning, F. (2001), pp. 277-281; Quick, R. (2012), pp. 248-249.

1493 Cf. Athanassakos, G. (2007), pp. 1405-1410; Burkert, M., Lueg, R. (2013), p. 18.

1494 Cf. Athanassakos, G. (2007), pp. 1401-1402; Peixoto, S. (2002), p. 9.

3.5.2 Classification of Studies Analysing Value Relevance of Key Figures

3.5.2.1 Objectives and Assumptions of Capital Market Research

One purpose of capital market research is to analyse, if accounting numbers contain information that investors use for determining Shareholder Value of a company[1496] and if the theoretically assumed relation between an accounting number and market value can be proved empirically.[1497] Apart from this aspect capital market research in accounting offers further topics of investigation like properties of analysts' forcecasts or test of market efficiency.[1498] The object of investigation is not single investors but instead the cumulative decisions of all market participants. The reaction of the capital market on disclosed information is assessed by using stock prices or returns which is the result of every single market participants' decision process.[1499] In other words: The stock price is a summary of investors' belief and reflects their assessment of the company and their expectations concerning the prospective development.[1500]

With respect to the presented actors on capital markets these studies focus on shareholders because their assessment of a company is directly reflected in the stock price. Statements for other capital market participants like information intermediaries cannot be made on the basis of these studies.[1501]

Furthermore, all studies imply a capital market equilibrium and do not further analyse in what way the formation of prices happens on the selected capital market.[1502] The first types of modern studies to which many later publications refer are published by Ball and Brown[1503] as well as by Beaver.[1504]

An accounting number is value relevant if it has an association with equity market values.[1505] The higher the value relevance of accounting numbers, the less investors have to analyse further information sources in order to receive the necessary information for their investment decision.[1506]

Value relevance is a term within the context of academic research. It is a construct to operationalise the criteria faithful presentation and relevance of the IFRS framework.[1507]

1495 Out of the analysed studies only Horváth, P., Minning, F. (2001) and Firk, S., Schrapp, S., Wolff, M. (2016) conduct a cross-national analysis.

1496 Cf. Barth, M. E., Beaver, W. H., Landsman, W. R. (2001), p. 78.

1497 Cf. Beaver, W. H. (2002), pp. 463-464.

1498 Cf. extensively for fields of capital market research and an overview of empirical studies Kothari, S. P. (2001).

1499 Cf. Bogajewskaja, J. (2007), p. 106.

1500 Cf. Barth, M. E. (2000), pp. 10-11; Barth, M. E., Beaver, W. H., Landsman, W. R. (2001), pp. 94-95.

1501 Cf. Schloemer, M. (2003), pp. 13-14.

1502 Cf. Barth, M. E., Beaver, W. H., Landsman, W. R. (2001), p. 82.

1503 Cf. extensively Ball, R., Brown, P. (1968).

1504 Cf. extensively Beaver, W. H. (1968).

1505 Cf. Barth, M. E., Beaver, W. H., Landsman, W. R. (2001), p. 79; Beaver, W. H. (2002), p. 459; Elbakry, A. E., Nwachukwu, J. C., Abdou, H. A., et al. (2017), p. 11; Rautiainen, A., Sippola, K., Mättö, T. (2017), p. 21.

1506 Cf. Clarkson, P., Hanna, J. D., Richardson, G. D., et al. (2011), p. 2.

1507 Cf. Barth, M. E., Beaver, W. H., Landsman, W. R. (2001), p. 80 who originally refer to the FASB framework. But the two named criteria are also fundamental characteristics of the IFRS framework, cf. Wagenhofer, A., Ewert, R. (2015), p. 118.

An accounting number is only value relevant if investors use this information[1508] and if the accounting number is measured free from errors and distortions.[1509] In the context of value relevance studies it is not possible to analyse separately the criteria of faithful presentation and relevance.[1510]

Value relevance studies do not investigate the decision usefulness criterion which is the overarching principle of IFRS accounting. In other words: It is not analysed if investors actually use the information for their investment decisions or if they fall back on other information sources.[1511]

The argumentation that underpins the necessity of analysing value relevance and explaining the link between an earning accounting number and stock prices consists of three steps: Firstly, current earnings contain information about future earnings. They are the basis for the forecast of prospective earnings for shareholders and are used to create expectations about the prospective development of earnings. Secondly, the current and forecasted profitability of a company determines its ability to pay dividends in future periods. Thirdly, the current share price includes as a present value these expected future dividends. Consequently, a disclosure of new earning information should change investors' expectation about future dividends which in turn leads to a change of the share price. So, information about profitability facilitates the prediction of future dividends and possible stock price developments.[1512]

On the basis of the illustrated coherence it is obvious that the degree of market efficiency is a decisive factor when having a look at value relevance.[1513]

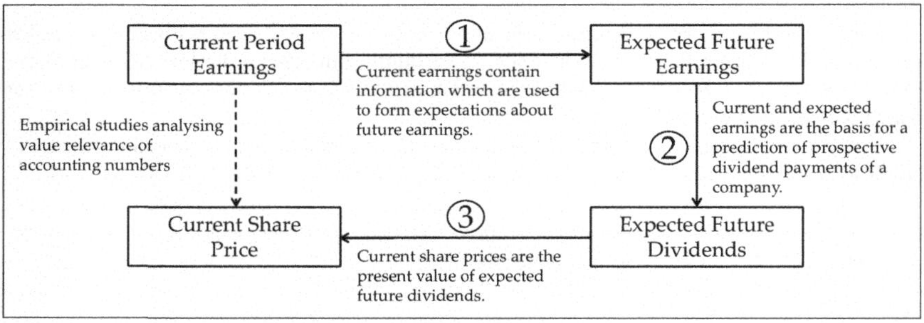

Source: Taken from: Nichols, D. C.; Wahlen, J. M. (2004), p. 266

Illustration 16: Links between earning numbers and stock prices

1508 Cf. IFRS Foundation (2016), Conceptual Framework QC 6, QC 7.

1509 Cf. IFRS Foundation (2016), Conceptual Framework QC 12.

1510 Cf. Barth, M. E. (2000), p. 17; Barth, M. E., Beaver, W. H., Landsman, W. R. (2001), p. 81; Wagenhofer, A., Dücker, H. (2007), p. 279.

1511 Cf. Barth, M. E., Beaver, W. H., Landsman, W. R. (2001), p. 80.

1512 Cf. Nichols, D. C., Wahlen, J. M. (2004), pp. 265-267; cf. for similar argumentation Lev, B. (1989), pp. 156-158.

1513 Cf. Möller, H. P., Hüfner, B. (2002), p. 407.

Capital market research is relevant for a broad audience. Beside other academics results of studies could be relevant for standards setters like the IASB and all capital market participants and information intermediaries which use accounting as a source of information.[1514] As all capital market participants use more or less accounting data for their investment decision as one source of information, results of such studies are relevant for them.[1515] Although insights from these studies might be relevant for standard setters, it is not the objective of value relevance studies to give direct recommendations concerning the designing of standards. The empirical studies base on certain assumptions which do not capture all aspects of reality.[1516] Rather more researchers aim to point out certain issues which then can be discussed by standard setters on the basis of the insights of an empirical study.[1517]

It is also important to delineate value relevance studies from corporate evaluation. It is not the aim to calculate company's value but instead to focus on selected accounting values and their influence on the market value of equity capital.[1518]

3.5.2.2 Capital Market Research Approaches

The studies can be classified into different approaches which are summarised in illustration 17.[1519]

Forecast relevance studies deal with the ability of accounting information to improve the forecast of investors concerning future profits, development of stock prices or further measures.[1520]

Decision relevance analyses if accounting information influences and change investment decisions of capital market participants.[1521] The typical form of studies are event studies which try to determine stock price reactions during disclosure of the selected information.[1522] The information content approach and valuation relevance approach can be allocated to this category. Information content studies are based on event studies structured like Beaver's event study.[1523] The decisions relevance is determined with the

1514 Cf. Barth, M. E., Beaver, W. H., Landsman, W. R. (2001), pp. 86-88.

1515 Cf. Lindemann, J. (2006), p. 968; cf. chapter 2.3.2.2.

1516 Cf. Barth, M. E., Beaver, W. H., Landsman, W. R. (2001), p. 88.

1517 Cf. Barth, M. E. (2000), pp. 8-9.

1518 Cf. Barth, M. E., Beaver, W. H., Landsman, W. R. (2001), p. 90.

1519 The following classification of accounting studies bases on Lo, K., Lys, T. Z. (2001) and Möller, H. P., Hüfner, B. (2002); cf. for a similar classification Dumontier, P., Raffournier, B. (2002), p. 120; cf. also for an overview Coenenberg, A. G., Haller, A., Schultze, W. (2014), pp. 1317-1334; Lindemann, J. (2004), pp. 107-140; Schloemer, M. (2003), pp. 15-21; Schmidt, M. (2005), pp. 99-115; cf. for different classification schemes: Holthausen, R. W., Watts, R. L. (2001) or Vorstius, S. (2004), pp. 121-126.

1520 Cf. Lindemann, J. (2006), pp. 969-970; Möller, H. P., Hüfner, B. (2002), pp. 412-413; examples for tools are discriminant analysis or artificial neural network for forecast of insolvencies, cf. therefore extensively Baetge, J., Kirsch, H.-J., Thiele, S. (2004), pp. 535-590.

1521 Cf. Möller, H. P., Hüfner, B. (2002), pp. 413-415; Rautiainen, A., Sippola, K., Mättö, T. (2017), p. 21.

1522 Cf. Kothari, S. P. (2001), p. 116; Lindemann, J. (2006), p. 970; Hüfner, B., Möller, H. P. (2002), pp. 142-143; cf. extensively for possible methodologies for event studies Brown, S. J., Warner, J. B. (1980).

1523 Cf. Kothari, S. P. (2001), p. 116; for the basic empirical study Beaver, W. H. (1968).

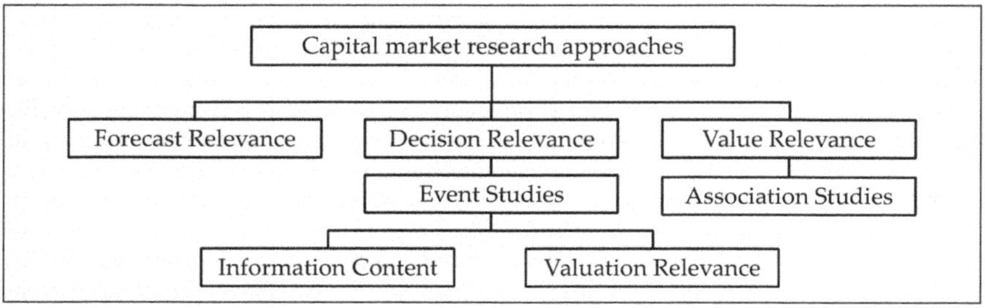

Source: In the style of: Lindemann, J. (2006), p. 970
Illustration 17: Overview of capital market research approaches

help of the extent of the stock price reaction at the point of disclosure of the accounting information independent from the direction of stock price movement.[1524] These studies can consider an amount of information, e.g. the publication of annual reports.[1525]

In contrast, valuation relevance studies investigate single accounting numbers.[1526] They focus on stock price reactions if accounting values derivate from the value capital market participants expected. In these studies the direction of stock price movements is considered. The basis for these studies is the publication of Ball and Brown.[1527]

Value relevance studies investigate the explanatory power of accounting information for stock prices or returns. In this case association studies aim to determine a correlation between the accounting information and a capital market measure.[1528] These studies want to determine to what extent accounting data can explain market values[1529] and analyse what is the contribution of accounting data for determining the fundamental value of a company.[1530] The underlying assumption is that accounting data is more informative if it has a higher association with stock prices[1531] and is able to capture most of the events included in stock prices.[1532] However, these studies do not assume that accounting information is the only source of information for investors. It is obvious that there are other more timely sources of information which investors can use.[1533]

Association studies do not deliver insights about the newness of information at time of disclosure[1534] or if investors actually use the accounting information.[1535] Thus, it is not

1524 Cf. Lo, K., Lys, T. Z. (2001), pp. 3-5.
1525 Cf. Lindemann, J. (2004), pp. 107-108.
1526 Cf. Lindemann, J. (2004), p. 108.
1527 Cf. Lo, K., Lys, T. Z. (2001), pp. 5-6; Möller, H. P., Hüfner, B. (2002); cf. also for this type of studies Ball, R., Brown, P. (1968).
1528 Cf. Lindemann, J. (2006), pp. 970-971; Lo, K., Lys, T. Z. (2001), pp. 6-7; cf. extensively for information about association studies Dumontier, P., Raffournier, B. (2002), pp. 128-131.
1529 Cf. Lindemann, J. (2006), p. 968; Möller, H. P., Hüfner, B. (2002), p. 415.
1530 Cf. Coenenberg, A. G., Haller, A., Schultze, W. (2014), p. 1325; Mölls, S. H., Strauß, M. (2007), pp. 957-958.
1531 Cf. Lang, M., Smith Raedy, J., Wilson, W. (2006), p. 264.
1532 Cf. Mölls, S. H., Strauß, M. (2007), p. 958.
1533 Cf. Kothari, S. P. (2001), p. 116.
1534 Cf. Beaver, W. H. (2002), p. 460.
1535 Cf. Lindemann, J. (2006), pp. 970-971; Mölls, S. H., Strauß, M. (2007), p. 958.

possible to draw conclusions with respect to causality between disclosure of an accounting number and a stock price.[1536]

In the context of association studies it has to be considered that accounting values will only be able to explain partly the stock prices because there is a time lag between accounting values and stock prices. Events which have been observed and assessed by the market in a prior period can influence the accounting values of the current period or events observed and assessed by the market in the current period do not influence the accounting values of this period.[1537] Beside the time lag of processing information, many other factors influence the market values.[1538]

So, much accounting information is anticipated by these other sources of information and consequently accounting information loses relevance. This argumentation alone is incomplete because it does not consider the cost of obtaining and getting access to these other information sources. Accounting information is relatively easy available.[1539] In the case that other information is available, the analysis of accounting information is still relevant and worthwhile because accounting information summarises information precisely so that it still can be analysed how well they fulfil this function for market participants.[1540]

A further criterion to divide studies is the analysed time horizon. Two kinds of measurement windows for capital market research exist: short and long term windows studies. Short window studies use daily or weekly capital market data while long term window studies are based commonly on annual periods. Event studies use a short window measuring the capital market number around the analysed event. Association studies are long term window studies.[1541]

3.5.2.3 Types of Statistical Tests for Determining Value Relevance

In the context of value relevance studies two types of value relevance respectively information content of key figures can be analysed: Relative information content and incremental information content.[1542] Relative information content studies deal with the question which key figure alone contains the greatest information content. So, it is a comparison between the explanatory power of single key figures.[1543] Incremental information content studies attempt to evaluate if a combination of key figures provides more information than a single key figure.[1544]

Studies which deal with relative information content can have three possible results which are illustrated below.

1536 Cf. Kothari, S. P. (2001), p. 116; Lo, K., Lys, T. Z. (2001), p. 12.
1537 Cf. Easton, P. D. (1999), pp. 400-401; Paulo, S. (2002), pp. 503-505.
1538 Cf. Lindemann, J. (2006), pp. 978-979.
1539 Cf. Beaver, W. H. (2002), pp. 460-462.
1540 Cf. Beaver, W. H. (2002), pp. 460-462; Collins, D. W., Kothari, S. P. (1989), p. 144.
1541 Cf. Bartov, E., Goldberg, S. R., Kim, M. (2005), p. 105; Lo, K., Lys, T. Z. (2001), pp. 15-16.
1542 Cf. basically for the differentiation between those two terms Biddle, G. C., Seow, G. S., Siegel, A. F. (1995).
1543 Cf. Biddle, G. C., Seow, G. S., Siegel, A. F. (1995), pp. 3-5.
1544 Cf. Biddle, G. C., Seow, G. S., Siegel, A. F. (1995), pp. 3-5; Francis, R. N. (2010), p. 836.

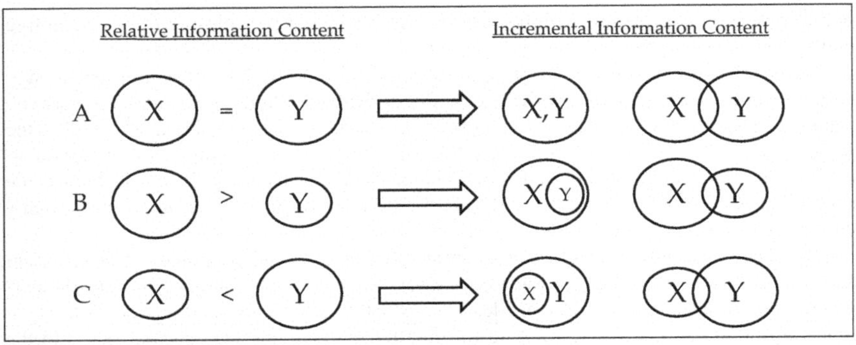

Source: In the style of: Biddle, G. C., Seow, G. S., Siegel, A. F. (1995), p. 4
Illustration 18: Differentiation between relative and incremental information content

Both key figures have the same level of relative information content, key figure X has a greater explanatory power than key figure Y or vice versa. These scenarios are named as A, B and C in the illustration. The areas covered by the circle represent the information content explained by the variables X and Y. Depending on the relative information content, the results for incremental information content are predefined. In the first scenario, A, both key figures can have a higher information content than key figures X or Y alone or the combination of the key figures does not deliver additional explanatory power. In scenario B it is only possible that key figure X has higher incremental information content than key figures X and Y together or both key figures have higher explanatory power than key figure X alone. In the third scenario the roles of key figures X and Y are exchanged.[1545]

3.5.3 *Value Relevance of Traditional and Value Based Performance Measures*

In recent years many scientific articles concerning the metric war have been published. Nearly all of the articles use the statistical method of the regression analysis in order to determine and compare the value relevance of selected key figures. In order to exemplarily demonstrate the contradicting results and different opinions of authors, some articles and their results are summarised in the following paragraphs.

Biddle, Bowen and Wallace conduct a comparative analysis of four key figures, EVA, residual income, net income before extraordinary items and Cash Flow from Operations, regarding their explanatory power of annual stock returns. Furthermore, they investigate the incremental information content of the single components of EVA. Their sample contains 773 firms. The investigation period is 1984–1993.[1546]

The dependent variable is market adjusted return, defined as the difference between a company's 12-month stock return and the 12-month market-wide return. Independent variables are the listed key figures.[1547]

1545 Cf. Biddle, G. C., Seow, G. S., Siegel, A. F. (1995), pp. 3-5.
1546 Cf. Biddle, G. C., Bowen, R. M., Wallace, J. S. (1997), pp. 307-311.
1547 Cf. Biddle, G. C., Bowen, R. M., Wallace, J. S. (1997), pp. 312-316.

The regression analysis shows that net income has the highest coefficient of determination with 12.8 %, followed by residual income (R^2 = 7.3 %), EVA (R^2 = 6.5 %) and Cash Flow from Operations (R^2 = 2.8 %). The authors conduct a second regression analysis with a panel in which they divide independent variables in positive and negative values. Considering prior empirical results, the explanatory power of accounting measures could vary with their sign. Although the second panel shows different coefficients of determination, the ranking of key figures remains unchanged.[1548]

Concerning the incremental information content of the single EVA components, the regression analysis shows that they contain little additional information which is not already included in net income before extraordinary items.[1549]

In the following, the authors extend their empirical study and modify the parameters of the regression analysis e.g. divide the sample into sub-periods, change the market adjusted returns calculation to a 24-month period. None of the modifications changes the summarised results above clearly so that the authors cannot support the claimed superiority of EVA.[1550]

Günther, Landrock and Muche compare the explanatory power of traditional performance measures, namely Return on Sales, Return on Equity and Return on Investment with the explanatory power of value based performance measures, EVA, CVA, DCF and Tobin's Q. As a database they chose 36 companies from the German DAX and MDAX in the time period 1989 – 1996.[1551]

As variables for the capital market development in their correlation analysis the authors chose the Total Shareholder Return for equity-based key figures and the Total Business Return for total capital based key figures. The Total Business Return is a calculated average return for all capital providers. It contains the Total Shareholder Return as the return for equity capital providers. The return of debt capital providers is the company's cost of debt capital. In order to compare the results for company of different sizes, all absolute key figures are divided by the invested capital.[1552]

As a result of their correlation analysis, the traditional performance measures explain in the long run the capital market development of companies significantly better than the value based performance measures. However, in the short run the value based performance measures EVA, CVA and DCF have higher R^2.[1553]

In total, the authors do not find a superior key figure or a superior category. Neither the traditional nor the value based performance key figures could explain completely the capital market development. But it is surprising that the traditional key figures have relatively high correlations. A reason for this could be that financial analysts use these key figures and therefore influence the stock price.[1554]

Schremper and Pälchen analyse the capital market relevance of traditional key figures as well as of value based performance measures. As dependent variables in their regression model they chose the Total Shareholder Return for equity-based key figures and the

1548 Cf. Biddle, G. C., Bowen, R. M., Wallace, J. S. (1997), pp. 316-318.
1549 Cf. Biddle, G. C., Bowen, R. M., Wallace, J. S. (1997), pp. 318-320.
1550 Cf. Biddle, G. C., Bowen, R. M., Wallace, J. S. (1997), pp. 330-331.
1551 Cf. Günther, T., Landrock, B., Muche, T. (2000a), pp. 129-130.
1552 Cf. Günther, T., Landrock, B., Muche, T. (2000b), p. 74.
1553 Cf. Günther, T., Landrock, B., Muche, T. (2000a), pp. 130-131.
1554 Cf. Günther, T., Landrock, B., Muche, T. (2000a), pp. 133.

Total Business Return for total capital based key figures. Analysed key figures are e.g. return on turnover, return on equity, two kinds of Cash Flow returns, Value Added, Delta-EVA or Delta-CVA. The S&P 400 is the data base for the empirical study. The data is analysed in the period between 1987 and 1998. The regression analysis is conducted for the periods of one, five and ten years.[1555]

The traditional key figures attain middle coefficients of determination. The key figure profit growth shows the highest capital market relevance, followed by turnover growth, return on capital and return on equity. The value based performance measures attain mostly similar coefficients of determination. The relative value added and the delta Cash Value Added have the highest values. Key figures based on the EVA concept have significantly lower results.[1556]

Based on the statistical results the authors draw two conclusions: Firstly, the value based performance measures are not superior to the traditional key figures. Secondly, it is not possible to identify a single superior key figure. In the analysis of the short period (five years) the CVA key figures are superior to the traditional key figures and in the long period (ten years) it is vice versa. But in total, the ranking of key figures does not change significantly dependent on the length of investigation period.[1557]

Worthington and West conduct a regression analysis in order to investigate the statistical explanatory power of earnings before extraordinary items, net cash flow from operations, residual income and EVA for Australian companies. The dependent variable is the annual stock return of a company. The independent variables are the above mentioned key figures. Their database are 110 Australian publicly listed companies in the period between 1992 and 1998.[1558]

EVA explains the stock returns best, followed by residual income, earnings before extraordinary items and net cash flow from operations. These results contradicts the results of Biddle, Bowen and Wallace. So, in contrast, Worthing and West show a high explanatory power of EVA.[1559]

As these results differ from other studies, the authors assume two reasons for the differences: At first, the differences between US GAAP and Australian GAAP might lead to different statistical results. Secondly, the differences in the design of the statistical analysis lead to different results, as in comparison to Biddle, Bowen and Wallace the variables are defined in a different way.[1560]

O'Byrne comes to similar results as Worthington and West. According to his results EVA explains the variation of market values better than NOPAT or FCF. His explanation for differences between the studies are conceptual mistakes within the structure of these studies.[1561]

Siebrecht, Heidorn and Klein focus on European companies. Their main findings are that positive EVA can better explain stock market performance better than negative

1555 Cf. Schremper, R., Pälchen Oliver (2001), pp. 546-549.
1556 Cf. Schremper, R., Pälchen Oliver (2001), pp. 549-554.
1557 Cf. Schremper, R., Pälchen Oliver (2001), pp. 550, 552, 555.
1558 Cf. Worthington, A. C., West, T. (2004), pp. 203-208.
1559 Cf. Worthington, A. C., West, T. (2004), pp. 214-215.
1560 Cf. Worthington, A. C., West, T. (2004), pp. 220-221.
1561 Cf. O'Byrne, S. F. (1997), p. 54.

ones,[1562] the explanatory power of EVA is higher for shorter time periods[1563] and that the EVA is not the appropriate key figure for companies in volatile industries.[1564]

Table fourteen summarises the results of the analysed articles and gives an overview of the current state of research concerning value relevance of key figures.

Table 14: Results of analysis of value relevance studies[1565]

Authors	Year of Publication	Source of data and data basis	Results / Insights
Biddle, G.; Bowen, R.; Wallace, J. S.	1997[1566]	Stern Stewart Performance 1000 database for the period 1984 - 1993	– Earnings outperform EVA. – The single components of EVA do not have economically relevant explanatory power.
O'Byrne, S. F.	1997	Stern Stewart Performance 1000 database for the period 1985 - 1993	– EVA explains changes in market value better than NOPAT or FCF. – Other studies have conceptual weaknesses.
Bacidore, J. M. et al.	1997	600 companies out of Stern Stewart 1000 database for the period 1982 - 1992	– Development of REVA as an improvement of EVA (a company's asset are calculated on the basis of market values). – REVA has a higher statistical expressiveness than EVA.
Bao, B.-H.; Bao, D.-H.[1567]	1998	Compustat, 166 companies in the years 1992 and 1993	– The authors cannot confirm the claimed superiority of EVA. – Value Added as the sum of profit, depreciation, wages, interest, dividends and taxes have the highest value relevance.
Ferguson, R.; Leistikow, D.	1998		– Reaction to the article of Bacidore, J. M. et al. – Criticism of the regression model and illustrated superiority of REVA over EVA.
Stark, A. W.; Thomas, H. M.	1998	Firms listed on the London Stock Exchange in the period from 1990 to 1994	– Residual Income has a stronger association with stock market development than earnings in conjunction with opening and closing book values and Research & Development expenditures.

1562 Cf. Siebrecht, F., Heidorn, T., Klein, H.-D. (2001), pp. 562-563.
1563 Cf. Siebrecht, F., Heidorn, T., Klein, H.-D. (2001), p. 563.
1564 Cf. Siebrecht, F., Heidorn, T., Klein, H.-D. (2001), pp. 563-564.
1565 Cf. also for an overview of empirical studies Ittner, C. D., Larcker, D. F. (2001), pp. 358-362.
1566 Cf. also Biddle, G. C., Bowen, R. M., Wallace, J. S. (1999). In this article the authors also present the most decisive results of their study.
1567 Cf. Bao, B.-H., Bao, D.-H. (1998).

Authors	**Year of Publication**	**Source of data and data basis**	**Results / Insights**
Garvey, G. T.; Milbourn, T. T.	2000	Compustat, CRSP, Stern Stewart Performance 1000, Approximately 540 companies in the time period 1978 - 1997	– EVA adoption should depend on the value relevance of the key figure for an individual company. – EVA does not deliver additional or only little additional information to companies. – Only a coherence between capital intensity and EVA adoption can be proved.
Günther, T.; Landrock, B.; Muche, T.	2000	36 companies of DAX and MDAX for the period 1989-1996	– Traditional performance measures have a higher explanatory power in the long run (8 years); value based ones in the short run (5 years). – A superior key figure cannot be detected.
Chen, S.; Dodd J. L.	2001	Stern Stewart 1,000 database and Compustat	– Operating income has the highest value relevance, followed by residual income and EVA. – Residual income and EVA provide additional incremental information in comparison to operating income.
Siebrecht, F.; Heidorn, T.; Klein, H.-D.	2001	Deutsche Bank Equity Research, 91 European companies in the time period 1992 - 2000	– Positive EVAs have a higher explanatory power than negative ones. – EVAs can better explain stock market performance of shorter periods. – EVA should not be used in volatile industries.
Schremper, R.; Pälchen, O.	2001	Companies of S&P 400 for the period 1987 - 1998	– Traditional and value based performance measures have nearly the same value relevance. – Ranking of key figures does not change over time. – EVA-based key figures have a low capital market relevance.
Machuga, S. M.; Pfeiffer, R. J.; Verma, K.[1568]	2002	Stern Stewart 1,000 database and Compustat; 232-362 firms per year in the period 1981-1996	– EVA adjustments have a high explanatory power in order to predict future EPS changes.
Lovata, L. M.,Costigan, M. L.	2002	LexisNexis and Compustat 115 US-companies adopting EVA	– Features of companies implementing EVA are a high concentration of institutional ownership and a cost-leadership strategy.

1568 Cf. Machuga, S. M., Pfeiffer, R. J., Verma, K. (2002).

Authors	Year of Publication	Source of data and data basis	Results / Insights
Paulo, S.	2002		– Comment to Chen and Dodd. – Critics on theoretical conception of EVA. – In general, accounting data have a declining value relevance.
Peixoto, S.	2002	39 Portuguese companies for the period 1995-1998	– Net income has a higher explanatory power than operating income and EVA. – EVA has a high value relevance if the company value is expressed by MVA.
Sparling, D.; Turvey, C. G.[1569]	2003	33 food companies of the Stern Stewart EVA database in the year 2000	– Only weak correlation between EVA and share performance on 3-, 5- and 10-year basis. – Same results apply for the correlation between changes in EVA and share performance.
Nichols, D. C.; Wahlen, J. M.[1570]	2004	Selected companies from NYSE, AMEX and NASDAQ	– The sign of annual earnings changes can better explain stock returns than changes in Cash Flow from Operations do.
Worthington, A. C., West, T.	2004	Australia's largest publicly listed non-financial 110 companies in the time period 1992 - 1998	– EVA explains the stock returns best. – EVA's typical accounting adjustments have a high statistical significance. – Results are contradictory to Biddle, Bowen and Wallace.
Ramana, D. V.[1571]	2005	243 Indian companies in the period 1999 - 2003	– Profit after Tax, Profit before interest and tax and NOPAT explain better the changes in MVA than EVA.
Mir, A. E.; Seboui, S.[1572]	2006	Database: Edgarscan and Yahoo Finance 252 firms in the period 1998 - 2004	– Low explanatory power of EVA for stock market returns. – EVA should not be used in technological industries and industries with high research and developments expenditures.

1569 Cf. Sparling, D., Turvey, C. G. (2003).
1570 Cf. Nichols, D. C., Wahlen, J. M. (2004).
1571 Cf. Ramana, D. V. (2005).
1572 Cf. Mir, A. E., Seboui, S. (2006).

Authors	Year of Publication	Source of data and data basis	Results / Insights
Kyriazis, D.; Anastassis, C.	2007	121 Greek non-financial firms for the period 1996 - 2003	– EVA has in comparison to operating income, net income and residual income the lowest explanatory power in describing changes in abnormal stock returns. – EVA typical adjustments do not contain more relevant information than traditional accounting measures.
Maditinos, D. I.; Sevic, Z.; Theriou, N. G.	2009	163 Greek companies in the period 1992 to 2001	– EPS have a higher explanatory power than EVA, ROI, SVA and ROE. – Combination of EVA and EPS delivers the highest degree of explanation of stock returns.
El-Sayed Ebaid, I.	2012	115 selected firms listed on the Egyptian capital market in the period of 1999-2009	– Only accounting-based key figures are investigated. – Net income and income before extraordinary items have the highest explanatory power while operating Cash Flow has the lowest.
Hawranek, B.; Öppinger, C.[1573]	2014	Companies of Euro Stoxx 50 in the period of 2006-2011	– Only accounting-based key figures are investigated. – Profit growth rate has the highest value relevance, followed by sales growth rate and return on capital. – Also Schremper and Pälchen receive a high value relevance for profit growth rate.
Wolf, R.; Hoffmann, H.	2017	Companies listed at London Stock Exchange in the period of 2011–2015	– Value based performance measures shows high significance. – Also the tradidtional key figures return on equity, EBT and return on capital have high signifiance values.

Source: Own table

1573 Cf. Hawranek, B., Öppinger, C. (2014).

On the basis of the selected articles the most important results regarding the explanatory power of vale based and traditional performance measures are the following ones:

- A superior key figure does not exist as the superiority of a key figure cannot be confirmed in many empirical studies. Thus, the theoretical assumed superiority of value based performance measures cannot be proved with the empirical studies.[1574] This insight also refers to the key figure EVA whose superiority has been claimed by Stern and Stewart[1575]
- Positive EVAs have a higher explanatory power than negative EVAs[1576] or in more general: The explanatory power of a key figure could vary with its sign[1577]
- Including cost of capital in a key figure increases (slightly) the value relevance of this key figure[1578]
- The value relevance of key figures can change due to the analysed time period.[1579]

1574 Cf. Maditinos, D. I., Sevic, Z., Theriou, N. G. (2009), p. 183; cf. exemplarily the contradictory result of Biddle, G. C., Bowen, R. M., Wallace, J. S. (1997) and Worthington, A. C., West, T. (2004) or Bacidore, J. M., Boquist, J. A., Milbourn, T. T., et al. (1997) and Ferguson, R., Leistikow, D. (1998); also Günther, T., Landrock, B., Muche, T. (2000a) cannot determine a superior key figure.

1575 Cf. Biddle, G. C., Bowen, R. M., Wallace, J. S. (1997); Chen, S., Dodd, J. L. (2001); Kyriazis, D., Anastassis, C. (2007).

1576 Cf. O'Byrne, S. F. (1997); Siebrecht, F., Heidorn, T., Klein, H.-D. (2001).

1577 Cf. Biddle, G. C., Bowen, R. M., Wallace, J. S. (1997), pp. 317-318.

1578 Cf. Biddle, G. C., Bowen, R. M., Wallace, J. S. (1997); Kyriazis, D., Anastassis, C. (2007) who only find little additional incremental information content by the capital charge Chen, S., Dodd, J. L. (2001); Worthington, A. C., West, T. (2004) prove a stronger incremental information content of adding capital cost to a key figure.

1579 Cf. Schremper, R., Pälchen Oliver (2001), p. 552; Siebrecht, F., Heidorn, T., Klein, H.-D. (2001), p. 563.

4 Application and Value Relevance of Value Based Performance Measures in Europe

4.1 Development of the Empirical Study

4.1.1 Research Questions, Research Hypotheses and Objectives of Empirical Study

4.1.1.1 Analysis of Application of Value Based Performance Measures in Europe

Value Added Reporting as one part of Value Reporting deals with the presentation and explanation of the increase of Shareholder Value of a company in one period.[1580] A way to explain and illustrate the Shareholder Value development is value based performance measures.[1581] Objectives of voluntary publication of value based performance measures are to reduce information asymmetries between capital market participants and management[1582] as well as to reduce the gap between intrinsic value and stock price.[1583] Reduced information asymmetries result in lower cost of capital.[1584] By reducing the gap between intrinsic value and the stock price, a company reduces the volatility of its shares on the stock market and achieves a fair assessment of the company.[1585] Also the Integrated Report as a kind of summary of the annual report puts an emphasis on the publication of key figures which underlines the importance of publication of carefully selected meaningful key figures for companies.[1586]

The analysis of the current state of research shows that more and more companies from the beginning of the century to the current time complement their reporting with the publication of value based performance measures.[1587] Most of the studies analysed focus on single countries.[1588] Cross-national investigations about publication behaviour are rare, but could result in new insights concerning the application of value based performance measures due to the diviergent economic area.[1589] Although, the publication behaviour throughout Europe has not been analysed intensively concerning the publication of value based performance measures. Many studies in the context of value based performance

1580 Cf. Fischer, T. M., Zirkler, B. (2008), pp. 589-590.
1581 Cf. Labhart, P. (1999), pp. 266-267; Pellens, B., Hillebrandt, F., Tomaszewski, C. (2000), pp. 184-185.
1582 Cf. Heumann, R. (2005), p. 5.
1583 Cf. Griewel, E. (2006), p. 78; cf. extensively chapter 2.4.4.1 for the objectives of Value Reporting.
1584 Cf. Bej, T. (2015), p. 109; cf. extensively chapter 2.2.5.
1585 Cf. Aders, C., Herbertinger, M., Wiedemann, F. (2003), pp. 357-358.
1586 Cf. Wulf, I., Niemöller, J., Rentzsch, N. (2014), p. 150.
1587 Cf. Gitt, N., Völl, W., Kettenring, T. (2013), pp. 101-102; Rapp, M. S., Schellong, D., Schmidt, M., et al. (2011), pp. 180-181; cf. for an overview of the current status of research chapter 3.5.1.
1588 Cf. exemplarily Aders, C., Herbertinger, M., Wiedemann, F. (2003); Laier, R. (2011); Malmi, S., Ikäheimo, S. (2003); Ruhwedel, F., Schultze, W. (2002) or the overview of the studies which deal with the application of value based performance measures, chapter 3.5.1, table 13.
1589 Cf. for cross-national studies Firk, S., Schrapp, S., Wolff, M. (2016); Horváth, P., Minning, F. (2001).

Electronic supplementary material The online version of this chapter (https://doi.org/10.1007/978-3-658-31429-3_4) contains supplementary material, which is available to authorized users.

N. Eikelmann, *Value Based Performance Measures*, FOM-Edition Research,
https://doi.org/10.1007/978-3-658-31429-3_4

measures refer to the Anglo-American region.[1590] Against the background of the current status of research and the available insights from scientific literature and with a focus on Europe three research questions arise in this context:

1. How many companies throughout Europe give voluntary information about value based performance measures?

Despite the existence of uniform accounting rules in Europe the publication behaviour and the extent of disclosed information differ from company to company.[1591] The latest empirical studies for Germany show that the majority of larger companies tend to publish information about voluntary key figures.[1592] The focus of the empirical study is on larger European companies listed at stock markets. Based on the results of the studies dealing with companies located in Germany and transferring them to the European level a high number of companies would disclose information about their value based performance measures. The empirical study of Firk, Schrapp and Wolff comes to lower application rates for European companies. What is striking is that there are large differences between the single countries. In this study an average share of 18 % of all European companies of the sample gives voluntary information about value based performance measures in the time period between 2005 and 2010. For this empirical study this average share of companies is taken as the basis for the later following hypothesis. It is assumed that the share of companies does not fluctuate strongly.[1593]

2. Which kind of information do companies give to external persons when disclosing a value based performance measure?

Only to reveal the name or the value of a value based performance measure is not sufficient. An explanation of calculation,[1594] forecasted target values[1595] and a variance analysis gives further insights for investors. A detailed calculation fosters the traceability and credibility of a presented value based performance measure.[1596] Especially in the context of VBM, costs of capital are important information because they are the hurdle rate for a company.[1597] The publication of the single components of the CAPM – the riskless rate of interest, the beta factor, the market risk premium[1598] – helps external persons to understand the cost of capital calculation. As companies know the information needs of investors, it is assumed that companies which give information about a value based performance measure do not only mention its name but give further accompanying information,[1599] in order to reduce communication gaps which might occur in the context

1590 Cf. Rapp, M. S., Schellong, D., Schmidt, M., et al. (2011), p. 174.
1591 Cf. Erkilet, G., Kholmy, K. (2016), p. 42.
1592 Cf. exemplarily the empirical studies of Gitt, N., Völl, W., Kettenring, T. (2013) and Quick, R. (2012) which proves that the majority of the largest German companies gives voluntarily information about value based performance measures.
1593 Cf. the empirical study of Firk, S., Schrapp, S., Wolff, M. (2016), p. 47.
1594 Cf. Fischer, T. M., Klöpfer, E. (2006), p. 8.
1595 Cf. Heumann, R. (2005), p. 137; Ruhwedel, F., Schultze, W. (2002), p. 624.
1596 Cf. Baetge, J., Solmecke, H. (2006), p. 24.
1597 Cf. Bej, T. (2015), p. 112.
1598 Cf. extensively for chapter 2.1.3 for information about the CAPM and a critical discussion.
1599 Cf. Fischer, T. M., Zirkler, B. (2008), pp. 590-591.

of Value Reporting. Especially the information gap is considered with this research question because it occurs if a company does not deliver sufficient information about a key figure.[1600]

3. Does the publication behaviour change during the time period of investigation?

At the beginning of the century the share of companies disclosing information about a value based performance measures was increasing.[1601] Recent empirical studies show that the share of companies remains relatively constant. For the following empirical study it is assumed that this continuity still exists and the total number of companies applying value based performance measures does not change overall.[1602]

Deriving from the current status of empirical research and the three posed research questions above the three following hypotheses are tested in this empirical study:[1603]

H1: More than 18 % of the companies of the sample publish information about the application of a value based performance measure in their company.[1604]

H2: The majority of companies (i.e. > 50 %) which applies a value based performance measure give additional information beyond the name of applied key figure.

H3: During the time period of investigation the share of companies applying a value based performance measure does not fluctuate more than 5 % in comparison to the first year of the investigation.

4.1.1.2 Standardised Calculation of a Value Based Performance Measure

A common problem in the context of publication of value based performance measures is that companies have individually adapted the concepts to their practical needs. Therefore, investors are not able to compare the performance of different companies.[1605] Even key figures with the same name can be calculated in many different ways. It is even elaborate because every value concept has to be analysed by an investor in order to comprehend the way of calculation. Due to this situation the following research question arises:[1606]

1600 Cf. Banzhaf, J. (2006), pp. 144-145; cf. also chapter 2.4.4.2 for an illustration of possible communication gaps in the context of Value Reporting.

1601 Cf. the empirical studies of Gitt, N., Völl, W., Kettenring, T. (2013); Rapp, M. S., Schellong, D., Schmidt, M., et al. (2011) and Schäffer, U., Lewerenz, U. (2011).

1602 Cf. Firk, S., Schrapp, S., Wolff, M. (2016), p. 47.

1603 The hypotheses are formulated in such a way that results from the research questions. For later tests the null-hypotheses are partly used. This approach corresponds to the typical procedure of critical rationalism issued by Karl Popper; cf. for further details Töpfer, A. (2012), pp. 113-116.

1604 The share of companies of 18 % bases on the empirical study of Firk, S., Schrapp, S., Wolff, M. (2016).

1605 Cf. Weber, J., Bramsemann, U., Heineke, C., et al. (2017), p. 239; Wolf, R. (2014), p. 5; Wolf, R. (2017), p. 206.

1606 Cf. Fischer, T. M., Rödl, K. (2005), p. 30; cf. Arbeitskreis Internes Rechnungswesen der Schmalenbach-Gesellschaft (2010) who analyse value concepts of five companies and carves out the differences between them; cf. Jacque, L. L., Vaaler, P. M. (2001), p. 817 who explains that over 160 possible conversions for EVA exist.

4. Which company out of the sample is the most successful one from the perspective of Value Based Management in the analysed period of time?

From the perspective of VBM a company is successful if it is able to cover all cost of capital.[1607] Only value based performance measures capture the profit after complete deduction of costs of capital.[1608] Thus, in order to answer this research question, it is necessary to calculate a value based performance measure with a uniform and standardised method of calculation for all companies of the sample. This procedure enables a comparison of performance of selected European companies.[1609]

4.1.1.3 Value Relevance of Value Based Performance Measures and Traditional Key Figures

Within scientific literature there are several controversial discussions about the quality and abilities of single key figures. The Metric War is still ongoing.[1610] In this context value relevance studies determine the value relevance of selected key figures.[1611] Many of these empirical studies deal with the EVA and its value relevance. This study uses the Value Added as the analysed value based performance measure instead.[1612] The focus of many relevance studies are American companies or companies of one country. Value relevance studies referring on a European cross-national database are rare, but could result in new insights due to the unique economic setting in Europe for the time period of investigation. Based on this current state of research three further research questions derive:[1613]

5. What is the value relevance of Value Added?
6. Does the development of Value Added correlate with the Shareholder Value development?

Studies analysing the value relevance of value based performance measures come to divergent results.[1614] This is surprising insofar as traditional key figures have been heavily criticised in the scientific literature.[1615] They do not consider the requirements of VBM in their calculation and ignore the cost of equity capital.[1616]

1607 Cf. Dillerup, R., Stoi, R. (2016), pp. 196-198.
1608 Cf. Zell, M. (2008), pp. 151-153.
1609 Cf. Weber, J., Bramsemann, U., Heineke, C., et al. (2017), p. 239; cf. for the approach of calculating a standardized value based performance measure Wolf, R. (2014); Wolf, R. (2017).
1610 Cf. Elgharbawy, A., Abdel-Kader, M. (2013), p. 104; cf. for the term "Metric War": Myers, R. (1996); cf. table 14 which summarizes the partly contradicting results of many empirical studies.
1611 Cf. basically for introduction to value relevance studies: Wagenhofer, A., Ewert, R. (2015), pp. 117-138; Wiederhold, P. (2008), pp. 135-138.
1612 Cf. Ittner, C. D., Larcker, D. F. (2001), p. 361; cf. for an overview of studies Gundel, T. (2012), pp. 158-160.
1613 Cf. table 14 and the analysed markets.
1614 Cf. exemplarily the results of the studies of Schremper, R., Pälchen Oliver (2001) and Worthington, A. C., West, T. (2004).
1615 Cf. exemplarily Knorren, N. (1998), pp. 10-16; Rappaport, A. (1986), pp. 19-49; cf. also chapter 3.2.2 for a listing of flaws of traditional key figures.
1616 Cf. Biddle, G. C., Bowen, R. M., Wallace, J. S. (1999), p. 70.

The Value Added includes in its calculation the cost of capital and shows if a company is successful in the sense of the VBM approach.[1617] A profit above the cost of capital indicates that the value of the company has increased and under the assumptions of capital markets in a semi-strong form the stock price will raise.[1618]

The economic environment in Europe with its low interest rates[1619] and the increasing importance of shares as asset class for investors offers a possibility to analyse what value relevance the Value Added as an example for a value based performance measure has under these special economic circumstances.[1620] Furthermore, the idea of value based performance measures exists for approximately 20 years so it can be assumed that capital market participants are aware of and familiar with this concept.[1621]

However, the Value Added is mainly based on accounting data and therefore its value relevance will be limited to a certain degree because investors get their information from several sources. Accounting data focuses mainly on past events. Nevertheless, the annual report enables investors a deep insight into the company's economic situation and has a high reliability due to the auditing process so that a certain degree of value relevance is ensured.[1622]

Based on the insights of VBM and the posed research questions the following hypothesis can be derived:

> H4: If the Value Added is larger than zero the Shareholder Value of a company increases. If the Value Added is below zero the Shareholder Value of a company decreases.[1623]

Due to the ongoing discussion in scientific literature the Value Added is not the only analysed key figure. In order to be able to assess the value relevance of the value based performance measure comprehensively and to have objects of comparisons, the study also determines the value relevance of five traditional key figures.

7. In comparison to the value relevance of the value based performance measure Value Added which value relevance do the key figures EPS, PER, ROI ROE and ROS have?

In the scientific literature there is no consensus, if value based performance measures are superior to traditional ones or vice versa. So, it is an open research question what proportion between these two kinds of key figures yields on a European level with the

1617 Cf. Bausch, A., Buske, A., Hagemeier, W. (2011), p. 365.

1618 Cf. Biddle, G. C., Bowen, R. M., Wallace, J. S. (1997), pp. 307-308.

1619 Cf. Eichler, S., Hielscher, K. (2012), pp. 554-555; Fiordelisi, F., Galloppo, G., Ricci, O. (2014), pp. 49-50.

1620 Cf. Schier, S. (03.12.2014), p. 26; Sommer, U. (15.12.2014), p. 1.

1621 Cf. Baum, H.-G., Coenenberg, A. G., Günther, T. (2013), p. 310, the VBM idea started to rise approximately at the end of the 80ies in Europe; cf. Ittner, C. D., Larcker, D. F. (2001), pp. 351-352 who date the starting in the mid of the 90s; for small and medium-sized companies the implementation rate is clearly lower: Günther, T., Gonschorek, T. (2011).

1622 Cf. Auer, K. v. (1999), pp. 178-180; cf. the study of Drake, M. S., Roulstone, D. T., Thornock, J. R. (2016) who finds evidence in their empirical study that accounting data is an important part within the information process of investors.

1623 Cf. for a similar empirical study analysing correlations: Günther, T., Landrock, B., Muche, T. (2000b) and Günther, T., Landrock, B., Muche, T. (2000a).

described economic situation.[1624] In order to compare value relevance between the listed key figures, a neutral position is taken and it is hypothesized the following:[1625]

H5a: The value relevance of Value Added is equal to EPS.
H5b: The value relevance of Value Added is equal to PER.
H5c: The value relevance of Value Added is equal to ROI.
H5d: The value relevance of Value Added is equal to ROE.
H5e: The value relevance of Value Added is equal to ROS.

The hypotheses show that in this empirical study only the relative information content is analysed. It is the appropriate research approach with reference to the research questions.

After introduction the research questions and hypotheses, the illustration below gives an overview of the corresponding methodologies which are applied in order to analyse the posed questions.

The study can be divided in three blocks. The first is the analysis of annual reports in order to receive more insights concnerning the publication behaviour of companies with respect to value based performance meausures. The second is the calculation of the standardised value based performance measures. This is a requirement for the association study as the third part of the study.

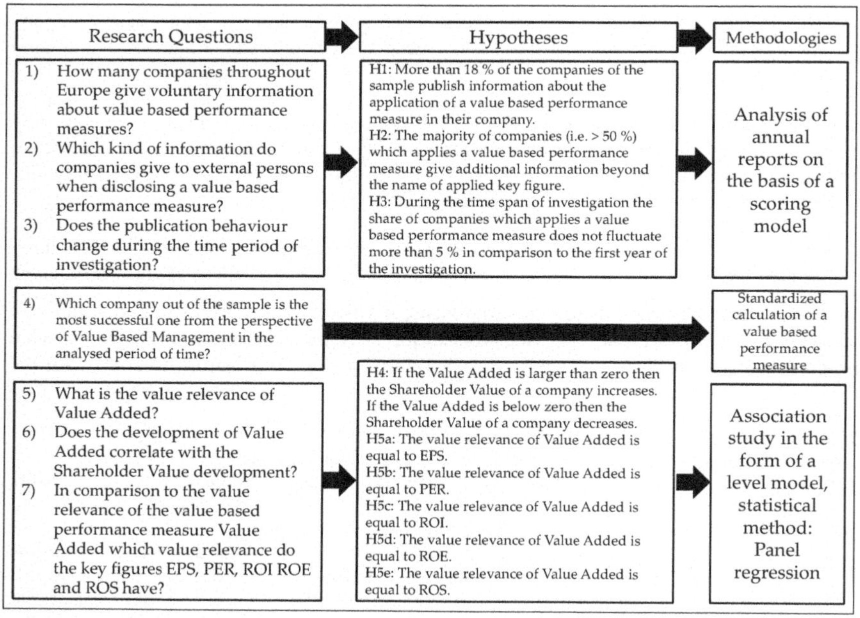

Source: Own illustration
Illustration 19: Overview of hypotheses and methodology of empirical study

1624 Cf. Elgharbawy, A., Abdel-Kader, M. (2013), p. 104.
1625 Cf. for equally hypothecating: Biddle, G. C., Bowen, R. M., Wallace, J. S. (1997), pp. 307-308.

4.1.2 *Methodology of the Study*

4.1.2.1 Analysis of Annual Reports

In order to test hypothesis H1, three research methods are available in general: Sending a questionnaire to companies included in the data base,[1626] conduct an interview with managers[1627] or analyse the annual report of these companies.[1628] In this empirical study the annual reports of the companies are analysed. Two reasons are crucial for this decision: Firstly, a study based on surveys or interviews has to deal to a higher degree with the problem of selection biases in comparision to the analysis on the basis of annual reports.[1629] Secondly, the annual report is still one of the most important mediums for companies for communicating with its shareholders and stakeholders.[1630] Especially for professional investors, the annual report is a widely used source of information.[1631] Much information within the annual report is audited so that this medium is a reliable source of information.[1632]

The information about applied value based performance measures has to be hand collected from the annual reports in order to ensure that data is gathered comprehensively and application of value based performance measures is assessed uniformly. For the analysis the annual reports of the selected companies are downloaded from the Internet. The research is conducted in two ways: On the one hand, pre-defined sections of annual reports are scanned for information about value based performance measures and on the other hand, the digital versions of the annual reports are searched for the key words listed in table fifteen.[1633]

In the context of this empirical study value based performance measures are defined as performance measures which consider all costs of capital in their calculation.[1634] The focus of the analysis is on value based performance measures focussing on a single period which enables shareholders, managers or possible investors to get an impression of the performance of the company in the last period.[1635] Consequently, MVA and DCF are excluded. Possible key figures are, amongst others, ROCE spread, Value added, CFROI spread or EVA. Also value based performance measures which were created by the companies themselves are included in the analysis. It is decisive that the key figure calculation includes a consideration of the total cost of capital. If a company states ROCE

1626 Cf. exemplarily the studies of Athanassakos, G. (2007); Günther, T., Gonschorek, T. (2011).
1627 Cf. exemplarily the studies of Malmi, S., Ikäheimo, S. (2003); Weber, J. (2009).
1628 Cf. exemplarily the studies of Ruhwedel, F., Schultze, W. (2002); Schultze, W., Steeger, L., Schabert, B. (2009).
1629 Cf. Rapp, M. S., Schellong, D., Schmidt, M., et al. (2011), p. 175.
1630 Cf. Pellens, B., Hillebrandt, F., Tomaszewski, C. (2000), p. 180.
1631 Cf. Gassen, J., Schwedler, K. (2010), pp. 501-502; Pro-Active Accounting Activities in Europe (PAAinE) (2009), p. 6; cf. also chapter 2.3.2.2 which analyses the information sources of investors.
1632 Cf. Wenzel, J. (2005), pp. 242-243.
1633 Cf. for a similar approach Firk, S., Schrapp, S., Wolff, M. (2016), pp. 46-48; Rapp, M. S., Schellong, D., Schmidt, M., et al. (2011).
1634 Cf. Biddle, G. C., Bowen, R. M., Wallace, J. S. (1999), p. 70; cf. definition of value based performance measures in chapter 3.2.1.
1635 Cf. Lachnit, L., Müller, S. (2012), pp. 255-256.

Table 15: Defined sections and search terms for analysis of annual reports

Sections in the annual report	Search terms
Financial position	Cash Flow Return on Investment
Business Performance	Cash Value Added
(Group) Financial Review	Cost of capital / WACC
Key figures overview	Economic Profit
Value Creation	Economic Report
Value Management	Economic Value Added
	Financial (Key) Performance Indicator
	Financial indicator
	Key Ratio
	KPI
	Management System
	Performance indicator
	Performance measurement
	Performance Ratio
	RAROC (Risk Adjusted Return on Capital)[1636]
	Shareholder Value Added
	Value (Based) Management
	Value Added

Source: Own table

and WACC separately from each other, the analysis does not assess this publication as a value based performance measure.[1637]

Insurance companies often disclose the key figure Embedded Value or Market Consistent Embedded Value (MCEV). These key figures are also not considered in the analysis because they refer to several periods and include – similar to MVA and DCF – a forecast of prospective developments.[1638]

Banks often use the key figure RAROC (Risk Adjusted Return on Capital) which is the result of the division of economic profit by economic capital. The term economic profit is a profit measure which considers costs for equity capital. In the sense of this work RAROC is a value based performance measure focussing on a single period. The annual reports of companies allocated to the supersector "Banks" are scanned for this key figure.[1639] The similar key figure RORAC (Return on Risk Adjusted Capital) does not

1636 This search term is only applied for companies allocated in the category "Finance."

1637 Cf. for an overview of various value based performance measures and their abilities chapters 3.3 and 3.4.

1638 Cf. extensively Wilson, T. C. (2015), pp. 101-124.

1639 Cf. Krause, H.-U., Arora, D. (2010), pp. 55-56; Lange, T. A. (2005), pp. 116-120.

include a hurdle rate in its calculation and is only assessed as value based performance measure if a difference of RORAC and a hurdle rate is calculated in an annual report.[1640]

In order to accept or refuse H2 and to determine additional delivered information by companies, this analysis uses a scoring model. Only those companies which mention a value based performance measure in their annual report are considered. It is assessed if the company gives accompanying information apart from the name of the key figure like the development of the key figure in the past and possible developments of it in the future.[1641]

In the context of Value Reporting investors are especially interested in information about future developments because it facilitates their prediction of future earnings and dividends. Often an outlook is done in a narrative form. But these outlooks cannot be assessed in the context of this scoring model.[1642] However, information concerning numbers is decisive. In order to assess investors' interest concerning concrete numbers accordingly, it is a separate question in the applied scoring model if companies state planned values of their value based performance measure.[1643]

Due to the important role of cost of capital additional points are allocated if the annual reports contain this information.[1644] For gaining points for cost of capital information, it is necessary that the costs of capital are mentioned in direct connection with the key figure and not separately in the annual report. [1645]

Illustration 19 gives an overview of the scoring model which is used for differentiating the quality of the publication of value based performance measures among the selected companies. The minimum number of points is zero if a company does not give any information in its annual report about a value based performance measure. The maximum number of points is six. In this case an investor will have a solid basis of information concerning the key figure.

A company can have one point according to the scoring scheme. This means that it simply mentions the name of the value based performance measure or gives some further verbal explanations. Beyond that, it does not mention any further figures. A result of two points indicates that a company provides the reader of the annual report with the name of the key figure and states the current value. Three points can be reached if a company gives information about the past development of the measure or gives estimated values for the future development. If both data are contained in the annual report, four points are given. Concerning the information about the cost of capital, two points can be achieved. Therefore, a company has to state a value of the cost of capital and to explain the calculation by listing single components.

To investigate possible changes in the publication behaviour of the companies, annual reports over four years are analysed. For companies with a fiscal year diverging from the calendar year, the fiscal year is allocated to that calendar year in which the majority of months is. This part of the analysis refers to H3.

1640 Cf. Krotsch, S. (2006), p. 118; Rudolph, B. (2005), pp. 47-48.

1641 Cf. Quick, R. (2012) and Schultze, W., Steeger, L., Schabert, B. (2009) who also used a scoring model for assessing the publication behaviour of companies.

1642 Cf. Athanasakou, V., Hussainey, K. (2014), pp. 227-229.

1643 Cf. Fischer, T. M., Zirkler, B. (2008), pp. 591-593.

1644 Bej, T. (2015), p. 112; Fischer, T. M., Klöpfer, E. (2006), p. 8.

1645 Cf. Langguth, H. (2008), pp. 217-218.

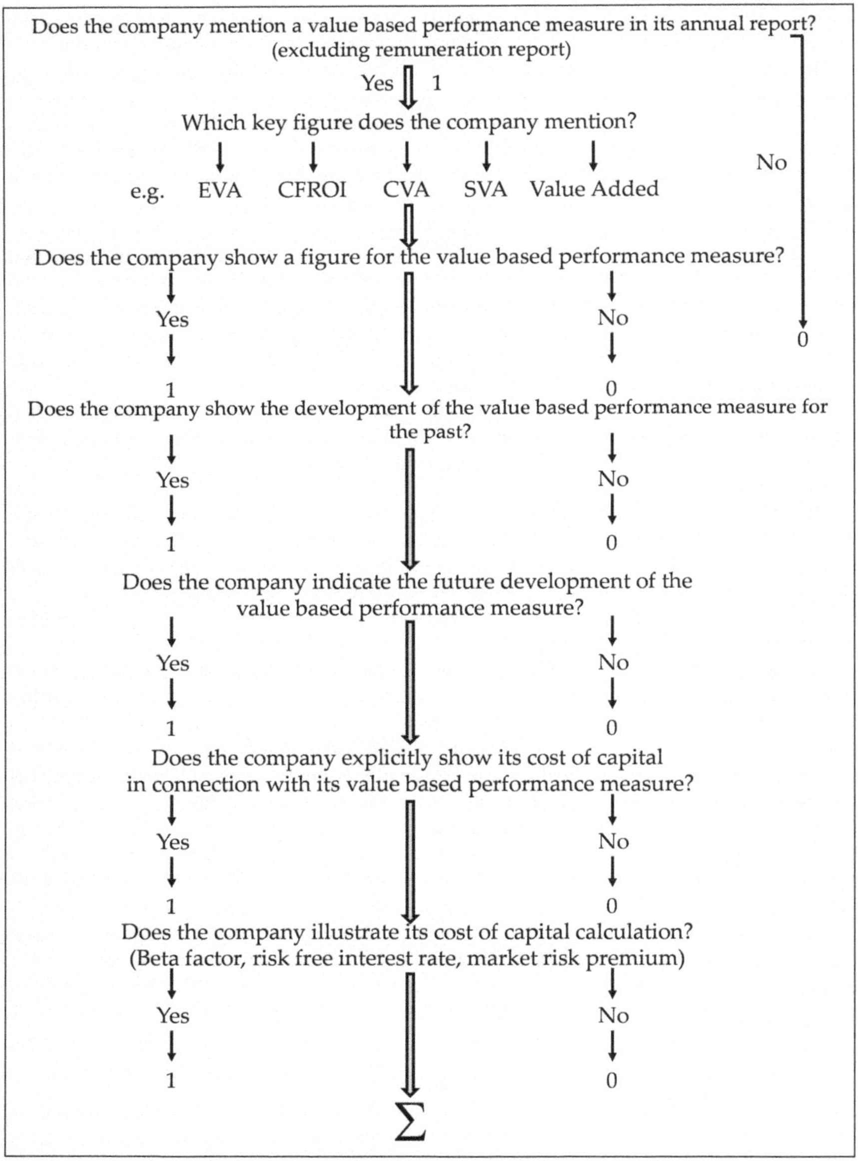

Source: In the style of: Quick, R. (2012), p. 247

Illustration 20: Scoring model for analysis of annual reports

To sum up: This analysis of annual reports can be classified as a disclosure index study with a binary measurement of items.[1646] It analyses the publication behaviour of companies concerning value based performance measures on an inter-company, inter-industry and cross-border level.[1647]

4.1.2.2 Standardised Calculation of ROCE, ROE Spread and Value Added

In order to answer research question 4) a value based performance measure has to be selected and to be calculated in a standardised way. The selection of an adequate value based performance measure is conducted on the basis of the evaluation criteria identified in chapter 3.2.3 and the presented value based performance measures in chapter 3.3.

The value based performance measures DCF and MVA are not adequate for answering the research question because these key figures refer to the total period. In contrast research question 4) refers to a limited period of time. Consequently, the selection process concentrates on the key figures ROCE Spread, EVA, CFROI and CVA.[1648]

The evaluation criteria for assessing the selected value based performance measures are: Including of of cost of capital, availability of data, quality of data, Present value of money, future orientation, considering risk and simplicity. [1649] Table 16 summarises the evaluation results.[1650]

The comparison of the evaluation results shows that all four key figures would be a possible key figure for the standardised calculation at first glance. In this empirical study the key figures ROCE Spread and Value Added are chosen due to three reasons. Firstly,

Table 16: Summary of evaluation of value based performance measures

Evaluation Criteria	ROCE Spread / Value Added	EVA	CFROI	CVA
Including of cost of capital	+	+	–	+
Data basis for calculation (Availability of data)	+	+	+ / –	+ / –
Data basis for calculation (Quality of data)	0	0 / +	+	+
Present value of money	–	–	–	–
Future orientation	–	–	–	–
Considering risk	+	+	–	+
Simplicity	+	0 / –	–	–

Source: In style of: Fiedler, R., Gräf, J. (2012), p. 339

1646 Cf. for an overview of possible approaches for analysing annual reports Beattie, V., McInnes, B., Fearnley, S. (2004), p. 209.
1647 Cf. Beattie, V., McInnes, B., Fearnley, S. (2004), pp. 208-211.
1648 Cf. the systematisation of value based performance measures in chapter 3.2.1.
1649 Cf. for an extensive description of evaluation criteria chapter 3.2.3.
1650 Cf. chapter 3.3.2.1.2 for evaluation of ROCE Spread / Value Added, chapter 3.3.2.2.3 for evaluation of EVA and chapter 3.3.3.3 for evaluation of CFROI and CVA.

they are the value based performance measure which can be calculated best on the basis of accounting data.[1651] The calculation of EVA, CVA, CFROI requires partly data which is not available for the public and external persons. In order to ensure a sufficient size of the sample for the standardised calculation the availability of data is important.[1652] Secondly, this study is a cross-national study. As the EVA is an after-tax key figure comparisions of performance on a cross-national basis could be distorted due to divergent tax laws in the European countries.[1653] Thirdly, especially the ROCE Spread is commonly used for comparisons between competitors over a period of time. So it is an appropriate key figure for comparing the performance of companies. EVA and CVA are absolute key figures so that the comparison between small and large companies would be distorted.[1654]

This and the following paragraphs describe the way of calculation for ROCE Spread and Value Added. For the calculation of ROCE the EBIT as a measure for the success of the operating activities of a company is chosen.[1655] As the EBIT is a pro-forma key figure, it is derived from the profit and loss statement starting with the annual profit or loss of a company. To take the EBIT directly from the companies' annual reports does not ensure a standardised calculation because companies use different ways of calculation or can change it over time.[1656]

The Capital Employed is computed via the liability side by adding interest bearing liabilities to the equity capital. All non-interest bearing liabilities are not considered in the Capital Employed calculation.[1657] Within the framework of calculation all non-current liabilities are assessed as part of Capital Employed. Exceptions are the deferred taxes which are always part of non-current liabilities in IFRS annual accounts. The non-current liabilities are reduced by deferred taxes.[1658] It is a balance sheet item which is not discounted and thus does not bear interest rates.[1659] The short-term / current liabilities are also not included in the Capital Employed calculation. These balance sheet items are not discounted and are assessed as non-interest bearing liabilities.[1660] The reason is that the current liabilities under IFRS are settled within the next twelve months.[1661] Further exceptions are the short-term financial liabilities which are added to the equity capital because companies are paying interest rates.[1662] In order to reduce the influence of outliners in balance sheet positions, the average value of the analysed year and the previous year of Capital Employed are the basis for ROCE calculation.[1663]

1651 Cf. Karrer, M. (2006), p. 159; cf. for an assessment of the quality of accounting data as the basis for key figure calculation chapter 2.4.3; cf. extensively for calculation and assessment of ROCE Spread and Value Added chapter 3.3.2.1.
1652 Cf. Baetge, J., Kirsch, H.-J., Thiele, S. (2004), p. 474; Gräfer, H., Gerenkamp, T. (2016), p. 148.
1653 Cf. Heier, K., Karsten, E., Müller-Wenzel, C., et al. (2015), pp. 13-14.
1654 Cf. Laier, R. (2011), pp. 51-52.
1655 Cf. Bode, D., Wiens, H. (2015), pp. 27-29.
1656 Cf. Ruhwedel, F., Thale, S. (2013), p. 388.
1657 Cf. Pape, U. (2015), pp. 277-278.
1658 Cf. Obst, H. (2009), p. 86; cf. contradictory Nowak, K. (2003), p. 151 who ignores passive deferred taxes by calculating the Capital Employed.
1659 Cf. IFRS Foundation (2016), IAS 12.53.
1660 Cf. Stauber, J. (2012), p. 620.
1661 Cf. Obst, H. (2009), p. 86.
1662 Cf. Schmidlin, N. (2013), p. 20.
1663 Cf. Ewert, R., Wagenhofer, A. (2000), p. 27.

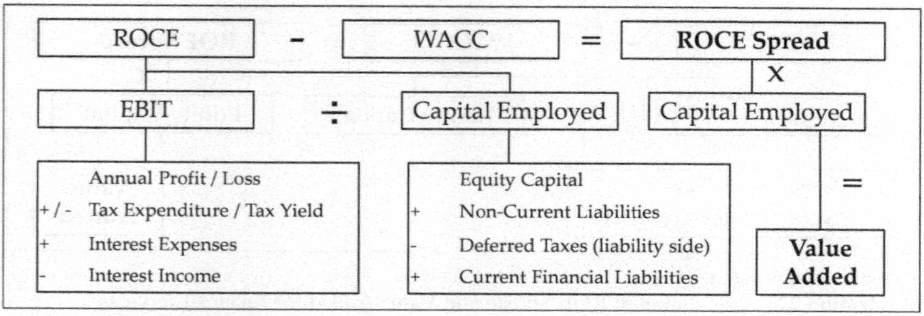

Source: Own illustration[1664]

Illustration 21: Calculation of ROCE Spread and Value Added for industry companies

The ROCE is a profit measure which determines the return before taxes. In order to calculate the ROCE spread correctly, a cost of capital rate before tax is used.[1665] The cost of capital rate bases on the WACC calculation scheme.[1666]

The ROCE Spread and Value Added are calculated on the balance sheet date of every single company. So ROCE as well as WACC are computed with the numbers available on that day.

The calculation scheme of ROCE Spread and Value Added used in this empirical study are partly simplified. The scientific literature contains ways of calculation which consider more balance sheet items. However, the objective of value based performance measures – to assess the success of a company in one period on the basis of the Shareholder Value approach – is fulfilled.[1667] Furthermore, there is no uniform definition for EBIT[1668] and Capital Employed in scientific literature.[1669]

The calculation of Value Added can be different according to the type of company. For banks, insurances or other companies which can be allocated to the financial services sector the calculation of Value Added has to be modified. These companies have different possibilites of refinancing in comparison to industrial companies. The costs of debt capital for these companies, especially for banks, is part of their business. In this respect they fundamentally differ from other industry companies for which debt capital is a way of receiving capital for further investments. Assets and liabilities may not be separated for financial services companies as easily as for companies in other industries.[1670] These

1664 Cf. for the calculation scheme of EBIT: Gladen, W. (2014), p. 66; cf. for the calculation scheme of Capital Employed: Guserl, R., Pernsteiner, H. (2015), p. 137; cf. for the calculation of ROCE Spread: Poeschl, H. (2013), p. 108; cf. for the calculation of Value Added: Alter, R. (2013), p. 74; Wolf, R. (2014), pp. 8-9.

1665 Cf. Pape, U. (2015), pp. 277-278.

1666 Cf. extensively for calculation of WACC and cost of capital chapter 2.1.3.

1667 Cf. exemplarily the calculation of Capital Employed in Guserl, R., Pernsteiner, H. (2015), p. 137.

1668 Cf. Wöltje, J. (2013), p. 237.

1669 Cf. Kajüter, P. (2007a), p. 444.

1670 Cf. Alter, R. (2013), pp. 74-75; Homburg, C., Lorenz, M., Sievers, S. (2011), pp. 122-123; Padberg, T. (2015), pp. 4-5.

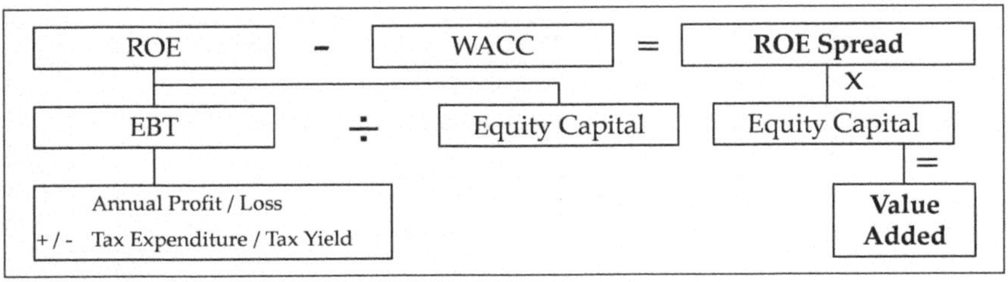

Source: Own illustration[1671]

Illustration 22: Calculation of ROE Spread and Value Added for financial services companies

peculiarities of their business lead to balance sheets and profit and loss statements which differ in structure from those of industry companies. Illustration 22 shows the way of ROE Spread and Value Added calculation for financial services companies.[1672]

The calculations of ROCE Spread and Capital Employed are adapted insofar that it is limited to the equity capital components. The ROCE Spread is modified to a ROE Spread. Consequently, the profit measure is the EBT instead of EBIT because debt capital providers have already settled their claims. Also the cost of capital has to be adopted. Instead of WACC, the cost of equity capital is deducted from the quotient of EBT and equity capital. The interpretation for the ROE Spread is the same as for the ROCE Spread. If a company is successful in covering the cost of equity, the ROE Spread is larger than zero.[1673]

4.1.2.3 Association Study in the Form of a Price Level Model

4.1.2.3.1 Price Level and Return Models as Possible Design Forms for Association Studies

The following chapters refer to the methodology which is used to investigate H4 and H5. According to the classification scheme of relevance studies this study is an association study analysing the relative information content of key figures.[1674] Value relevance studies differentiate between two models: Price level or return regressions.[1675] It depends on the research question and econometric issues which form is appropriate. Using price level regressions implies to investigate what factors are influencing stock prices. Return regressions are focussed on determining factors that trigger the change in stock prices.[1676]

1671 Cf. for calculation of EBT: Wöltje, J. (2016b), p. 219; cf. for calculation of ROE: Hax, A. C., Majluf, N. S. (1991), pp. 231-232; cf. for calculation of Value Added: Alter, R. (2013), p. 74.

1672 Cf. Padberg, T. (2015), pp. 32-33.

1673 Cf. Hax, A. C., Majluf, N. S. (1991), pp. 231-232; Landsmann, C. (1999), p. 158; Reitwiesner, B. (2001), pp. 35-36.

1674 Cf. for an overview of systematisation of relevance studies 3.5.2.

1675 Cf. for an exemplarily study which uses both models: Joos, P., Lang, M. (1994); cf. for an overview of price and return models Schloemer, M. (2003), pp. 46-60.

1676 Cf. Barth, M. E., Beaver, W. H., Landsman, W. R. (2001), pp. 95-96; Barth, M. E., Clinch, G. (2009), p. 282; Landsman, W. R., Magliolo, J. (1988), pp. 586-587; Lo, K., Lys, T. Z. (2001), pp. 16-17.

The focus is more on the timing of information[1677] and if accounting information contains new information at time of its disclosure.[1678] For this purpose changes in accounting numbers are investigated with changes in market prices. In contrast, level studies combine levels of accounting numbers with levels of stock prices.[1679] It has to be noted that both models can cause econometric problems. In general, by applying price models more caution concerning statistical issues is necessary.[1680] Examples for possible statistical problems are correlated omitted variables or heteroscedasticity.[1681]

The research question should primarily influence the choice of model as both have different research aims.[1682] Under consideration of the research questions and that both models may cause econometric problems,[1683] a price model is the appropriate choice because the study aims to determine the value relevance of different key figures and does not deal with the timing of information disclosure.[1684] Furthermore, price models are more appropriate when assessing the value relevance of balance sheet items. Most of the analysed key figures mostly contain items of the balance sheet.[1685]

In comparison to return models price level regressions have a common disadvantage. They suffer under the statistical problem of scale effects.[1686] The term scale effects summarises the influence large firms have on the regression results.[1687] Large companies have a large market capitalisation, large book values and large earning numbers. For small companies the opposite is valid. Due to this effect statistical results could be misinterpreted because they do not capture other effects than scale effects.[1688] But it is often difficult to differentiate between the variations in size per se and scale effects.[1689] Five kinds of scale effects can be distinguished:[1690]

- Multiplicative Scale Effects: Each variable of the regression equation can be expressed as a product of the variable itself and a common scale factor.[1691]
- Additive Scale Effects: These scale effects might occur, if firms raise new equity capital. Then the market value to book value relationship is distorted.[1692]
- Scale-varying coefficients: The coefficients vary with the size of the companies. This can be caused because larger firms tend to operate in more mature and stable markets,

1677 Cf. Beaver, W. H. (2002), pp. 461-462.
1678 Cf. Barth, M. E., Clinch, G. (2009), p. 282.
1679 Cf. Landsman, W. R., Magliolo, J. (1988), p. 586.
1680 Cf. Christie, A. A. (1987), p. 232; Kothari, S. P., Zimmerman, J. L. (1995), p. 157.
1681 Cf. Barth, M. E., Beaver, W. H., Landsman, W. R. (2001), p. 96.
1682 Cf. Gu, Z. (2005), p. 73.
1683 Cf. the conclusion of Kothari, S. P., Zimmerman, J. L. (1995), p. 183 who do not recommend a price or a return model; Schmidt, M. (2005), pp. 112-113.
1684 Cf. Beaver, W. H. (2002), pp. 461-462; Gabriel, A. (2015), pp. 107-108.
1685 Cf. Gjerde, Ø., Knivsflå, K., Sættem, F. (2011), pp. 117-118.
1686 Cf. Dumontier, P., Raffournier, B. (2002), p. 131.
1687 Cf. Easton, P. D., Sommers, G. A. (2003), pp. 25-27.
1688 Cf. Barth, M. E., Kallapur, S. (1996), p. 528; Easton, P. D. (1999), p. 404.
1689 Cf. Barth, M. E., Clinch, G. (2009), pp. 253-255.
1690 The kinds of scale effects bases on: Barth, M. E., Clinch, G. (2009), pp. 256-259.
1691 Cf. Barth, M. E., Clinch, G. (2009), pp. 256-257.
1692 Cf. Barth, M. E., Clinch, G. (2009), p. 257.

thus the accounting values like earnings and book value of equity are more constant figures.[1693]

- Survivorship effects: In general, the larger the firm, the less is the probability that it fails. This effect leads to statistical distortions.
- Scale-related heteroscedasticity: Heteroscedasticity describes the fact that the variance of the error term is not equally distributed.[1694]

There are econometrical tests for identifying scale effects in the sample[1695] but the problem is that these tests are often ineffective or indicate wrong results. Only the White test for heteroscedasticity is assessed as effective.[1696] Due to the fact that most statistical tests for scale effects are not effective or respectively scientific literature does not provide researchers with a superior way of dealing with it,[1697] it should be ensured in advance that scale effects do not exist in the sample or are at least reduced. In a large data sample without scale effects the standard deviation of market value of equity is 3,985.6 which can be taken as a reference value for this study.[1698]

For empirical studies researchers regularly use three possibilities for dealing with scale problems: Deflate regression variables with a scale proxy, including a scale proxy as an independent variable and White's heteroscedasticity-consistent standard errors.[1699] Possible deflators are number of shares outstanding, total assets, sales, book value of equity, net income and share price[1700] or market capitalisation.[1701] The most common deflator is to divide the variables by the numbers of shares outstanding in order to mitigate scale effects.[1702] The intercept of the regression equation is not deflated,[1703] but the dependent and all independent variables.[1704] By scaling variables, two points have to be considered. Firstly, it should be checked if other statistical methods are available, in order to avoid heteroscedasticity. Secondly, all variables have to be scaled with the same deflator.[1705]

Barth and Clinch show in their analysis of scale effects that the deflator "number of shares outstanding" is quite effective for many scale effects or their combinations. A first advantage is that variables are insensitive to an increase in capital because market capitalisation as well as number of shares is increasing. A second advantage is that the

---

1693 Cf. Barth, M. E., Clinch, G. (2009), pp. 257-258.
1694 Cf. Barth, M. E., Clinch, G. (2009), p. 258.
1695 Cf. extensively Barth, M. E., Clinch, G. (2009), pp. 262-265.
1696 Cf. Barth, M. E., Clinch, G. (2009), pp. 265-268; cf. Barth, M. E., Kallapur, S. (1996) who also assess the White test as effective.
1697 Cf. Oliveira, L., Rodrigues, L. L., Craig, R. (2010), p. 246.
1698 Cf. Barth, M. E., Clinch, G. (2009), p. 268.
1699 Cf. Barth, M. E., Kallapur, S. (1996), p. 528.
1700 Cf. Barth, M. E., Kallapur, S. (1996), pp. 528-529.
1701 Cf. Easton, P. D., Sommers, G. A. (2003).
1702 Cf. Barth, M. E., Clinch, G. (2009), p. 281; Lo, K., Lys, T. Z. (2001), p. 21; cf. exemplarily the studies of Barth, M. E., Landsman, W. R., Lang, M. H. (2008), pp. 486-487; Fields, T. D., Rangan, S., Thiagarajan, S. R. (1998), p. 113; Kothari, S. P., Zimmerman, J. L. (1995), p. 164; Tsalavoutas, I., André, P., Evans, L. (2012), p. 268; Worthington, A. C., West, T. (2004), p. 206.
1703 Cf. Barth, M. E., Kallapur, S. (1996), p. 532.
1704 Cf. Christie, A. A. (1987), p. 240.
1705 Cf. Landsman, W. R., Magliolo, J. (1988), pp. 591-592.

number of shares is a more constant figure in contrast to other possible deflators like market value of equity or book value of equity which are strongly influenced by economic development.[1706] But the number of shares has also a disadvantage: Management can influence the number of shares by e.g. a stock split. This split changes the results of the regression without a change of the situation in the economic context.[1707] Despite the division by the number of shares scale effects cannot totally be eliminated because the resulting quotient is based on data which is affected by scale effects and a division does not completely eliminate these effects.[1708]

Another possibility is to deflate the dependent variable, the stock price of the current period and independent variables by the stock price of the previous period.[1709] This procedure is based on the assumption that prices lead earnings. Due to accounting conservatism and historical cost approach accounting does not or only in a limited way reflect the future expectations of market participants while stock prices do contain these expectations.[1710] Annual earnings consist of an anticipated and an unanticipated component. Only the unanticipated component can explain the stock price as dependent variable. Dividing earnings by the stock price of the previous period, the anticipated part of earnings is at least partly eliminated thus the slope coefficient of this variable is less biased and total explanatory power of regression increases.[1711] In other words: The part of the earnings which is already captured by the stock price of the previous periods does not lead to price reactions in the current period and can be eliminated.[1712] Kothari shows that under the assumption that price leads earnings and the earnings variable is deflated by stock price of previous period, the level regression is superior to the return regression yielding less biased coefficients and higher R^2.[1713]

By testing the effectiveness of scale effects reducing possibilities, Barth and Kallapur come to the conclusion that including the scale proxy as an additional independent variable is the best solution. Furthermore, they recommend the use of White's standard errors.[1714]

The removal of the companies with the largest market capitalisation is not a solution for overcoming scale effects because within the sample there will always be companies with a large market capitalisation in comparison to the rest.[1715]

1706 Cf. Barth, M. E., Clinch, G. (2009), pp. 281-282.

1707 Cf. Brown, S., Lo, K., Lys, T. (1999), p. 84; Easton, P. D. (1999), p. 404.

1708 Cf. Brown, S., Lo, K., Lys, T. (1999), pp. 87-88; Oliveira, L., Rodrigues, L. L., Craig, R. (2010), p. 246.

1709 Cf. exemplarily Kyriazis, D., Anastassis, C. (2007), pp. 76-77; Machuga, S. M., Pfeiffer, R. J., Verma, K. (2002), pp. 62-64 who scaled the independent variables with the stock price of the previous period.

1710 Cf. Kothari, S. P. (1992), pp. 180-181.

1711 Cf. Kothari, S. P. (1992), p. 175.

1712 Cf. Brown, S., Lo, K., Lys, T. (1999), p. 104.

1713 Cf. Kothari, S. P. (1992), p. 198; cf. contradictory Gu, Z. (2005), pp. 82-83; cf. confirmatory Brown, S., Lo, K., Lys, T. (1999), pp. 103-107.

1714 Cf. Barth, M. E., Kallapur, S. (1996), pp. 555-556; cf. the empirical study of Harris, M. S., Muller, K. A. (1999) who implement an additional variable in order to control scale effects.

1715 Cf. Easton, P. D., Sommers, G. A. (2003), pp. 27-28, 40.

As all solutions have advantages and disadvantages, this study uses the most common method for avoiding scale effects and divide all absolute variables by the number of shares outstanding.

4.1.2.3.2 Ohlson Model as Theoretical Basis for the Regression Equation

The regression equations for value relevance studies typically consist of a market value as dependent variable and numbers from accounting as independent variables.[1716] A number of valuation models exist on which association studies base. The most prominent and common models are the Ohlson model[1717] or the modified Feltham Ohlson model.[1718]

These models are commonly used as theoretical concept for value relevance studies. They have a high importance within scientific literature[1719] because they prove a coherence between book values and market value of equity capital.[1720]

The Ohlson model is based on three assumptions: Dividend Discount Model, Clean Surplus Relation and linear information dynamics.[1721] Beyond that, perfect capital markets but imperfect product markets are assumed.[1722] The Dividend Discount Model expresses that the present value of future dividends yields the current market value of a company.[1723] The Clean Surplus Relation ensures that dividends only influence the book value of equity and not current earnings.[1724] Under the validity of the Clean Surplus Relation and in combination with the Dividend Discount model the current stock price can be explained by the current book value of equity and the present value of abnormal earnings. The Ohlson model only considers abnormal earnings and no dividends.[1725] The residual income valuation formula is an essential part of both models[1726] expressed by the following equation:[1727]

1716 Cf. Schmidt, M. (2005), p. 108.

1717 Cf. extensively Ohlson, J. A. (1995).

1718 Cf. Easton, P. D. (1999), p. 402; Mölls, S. H., Strauß, M. (2007), p. 958; cf. extensively Feltham, G. E., Ohlson, J. A. (1995). There are two further models commonly used: Balance Sheet Model and Earnings Model, cf. extensively Bastini, K. (2015), pp. 71-77; Lindemann, J. (2004), pp. 118-130.

1719 Cf. Beaver, W. H. (2002), p. 457, who describes the models as "one of the most important research developments in the last ten years"; Bernard, V. L. (1995), p. 733 assess the model as "the most important developments in capital market research in the last several years"; Lundholm, R. J. (1995), p. 749 describes the model as "landmark works in financial accounting."

1720 Cf. Bastini, K. (2015), p. 75.

1721 Cf. Bastini, K. (2015), pp. 73-77; Beaver, W. H. (2002), p. 457.

1722 Cf. Barth, M. E., Beaver, W. H., Landsman, W. R. (2001), p. 91.

1723 Cf. Feltham, G. E., Ohlson, J. A. (1995), p. 696.

1724 Cf. Wassermann, H. (2011), p. 39.

1725 Cf. Ohlson, J. A. (1995), p. 664.

1726 Cf. Lindemann, J. (2004), p. 85; cf. extensively chapter 3.3.1.

1727 Cf. chapter 3.3.1. This equation is the result of the Preinreich-Lücke theorem. The following equations are directly adapted from original literature sources and for reason of a better confirmability the original notation of variables is not changed.

$$P_t = y_t + \sum_{\tau}^{\infty} R_f^{-\tau} E_t\left[\tilde{x}_{t+\tau}^a\right]$$

Source: Ohlson, J. A. (1995), p. 667
Formula 41: Preinreich-Lücke theorem in the context of Ohlson's model

with
P_t = market value of equity capital in period t
y_t = book value of equity capital in period t
$R_f^{-\tau}$ = risk free interest rate increased by factor one
$\tilde{x}^a$ = estimated residual earnings in future periods

As formula 41 shows, the development of residual earnings has a significant influence on market value of equity capital. For describing the development of abnormal returns in the future, the Ohlson model uses linear information dynamics which is a stochastic process.[1728]

$$\tilde{x}_{\tau+1}^a = \omega x_t^a + v_t + \tilde{\varepsilon}_{1t+1}$$

$$\tilde{v}_{t+1} = \gamma v_t + \tilde{\varepsilon}_{2t+1}$$

where
$E_t\left[\tilde{\varepsilon}_{kt+\tau}\right] = 0; k = 1,2; \tau \geq 1$
$\omega, \gamma \in [0; 1[$
Source: Ohlson, J. A. (1995), p. 668
Formula 42: Stochastic process of linear information dynamics

with
x_t^a = residual earning in period t
v_t = information variable / other information than abnormal earnings
$\tilde{\varepsilon}$ = standard normal distributed disturbance terms

Ohlson uses this autoregressive process in his model in order to predict future abnormal earnings.[1729] Three variables influence the prospective abnormal earnings in the stochastic process: The abnormal earnings of the current period, other information which are not contained in residual earnings and accounting figures and a disturbance term.[1730] This means that the complete development of future abnormal earnings can be computed on the basis of the current abnormal earnings in the Ohlson model.[1731]

v_t is a variable which summarises all events that influence the value of a company beside the information contained in abnormal earnings as well as in accounting figures. The other information is included in the current stock price but is not yet captured by the

1728 Cf. Lundholm, R. J. (1995), p. 752.
1729 Cf. Henschke, S. (2009), pp. 18-19; Hüfner, B., Möller, H. P. (2002), p. 143.
1730 Cf. Ohlson, J. A. (1995), pp. 667-668.
1731 Cf. Hesselmann, C. (2006), p. 130.

balance sheet or profit and loss statement.[1732] A reason could be accounting rules like prudence principle that avoid an illustration of an issue on balance sheet or in the profit and loss statement.[1733] Examples are investments which are made in the current period but only have effects upon the results in upcoming periods.[1734]

ω and γ are named persistence parameters.[1735] Persistence parameter ω expresses for how long a company can generate abnormal earnings. It can also be interpreted as a sign for intensity of competition on the market on which the company is active. The lower the value, the more intensive the competition and the shorter the time period in which a company is able to generate abnormal earnings.[1736] The Ohlson model assumes that at some point in the future abnormal earnings of a company are reduced due to increasing competition.[1737]

The second persistence parameter γ describes how fast the additional information is processed and then shown in the accounting documents. The faster the processing is, the lower the persistence parameter.[1738] The disturbance terms in both equations captures uncertainty concerning non-predictable developments.[1739]

The final equation of the Ohlson model is formed by combining formula 41 and 42.[1740]

$$P_t = y_t + \alpha_1 x_t^a + \alpha_2 v_t$$

where

$$\alpha_1 = \frac{\omega}{R_f - \omega} \geq 0$$

$$\alpha_2 = \frac{R_f}{(R_f - \omega)(R_f - \gamma)} > 0$$

Source: Ohlson, J. A. (1995), p. 669
Formula 43: Equation of the Ohlson model

According to the Ohlson model the market value depends on two factors. On the one hand the current abnormal earnings and on the other the term other information which expresses the prospective development of abnormal earnings.[1741] The parameters α_1 and α_2 determine the share abnormal earnings and other information have in explaining the market value of equity capital.[1742] The Ohlson model is independent from current or

1732 Cf. Beaver, W. H. (2002), p. 457; Ohlson, J. A. (1995), p. 668; Zhang, G. (2014), p. 20.
1733 Cf. Lindemann, J. (2004), p. 131.
1734 Cf. Hesselmann, C. (2006), p. 132.
1735 Cf. Bastini, K. (2015), p. 74.
1736 Cf. Lindemann, J. (2004), pp. 131-132; Zhang, G. (2014), p. 20.
1737 Cf. Kothari, S. P. (2001), p. 176.
1738 Cf. Hesselmann, C. (2006), p. 132.
1739 Cf. Ohlson, J. A. (1995), p. 670; Wassermann, H. (2011), p. 40.
1740 An extensive mathematical derivation can be taken out of Ohlson, J. A. (1995), pp. 682-685.
1741 Cf. Ohlson, J. A. (1995), p. 669.
1742 Cf. Lindemann, J. (2004), p. 133.

prospective dividend payments.[1743] This model proves coherence between accounting data and market value. Consequently, it is the theoretical justification for conducting value relevance studies.[1744]

4.1.2.3.3 Feltham Ohlson model as extension of the Ohlson model

The Feltham Ohlson model is an extension of the Ohlson model.[1745] The book value of equity capital which is part of the previous presented Ohlson model is divided into operating and financial assets. The reason for splitting up the book value of equity into two groups is that financial assets are traded on almost perfect markets so that their market and book value nearly correspond. In contrast operating assets are not traded on nearly perfect markets so that differences between their market and book values exist.[1746] Financial assets are the difference of financial assets (marketable securities) and debt (bonds payable). Operating assets summarise all assets which do not generate interest, revenues or interest expenses. Examples are property, plant and equipment or accounts receivable.[1747]

The factor ω_{11} is the previously introduced persistence parameter.[1748] The factor ω_{12} is an extension and is named as conservatism parameter. It shows the distortion of accounting by conservatism which leads to lower assets values. Lower assets values reduce costs of capital and give companies the possibility to generate a higher residual income. The third factor ω_{22} captures the growth of operating assets. Asset growth influences residual income only in cases where accounting is conservative.[1749] To sum up the meaning of the parameters: The parameter ω_{11} captures the persistence of abnormal earnings and the parameter ω_{12} the conservatism contained in accounting. ω_{22} illustrates the growth in book values.[1750]

It is assumed that financial assets do not generate a return above the risk-free interest rate.[1751] Thus, all abnormal earnings can be attributed to the operating assets. Conservative accounting only has an influence on the book value of operating assets and the level of abnormal earnings.[1752] Similar to the Ohlson model the abnormal earnings are determined by operating assets, current abnormal operating earnings and other information.[1753]

As financial assets equal their market value, they do not have to be considered in the final equation. Only operating assets are considered to generate abnormal earnings.[1754] The central valuation equation of the Feltham Ohlson model is expressed as following:[1755]

1743 Cf. Wassermann, H. (2011), p. 41.
1744 Cf. Bastini, K. (2015), p. 75.
1745 Cf. Stromann, H. (2003), p. 27; cf. extensively Feltham, G. E., Ohlson, J. A. (1995).
1746 Cf. Feltham, G. E., Ohlson, J. A. (1995), pp. 690-691.
1747 Cf. Feltham, G. E., Ohlson, J. A. (1995), pp. 694-695.
1748 Cf. chapter 4.1.2.3.2.
1749 Cf. Zhang, G. (2014), pp. 28-29.
1750 Cf. Myers, J. N. (1999), p. 9.
1751 Cf. Stromann, H. (2003), p. 28; Lo, K., Lys, T. Z. (2000), p. 351.
1752 Cf. Feltham, G. E., Ohlson, J. A. (1995), pp. 700-701.
1753 Cf. Feltham, G. E., Ohlson, J. A. (1995), p. 702.
1754 Cf. Trautwein, A. (2007), p. 112.
1755 Cf. for a comprehensive derivation of the equation Feltham, G. E., Ohlson, J. A. (1995); cf. also for explanation Stromann, H. (2003), pp. 11-42.

$$P_t = y_t + \alpha_1 ox_t^a + \alpha_2 oa_t + \beta v_t$$

where

$$\alpha_1 = \frac{\omega_{11}}{R_f - \omega_{11}}$$

$$\alpha_2 = \frac{\omega_{12} R_f}{(R_f - \omega_{22})(R_f - \omega_{11})}$$

and

$$ß = (ß_1, ß_2) = \left[\frac{R_f}{(R_f - \omega_{11})(R_f - \gamma_1)}, \frac{\alpha_2}{(R_f - \gamma_2)}\right]$$

with
ox_t^a = operating earnings for period t
oa_t = operating assets at date t

Source: Feltham, G. E., Ohlson, J. A. (1995), p. 705
Formula 44: Equation of the Feltham Ohlson model

Following the equation of Feltham Ohlson model, the market value of equity depends on the following factors: Book value of equity capital, book value of operating assets, residual earnings of the current period and prospective development of residual earnings expressed by the term v_t for other information.[1756]

Also the Feltham Ohlson model uses linear information dynamics to estimate the abnormal earnings. In addition, this model is able to differentiate between unbiased and conservative accounting. In the case of unbiased accounting the Feltham Ohlson model equals the Ohlson model. In the case of conservative accounting the Feltham Ohlson model considers residual earnings resulting out of accounting conservatism.[1757]

It is important to note that the Ohlson model is independent from a certain accounting standard as long as the Clean Surplus Relation holds.[1758] Critiques of Ohlson and Feltham Ohlson model refer to the assumption upon which the model is based. There are no information asymmetries included and hence accounting is not used strategically by management as this might be the case in reality.[1759] For empirical studies this flaw is not considered serious because the effects on value relevance are assessed as low.[1760] Concerning the Feltham Ohlson model, the assumption that financial assets do not generate a return above the risk-free interest rate is unrealistic because a certain return can be reached by financial assets.[1761] Also the linear information dynamics are criticised

1756 Cf. Trautwein, A. (2007), p. 116.
1757 Cf. Henschke, S. (2009), pp. 22-23.
1758 Cf. Wassermann, H. (2011), p. 41.
1759 Cf. Beaver, W. H. (2002), p. 458.
1760 Cf. Schloemer, M. (2003), pp. 87-88.
1761 Cf. Stromann, H. (2003), p. 40.

because the calculation of persistence parameters is difficult in practice.[1762] Analysis of persistence parameters yields to the result that persistence parameters calculated with the models differ from empirical estimated parameters.[1763] This flaw is associated with the assumption that the residual income converges in the far future towards zero because companies are not able to preserve residual incomes in a competitive environment forever. However, empirical insights cannot confirm this theoretical assumption of linear information dynamics.[1764]

But despite all critics the models are frequently used in accounting studies.[1765] In the style of several previous studies the Ohlson model is the theoretical basis and justification for the following regression equation because it proves the coherence between accounting numbers and valuation process on capital markets.[1766]

4.1.2.3.4 Derivation of the equation for panel regression

Based on formula 44 which expresses the equation of the Feltham Ohlson model, the equation used in the empirical study is derived. The model term y for equity capital in period t and the regression coefficients α are substituted by the expression bv_t and the regression coefficients ß. The whole equation is complemented with the term ε which includes the regression error. Thus, the equation for the panel regression is as follows:[1767]

$$P_{i,t} = \beta_0 + \beta_1 bv_t + \beta_2 ox^a_{i,t} + \beta_3 oa_{i,t} + \beta_4 v_{i,t} + \varepsilon_{i,t}$$

with
bv_t = book value of company in period t

Source: Gabriel, A. (2015), p. 110
Formula 45: Empirical formulation of the Feltham Ohlson model

The Feltham Ohlson model assumes the validity of the Clean Surplus Relation. As described earlier, the IFRS do not fulfil this condition so that this assumption of the model is violated.[1768] For empirical studies the violation of clean surplus accounting is not considered serious because the effects on value relevance are assessed as low.[1769] Beyond the violation of this assumption, the linear information dynamics which Feltham and

1762 Cf. Bastini, K. (2015), p. 75; cf. also for a critique of linear information dynamics Lo, K., Lys, T. Z. (2000), pp. 347-348.
1763 Cf. Beaver, W. H. (2002), p. 459; Lindemann, J. (2004), pp. 138-139.
1764 Cf. Zhang, G. (2014), p. 20.
1765 Cf. Beaver, W. H. (2002), p. 459.
1766 Cf. Lo, K., Lys, T. Z. (2000), p. 338.
1767 Cf. for similar derivation of an equation for empirical purposes on the basis of the Ohlson or Feltham-Ohlson model Barth, M. E., Clinch, G. (2009), p. 255; Dahmash, F. N., Durand, R. B., Watson, J. (2009), pp. 124-127; Elshandidy, T. (2014), p. 180; Fields, T. D., Rangan, S., Thiagarajan, S. R. (1998), p. 115; Frankel, R., Lee, C. M. (1998), p. 288; Gabriel, A. (2015), pp. 109-110; Kaspereit, T., Lopatta, K. (2016), pp. 7-9; Lo, K., Lys, T. Z. (2001), p. 21; Möller, H. P., Hüfner, B. (2002), p. 430; Schloemer, M. (2003), pp. 51-55; Schmidt, M. (2005), p. 110; Trautwein, A. (2007), pp. 116-119; Tsalavoutas, I., André, P., Evans, L. (2012), p. 267; Vorstius, S. (2004), p. 140.
1768 Cf. Bogajewskaja, J. (2007), p. 109.
1769 Cf. Holler, A. (2009), p. 125; Schloemer, M. (2003), pp. 87-88.

Ohlson use to predict abnormal earnings of future periods are not transferred to the empirical formulation of the model in this study.[1770] The linear information dynamics are a necessary part of the theoretical model of Feltham and Ohlson but have not been directly created for empirical studies.[1771] Moreover, also this construct was often not able to capture the market valuation process appropriately in previous empirical studies.[1772]

In order to use the Feltham Ohlson model in the context of an empirical study, it is necessary to operationalise the variables and to make simplifying assumptions. Nevertheless, the operationalisation of the variables should be as close to the theoretic model as possible in order to reduce the derivation.[1773]

Under consideration of the availability of price level and return models for value relevance studies, the applied equation in this study is a level specification.[1774] The majority of value relevance studies are conducted with a level specification. Nevertheless, a return specification would also be possible.[1775] A further feature of value relevance studies is that they are long window studies analysing accounting figures over several years which is also valid for this study.[1776]

4.1.2.3.5 Definition of Endogenous Variable

Association studies analyse the relationship between market values and accounting data. Consequently, the dependent variable has to reflect the assessment of a company by the market.[1777] As the dependent variable is a number derived from market values, it is necessary that the market has a certain degree of efficiency in order to ensure that market values reflect capital market participants' assessments of a company. Then it is possible to analyse if accounting numbers contain parts of these assessments.[1778] Association studies typically assume efficiency in the semi-strong form in order to use the stock price as an appropriate proxy for the intrinsic value. In the context of this part of the study it is also assumed that capital markets are semi-efficient.[1779]

However, this assumption is limited to the third part of the empirical study. Otherwise, the analysis of publication of value based performance measures in the first part and the calculation of a standardised key figure in the second part would be senseless. At a market with efficiency in the semi strong form capital market prices would already contain all public available information and reporting would be without benefit.[1780]

1770 Cf. exemplarily the studies of Gabriel, A. (2015), pp. 109-110; Kaspereit, T., Lopatta, K. (2016), pp. 7-9; Trautwein, A. (2007), pp. 116-119 which also do not consider the linear information dynamics.

1771 Cf. Bar-Yosef, S., Callen, J. L., Livnat, J. (1996), p. 222.

1772 Cf. Myers, J. N. (1999), p. 26.

1773 Cf. Trautwein, A. (2007), p. 117.

1774 Cf. the way of argumentation in chapter 4.1.2.3.1 for choosing the level specification.

1775 Cf. Lo, K., Lys, T. Z. (2001), pp. 16-17.

1776 Cf. Collins, D. W., Kothari, S. P. (1989), p. 144; Lo, K., Lys, T. Z. (2001), pp. 15-16.

1777 Cf. Aboody, D., Hughes, J., Liu, J. (2002), p. 966; Fiordelisi, F., Molyneux, P. (2006), p. 83.

1778 Cf. Holthausen, R. W., Watts, R. L. (2001), p. 18; Vorstius, S. (2004), p. 101.

1779 Cf. exemplarily empirical studies of Aboody, D., Hughes, J., Liu, J. (2002), p. 966; Fields, T. D., Rangan, S., Thiagarajan, S. R. (1998), p. 104 for the same assumption; cf. extensively for information about the level of market efficiency chapter 2.3.1.

1780 Cf. argumentation in chapter 2.3.1.2.

Based on the Feltham Ohlson model the dependent variable is the market value of equity capital which reflects the present value of expected dividends.[1781] This choice of variable also fits to the research questions because it ensures that the analysed performance measures are assessed concerning their ability to capture information of the complete shareholder wealth. A return figure as dependent variable would focus on a performance measure's ability to explain the variation in the stock price.[1782]

The proxy used for the market value of a company is its market capitalisation at the stock market[1783] which is defined as the product of stock price of a company multiplied by its number of outstanding shares.[1784] The market capitalisation considers movement of the stock price due to dividend payments or stock splits.[1785]

A further point of discussion is the point in time at which the market capitalisation is measured. Many empirical studies use a lagged dependent variable in order to consider the publication of annual results and their impact on stock price.[1786] In the context of this empirical study using market values with time lag would not correspond to the posed research questions. The objective is to determine the value relevance of Value Added and further traditional key figures for certain fiscal years and to what extent these accounting numbers can explain the stock prices in those fiscal years.[1787] By using market values with a time lag, further events that happen after the end of a fiscal year are included in the stock price.[1788] Beside the annual report investors have various sources of information, so that it can be assumed that many parts of information conveyed by accounting numbers are already included in the stock price before final release of annual reports.[1789] If the stock price includes already private information or information about earnings which the company announced before in another medium, the stock price reaction to final disclosure of annual reports is reduced.[1790] Thus, the disclosure of the annual report is just a conformation of expectation of capital market participants. The stock price only changes by a significant derivation of companies' earnings from their expectations.[1791] In addition, it should be noted that the market is able to anticipate disclosed earnings. Up to 12 months before the earnings announcement, stock prices show a reaction. A large derivation in the month of announcement does not exist.[1792] In addition to the named reasons it is difficult

1781 Cf. Feltham, G. E., Ohlson, J. A. (1995), p. 690.

1782 Cf. Fiordelisi, F., Molyneux, P. (2006), pp. 91-92.

1783 Cf. also the following studies which all used market capitalization as dependent variable Clout, V. J., Willett, R. J. (2016), p. 226; Dahmash, F. N., Durand, R. B., Watson, J. (2009), p. 126; Gabriel, A. (2015), p. 110; Henschke, S. (2009), p. 106; Trautwein, A. (2007), pp. 163-164; Vorstius, S. (2004), pp. 181-182.

1784 Cf. Brealey, R. A., Myers, S. C., Allen, F. (2011), p. 32.

1785 Cf. Schloemer, M. (2003), p. 125.

1786 Cf. exemplarily Bartov, E., Goldberg, S. R., Kim, M. (2005); Biddle, G. C., Bowen, R. M., Wallace, J. S. (1997), p. 312; Elbakry, A. E., Nwachukwu, J. C., Abdou, H. A., et al. (2017), p. 14; El-Sayed Ebaid, I. (2011), p. 78; Schloemer, M. (2003), pp. 123-125.

1787 Cf. Francis, J., Schipper, K., Vincent, L. (2003), p. 162.

1788 Cf. Francis, J., Schipper, K., Vincent, L. (2003), p. 162; Wagenhofer, A., Ewert, R. (2015), p. 121.

1789 Cf. Auer, K. v. (1999), pp. 190-191; Dumontier, P., Raffournier, B. (2002), p. 129.

1790 Cf. Beaver, W. H. (2002), pp. 460-461.

1791 Cf. Coenenberg, A. G., Haller, A., Schultze, W. (2014), pp. 1326-1329; Wagenhofer, A., Ewert, R. (2015), p. 99.

1792 Cf. Vollmer, R. (2008), pp. 81-82.

in practice to determine an exact announcement date for single companies.[1793] Due to the listed disadvantages by using a time lag this study uses the market value at the end of a fiscal year of a company.[1794]

4.1.2.3.6 Definition of Explanatory Variables

The empirical formulation of the Feltham Ohlson model contains a variable which represents abnormal earnings for operating activities.[1795] This earning figure of the model is used to implement chosen performance measures in the regression equation in order to determine their relative information content.[1796]

The accounting numbers for which the relative information content is analysed are Value Added, Price Earnings Ratio (PER), Earnings per Share (EPS), Return on Investment (ROI), Return on Equity (ROE) and Return on Sales (ROS). For each of these key figures a separate panel regression is conducted leaving all other variables unchanged. The adjusted coefficients of determination of six panel regressions and five annual regressions per key figure are compared in order to determine the key figure with the highest value relevance. Table 17 summarises the calculation of selected performance measures.

The Value Added values used in the panel regression correspond to those which are used for the performance comparison of companies in the second part of the empirical study.[1797] As the calculation scheme reveals, extraordinary items are not excluded from EBIT calculation.[1798]

All traditional key figures are common key figures and are also analysed in comparable studies. Thus, implementing them in this study enables a comparison of the determined explanatory power not only with the other key figures analysed in this study but also to compare their value relevance with the results of further studies.[1799]

All key figures are profitability key figures. The higher e.g. the Value Added is, the better is the performance of a company in a period. Therefore, a positive sign for all five explanatory variables is expected.[1800] Concerning the PER, a negative sign is expected because companies with a higher stock price have a lower PER.[1801]

1793 Cf. Bartov, E., Goldberg, S. R., Kim, M. (2005), p. 105.

1794 Cf. Abrahams, T., Sidhu, B. K. (1998), p. 172, the authors state that results are similar if market capitalization is measured with a time lag of three months; cf. also the following studies for the same approach Clarkson, P., Hanna, J. D., Richardson, G. D., et al. (2011), p. 6; Clout, V. J., Willett, R. J. (2016), p. 226; Gjerde, Ø., Knivsflå, K., Sættem, F. (2011), p. 117; Tahat, Y. A., Alhadab, M. (2017), p. 4.

1795 Cf. Koch, J. (2005), p. 64.

1796 Cf. exemplarily the studies of Clarkson, P., Hanna, J. D., Richardson, G. D., et al. (2011); Elbakry, A. E., Nwachukwu, J. C., Abdou, H. A., et al. (2017); Elshandidy, T. (2014) which also uses the earnings variable of the Ohlson or Feltham Ohlson model to implement different earnings or return figures in the regression equation.

1797 Cf. extensively chapter 4.1.2.2 for an illustration of Value Added calculation scheme.

1798 Cf. Dahmash, F. N., Durand, R. B., Watson, J. (2009), p. 125; Dechow, P., Hutton, A. P., Sloan, R. G. (1999), p. 14.

1799 Cf. the studies of Maditinos, D. I., Sevic, Z., Theriou, N. G. (2009); Hawranek, B., Öppinger, C. (2014); Schremper, R., Pälchen Oliver (2001) which analyses among others the key figures Return on Equity and Return on Sales.

1800 Cf. Rutherford, B. A. (2002), p. 74.

1801 Cf. Schmidlin, N. (2013), pp. 112-113.

Table 17: Chosen performance measures for panel regression as explanatory variables

Name of performance measure	Kind of performance measure	Calculation
Value Added[1802]	Value based performance measure	$Value\ Added = (ROCE - WACC) \times Capital\ Employed$
Earnings per Share[1803]	Traditional key figure	$\frac{Annual\ profit\ (loss)}{Number\ of\ shares\ outstanding}$
Price Earnings Ratio[1804]	Traditional key figure	$\frac{Market\ price\ per\ share}{Earnings\ per\ share}$
Return on Investment[1805]	Traditional key figure	$\frac{Annual\ profit\ (losses) + Tax\ paid + Interest\ expenses}{Total\ capital}$
Return on Equity[1806]	Traditional key figure	$\frac{EBT}{Equity\ Capital}$
Return on Sales[1807]	Traditional key figure	$\frac{EBIT}{Turnover}$

Source: Own table

4.1.2.3.7 Definition of Control Variables

Beside market value of equity capital and operating earnings the Feltham Ohlson model contains book value of equity capital and operating assets as further variables. In this empirical study these variables are classified as control variables because the focus of the study is on determining the relative information content of presented performance measures.[1808]

The variable book value of equity (BVE) is taken identically in the regression equation. The values are taken from the company's balance sheet at the end of the fiscal year.[1809] The higher the equity capital, the lower the risk of insolvency and the easier it is for a company to acquire additional debt capital. In contrast to that, a too large share of equity capital could also be disadvantageous due to the expected return of equity capital

1802 Cf. extensively chapter 3.3.2.1; formula taken from: Alter, R. (2013), p. 74.
1803 Cf. extensively chapter 3.1.2; formula taken from: Krause, H.-U., Arora, D. (2010), p. 43.
1804 Cf. extensively chapter 3.1.2; formula taken from: Garrison, R. H., Noreen, E. W., Brewer, P. C. (2012), p. 687.
1805 Cf. extensively chapter 3.1.4; the ROI can also be calculated with the formula of return on capital, cf. Hauerdinger, M., Probst, H.-J. (2006), p. 189. Formula taken from: Baetge, J., Kirsch, H.-J., Thiele, S. (2004), p. 370.
1806 Cf. extensively chapter 3.1.3; formula taken from: Baetge, J., Kirsch, H.-J., Thiele, S. (2004), p. 357.
1807 Cf. extensively chapter 3.1.3; formula taken from: Küting, K., Weber, C.-P. (2015), p. 330.
1808 Cf. Koch, J. (2005), p. 64.
1809 Cf. exemplarily the studies of Clarkson, P., Hanna, J. D., Richardson, G. D., et al. (2011); Elshandidy, T. (2014) which uses the same approach.

Table 18: Calculation of net operating assets

Calculation of operating assets
Total assets
– Financial assets
– Assets to be disposed (including discontinued operations)
= Operating assets
– Operating liabilities
= Net Operating Assets

Source: In the style of: Penman, S. H. (2013), p. 295; Coenenberg, A.G., Haller, A., Schultze, W. (2014), p. 1042

providers and the non-deductibility of costs for equity capital. Consequently, a distinct sign for the variable BVE cannot be predicted before the panel regression.[1810]

The second variable given by the Feltham Ohlson model is operating assets. The distinction of operating and financial assets which is used in the model is difficult to transfer to empirical studies because financial statements do not separate assets into operating assets and financial ones.[1811] Operating assets are defined as assets which are necessary for producing and selling products to customers.[1812] Therefore, a calculation scheme which derives net operating assets coming from total assets is used.[1813] All financial assets and assets allocated to businesses which are not continued are deducted. Cash is included in the Net Operating Assets because a minimum of cash is necessary for conducting the business. It is assumed that operating liabilities mainly contain trade payables.[1814] They are deducted from Operating assets in order to receive the variable Net Operating Assets (NOA).[1815]

The sign of the variable NOA is difficult to predict because it depends on how profitable a company is using its assets. In general, it can be assumed that the more operating assets a company has, the higher are the earnings and the stock price increases. Therefore, a positive sign for this variable is expected.[1816]

Beside the named accounting numbers it is necessary to consider additional variables. Earnings or related numbers alone cannot explain the stock price of a company. The reason why accounting figures alone cannot explain the stock price is that value relevant events occurred in a previous period which have already influenced the share price of this previous period but they may influence the earnings of the current period as well. A second possible scenario is that value relevant events of the current period influence the market price but do not have an influence on accounting numbers of this period. It has to be considered that there can be time lags in reporting in comparison to stock price

1810 Cf. Küting, K., Weber, C.-P. (2015), pp. 139-141.
1811 Cf. Callen, J. L., Segal, D. (2005), pp. 412-413; Küting, K., Weber, C.-P. (2015), pp. 330-331.
1812 Cf. Penman, S. H. (2013), p. 241.
1813 Cf. for similar proxies for Operating Assets Dahmash, F. N., Durand, R. B., Watson, J. (2009), p. 126; Kaspereit, T., Lopatta, K. (2016), p. 8; Trautwein, A. (2007), pp. 167-169.
1814 Cf. Coenenberg, A. G., Haller, A., Schultze, W. (2014), p. 1042.
1815 Cf. Penman, S. H. (2013), p. 241.
1816 Cf. Baetge, J., Kirsch, H.-J., Thiele, S. (2004), pp. 373-376.

development.[1817] Previous studies show that especially additional variables which contain non earnings information increase strongly the explanatory power of regression equations between stock price and accounting numbers.[1818] Furthermore, additional variables might reduce scale effects, a common problem of price level regressions.[1819]

The term $v_{i,t}$ summarises all information not included in the abnormal earnings but factors that will influence abnormal earnings of future periods.[1820] In the context of empirical studies this term is the justification for adding further variables to the model which reflect factors that also influence the stock price of a company.[1821] This is possible because within the framework of the Feltham Ohlson model this term is unknown a priori.[1822] A common proxy for the other information term are analysts' forecasts.[1823] This study does not follow this approach because the data availability is limited especially concerning the smaller companies within the data set. Using analysts' forecasts would lead to a further reduction of the data set.[1824]

Dividend policy is another factor which influences stock prices.[1825] The impact could also be vice versa that changes in stock prices lead to a variation of future dividends.[1826] The inclusion of a dividend number in the regression equation is also supported by the fact that dividends play an important role in the context of the Clean Surplus Relation which is one of the assumptions of the Ohlson model.[1827] In this study the dividend paid in one fiscal year is a proxy for the dividend policy and its influence on stock price.[1828] On the basis of the dividend discount model which expresses the current share price as the present value of future dividend payments, a positive sign for the variable Dividend payed within a fiscal year (DIV) is expected.[1829]

An important factor which influences the assessment of a company by an investor is the capital structure.[1830] Deriving from this, shareholders make conclusions about a company's financial stability and its ability to settle interest rates. The influence of capital structure on enterprise value is shown by capital structure theories like Pecking Order or

---

1817 Cf. Easton, P. D. (1999), pp. 400-401.

1818 Cf. Dechow, P., Ge, W., Schrand, C. (2010), pp. 369-370; Dumontier, P., Raffournier, B. (2002), p. 139.

1819 Cf. Barth, M. E., Clinch, G. (2009), p. 283.

1820 Cf. Hesselmann, C. (2006), p. 132.

1821 Cf. Barth, M. E. (2000), pp. 16-17; cf. for similar procedure Elbakry, A. E., Nwachukwu, J. C., Abdou, H. A., et al. (2017), pp. 14-15; Gabriel, A. (2015), p. 113; Kaspereit, T., Lopatta, K. (2016), p. 7.

1822 Cf. Callen, J. L., Segal, D. (2005), p. 411.

1823 Cf. Easterday, K., Sen, P. K., Stephan, J. A. (2011), p. 1124; Lindemann, J. (2004), p. 132; cf. exemplarily Dechow, P., Hutton, A. P., Sloan, R. G. (1999), pp. 6-7.

1824 Cf. for similar argumentation: Dahmash, F. N., Durand, R. B., Watson, J. (2009), p. 126.

1825 Cf. Elbakry, A. E., Nwachukwu, J. C., Abdou, H. A., et al. (2017), p. 14; cf. chapter 3.5.2.1 and the coherence between earnings, stock prices and dividends.

1826 Cf. Cesari, A. de, Huang-Meier, W. (2015), p. 16.

1827 Cf. Frankel, R., Lee, C. M. (1998), p. 286.

1828 Cf. the studies of Easterday, K., Sen, P. K., Stephan, J. A. (2011), pp. 1143-1144; Elbakry, A. E., Nwachukwu, J. C., Abdou, H. A., et al. (2017), pp. 14-15; Hüfner, B., Möller, H. P. (2002), p. 147 which includes dividend policy as a factor in their regression equations.

1829 Cf. Nichols, D. C., Wahlen, J. M. (2004), pp. 266-267.

1830 Cf. Coenenberg, A. G., Schultze, W. (2003), pp. 129-131.

Trade-off theory.[1831] A key figure for determing the capital structure and financial stability is the leverage ratio, computed as debt capital divided by equity capital.[1832] Against the background of accounting studies it can be assumed that investors consider the capital structure in their calculation of a possible return of their investment. The leverage ratio of a company does not influence the value relevance of an earning figure directly but it has influence on the relation of earnings and returns.[1833] The higher the leverage ratio of a company, the higher the financial risk. Therefore, the leverage ratio is negatively associated with stock returns. It is included in the regression equation as a further variable, Leverage Ratio (LEV). Due to the increasing financial risk with a higher leverage ratio a negative sign is expected.[1834] However, it could be the case that companies with a high leverage ratio tend to use more intensively accounting policy in order to improve the weak performance. These kinds of actions would reduce the value relevance of accounting numbers because they do not reflect the company's performance assessment by the capital market.[1835]

Due to the chosen design of study as level study and possible occurring scale effects[1836] a variable that captures the size of a company is important. With the help of such a variable it is possible to control if the company's size plays an important role in explaining the dependent variable.[1837] For this purpose the variable Total Assets (ASS) is part of the regression equation.[1838] Larger companies regularly have more stable Cash Flows expressed by the fact that credit ratings are influenced by a company's size. Another effect is that large companies are more diversified than smaller firms and can better distribute their risk. Thus, a positive sign is expected for the variable ASS.[1839]

The stock price depends on the current and assumed prospective development of the company.[1840] Closely connected with this issue is the question of how the company's sales develop. As the companies of the sample may be in different life cycle stages, the development of their sales is different. Companies in the growth stages increase their turnovers while companies in the mature stage do not experience large changes in sales. Thus, the information contained in the change of sales has relative importance for

1831 Cf. Hermanns, J. (2006), pp. 1-2.
1832 Cf. Krause, H.-U., Arora, D. (2010), pp. 65-66.
1833 Cf. Dechow, P., Ge, W., Schrand, C. (2010), p. 369.
1834 Cf. Penman, S. H., Richardson, S. A., Tuna, I. (2007), p. 429; cf. the studies of Barth, M. E., Landsman, W. R., Lang, M. H. (2008), p. 482; Lang, M., Raedy, J. S., Yetman, M. H. (2003), p. 370; Tahat, Y. A., Alhadab, M. (2017), p. 4 which includes the leverage as a factor in their regression analysis.
1835 Cf. Dechow, P., Ge, W., Schrand, C. (2010), pp. 379-380.
1836 Cf. extensively chapter 4.1.3.3.1 for scale effects in value relevance studies.
1837 Cf. Gabriel, A. (2015), pp. 123-124.
1838 Cf. exemplarily the studies of Athanassakos, G. (2007), p. 1406; Bartov, E., Goldberg, S. R., Kim, M. (2005), pp. 105-106; Garvey, G. T., Milbourn, T. T. (2000), p. 229; Kaspereit, T., Lopatta, K. (2016), p. 8; Mir, A. E., Seboui, S. (2006), p. 250; Rapp, M. S., Schellong, D., Schmidt, M., et al. (2011), p. 178 which includes total assets as a size variable in their regression equation.
1839 Cf. Shivdasani, A., Zenner, M. (2005), pp. 26-28, 32.
1840 Cf. Nichols, D. C., Wahlen, J. M. (2004), p. 265.

explaining stock prices.[1841] The turnovers and also the change in turnover can be interpreted as a sign for market power of a company.[1842] The information contained in change in turnovers is captured in the regression equation with the variable Change in Sales (ΔSALES), expressed by the percentage change in turnovers per period. A positive sign is expected for this variable.[1843]

Variations in the stock price of a company cannot only be explained with the help of firm specific variables. There also may be macroeconomic and country-specific factors that influence stock prices of companies.[1844] Empirical studies indicate that the value relevance of key figures depends on country-specific factors and that due to these factors the value relevance of key figures can differ from country to country. For this reason the variable COUNTRY is included in order to capture country-specific effects that might influence the key figure's value relevance. It contains the country in which a company is located.[1845] Apart from differences concerning the value relevance of key figures, this variable stresses that there are differences in investor protection and corporate governance mechanisms in the invested countries. These differences may have effects on capital markets and behaviour of investors.[1846]

Beside the country also the industry in which a company conducts its business may have an influence on the stock price. For this purpose the variable INDUSTRY is a further variable in the regression equation. It reflects the industry in which the company conducts its business.[1847]

The stock price is also influenced by a company's risk which is connected with a purchase of its shares.[1848] In order to gather the risk assessment of investors, the variable RISK is added to the regression equation. The applied risk factor is similar to the beta of the CAPM model. It is the quotient of the percentage change in the price of a share at the stock market and the corresponding percentage change in its national index in which it is

1841 Cf. Anthony, J. H., Ramesh, K. (1992), pp. 205-206; cf. extensively the empirical study of Anthony, J. H., Ramesh, K. (1992) who proves that changes in sales differ according to life cycle phase of a company.

1842 Cf. Vorstius, S. (2004), p. 111.

1843 Cf. exemplarily the studies of Barth, M. E., Landsman, W. R., Lang, M. H. (2008), p. 482; Lang, M., Raedy, J. S., Yetman, M. H. (2003), p. 370; Rapp, M. S., Schellong, D., Schmidt, M., et al. (2011), p. 178; Schremper, R., Pälchen Oliver (2001), p. 548 which also includes sales growth as variable in the regression equation; another possibility to capture future growth possibilities in a regression equation is the divisions of research and development expenditures to total sales, cf. Mir, A. E., Seboui, S. (2006), pp. 250-251.

1844 Cf. Dechow, P., Ge, W., Schrand, C. (2010), p. 370; Elbakry, A. E., Nwachukwu, J. C., Abdou, H. A., et al. (2017), p. 11.

1845 Cf. Barton, J., Hansen, T. B., Pownall, G. (2010), p. 771; Dechow, P., Ge, W., Schrand, C. (2010), p. 370; Frost, C. A., Gordon, E. A., Hayes, A. F. (2006), pp. 437-441.

1846 Cf. Frost, C. A., Gordon, E. A., Hayes, A. F. (2006), pp. 437-441; La Porta, R., Lopez-de-Silanes, F., Shleifer, A., et al. (2000), pp. 3-6.

1847 Cf. for similar procedure the empirical studies of Gabriel, A. (2015), pp. 120-123; Kaspereit, T., Lopatta, K. (2016), p. 7 which implements country and industry specific variables in their regression equations; cf. also Vorstius, S. (2004), p. 176 who divides its sample according to industries and compares the value relevance.

1848 Cf. Lueg, R., Schäffer, U. (2010), pp. 9-10.

listed.[1849] A change in risk can be connected with a change of risk factors which are outside the company or with a company-specific risk factor. For this variable no sign is predicted.[1850]

A challenge for association studies is to define all necessary variables which explain the stock market variable. Correlated omitted variables might derivate the results.[1851] All influence factors which are not covered by the explanatory variable or control variables are contained in the term $\varepsilon_{i,t}$ of the regression equation.[1852]

On basis of previous remarks the six following regression equations are formed. The value relevance of the key figures can be compared because only the analysed performance measure is exchanged in each equation. All other variables do not change.[1853] In order to avoid scale effects, all variables which are absolute numbers are deflated by the numbers of shares outstanding. These are the variables $BVE_{i,t}$, $VA_{i,t}$, $NOA_{i,t}$, $DIV_{i,t}$, $LEV_{i,t}$ and $ASS_{i,t}$.[1854]

$$P_{i,t} = \beta_0 + \beta_1 BVE_{i,t} + \beta_2 VA_{i,t} + \beta_3 NOA_{i,t} + \beta_4 DIV_{i,t} + \beta_5 LEV_{i,t} + \beta_6 ASS_{i,t} + \beta_7 \Delta SALES_{i,t} + \beta_8 COUNTRY_{i,t} + \beta_9 INDUSTRY_{i,t} + \beta_{10} RISK_{i,t}$$

Formula 46: Determination of relative information content for performance measure Value Added

$$P_{i,t} = \beta_0 + \beta_1 BVE_{i,t} + \beta_2 PER_{i,t} + \beta_3 NOA_{i,t} + \beta_4 DIV_{i,t} + \beta_5 LEV_{i,t} + \beta_6 ASS_{i,t} + \beta_7 \Delta SALES_{i,t} + \beta_8 COUNTRY_{i,t} + \beta_9 INDUSTRY_{i,t} + \beta_{10} RISK_{i,t}$$

Formula 47: Determination of relative information content for performance measure Price Earnings Ratio

$$P_{i,t} = \beta_0 + \beta_1 BVE_{i,t} + \beta_2 EPS_{i,t} + \beta_3 NOA_{i,t} + \beta_4 DIV_{i,t} + \beta_5 LEV_{i,t} + \beta_6 ASS_{i,t} + \beta_7 \Delta SALES_{i,t} + \beta_8 COUNTRY_{i,t} + \beta_9 INDUSTRY_{i,t} + \beta_{10} RISK_{i,t}$$

Formula 48: Determination of relative information content for performance measure Earnings per Share

$$P_{i,t} = \beta_0 + \beta_1 BVE_{i,t} + \beta_2 ROI_{i,t} + \beta_3 NOA_{i,t} + \beta_4 DIV_{i,t} + \beta_5 LEV_{i,t} + \beta_6 ASS_{i,t} + \beta_7 \Delta SALES_{i,t} + \beta_8 COUNTRY_{i,t} + \beta_9 INDUSTRY_{i,t} + \beta_{10} RISK_{i,t}$$

Formula 49: Determination of relative information content for performance measure Return on Investment

1849 Cf. for a similar approach the empirical study of Lovata, L. M., Costigan, M. L. (2002), pp. 218-219 who include a beta factor in their regression equation.

1850 Cf. Lovata, L. M., Costigan, M. L. (2002), p. 219.

1851 Cf. Lindemann, J. (2006), p. 972; Schmidt, M. (2005), p. 113.

1852 Cf. Gabriel, A. (2015), p. 113.

1853 Cf. for similar procedure for testing relative information content Biddle, G. C., Bowen, R. M., Wallace, J. S. (1997), p. 310; Chen, S., Dodd, J. L. (2001); El-Sayed Ebaid, I. (2011), pp. 77-78; Holler, A. (2009), pp. 137-146.

1854 Cf. extensively for an argumentation for deflating with the numbers of shares outstanding chapter 4.1.2.3.1.

$$P_{i,t} = \beta_0 + \beta_1 BVE_{i,t} + \beta_2 ROE_{i,t} + \beta_3 NOA_{i,t} + \beta_4 DIV_{i,t} + \beta_5 LEV_{i,t} + \beta_6 ASS_{i,t} + \beta_7 \Delta SALES_{i,t} + \beta_8 COUNTRY_{i,t} + \beta_9 INDUSTRY_{i,t} + \beta_{10} RISK_{i,t}$$

Formula 50: Determination of relative information content for performance measure Return on Equity

$$P_{i,t} = \beta_0 + \beta_1 BVE_{i,t} + \beta_2 ROS_{i,t} + \beta_3 NOA_{i,t} + \beta_4 DIV_{i,t} + \beta_5 LEV_{i,t} + \beta_6 ASS_{i,t} + \beta_7 \Delta SALES_{i,t} + \beta_8 COUNTRY_{i,t} + \beta_9 INDUSTRY_{i,t} + \beta_{10} RISK_{i,t}$$

Formula 51: Determination of relative information content for performance measure Return on Sales

Table 19 gives an overview of all variables used.

Table 19: Overview of variables of panel regression

Variable	Proxy for	Expected sign	Definition	Notation
Market Capitalisation divided by number of shares / Stock price	Market value of equity capital	Dependent variable	Product of stock price at a company's fiscal year end and number of shares	P
Value Added Price Earnings Ratio Earnings per Share Return on Investment Return on Equity Return on Sales		Positive, exception: Price Earnings Ratio, negative sign expected	Cf. chapters 3.1 and 3.3.2	VA EPS PER ROI ROE ROS
Book Value of Equity Capital	Book Value of Equity Capital	No prediction	Book value of a company's equity capital at the end of a fiscal year	BVE
Net Operating Assets	Operating Assets	Positive	Cf. chapter 4.1.2.3.7	NOA
Dividend paid within a fiscal year	Dividend policy	Positive	Total dividend divided by number of shares	DIV
Leverage Ratio	Capital structure and financial stability	Negative	Total debt capital divided by total equity capital	LEV
Total Assets	Size of company	Independent Variable	Balance sheet total	ASS
Change in Sales	Growth	Positive	Difference between turnover of the current period and turnover of the previous period divided by turnover of the previous period	ΔSALES

Variable	Proxy for	Expected sign	Definition	Notation
Country	Country-specific factors	Time invariant Variable – no sign expected	Differentiation of country is conducted by consecutive numbering	COUNTRY
Industry	Industry-specific factors	Time invariant Variable – no sign expected	Differentiation of industry is conducted by consecutive numbering	INDUSTRY
Risk	Risk that investor bears inherent with investment	No prediction	Division of percentage change in the price of a share and the percentage change of the national index	RISK

Source: Own table

4.1.2.3.8 Panel Regression as the Applied Statistical Method

Association studies typically use regression analysis or panel regressions as a tool for determining the value relevance of key figures or book values.[1855] The regression analysis explains a dependent variable with one or more independent variables.[1856] It considers several objects in one year on the basis of cross-sectional data or one object over several years on the basis of longitudinal data.[1857] Panel data is defined as a data set which observes several objects over several years.[1858] So it is a combination of cross-sectional and time series data.[1859] Using panel data leads to a higher efficiency in analysing data due to the higher amount of information contained in the data. More sophisticated models can be tested in comparison to cross-sectional or longitudinal data sets.[1860]

Two kinds of panels exist: Balanced and unbalanced ones. Balanced panels are panels in which every subject is observed during the complete time. Unbalanced panels do not contain data for every subject in every period of observation.[1861] The same statistical techniques can be used in both cases.[1862]

It is often the case that this heterogeneity cannot be observed with the help of variables. Due to the structure of panel data heterogeneity of analysed objects can be considered statistically.[1863]

Panel regressions can be conducted with three different models: Pooled regression, fixed effects model (FEM) and random effects model (REM).[1864] The pooled regression

1855 Cf. Gow, I. D., Ormazabal, G., Taylor, D. J. (2010), p. 484; Lindemann, J. (2006), p. 972.
1856 Cf. Schloemer, M. (2003), p. 26.
1857 Cf. Annacker, D. (2011), p. 73; Bauer, T. K., Fertig, M., Schmidt, C. M. (2009), pp. 69-78.
1858 Cf. Baltagi, B. H. (2013), p. 1; Petersen, M. A. (2008), p. 435.
1859 Cf. Bauer, T. K., Fertig, M., Schmidt, C. M. (2009), p. 76.
1860 Cf. Oliveira, L., Rodrigues, L. L., Craig, R. (2010), p. 246; cf. also for the advantages of panel data Gujarati, D. N., Porter, D. C. (2009), pp. 592-593; Hsiao, C. (2003), pp. 1-8.
1861 Cf. Baltagi, B. H. (2013), p. 187; Greene, W. H. (2012), p. 388.
1862 Cf. Brooks, C. (2014), p. 529.
1863 Cf. Baltagi, B. H. (2013), p. 13; Schröder, A. (2009), p. 316.
1864 Cf. Asteriou, D., Hall, S. G. (2011), pp. 417-420; Greene, W. H. (2012), pp. 386-387; Varmaz, A. (2006), p. 163.

ignores the existing heterogeneity of objects. The residual term contains it. Additionally pooled regressions ignore the existence of cross-sectional and time-series attributes of panel data.[1865] So, this method does not consider which observed value is allocated to which object.[1866] Providing that heterogeneity exists, the pooled regression results in distorted regression coefficients.[1867]

FEM and REM consider unobservable heterogeneity between the different objects of a sample which cannot be described with a variable.[1868] These models base on the assumption that every object has an individual unobserved effect on the dependent variable. The difference between FEM and REM is that these object specific influence factors or effects are considered as random or as fixed.[1869]

In other words: The residual term contains so far the unobservable heterogeneity which can be divided into individual, time and common effects. In general, the FEM model is used if individual or time effects correlate with the independent variables. The REM model is applied if no correlation exists.[1870] Both models assume that influence factors are constant over time.[1871]

The FEM model uses the Least Square Dummy Variable (LSDV) as a method for determining the regression parameters.[1872] Often the so-called within transformation is used in order to reduce time necessary for computing. The within transformation deducts from every variable of the equation the time mean of each object. Individual influences are eliminated (demeaned values).[1873] REM normally uses the Generalized Least Square (GLS) approach for calculating regression coefficients.[1874]

By analysing panel data, it is an important question which method is applied. The econometric literature offers tests which help to identify the appropriate method for samples used in empirical studies. Illustration 23 summarises the approach used in this empirical study for identifying the model for panel regression.[1875]

The first question to answer is: Do object specific influence factors occur in the sample? On the basis of an F test the pooled regression and the FEM are compared. Rejecting the null hypothesis that no heterogeneity occurs, the application of pooled regression technique is obsolete.[1876] Accepting the null hypothesis means that no heterogeneity exists in the panel data or existing heterogeneity can be completely explained with the help of variables.[1877]

1865 Cf. Gujarati, D. N., Porter, D. C. (2009), pp. 594-595; Varmaz, A. (2006), pp. 163-164.

1866 Cf. Aßmann, C., Rässler, S., Wolf, K. (2012), p. 155; Jaeger, S. (2012), p. 76.

1867 Cf. Varmaz, A. (2006), p. 164.

1868 Cf. Dorfard, A. (2014), p. 104.

1869 Cf. Aßmann, C., Rässler, S., Wolf, K. (2012), pp. 155-156; Jaeger, S. (2012), p. 76.

1870 Cf. Köster, C. (2015), p. 77; Schröder, A. (2009), pp. 317-318.

1871 Cf. Aßmann, C., Rässler, S., Wolf, K. (2012), p. 156.

1872 Cf. Dreger, C., Kosfeld, R., Eckey, H.-F. (2014), p. 264; Hsiao, C. (2003), p. 32.

1873 Cf. Brooks, C. (2014), p. 530; Gujarati, D. N., Porter, D. C. (2009), pp. 599-602.

1874 Cf. Brooks, C. (2014), p. 536; Schröder, A. (2009), p. 318.

1875 Cf. Varmaz, A. (2006), p. 167; cf. basically for the following approach of model decision: Annacker, D. (2011), pp. 92-94; Dreger, C., Kosfeld, R., Eckey, H.-F. (2014), pp. 272-274; Jaeger, S. (2012), pp. 95-100; Lippe, P. von (2011), http://www.von-der-lippe.org/dokumente/Taupool.pdf.

1876 Cf. Asteriou, D., Hall, S. G. (2011), pp. 418-419; Dreger, C., Kosfeld, R., Eckey, H.-F. (2014), pp. 260-262, 265; Varmaz, A. (2006), pp. 164-165.

1877 Cf. Schröder, A. (2009), p. 317.

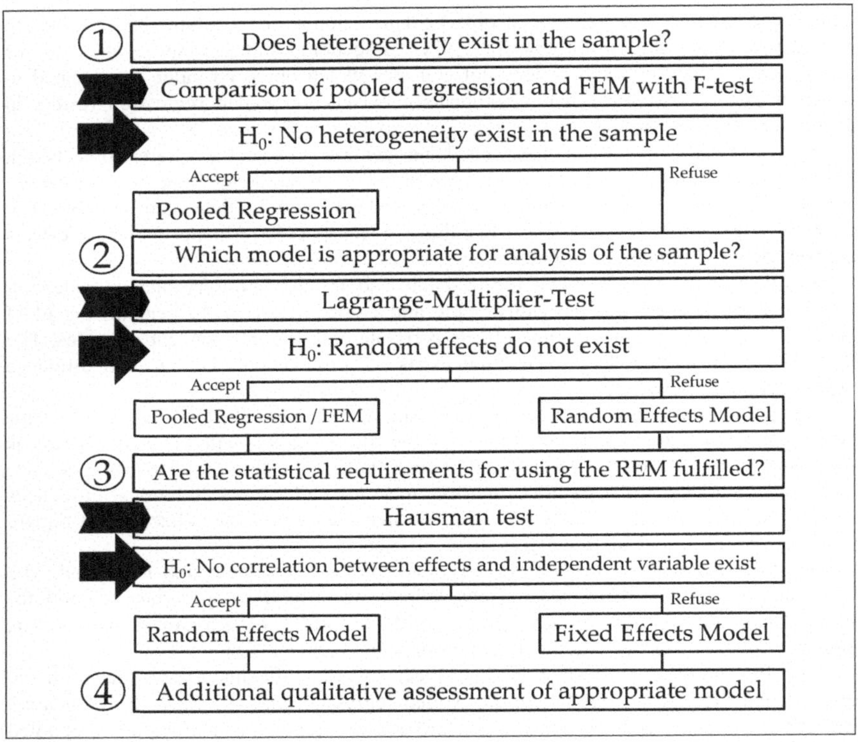

Source: In the style of: Jaeger, S. (2012), p. 97; Lippe, P. von der (2011), S. 3; Wolf, R., Hoffmann, H. (2017), p. 382
Illustration 23: Decision model for selecting the appropriate panel model

If the F test reveals that heterogeneity exists, the Lagrange-Multiplier-test (LM-test) delivers additional insights if the pooled regression or REM is the appropriate model.[1878] The null hypothesis of the test is that no random effects exist. Rejecting the null hypothesis that no random effects exist indicates that the REM will lead to better computed parameters. Vice versa the pooled regression or FEM should be preferred.[1879]

However, a requirement for applying the REM is that effects contained in the data do not correlate with independent variables.[1880] The Hausman test examines the illustrated issue and determines if FEM or REM is the convenient model.[1881] The null hypothesis is

1878 Cf. Annacker, D. (2011), pp. 92-93; Schröder, A. (2009), pp. 322-323.
1879 Cf. Dreger, C., Kosfeld, R., Eckey, H.-F. (2014), p. 271; Greene, W. H. (2012), pp. 416-419.
1880 Cf. Köster, C. (2015), p. 77.
1881 Cf. Dreger, C., Kosfeld, R., Eckey, H.-F. (2014), p. 272; Giesselmann, M., Windzio, M. (2012), p. 109; Greene, W. H. (2012), pp. 419-420.

that no correlation between effects and independent variable exists and the REM is the most efficient method.[1882] Rejecting the null hypothesis of the Hausman test indicates the application of the FEM. Otherwise the REM should be preferred.[1883]

Beside the two statistical tests further qualitative criteria can be used in order to make a decision if the FEM or REM is the appropriate model:[1884]

1. Do the effects result from randomly distributed influence factors (REM) or do they result from the characteristics of selected objects (FEM)?

It is assumed that the effects result from the different characteristics of the companies in the sample.[1885]

2. How is the relation between the number of objects and the observed values per object? A high number of objects would result in a loss of degrees of freedom by applying the FEM.[1886]

The number of objects is relatively small in comparison to the observed values per objects. This would result in a loss of degrees of freedom by applying the FEM.[1887]

3. Does the sample consider nearly all objects of the basic population (FEM) or is it a relatively small sample (REM)?

The sample contains 410 companies with large market capitalisation throughout the European Union. However, the basic population is a multiple of the sample because there are several companies on stock markets at the European Union which are not part of the sample. This indicates an application of the REM.

4. Are the insights from the study limited to the objects of the sample (FEM) or should the results be transferred to all objects of the basic population (REM)?[1888]

The insights should be transferred to the basic population.

The criterion 1) indicates an application of the FEM while criteria 2), 3) and 4) recommend an application of the REM. Thus, the REM is used for the panel regression.

4.1.3 Description of Data Base

4.1.3.1 Analysis of Annual Reports

In order to take all research questions into account, a collocation of European companies is necessary, in order to adequately answer them. To be more precise, the population are

1882 Cf. Köster, C. (2015), p. 77; Schröder, A. (2009), p. 322.
1883 Cf. Baltagi, B. H. (2013), p. 79.
1884 Cf. Jaeger, S. (2012), p. 96; Klodt, T. (2000), pp. 109-111; Wenzel, A. (2006), p. 250; cf. also Gujarati, D. N., Porter, D. C. (2009), pp. 606-607 and Hsiao, C. (2003), pp. 43-44 who recommend to consider also qualitative aspects by choosing the appropriate model.
1885 Cf. Jaeger, S. (2012), p. 98; Wenzel, A. (2006), p. 250.
1886 Cf. Asteriou, D., Hall, S. G. (2011), p. 419; Baltagi, B. H. (2013), p. 15.
1887 Cf. Jaeger, S. (2012), p. 99; Wenzel, A. (2006), p. 250.
1888 Cf. also Baltagi, B. H. (2013), p. 14.

companies located in Europe which are listed on a capital market. On the basis of the population the sample for the empirical study has been defined.[1889]

The starting point for all parts of the empirical study is the Stoxx Europe 600 in its composition at 31st July 2015. The Stox Europe 600 contains 600 companies from 17 countries of the European region. According to their market capitalisation they can be classified as large, mid-size and small companies. Later changes of composition of the index are not considered in the data base of the empirical study.[1890]

The data base contains relatively large companies in terms of market capitalisation in order to ensure a certain degree of quality of their financial statements. All financial statements of these companies are controlled by an auditor company which reduces the probability of violation of accounting rules.[1891]

The composition of the index is taken from the financial service information provider Bloomberg. As it is important to be able to differentiate the sample companies according to their origin, the country classification of Bloomberg is also part of the database for the empirical study.[1892]

A further classification criterion is the industry sector in which a company operates. Therefore, the supersector classification of Stoxx is used which enables the allocation of companies to 19 sectors in total. The classification scheme is based on the Industry Classification Benchmark.[1893] Each company has a subsector code which consists of four digits. The first two digits contain the information about the Supersector.[1894]

On the basis of the supersectors companies are grouped for the empirical study into two categories: Finance or Industry. The category "Finance" mostly contains banks and insurance companies. The category "Industry" contains all other companies which do not focus their business on providing capital or financial services to other companies. Illustration 24 gives an overview of the supersectors and their category.

Due to mergers and acquisitions during the time period of the analysis some exceptions concerning the annual report analysis have to be taken into account. Furthermore, some annual reports are not available via the Internet such that for these companies and the respective fiscal years, they are not part of the analysis.[1895] For analysing the annual reports, the sample in table 20 out of the 600 companies of the Stoxx Europe 600 is taken for the time period 2012–2015.

1889 Cf. for similar argumentation for sample selection Vorstius, S. (2004), pp. 152-153.

1890 Cf. https://www.stoxx.com/index-details?symbol=SXXP , access at 12th July 2017; cf. for a complete list of the companies of the Stoxx Europe 600 appendix 1 (The appendices are available for download free of charge online on SpringerLink (see URL at the beginning of this chapter)).

1891 Cf. Dechow, P., Ge, W., Schrand, C. (2010), p. 383.

1892 Cf. for further information www.bloomberg.com.

1893 Cf. Stoxx (2015), p. 40; cf. for an overview of the Stoxx Europe 600 classification Stoxx (2015), pp. 147-148.

1894 Stoxx customer service provided the data for Supersector classification; cf. for a complete allocation of supersectors to single companies of Stoxx Europe 600 appendix 2.

1895 Cf. for an overview of all special cases or omitted reports appendix 3.

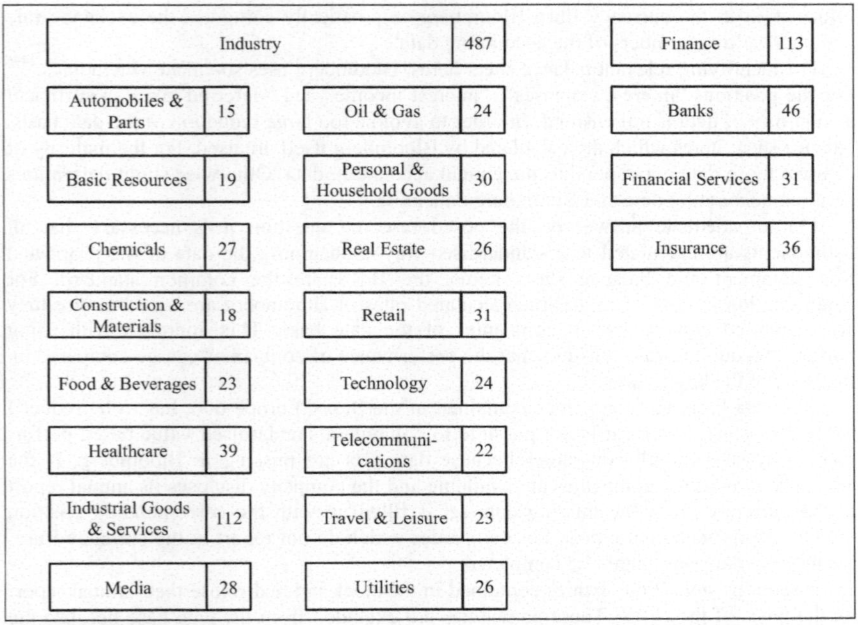

Source: Own illustration

Illustration 24: Supersectors of Stoxx Europe 600 and allocation to category Industry or Finance

Table 20: Composition of data base for analysing annual reports

Fiscal year	Annual reports of companies of category industry	Annual reports of companies of category finance	Annual report not available	Companies in total
2012	480	113	7	600
2013	483	113	4	600
2014	487	113	0	600
2015	482	113	5	600
Σ	1,932	452	16	2,400

Source: Own table

4.1.3.2 Standardised Calculation of ROCE, ROE Spread and Value Added

The division of all companies into the categories "Industry" and "Finance" is important for the second part of the empirical study, the standardised calculation of ROCE Spread, ROE spread and Value Added. The key figures are computed on the basis of public available accounting data. According to the presented calculation scheme the relevant accounting data is taken from Bloomberg. For companies which do not disclose financial information in the currency Euro Bloomberg automatically computes the exchange rate and the resulting numbers of the accounting data.

For identifying relevant balance sheet items, Bloomberg uses so-called Mnemonics.[1896] For the positions "interest expenses", "interest income" and "deferred taxes" a sufficient availability of data is not ensured. In order to avoid a too large reduction of the data basis, balance sheet items which are calculated by Bloomberg itself are used. For the majority of datasets these data correspond to the annual accounting data. Otherwise slight derivations between accounting data and Bloomberg data exist.

For an adequate answer on the posed research question it is necessary that all components are calculated in a standardised way. Concerning the data of the profit and loss statement and balance sheet items, the IFRS are the common standard. For determination of cost of capital the calculated rates of Bloomberg are used because they are computed equally for all companies of the data base. This approach with using uniform accounting rules ensures that the performance of companies can be compared on the basis of the key figures.

The data base, the companies contained in the Stoxx Europe 600, has to be reduced for two reasons. Firstly, it is not possible to compute a standardised value based performance measure for all companies because data sets are missing in Bloomberg. If the annual reports of the companies are available and the company discloses its annual report in the currency Euro, the missing data set is filled up with the corresponding position directly from the annual report. For companies which do not report in the currency Euro, the missing data sets cannot be completed.

Secondly, not all companies contained in the stock index disclose their annual report on the basis of the IFRS. These companies are excluded from the data base because the application of other accounting principles might lead to derivations by comparing the performance of companies. The applied accounting standard is also identified with the help of Bloomberg.

It was noted that the introduction of IFRS is not a guarantee for accounting quality and complete cross-country comparability.[1897] However, the quality of accounting data

Table 21: Composition of data base for standardised key figure calculation

Fiscal year	Number of companies with complete data sets	Number of companies with incomplete data sets	Number of companies not disclosing on the basis of IFRS	Companies in total
2012	517	66	17	600
2013	525	58	17	600
2014	544	39	17	600
2015	555	28	17	600
2016	543	39	18	600
Σ	2,684	230	86	3,000

Source: Own table

1896 Cf. appendix 4 which contains a list of used Bloomberg Mnemonics.
1897 Cf. extensively the discussion in chapter 2.4.3.

can be assumed as relatively high due to initiatives of the European Union in order to ensure a strong enforcement and a uniform application of accounting rules.[1898] Furthermore, the IFRS are able to improve the informativeness of accounting numbers independent from the former accounting system and at least align possible remaining national differences. It can be concluded that the IFRS enable investors to compare performance of companies from different countries in a better way than on the basis of national accounting standards.[1899]

4.1.3.3 Value Relevance Analysis

The data base for the third part of the empirical study also uses available data in Bloomberg. For the calculation of operating assets data from Bloomberg is used, in order to receive the results according to the presented calculation scheme.[1900] Beside typical financial assets and assets which will be disposed respectively belong to discontinued operations the category non-operating assets is added to the calculation scheme of the variable NOA. This category and the corresponding data fields of Bloomberg summarise non-current and current assets which are not classified under the typical balance sheet items. These assets are deducted because they are assessed as unnecessary for the company's operations.[1901]

Companies belonging to the category "Finance" are excluded from the panel regression due to the divergent rules for disclosure. That means that banks, insurance and financial services companies are not further considered in this part of the study.[1902]

Table 22: Composition of data base for panel regression analysis

Fiscal year	**Number of companies with complete data sets**	**Removal of companies of category Bank / Insurance**	**Number of companies with incomplete data sets**	**Compa-nies which do not report on the basis of IFRS**	**Extreme observa-tions**	**Compa-nies in total**
2012	372	113	105	10	0	600
2013	386	113	91	10	0	600
2014	402	113	75	10	0	600
2015	410	113	67	10	0	600
2016	401	113	77	9	0	600
Σ	1,971	565	415	49	0	3,000

Source: Own table

1898 Cf. Daske, H., Hail, L., Leuz, C., et al. (2008), pp. 1093-1094.

1899 Cf. Elbakry, A. E., Nwachukwu, J. C., Abdou, H. A., et al. (2017), p. 11.

1900 Cf. appendix 5 which contains a list of used Bloomberg Mnemonics.

1901 Cf. Baetge, J., Kirsch, H.-J., Thiele, S. (2004), p. 374 who also assess these assets as not necessary for a company's operation; cf. Trautwein, A. (2007), p. 170 who also deducts other assets for the calculation of operating assets.

1902 Cf. for the same procedure in the context of regression analysis Elbakry, A. E., Nwachukwu, J. C., Abdou, H. A., et al. (2017), p. 13; Mir, A. E., Seboui, S. (2006), p. 245; Wagenhofer, A., Dücker, H. (2007), p. 282; Worthington, A. C., West, T. (2004), p. 207.

4.2 Results of the Empirical Study

4.2.1 Analysis of Annual Reports

The analysis of the annual reports reveals that approximately the share of those companies which mentions at least a value based performance measure in their annual report fluctuates between 11 % and 13 % during the investigation period. Hypothesis H1 is rejected as in every year the relative share of companies is clearly below the expected 18 %.[1903]

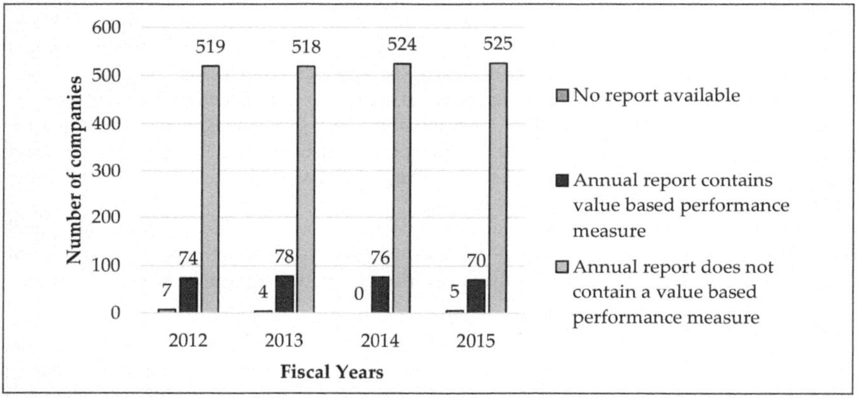

Source: Own illustration

Illustration 25: Number of companies with value based performance measures in their annual business reports

Having a closer look at the companies which mention a value based performance measure indicates that companies from the countries Germany, Great Britain and Switzerland dominate. They tend to mention a key figure in their annual report more frequently than companies in other countries. From the 70 companies in 2015 which have at least one point on the basis of the used ranking scheme, 47 companies have as an origin country Germany, Great Britain or Switzerland. In Austria, Finland and Greece, none of the companies receive at least one point. But it has to be considered that only 6 companies from Austria and 3 companies from Greece are part of the analysis.

Among all countries, Germany is the only country in which consistently over the time period over 20 companies mention a value based performance measure in the annual reports. This is twice the incidence as in Great Britain or Switzerland except the year 2013 for Great Britain.

1903 Cf. chapter 4.1.1.1 for hypotheses for the analysis of annual reports.

Table 23: Number of companies which mentioned a value based performance measure sorted by their countries of origin

Country of origin	2012	2013	2014	2015
Austria	1	1	1	0
Belgium	1	1	1	1
Czech	0	0	0	0
Denmark	1	2	2	2
Finland	1	0	1	0
France	3	3	3	3
Germany	26	27	26	25
Great Britain	13	15	13	11
Greece	1	0	0	0
Ireland	2	2	2	2
Italy	2	2	2	2
Luxembourg	1	2	2	2
Netherlands	2	2	2	2
Norway	0	1	1	1
Portugal	0	0	0	0
Spain	1	1	1	2
Sweden	6	6	6	6
Switzerland	13	13	13	11
Σ	74	78	76	70

Source: Own table

The dominant supersectors are Industrial Goods & Services in which 18 up to 20 companies conduct Value Added Reporting and companies allocated to the supersector Bank in which 12 or 13 companies inform their readers about the defined key figures. These are the only two supersectors which contain a double-digit number of companies. It is striking that in three supersectors, Basic Resources, Real Estate and Technology companies do not give any information about a value based performance measure. Regarding companies in the supersectors Construction & Materials, Financial Services, Oil & Gas and Telecommunications only a small number of companies get one point. Thus, many companies in the listed supersectors give no information concerning the further application and calculation of the value based performance measures they use.

Table 24: Number of companies which mentioned a value based performance measure sorted by their Supersector

Supersector	2012	2013	2014	2015
Automobiles & Parts	4	4	4	4
Banks	12	13	12	13
Basic Resources	0	0	0	0
Chemicals	9	8	8	8
Construction & Materials	0	0	0	1
Financial Services	1	1	1	1
Food & Beverages	3	3	2	2
Healthcare	5	7	7	6
Industrial Goods & Services	18	19	20	18
Insurance	6	6	5	5
Media	1	2	2	2
Oil & Gas	1	1	1	0
Personal & Household Goods	3	3	2	2
Real Estate	0	0	0	0
Retail	4	3	4	2
Technology	0	0	0	0
Telecommunications	0	1	1	0
Travel & Leisure	4	3	3	2
Utilities	3	4	4	4
Σ	74	78	76	70

Source: Own table

Among the companies which give information about a value based performance measure, key figures which are based on the Value Added, EVA or Economic profit concept dominate. Many companies also give individual names to their key figures like RTL Value Added or Fraport Value Added. Only two companies, Bayer and Lufthansa, use the CVA. While Lufthansa changes its value based performance measure during the investigation period from CVA to Earnings after cost of capital, Bayer continues to use the CVA. Four companies use the CFROI. In comparison to the value based performance measures which base on earnings figures, this is relatively low. Table 23 summarises the applied value based performance measures and gives an indication about their frequency of application.

Table 25: Applied value based performance measure by companies of Stoxx Europe 600

Value Based Performance Measure	Companies applying
Adecco EVA	Adecco
Cash Flow Return on Investment	Glaxosmithkline, Kerry Group, Solvay, Syngenta
Cash Value Added	Bayer, Deutsche Lufthansa
Continental Value Contribution	Continental
Contribution after capital charge	Adidas
Earnings after cost of capital	Deutsche Lufthansa
EBIT after asset charge	Deutsche Post
EBIT after cost of capital	BASF, Metro
Economic Profit	Banco Bilbao Vizcaya Argenta, Cable & Wireless Communications, Capita, Centrica, Diageo, HSBC Holdings, Julius Baer Group, Lloyds Banking Group, Nordea Bank, Novozymes, Royal Bank of Scotland Group, Spectris, Zurich Insurance Group
Economic Profit after tax	Legrand
Economic Value Added	Accor, Adecco, Atlas Copco, Aviva, Baloise Holding, Barry Callebaut, Commerzbank, Duerr, Evonik Industries, Finmeccanica, Halma, Henkel, Hermes International, IMI, Investec, Kesko, Lonza, OMV, OPAP, Randstad Holding, SES, SGS, Siemens, Unicredit
Economic Value Management Profit	Swiss RE
Fraport Value Added	Fraport
Fuchs Value Added	Fuchs Petrolub
Galencia Economic Profit	Galencia
Intrinsic Value Creation	Hannover Rueck
Kingfisher Economic Profit	Kingfisher
Merck Value Added	Merck
Novartis Economic Value Added	Novartis
Oerlikon Value Added	Oerlikon
Qiagen Value Added	Qiagen
Risk Adjusted Return on Capital	Banco de Sabadell, Bank of Ireland, Credit Agricole, DNB, ING Groep, Jyske Bank, Swedbank
ROCE Spread	Vinci, Weir Group
ROCE with cost of capital	MAN
RTL Group Value Added	RTL Group
Sandvik Value Added	Sandvik
Thyssenkrupp Value Added	Thyssenkrupp

Value Based Performance Measure	Companies applying
Total Value Added	SKF
Value Added	BMW, Bilfinger, Daimler, EON, K+S, Muenchener Rückversicherung, National Grid, RWE, Straumann Holding, TUI
Value Contribution	Volkswagen
Value Creation	Husqvarna

Source: Own table

Some companies are not included in the ranking as they only show e.g. ROCE and WACC in their annual report but do not calculate the difference, e.g. Boliden, Atlas Copco, Croda or Halma.[1904] In addition, a graphical comparison of ROCE and WACC is not assessed as value based performance measure in the sense of this study.[1905]

Some companies inform about the cost of capital but they only provide the reader with the after tax cost of capital. As ROCE is a key figure which is usually calculated without tax influence, the ROCE spread or Value Added has to be calculated with cost of capital before tax.[1906] Atlas Copco is an example for such a disclosure.[1907]

The second research question and hypothesis deal with the amount of accompanying information companies add if they mention a value based performance measure in their annual business report. For analysing and testing this hypothesis, the presented scoring scheme is used. If a company has more than one point, it gives additional information to the reader like the absolute value of the key figure, past values or explains the cost of capital calculation.

Hypothesis H2 can be accepted because in every year more than 50 % of the companies give the reader more information than just the name of the key figure. Many companies deliver the current value of the key figure and at least the value of the previous year so that investors have a point of comparison. However, it has to be noted that none of the companies is successful in receiving the maximum number of points. The reason for this result is that no company gives information about the estimated future development of a key figure in the business report. Also the number of companies with five points decreases during the time period from 11 companies in 2012 to 7 companies in 2015, whereas the number of companies with three or four points remains constant. Approximately a third of the companies publishing value based performance measures provide the reader at least with an information about the level of the cost of capital.

The third research question refers to changes in publication behaviour of the companies. Hypothesis H3 defines a change as a fluctuation of more than 5 % in comparison to the first year of the investigation, 2012. On the basis of the analysis of the annual reports the hypothesis has to be rejected because the limit of 5 % is exceeded in two years as shown in table 26.

1904 Cf. the annual reports of the companies: Atlas Copco (2015), p. 18; Boliden (2014), p. 20; Croda International (2015), p. 117.
1905 Cf. the annual report of TGS Nopec Geophysical (2013), p. 113.
1906 Cf. Pape, U. (2015), pp. 277-278.
1907 Cf. Atlas Copco (2015), p. 18.

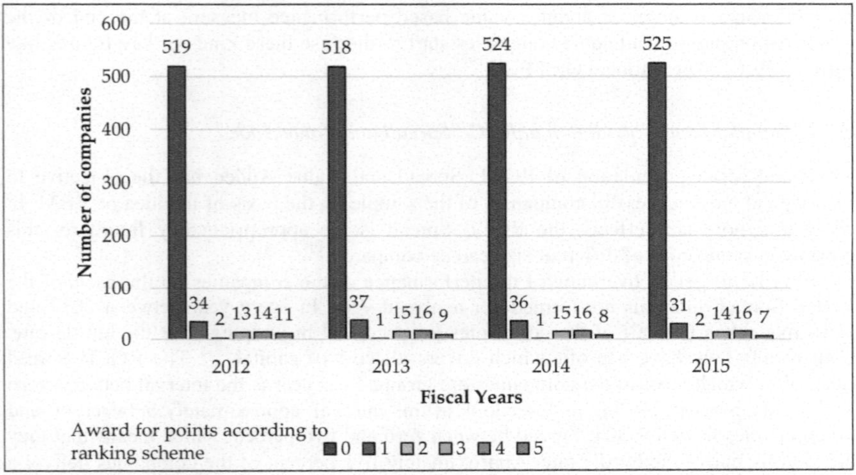

Source: Own illustration

Illustration 26: Assessment of companies' annual business reports

In total, the share of companies which applies a value based performance measure decreases by 5.41 %. This aspect of the analysis shows that the number of companies presenting information about their value concepts or applying them slightly decreases during the investigation period. Companies like Symrise AG[1908] or Imi PLC[1909] do not

Table 26: Relative change of companies applying value based performance measures

Year	Number of companies with at least one point	Relative change referring to starting year (2012)	Relative change referring to previous year
2012	74	–	–
2013	78	+5,41 %	+5,41 %
2014	76	+2,70 %	–2,56 %
2015	70	–5,41 %	–7,89 %

Source: Own table

1908 Cf. the annual report of Symrise (2012) in which a value based performance measure is mentioned and the annual reports in the following years in which information about the key figure is no longer disclosed.

1909 Cf. the annual reports of Imi (2012), Imi (2013), Imi (2014) in which a value based performance measure is mentioned and the annual report of the year 2015 in which information about the key figure is no longer disclosed.

give information anymore about a value based performance measure at the end of the investigation period. But some companies start to disclose these kinds of key figures like Spectris PLC[1910] or National Grid PLC.[1911]

4.2.2 Standardised Calculation of ROCE Spread and Value Added

The standardised calculation of ROCE Spread and Value Added has the objective to identify the most successful companies of the sample on the basis of the idea of VBM. In order to ignore size effects, the ROCE Spread is the appropriate key figure for this purpose as companies of different size can be compared.[1912]

In order to get an overview of the performance of the companies on the basis of the ROCE Spread, intervals are formed per analysed year. In every year between 2012 and 2016 more than the half of the companies is successful in jumping over the hurdle rate. That means they have a profit which covers all cost of capital.[1913] The ROCE Spread interval in which most of the companies are grouped per year is the interval between zero and twenty percent. Having a closer look at this interval, approximately between 60 and 70 companies have a ROCE Spread between zero and two percent which means that they are slightly above the hurdle rate. Approximately five percent of the companies deliver a ROCE Spread between 20 and 39 %. This is a strong decrease in comparison to the previous interval. The further intervals contain companies with very high ROCE spreads. The number of companies in these intervals is very low and fluctuates between eight and fourteen.

To summarise: During the time period of investigation the numbers of companies in the single intervals does not fluctuate in a significant way and that the distribution of performance of the companies is similar in each year. Illustration 27 gives an overview of the number of companies in the ROCE Spread intervals for the single years.[1914]

When focussing on single companies, it can be detected that the company Rightmove Plc is the most successful company in terms of ROCE Spread. The company has in every year of the investigation period a spread which is clearly above 100 %. With these values this company has in every year the highest ROCE Spread of the complete sample. Among the most ten successful companies the companies Rightmove Plc, Hargreaves Landsown Plc and Edenred are part of it in every year. The companies Admiral Group Plc and Next Plc are four times contained in the group of the ten best performing companies.[1915]

1910 Cf. the annual report of Spectris (2012) in which information about a value based performance measure is missing. In the annual reports for the following fiscal years the company gives information about its value based performance measure.

1911 Cf. the annual report of National Grid (2012) in which information about a value based performance measure is missing. In the annual reports for the following fiscal years the company gives information about its value based performance measure.

1912 Cf. Krause, H.-U., Arora, D. (2010), p. 51; Wöltje, J. (2011), p. 221.

1913 Cf. for the importance of covering the cost of capital chapter 2.1.1.2.

1914 Analysis of ROCE Spread bases on the results of the calculation of this key figure for every company of the data sample for the investigation period.

1915 Cf. appendix 6.

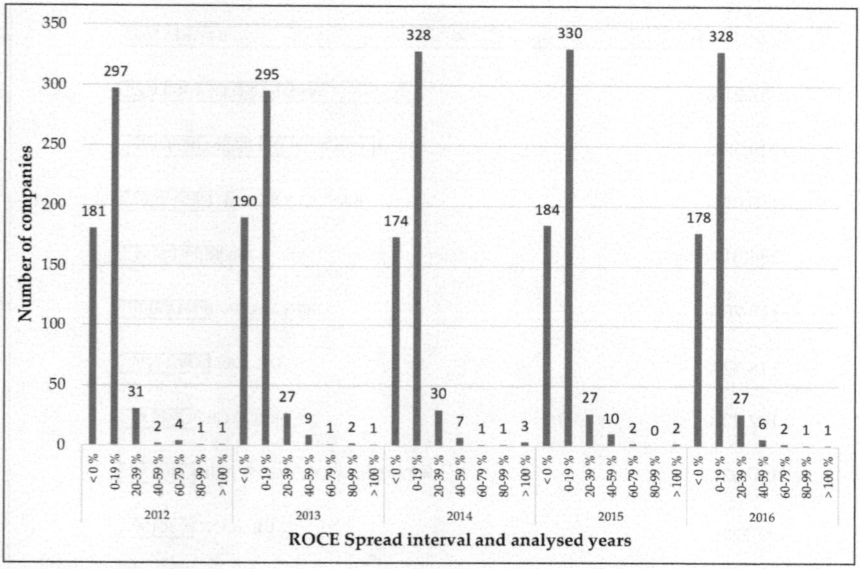

Source: Own illustration
Illustration 27: Ranking of companies on the basis of the ROCE Spread

The group of the companies with the lowest ROCE Spread consists of 50 % of companies which are allocated to the category "Finance" referring to the ten companies with the lowest value of the computed key figure. Exception is the year 2014. In contrast, 9 out of 10 companies of the group of the worst performing companies are allocated to the mentioned category in the year 2013. The company National Bank of Greece is part of the group of the ten companies with lowest ROCE spread in every year of the empirical study. The company Bance Monte dei Paschi Siena is represented four times in this group. All other companies are at least three times or less part of this group.[1916]

For 491 companies of the sample it is possible to calculate the ROCE Spread for the whole period between 2012 and 2016. Therefore, a cumulative ROCE Spread for this subgroup can be calculated over the five periods in order to determine which companies have the highest and lowest ROCE Spreads during a longer time period. For this purpose the ROCE Spreads of every year are added. The results are shown in the illustrations 28 and 29.

1916 Cf. appendix 6.

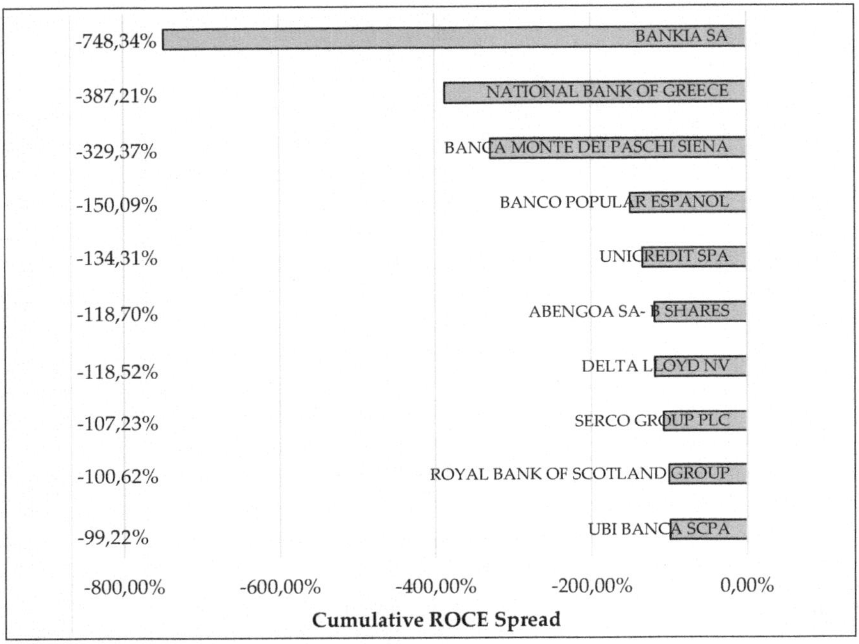

Source: Own illustration
Illustration 28: Ten companies with the lowest cumulative ROCE Spread

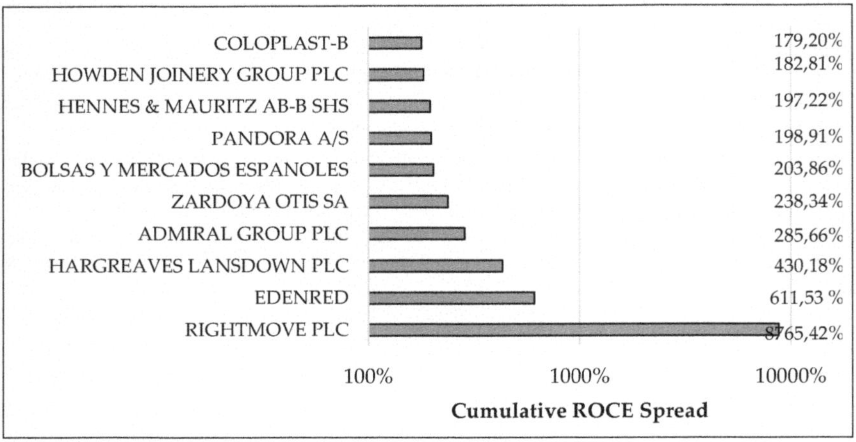

Source: Own illustration
Illustration 29: Ten companies with the highest cumulative ROCE Spread

The best performing company, Righmove Plc has a cumulative ROCE Spread of 8,765 % whereas the second best company has a cumulative ROCE Spread of 612 %. The lowest ROCE Spread during the investigation period has the company Bankia SA with a negative ROCE Spread of 748 %. Illustrations 28 and 29 summarise the results of cumulative ROCE Spread calculation.[1917]

4.2.3 *Value Relevance of Value Added in Comparison to Selected Traditional Key Figures*

4.2.3.1 Descriptive Statistics

4.2.3.1.1 Descriptive Statistics of Dependent Variable and Analysed Key Figures

This chapter aims to give an overview of the data set used for the association studies. Therefore, every variable is analysed per year with the help of typical descriptive statistic measures.

The data set is an unbalanced panel because it does not contain a period observation for every subject.[1918]

The dependent variable is the market capitalisation of companies divided by the number of shares. In other words: The stock price at the end of a fiscal year of a company. The difference between minima and maxima values demonstrates the heterogeneity between the companies of the sample. Median and arithmetic mean show that the average stock price is relatively stable during the time period of investigation.

The independent variable of the first regression equation, the Value Added, is widely spread. This is demonstrated by large differences between the minima and maxima. Referring to the calculation of Value Added and the illustration in the previous chapter, this is not surprising because already in this analysis the gap between top and worst

Table 27: Descriptive statistics of the dependent variable Stock price

Market capitalisation per share / Stock price in EUR					
Year	**2012**	**2013**	**2014**	**2015**	**2016**
Min	0.2195383	0.0186400	0.0041870	0.0050370	0.0020540
1st Quartile	8.649679	9.990240	10.118054	10.206283	9.668124
Median	19.84448	22.21725	23.80366	24.59500	23.61316
3rd Quartile	43.05431	49.53125	49.41000	56.11693	54.36755
Max	5710.366	7889.465	2441.684	3351.265	4559.856
Mean	61.78246	74.27288	58.27963	64.18316	65.33635
SD	325.5885	434.8380	193.8153	222.6866	267.3851
N	372	386	402	410	401

Source: Own table

1917 Cf. appendix 7.
1918 Cf. Baltagi, B. H. (2013), p. 187; Greene, W. H. (2012), p. 388.

Table 28: Descriptive statistics of the variable Value Added

Value Added in EUR					
Year	**2012**	**2013**	**2014**	**2015**	**2016**
Min	-11,882,322,450	-49,908,250,738	-49,803,499,884	-24,472,596,306	-20,370,997,180
1st Quartile	-16,961,213	-102,740,521	-37,783,472	-51,353,311	-33,835,862
Median	132,337,689	114,724,843	109,674,757	119,591,727	152,226,988
3rd Quartile	381,917,241	335,565,234	320,821,164	344,691,713	430,005,910
Max	25,345,838,823	40,986,096,517	9,786,949,718	11,376,063,651	8,544,236,246
Mean	386,029,833	197,343,997	76,823,234	-53,485,125	9,989,728
SD	2,692,063,637	3,819,929,431	2,926,212,301	2,539,086,970	2,229,154,334
N	372	386	402	410	401

Source: Own table

performing companies is very large.[1919] The high standard derivation as well as the differences between median and arithmetic mean also indicate the large dispersion of the variable.[1920] Also during the years included in this panel regression the Value Added fluctuates strongly documented by the changes in minima and maxima per year. The standard derivation is lower in 2016 in comparison to the other analysed years.

Concerning a comparison of median and arithmetic mean, it is striking that the median is below the arithmetic mean in every period. This indicates that lower or negative values of Value Added per share dominate the sample because the median is the value which divides the sample in two halves.[1921] In addition, a difference between median and arithmetic mean is a hint for some outliers because the median is more insensitive to outliers than the arithmetic mean.[1922] Median and arithmetic mean are positive for the whole periods of five years. This shows that the majority of companies is able to cover their cost of capital.[1923]

The inhomogeneity concerning the economic performance of the companies contained in the sample is confirmed by the second dependent variable EPS. This key figure exhibits similar features in comparison to the Value Added variable. That means large differences between minima and maxima, large differences between arithmetic mean and median and a high volatility of values during the years. An exception is the standard derivation which is relatively constant in the last two years.

1919 Cf. for a detailed analysis of the performance of companies on the basis of a value based performance measure chapter 4.2.2.
1920 Cf. Eckstein, P. (2016), p. 121.
1921 Cf. Kohn, W., Öztürk, R. (2017), pp. 45-46.
1922 Cf. Zwerenz, K. (2015), p. 111.
1923 Cf. Holler, A. (2009), p. 174 for similar conclusions on the basis of descriptive statistics of value based performance measures and the analysis of ROCE Spread in chapter 4.2.2.

Table 29: Descriptive statistics of the variable EPS

Earnings per Share					
Year	**2012**	**2013**	**2014**	**2015**	**2016**
Min	-13.873507	-6.275909	-6.766472	-11.925420	-82.685097
1st Quartile	0.4261162	0.3643494	0.3609096	0.3495012	0.3625508
Median	1.260444	1.155265	1.073127	1.109289	1.215025
3rd Quartile	2.778871	2.751993	2.361871	2.605046	2.805791
Max	719.8855	667.3198	181.5548	508.6298	445.2622
Mean	4.525341	4.374652	3.038507	4.018322	3.776858
SD	37.88858	34.73545	12.63113	27.09085	25.20221
N	372	386	402	410	401

Source: Own table

As the key figure PER depends on the previous presented key figure EPS and on the stock price of companies, it is very volatile. For this key figure the low value in 2016 is striking because it is clearly below all other minima during the five years. It results from the company MAN SE. This company makes a slight loss in this fiscal year and has an EPS which is slightly below zero and a stock price of 94.33 EUR which results in a very negative PER. The maximum value in 2013 results from the company Axel Springer SE. The reason is again the method of calculation. The stock price of Axel Springer SE is 46.70 EUR but the EPS is exactly zero due to rounding differences. This leads to a very high PER.

Table 30: Descriptive statistics of the variable PER

Price Earnings Ratio					
Year	**2012**	**2013**	**2014**	**2015**	**2016**
Min	-606.5265	-543.4754	-661.4927	-192.4904	-1,981.4691
1st Quartile	10.33443	12.84370	13.86556	13.77784	13.08478
Median	15.66683	19.00488	19.23872	20.22850	19.07612
3rd Quartile	20.88835	25.13421	25.55850	27.25228	25.14665
Max	1,174.08	25,812,838.43	12,559.92	10,322.35	745.59
Mean	18.11603	66,896.27504	51.91277	50.41551	16.53574
SD	74.6270	1,313,837.6796	628.6081	512.0653	133.5233
N	372	386	402	410	401

Source: Own table

Table 31: Descriptive statistics of the variable ROI

Return on Investment					
Year	**2012**	**2013**	**2014**	**2015**	**2016**
Min	-0.2645351	-0.1831577	-0.5698107	-0.2799405	-0.2585475
1st Quartile	0.05188595	0.05073384	0.04625044	0.04543254	0.04545699
Median	0.08188361	0.07800814	0.07284097	0.07343292	0.07036917
3rd Quartile	0.1238880	0.1209688	0.1137971	0.1093226	0.1058368
Max	2.069944	2.467840	2.725363	2.766101	2.795017
Mean	0.09669785	0.09999135	0.09221694	0.08868762	0.08768481
SD	0.1274184	0.1421849	0.1555121	0.1542008	0.1559363
N	372	386	402	410	401

Source: Own table

It is striking that the median, arithmetic mean and standard derivation of ROI does not fluctuate with the same intensity as the other key figures analysed. The median and arithmetic mean fluctuates between 7 and 9 %. From the perspective of ROI the range of the economic performance of the companies is relatively constant. The ROI data shows an outliner in 2014 with a negative ROI of 56.98 %. The company Serco Group PLC has a large loss in this year which consequently leads to a negative ROI.

The ROE values demonstrate gaps between the worst and the best performing companies. In 2016, the lowest ROE during the whole investigation period is reached with -1,108 %. The company E.ON SE has a very negative EBIT and only a low equity capital so that the ROE is clearly negative. In contrast, the highest ROE amounts to 4,799 % in 2014. The company Rightmove PLC has an EBIT which is 50 times higher than its equity capital. In contrast to the key figures before, the median is constant during the five years and fluctuates between 18.98 % and 21.93 %. The high standard derivation also indicates the large spread of values contained in the sample as well as the differences between median and arithmetic mean in many years.

The last dependent variable, ROS, demonstrates again the broad range of performance spectrum of companies. In 2015, the difference between the minimum with -238 % and the maximum with 550 % is striking. Both values seem to be outliers. The standard derivation is constant with the exception of the year 2015.

Table 32: Descriptive statistics of the variable ROE

Return on Equity					
Year	**2012**	**2013**	**2014**	**2015**	**2016**
Min	-1.688623	-8.420232	-1.077505	-1.097087	-12.095571
1st Quartile	0.10612009	0.10629858	0.09715120	0.08808463	0.09756098
Median	0.1929788	0.1753089	0.1609770	0.1717308	0.1724654
3rd Quartile	0.2831646	0.2642616	0.2484386	0.2486113	0.2610358
Max	11.09554	10.66970	48.04009	20.98603	21.01094
Mean	0.2562350	0.2014725	0.4000829	0.2867098	0.1827905
SD	0.8101465	0.7734697	2.6588493	1.2763501	1.2813933
N	372	386	402	410	401

Source: Own table

Table 33: Descriptive statistics of the variable ROS

Return on Sales					
Year	**2012**	**2013**	**2014**	**2015**	**2016**
Min	-0.2614186	-0.2416605	-0.8873424	-2.3866151	-1.2234992
1st Quartile	0.05793274	0.05396259	0.05085823	0.04805264	0.05486415
Median	0.1066167	0.1103337	0.1065445	0.1048890	0.1055493
3rd Quartile	0.1882673	0.1871043	0.1887913	0.1797344	0.1764327
Max	0.6949525	1.3344172	0.8373288	5.5051704	1.5113796
Mean	0.1306160	0.1401739	0.1320841	0.1356898	0.1252928
SD	0.1214718	0.1468853	0.1391864	0.3290573	0.1697960
N	372	386	402	410	401

Source: Own table

4.2.3.1.2 Descriptive Statistics of Independent Variables

The variable BVE surprisingly has some negative values in every year. It can be concluded that companies with a negative equity capital are in a bad economic situation because constant losses have consumed the equity capital of the company.[1924] This is not the majority of companies because median and arithmetic mean constantly show positive values. The high standard derivation and the differences between median and arithmetic mean point out that the sample consists of companies with divergent equity capital resources. By comparing the median and arithmetic mean over time, the equity capital of companies slightly increased.

1924 Cf. Auer, B. (2008), pp. 34-35.

Table 34: Descriptive statistics of the variable Book Value of Equity Capital

Book Value of Equity Capital in EUR					
Year	**2012**	**2013**	**2014**	**2015**	**2016**
Min	-1,576,826,629	-1,481,012,000	-3,000,540,397	-2,565,727,935	-2,339,600,000
1st Quartile	1,166,466,500	1,182,017,184	1,205,671,750	1,379,134,022	1,471,056,325
Median	2,364,962,458	2,436,655,609	2,528,703,500	2,743,949,908	2,875,154,831
3rd Quartile	7,289,946,693	7,114,079,407	7,060,425,000	6,963,250,000	7,354,369,917
Max	133,502,000,000	131,371,000,000	142,798,000,000	151,041,000,000	178,734,000,000
Mean	7,693,840,515	7,581,619,232	7,438,330,341	7,971,970,438	8,360,870,228
SD	14,680,774,046	14,571,801,487	14,357,508,218	15,100,081,164	16,351,842,538
N	372	386	402	410	401

Source: Own table

The insights gained so far concerning the heterogeneity of the sample are confirmed by the descriptive statistics of the variable NOA, proven by the wide range between minima and maxima values. This also indicates that the sample contains small and large companies. Over time, companies enlarge in average their assets necessary for operations documented by an increasing median and arithmetic mean. For 2013, the sample shows a large negative outliers (Hugo Boss AG). The analysis of data from Bloomberg shows a higher value of assets to be disposed than the total sum of assets. According to the calculation scheme of Net Operating Assets the value is negative.

Table 35: Descriptive statistics of the variable Net Operating Assets

Net Operating Assets in EUR					
Year	**2012**	**2013**	**2014**	**2015**	**2016**
Min	43,000,624	-1,048,212,000	51,755,961	58,100,720	60,713,711
1st Quartile	2,363,814,354	2,376,394,812	2,544,775,000	2,990,700,665	3,142,963,871
Median	5,324,716,500	5,219,396,771	5,540,718,171	5,914,699,539	6,166,000,000
3rd Quartile	18,384,115,475	17,423,438,796	17,054,750,000	18,315,250,000	19,179,900,000
Max	246,898,000,000	256,493,000,000	272,877,000,000	325,591,000,000	349,310,000,000
Mean	17,933,306,237	17,154,250,027	17,357,975,099	18,849,239,636	19,952,284,215
SD	33,111,817,885	32,110,631,318	32,509,485,542	35,941,783,552	39,584,895,421
N	372	386	402	410	401

Source: Own table

The minima values of the variable dividends are zero in every year. That means that in every year some companies do not pay a dividend to their shareholders. Another fact is that the maximum dividend payment constantly increases. Also median and arithmetic mean are higher at the end of fiscal year 2016 than at the beginning of the investigation period. Higher dividend payments could be an evidence for a better economic situation for the companies of the sample.

Table 36: Descriptive statistics of the variable Dividend

Dividends in EUR					
Year	**2012**	**2013**	**2014**	**2015**	**2016**
Min	0	0	0	0	0
1st Quartile	64,749,216	65,047,250	59,475,000	78,098,095	78,075,826
Median	154,700,000	154,137,332	160,199,500	175,762,439	190,000,000
3rd Quartile	449,357,515	441,047,548	462,500,000	489,006,100	485,000,000
Max	5,901,185,036	6,018,755,898	7,120,669,342	8,447,115,385	8,747,590,910
Mean	526,082,141	511,877,982	512,186,249	566,052,752	554,303,655
SD	988,226,617	979,779,189	989,023,908	1,120,087,123	1,078,803,077
N	372	386	402	410	401

Source: Own table

In accordance with the development of dividends also the variable ΔSALES indicates a better economic environment for the companies at the end of period of investigation. The minimum in 2016 of 53.17 % is the lowest during the sample period. However, arithmetic mean and median do not support this assumption because they are decreasing.

Table 37: Descriptive statistics of the variable Sales

ΔSales					
Year	**2012**	**2013**	**2014**	**2015**	**2016**
Min	-0.6016452	-0.7174996	-0.7670274	-0.7491749	-0.5317063
1st Quartile	0.02889544	-0.04775149	-0.02057012	0.02631391	-0.04374624
Median	0.078344190	-0.003650943	0.023945927	0.083591455	0.009871373
3rd Quartile	0.13324687	0.04297631	0.07259551	0.15359935	0.05428443
Max	0.657993	23.046775	2.057585	2.698056	2.026992
Mean	0.08191889	0.05632079	0.03643525	0.09562847	0.01719927
SD	0.1209492	1.1788811	0.1607861	0.2032723	0.1622414
N	372	386	402	410	401

Source: Own table

The variable LEV, which represents the leverage ratio of the analysed companies and their capital structure documents that the companies of the sample are very inhomogeneous because the lowest leverage ratio amounts to -42 while the company with the highest leverage ratio has a value of 111. Negative leverage ratios result because these companies have a negative equity capital. Therefore, also leverage ratios below zero demonstrate that capital structures of these companies are not optimal.

Table 38: Descriptive statistics of the variable Leverage Ratio

Leverage Ratio					
Year	**2012**	**2013**	**2014**	**2015**	**2016**
Min	-16.53616	-42.44595	-36.59112	-11.92718	-35.36998
1st Quartile	1.0326530	0.9756184	0.9454251	0.9504567	0.9778139
Median	1.544002	1.492731	1.552558	1.525335	1.446828
3rd Quartile	2.526477	2.527937	2.478177	2.465496	2.400979
Max	111.55215	21.56620	58.40143	84.47619	48.49417
Mean	2.333569	1.795914	2.187717	2.416184	2.030904
SD	6.194385	3.327675	5.157466	5.797376	4.646271
N	372	386	402	410	401

Source: Own table

The heterogeneity concerning the economic performance has been demonstrated by the descriptive analysis of the dependent variables. The variable ASS which represents the size of the companies underlines that the companies differ in their size, too. The sample contains small companies as well as large companies which conduct their business worldwide. Furthermore, the minima values are constantly growing per year which indicates that the sample consists of high growth companies as well as established companies.[1925]

Table 39: Descriptive statistics of the variable Total Assets

Total Assets in EUR					
Year	**2012**	**2013**	**2014**	**2015**	**2016**
Min	49,564,130	46,306,469	55,564,936	68,278,652	70,759,897
1st Quartile	3,176,826,692	3,122,173,690	3,369,099,884	3,749,930,758	4,067,304,447
Median	6,905,709,593	6,644,292,522	7,070,400,000	7,241,878,719	7,739,265,407
3rd Quartile	22,658,750,000	22,742,500,000	21,381,750,000	22,656,000,000	23,344,000,000
Max	309,518,000,000	324,333,000,000	351,209,000,000	381,935,000,000	409,732,000,000
Mean	21,949,974,318	21,058,333,859	21,385,660,059	22,846,554,727	24,186,287,880
SD	39,984,109,706	38,654,497,590	39,588,145,274	42,703,241,587	46,763,083,367
N	372	386	402	410	401

Source: Own table

The risk variable indicates that the risk for investors slightly decreases during the investigation period for the companies of the sample. Median and arithmetic mean are very close so that extreme values are rare for this variable. Most of the companies will have a risk value between seven and nine. However, the difference between minima and maxima gives a further indication of heterogeneity contained in the sample.

1925 Cf. Jaeger, S. (2012), p. 109 for similar conclusions on the basis of descriptive statistics of variable for company size.

Table 40: Descriptive statistics of the variable Risk

Risk					
Year	**2012**	**2013**	**2014**	**2015**	**2016**
Min	2.5028	-0.7839	0.7595	1.5202	1.3598
1st Quartile	6.980475	6.128125	7.387725	7.311425	6.836100
Median	8.70520	7.38370	8.79030	8.43865	8.24570
3rd Quartile	10.429600	9.075250	10.068650	9.928675	9.695300
Max	23.6264	24.2738	22.1128	21.2347	19.2459
Mean	8.943656	7.873234	8.922081	8.652890	8.550063
SD	2.685478	2.783263	2.504046	2.096565	2.402738
N	372	386	402	410	401

Source: Own table

The variables Industry and Country are implemented as factors or categorical variables within the regression equation.[1926] They have 16 and 18 manifestations respectively. They demonstrate the diversified sample which contains companies from different countries of Europe and industries. Both tables below summarise how many data sets of each industry or country are part of the sample.[1927]

Table 41: Descriptive statistics of the variable Industry

Industry	**Number of data sets**
Automobiles & Parts	64
Basic Resources	92
Chemicals	122
Construction & Materials	90
Food & Beverages	106
Healthcare	146
Industrial Goods & Services	473
Media	130
Oil & Gas	99
Personal & Household Goods	124
Real Estate	12
Retail	123
Technology	88
Telecommunications	94
Travel & Leisure	92
Utilities	116

Source: Own table

1926 Cf. for the implementation of factors in regression equations Stoetzer, M.-W. (2017), pp. 94-96; Wollschläger, D. (2017), pp. 59-60.

1927 Cf. for further information about the classification of companies according to industry and country chapter 4.1.3.1.

Table 42: Descriptive statistics of the variable Country

Country	**Number of data sets**
Austria	17
Belgium	43
Czech	5
Denmark	61
Finland	70
France	331
Germany	252
Great Britain	568
Greece	10
Ireland	35
Italy	71
Luxembourg	10
Netherlands	104
Norway	40
Portugal	15
Spain	82
Sweden	132
Switzerland	125

Source: Own table

4.2.3.2 Selection of Panel Model

Before analysing the requirements for the regression analysis, it is necessary to specify the model used for panel regressions.[1928] In the context of the following statistical tests the p value is often used for deciding if the null hypothesis can be rejected. If the p value is below the determined significance level, the null hypothesis can be rejected.[1929] In order to minimise the Alpha error, the significance level in this study is 5 %.[1930]

The first step is to compare the pooled regression with the FEM model. For this purpose an F test for individual effects is conducted. The null hypothesis – stating that no individual effects exist – can be rejected. Thus, the LM test, the Hausman test and the qualitative criteria are used for a decision between the FEM and REM.

1928 Cf. for an overview of the scheme used for the model decision chapter 4.1.2.3.8.

1929 Cf. Auer, L. v. (2016), pp. 130-132.

1930 Cf. Auer, L. v. (2016), p. 135; the Alpha error is the error that the null hypothesis is rejected although it is correct, cf. extensively Auer, L. v. (2016), pp. 132-137.

Table 43: Results of the F test for individual effects

Test summary	P Value
VA_rel	< 0.0001
EPS	< 0.0001
PER	< 0.0001
ROI	< 0.0001
ROE	< 0.0001
ROS	< 0.0001

Source: Own table

The second step is to conduct the LM-test. This test delivers insight if individual effects exist.

Table 44: Results of the Lagrange-Multiplier-test (Breusch Pagan) for panel regression scenarios

Dependent variable	P value
VA_rel	< 0.0001
EPS	< 0.0001
PER	< 0.0001
ROI	< 0.0001
ROE	< 0.0001
ROS	< 0.0001

Source: Own table

The LM test indicates the application of the REM model. For every six panel regressions the null hypothesis that no random effects existed can be rejected. Thus, the REM model should be used on the basis of this test.[1931]

A test for the decision between REM and FEM is the Hausman test. A p value below 0.05 indicates that the FEM model should be used. The results of the LM and Hausman test are contradictory for two of the six panel regressions.

To sum up: The Hausman test indicates for six regressions an application of the REM while the LM test indicates that the REM is the convenient model for all panel regressions. The qualitative criteria recommend the application of the REM.[1932]

Ultimately, the REM is used for the statistical analysis due to its characteristics. For short panel data sets the REM delivers more efficient results. The requirements for applying this model are fulfilled and supported by the LM test. Furthermore, the REM is

1931 Cf. Dreger, C., Kosfeld, R., Eckey, H.-F. (2014), p. 271; Greene, W. H. (2012), pp. 416-419.
1932 Cf. for the assessment of the qualitative criteria chapter 4.1.2.3.8.

Table 45: Results of the Hausman test for panel regression scenarios

Dependent variable	P value
VA_rel	< 0.0001
EPS	< 0.0001
PER	< 0.0001
ROI	< 0.0001
ROE	< 0.0001
ROS	< 0.0001

Source: Own table

able to include the time invariant variables COUNTRY and INDUSTRY.[1933] The FEM does not include these variables in its calculation because it is not able to consider time invariant variables. Thus, its application would lead to a loss of variables.[1934] In addition, many value relevance studies use the Ordinary Least Square technique which often causes misspecification errors.[1935] This study uses the GLS approach due to the application of the REM.[1936]

4.2.3.3 Analysis of Regression Requirements

For panel regressions the same requirements are valid as for simple or multiple regressions.[1937] It is the purpose of the following analysis to identify possible problems within the data and apply appropriate methods to mitigate these statistical problems.[1938]

Regression analysis bases on certain assumptions. These are:[1939]

I. The regression equation contains all relevant variables and the variables included are not irrelevant (avoidance of omitted variable bias).
II. The coherence between dependent and independent variables is linear.
III. The error term for all observations has a mean of zero.
IV. The error term has for all observations a constant variance (homoscedasticity).
V. The error terms are not correlated with each other (no autocorrelation).
VI. The error term has a normal distribution.
VII. There is no multicollinearity, i.e. between the independent variables do not exist a linear dependency.
VIII. Between independent variables and error term correlations do not exist.

1933 Cf. Asteriou, D., Hall, S. G. (2011), p. 419; Dorfard, A. (2014), p. 105; Giesselmann, M., Windzio, M. (2012), pp. 107,109-110; Wooldridge, J. M. (2013), pp. 467, 475.
1934 Cf. Asteriou, D., Hall, S. G. (2011), p. 419; Dorfard, A. (2014), p. 105; Wooldridge, J. M. (2013), p. 467.
1935 Cf. Elbakry, A. E., Nwachukwu, J. C., Abdou, H. A., et al. (2017), pp. 11-12; cf. exemplarily for studies applying OLS regressions Clarkson, P., Hanna, J. D., Richardson, G. D., et al. (2011); Elshandidy, T. (2014).
1936 Cf. Brooks, C. (2014), p. 536.
1937 Cf. Greene, W. H. (2012), p. 388.
1938 Cf. Cooke, T. E. (1998), p. 209.
1939 Cf. extensively Auer, L. v. (2016), pp. 160-167.

The dependent variable is the stock price of a company at the end of its fiscal year. As illustrated before, many factors influence stock prices. The regression equations include many control variables in order to explain most of the relevant factors. Thus, assumption I is assessed as fulfilled.[1940]

A further requirement for regression analysis is linearity (assumption II). The basis for the regression equation is the Feltham Ohlson model that illustrates linear coherences between market and book values. Therefore, it is assumed that the coherence between dependent and independent variable is mostly linear. Assumption II is fulfilled.[1941] It has to be added that the assumption of linearity is not a critical assumption. In practice, many regression equations deal with issues that are not based on a linear coherence.[1942]

Regression analysis assumes that the mean of error terms is zero. If the model is specified correctly and completely, all random influences are gathered in the error term and balance each other. It is not possible to directly analyse this assumption. Causes for violation are often measurement errors or a misspecification of the model. For the further procedure assumption III is assessed as fulfilled.[1943]

In the context of panel data heteroscedasticity can be a problem by analysing statistically the data sample. Heteroscedasticity leads to a violation of assumption IV.[1944] The Breusch-Pagan test is applied in order to detect possible heteroscedasticity.[1945] The null hypothesis of this test is that homoscedasticity exists. The p value of the Breusch-Pagan test has a value of zero. If the p value is below the level of significance, heteroscedasticity exists.[1946] Thus, the null hypothesis is rejected. Assumption IV is not fulfilled.

Table 46: Results of the Breusch-Pagan test for heteroscedasticity for panel regression

Panel regression with analysed key figure	**P Value**
VA_rel	< 0.0001
EPS	< 0.0001
PER	< 0.0001
ROI	< 0.0001
ROE	< 0.0001
ROS	< 0.0001

Source: Own table

1940 Cf. for the definition of variables extensively chapters 4.1.2.3.5 – 4.1.2.3.7.
1941 Cf. for similar argumentation Vorstius, S. (2004), pp. 155-156.
1942 Cf. Auer, L. v. (2016), p. 334.
1943 Cf. Wenzelburger, G., Jäckel, S., König, P. (2014), p. 28.
1944 Cf. Baltagi, B. H. (2013), p. 91.
1945 Cf. Asteriou, D., Hall, S. G. (2011), pp. 130-132, 136; Auer, L. v. (2016), pp. 434-436.
1946 Cf. Poodig, T., Dichtl, H., Petersmeier, K. (2008), p. 327; cf. for an extensive description of the Breusch Pagan test and its assumptions Poodig, T., Dichtl, H., Petersmeier, K. (2008), pp. 322-328.

Table 47: Results of the Breusch-Godfrey test for autocorrelation for panel regression

Panel regression with analysed key figure	P Value
VA_rel	< 0.0001
EPS	< 0.0001
PER	< 0.0001
ROI	< 0.0001
ROE	< 0.0001
ROS	< 0.0001

Source: Own table

The Breusch-Godfrey test is a test for autocorrelation contained in panel data. If the p value is below the significance level, autocorrelation exists within the sample. As the results summarised in table 46 show, the tests indicate that autocorrelation exists. Assumption five cannot be accepted.[1947]

A requirement for regression analysis is the normal distribution of residua. According to the central limit theorem a normal distribution can be assumed if the number of objects investigated is large enough. As this condition is fulfilled for this empirical study, an empirical examination of normal distribution of residua is omitted.[1948] Regularly, the assumption of normal distribution of residua is not a critical one for conducting panel analysis.[1949] In this context an examination of skewness and kurtosis is skipped due to the assumption of normal distribution.[1950]

The correlation matrix which is illustrated in figure 30 reveals that multicollinearity exists. A high correlation exists between the variables NOA_rel and ASS_rel between BVE_rel and ASS_rel and BVE_rel and NOA_rel. In order to avoid multicollinearity, the variables ASS_rel and NOA_rel are removed from the regression equation. It is expected that no loss of statistical power results from this variable reduction because the removed variables are mostly explained by the variable BVE_rel which is still contained in the regression equation.[1951]

1947 Cf. Gujarati, D. N., Porter, D. C. (2009), pp. 438-440.

1948 Cf. for this argumentation Poodig, T., Dichtl, H., Petersmeier, K. (2008), pp. 331-333; Schloemer, M. (2003), p. 136; Schremper, R., Pälchen Oliver (2001), p. 554; Vorstius, S. (2004), p. 158.

1949 Cf. Poodig, T., Dichtl, H., Petersmeier, K. (2008), p. 331.

1950 Cf. Stoetzer, M.-W. (2017), pp. 154-155.

1951 Cf. Auer, L. v. (2016), pp. 574-575; Poodig, T., Dichtl, H., Petersmeier, K. (2008), p. 383.

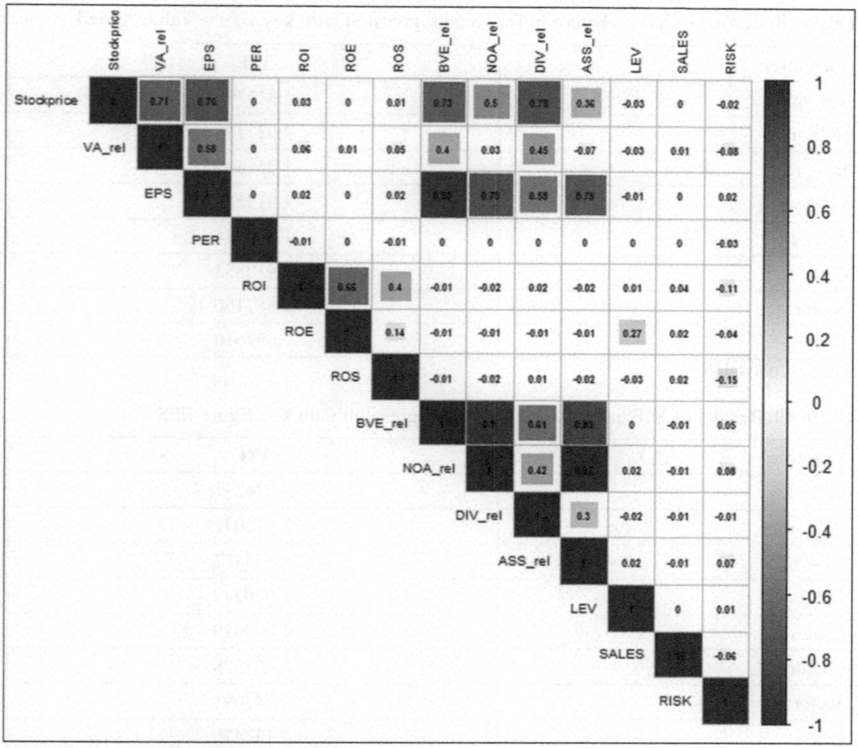

Source: Generated with statistic software R

Illustration 30: Correlation matrix

For the adapted regression equation without the two removed variables the existence of multicollinearity is analysed with the Variance Influence Factor (VIF).[1952] It is assumed that multicollinearity exists, if the VIF has a value above ten.[1953] A calculation of VIF shows that there is no multicollinearity. The detailed results of the VIF calculation are listed in tables 48-53.

Multicollinearity does not influence R^2 which is the measure for degree of value relevance. It distorts the regression coefficients. Thus, for this empirical study the avoidance of multicollinearity is not a critical issue.[1954]

1952 Cf. Poodig, T., Dichtl, H., Petersmeier, K. (2008), p. 380.
1953 Cf. Oliveira, L., Rodrigues, L. L., Craig, R. (2010), p. 247.
1954 Cf. Schloemer, M. (2003), p. 137.

Table 48: Results of VIF calculation for panel regression with key figure Value Added

Variables	VIF
VA_rel	1.813790
BVE_rel	2.037338
DIV_rel	1.251503
LEV	1.013523
ΔSales	1.006254
Country	2.919852
Sector	2.687160
Risk	1.097610

Source: Own table

Table 49: Results of VIF calculation for panel regression with key figure EPS

Variables	VIF
EPS	7.074231
BVE_rel	7.712077
DIV_rel	1.373871
LEV	1.020249
ΔSales	1.009419
Country	3.007578
Sector	2.743091
Risk	1.132479

Source: Own table

Table 50: Results of VIF calculation for panel regression with key figure PER

Variables	VIF
PER	1.003452
BVE_rel	1.224684
DIV_rel	1.250205
LEV	1.013190
ΔSales	1.006070
Country	2.821394
Sector	2.669039
Risk	1.088316

Source: Own table

Table 51: Results of VIF calculation for panel regression with key figure ROI

Variables	VIF
ROI	1.069997
BVE_rel	1.212899
DIV_rel	1.236976
LEV	1.012568
ΔSales	1.007288
Country	2.857386
Sector	2.772545
Risk	1.087975

Source: Own table

Table 52: Results of VIF calculation for panel regression with key figure ROE

Variables	VIF
ROE	1.077691
BVE_rel	1.212951
DIV_rel	1.237082
LEV	1.077903
ΔSales	1.005758
Country	2.814574
Sector	2.684053
Risk	1.082531

Source: Own table

Table 53: Results of VIF calculation for panel regression with key figure ROS

Variables	VIF
ROS	1.048178
BVE_rel	1.213140
DIV_rel	1.237269
LEV	1.012737
ΔSales	1.005988
Country	2.844813
Sector	2.732599
Risk	1.086673

Source: Own table

Assumption VIII, no correlations between independent variables and error terms, is similar to assumption III not directly testable. In general, the way of calculation of the regression equation avoids a violation of this assumption. Thus, assumption VIII is assessed as fulfilled.[1955]

The analysis of regression requirements leads to the result that three assumptions are violated. Heteroscedasticity, autocorrelation and multicollinearity exist. The multicollinearity can be avoided by removing the variables NOA_rel and ASS_rel from the regression equation. Thus, each of the regression equations has the following structure.

$$P_{i,t} = \beta_0 + \beta_1 BVE_{i,t} + \beta_2 key\ figure\ analysed_{i,t} + \beta_4 DIV_{i,t} + \beta_5 LEV_{i,t} \\ + \beta_7 \Delta SALES_{i,t} + \beta_8 COUNTRY_{i,t} + \beta_9 INDUSTRY_{i,t} + \beta_{10} RISK_{i,t}$$

Formula 52: Adapted determination of relative information content for performance measures

For solving the problem of heteroscedasticity and autocorrelation heteroscedasticity and autocorrelation consistent (HAC) estimators are used. These estimators are able to handle these two statistical problems and are still expressive under the described circumstances.[1956]

By analysing the data, some outliers can be identified.[1957] Outliers could be critical points within a data sample because they might distort the results calculated with the regression analysis.[1958] It is a common practice in similar studies to remove observations which derivate more than four standard derivations from mean values.[1959] In the following panel regressions outliers are not removed from the data sample because their number in total is low and their influence on the results of the regression limited. Furthermore, outliers are part of capital market data, so in order to give a comprehensive answer to the research questions, the outliers remain part of the sample.[1960]

For the annual regressions also an analysis of fulfilment of regression requirements is conducted. The Breusch-Pagan test is used again for determining heteroscedasticity. The applied test for autocorrelation is the Durbin Watson test. A resulting value of 2 indicates that there is no autocorrelation.[1961] The test for multicollinearity is same as for the panel regression. If the VIF exceeds the value of ten, multicollinearity exists. The results of the analysis are summarised in the table below.

It reveals that heteroscedasticity and autocorrelation are also present in the annual regression analysis. In order to reduce the possible distortions from heteroscedasticity, White standard errors are used in the annual regression equations.[1962]

1955 Cf. Wenzelburger, G., Jäckel, S., König, P. (2014), p. 28.

1956 Cf. Brüderl, J. (2010), pp. 977-978; Komlos, J., Süssmuth, B. (2010), p. 94; cf. about the implementation in the statistic software R Zeileis, A. (2004).

1957 Cf. chapters 4.2.3.1.1 and 4.2.3.1.2 and the analysis of the minima and maxima values.

1958 Cf. James, G., Witten, D., Hastie, T., et al. (2013), pp. 96-97.

1959 Cf. exemplarily Schloemer, M. (2003), pp. 139-141; Vorstius, S. (2004), p. 161.

1960 Cf. James, G., Witten, D., Hastie, T., et al. (2013), pp. 96-97.

1961 Cf. Asteriou, D., Hall, S. G. (2011), pp. 156-158; Gujarati, D. N., Porter, D. C. (2009), pp. 434-438; cf. for an extensive description of the Durbin Watson test Auer, L. v. (2016), pp. 469-472.

1962 Cf. Auer, L. v. (2016), pp. 442-444; Gow, I. D., Ormazabal, G., Taylor, D. J. (2010), p. 487.

Table 54: Analysis of regression requirements for annual regression analysis

Year	Analysed key figure	Heteroscedasticity	Autocorrelation	Multicollinearity
2012	VA_rel	Yes	Yes	Yes
2012	EPS	Yes	Yes	Yes
2012	PER	Yes	Yes	No
2012	ROI	Yes	Yes	No
2012	ROE	Yes	Yes	No
2012	ROS	Yes	Yes	No
2013	VA_rel	Yes	Yes	Yes
2013	EPS	Yes	Yes	Yes
2013	PER	Yes	Yes	No
2013	ROI	Yes	Yes	No
2013	ROE	Yes	Yes	No
2013	ROS	Yes	Yes	No
2014	VA_rel	Yes	Yes	No
2014	EPS	Yes	Yes	No
2014	PER	Yes	Yes	No
2014	ROI	Yes	Yes	No
2014	ROE	Yes	Yes	No
2014	ROS	Yes	Yes	No
2015	VA_rel	Yes	No	No
2015	EPS	Yes	Yes	Yes
2015	PER	Yes	Yes	No
2015	ROI	Yes	Yes	No
2015	ROE	Yes	Yes	No
2015	ROS	Yes	Yes	No
2016	VA_rel	Yes	Yes	No
2016	EPS	Yes	Yes	No
2016	PER	Yes	Yes	No
2016	ROI	Yes	Yes	No
2016	ROE	Yes	Yes	No
2016	ROS	Yes	Yes	No

Source: Own table

4.2.3.4 Value Relevance Analysis

A measure for the degree of value relevance is the adjusted coefficient of determination, R^2.[1963] It shows to what extent the regression equation is able to explain changes of the dependent variable. As a multiple regression is used in the context of this empirical study, the adjusted coefficient of determination is used for assessing the quality because it is independent from the number of variables included in the regression model.[1964] The higher the R^2, the higher is the key figure's value relevance.[1965]

For using the adjusted R^2, it is necessary that three conditions are fulfilled: All models must have the same endogenous variable, the number of exogenous variables is the same and the models have an intercept. These conditions are fulfilled so that a comparison based on R^2 is possible.[1966]

The results of the six panel regressions are illustrated in the tables 55-60.

Table 55: Results of panel regression with VA_rel as independent variable[1967]

Analysed key figure	**VA_rel**			
Independent variables	**Coefficients**	**T value**	**P value**	
VA_rel	4.212675	27.4103	< 0.0001	***
BVE_rel	0.484769	31.1496	< 0.0001	***
DIV_rel	6.672461	16.8899	< 0.0001	***
LEV	-0.033883	-0.0729	0.9418657	
SALES	-0.885004	-0.2201	0.8258072	
RISK	-0.098328	-0.0894	0.9287450	
Adj. R²	78.62 %			
F statistic	191.588			
P value	< 0.0001			
Explanation	. = significant at level of 10 %, * = significant at level of 5 %, ** = significant at level of 1 %, *** = significant at level of 0.01 %			

Source: Own table

1963 Cf. Bao, B.-H., Bao, D.-H. (1998), p. 251; Barton, J., Hansen, T. B., Pownall, G. (2010), p. 771; Hüfner, B., Möller, H. P. (2002), p. 144.
1964 Cf. Schloemer, M. (2003), pp. 27-29.
1965 Cf. Gu, Z. (2005), p. 72.
1966 Cf. Auer, L. v. (2016), pp. 312-313.
1967 For reasons of clarity the factor variables country and sector are not listed in the result tables.

Table 56: Results of panel regression with EPS as independent variable

Analysed key figure	EPS			
Independent variables	**Coefficients**	**T value**	**P value**	
EPS	2.171898	7.2912	< 0.0001	***
BVE_rel	0.442486	12.3455	< 0.0001	***
DIV_rel	9.372535	19.2395	< 0.0001	***
LEV	-0.302191	-0.5097	0.6102982	
SALES	0.260551	0.0500	0.9601630	
RISK	-3.100951	-2.2495	0.0245921	*
Adj. R^2	70.32 %			
F statistic	123.848			
P value	< 0.0001			
Explanation	. = significant at level of 10 %, * = significant at level of 5 %, ** = significant at level of 1 %, *** = significant at level of 0.01 %			

Source: Own table

Table 57: Results of panel regression with PER as independent variable

Analysed key figure	PER			
Independent variables	**Coefficients**	**T value**	**P value**	
PER	-0,000000	-0.0690	0.9450035	
BVE_rel	0,000000	53.1053	< 0.0001	***
DIV_rel	0,000000	14.1177	< 0.0001	***
LEV	-0,000000	-0.4335	0.6646890	
SALES	0,000000	0.0983	0.9217107	
RISK	-0,000000	-2.2462	0.0248026	*
Adj. R^2	70.32 %			
F statistic	123.82			
P value	< 0.0001			
Explanation	. = significant at level of 10 %, * = significant at level of 5 %, ** = significant at level of 1 %, *** = significant at level of 0.01 %			

Source: Own table

Table 58: Results of panel regression with ROI as independent variable

Analysed key figure	**ROI**			
Independent variables	**Coefficients**	**T value**	**P value**	
ROI	57.525485	1.8991	0.0577047	.
BVE_rel	0.764110	54.2962	< 0.0001	***
DIV_rel	6.259172	13.5880	< 0.0001	***
LEV	-0.234645	-0.4357	0.6631185	
SALES	0.060869	0.0131	0.9895680	
RISK	-2.622969	-2.0575	0.0397744	*
Adj. R^2	70.59 %			
F statistic	125.451			
P value	< 0.0001			
Explanation	. = significant at level of 10 %, * = significant at level of 5 %, ** = significant at level of 1 %, *** = significant at level of 0.01 %			

Source: Own table

Table 59: Results of panel regression with ROE as independent variable

Analysed key figure	**ROE**			
Independent variables	**Coefficients**	**T value**	**P value**	
ROE	1.065812	0.4991	0.6177901	
BVE_rel	0.764192	54.2517	< 0.0001	***
DIV_rel	6.262996	13.5834	< 0.0001	***
LEV	-0.288843	-0.5193	0.6036171	
SALES	0.397150	0.0853	0.9320313	
RISK	-2.795712	-2.1964	0.0281825	*
Adj. R^2	71.11 %			
F statistic	125.133			
P value	< 0.0001			
Explanation	. = significant at level of 10 %, * = significant at level of 5 %, ** = significant at level of 1 %, *** = significant at level of 0.01 %			

Source: Own table

The regression model with the Value Added has the highest R^2 with 78.62 %. This is a clear gap to the other regression models which contain the traditional key figures. Among the traditional key figures, clear differences cannot be detected. The R^2 for these regression analyses is between 70 % and 71 %.

Table 60: Results of panel regression with ROS as independent variable

Analysed key figure	**ROS**			
Independent variables	**Coefficients**	**T value**	**P value**	
ROS	16.634906	1.0625	0.2881516	
BVE_rel	0.763998	54.2426	< 0.0001	***
DIV_rel	6.267026	13.5935	< 0.0001	***
LEV	-0.209971	-0.3895	0.6969797	
SALES	0.331631	0.0712	0.9432301	
RISK	-2.714198	-2.1285	0.0334253	*
Adj. R^2	70.55 %			
F statistic	125.194			
P value	< 0.0001			
Explanation	. = significant at level of 10 %, * = significant at level of 5 %, ** = significant at level of 1 %, *** = significant at level of 0.01 %			

Source: Own table

Analysing the level of significance in the panel regressions, the key figures Value Added and EPS are significant on the level of 0.001 %. This confirms their important role in explaining stock prices. The key figure ROI is significant on the 0.1 % level which also indicates a certain part of explaining stock prices. All remaining key figures are not significant.

Beyond the analysed key figures the control variables book value of equity and dividends have in every panel regression a significance of 0.01 %. The variable risk has in five of six equations a significance of 0.1 %. That means that these three control variables are also important for explaining the share price. For the variables leverage and sales no significance can be detected.[1968]

The F test analyses the relevance of the complete regression equation. In general, the higher the F value, the higher the probability that the null hypothesis that the model is invalid can be rejected.[1969] The F test provides insights if the results of the regression model and the sample can be transferred to the population. The F values of all regression equations exceed clearly the critical F values so that it is possible to transfer the results of these models to the basic population.[1970]

The t values show if the influence of one independent variable on the dependent variable is significant.[1971] Similar to the F test the empirical t values are compared to the values of t tables. If the empirical values exceed the critical values, it can be assumed that

1968 Cf. Backhaus, K., Erichson, B., Plinke, W., et al. (2016), p. 95.
1969 Cf. Poodig, T., Dichtl, H., Petersmeier, K. (2008), p. 303; cf. exemplarily for the steps in the context of an F test Poodig, T., Dichtl, H., Petersmeier, K. (2008), pp. 304-307.
1970 Cf. Backhaus, K., Erichson, B., Plinke, W., et al. (2016), pp. 90-91; Kuhne, D. (2015), p. 21.
1971 Cf. Poodig, T., Dichtl, H., Petersmeier, K. (2008), p. 293; cf. extensively Poodig, T., Dichtl, H., Petersmeier, K. (2008) for a description of t-test pp. 293-302.

the independent variables have a significant influence on the dependent variable.[1972] Alternatively, the p values can be analysed. If $p < \alpha$, the null hypothesis can be rejected and the variable is significant.[1973]

Analysing the p values only the panel regressions with the variables VA_rel and EPS have p values below the determined significance level of 0.05. Both key figures, Value Added and EPS are significant on the level of 0.001 %. This confirms their important role in explaining stock prices. The panel regression with the key figure ROI has a p value which is slightly above the significance level. It is significant on the 0.1 % level which also indicates a certain part of explaining stock prices. All remaining key figures have p values which are above the significance level and are not significant.

Beyond the analysed key figures the control variables book value of equity and dividends have a p value near zero which results in a significance on the level of 0.01 % in every panel regression. The variable risk has a significance of 0.1 % in five of six equations. That means that these three control variables are also important for explaining the share price. For the variables "leverage" and "sales no significance can be detected.

The regression coefficients have the predicted signs. That means that an increase of the stock price or market capitalisation of a company leads to an increase of the key figures Value Added, EPS, ROI, ROE and ROS. The interdepency is inverse for the key figure PER. Also this sign has been expected.[1974]

The control variables also have the expected signs. An exception is the sign for the variable ΔSALES in the panel regression with Value Added as analysed key figures. In this equation the variable has negative coherence to the stock price in contrast to the assumed positive coherence and to all other regression equations. The sign for the variable BVE has not been predicted but due to the results a positive coherence between equity capital and stock price can be assumed. The other control variables which have a positive coherence are DIV and ΔSALES. The leverage of a company as well as the risk of an investment have a negative coherence to the stock price which also corresponds to the expectations.[1975]

On the basis of the results of the panel regression hypothesis H4 can be accepted. The coefficient of the key figure Value Added is positive which confirms the coherence between Shareholder Value and Value Added. So, if the Value Added increases, the Shareholder Value will increase. Furthermore, the p value shows that the variable is highly significant.[1976]

Hypotheses H5b to H5e cannot be accepted because the panel regressions reveal a difference in the value relevance of Value Added and the traditional key figures. The R^2 of Value Added exceeds the R^2 of all traditional key figures selected clearly. Only the key figure EPS has a significance which is comparable to the significance of Value Added, although the R^2 of this panel regression is below the R^2 of the Value Added panel regression. Due to the low p value of the variable EPS hypothesis H5a is accepted.[1977]

1972 Cf. Kuhne, D. (2015), pp. 23-24.
1973 Cf. Backhaus, K., Erichson, B., Plinke, W., et al. (2016), pp. 91-95.
1974 Cf. table 19.
1975 Cf. table 19 which contains the assumed signs for the variables and tables 55 to 60 which presents the results of the panel regressions.
1976 Cf. chapter 4.1.1.3 for hypothesis H4.
1977 Cf. chapter 4.1.1.3 for hypotheses H5a to H5e.

Beside the panel regressions which consider the whole investigation period annual regressions have been conducted. In general, the results from the panel regressions can be confirmed despite some derivations. The key figure Value Added is apart from the year 2012 significant in every year, at least at a 10 % level. The p value is in the years 2013, 2014 and 2015 below the determined significance level.[1978] The Value Added has in every year a high adjusted R^2 in comparison to most of the other traditional key figures. In 2012, the coefficient of Value Added is negative which contradicts to the predicted sign.

It is striking that the adjusted R^2 do not differ strongly between the single key figures in the year 2012, and 2013. Since 2014 the differences between the key figures become more clearly. In 2015, the adjusted R^2 of the key figures PER, ROI, ROE and ROS are reduced by half while in 2016 they increase nearly to the previous level.

The EPS shows in four of five regression equations significance. In three of five years the p value is below the significance level of 5 %. The adjusted R^2 of this key figure are also relatively high and on one level with the R^2 of the key figure Value Added in the majority of the analysed years. This is different to the panel regressions. The panel regression with the key figure Value Added has higher value relevance than the other panel regressions with traditional key figures.

In the years 2012 and 2013, the adjusted R^2 of the PER regression equations is on one level with the key figures Value Added and EPS. In the following years differences concerning the level of R^2 exist. The PER is only in one of the analysed years significant which corresponds to the results of the panel regression. The expected sign of the coefficient deviates in four of five years from the expected sign. The coefficient is relatively close to zero which is also in line with the results of the panel regression analysis.

In the first two years the value relevance of the ROI corresponds to those of the other key figures. In the latter years the ROI has the same explanatory power with reference to the adjusted R^2 as the key figures PER, ROE and ROS. ROI does not show any significance in the annual regression analysis. It has a non-expected sign for its coefficient in the years 2012 and 2014.

The annual regressions for the ROE show higher value relevance than the panel regression. In the years 2013 and 2015, the key figure is significant at least at 5 % level. In the panel regression no significance can be proved. Concerning the adjusted R^2, the statements from the previous key figure can be transferred. The ROE has a negative coefficient in 2012.

The adjusted R^2 of the ROS is apart from the first two years on the same level as for the key figures PER, ROI and ROE. The annual regression analysis shows significance on the 10 % level for the annual regression in the year 2012. The p value is clearly above the significance level of 5 % in the further years. This result is congruent with the result of the panel regression. The ROS has only in the year 2015 the predicted positive sign. In all other years the coefficient is negative.

The annual panel regressions do not change the previous acceptance of hypothesis H4. Apart from the year 2012, the positive coherence between the key figure Value Added and the Shareholder Value can be confirmed.

The assessment of hypothesis H5a does change on the basis of annual regressions. EPS and Value Added have a similar significance and a similar level of adjusted R^2. This

1978 Cf. the results of annual regressions in table 61.

indicates that the value relevance of both key figures is equal. Thus, the insights gained from the panel regressions can be confirmed.

All other key figures have value relevance below the value relevance of Value Added. Thus, hypotheses 5b to 5e are also rejected on the basis of annual regressions. The results of the annual regressions are summarised in table 61.

Table 61: Results of annual regression analysis

Year	Analysed key figure	Coefficients	T value	P value		Adj. R²
2012	Value Added	-0.1419621	-0.0631	0.94972		97.68 %
2013	Value Added	1.26774	2.5059	0.01268	*	97.90 %
2014	Value Added	3.744901	2.3991	0.01694	*	94.32 %
2015	Value Added	16.994614	21.0394	< 0.0001	***	93.05 %
2016	Value Added	4.01113	1.9582	0.05098	.	88.37 %
2012	EPS	2.1497459	1.2404	0.21569		97.70 %
2013	EPS	8.925054	7.6064	< 0.0001	***	98.29 %
2014	EPS	5.8424341	2.6963	0.007339	**	94.75 %
2015	EPS	21.23091	5.6229	< 0.0001	***	84.48 %
2016	EPS	2.194635	1.3566	0.17576		85.38 %
2012	PER	0.0084381	0.6976	0.48593		97.68 %
2013	PER	< 0.0001	0.0882	0.92975		97.53 %
2014	PER	<- 0.0001	-1.0237	0.306648		92.20 %
2015	PER	< 0.0001	0.7617	0.44674		44.91 %
2016	PER	<- 0.0001	-2.2136	0.02748	*	84.23 %
2012	ROI	-9.2694290	-0.9503	0.34263		97.68 %
2013	ROI	5.120264	0.3293	0.74215		97.53 %
2014	ROI	-3.78880	-0.3224	0.747339		92.20 %
2015	ROI	66.790244	1.4929	0.13632		45.11 %
2016	ROI	17.818092	1.2696	0.20505		84.21 %
2012	ROE	-1.305434	-0.8249	0.41004		97.68 %
2013	ROE	4.71736	2.8113	0.005214	**	97.54 %
2014	ROE	0.285416	1.1983	0.23160		92.20 %
2015	ROE	3.641532	2.4103	0.016426	*	44.95 %
2016	ROE	1.933637	1.5010	0.13423		84.21 %
2012	ROS	-35.073713	-1.8355	0.06733	.	97.69 %
2013	ROS	-11.691033	-0.7318	0.46476		97.53 %
2014	ROS	-13.699749	-0.7937	0.427861		92.21 %
2015	ROS	9.346493	1.2214	0.22273		44.92 %
2016	ROS	-11.437915	-0.6039	0.54630		84.21 %
Explanation	. = significant at level of 10 %, * = significant at level of 5 %, ** = significant at level of 1 %, *** = significant at level of 0.01 %					

Source: Own table

4.3 Interpretation of Results

4.3.1 Analysis of Annual Reports

As not many investigations so far deal with the application rate of value based performance measures on a European level, objects of comparisons are rare. Firk et al. also conduct an analysis at a European level and come to an average application rate of 18 %. Hence, their rate is slightly higher than the rate of the analysis of the companies of the Stoxx Europe 600. Probably two factors explain the differences: Firstly, the analysis refers to a different time period, 2005 to 2010. Secondly, differences might occur due to another database. The study of Firk et al. contains companies of the MSCI Europe and S&P 500 so that American companies are also included. Comparable to this analysis, the authors detect a slight decrease of application of value based performance measures at the end of analysed period. Independent from diverging application rates, both studies come to similar results concerning the disclosure behaviour of German companies. Companies located in Germany tend to disclose more often value based performance measures in their annual reports than companies in other countries.[1979]

The study of Horvath et al. comes to different application rates by interviewing managers in Germany, Great Britain, France and Italy. 54 % of Italian companies, 43 % of French ones, 34 % German ones and 14 % of British ones use the EVA. The application rate for value based performance measures in these countries is clearly higher than those determined in this analysis and also contradicts the results of Firk et al.[1980] A reason for the clear deviation could be the applied methodology of survey on the basis of the questionnaire. Companies are not forced by accounting standards or laws to disclose information about value based performance measures. Consequently, companies might apply such a key figure without informing the readers of its annual report.[1981]

This study detects a high application rate of value based performance measures for German companies in contrast to the application rate in the other analysed European countries. Several other studies referring to the German market confirm the high application rates of value based performance measures in Germany.[1982]

An explanation for the diverging reporting behaviour of German companies could be the high significance of the topic within the German scientific community. The high number of empirical studies in the German language or referring to the German market proves the scientific importance of this topic.[1983] A further explanation for the diverging results between Germany and the rest of Europe could be the applied methodology of the study. So far, it can be concluded that companies only apply internally a value based performance measure, if they publish information in their annual report. For companies outside Germany a higher application rate could be possible by using a different methodology, e.g. a questionnaire or conducting interviews with managers. The study of

1979 Cf. Firk, S., Schrapp, S., Wolff, M. (2016), pp. 47, 51, 54.

1980 Cf. Horváth, P., Minning, F. (2001), pp. 277-281.

1981 Cf. chapter 2.4.4 about Value Reporting.

1982 Cf. exemplarily the empirical studies of Gitt, N., Völl, W., Kettenring, T. (2013); Laier, R. (2011); Weber, J. (2009).

1983 Cf. table 13 in which many articles are taken from German journals or are referring to the German market.

Horvath et al. determines significantly higher application rates. Malmi and Ikäheimo conduct interviews with five Finnish managers and three of the interviewed persons state that value based performance measures are used in their company.[1984]

The analysis reveals that especially companies in the supersector Industrial Goods & Services use value concepts. The coherence between industry and application of value concepts is also a topic in other empirical studies.[1985] Especially in capital intensive industries, companies tend to implement value based performance measures because capital is an extremly scarce resource for them.[1986] The study can partly confirm this assumption with the number of adopters within the supersector Industrial Goods & Services. However, as a contradiction to this, companies in the supersectors of Oil & Gas which can also be assessed as a capital intensive industry do not implement such key figures in the same way.[1987]

Concerning the kind of value based performance measures, the problems identified within scientific literature so far are confirmed. Companies use many different kinds of value based performance measures.[1988] Some companies use their own value concepts or adapt the calculation schemes to their individual needs.[1989] In this context it can be assumed that all companies listed as EVA users do not calculate the EVA in a uniform way and use different conversions.[1990]

The theoretical concepts offer many modifications companies can use in order to calculate value based performance measures. In practice, many of these modifications are ignored. One reason is increasing complexity. But from the point of view of the Principal Agent Theory, the managers as agents have the advantage that only they know in detail what modifications have to be conducted, e.g. hidden fundings. For shareholders it is very difficult to get all necessary information for calculating a value based performance measure with all modifications.[1991]

This leads in the end to the fact that the performances of companies are not comparable on the basis of the disclosed value based performance measures.[1992] It is important to know the exact calculation scheme in order to be able to compare the performance of a company on the basis of selected key figures properly.[1993] Due to this non standardised application the advantages of Value Reporting are limited because investors do not receive as much information as would be possible with a standardised calculation or at

1984 Cf. the empirical studies of Horváth, P., Minning, F. (2001) and Malmi, S., Ikäheimo, S. (2003).

1985 Cf. for identified coherence between industry characteristics and the application of value based performance measure: Athanasakou, V., Hussainey, K. (2014); Gitt, N., Völl, W., Kettenring, T. (2013); Ruhwedel, F., Schultze, W. (2002), pp. 620, 622.

1986 Cf. Firk, S., Schmidt, T., Wolff, M. (2018); Gitt, N., Völl, W., Kettenring, T. (2013), pp. 102-103; Ruhwedel, F., Schultze, W. (2002), pp. 620, 622.

1987 Cf. table 24 which gives an overview of companies applying value based performance measures per supersector.

1988 Cf. table 25 in which the kind of applied value concepts are listed.

1989 Cf. the exemplarily analysis of five value concepts and the identified differences in Arbeitskreis Internes Rechnungswesen der Schmalenbach-Gesellschaft (2010). Cf. also table 25 and the names companies invent for their value based performance measures.

1990 Cf. Hostettler, S. (2003), pp. 119-120; Zirkler, B. (2002), p. 99.

1991 Cf. Weißenberger, B. E. (2003), pp. 259-260.

1992 Cf. Beck, R. (2003), p. 193; Fischer, T. M., Rödl, K. (2005), p. 30.

1993 Cf. Pape, U. (2015), p. 278.

least minimum information requirements.[1994] Actually, investors are not able to use value based performance measures for their main purpose, namely the measurement and comparison of performance of companies.[1995]

The scoring scheme also reveals that many companies only mention the name of the value based performance measure and do not to give the reader further information about the applied key figure.[1996] So the Value Reporting of companies concerning value based performance measures exhibits information gaps.[1997] These gaps lead to the circumstance that readers of annual reports are not able to assess and to use this information for further purposes.[1998] Especially against the background that companies adapt individually the calculation to their purposes, accompanying information about key figure calculation would be helpful for investors.[1999] Also the fact that none of the companies report about calculated target values for prospective periods is surprising because scientific literature as well as the information needs of the financial community have a clear expectation concerning this point.[2000]

Three points can be stressed after the analysis of the annual reports: Firstly, many companies do not use the advantages of this part of Value Reporting / Integrated Reporting and do not give investors voluntary information about the applied value based performance measure.[2001] They miss the opportunity to reduce information asymmetry and decrease cost of capital[2002] as well as reduce volatility of their share price by aligning external and internal company value.[2003] Secondly, the disclosed information could be more detailed. Many companies only give verbal information about the key figure they use[2004] or do not give information about the prospective development of the key figure.[2005] Thirdly, investors are forced to read carefully the information about value based performance measures because companies adapt these key figures to their individual needs. Comparability of performance is restricted.[2006]

1994 Cf. Fischer, T. M., Rödl, K. (2005), p. 30.

1995 Cf. Coenenberg, A. G., Mattner, G. R., Schultze, W. (2003), p. 2; Lachnit, L., Müller, S. (2012), pp. 255-256.

1996 Cf. chapter 4.2.1.

1997 Cf. Mikołajek-Gocejna, M. (2014), p. 99.

1998 Cf. Banzhaf, J. (2006), pp. 144-145; cf. extensively for communication gaps in the context of Value Reporting chapter 2.4.4.2.

1999 Cf. Baetge, J., Solmecke, H. (2006), p. 24; Müller, M. (1998), p. 132.

2000 Cf. Heumann, R. (2005), p. 137; Pellens, B., Hillebrandt, F., Tomaszewski, C. (2000), p. 186; cf. concerning the information needs chapter 2.3.2.2.2.

2001 Cf. affirmatively: Aders, C., Herbertinger, M., Schaffer, C., et al. (2003), p. 724; Schultze, W., Steeger, L., Schabert, B. (2009), pp. 20-21.

2002 Cf. Bej, T. (2015), p. 109.

2003 Cf. Banzhaf, J. (2006), pp. 141-143.

2004 Cf. illustration 26 which shows that many companies receive only one point in the scoring model. This means that they use a certain value based performance measure but do not give further information.

2005 Cf. chapter 4.2.1 with the result of the analysis. None of the companies receive the maximum number of points because no information about the prospective development of the key figure is given in the annual reports; cf. affirmatively: Ruhwedel, F., Schultze, W. (2002), p. 629; Schultze, W., Steeger, L., Schabert, B. (2009), p. 20.

2006 Cf. Hahn, G. J., Burger, A., Kuhn, H. (2011), p. 310; Schäffer, U., Lewerenz, U. (2011), p. 298.

4.3.2 Standardised Calculation of ROCE Spread and Value Added

The standardised calculation enables an easy comparison of performance of companies for capital market participants. In this context it has to be stressed that the way of presentation of accounting information influences its perception by recipients. Consequently, the analysis of ROCE Spread or Value Added might change the assessment of a company by investors.[2007]

The standardised ROCE Spread calculation delivers new information about the company's financial performance and clearly shows the profit or loss after complete deduction of cost capital. The key figure contains information which is not directly observable on the capital market and therefore enlarges the knowledge of capital market participants about the company's performance.[2008]

Analysing the resulting numbers, the first conclusion is that the majority of companies are able to jump over the hurdle rate. However, large differences to the hurdle rate are rare so many companies only have a ROCE Spread which is relatively near to zero.[2009] Companies that constantly do not jump over the hurdle rate have to be aware that problems concerning the acquisition of additional capital for new investment possibilities might occur in the future.[2010] The distribution of companies reveals that the majority of companies is in the group which has a ROCE Spread between zero and twenty percent.[2011] This circumstance indicates that these companies are acting on markets with strong competition so that high excess returns are not possible.[2012]

It is striking that among the top performing companies often the same companies are represented during the investigation period. The group of the companies with the highest ROCE Spread fluctuates less than the group of companies with the lowest ROCE Spread.[2013] An explanation for the constancy in the group of the best performing companies could be that these companies do not have any or only a few competitors. The consequences of the sovereign debt crisis which occurs during the time period of investigation are reflected in the fact that many companies with the lowest ROCE Spreads are allocated to the category "Finance".[2014]

2007 Cf. Pfaff, D., Bärtl, O. (1998), pp. 770-771.
2008 Cf. Dechow, P., Ge, W., Schrand, C. (2010), p. 344.
2009 Cf. illustration 27 which gives an overview of performance of companies measured by ROCE Spread.
2010 Cf. Weiß, M. (2006), p. 1.
2011 Cf. illustration 27.
2012 Cf. Mondello, E. (2015), pp. 10-17.
2013 Cf. chapter 4.2.2 and appendix six which gives an overview of the ten companies with the highest and lowest ROCE Spread per year.
2014 Cf. exemplarily Allegret, J.-P., Raymond, H., Rharrabti, H. (2017) for the effects of the sovereign debt crisis on banks.

4.3.3 *Value Relevance Analysis*

By analysing and interpreting the results of the value relevance study, it has to be considered that these results depend on the one hand on the information content of the selected accounting variable and on the other hand on the underlying valuation model. As it is a joint test, both factors cannot be assessed separately.[2015]

A second feature of the empirical study is that the sample is a cross-national one. An advantage is that the number of companies is significantly larger and results can also be interpreted cross-nationally.[2016] The data reflects a greater heterogeneity. Thus, the acceptance or refusal of each hypothesis is made on a broader basis. A factor that may have a negative impact are the variations due to the cross-country sample which are not described by the selected variables like level of economic development or cultural differences which can result in more or less trust in stock market development.[2017] In order to mitigate these effects, the factor variables Country and Industry are included within the regression equation.[2018]

The third feature of the study is that only companies are included which disclose their results according to the IFRS. It is probable that the IFRS ensures that the association between stock prices and accounting measures is higher in comparison to studies which focus on value relevance of national GAAPs.[2019]

The fourth feature is that this study considers Value Added as the only value based performance measure. By comparing value relevance of value based performance measures with each other and across different empirical studies, it has to be considered that due to several assumptions for calculation it is not possible to comprehensively compare the results.[2020]

The panel as well as the annual regressions reveal that the key figures Value Added and EPS have high value relevance and are significant in explaining the Shareholder Value.[2021] Usually the value relevance of key figures is compared on the basis of the adjusted R^2. Illustration 31 summarises the R^2 of the planel regressions. It demonstrates that the key figure Value Added has the highest R^2 in comparison to the other analysed key figures.

The value based performance measure Value Added is comparable to the key figure Residual Income which is also analysed in other association studies. It is defined as the result of adding interest expense to earnings and reduction of this sum by a charge on capital.[2022] Similar to the Value Added it is a key figure which captures the profit of a company after cost of capital deduction.[2023] In these studies the Residual Income has a

2015 Cf. Hüfner, B., Möller, H. P. (2002), p. 150.
2016 Cf. Hawranek, B., Öppinger, C. (2014), p. 102.
2017 Cf. Dechow, P., Ge, W., Schrand, C. (2010), p. 377.
2018 Cf. chapter 4.1.2.3.7 and the justification for implementing these two variables in the regression equation.
2019 Cf. Barth, M. E., Landsman, W. R., Lang, M. H. (2008), p. 496.
2020 Cf. Günther, T., Landrock, B., Muche, T. (2000a), p. 133.
2021 Cf. chapter 4.2.3.4.
2022 Cf. Biddle, G. C., Bowen, R. M., Wallace, J. S. (1997), p. 313.
2023 Cf. the definition of Value Added in this study in chapter 4.1.2.2.

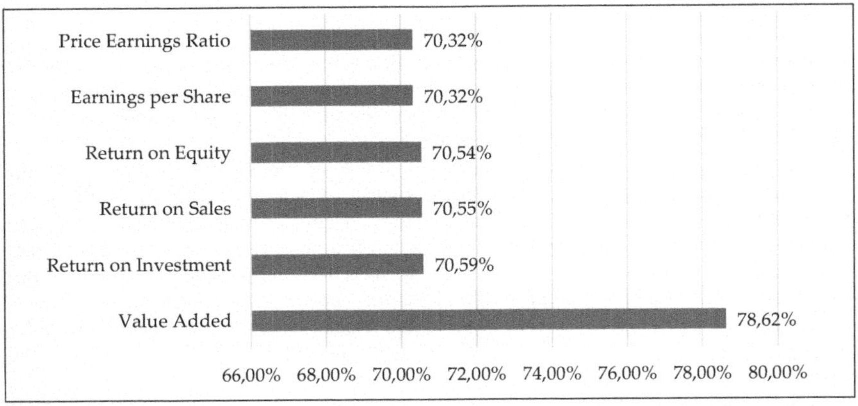

Source: Own illustration
Illustration 31: Comparison of R^2 of panel regression

similar explanatory power like earning key figures.[2024] This empirical study comes to comparable results because Value Added and EPS have value relevance on a comparable level.[2025]

In previous studies value based performance measures do not dominate so clearly traditional ones. An explanation for a change could be that today capital market participants are more strongly guided by the principles of VBM and Shareholder Value approach in contrast to the time periods in which the previous studies analyse the value relevance.[2026] An important factor that could be responsible for the higher value relevance is the cost of capital which might provide additional information in comparison to all traditional key figures.[2027] One further reason for diverging results could be the accounting standard IFRS. Many studies refer to the American market and use data based on US GAAP. In addition, the definition of the variables used is different to other studies and could result in differences concerning the statistical results.[2028] It might also play an important role that the Clean Surplus Relation of the Feltham Ohlson model is violated[2029] and that the autoregressive process of linear information dynamics is not applied in this association study.[2030]

2024 Cf. exemplarily the studies of Biddle, G. C., Bowen, R. M., Wallace, J. S. (1997), p. 317; Chen, S., Dodd, J. L. (2001); Holler, A. (2009), p. 176; Stark, A. W., Thomas, H. M. (1998), pp. 457-458.

2025 Cf. chapter 4.2.3.4.

2026 Cf. Biddle, G. C., Bowen, R. M., Wallace, J. S. (1997), p. 333; Günther, T., Landrock, B., Muche, T. (2000a), p. 133.

2027 Cf. Wolf, R., Hoffmann, H. (2017), p. 384; cf. also the empirical study of Kerstein, J., Kim, S. (1995) which demonstrates that cost of capital might provide value relevant information under certain circumstances.

2028 Cf. for similar argumentation for diverging results Worthington, A. C., West, T. (2004), pp. 220-221.

2029 Cf. Bogajewskaja, J. (2007), p. 109.

2030 Cf. argumentation in chapter 4.1.2.3.4.

The value based performance measures enable market participants to assess the performance of a company from the perspective of VBM[2031] which plays an important role in today's business world.[2032] Traditional key figures are not able to deliver this kind of information.[2033] A further reason might be that market participants have a better and more comfortable access to the available data for calculation of this key figure which is a prerequisite for using it.[2034] The assumptions of scientific literature that value based performance measures are able to summarise the performance of companies can be confirmed with this empirical study referring to the value based performance measure Value Added.[2035]

The distinguishing feature between traditional key figures and value based ones is that the latter include costs of capital in their calculation.[2036] However, it seems that an accurate calculation of cost of capital is not decisive for the value relevance of value based performance measures. In this study the cost of capital taken from the data provider Bloomberg has been used. So, an individual verification of the calculated cost of capital for each company has not been conducted.[2037] Another study comes to similar conclusions.[2038]

Although there is a high association between stock returns and Value Added, it cannot automatically be concluded that value based performance measures are superior to traditional key figures. Internal and external significance can vary extremely. That means that a key figure provides managers internally with helpful insights but for capital market participants no new information is really transferred.[2039] From a manager's point of view it is important that a key figure fosters internal decision-making in the sense of shareholders and improves organisational performance. The direct coherence to stock prices is secondary for them as a better organisational performance will influence the stock prices positively in the long-term.[2040] To sum up: Association studies do not analyse if key figures are really used by managers or investors.[2041]

Overall, the traditional key figures have a lower value relevance and significance than the Value Added in this empirical study. A reason for this might be that the data contained in this key figure has already been anticipated by the stock market, so that this information is already included in the stock price. Consequently at the end of a fiscal year, the relationship between traditional key figures and stock prices does not reveal any significant association.[2042] A further explanation for the low significance of the traditional key figures or a possible distorted high value relevance of Value Added and EPS might

2031 Cf. Holler, A. (2009), p. 192.
2032 Cf. for the importance of VBM chapter 2.1.1.
2033 Cf. extensively chapter 3.2.2 which illustrates the advantages of value based performance measures in contrast to traditional ones.
2034 Cf. Biddle, G. C., Bowen, R. M., Wallace, J. S. (1997), p. 332.
2035 Cf. Günther, T. (2002), p. 97; Hoffjan, A., Schroll, S. (2010), p. 410.
2036 Cf. Behringer, S. (2014), pp. 100-102.
2037 Cf. chapter 4.1.3.2 for the explanation which data has been used for calculation of Value Added.
2038 Cf. Günther, T., Landrock, B., Muche, T. (2000a), pp. 133-134.
2039 Cf. Biddle, G. C., Bowen, R. M., Wallace, J. S. (1999), p. 79.
2040 Cf. Ittner, C. D., Larcker, D. F. (1998), pp. 211-212.
2041 Cf. Barth, M. E. (2000), pp. 10-11; cf. chapter 3.5.2.2 concerning the objective of association studies.
2042 Cf. Biddle, G. C., Bowen, R. M., Wallace, J. S. (1997), p. 332.

result from the level of efficiency of European capital markets. In comparison to Anglo American capital markets the efficiency of European ones could be lower and leads to different results.[2043]

The key figure EPS is the only traditional key figure which has a comparable value relevance than the Value Added.[2044] The high explanatory power of EPS is a comparable result to other association studies. These studies also detect a high explanatory power respectively value relevance of earnings or key figures which contain earnings.[2045] In other words: For capital market participants this key figure or key figures which base on earnings have a very high importance.[2046]

The high results for the traditional key figures in the first two years and for the EPS for all years of the study may also result from their application due to information intermediaries. Their analyses influence the price formation on stock markets[2047] because many market participants use such analysis as one important source of information for coming to an investment decision.[2048]

The gap between EPS and the other traditional key figures might be explained by the fact that capital market participants focus on earning key figures and that the other traditional key figures do not convey so much new information.[2049] A further reason could also be the used stock prices. They are the stock prices at the end of a fiscal year and not average prices. In the annual regressions the influence of reference date prices could distort the results. For the panel regression which includes a period of five years the influence of reference date prices is probably clearly smaller.[2050] Another reason for low association between stock prices and traditional accounting numbers could be that the capital markets are not as efficient as assumed and distort especially the value relevance of the traditional key figures.[2051]

The annual regression shows that the explanatory power of the variables vary over time which is consistent with prior research.[2052] In this empirical study it is striking that the explanatory power of traditional key figures decreases significantly during the investigation period. Often an explanation of declining value relevance is a critical economic situation. In general, negative key figures have a clear reduced explanatory power.[2053] On the basis of the analysis of the key figure Value Added a significant deviation cannot be detected. The number of companies with a negative Value Added is relatively constant.[2054] However, having a look at the key figure EPS signs for earnings management exist. The number of companies which have an EPS between zero and 0.5 is

2043 Cf. Günther, T., Landrock, B., Muche, T. (2000a), p. 133.
2044 Cf. chapter 4.2.3.4.
2045 Cf. exemplarily the studies of Biddle, G. C., Bowen, R. M., Wallace, J. S. (1997), p. 317; Chen, S., Dodd, J. L. (2001); Holler, A. (2009), p. 176; Kyriazis, D., Anastassis, C. (2007), p. 82; Maditinos, D. I., Sevic, Z., Theriou, N. G. (2009); p. 192; Vorstius, S. (2004), pp. 216-217.
2046 Cf. Biddle, G. C., Bowen, R. M., Wallace, J. S. (1999), pp. 78-79; Vorstius, S. (2004), p. 216.
2047 Cf. Günther, T., Landrock, B., Muche, T. (2000a), p. 133.
2048 Cf. chapter 2.3.2.1 and the introduction of actors on capital markets and their information needs.
2049 Cf. Biddle, G. C., Bowen, R. M., Wallace, J. S. (1999), p. 79.
2050 Cf. Schremper, R., Pälchen Oliver (2001), pp. 552-554.
2051 Cf. Dumontier, P., Raffournier, B. (2002), p. 145.
2052 Cf. exemplarily Hüfner, B., Möller, H. P. (2002), p. 161.
2053 Cf. Vorstius, S. (2004), pp. 203-208.
2054 Cf. chapter 4.2.2.

in the years 2012 and 2013 are 74 and 77. In the following years the number increases by approximately 18 % to 91 in 2014 and remains for the following years at this level. This is an indication that companies try to avoid small losses and conduct earnings management in order to disclose a positive result. This fact can be an explanation for the declining value relevance of most traditional key figures. The Value Added is not influenced in the same degree by earnings management because the deduction of cost of capital leads to a negative Value Added for companies which only have earnings slightly above zero.[2055] Although capital market participants are aware of the possibilities of earnings management which can be concluded by the declining value relevance of the traditional key figures, key figures based on earnings are preferred and have high value relevance despite earnings management.[2056]

Neither the value based performance measure nor traditional key figures have superior value relevance. In the context of the special economic situation during the investigation period in Europe both kinds of key figures have comparable value relevance. Previous research data does not include this economic situation but comes to similar results. Overall, this study confirms the results of prior value relevance research.[2057]

It has to be taken into account that the value relevance of accounting data is per se limited because investors have several sources of information and accounting data focuses on past periods whereas for investors the prospective development of the company is more important.[2058] A cause for the limited value relevance of accounting is the growing importance of intangible factors like know-how which are not all disclosed on balance sheet. The increasing speed of economic change that forces investors and information intermediaries to have access to current sources of information and process them quickly also limits the value relevance of accounting information because it is available only per quarter.[2059] Under these circumstances the Internet provides investors faster with information. Investors already know so much information when annual reports are disclosed. The influence of accounting on shares prices has decreased in the last decades due to this development.[2060]

4.4 Limitations

4.4.1 Analysis of Annual Reports

The empirical study has some limitations due to the applied methodology and the selected data base. For identifying the limitations, the three parts of the study are assessed separately.

Concerning the analysis of the annual reports, an essential assumption is important: Companies which use a value concept disclose information about it in the annual report and information about such a key figure within the annual report means that a company

2055 Cf. for similar interpretation Vorstius, S. (2004), pp. 207-208.
2056 Cf. Vorstius, S. (2004), p. 217.
2057 Cf. chapter 3.5.3 for an overview of the current state of research.
2058 Cf. Auer, K. v. (1999), pp. 178-179; Kothari, S. P. (2001), p. 109.
2059 Cf. Kothari, S. P. (2001), pp. 117-118; Lindemann, J. (2006), p. 969.
2060 Cf. Kothari, S. P. (2001), pp. 129-130; Vorstius, S. (2004), pp. 106-109.

actually uses this value concept.[2061] If the assumption is not fulfilled, this means that companies use a value based performance measure, but do not report about this in the annual business report. In order to avoid this problem, a robustness check in type of a survey would be necessary.[2062] In order to get access to a large database at a European level, there is no alternative to analysing annual reports.[2063]

The analysis of publication behaviour concerning value based performance measures uses a self-constructed ranking scheme. Due to this fact it is difficult to compare the results in detail with other studies. The data base also limits the insights from this study as it assesses the information contained in annual reports. Beyond this information source companies may give additional information about value based performance measures in conference calls or similar events. The data source annual report also does not indicate how intensively companies are applying the value concepts in daily business.[2064]

4.4.2 Standardised Calculation of ROCE Spread and Value Added

The ROCE Spread as a value based performance measure has some flaws which have to be taken into account by comparing the performance of companies. The performance comparison on the basis of the ROCE / ROE Spread is linked with the strengths and weaknesses of these two key figures. The two decisive flaws are: They are influenced by accounting policy and give companies an advantage with depreciated assets. The chosen profit measure EBIT can contain extraordinary profits or losses which might distort the performance of one period.[2065]

A listed disadvantage of using accounting data is that it may be influenced by management's accounting policy and the values are biased upwards or downwards which influences the key figure calculation.[2066] The annual business reports are audited so that it is ensured that accounting follows the IFRS rules and a certain level of quality standard can be expected. A complete exclusion from accounting policy is not possible. This is an inherent problem by using accounting data.[2067] However, the IFRS contain less discretion for accounting policy than most local GAAPs.[2068]

A second problem could be that accounting values are biased due to accounting conservatism meaning losses are shown earlier than profits.[2069] This point of criticism is mitigated within the context of IFRS because the analysis of IFRS accounting quality revealed that market participants experience an increase in accounting quality documented by a decrease in analysts' forecast error.[2070]

2061 Cf. Rapp, M. S., Schellong, D., Schmidt, M., et al. (2011), p. 180.
2062 Cf. exemplarily for empirical studies based on surveys: Malmi, S., Ikäheimo, S. (2003) and Weber, J. (2009).
2063 Cf. Firk, S., Schrapp, S., Wolff, M. (2016), p. 56.
2064 Cf. Firk, S., Schrapp, S., Wolff, M. (2016), pp. 56-57.
2065 Cf. for an extensive assessment of the ROCE and ROCE Spread chapter 3.3.2.1.2.
2066 Cf. Holthausen, R. W., Watts, R. L. (2001), pp. 28-29.
2067 Cf. Dechow, P., Ge, W., Schrand, C. (2010), p. 368; Gantzhorn, A. (2016), pp. 116-118.
2068 Cf. Daske, H., Hail, L., Leuz, C., et al. (2008), pp. 1091-1092.
2069 Cf. Holthausen, R. W., Watts, R. L. (2001), pp. 37-38.
2070 Cf. Chalmers, K., Clinch, G., Godfrey, J. M., et al. (2012), pp. 704-707; Erkilet, G., Kholmy, K. (2016), pp. 50-60.

4.4.3 *Value Relevance Analysis*

The third part of the empirical study uses the statistical method of regression analysis. It is important to stress that regression analysis is able to prove mathematical correlations. But these correlations do not automatically lead to causality between the variables.[2071]

Transferred to the association study, this means: The identified statistical associations do not mean that accounting data induced the change in stock prices.[2072] In other words: A cause-effect relationship is missing. The association between a key figure and a stock price has not been causal for a stock price change. Stock prices include many other factors so that a high association between a key figure and a stock price does not indicate automatically a corresponding information effect of this key figure for investors.[2073]

Many statistical approaches like the regression analysis assume a linear form.[2074] Despite theoretical foundation it is doubtful that such complexes coherences show a linear form in reality. Therefore, it is a claim in the scientific literature to investigate the problems with more sophisticated statistical approaches which do not assume or base on linear models.[2075]

Beside the mathematical method and the data base the applied kind of value relevance study, an association study, is criticised in the scientific literature.[2076] The empirical study compares the value relevance of different key figures with the objective to deliver further insights to the controversial discussion about convenient and meaningful key figures. But association studies only consider one of several aspects of key figures, namely its association with stock returns. They do not deliver information how successful the key figures are for internal control purposes or if one of the key figures is well suited for forecasting a company's insolvency.[2077]

Consequently, R^2 does not measure the complete usefulness of a key figure. It does not capture for what purposes the key figure is used within companies beyond its coherence to stock price development. Further possible applications are prediction of bankruptcy, implementing it as a part of manager's compensation system or as a benchmark within credit contracts.

In addition, possible costs due to the application of a key figure are not contained within the analysis of R^2. Examples are costs of preparing the data base for the key figure calculation in the company and the cost for communicating it to the public.[2078]

On the basis of the level of information efficiency on capital markets the aggregation of information in stock prices and their use in value relevance studies can be assessed critically. This study uses stock prices as dependent variable. Therefore, some flaws of

---

2071 Cf. Coenenberg, A. G., Haller, A., Schultze, W. (2014), p. 1314.
2072 Cf. Wagenhofer, A., Ewert, R. (2015), p. 131.
2073 Cf. Bogajewskaja, J. (2007), p. 109.
2074 Cf. chapter 4.2.3.3 in which the requirements for regression analysis are explained.
2075 Cf. Ittner, C. D., Larcker, D. F. (2001), pp. 400-402.
2076 Cf. for an overview of points of criticism for associations studies Bogajewskaja, J. (2007), pp. 108-113; cf. for points of criticism for value relevance studies in general Holthausen, R. W., Watts, R. L. (2001).
2077 Cf. Chen, S., Dodd, J. L. (2001).
2078 Cf. Lev, B. (1989), pp. 157-158.

this variable have to be taken into account.[2079] In addition to that it has to be considered that the objective of a performance measure has to be taken into account when determining their value relevance. For example debt capital providers are not interested in increasing market capitalization so that using stock prices as dependent variable might lead to misleading results and insights.[2080]

Market values are closely connected to the current economic situation in Europe.[2081] A distortion of stock prices can result from the European debt crisis and the low interest rate environment across Europe during the investigation period. Consequently, the results could change if a different capital market or different time period is selected.[2082]

A further assumption of association studies is that capital markets are efficient in the semi strong form and stock prices are formed under the validity of this assumption. This is problematic insofar as some empirical studies prove capital market anomalies which would normally not occur at this level of information, e.g. the post earnings announcement drift.[2083] It is probable that the efficiency of capital market is not semi-strong. Consequently, the used stock prices might be distorted due to capital market anomalies.[2084] These anomalies might influence the stock prices of the companies of the sample in different extents. The stock prices of smaller companies might be influenced more than the stock prices of larger ones.[2085] In total, a lower degree of information efficiency of a capital market distorts value relevance results from the association study and might lead to wrong conclusions.[2086]

Beside the information efficiency of stock markets it has to be considered that stock prices are not only influenced by information available but also by the behaviour of capital market participants.[2087] The information content of stock prices declines if non-information based trading occurs or even increases.[2088] Noise traders influence the stock price which then deviates from its fundamental value. In order to mitigate the effects of noise traders, hybrid approaches can be used. They mix market and accounting information for the dependent variable and reduce the influence of noise traders.[2089] This study does not consider the mixed approach and takes only the market values as dependent

---

2079 Cf. for an extensive analysis of using stock prices in value relevance studies Donoth, A., Radhakrishnan, S., Ronen, J. (2007).

2080 Cf. Kothari, S. P. (2001), pp. 169-170.

2081 Cf. Chen, C. J. P., Chen, S., Su, X. (2001), p. 19.

2082 Cf. for similar argumentation Hawranek, B., Öppinger, C. (2014), p. 102 who argues that their results can be distorted due to the financial crisis in 2007 and 2008 and Lindemann, J. (2006), p. 983.

2083 Cf. Dumontier, P., Raffournier, B. (2002), p. 126; Wagenhofer, A., Ewert, R. (2015), pp. 105-106, cf. extensively chapter 2.3.1.2 and 2.3.1.3.

2084 Cf. confirmatory Kothari, S. P. (2001), p. 120; Mölls, S. H., Strauß, M. (2007), p. 978; Nichols, D. C., Wahlen, J. M. (2004), p. 265.

2085 Cf. Donoth, A., Radhakrishnan, S., Ronen, J. (2007), pp. 6-7.

2086 Cf. the study of Aboody, D., Hughes, J., Liu, J. (2002) which compares the results of value relevance analysis on efficient and inefficient markets.

2087 Cf. Dumontier, P., Raffournier, B. (2002), p. 140.

2088 Cf. Donoth, A., Radhakrishnan, S., Ronen, J. (2007), pp. 5, 38. Non-information based trading summarizes all trading actions at stock markets which are not executed on the basis of information.

2089 Cf. Lee, C. M. (2001), pp. 249-250.

variable. It could be the case that the stock prices used are distorted due to noise traders.[2090]

In reality the individual information needs are more diverse than expressed by stock prices. Furthermore, no investor probably has as much information as contained in stock prices. These two circumstances lead to derivation of stock prices from individual investors' valuation models. Stock prices do not reflect this diversity of valuation models.[2091]

It might be that the association determined within the study is random because so many possible factors may influence the stock price. That means that at the same time investors react on other information than accounting. Then accounting information is not the cause for the change in stock price but the value relevance study has as a result a high R^2.[2092] It could be the case that the market price is influenced by factors beyond the company's control which results in derivation from the inner and true company value. Furthermore, investors can use several information channels through which they get information earlier in comparison to accounting data. In the end, accounting data will only partly be able to explain market prices.[2093] A limitation of the study is that the results do not deliver information which information sources substitute accounting data.[2094]

Due to the focus on market values and the choice of stock price as dependent variable the association study is completely focussed on the capital market and does not consider further stakeholder groups which are also interested in the annual report and accounting figures.[2095] By determing the association between stock prices and accounting numbers, only the value relevance of accounting values with reference to capital market values is assessed. Explanatory power of accounting values might derivate for members of compensation committee or bondholders because they have different criteria for making their decisions.[2096] Therefore, further insights concerning the value relevance of the analysed key figures might come up if further stakeholder groups are considered.[2097] The focus on shareholders is criticised but corresponds to the IFRS framework which is primarily orientated at the information needs of equity capital providers.[2098]

Concerning the independent variables, especially the key figures analysed and some of the control variables might be influenced by a company's accounting policy. It is a common disadvantage of accounting figures that the information content and accounting policy could not be assessed separately. Results of the association study might be distorted due to effects of accounting policy on the selected variables.[2099]

The key figure Value Added considers the cost of capital. But the cost of capital calculation from Bloomberg might derivate from the cost of capital calculation of capital market participants. The Value Added numbers used might be distorted due to the used

2090 Cf. chapter 4.1.2.3.5.
2091 Cf. Holthausen, R. W., Watts, R. L. (2001), p. 27.
2092 Cf. Wagenhofer, A., Ewert, R. (2015), pp. 129-130.
2093 Cf. Bogajewskaja, J. (2007), p. 109; Mölls, S. H., Strauß, M. (2007), p. 977.
2094 Cf. Schloemer, M. (2003), p. 197; Vorstius, S. (2004), pp. 235-236.
2095 Cf. Bogajewskaja, J. (2007), pp. 108-109; Mölls, S. H., Strauß, M. (2007), p. 978.
2096 Cf. Dechow, P., Ge, W., Schrand, C. (2010), p. 367.
2097 Cf. Coenenberg, A. G., Haller, A., Schultze, W. (2014), p. 1317.
2098 Cf. Bogajewskaja, J. (2007), pp. 111-112.
2099 Cf. Wagenhofer, A., Dücker, H. (2007), p. 293.

cost of capital. This distortion might lead to a different value relevance of Value Added.[2100]

Many other important factors are probably not considered sufficiently in the regression equation, e.g. auditing quality, corporate governance or analyst coverage. Therefore, additional variables could have been included.[2101]

The theoretical construct of the regression equation is the Feltham Ohlson model which bases on assumptions like the clean surplus relation which are not fulfilled in reality. In addition, this study simplifies the theoretical model. Due to the violation of assumptions and used simplifications the results might be distorted.[2102]

For setting up the regression equation on the basis of the Feltham Ohlson model the study uses a price model. An alternative would be the return model which has been excluded due to the posed research question. The choice of the model has also influenced the results and a return model might deliver divergent insights.[2103]

Due to the application of the price model the R^2 might be distorted due to scale effects. The high level of R^2 indicates that despite the division of all variables by total numbers of shares outstanding scale effects could not completely be avoided.[2104]

Also the data base causes some limitations of the study and the interpretation of its results. The data could be partly distorted due to a survivorship bias. The index composition of Stoxx Europe 600 at 31st July 2015 is the data base. As also periods from 2012 to 2014 are included in the statistical analysis the data base contains only companies which survive. A possible bias is limited to these periods. During the periods 2015 and 2016 some companies are not included in the data base anymore due to insolvency or merger & acquisitions.[2105]

The data base may cause a further statistical problem. The sample of the study bases on a stock index and the assumption that the companies within this stock index have similar characteristics as the basic population. It could be the case that the characteristics of the sample companies do not correspond completely to the characteristic of the companies of the population and that these characteristics change over time.[2106]

The data base includes companies from several countries of Europe. Studies that are analysing stock returns across countries have a common disadvantage. They assume that capital market structures and resulting pricing mechanisms are identical across countries although empirical studies conducted so far show the opposite.[2107] Thus, results can be influenced by national economic factors like diverging levels of information efficiency on national capital markets[2108] or further economic environment conditions which diverge

2100 Cf. Biddle, G. C., Bowen, R. M., Wallace, J. S. (1997), p. 332.

2101 Cf. Barth, M. E., Landsman, W. R., Lang, M. H. (2008), p. 482; Chen, C. J. P., Chen, S., Su, X. (2001), p. 19.

2102 Cf. Bogajewskaja, J. (2007), p. 111; cf. extensively for the derivation of the Feltham Ohlson model for this emprical study chapter 4.1.2.3.2.

2103 Cf. Schmidt, M. (2005), p. 113.

2104 Cf. Schloemer, M. (2003), p. 143; cf. extensively the discussion in chapter 4.1.2.3.1 for advantages and disadvantages of price models and possible occuring scale effects.

2105 Cf. Hesselmann, C. (2006), p. 185; Holler, A. (2009), p. 135.

2106 Cf. Schneider, N. C. (2007), pp. 189-190.

2107 Cf. Bartov, E., Goldberg, S. R., Kim, M. (2005), p. 100.

2108 Cf. Möller, H. P., Hüfner, B. (2002), p. 452.

between the countries.[2109] One limitation of the regression equation is that it does not consider these macroeconomic factors, e.g. the long-term interest rate or the inflation rate which also have an influence on share prices.[2110]

2109 Cf. Mölls, S. H., Strauß, M. (2007), p. 964.
2110 Cf. Elbakry, A. E., Nwachukwu, J. C., Abdou, H. A., et al. (2017), pp. 22-23.

5 Conclusion

5.1 Summary

Companies' actions are determined by VBM and Shareholder Value approach. Thus, they strive to earn a profit which covers the total cost of capital. The costs of capital play an important role as they are the hurdle rate for companies.[2111] The widely used method of CAPM for cost of capital calculation is controversially discussed in the scientific literature and shows some flaws in its practical application.[2112]

Due to the separation of ownership and control the Shareholder Value maximation is the primary goal of companies. The Principal Agent Theory is used to describe the behaviour of managers and shareholders under these circumstances. Both parties act opportunistically and due to information asymmetries managers can harm shareholders. In order to reduce information asymmetries and limit opportunistic behaviour monitoring, screening, self-selection, incentive systems and control systems are possible solutions.[2113] In this context key figures are an instrument as they help to reduce agency problems before and during an investment. They can be used for monitoring and controlling the actions of managers. The voluntary publication of value based performance measures can be seen as a signal in order to increase trust into mangement's abilities and behaviour. Key figures are also part of control and incentive systems within a company.[2114]

Beside the relationship between managers and shareholders it is important to point out how the capital market processes information. The theory of efficient capital markets stresses that the delivery of information plays an important role as the efficiency of a capital market is determined by the information contained in prices. It can be assumed that capital markets are regularly nearly semi-efficient. Thus, the prices contain mostly all public available information but can be distorted by capital market anomalies or the behaviour of individuals. The accounting of companies is an important part for price setting on capital markets as it contains reliable information for investors about a companies' performance.[2115]

The analysis of information needs of the most important actors on capital markets confirms the important role of accounting. Most relevant information sources for investors are personal contacts to management and the annual accounts published by a company. Key figures summarise the information contained in annual accounts and are used in the context of fundamental analysis which many professional investors conduct. Analysts also use key figures for performance analysis, rating agencies for an assessment of creditworthiness. For private investors key figures play a minor important role.[2116]

Taking insights from Principal Agent Theory, theory of efficient capital markets and analysis of information sources of capital market participants together accounting fulfils a

2111 Cf. chapters 2.1.1 and 2.1.2.
2112 Cf. chapter 2.1.3.
2113 Cf. chapters 2.2.1, 2.2.2, 2.2.3 and 2.2.4.1.
2114 Cf. chapter 2.2.4.2.
2115 Cf. chapter 2.3.1.
2116 Cf. chapter 2.3.2.2.

N. Eikelmann, *Value Based Performance Measures*, FOM-Edition Research,
https://doi.org/10.1007/978-3-658-31429-3_5

stewardship role, is a common basis for investment decisions and thus is an important part of information which influences price formation on capital markets.[2117]

The annual accounts are set up on the basis of IFRS rules. IFRS accounting rules focus on equity and debt capital providers. They strive to provide the addressees with decision-useful information. Despite several advantages and an overwhelming objective which corresponds to the objectives of VBM and Shareholder Value approach, the legal reporting is not sufficient to satisfy comprehensively the information needs of investors.[2118]

Therefore, companies often give voluntarily additional information to their capital providers. This behaviour is summarised under the term Value Reporting which has the objectives to adapt the stock price to the intrinsic value as well as to reduce information asymmetries between the company and investors and creditors. Reduction of information asymmetries leads to decreasing costs of capital.[2119]

Key figures are an important part of Value Reporting. They document and summarise the performance of a company. Especially value based performance measures play an important role because they are able to give shareholders an indication about the success of a company in a period on the basis of the Shareholder Value approach.[2120]

The latest initiative is the integrated reporting framework which strives to create a standardised and summarised report containing the most important information. In this context key figures also play an important role for delivering summarised information to recipients of integrated reports. Illustration 32 summarises in simplified terms the framework conditions for the application of value based management.[2121]

In the context of the framework conditions illustrated companies use and disclose information about traditional key figures like PER, EPS, ROE, ROS or ROI. Independent from individual strength and weaknesses of these key figures, traditional key figures do not include the cost of capital in their calculation.[2122] Due to the occurring dissatisfaction with traditional key figures value based performance measures have been developed. These key figures have the objective to reduce the flaws of traditional key figures, e.g. no consideration of cost of equity capital, many possibilities for manipulation or low correlation with the developments at capital markets.[2123]

Value based performance measure can be classified with the help of three criteria: Data basis, time horizon and type of key figure. They can be calculated on the basis of earnings or Cash Flows. Independent from the data basis is the focus of a key figure. It can assess the performance of a single period or of the total period. The criterion type of key figure includes the differentiation between absolute and relative numbers.[2124]

2117 Cf. chapter 2.4.1.
2118 Cf. chapters 2.4.2 and 2.4.3.
2119 Cf. chapters 2.4.4.1, 2.4.4.2 and 2.4.4.3.
2120 Cf. chapter 2.4.4.4.
2121 Cf. chapter 2.4.4.5.
2122 Cf. chapter 3.1.
2123 Cf. chapter 3.2.2.
2124 Cf. chapter 3.2.1.

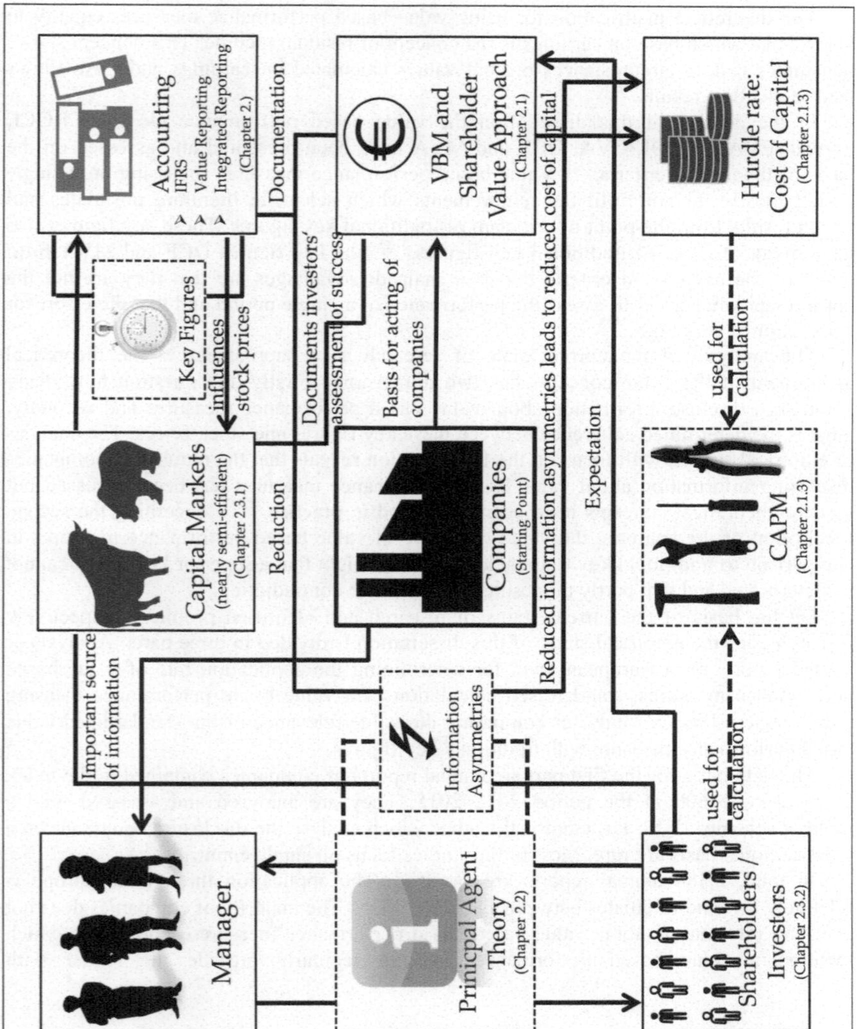

Source: Own illustration

Illustration 32: Framework conditions for the application of value based performance measures

The theoretical justification for using value based performance measures equally to key figures which base on earnings is the concept of residual income. This concept shows that under certain circumstances present values calculated on earnings and Cash Flows lead to identical results.[2125]

In the context of this dissertation the value based performance measures ROCE Spread, EVA, CFROI, CVA, DCF and MVA have been presented and assessed on the basis of theoretical criteria.[2126] Value based performance measures focussing on a single period mostly do not fulfil the requirements which scientific literature postulates and which results from the point of criticism of traditional key figures. These key figures also have many of flaws of traditional key figures.[2127] The key figures DCF and MVA fulfil many of the assessment criteria but their main disadvantages are that they are not the appropriate key figures to assess the performance of a single period and that the effort for calculation is very high.[2128]

The analysis of the current state of research as a supplement to the theoretical assessment of the value concepts has two dimensions: Firstly, the question how many companies disclose information about value based performance measures and secondly, what is the determined coherence between these key figures and stock prices. The analysis of empirical studies with focus on the first question reveals that the number of companies disclosing information about value based performance measures has been increased but that the theoretical concepts have been simplified in practice.[2129] Concerning the second focal point of the analysis, the value relevance of value based performance measures in comparison to traditional key figures, leads to the insight that a superior key figure cannot be determined and that partly the results of studies are contradicting.[2130]

On the basis of the current status of research and identified problems respectively research gaps the empirical study of this dissertation is divided in three parts: Analysis of annual reports on a European level for determining the application rate of value based performance measures, standardised calculation of a value based performance measure and a value relevance study for comparing the value relevance of the standardized value based performance measure with traditional key figures.

The data basis for the first part are annual reports of companies contained in the index Stoxx Europe 600 in the period 2012–2015. They are analysed and assessed with a ranking scheme.[2131] So far, empirical studies which analyse the disclosure behaviour on a cross-national basis are rare. Most of the studies focus on single countries.[2132]

In total, 2,384 annual reports are assessed. The application throughout Europe is relatively low and fluctuates between 11 % and 13 %. The majority of companies does not give any information about value based based performance measures. Companies which mention a value based performance measure regularly provide the reader with

2125 Cf. chapter 3.3.1.
2126 Cf. chapter 3.2.3, 3.3 and 3.4.
2127 Cf. chapter 3.3.2 and 3.3.3; Weber, J., Schäffer, U. (2016), p. 184.
2128 Cf. chapter 3.4.
2129 Cf. chapter 3.5.1.
2130 Cf. chapter 3.5.3.
2131 Cf. chapters 4.1.1.1, 4.1.2.1 and 4.1.3.1.
2132 Cf. the analysis of the current state of research in chapter 3.5.1.

Research Questions	Hypotheses	Results
1) How many companies throughout Europe give voluntary information about value based performance measures?	H1: More than 18 % of the companies of the sample publish information about the application of a value based performance measure in their company.	**Rejected** Between 11 and 13 % of the companies at least mention a value based performance measure in their annual report.
2) Which kind of information do companies give to external persons when disclosing a value based performance measure?	H2: The majority of companies (i.e. > 50 %) which applies a value based performance measure give additional information beyond the name of applied key figure.	**Fail to Reject** Many companies give the reader accompanying information to the name of the value based performance measure.
3) Does the publication behaviour change during the time period of investigation?	H3: During the time span of investigation the share of companies which applies a value based performance measure does not fluctuate more than 5 % in comparison to the first year of the investigation.	**Rejected** In two of four analysed years the share of companies fluctuates more than 5 %.

Source: Own illustration

Illustration 33: Overview of results of first part of empirical study

accompanying information. In total, the number of companies which disclose their value concept in the annual report slightly decreases in the investigation period.[2133]

Most striking is the difference of the application rate of value based performance measures between Germany and the rest of Europe. A possible explanation could be the high significance of the topic within the German scientific community. Also the methodology could be a cause for the difference. Another method, e.g. interview with managers, could lead to higher application rates in other countries. Apart from this peculiarity it can be summarised that it is surprising how many companies do not provide the reader of annual reports with information about a value based performance measure.[2134] A short overview of the results of the first part of the study is given in illustration 33.

The analysis of current state of research in combination with the theoretical assessment of value concepts reveal that the number of value based performance measures out of which companies can select is very high and that companies adapt the calculation to their individual needs. In order to be able to compare the performance of companies independently from size, the ROCE Spread and ROE Spread are computed for the period 2012 – 2016.[2135] The posed research question and corresponding answer is illustrated below.

2133 Cf. chapter 4.2.1.
2134 Cf. chapter 4.3.1.
2135 Cf. chapters 4.1.1.2, 4.1.2.2 and 4.1.3.2.

Research Questions	Hypotheses	Results
4) Which company out of the sample is the most successful one from the perspective of Value Based Management in the analysed period of time?	No hypothesis	The company Rightmove Plc is the most successful company in the analysed period of time.

Source: Own illustration

Illustration 34: Overview of results of second part of empirical study

The analysis shows that the majority of companies in the sample are able to generate a profit above the hurdle rate of the cost of capital. However, many companies have a profit which is only slightly above their cost of capital. By analysing the top performers within the investigation period, five companies are part of this group every year. The companies with lowest ROCE Spread are often banks or financial institutions.[2136]

These results indicate that many companies act in markets with strong competition because they have hurdle rates slightly above zero. In contrast, the top performing companies probably act in markets with less strong competition.[2137]

The last part of the study is a value relevance analysis in the form of an association study.[2138] Despite several empirical studies a superior key figure cannot be determined. Many of these studies focus on Anglo American markets or deal with the EVA. Furthermore, the study is conducted in a unique economic environment due to the period of low interest rates in Europe. It deals with the question what is the relative information content of the Value Added as an example for a value based performance measure in comparison to common traditional figures EPS, PER, ROI, ROE and ROS. The used regression equation is an equation based on the price level approach and derived from the Feltham Ohlson model.[2139]

The results show that the regression equation with the value based performance measure Value Added and the traditional key figure EPS have the highest coefficient of determination. The other traditional key figures have R^2 below the R^2 of Value Added and EPS.[2140] Illustration 35 contains a short overview of the most important results.

In comparison to previous studies the difference between traditional key figures and value based performance measures is lower and partly reverse. Reasons for diverging results could be the continuous dissemination of VBM and Shareholder Value approach which fosters the value relevance of key figures like Value Added. The high value relevance of EPS can be explained with the focus of all capital market participants on earnings. In total, the value relevance analysis confirms the results of previous studies and a uniform superior key figure cannot be determined.[2141]

2136 Cf. chapter 4.2.2.
2137 Cf. chapter 4.3.2.
2138 Cf. chapter 3.5.2.
2139 Cf. chapters 4.1.1.3, 4.1.2.3, 4.1.3.3.
2140 Cf. chapter 4.2.3.
2141 Cf. chapter 4.3.3.

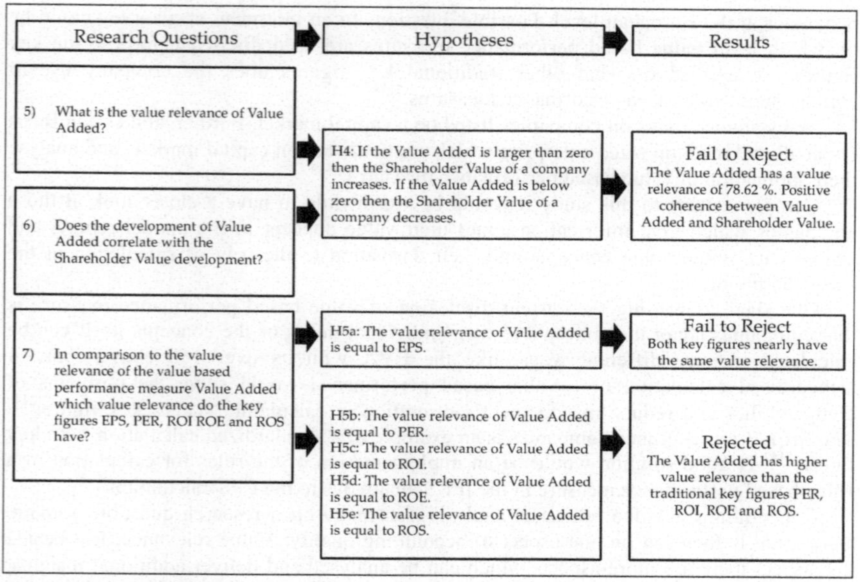

Source: Own illustration
Illustration 35: Overview of results of third part of empirical study

5.2 Outlook

The empirical study in this dissertation aims to contribute to open research questions in the context of value based performance measures. On the basis of the study's design two fields of research can be identified: The analysis of application of value concepts by companies and value relevance analysis.

Analysing the reporting behaviour of companies at a European level concerning the implementation of value based performance measures is a field which is fairly less explored. This study is only one of a few studies so far which reviews the disclosure of value based performance measures at a European level. It would be an interesting question whether the results of this analysis can be confirmed with another data base at a European level.[2142]

This study comes to the result that the application rates are slightly decreasing. It would be an interesting question if this trend can be confirmed for future periods at a European level or if certain volatility is constantly given.

Also the methodology of the analysis could be changed and could lead to new fruitful insights on the reporting behaviour. A survey or interviews with managers at the European level could lead to divergent application rates or confirm the results of the analysis of annual reports. Beyond that it would result in a more detailed picture about the reporting

2142 Cf. chapter 3.5.1 for an overview of existing studies.

behaviour at the European level. Possible questions in an interview or a survey could be on which level value based performance measures are used, for what purpose the key figures are applied or what other traditional key figures does the company use to complement value based performance measures.[2143]

Many studies focus on companies listed on a capital market. Further studies can focus on small and medium sized enterprise which are not listed on capital markets and analyse their application of value based performance measures.[2144]

Complementary to this study it would be worthwhile to have a closer look at those companies which give information about their value concept in the annual reports and analyse the single value concepts and their derivation to the way of calculation in the scientific literature.[2145]

One flaw concerning the current disclosing of value based performance measure is that companies adapt the concepts to their individual needs or the concepts itself can be calculated in very different ways, like the EVA with its over 160 conversions. A standardised calculation of a value based performance would solve the problems of comparability and reduce management's discretion in calculating such a key figure.[2146] The MCEV for insurance companies is an example of a standardized calculation for a key figure.[2147] A good solution would be an implementation of the rules for calculation of a value based performance measure in the IFRS analogous to the EPS calculation.[2148]

Concerning the value relevance analysis also many open research questions remain. This study is focusing on one aspect of accounting quality: Value relevance. But beside this aspect there are more aspects which can be analysed and deliver additional insights, e.g. persistence, predictability, volatility or timeliness.[2149] In addition to that prospective studies can explore the advantages and disadvantages of the selected key figures concerning its forecast quality or its reaction to certain events.[2150]

Value relevance studies use capital market measures as dependent variables although it is obvious that many markets are not efficient in the semi-strong form. It is an open task for researchers to search for better proxies for a company's intrinsic value and analyse the effect on value relevance.[2151]

Regularly, the regression analysis is the typical statistical method which is used in order to determine value relevance of key figures. It would be an interesting question if the results available so far in scientific literature can be confirmed with other more advanced statistical methods.[2152]

2143 Cf. exemplarily for survey or interviews the studies of Malmi, S., Ikäheimo, S. (2003); Weber, J. (2009).

2144 Cf. exemplarily Brück, C., Ludwig, J., Schwering, A. (2018); Tappe, R. (2009) and Günther, T., Gonschorek, T. (2011) who focus on small and medium sized companies.

2145 Cf. exemplarily for such an analysis Arbeitskreis Internes Rechnungswesen der Schmalenbach-Gesellschaft (2010), p. 798.

2146 Cf. Fischer, T. M., Rödl, K. (2005), p. 30.

2147 Cf. Wilson, T. C. (2015), pp. 102-104.

2148 Cf. IFRS Foundation (2016), IAS 33.

2149 Cf. for an overview of further aspects of accounting quality Wagenhofer, A., Dücker, H. (2007), pp. 270-280.

2150 Cf. Chen, S., Dodd, J. L. (2001).

2151 Cf. Schloemer, M. (2003), p. 198.

2152 Cf. Ittner, C. D., Larcker, D. F. (2001), pp. 400-402.

For drawing further conclusions about the value relevance of key figures and its coherence to investors' decisions, a survey or an experiment would be appropriate methods to gain additional insight.[2153]

There is already a high number of value relevance studies dealing with the EVA. This study instead uses the Value Added as the analysed value based performance measure. For future research it would be interesting to analyse the value relevance of further value based performance measures, e.g. CVA or CFROI in comparison to traditional key figures.[2154]

Studies with a direct comparison of value relevance of value based performance measures with traditional key figures are rare. So, this is a further field of research which offers possibilities for prospective studies.[2155]

Similar to the analysis of application of value based performance measures the data base of many studies focuses on Anglo American companies. Cross national studies analysing value relevance are also rare.[2156]

The outlook stresses that the reasearch field of value concepts or value based performance measures offers a broad variety for prospective research activities and that probably many interesting studies can be expected in the near future which try to solve the Metric War or at least specifies the knowledge about the abilities and characteristics of value based performance measures.

2153 Cf. Bastini, K., Kasperzak, R. (2013), pp. 623-624; cf. extensively for information about experimental studies Bastini, K., Kasperzak, R. (2013).

2154 Cf. Ittner, C. D., Larcker, D. F. (2001), p. 361.

2155 Cf. Schremper, R., Pälchen Oliver (2001), p. 543.

2156 Cf. Rapp, M. S., Schellong, D., Schmidt, M., et al. (2011), p. 174.

List of Literature

Abergel, F., Politi, M. (2013): Optimizing a basket against the efficient market hypothesis, in: Quantitative Finance, 13th vol., 2013, No. 1, pp. 13–23

Aboody, D., Hughes, J., Liu, J. (2002): Measuring Value Relevance in a (Possibly) Inefficient Market, in: Journal of Accounting Research, 40th vol., 2002, No. 4, pp. 965–986

Abrahams, T., Sidhu, B. K. (1998): The Role of R&D Capitalisations in Firm Valuation and Performance Measurement, in: Australian Journal of Management, 23rd vol., 1998, No. 2, pp. 169–183

Achleitner, A.-K., Bassen, A., Pietzsch, L., Wichels, D. (2002): Effiziente Kapitalmarktkommunikation mit Finanzanalysten - Gestaltungsempfehlungen für Wachstumsunternehmen, in: Finanz Betrieb, 4th vol., 2002, No. 1, pp. 29–44

Aders, C., Herbertinger, M., Schaffer, C., Wiedemann, F. (2003): Shareholder Value-Konzepte - Umsetzung bei den DAX100-Unternehmen, in: Finanz Betrieb, 5th vol., 2003, No. 11, pp. 719–725

Aders, C., Herbertinger, M., Wiedemann, F. (2003): Value Based Management (VBM): Lösungsansätze zur Schließung von Implementierungslücken, in: Finanz Betrieb, 5th vol., 2003, No. 6, pp. 356–372

Aharony, J., Barniv, R., Falk, H. (2010): The Impact of Mandatory IFRS Adoption on Equity Valuation of Accounting Numbers for Security Investors in the EU, in: European Accounting Review, 19th vol., 2010, No. 3, pp. 535–578

Akerlof, G. A. (1970): The market for "Lemons": quality uncertainty and the market mechanism, in: The Quarterly Journal of Economics, 84th vol., 1970, No. 84, pp. 488–500

Allegret, J.-P., Raymond, H., Rharrabti, H. (2017): The impact of the European sovereign debt crisis on banks stocks - some evidence of shift contagion in Europe, in: Journal of Banking & Finance, 74th vol., 2017, pp. 24–37

Allen, B., Chan, K. K., Milne, A., Thomas, S. (2012): Basel III: Is the cure worse than the disease?, in: International Review of Financial Analysis, 25th vol., 2012, pp. 159–166

Almazan, A., Hartzell, J., Starks, L. T. (2005): Active Institutional Shareholders and Costs of Monitoring: Evidence from Executive Compensation, in: Financial Management, 34th vol., 2005, No. 4, pp. 5–34

Alparslan, A. (2006): Strukturalistische Prinzipal-Agent-Theorie - eine Reformulierung der Hidden-Action-Modelle aus der Perspektive des Strukturalismus, Wiesbaden 2006

Alter, R. (2013): Strategisches Controlling - Unterstützung des strategischen Managements, 2nd edition, Munich 2013

Altman, M. (2010): Prospect Theory and Behavioral Finance, in: Baker, H. K., Nofsinger, J. R. (editors), Behavioral Finance - Investors, Corporations and Markets, Hoboken 2010

American Institute of Certified Public Accountants (AICPA) (1994): Improving Business Reporting - A Customer Focus, New York 1994

Amihud, Y., Mendelson, H. (1986): Asset Pricing and the Bid-Ask Spread, in: Journal of Financial Economics, 17th vol., 1986, No. 2, pp. 223–249

Anheuser-Busch InBev (2013): Annual Report 2013

Annacker, D. (2011): Unbeobachtbare Einflussgrößen in der strategischen Erfolgsfaktorforschung - Ein kausalanalytischer Ansatz auf der Basis von Paneldaten, dissertation, Wiesbaden 2011

Anthony, J. H., Ramesh, K. (1992): Association between accounting performance measures and stock prices, in: Journal of Accounting and Economics, 15th vol., 1992, No. 2-3, pp. 203–227

Arbeitskreis Externe Unternehmensrechnung der Schmalenbach-Gesellschaft (2002): Grundsätze für das Value Reporting, in: Der Betrieb, 55th vol., 2002, No. 45, pp. 2337–2340

N. Eikelmann, *Value Based Performance Measures*, FOM-Edition Research,
https://doi.org/10.1007/978-3-658-31429-3

Arbeitskreis Internes Rechnungswesen der Schmalenbach-Gesellschaft (2010): Vergleich von Praxiskonzepten zur wertorientierten Unternehmenssteuerung, in: Zeitschrift für betriebswirtschaftliche Forschung (zfbf), 62nd vol., 2010, No. 7, pp. 797–820

Arrow, K. J. (1986): Agency and the market, in: Arrow, K. J., Intriligator, M. D. (editors), Handbook of mathematical economics - Volume III, Amsterdam, New York, Oxford, Tokyo 1986

Aßmann, C., Rässler, S., Wolf, K. (2012): Ökonometrische Prognoseverfahren für Paneldaten, in: Mertens, P., Rässler, S. (editors), Prognoserechnung, 7th edition, Berlin, Heidelberg 2012, pp. 153–166

Asteriou, D., Hall, S. G. (2011): Applied Econometrics, 2nd edition, Basingstoke 2011

Athanasakou, V., Hussainey, K. (2014): The perceived credibility of forward-looking performance disclosures, in: Accounting and Business Research, 44th vol., 2014, No. 3, pp. 227–259

Athanassakos, G. (2007): Value-based management, EVA and stock price performance in Canada, in: Management Decision, 45th vol., 2007, No. 9, pp. 1397–1411

Atlas Copco (2015): Annual Report

Auer, B. (2008): Grundkurs Buchführung, 2nd edition, Wiesbaden 2008

Auer, K. von (1999): International harmonisierte Rechnungslegungsstandards aus Sicht der Aktionäre, 2nd edition, Wiesbaden 1999

Auer, L. von (2016): Ökonometrie - Eine Einführung, 7th edition, Wiesbaden 2016

Auer, M. (2007): Risiko-/ertragsorientierte Steuerungsmaße, in: Kaiser, T. (editor), Wettbewerbsvorteil Risikomanagement – erfolgreiche Steuerung der Strategie-, Reputations- und operationellen Risiken, Berlin 2007, pp. 293–306

Bacidore, J. M., Boquist, J. A., Milbourn, T. T., Thakor, A. V. (1997): The search for the best financial performance measure, in: Financial Analysts Journal, 53rd vol., 1997, No. 3, pp. 11–20

Backhaus, K., Erichson, B., Plinke, W., Weiber, R. (2016): Multivariate Analysemethoden - Eine anwendungsorientierte Einführung, 14th edition, Berlin, Heidelberg 2016

Badertscher, B., Shroff, N., White, H. D. (2013): Externalities of public firm presence: Evidence from private firms' investment decisions, in: Journal of Financial Economics, 109th vol., 2013, No. 3, pp. 682–706

Baetge, J., Kirsch, H.-J., Thiele, S. (2004): Bilanzanalyse, 2nd edition, Düsseldorf 2004

Baetge, J., Kümmel, J. (2003): Shareholder Value Reporting mit Hilfe wertorientierter Unternehmenskennzahlen, in: Rathgeber, A., Steiner, M., Tebroke, H.-J., Wallmeier, M. (editors), Finanzwirtschaft, Kapitalmarkt und Banken, Stuttgart 2003, pp. 47–66

Baetge, J., Niemeyer, K., Kümmel, J., Schulz, R. (2015): Darstellung der Discounted Cashflow-Verfahren, in: Peemöller, V. H. (editor), Praxishandbuch der Unternehmensbewertung, 6th edition, Herne 2015, pp. 353–508

Baetge, J., Solmecke, H. (2006): Grundsätze und Konzeption des Value Reportings, in: Zeitschrift für Controlling & Management (ZfCM), 2006, Special Issue 3, pp. 16–30

Baghai, R. P., Servaes, H., Tamayo, A. (2014): Have Rating Agencies Become More Conservative? Implications for Capital Structure and Debt Pricing, in: Journal of Finance, 69th vol., 2014, No. 5, pp. 1961–2005

Baiman, S., Verrecchia, R. E. (1996): The Relation among Capital Markets, Financial Disclosure, Production Efficiency and Insider Trading, in: Journal of Accounting Research, 34th vol., 1996, No. 1, pp. 1–22

Baker, H. K., Nofsinger, J. R. (2010): Behavioral Finance: An Overview, in: Baker, H. K., Nofsinger, J. R. (editors), Behavioral Finance - Investors, Corporations and Markets, Hoboken 2010, pp. 3–21

Ball, R. (2006): International Financial Reporting Standards (IFRS): pros and cons for investors, in: Accounting and Business Research, 36th vol., 2006, Special Issue, pp. 5–27

Ball, R., Brown, P. (1968): An Empirical Evaluation of Accounting Income Numbers, in: Journal of Accounting Research, 6th vol., 1968, No. 2, pp. 159–178

Ball, R., Jayaraman, S., Shivakumar, L. (2012): Audited financial reporting and voluntary disclosure as complements: A test of the Confirmation Hypothesis, in: Journal of Accounting and Economics, 53rd vol., 2012, No. 1, pp. 136–166

Ball, R., Kothari, S. P., Robin, A. (2000): The effect of international institutional factors on properties of accounting earnings, in: Journal of Accounting and Economics, 29th vol., 2000, No. 1, pp. 1–51

Ball, R., Robin, A., Wu, J. S. (2003): Incentives versus standards: properties of accounting income in four East Asian countries, in: Journal of Accounting and Economics, 36th vol., 2003, No. 1-3, pp. 235–270

Ball, R., Shivakumar, L. (2005): Earnings quality in UK private firms: comparative loss recognition timeliness, in: Journal of Accounting and Economics, 39th vol., 2005, pp. 83–128

Ballwieser, W. (2009): Shareholder Value als Element von Corporate Governance, in: Zeitschrift für betriebswirtschaftliche Forschung (zfbf), 61st vol., 2009, No. 1, pp. 93–101

Ballwieser, W., Hachmeister, D. (2016): Unternehmensbewertung - Prozesse, Methoden und Probleme, 5th edition, Stuttgart 2016

Balsam, S., Lipka, R. (1998): Share Prices and Alternative Measures of Earnings per Share, in: Accounting Horizons, 12th vol., 1998, No. 3, pp. 234–249

Baltagi, B. H. (2013): Econometric Analysis of Panel Data, 5th edition, Chichester 2013

Banz, R. W. (1981): The Relationship Between Return And Market Value Of Common Stocks, in: Journal of Financial Economics, 9th vol., 1981, No. 1, pp. 3–18

Banzhaf, J. (2006): Wertorientierte Berichterstattung (Value Reporting), dissertation, Frankfurt on the Main 2006

Bao, B.-H., Bao, D.-H. (1998): Usefulness of Value Added and Abnormal Economic Earnings: an empirical examination, in: Journal of Business Finance & Accounting, 25th vol., 1998, No. 1 - 2, pp. 251–264

Barker, R. G. (1999): The role of dividends in valuation models used by analysts and fund managers, in: The European Accounting Review, 8th vol., 1999, No. 2, pp. 195–218

Barry, C. B., Brown, S. J. (1985): Differential Information and Security Market Equilibrium, in: Journal of Financial and Quantitative Analysis, 20th vol., 1985, No. 4, pp. 407–422

Barth, M. E. (2000): Valuation-based accounting research: Implications for financial reporting and opportunities for future research, in: Accounting and Finance, 40th vol., 2000, No. 1, pp. 7–32

Barth, M. E., Beaver, W. H., Landsman, W. R. (2001): The relevance of the value relevance literature for financial accounting standard setting: another view, in: Journal of Accounting and Economics, 31st vol., 2001, No. 1-3, pp. 77–104

Barth, M. E., Clinch, G. (2009): Scale Effects in Capital Markets-Based Accounting Research, in: Journal of Business Finance & Accounting, 36th vol., 2009, No. 3-4, pp. 253–288

Barth, M. E., Kallapur, S. (1996): The Effects of Cross-Sectional Scale Differences on Regression Results in Empirical Accounting Research, in: Contemporary Accounting Research, 13th vol., 1996, No. 2, pp. 527–567

Barth, M. E., Landsman, W. R., Lang, M. H. (2008): International Accounting Standards and Accounting Quality, in: Journal of Accounting Research, 46th vol., 2008, No. 3, pp. 467–498

Barth, M. E., Landsman, W. R., Young, D., Zhuang, Z. (2014): Relevance of Differences between Net Income based on IFRS and Domestic Standards for European Firms, in: Journal of Business Finance & Accounting, 41st vol., 2014, No. 3-4, pp. 297–327

Barth, T., Barth, D. (2008): Controlling, 2nd edition, Munich 2008

Barton, J., Hansen, T. B., Pownall, G. (2010): Which Performance Measures Do Investors Around the World Value the Most—and Why?, in: The Accounting Review, 85th vol., 2010, No. 3, pp. 753–789

Bartov, E., Goldberg, S. R., Kim, M. (2005): Comparative Value Relevance Among German, U.S., and International Accounting Standards: A German Stock Market Perspective, in: Journal of Accounting, Auditing & Finance, 20th vol., 2005, No. 2, pp. 95–119

Bar-Yosef, S., Callen, J. L., Livnat, J. (1996): Modeling dividends, earnings, and book value equity: An empirical investigation of the Ohlson valuation dynamics, in: Review of Accounting Studies, 1st vol., 1996, No. 3, pp. 207–224

Bassen, A. (2002): Institutionelle Investoren und Corporate Governance - Analyse der Einflussnahme unter besonderer Berücksichtigung börsennotierter Wachstumsunternehmen, Wiesbaden 2002

Bassen, A., Frank, R., Madsen, O., Bojanic, T., Laskavaya, E. (2012): Ausweis von Pro-Forma-Kennzahlen kapitalmarktorientierter Unternehmen, in: KoR: Internationale und kapitalmarktorientierte Rechnungslegung, 12th vol., 2012, No. 7/8, pp. 360–365

Bastini, K. (2015): Gestaltung der Erfolgsrechnung nach IFRS – Experimentelle Analyse der Entscheidungsprozesse nichtprofessioneller Investoren, dissertation, Wiesbaden 2015

Bastini, K., Kasperzak, R. (2013): Erkenntnisfortschritt in der Rechnungslegung durch experimentelle Forschung? - Diskussion methodischer Grundsatzfragen anhand der Entscheidungsnützlichkeit des Performance Reporting, in: Zeitschrift für betriebswirtschaftliche Forschung (zfbf), 65th vol., 2013, No. 8, pp. 622–660

Bauer, T. K., Fertig, M., Schmidt, C. M. (2009): Empirische Wirtschaftsforschung - Eine Einführung, Berlin, Heidelberg 2009

Baum, H.-G., Coenenberg, A. G., Günther, T. (2013): Strategisches Controlling, 5th edition, Stuttgart 2013

Baumann, S. (2008): Projektfinanzierung in Supply Chain Netzwerken – eine neo-institutionenökonomische Analyse am Beispiel der Automobilindustrie, dissertation, Wiesbaden 2008

Bausch, A., Buske, A., Hagemeier, W. (2011): Performance-Messung zur Steuerung von Unternehmen, in: Funk, W., Rossmanith, J. (editors), Internationale Rechnungslegung und Internationales Controlling - Herausforderungen - Handlungsfelder - Erfolgspotenziale, 2nd edition, Wiesbaden 2011, pp. 355–386

Beattie, V., McInnes, B., Fearnley, S. (2004): A methodology for analysing and evaluating narratives in annual reports: a comprehensive descriptive profile and metrics for disclosure quality attributes, in: Accounting Forum, 28th vol., 2004, No. 3, pp. 205–236

Beaver, W. H. (1968): The Information Content of Annual Earnings Announcements, in: Journal of Accounting Research, 6th vol., 1968, Empirical Research in Accounting: Selected Studies 1968, pp. 67–92

Beaver, W. H. (2002): Perspectives on Recent Capital Market Research, in: The Accounting Review, 77th vol., 2002, No. 2, pp. 453–474

Beck, R. (2003): Erfolg durch wertorientiertes Controlling - Entscheidungen unterstützende Konzepte, Berlin 2003

Becker, H. P. (2016): Investition und Finanzierung - Grundlagen der betrieblichen Finanzwirtschaft, 7th edition, Wiesbaden 2016

Beekes, W., Brown, P., Zhan, W., Zhang, Q. (2016): Corporate Governance, Companies' Disclosure Practices and Market Transparency: A Cross Country Study, in: Journal of Business Finance & Accounting, 43rd vol., 2016, No. 3-4, pp. 263–297

Behringer, S. (2014): Konzerncontrolling, 2nd edition, Wiesbaden 2014

Bej, T. (2015): Die Kapitalflussrechnung im wertorientierten Controlling - Unternehmen auf Basis von Free Cash Flows steuern, Wiesbaden 2015

Berger, S. (2012): Die Vernetzung der Finanzdienstleister - eine Analyse am Beispiel des Asset Management, dissertation, Wiesbaden 2012

Berk, J. B., DeMarzo, P. M. (2011): Grundlagen der Finanzwirtschaft - Analyse, Entscheidung und Umsetzung, Munich 2011

Berlien, O., Kirsten, A. S., Oelert, J., Schutt, R. (2006): Wertsteigerung durch das Konzernprogramm best bei ThyssenKrupp, in: Schweickart, N., Töpfer, A. (editors), Wertorientiertes Management - Werterhaltung - Wertsteuerung - Wertsteigerung ganzheitlich gestalten, Berlin, Heidelberg 2006, pp. 597–608

Bernard, V. L. (1995): The Feltham-Ohlson Framework: Implications for Empiricists, in: Contemporary Accounting Research, 11th vol., 1995, No. 2, pp. 733–747

Bernard, V. L., Thomas, J. K. (1989): Post-Earnings-Announcement Drift: Delayed Price Response or Risk Premium?, in: Journal of Accounting Research, 27th vol., 1989, Supplement, pp. 1–36

Bernard, V. L., Thomas, J. K. (1990): Evidence That Stock Prices Do Not Fully Reflect The Implications Of Current Earnings For Future Earnings, in: Journal of Accounting and Economics, 13th vol., 1990, No. 4, pp. 305–340

Bernheim, D., Whinston, M. D. (1986): Common Agency, in: Econometrica, 54th vol., 1986, No. 4, pp. 923–942

Bessembinder, H., Chan, K. (1998): Market Efficiency and the Returns to Technical Analysis, in: Financial Management, 27th vol., 1998, No. 2, pp. 5–17

Beyer, A., Cohen, D. A., Lys, T. Z., Walther, B. R. (2010): The financial reporting environment: Review of the recent literature, in: Journal of Accounting and Economics, 50th vol., 2010, No. 2-3, pp. 296–343

Bezemer, P.-J., Zajac, E. J., Naumovska, I., van den Bosch, F. A. J., Volberda, H. W. (2014): Power and Paradigms: The Dutch Response to Pressures for Shareholder Value, in: Corporate Governance : An International Review, 22nd vol., 2014, pp. 1-16

Bhat, G., Callen, J. L., Segal, D. (2014): Credit Risk and IFRS: The Case of Credit Default Swaps, in: Journal of Accounting, Auditing & Finance, 29th vol., 2014, No. 2, pp. 129–162

Biddle, G. C., Bowen, R. M., Wallace, J. S. (1997): Does EVA beat earnings? Evidence on associations with stock returns and firm values, in: Journal of Accounting and Economics, 24th vol., 1997, No. 3, pp. 301–336

Biddle, G. C., Bowen, R. M., Wallace, J. S. (1999): Evidence on EVA, in: Journal of Applied Corporate Finance, 12th vol., 1999, No. 2, pp. 69–79

Biddle, G. C., Seow, G. S., Siegel, A. F. (1995): Relative versus incremental information content, in: Contemporary Accounting Research, 12th vol., 1995, No. 1, pp. 1–23

Bieg, H., Kußmaul, H. (2011): Investition, 2nd edition, Munich 2011

Bieg, H., Kußmaul, H., Waschbusch, G. (2016): Finanzierung, 3rd edition, Munich 2016

Bizenberger, R. (2008): Informal Private Debt - ein Beitrag zur innovativen Finanzwirtschaft von Unternehmen, dissertation, Wiesbaden 2008

Black, F. (1986): Noise, in: Journal of Finance, 41st vol., 1986, No. 3, pp. 529–543

Blum, U., Dudley, L., Leibbrand, F., Weiske, A. (2005): Angewandte Institutionenökonomik - Theorien - Modelle - Evidenz, Wiesbaden 2005

Blyth, M. L., Friskey, E. A., Rappaport, A. (1986): Implementing the Shareholder Value approach, in: Journal of Business Strategy, 6th vol., 1986, No. 3, pp. 48–58

Böcking, H.-J. (1998): Zum Verhältnis von Rechnungslegung und Kapitalmarkt: Vom "financial accounting" zum "business reporting", in: Zeitschrift für betriebswirtschaftliche Forschung (zfbf), 50th vol., 1998, Special issue 40, pp. 17–53

Böcking, H.-J., Nowak, K. (1999): Das Konzept des Economic Value Added, in: Finanz Betrieb, 1st vol., 1999, No. 10, pp. 281–288

Bode, D., Wiens, H. (2015): Die Return-on-Capital-Employed Konzeption im Krankenhaus, in: Zapp, W. (editor), Wertorientierte Konzeptionen im Krankenhaus – Analyse – Verfahren – Praxisbeispiele, Wiesbaden 2015, pp. 23–46

Bogajewskaja, J. (2007): Reporting Financial Performance – Konzeption und Darstellung der Erfolgsrechnung nach Vorschriften des ASB, FASB und IASB, dissertation, Wiesbaden 2007

Boland, L. A., Gordon, I. M. (1992): Criticizing positive accounting theory, in: Contemporary Accounting Research, 9th vol., 1992, No. 1, pp. 142–170

Boliden (2014): Annual Report

Borchers, S. (2006): Integriertes Wertmanagement im Bayer-Konzern, in: Wagenhofer, Alfred (editor), Controlling und IFRS-Rechnungslegung - Konzepte, Schnittstellen, Umsetzung, Berlin 2006, pp. 267–288

Borm, M., Britzelmaier, B., Kraus, P., Nguyen-Noc, B. (2012): Wertorientierte Unternehmensführung in den DAX 30-Unternehmen - eine Untersuchung auf Basis der Geschäftsberichte 2010, in: Controller Magazin, 37th vol., 2012, No. 2, pp. 26–28

Borowicz, F. (2006): M&A-Management zwischen Stakeholder-Erwartungen und Shareholder Ansprüchen, in: Borowicz, F., Mittermair, K. (editors), Strategisches Management von Mergers & Acquisitions - State of the Art in Deutschland und Österreich, Wiesbaden 2006, pp. 3-20

Botosan, C. A. (1997): Disclosure Level and the Cost of Equity Capital, in: The Accounting Review, 72nd vol., 1997, No. 3, pp. 323–349

Botosan, C. A. (2006): Disclosure and the cost of capital: what do we know?, in: Accounting and Business Research, 36th vol., 2006, Special issue: International Accounting Policy Forum, pp. 31–40

Bouwens, J., Lent, L. von (2007): Assessing the performance of business unit managers, in: Journal of Accounting Research, 45th vol., 2007, No. 4, pp. 667–697

Bowen, R. M., Noreen, E. W. (1981): Determinants of the corporate decision to capitalize interest, in: Journal of Accounting and Economics, 3rd vol., 1981, No. 2, pp. 151–179

Brealey, R. A., Myers, S. C., Allen, F. (2011): Principles of Corporate Finance, 10th edition, New York 2011

Brecht, U. (2012): Controlling für Führungskräfte - Was Entscheider im Unternehmen wissen müssen, 2nd edition, Wiesbaden 2012

Breuer, W. (2013): Finanzierung - eine systematische Einführung, 3rd edition, Wiesbaden 2013

Bris, A., Koskinen, Y., Nilsson, M. (2014): The euro and corporate financing before the crisis, in: Journal of Financial Economics, 114th vol., 2014, No. 3, pp. 554–575

Britzelmaier, B. (2013a): Controlling, München 2013

Britzelmaier, B. (2013b): Wertorientierte Unternehmensführung, 2nd edition, Herne 2013

Brock, W., Lakonishok, J., LeBaron, B. (1992): Simple Technical Trading Rules and the Stochastic Properties of Stock Returns, in: Journal of Finance, 47th vol., 1992, No. 5, pp. 1731–1764

Bromwich, M., Walker, M. (1998): Residual income past and future, in: Management Accounting Research, 9th vol., 1998, No. 4, pp. 391–419

Brooks, C. (2014): Introductory Econometrics for Finance, 3rd edition, Cambridge 2014

Brösel, G. (2014): Bilanzanalyse - Unternehmensbeurteilung auf der Basis von HGB- und IFRS-Abschlüssen, 15th edition, Berlin 2014

Brown, L. D., Call, A. C., Clement, M. B., Sharp, N. Y. (2015): Inside the "Black Box" of Sell-Side Financial Analysts, in: Journal of Accounting Research, 53rd vol., 2015, No. 1, pp. 1–47

Brown, P. (2011): International Financial Reporting Standards: what are the benefits?, in: Accounting and Business Research, 41st vol., 2011, No. 3, pp. 269–285

Brown, P., Walter, T. (2013): The CAPM: Theoretical Validity, Empirical Intractability and Practical Applications, in: Abacus, 49th vol., 2013, pp. 44–50

Brown, S., Lo, K., Lys, T. (1999): Use of R2 in accounting research: measuring changes in value relevance over the last four decades, in: Journal of Accounting and Economics, 28th vol., 1999, No. 2, pp. 83–115

Brown, S. J. (2011): The efficient market hypothesis: The demise of the demon of chance?, in: Accounting and Finance, 51st vol., 2011, No. 1, pp. 79–95

Brown, S. J., Warner, J. B. (1980): Measuring Security Price Performance, in: Journal of Financial Economics, 8th vol., 1980, No. 3, pp. 205–258

Brück, C., Ludwig, J., Schwering, A. (2018): The use of value-based management in family firms, in: Journal of Management Control, 28th vol., 2018, No. 4, pp. 383–416

Brüderl, J. (2010): Kausalanalyse mit Paneldaten, in: Wolf, Christof, Best, H. (editors), Handbuch der sozialwissenschaftlichen Datenanalyse, Wiesbaden 2010, pp. 963–994

Brüggemann, U., Hitz, J.-M., Selhorn, T. (2013): Intended and Unintended Consequences of Mandatory IFRS Adoption: A Review of Extant Evidence and Suggestions for Future Research, in: European Accounting Review, 22nd vol., 2013, No. 1, pp. 1–37

Brühl, R. (2016): Controlling - Grundlagen einer erfolgsorientierten Unternehmenssteuerung, 4th edition, Munich 2016

Brunnermeier, M. K. (2001): Asset Pricing under Asymmetric Information, Oxford, New York 2001

Bughin, J., Copeland, T. E. (1997): The virtuous cycle of Shareholder Value creation, in: The McKinsey Quarterly, 1997, No. 2, pp. 156–167

Bühren, C., Pleßner, M. (2015): Rating Agencies - An Experimental Analysis of Their Remuneration Model, in: German Economic Review, 16th vol., 2015, No. 3, pp. 324–342

Bültel, N. (2011): Starmanager - Medienprominenz, Reputation und Vergütung von Top-Managern, dissertation, Wiesbaden 2011

Burger, A., Ulbrich, P., Ahlemeyer, N. (2010): Beteiligungscontrolling, 2nd edition, Munich 2010

Burgstahler, D. C., Hail, L., Leuz, C. (2006): The Importance of Reporting Incentives: Earnings Management in European Private and Public Firms, in: The Accounting Review, 81st vol., 2006, No. 5, pp. 983–1016

Burkert, M., Lueg, R. (2013): Differences in the sophistication of Value-based Management - The role of top executives, in: Management Accounting Research, 24th vol., 2013, No. 1, pp. 3–22

Buschmeier, A. (2011): Ratingagenturen – Wettbewerb und Transparenz auf dem Ratingmarkt, dissertation, Wiesbaden 2011

Busse, D. (2012): Nachhaltigkeitsaspekte in Theorie und Praxis der Entscheidungsfindung - Perspektiven institutioneller Steuerung in der Immobilienwirtschaft, Wiesbaden 2012

Busse, F.-J. (2003): Grundlagen der betrieblichen Finanzwirtschaft, 5th edition, Munich 2003

Busse, J. A., Green, T. C. (2002): Market efficiency in real time, in: Journal of Financial Economics, 65th vol., 2002, No. 3, pp. 415–437

Byard, D., Li, Y., Yu, Y. (2011): The Effect of Mandatory IFRS Adoption on Financial Analysts' Information Environment, in: Journal of Accounting Research, 49th vol., 2011, No. 1, pp. 69–96

Cabral, R. (2013): A perspective on the symptoms and causes of the financial crisis, in: Journal of Banking & Finance, 37th vol., 2013, No. 1, pp. 103–117

Cai, C. X., Clacher, I., Keasey, K. (2013): Consequences of the Capital Asset Pricing Model (CAPM)-a Critical and Broad Perspective, in: Abacus, 49th vol., 2013, pp. 51–61

Callen, J. L., Fang, X. (2013): Institutional investor stability and crash risk: Monitoring versus short-termism?, in: Journal of Banking & Finance, 37th vol., 2013, No. 8, pp. 3047–3063

Callen, J. L., Segal, D. (2005): Empirical Tests of the Feltham–Ohlson (1995) Model, in: Review of Accounting Studies, 10th vol., 2005, No. 4, pp. 409–429

Camphausen, B. (2013): Strategisches Management - Planung, Entscheidung, Controlling, 3rd edition, Munich 2013

Cesari, A. de, Huang-Meier, W. (2015): Dividend changes and stock price informativeness, in: Journal of Corporate Finance, 35th vol., 2015, pp. 1–17

CFA Institute Centre for Financial Market Integrity (2007): A Comprehensive Business Reporting Model: Financial Reporting for Investors

Chalmers, K., Clinch, G., Godfrey, J. M., Wei, Z. (2012): Intangible assets, IFRS and analysts' earnings forecasts, in: Accounting & Finance, 52nd vol., 2012, No. 3, pp. 691–721

Chan, L. K. C., Hamao, Y., Lakonishok, J. (1991): Fundamentals and Stock Returns in Japan, in: Journal of Finance, 46th vol., 1991, No. 5, pp. 1739–1764

Chari, L. (2009): Measuring value enhancement through Economic Value Added: evidence from literature, in: ICFAI - Journal of applied finance, 15th vol., 2009, No. 9, pp. 46–62

Chen, C., Young, D., Zhuang, Z. (2013): Externalities of Mandatory IFRS Adoption: Evidence from Cross-Border Spillover Effects of Financial Information on Investment Efficiency, in: The Accounting Review, 88th vol., 2013, No. 3, pp. 881–914

Chen, S., Dodd, J. L. (2001): Operating Income, Residual Income and EVA: Which Metric is more value relevant?, in: Journal of Managerial Issues, 13th vol., 2001, No. 1, pp. 65–86

Chen, X., Harford, J., Li, K. (2007): Monitoring: Which institutions matter?, in: Journal of Financial Economics, 86th vol., 2007, No. 2, pp. 279–305

Chen, C. J. P., Chen, S., Su, X. (2001): Is accounting information value-relevant in the emerging Chinese stock market?, in: Journal of International Accounting, Auditing & Taxation, 10th vol., 2001, No. 1, pp. 1–22

Cheung, Y.-L., Jiang, P., Tan, W. (2010): A transparency Disclosure Index measuring disclosures: Chinese listed companies, in: Journal of Accounting and Public Policy, 29th vol., 2010, No. 3, pp. 259–280

Chiwamit, P., Modell, S., Yang, C. L. (2014): The societal relevance of management accounting innovations: economic value added and institutional work in the fields of Chinese and Thai state-owned enterprises, in: Accounting and Business Research, 44th vol., 2014, No. 2, pp. 144–180

Christensen, B. E., Glover, S. M., Wood, D. A. (2012): Extreme Estimation Uncertainty in Fair Value Estimates: Implications for Audit Assurance, in: Auditing: A Journal of Practice & Theory, 31st vol., 2012, No. 1, pp. 127–146

Christensen, H. B., Hail, L., Leuz, C. (2013): Mandatory IFRS reporting and changes in enforcement, in: Journal of Accounting and Economics, 56th vol., 2013, No. 2-3, pp. 147–177

Christensen, H. B., Hail, L., Leuz, C. (2016): Capital-Market Effects of Securities Regulation: Prior Conditions, Implementation, and Enforcement, in: Review of Financial Studies, 29th vol., 2016, No. 11, pp. 2885–2924

Christensen, P. O., de la Rosa, L. E., Feltham, G. E. (2010): Information and the Cost of Capital: An Ex Ante Perspective, in: The Accounting Review, 85th vol., 2010, No. 3, pp. 817–848

Christie, A. A. (1987): On cross-sectional analysis in accounting research, in: Journal of Accounting and Economics, 9th vol., 1987, No. 3, pp. 231–258

Clarkson, P., Hanna, J. Douglas, Richardson, G. D., Thompson, R. (2011): The impact of IFRS adoption on the value relevance of book value and earnings, in: Journal of Contemporary Accounting & Economics, 7th vol., 2011, No. 1, pp. 1–17

Clinch, G. (2013): Disclosure quality, diversification and the cost of capital, in: Australian Journal of Management, 38th vol., 2013, No. 3, pp. 475–489

Clout, V. J., Willett, R. J. (2016): Earnings in firm valuation and their value relevance, in: Journal of Contemporary Accounting & Economics, 12th vol., 2016, No. 3, pp. 223–240

Coenenberg, A. G., Federspieler, C. (1999): Zwischenberichtspublizität in Europa - Der Informationsgehalt der Zwischenberichterstattung deutscher, britischer und französischer Unternehmen, in: Zeitschrift für betriebswirtschaftliche Forschung (zfbf), 1999, Special issue 41, pp. 167–198

Coenenberg, A. G., Fischer, T. M., Günther, T. (2012): Kostenrechnung und Kostenanalyse, 8th edition, Stuttgart 2012

Coenenberg, A. G., Haller, A., Schultze, W. (2014): Jahresabschluss und Jahresabschlussanalyse, 23rd edition, Stuttgart 2014

Coenenberg, A. G., Mattner, G. R., Schultze, W. (2003): Wertorientierte Steuerung: Anforderungen, Konzepte, Anwendungsprobleme, in: Rathgeber, A., Steiner, M., Tebroke, H.-J., Wallmeier, M. (editors), Finanzwirtschaft, Kapitalmarkt und Banken, Stuttgart 2003, pp. 1–24

Coenenberg, A. G., Salfeld, R. (2007): Wertorientierte Unternehmensführung - vom Strategieentwurf zur Implementierung, 2nd edition, Stuttgart 2007

Coenenberg, A. G., Schultze, W. (2002): Unternehmensbewertung: Konzeptionen und Perspektiven, in: Die Betriebswirtschaft (DBW), 62nd vol., 2002, No. 6, pp. 597–621

Coenenberg, A. G., Schultze, W. (2003): Residualgewinn- vs. Ertragswertmethode in der Unternehmensbewertung, in: Richter, F., Schüler, A. (editors), Kapitalgeberansprüche, Marktwertorientierung und Unternehmenswert - Festschrift für Prof. Dr. Dr. h.c. Jochen Drukarczyk zum 65. Geburtstag, Munich 2003, pp. 117–142

Coles, J. L., Loewenstein, U. (1988): Equilibrium Pricing and Portfolio Composition in the Presence of uncertain Parameters, in: Journal of Financial Economics, 22nd vol., 1988, pp. 279–303

Coles, J. L., Loewenstein, U., Suay, J. (1995): On Equilibrium Pricing under Parameter Uncertainty, in: Journal of Financial and Quantitative Analysis, 30th vol., 1995, No. 3, pp. 347–364

Collin, S.-O. Y., Tagesson, T., Andersson, A., Joosefin, C., Hansson, K. (2009): Explaining the choice of accounting standards in municipal corporations: Positive accounting theory and institutional theory as competitive or concurrent theories, in: Critical Perspectives on Accounting, 20th vol., 2009, No. 2, pp. 141–174

Collins, D. W., Kothari, S. P. (1989): An Analysis of Intertemporal And Cross-Sectional Determinants Of Earnings Response Coefficients, in: Journal of Accounting and Economics, 11th vol., 1989, No. 2-3, pp. 143–181

Cooke, T. E. (1998): Regression Analysis in Accounting Disclosure Studies, in: Accounting and Business Research, 28th vol., 1998, No. 3, pp. 209–224

Cooper, S. (2006): Discussions of "Disclosure and the cost of capital: what do we know?", in: Accounting and Business Research, 36th vol., 2006, Special issue: International Accounting Policy Forum, pp. 41–42

Copeland, T. E., Galai, D. (1983): Information Effects on the Bid-Ask Spread, in: Journal of Finance, 38th vol., 1983, No. 5, pp. 1457–1469

Copeland, T. E., Koller, T., Murrin, J. (1991): Valuation - Measuring and managing the value of companies, New York 1991

Cornett, M. M., Marcus, A. J., Saunders, A., Tehranian, H. (2007): The impact of institutional ownership on corporate operating performance, in: Journal of Banking & Finance, 31st vol., 2007, No. 6, pp. 1771–1794

Cour-Thimann, P., Winkler, B. (2012): The ECB's non-standard monetary policy measures: the role of institutional factors and financial structure, in: Oxford Review of Economic Policy, 28th vol., 2012, No. 4, pp. 765–803

Croda International (2015): Annual Report

Cuijpers, R., Buijink, W. (2005): Voluntary adoption of non-local GAAP in the European Union: A study of determinants and consequences, in: European Accounting Review, 14th vol., 2005, No. 3, pp. 487–524

Dahlhaus, C. (2009): Investitions-Controlling in dezentralen Unternehmen - Anreizsysteme als Instrument zur Verhaltenssteuerung im Investitionsprozess, dissertation, Wiesbaden 2009

Dahmash, F. N., Durand, R. B., Watson, J. (2009): The value relevance and reliability of reported goodwill and identifiable intangible assets, in: The British Accounting Review, 41st vol., 2009, No. 2, pp. 120–137

Damant, D. (2006): Discussion of International Financial Reporting Standards (IFRS): pros and cons for investors', in: Accounting and Business Research, 36th vol., 2006, Special issue: International Accounting Policy Forum, pp. 29–30

Daske, H., Gebhardt, G. (2006): International financial reporting standards and experts' perceptions of disclosure quality, in: Abacus, 42nd vol., 2006, No. 3-4, pp. 461–498

Daske, H., Hail, L., Leuz, C., Verdi, R. (2008): Mandatory IFRS Reporting around the World: Early Evidence on the Economic Consequences, in: Journal of Accounting Research, 46th vol., 2008, No. 5, pp. 1085-1142

Daske, H., Hail, L., Leuz, C., Verdi, R. (2013): Adopting a Label: Heterogeneity in the Economic Consequences Around IAS/IFRS Adoptions, in: Journal of Accounting Research, 51st vol., 2013, No. 3, pp. 495–547

Davis, G. F. (2008): A new finance capitalism? Mutual funds and ownership re-concentration in the United States, in: European Management Review, 5th vol., 2008, No. 1, pp. 11–21

Dechow, P., Ge, W., Schrand, C. (2010): Understanding earnings quality: A review of the proxies, their determinants and their consequences, in: Journal of Accounting and Economics, 50th vol., 2010, No. 2-3, pp. 344–401

Dechow, P., Hutton, A. P., Sloan, R. G. (1999): An empirical assessment of the residual income valuation model, in: Journal of Accounting and Economics, 26th vol., 1999, No. 1-3, pp. 1–34

Deckow, F. (2006): Vertrauen durch Kompetenzmarketing - ein ganzheitlicher Ansatz zur Vermarktung von Kontraktgütern, dissertation, Wiesbaden 2006

Dekker, H. C., Groot, T., Schoute, M., Wiersma, E. (2012): Determinants of the use of value-based performance measures for managerial performance evaluation, in: Journal of Business Finance & Accounting, 39th vol., 2012, No. 9 & 10, pp. 1214–1239

Demirakos, E. G., Strong, N., Walker, M. (2004): What Valuation Model Do Analysts Use?, in: Accounting Horizons, 18th vol., 2004, No. 4, pp. 221–240

Derenthal, K. (2009): Innovationsorientierung von Unternehmen - Messung, Determinanten und Erfolgswirkungen, dissertation, Wiesbaden 2009

Devalle, A., Onali, E., Magarini, R. (2010): Assessing the value relevance of accounting data after the introduction of IFRS in Europe, in: Journal of International Financial Management and Accounting, 21st vol., 2010, No. 2, pp. 85–119

Diamond, D. W., Verrecchia, R. E. (1991): Disclosure, Liquidity and the Cost of Capital, in: Journal of Finance, 46th vol., 1991, No. 4, pp. 1325–1359

Didier, T., Schmukler, S. L. (2013): The financing and growth of firms in China and India: Evidence from capital markets, in: Journal of International Money and Finance, 39th vol., 2013, pp. 111–137

Diedrich, R., Dierkes, S. (2015): Kapitalmarktorientierte Unternehmensbewertung, Stuttgart 2015

Dietrich, A., Hess, K., Wanzenried, G. (2014): The good and bad news about the new liquidity rules of Basel III in Western European countries, in: Journal of Banking & Finance, 44th vol., 2014, pp. 13–25

Dillerup, R., Stoi, R. (2016): Unternehmensführung - Management und Leadership, 5th edition, Munich 2016

Dinstuhl, V. (2003): Konzernbezogene Unternehmensbewertung - DCF-orientierte Konzern- und Segmentbewertung unter Berücksichtigung der Besteuerung, dissertation, Wiesbaden 2003

Dobbs, R., Kim, A., Lund, S. (2011): Growth in a capital constrained world, in: McKinsey Quarterly, without volume, 2011, No. 2, pp. 82–93

Donaldson, T., Preston, L. E. (1995): The stakeholder theory of the corporation: concepts, evidence and implications, in: Academy of Management Review, 20th vol., 1995, No. 1, pp. 65–91

Donoth, A., Radhakrishnan, S., Ronen, J. (2007): Is stock price a good measure for assessing value-relevance of earnings? An empirical test, in: Review of managerial science, 1st vol., 2007, No. 1, pp. 3–45

Dorfard, A. (2014): Kosteneffizienzen und Einsparungspotenziale durch Fusionen - Eine Anwendung auf die Kommunal- und Verwaltungsreform in Rheinland-Pfalz, dissertation, Wiesbaden 2014

Doyle, J. T., Jennings, J. N., Soliman, M. T. (2013): Do managers define non-GAAP earnings to meet or beat analyst forecasts?, in: Journal of Accounting and Economics, 56th vol., 2013, No. 1, pp. 40–56

Drake, M. S., Roulstone, D. T., Thornock, J. R. (2016): The usefulness of historical accounting reports, in: Journal of Accounting and Economics, 61st vol., 2016, No. 2-3, pp. 448–464

Dreger, C., Kosfeld, R., Eckey, H.-F. (2014): Ökonometrie - Grundlagen - Methoden - Beispiele, 5th edition, Wiesbaden 2014

Dreher, M. (2010): Unternehmenswertorientiertes Beteiligungscontrolling, dissertation, Cologne 2010

Drukarczyk, J., Schüler, A. (2016): Unternehmensbewertung, 7th edition, Munich 2016

Dück-Rath, M. (2005): Unternehmensbewertung mit Hilfe von DCF-Methoden und ausgewählten Realoptionsansätzen, dissertation, Frankfurt on the Main 2005

Dumontier, P., Raffournier, B. (2002): Accounting and capital markets: a survey of the European evidence, in: The European Accounting Review, 11th vol., 2002, No. 1, pp. 119–151

Düsterloh von, E. (2003): Das Shareholder-Value-Konzept - Methodik und Anwendung im strategischen Management, dissertation, Wiesbaden 2003

Dyckman, T. R., Morse, D. (1986): Efficient Capital Markets and Accounting: A Critical Analysis, 2nd edition, Englewood Cliffs 1986

Easley, D., Hvidkjaer, S., O'Hara, M. (2002): Is Information Risk a Determinant of Asset Returns?, in: Journal of Finance, 57th vol., 2002, No. 5, pp. 2185–2221

Easley, D., O'Hara, M. (2004): Information and the Cost of Capital, in: Journal of Finance, 59th vol., 2004, No. 4, pp. 1553–1583

Easterday, K., Sen, P. K., Stephan, J. A. (2011): Another specification of Ohlson's "Other Information" term for the earnings / returns association: theory and some evidence, in: Journal of Business Finance & Accounting, 38th vol., 2011, No. 9&10, pp. 1123–1155

Easton, P. D. (1999): Security returns and the value relevance of accounting data, in: Accounting Horizons, 13th vol., 1999, No. 4, pp. 399–412

Easton, P. D., Sommers, G. A. (2003): Scale and the Scale Effect in Market-based Accounting Research, in: Journal of Business Finance & Accounting, 30th vol., 2003, No. 1&2, pp. 25–56

Ebeling, C. (2007): Erfolgsfaktoren einer wertorientierten Unternehmensführung, dissertation, Wiesbaden 2007

Eccles, R. G., Herz, R. H., Keegan, E. M., Phillips, D. M. H. (2001): The Value Reporting Revolution - Moving beyond the earnings game, New York, Chichester, Weinheim 2001

Eckstein, P. (2016): Statistik für Wirtschaftswissenschaftler - Eine realdatenbasierte Einführung mit SPSS, 5th edition, Wiesbaden 2016

Edwards, E. O., Bell, P. W. (1961): The Theory and Measurement of Business Income, Berkeley, Los Angeles, London 1961

Eichler, S., Hielscher, K. (2012): Does the ECB act as a lender of last resort during the subprime lending crisis?: Evidence from monetary policy reaction models, in: Journal of International Money and Finance, 31st vol., 2012, No. 3, pp. 552–568

Eidel, U. (1999): Moderne Verfahren der Unternehmensbewertung und Performance-Messung, 2nd edition, Herne, Berlin 1999

Eilenberger, G., Ernst, D., Toebe, M. (2013): Betriebliche Finanzwirtschaft - Einführung in Investition und Finanzierung, Finanzpolitik und Finanzmanagement von Unternehmungen, 8th edition, Munich 2013

Eisenhardt, K. M. (1989): Agency Theory: an assessment and review, in: Academy of Management Review, 14th vol., 1989, No. 1, pp. 57–74

Elbakry, A. E., Nwachukwu, J. C., Abdou, H. A., Elshandidy, T. (2017): Comparative evidence on the value relevance of IFRS-based accounting information in Germany and the UK, in: Journal of International Accounting, Auditing and Taxation, 28th vol., 2017, pp. 10–30

Elgharbawy, A., Abdel-Kader, M. (2013): Enterprise governance and value-based management: a theoretical contingency framework, in: Journal of Management & Governance, 17th vol., 2013, No. 1, pp. 99–129

Elliot, R. K., Jacobson, P. D. (1994): Costs and Benefits of Business Information Disclosure, in: Accounting Horizons, 8th vol., 1994, No. 4, pp. 80–96

El-Sayed Ebaid, I. (2011): The value relevance of accounting-based performance measures in emerging economies, in: Management Research Review, 35th vol., 2011, No. 1, pp. 69–88

Elschen, R. (1991): Gegenstand und Anwendungsmöglichkeiten der Agency-Theorie, in: Zeitschrift für betriebswirtschaftliche Forschung (zfbf), 43rd vol., 1991, No. 11, pp. 1002–1012

Elshandidy, T. (2014): Value relevance of accounting information: Evidence from an emerging market, in: Advances in Accounting, 30th vol., 2014, No. 1, pp. 176–186

Elton, E. J., Gruber, M. J., Brown, M. J., Goetzmann W. (2011): Modern Portfolio Theory And Investment Analysis, 8th edition, Hoboken 2011

Elyasiani, E., Mester, L. J., Pagano, M. S. (2014): Large capital infusions, investor reactions, and the return and risk-performance of financial institutions over the business cycle, in: Journal of Financial Stability, 11th vol., 2014, without number, pp. 62–81

Endres, K. (2007): Die Gestaltung von Anreizsystemen zur wertorientierten Steuerung von Versicherungskonzernen, dissertation, Lohmar, Cologne 2007

Erkilet, G., Kholmy, K. (2016): Implikationen der IFRS-Einführung auf die Informationsbasis und Prognosequalität von Finanzanalysten: State of the Art der empirischen Kapitalmarktforschung, in: Management Review Quarterly, 66th vol., 2016, No. 1, pp. 33–73

Ernst, D., Schneider, S., Thielen, B. (2010): Unternehmensbewertung erstellen und verstehen - Ein Praxisleitfaden, 4th edition, Munich 2010

Ernst, E., Gassen, J., Pellens, B. (2009): Verhalten und Präferenzen deutscher Aktionäre - Eine Befragung von privaten und institutionellen Anlegern zum Informationsverhalten, zur Dividendenpräferenz und zur Wahrnehmung von Stimmrechten, in: Studien des Deutschen Aktieninstituts, 2009, No. 42, pp. 1–141

Ernst & Young (2018): International GAAP 2016, Chichester 2018

Ewert, R. (1989): The financial theory of agency as a tool for analysis of problems in external accounting, in: Bamberg, G., Spremann, K. (editors), Agency theory, information, and incentives, Corrected reprint of the 1st edition, Berlin 1989, pp. 281–309

Ewert, R., Wagenhofer, A. (2000): Rechnungslegung und Kennzahlen für das wertorientierte Management, in: Wagenhofer, A., Hrebicek, G. (editors), Wertorientiertes Management - Konzepte und Umsetzungen zur Unternehmenswertsteigerung, Stuttgart 2000, pp. 3–64

Ewert, R., Wagenhofer, A. (2014): Interne Unternehmensrechnung, 8th edition, Wiesbaden 2014

Fabozzi, F. J. (2015): Capital Markets - Institutions, Instruments and Risk Management, 5th edition, London 2015

Faccio, M., Lang, L. H. P. (2002): The ultimate ownership of Western European corporations, in: Journal of Financial Economics, 65th vol., 2002, No. 3, pp. 365–395

Fackler, M., Wimschulte, J. (2009): Residualgewinnverfahren zur Unternehmensbewertung und -steuerung - Am Beispiel des Economic Value Added, in: Schacht, U., Fackler, M. (editors), Praxishandbuch Unternehmensbewertung - Grundlagen, Methoden, Fallbeispiele, 2nd edition, Wiesbaden 2009, pp. 313–334

Falkman, P., Tagesson, T. (2008): Accrual accounting does not necessarily mean accrual accounting: Factors that counteract compliance with accounting standards in Swedish municipal accounting, in: Scandinavian Journal of Management, 24th vol., 2008, No. 3, pp. 271–283

Faltz, F. (1999): Investor Relations und Shareholder Value - die Kommunikation zwischen Unternehmen und Investoren, Wiesbaden 1999

Fama, E. F. (1970): Efficient Capital Markets: A Review of Theory and Empirical Work, in: Journal of Finance, 25th vol., 1970, No. 2, pp. 383–417

Fama, E. F. (1980): Agency problems and the theory of the firm, in: Journal of Political Economy, 88th vol., 1980, No. 2, pp. 288–307

Fama, E. F. (1991): Efficient Capital Markets: II, in: Journal of Finance, 46th vol., 1991, No. 5, pp. 1575–1617

Fama, E. F., Blume, M. E. (1966): Filter Rules and Stock-Market Trading, in: Journal of Business, 39th vol., 1966, No. 1, pp. 226–241

Fama, E. F., French, K. R. (1992): The Cross-Section of Expected Stock Returns, in: Journal of Finance, 47th vol., 1992, No. 2, pp. 427–465

Fama, E. F., French, K. R. (1993): Common risk factors in the returns on stock and bonds, in: Journal of Financial Economics, 33rd vol., 1993, No. 1, pp. 3–56

Fama, E. F., French, K. R. (2002): The Equity Premium, in: Journal of Finance, 57th vol., 2002, No. 2, pp. 637–659

Fama, E. F., Jensen, M. C. (1983a): Agency problems and residual claims, in: The Journal of Law & Economics, 26th vol., 1983, No. 2, pp. 327–349

Fama, E. F., Jensen, M. C. (1983b): Separation of ownership and control, in: Journal of Law and Economics, 26th vol., 1983, No. 2, pp. 301–325

Fama, E. F., Lawrence, F., Jensen, M. C., Roll, R. (1969): The Adjustment of Stock Prices to New Information, in: International Economic Review, 10th vol., 1969, No. 1, pp. 1–21

Fama, E. F., MacBeth, J. D. (1973): Risk, Return and Equilibrium: Empirical Tests, in: Journal of Political Economy, 81st vol., 1973, No. 3, pp. 607–636

Feltham, G. E., Ohlson, J. A. (1995): Valuation and Clean Surplus Accounting for Operating and Financial Activities, in: Contemporary Accounting Research, 11th vol., 1995, No. 2, pp. 689–731

Ferguson, R., Leistikow, D. (1998): Search for the best financial performance measure, in: Financial Analysts Journal, 54th vol., 1998, No. 1, pp. 81–85

Ferreira, M. A., Matos, P. (2008): The colors of investors' money: The role of institutional investors around the world, in: Journal of Financial Economics, 88th vol., 2008, No. 3, pp. 499–533

Fiedler, R., Gräf, J. (2012): Einführung in das Controlling - Methoden, Instrumente und IT-Unterstützung, 3rd edition, Munich 2012

Fields, T. D., Lys, T. Z., Vincent, L. (2001): Empirical research on accounting choice, in: Journal of Accounting and Economics, 31st vol., 2001, No. 1, pp. 255–307

Fields, T. D., Rangan, S., Thiagarajan, S. R. (1998): An Empirical Evaluation of the Usefulness of Non-GAAP Accounting Measures in the Real Estate Investment Trust Industry, in: Review of Accounting Studies, 3rd vol., 1998, No. 1/2, pp. 103–130

Filzen, J. J., Peterson, K. (2015): Financial Statement Complexity and Meeting Analysts' Expectations, in: Contemporary Accounting Research, 32nd vol., 2015, No. 4, pp. 1560–1594

Fiordelisi, F., Galloppo, G., Ricci, O. (2014): The effect of monetary policy interventions on interbank markets, equity indices and G-SIFIs during financial crisis, in: Journal of Financial Stability, 11th vol., 2014, without number, pp. 49–61

Fiordelisi, F., Molyneux, P. (2006): Shareholder Value in Banking, New York 2006

Firk, S., Schmidt, T., Wolff, M. (2018): Exploring Value-Based Management Sophistication: The Role of Potential Economic Benefits and Institutional Influence, in: Contemporary Accounting Research, 2018

Firk, S., Schrapp, S., Wolff, M. (2016): Drivers of value creation—The role of value-based management and underlying institutions, in: Management Accounting Research, 33rd vol., 2016, pp. 42–60

Firk, S., Wolff, M. (2018): Wertorientierung kann sich lohnen, in: Controlling & Management Review, 62nd vol., 2018, No. 2, pp. 52–57

Fischbach, R., Wollenberg, K. (2007): Volkswirtschaftslehre 1 - Einführung und Grundlagen, 13th edition, Munich, Vienna 2007

Fischer, A. (2003): Shareholder Value Reporting mittels jahresabschlussergänzenden Angaben - Untersuchung ökonomischer Wirkungsweisene der Investor Relations im Rahmen einer wertorientierten Unternehmensführung, dissertation, Bern, Stuttgart, Vienna 2003

Fischer, T. M., Becker, S., Wenzel, J. (2001): Internetbasierte wertorientierte Berichterstattung (Web-Based Value Reporting) - Eine empirische Untersuchung der DAX 30-Unternehmen, in: Der Betrieb, 54th vol., 2001, No. 38, pp. 2001–2007

Fischer, T. M., Klöpfer, E. (2006): Entwicklung und Perspektiven des Value Reportings, in: Zeitschrift für Controlling & Management (ZfCM), 50th vol., 2006, Special Issue 3, pp. 4–14

Fischer, T. M., Rödl, K. (2005): Value Added Reporting: Publizität wertorientierter Managementkonzepte in den Geschäftsberichten der DAX-30 Unternehmen, in: Controlling, 17th vol., 2005, No. 1, pp. 23–32

Fischer, T. M., Wenzel, J. (2002): DBW-Stichwort Value Reporting, in: Die Betriebswirtschaft (DBW), 62nd vol., 2002, No. 3, pp. 327–332

Fischer, T. M., Wenzel, J., Kühn, C. (2001): Value Reporting - Wertorientierte Berichterstattung in den Nemax 50-Unternehmen, in: Der Betrieb, 54th vol., 2001, No. 23, pp. 1209–1216

Fischer, T. M., Zirkler, B. (2008): Lagebericht - Value Reporting, in: Freidank, C.-C.; Peemöller, V. H. (editors), Corporate Governance und Interne Revision - Handbuch für Neuausrichtung des Internal Auditing, Berlin 2008, pp. 579–604

Fiss, P. C., Zajac, E. J. (2004): The Diffusion of Ideas over Contested Terrain: The (Non)adoption of a Shareholder Value Orientation among German Firms, in: Administrative Science Quarterly, 49th vol., 2004, No. 4, pp. 501–534

Florou, A., Kosi, U. (2015): Does mandatory IFRS adoption facilitate debt financing?, in: Review of Accounting Studies, 20th vol., 2015, No. 4, pp. 1407–1456

Fochler, R. (2000): Investor Relations als Teil des wertorientierten Managements am Beispiel der Böhler-Uddeholm AG, in: Wagenhofer, A., Hrebicek, G. (editors), Wertorientiertes Management - Konzepte und Umsetzungen zur Unternehmenswertsteigerung, Stuttgart 2000, pp. 311–332

Foster, G., Olsen, C., Shevlin, T. (1984): Earnings Releases, Anomalies and the Behavior of Security Returns, in: The Accounting Review, 59th vol., 1984, No. 4, pp. 574–603

Francis, J., Schipper, K., Vincent, L. (2003): The relative and incremental explanatory power of earnings and alternatives (to earnings) performance measures for returns, in: Contemporary Accounting Research, 20th vol., 2003, No. 1, pp. 121–164

Francis, R. N. (2010): The relative information content of operating and financing cash flow in the proposed cash flow statement, in: Accounting and Finance, 50th vol., 2010, No. 4, pp. 829–851

Franco, G. de, Hope, O.-K., Vyas, D., Zhou, Y. (2015): Analyst Report Readability, in: Contemporary Accounting Research, 32nd vol., 2015, No. 1, pp. 76–104

Franco-Santos, M., Lucianetti, L., Bourne, M. (2012): Contemporary performance measurement systems: A review of their consequences and a framework for research, in: Management Accounting Research, 23rd vol., 2012, No. 2, pp. 79–119

Franke, G., Hax, H. (2009): Finanzwirtschaft des Unternehmens und Kapitalmarkt, 6th edition, Berlin, Heidelberg, New York 2009

Frankel, R., Lee, C. M. (1998): Accounting valuation, market expectation and cross-sectional stock returns, in: Journal of Accounting and Economics, 25th vol., 1998, No. 3, pp. 283–319

Freeman, R. E. (2010): Strategic management: a stakeholder approach, reissue edition, New York 2010

Freidank, C.-C., Reibis, C. (2008): Weiterentwicklung der simultanen internationalen Rechnungslegungspolitik, in: Freidank, C.-C., Peemöller, V. H. (editors), Corporate Governance und Interne Revision - Handbuch für Neuausrichtung des Internal Auditing, Berlin 2008, pp. 283–304

Freidank, C.-C., Weber, S. C. (2009): Entwicklung erster Ansätze zur konzeptionellen Ausgestaltung des externen Corporate Governance-Reporting, in: Freidank, C.-C. (editor), Das Gesetz zur Modernisierung des Bilanzrechts - Neue Herausforderungen für Rechnungslegung und Corporate Governance, Berlin 2009, pp. 303–340

French, K. R. (1980): Stock Returns And The Weekend Effect, in: Journal of Financial Economics, 8th vol., 1980, No. 1, pp. 55–69

Friedrich, N. (2007): Die Rolle von Analysten bei der Bewertung von Unternehmen am Kapitalmarkt - das Beispiel der Telekommunikationsindustrie, dissertation, Lohmar, Cologne 2007

Frings, G. W., Frings, M. C., Mastilak, C. (2012a): Does IFRS stand for Information Risk?, in: Financial Analysts Journal, 68th vol., 2012, No. 3, pp. 17–21

Frings, G. W., Frings, M. C., Mastilak, C. (2012b): Does IFRS stand for information risk?: Author Response, in: Financial Analysts Journal, 68th vol., 2012, No. 6, pp. 13–14

Frost, C. A., Gordon, E. A., Hayes, A. F. (2006): Stock Exchange Disclosure and Market Development: An Analysis of 50 International Exchanges, in: Journal of Accounting Research, 44th vol., 2006, No. 3, pp. 437–483

Fruhan, W. (1979): Financial Strategy: Studies in the creation, transfer and destruction of Shareholder Value, Homowood, Illinois 1979

Fülbier, R. U. (1998): Regulierung der Ad-hoc-Publizität - Ein Beitrag zur ökonomischen Analyse des Rechts, dissertation, Wiesbaden 1998

Funk, W., Fredrich, I. (2011): Auswirkungen einer Rechnungslegung nach IAS / IFRS auf die wertorientierte Unternehmensführung, in: Funk, W., Rossmanith, J. (editors), Internationale Rechnungslegung und Internationales Controlling - Herausforderungen - Handlungsfelder - Erfolgspotenziale, 2nd edition, Wiesbaden 2011, pp. 445–477

Funk, W., Rossmanith, J. (2008): Rechtliche Rahmenbedingungen und Umsetzung der Corporate Governance in Deutschland, in: Brauweiler, H.-C. (editor), Unternehmensführung heute, Munich 2008, pp. 279–300

Gabriel, A. (2015): Freiwillige Veröffentlichung und Prüfung von GRI-Nachhaltigkeitsberichten - Eine empirische Analyse auf dem europäischen Kapitalmarkt, dissertation, Wiesbaden 2015

Gantzhorn, A. (2016): Determinanten und Auswirkungen der freiwilligen prüferischen Durchsicht von Halbjahresfinanzberichten nach § 37w WpHG - Eine empirische Analyse für den deutschen Kapitalmarkt, dissertation, Wiesbaden 2016

Garcia-Appendini, E., Montoriol-Garriga, J. (2013): Firms as liquidity providers : evidence from the 2007 - 2008 financial crises, in: Journal of Financial Economics, 109th vol., 2013, No. 1, pp. 272–291

Garrison, R. H., Noreen, E. W., Brewer, P. C. (2012): Managerial Accounting, 14th edition, New York 2012

Garvey, G. T., Milbourn, T. T. (2000): EVA versus Earnings: Does it matter which is more highly correlated with stock returns?, in: Journal of Accounting Research, 38th vol., 2000, Supplement: Studies on Accounting, pp. 209–245

Gassen, J., Schwedler, K. (2010): The Decision Usefulness of Financial Accounting Measurements Concepts: Evidence from an Online Survey of Professional Investors and their Advisors, in: European Accounting Review, 19th vol., 2010, No. 3, pp. 495–509

Geiersbach, K. (2011): Der Beitrag der Internen Revision zur Corporate Governance, dissertation, Wiesbaden 2011

George, E. T. de, Li, X., Shivakumar, L. (2016): A review of the IFRS adoption literature, in: Review of Accounting Studies, 21st vol., 2016, No. 3, pp. 898–1004

Gibbons, M. R., Hess, P. (1981): Day of the Week Effects and Asset Returns, in: Journal of Business, 54th vol., 1981, No. 4, pp. 579–596

Gibson, C. H. (2013): Financial Reporting & Analysis - Using Financial Accounting Information, Mason 2013

Giesselmann, M., Windzio, M. (2012): Regressionsmodelle zur Analyse von Paneldaten, Wiesbaden 2012

Girmes, D. H., Benjamin, A. E. (1975): Random Walk Hypothesis for 543 Stocks and Shares Registered on the London Stock Exchange, in: Journal of Business Finance & Accounting, 2nd vol., 1975, No. 1, pp. 135–145

Gitt, N., Völl, W., Kettenring, T. (2013): Anwendung wertorientierter Steuerungskennzahlen in deutschen HDAX-Unternehmen - aktueller Stand und Entwicklungen, in: Controlling, 25th vol., 2013, No. 2, pp. 100–108

Gjerde, Ø., Knivsflå, K., Sættem, F. (2011): The value relevance of financial reporting in Norway 1965–2004, in: Scandinavian Journal of Management, 27th vol., 2011, No. 1, pp. 113–128

Gjesdal, F. (1981): Accounting for stewardship, in: Journal of Accounting Research, 19th vol., 1981, No. 1, pp. 208–231

Gladen, W. (2014): Performance Measurement - Controlling mit Kennzahlen, 6th edition, Wiesbaden 2014

Glaum, M., Friedrich, N. (2006): After the "Bubble": Valuation of Telecommunications Companies by Financial Analysts, in: Journal of International Financial Management and Accounting, 17th vol., 2006, No. 2, pp. 160–174

Glosten, L. R., Milgrom, P. (1985): Bid, Ask and Transaction Prices in a specialist market with heterogeneously informed traders, in: Journal of Financial Economics, 14th vol., 1985, No. 1, pp. 71–100

Gong, J. J. (2011): Examining Shareholder Value Creation over CEO Tenure: A New Approach to Testing Effectiveness of Executive Compensation, in: Journal of Management Accounting Research, 23rd vol., 2011, No. 1, pp. 1–28

Goodman, T. H., Neamtiu, M., Shroff, N., White, H. D. (2014): Management Forecast Quality and Capital Investment Decisions, in: The Accounting Review, 89th vol., 2014, No. 1, pp. 331–365

Götze, U. (2008): Investitionsrechnung - Modelle und Analysen zur Beurteilung von Investitionsvorhaben, 6th edition, Berlin, Heidelberg 2008

Gow, I. D., Ormazabal, G., Taylor, D. J. (2010): Correcting for Cross-Sectional and Time-Series Dependence in Accounting Research, in: The Accounting Review, 85th vol., 2010, No. 2, pp. 483–512

Gräfer, H., Gerenkamp, T. (2016): Bilanzanalyse, 13th edition, Herne 2016

Grammatikos, T., Vermeulen, R. (2012): Transmission of the financial and sovereign debt crises to the EMU: Stock prices, CDS spreads and exchange rates, in: Journal of International Money and Finance, 31st vol., 2012, No. 3, pp. 517–533

Graumann, M. (2014): Controlling - Begriffe, Elemente, Methoden und Schnittstellen, 4th edition, Herne 2014

Greene, W. H. (2012): Econometric Analysis, 7th edition, Harlow 2012

Greiling, D. (2009): Performance Measurement in Nonprofit-Organisationen, dissertation, Wiesbaden 2009

Grichnik, D. (2000): Bankenverbände - strategisches Netzwerkmanagement in der Bankenwirtschaft, dissertation, Wiesbaden 2000

Griewel, E. (2006): Ad hoc-Publizität und Zwischenberichterstattung im deutschen Corporate Governance-System - Eine Analyse vor dem Hintergrund europäischer Harmonisierungsbestrebungen, dissertation, Wiesbaden 2006

Grimpe, C. (2005): Post Merger Integration der Forschung und Entwicklung, dissertation, Wiesbaden 2005

Groll, K.-H. (2000): Das Kennzahlensystem zur Bilanzanalyse, 2nd edition, Munich, Vienna 2000

Groll, K.-H. (2003): Kennzahlen für das wertorientierte Management - ROI, EVA and CFROI im Vergleich - Ein neues Konzept zur Steigerung des Unternehmenswertes, Munich, Vienna 2003

Gronwald, T., Nasev, J. (2013): Value Reporting in der Finanzkrise, in: Controlling & Management Review, 57th vol., 2013, No. 6, pp. 50–59

Gros, M. (2010): Rechnungslegung in Deutschland und den USA - Implikationen für eine zweckadäquate Fortentwicklung der deutschen Rechnungslegungskonzeption, dissertation, Wiesbaden 2010

Grossman, S. J. (1976): On the efficiency of competitive stock markets where traders have diverse information, in: Journal of Finance, 31st vol., 1976, No. 2, pp. 573–585

Grossman, S. J., Hart, O. D. (1983): An analysis of the principal-agent problem, in: Econometrica, 51st vol., 1983, No. 1, pp. 7–45

Grossman, S. J., Stiglitz, J. E. (1980): On the Impossibility of Informationally Efficient Markets, in: The American Economic Review, 70th vol., 1980, No. 3, pp. 393–408

Grüning, M. (2011a): Capital market implications of corporate disclousure: German evidence, in: BuR - Business Research, 4th vol., 2011, No. 1, pp. 48–72

Grüning, M. (2011b): Publizität börsennotierter Unternehmen, dissertation, Wiesbaden 2011

Gu, Z. (2005): Scale Factor, R^2 and the choice of Levels versus Return Models, in: Journal of Accounting, Auditing & Finance, 20th vol., 2005, No. 1, pp. 71–91

Gujarati, D. N., Porter, D. C. (2009): Basic Econometrics, 5th edition, Boston, Burr Ridge, Dubuque 2009

Gultekin, M. N., Gultekin, N. B. (1983): Stock Market Sesonality - International Evidence, in: Journal of Financial Economics, 12th vol., 1983, No. 4, pp. 469–481

Gundel, T. (2012): Der EVA als Management und Bewertungsinstrument, dissertation, Wiesbaden 2012

Günther, T. (1997): Unternehmenswertorientiertes Controlling, Munich 1997

Günther, T. (2002): Wertorientierte Kennzahlen zur Steuerung mittelständischer Unternehmen, in: Kostenrechnungspraxis, 2002, Special Edition No. 1, pp. 89–97

Günther, T. (2004): Theoretische Einbettung des Controllings in die Methodologie der Unternehmensüberwachung und -steuerung, in: Freidank, C.-C. (editor), Corporate Governance und Controlling, Heidelberg 2004, pp. 25–50

Günther, T., Beyer, D. (2001): Value Based Reporting - Entwicklungspotenziale der externen Unternehmensberichterstattung, in: Betriebs-Berater (BB), 56th vol., 2001, No. 32, pp. 1623–1630

Günther, T., Gonschorek, T. (2011): Wertorientierte Unternehmensführung im deutschen Mittelstand: Ergebnisse einer empirischen Studie, in: Controlling, 23rd vol., 2011, No. 1, pp. 18–27

Günther, T., Landrock, B., Muche, T. (2000a): Gewinn- versus unternehmenswertorientierte Performancemaße - eine empirische Untersuchung auf Basis der Korrelation von Kapitalmarktrenditen - Teil II: Datenaufbereitung, Ergebnisse und Schlussfolgerungen, in: Controlling, 12th vol., 2000, No. 3, pp. 129–134

Günther, T., Landrock, B., Muche, T. (2000b): Gewinn- versus unternehmenswertorientierte Performancemaße - eine empirsiche Untersuchung auf Basis der Korrelation von Kapitalmarktrenditen - Teil I: Grundlagen und Design der Studie, in: Controlling, 12th vol., 2000, No. 2, pp. 69–76

Guserl, R., Pernsteiner, H. (2015): Finanzmanagement - Grundlagen - Konzepte - Umsetzung, 2nd edition, Wiesbaden 2015

Hachmeister, D. (1997): Der Cash Flow Return on Investment als Erfolgsgröße einer wertorientierten Unternehmensführung, in: Zeitschrift für betriebswirtschaftliche Forschung (zfbf), 49th vol., 1997, No. 6, pp. 556–579

Hachmeister, D. (2003): Gestaltung von Wertbeitragskennzahlen in der Theorie der Unternehmensrechnung, in: Franck, E., Arnoldussen, L., Jungwirth, C. (editors), Marktwertorientierte Unternehmensführung – Anreiz- und Kommunikationsaspekte, Düsseldorf, Frankfurt on the Main 2003, pp. 97–119

Hachmeister, D. (2009): Methoden der Unternehmensbewertung im Überblick, in: Zeitschrift für Controlling & Management (ZfCM), 53rd vol., 2009, Supplement 1, pp. 64–74

Haeger, B. (2006): Harmonisierung von Rechnungswesen und Controlling bei E.ON, in: Wagenhofer, A. (editor), Controlling und IFRS-Rechnungslegung - Konzepte, Schnittstellen, Umsetzung, Berlin 2006, pp. 243–266

Haenelt, T. (2009): Die Zwischenberichterstattung nach IFRS - Eine empirische Analyse der gesetzlichen Vorschriften und der Anforderungen des Kapitalmarktes, dissertation, Cologne 2009

Hahn, D., Hintze, M. (2006): Konzepte wertorientierter Unternehmensführung, in: Hahn, D., Taylor, B. (editors), Strategische Unternehmensplanung - Strategische Unternehmensführung, 9th edition, Berlin, Heidelberg, New York 2006, pp. 83–113

Hahn, G. J., Burger, A., Kuhn, H. (2011): Wertorientierte Unternehmensplanung - Ein optimierungsbasierter Ansatz für das wertorientierte Performance- und Risiko-Management, in: Funk, W., Rossmanith, J. (editors), Internationale Rechnungslegung und Internationales Controlling - Herausforderungen - Handlungsfelder - Erfolgspotenziale, 2nd edition, Wiesbaden 2011, pp. 307–332

Hamilton, J., Rahman, S., Lee, A. C. (2009): EVA: Does Size Matter?, in: Review of Pacific Basin Financial Markets and Policies, 12th vol., 2009, No. 2, pp. 267–287

Hanauer, M., Kaserer, C., Rapp, M. Steffen (2013): Risikofaktoren und Multifaktormodelle für den deutschen Aktienmarkt, in: Betriebswirtschaftliche Forschung und Praxis, 65th vol., 2013, No. 5, pp. 469–492

Handa, P., Linn, S. C. (1993): Arbitrage Pricing with Estimation Risk, in: Journal of Financial and Quantitative Analysis, 28th vol., 1993, No. 1, pp. 81–100

Harris, M. S., Muller, K. A. (1999): The market valuation of IAS versus US-GAAP accounting measures using Form 20-F reconciliations, in: Journal of Accounting and Economics, 26th vol., 1999, No. 1-3, pp. 285–312

Hartzell, J., Starks, L. T. (2003): Institutional Investors and Executive Compensation, in: Journal of Finance, 58th vol., 2003, No. 6, pp. 2352–2374

Hartzell, J., Sun, L., Titman, S. (2014): Institutional investors as monitors of corporate diversification decisions: evidence from real estate investment trusts, in: Journal of Corporate Finance, 25th vol., 2014, without number, pp. 61–72

Hasan, M. S. (2004): On The Validity Of The Random Walk Hypothesis Applied To The Dhaka Stock Exchange, in: International Journal of Theoretical and Applied Finance, 7th vol., 2004, No. 8, pp. 1069–1085

Hasler, P. T. (2011): Aktien richtig bewerten - Theoretische Grundlagen praktisch erklärt, Berlin, Heidelberg 2011

Haspeslagh, P., Noda, T., Boulos, F. (2001): It's not just about the numbers, in: Harvard business review, 79th vol., 2001, No. 7, pp. 65–73

Hauer, G., Ultsch, M. (2010): Unternehmensführung kompakt, Munich 2010

Hauerdinger, M., Probst, H.-J. (2006): Finanz- und Liquiditätsplanung in kleineren und mittleren Unternehmen, Planegg 2006

Hauschildt, J. (1996): Erfolgs-, Finanz- und Bilanzanalyse, 3rd edition, Cologne 1996

Hauser, S. E. (2003): Informationsverarbeitung am Neuen Markt - Eine empirische Analyse der Determinanten von Kursreaktionen auf Ad-hoc-Meldungen, dissertation, Wiesbaden 2003

Hawawini, G., Viallet, C. (2011): Finance for Executives - Managing for Value Creation, 4th edition, Mason 2011

Hawranek, B., Öppinger, C. (2014): Wertrelevanz rechnungswesenbasierter Erfolgskennzahlen, in: KoR: Internationale und kapitalmarktorientierte Rechnungslegung, 14th vol., 2014, No. 2, pp. 95–102

Hax, A. C., Majluf, N. S. (1991): Strategisches Management - Ein integratives Konzept aus dem MIT, Frankfurt on the Main 1991

Healy, P. M., Hutton, A. P., Palepu, K. G. (1999): Stock Performance and Intermediation Changes Surrounding Sustained Increases in Disclosure, in: Contemporary Accounting Research, 16th vol., 1999, No. 3, pp. 485–520

Healy, P. M., Palepu, K. G. (2001): Information asymmetry, corporate disclosure and the capital markets: a review of the eimpirical disclosure literature, in: Journal of Accounting and Economics, 31st vol., 2001, No. 1, pp. 405–440

Heese, V. (2011): Aktienbewertung mit Kennzahlen - Kurschancen und -risiken fundiert beurteilen, Wiesbaden 2011

Hehn, M. (2011): Auswirkung der Beteiligung von Private Equity Gesellschaften auf die Governance von Familienunternehmen in Deutschland, Lohmar, Cologne 2011

Heiden, M. (2006): Pro-forma Berichterstattung - Reporting zwischen Information und Täuschung, dissertation, Berlin 2006

Heier, K., Karsten, E., Müller-Wenzel, C., Zapp, W. (2015): EVAluation, die sich lohnt - Der Ansatz des Economic Value Added im wertorientierten Management, in: Zapp, W. (editor), Wertorientierte Konzeptionen im Krankenhaus - Analyse - Verfahren - Praxisbeispiele, Wiesbaden 2015, pp. 1–21

Heilbron, J., Verheul, J., Quak, S. (2014): The origins and early diffusion of "shareholder value" in the United States, in: Theory and Society, 43rd vol., 2014, pp. 1–22

Heim, F.-B. (2015): Erfolgsfaktoren für Internal Corporate Venturing in Großunternehmen - eine empirische Analyse, dissertation, Lohmar, Cologne 2015

Hens, T., Rieger, M. O. (2016): Financial Economics - A Concise Introduction to Classical and Behavioral Finance, 2nd edition, Berlin, Heidelberg 2016

Henschke, S. (2009): Towards a more accurate equity valuation - An empirical analysis, dissertation, Wiesbaden 2009

Henselmann, K. (2005): Value Reporting und Konkurrenzanalyse, in: Betriebswirtschaftliche Forschung und Praxis, 57th vol., 2005, No. 3, pp. 296–305

Herbertinger, M. (2002): Wertsteigerungsmaße - Eine kritische Analyse, dissertation, Frankfurt on the Main 2002

Hermanns, J. (2006): Optimale Kapitalstruktur und Market Timing - empirische Analyse börsennotierter deutscher Unternehmen, dissertation, Wiesbaden 2006

Hesselmann, C. (2006): Residualgewinnkonzepte zur externen Aktienanalyse, dissertation, Wiesbaden 2006

Heumann, R. (2005): Value Reporting in IFRS-Abschlüssen und Lageberichten, dissertation, Düsseldorf 2005

Heusinger von Waldegge, S. (2009): Steigerung des Unternehmenswertes - Entwicklung und Einsatz eines Controlling-Instrumentes, dissertation, Wiesbaden 2009

Hielscher, U. (1999): Investmentanalyse, 3rd edition, Munich 1999

Hienerth, C. (2010): Kennzahlenmodell zur Erfolgsbewertung des E-Commerce - Analyse am Beispiel eines Mehrkanaleinzelhändlers, dissertation, Wiesbaden 2010

Hilpisch, Y. (2005): Kapitalmarktorientierte Unternehmensführung - Grundlagen der Finanzierung, Wertorientierung und Corporate Governance, Wiesbaden 2005

Hippel, B. (2011): Konzernlagebericht und Kapitalmarkt - Eine empirische Analyse der Berichtspflichten nach HGB und DRS, dissertation, Düsseldorf 2011

Hirsch, B. (2006): Implementierungsprobleme der wertorientierten Unternehmenssteuerung - Stand der empirischen Literatur und Konsequenzen für die Forschung, in: zfo - Zeitschrift Führung und Organisation, 75th vol., 2006, No. 5, pp. 270–277

Hodge, F., Pronk, M. (2006): The Impact of Expertise and Investment Familiarity on Investors' Use of Online Financial Report Information, in: Journal of Accounting, Auditing and Finance, 21st vol., 2006, No. 3, pp. 267–292

Hodge, F. D. (2003): Investors' Perceptions of Earnings Quality, Auditor Independence and the Usefulness of Audited Financial Information, in: Accounting Horizons, 17th vol., 2003, Supplement, pp. 37–48

Hoffjan, A., Schroll, S. (2010): Modell zur wertorientierten Unternehmenssteuerung und seine Anwendung im Anlagenbau, in: Bandow, G., Holzmüller, H. H. (editors), "Das ist gar kein Modell!" - Unterschiedliche Modelle und Modellierungen in Betriebswirtschaftslehre und Ingenieurwissenschaften, Wiesbaden 2010, pp. 407–428

Hoffmann, W. (2011): Turnaround Equity – Erfolgsfaktoren im Transaktionsprozess bei Turnaround-Investitionen in Deutschland, dissertation, Cologne 2011

Hofmann, J., Schmolz, S. (2014): Controlling und Basel III in der Unternehmenspraxis - Strategien zur Bewältigung erhöhter Bonitätsanforderungen, Wiesbaden 2014

Holler, A. (2009): New Metrics for Value-Based Management - Enhancement of Performance Measurement and Empirical Evidence on Value Relevance, dissertation, Wiesbaden 2009

Holmstrom, B. (1979): Moral hazard and observability, in: The Bell Journal of Economics, 10th vol., 1979, No. 1, pp. 74–91

Hölscher, R. (2010): Investition, Finanzierung und Steuern, Munich 2010

Holthausen, R. W. (1981): Evidence on the effect of bond covenants and management compensation contracts on the choice of accounting techniques - The case of depreciation switch-back, in: Journal of Accounting and Economics, 3rd vol., 1981, No. 1, pp. 73–109

Holthausen, R. W., Leftwich, R. W. (1983): The economic consequences of accounting choice - Implications of costly contracting and monitoring, in: Journal of Accounting and Economics, 5th vol., 1983, pp. 77–117

Holthausen, R. W., Watts, R. L. (2001): The relevance of the value-relevance literature for financial accounting standard setting, in: Journal of Accounting and Economics, 31st vol., 2001, No. 1-3, pp. 3–75

Homburg, C. (2017): Marketingmanagement - Strategie-Instrumente-Umsetzung-Unternehmensführung, 6th edition, Wiesbaden 2017

Homburg, C., Lorenz, M., Sievers, S. (2011): Unternehmensbewertung in Deutschland: Verfahren, Finanzplanung und Kapitalkostenermittlung, in: ZfCM - Zeitschrift für Controlling & Management, 55th vol., 2011, No. 2, pp. 119–130

Horster, J., Knauer, T. (2012): Eignung und Einsatz finanzieller Steuerungskennzahlen zur wertorientierten Unternehmenssteuerung, in: Zeitschrift für Controlling & Management (ZfCM), 56th vol., 2012, No. 2, pp. 118–124

Horton, J., Serafeim, G., Serafeim, I. (2013): Does Mandatory IFRS Adoption Improve the Information Environment?, in: Contemporary Accounting Research, 30th vol., 2013, No. 1, pp. 388–423

Horváth, P. (2011): Controlling, 12th edition, Munich 2011

Horváth, P., Gleich, R., Voggenreiter, D. (2012): Controlling umsetzen - Fallstudien, Lösungen und Basiswissen, 5th edition, Stuttgart 2012

Horváth, P., Minning, F. (2001): Wertorientiertes Management in Deutschland, Großbritannien, Italien und Frankreich - eine empirische Analyse, in: Controlling, 13th vol., 2001, No. 6, pp. 273–282

Horzella, A. (2010): Wertsteigerung im M&A-Prozess - Erfolgsfaktoren - Instrumente - Kennzahlen, dissertation, Wiesbaden 2010

Hostettler, S. (2002): Economic Value Added (EVA) - Darstellung und Anwendung auf Schweizer Aktiengesellschaften, 5th edition, Bern, Stuttgart, Vienna 2002

Hostettler, S. (2003): Economic Value Added - Lektionen aus der Praxis, in: Der Schweizer Treuhänder, 77th vol., 2003, No. 3, pp. 117–122

Hristov, N., Hülsewig, O., Wollmershäuser, T. (2012): Loan supply shocks during the financial crisis: Evidence for the Euro area, in: Journal of International Money and Finance, 31st vol., 2012, No. 3, pp. 569–592

Hsiao, C. (2003): Analysis of Panel Data, 2nd edition, Cambridge, New York, Melbourne 2003

Huchzermeier, M. (2006): Investor Relations beim Börsengang - Konzept für mittelständische Unternehmen, dissertation, Wiesbaden 2006

Hüfner, B., Möller, H. P. (2002): On the "Superiority" of German Financial Analyst's Earnings Over Reported Earnings for the Valuation of German Stocks, in: Schmalenbach Business Review, Special Issue, 2002, No. 1, pp. 135–170

Hughes, J. S., Liu, J. (2007): Information Asymmetry, Diversification and Cost of Capital, in: The Accounting Review, 82nd vol., 2007, No. 3, pp. 705–729

IFRS Foundation (2016): International Financial Reporting Standards - A Guide through IFRS, London 2016

Imberger, K. (2003): Wertorientierte Anreizgestaltung, dissertation, Lohmar, Cologne 2003

Imi (2012): Annual Report

Imi (2013): Annual Report

Imi (2014): Annual Report

International Integrated Reporting Council (IIRC) (2013): The International IR Framework, URL: http://integratedreporting.org/resource/international-ir-framework/, last accessed: 11.01.2017

Ittner, C. D., Larcker, D. F. (1998): Innovations in Performance Measurement: Trends and Research Implications, in: Journal of Management Accounting Research, 10th vol., 1998, pp. 205–238

Ittner, C. D., Larcker, D. F. (2001): Assessing empirical research in managerial accounting: a value-based management perspective, in: Journal of Accounting and Economics, 32nd vol., 2001, No. 1-3, pp. 349–410

Ittner, C. D., Larcker, D. F., Randall, T. (2003): Performance implications of strategic performance measurement in financial services firms, in: Accounting, Organizations and Society, 28th vol., 2003, No. 7-8, pp. 715–741

Jacque, L. L., Vaaler, P. M. (2001): The International Control Conundrum with Exchange Risk: An EVA Framework, in: Journal of International Business Studies, 32nd vol., 2001, No. 4, pp. 813–832

Jaeger, S. (2012): Kapitalstrukturpolitik deutscher börsennotierter Aktiengesellschaften - Eine empirische Analyse von Kapitalstrukturdeterminanten, Wiesbaden 2012

Jähnchen, S. (2009): Kapitalkosten von Versicherungsunternehmen - Fundamentale Betafaktoren als ein Erklärungsbeitrag zur Erfassung der Renditeforderungen der Eigenkapitalgeber, dissertation, Wiesbaden 2009

James, G., Witten, D., Hastie, T., Tibshirani, R. (2013): An Introduction to Statistical Learning with Applications in R, New York 2013

Janakiraman, S., Radhakrishnan, S., Tsang, A. (2010): Institutional Investors, Managerial Ownership and Executive Compensation, in: Journal of Accounting, Auditing and Finance, 25th vol., 2010, No. 4, pp. 673–707

Janocha, M. (2014): Vergütung mittels Bonusbanken - eine agency-theoretische Perspektive, dissertation, Wiesbaden 2014

Jeanjean, T., Stolowy, H. (2008): Do accounting standards matter? An exploratory analysis of earnings management before and after IFRS adoption, in: Journal of Accounting and Public Policy, 27th vol., 2008, No. 6, pp. 480–494

Jensen, M. C. (1983): Organization theory and methodology, in: The Accounting Review, 58th vol., 1983, No. 2, pp. 319–339

Jensen, M. C. (2002): Value maximization, stakeholder theory, and the corporate objective function, in: Business ethics quarterly, 12th vol., 2002, No. 2, pp. 235–256

Jensen, M. C., Benington, G. A. (1970): Random Walks and Technical Theories: Some Additional Evidence, in: Journal of Finance, 25th vol., 1970, No. 2, pp. 469–482

Jensen, M. C., Meckling, W. H. (1976): Theory of the firm: managerial behavior, agency costs and ownerhsip structure, in: Journal of Financial Economics, 3rd vol., 1976, No. 4, pp. 305–360

Jensen, M. C., Murphy, K. J. (1990): Performance pay and top-management incentives, in: Journal of Political Economy, 98th vol., 1990, No. 2, pp. 225–264

Jermakowicz, E. K., Prather-Kinsey, J., Wulf, I. (2007): The Value Relevance of Accounting Income Reported by DAX-30 German Companies, in: Journal of International Financial Management and Accounting, 18th vol., 2007, No. 3, pp. 151–191

Johnson, R. A., Schnatterly, K., Johnson, S. G., Chiu, S.-C. (2010): Institutional Investors and Institutional Environment: A Comparative Analysis and Review, in: Journal of Management Studies, 47th vol., 2010, No. 8, pp. 1590–1613

Jones, S., Finley, A. (2011): Have IFRS made a difference to intra-country financial reporting diversity?, in: The British Accounting Review, 43rd vol., 2011, No. 1, pp. 22–38

Joos, P., Lang, M. (1994): The Effects of Accounting Diversity: Evidence from the European Union, in: Journal of Accounting Research, 32nd vol., 1994, pp. 141-168

Jost, P.-J. (2001): Die Prinzipal-Agenten-Theorie im Unternehmenskontext, in: Jost, P.-J. (editor), Die Prinzipal-Agenten-Theorie in der Betriebswirtschaftslehre, Stuttgart 2001, pp. 11–43

Junginger, M. (2005): Wertorientierte Steuerung von Risiken im Informationsmanagement, dissertation, Wiesbaden 2005

Käfer, T. M. (2006): Dezentralisierung im Konzern - eine Mehr-Ebenen-Analyse strategischer Restrukturierungen, dissertation, Wiesbaden 2006

Kahle, H. (2003): Unternehmenssteuerung auf Basis internationaler Rechnungslegungsstandards?, in: Zeitschrift für betriebswirtschaftliche Forschung (zfbf), 55th vol., 2003, No. 8, pp. 773–789

Kahle, K. M., Stulz, R. M. (2013): Access to capital, investment, and the financial crisis, in: Journal of Financial Economics, 110th vol., 2013, No. 2, pp. 280–299

Kahlenberg, M. (2009): Was erwarten Finanzanalysten von guter IR-Arbeit?, in: Kirchhoff, K. R., Piwinger, M. (editors), Praxishandbuch Investor Relations - das Standardwerk der Finanzkommunikation, 2nd edition, Wiesbaden 2009, pp. 491–498

Kahneman, D., Tversky, A. (1979): Prospect Theory: An Analysis of Decision under Risk, in: Econometrica, 47th vol., 1979, No. 2, pp. 263–292

Kajüter, P. (2007a): Wertorientierte Performancemessung, in: Busse von Colbe, W., Coenenberg, A. G., Kajüter, P., Linnhoff, U., Pellens, B. (editors), Betriebswirtschaft für Führungskräfte - Eine Einführung für Ingenieure, Naturwissenschaftler, Juristen und Geisteswissenschaftler, Stuttgart 2007, pp. 437–456

Kajüter, P. (2007b): Wertorientierte Unternehmensführung, in: Busse von Colbe, W., Coenenberg, A. G., Kajüter, P., Linnhoff, U., Pellens, B. (editors), Betriebswirtschaft für Führungskräfte - Eine Einführung für Ingenieure, Naturwissenschaftler, Juristen und Geisteswissenschaftler, Stuttgart 2007, pp. 27–46

Karamanou, I., Nishiotis, G. P. (2009): Disclosure and the Cost of Capital: Evidence from the Market's Reaction to Firm Voluntary Adoption of IAS, in: Journal of Business Finance & Accounting, 36th vol., 2009, No. 7-8, pp. 793–821

Karrer, M. (2006): Supply Chain Performance Management - Entwicklung und Ausgestaltung einer unternehmensübergreifenden Steuerungskonzeption, dissertation, Wiesbaden 2006

Kaspereit, T., Lopatta, K. (2016): The value relevance of SAM's corporate sustainability ranking and GRI sustainability reporting in the European stock markets, in: Business Ethics: A European Review, 25th vol., 2016, No. 1, pp. 1–24

Kato, K., Schallheim, J. S. (1985): Seasonal and Size Anomalies in the Japanese Stock Market, in: Journal of Financial and Quantitative Analysis, 20th vol., 1985, No. 2, pp. 243–260

Kausar, A., Shroff, N., White, H. (2016): Real effects of the audit choice, in: Journal of Accounting and Economics, 62nd vol., 2016, No. 1, pp. 157–181

Ke, B., Huddart, S., Petroni, K. (2003): What insiders know about future earnings and how they use it: Evidence from insider trades, in: Journal of Accounting and Economics, 35th vol., 2003, No. 3, pp. 315–346

Keay, A., Adamopoulou, R. (2012): Shareholder Value and UK Companies: A Positivist Inquiry, in: European Business Organization Law Review, 13th vol., 2012, No. 1, pp. 1–29

Keim, D. B. (1983): Size-Related Anomalies And Stock Return Seasonality - Further Empirical Evidence, in: Journal of Financial Economics, 12th vol., 1983, No. 1, pp. 13–32

Keim, D. B. (1989): Trading Patterns, Bid-Ask Spreads, And Estimated Security Returns: The Case of Common Stocks at Calendar Turning Points, in: Journal of Financial Economics, 25th vol., 1989, No. 1, pp. 75–97

Kerstein, J., Kim, S. (1995): The Incremental Information Content of Capital Expenditures, in: The Accounting Review, 70th vol., 1995, No. 3, pp. 513–526

Khakad, F. (2009): Die Bedeutung von Financial Covenants in der internationalen Finanzkrise, dissertation, Cologne 2009

King, M. R. (2013): The Basel III Net Stable Funding Ratio and bank net interest margins, in: Journal of Banking & Finance, 37th vol., 2013, No. 11, pp. 4144–4156

Kirchhoff, K. R. (2009): Grundlagen der IR, in: Kirchhoff, K. R., Piwinger, M. (editors), Praxishandbuch Investor Relations - das Standardwerk der Finanzkommunikation, 2nd edition, Wiesbaden 2009, pp. 35–61

Kirchhoff, K. R., Piwinger, M. (2014): Kommunikation mit Kapitalgebern: Grundlagen der Investor Relations, in: Zerfass, A., Piwinger, M. (editors), Handbuch Unternehmenskommunikation - Strategie, Management, Wertschöpfung, 2nd edition, Wiesbaden 2014, pp. 1079–1098

Klein, J. (2008): Anforderungen an Sanierungskonzepte - Analyse bestehender Anforderungen und Leitfaden zur zukünftigen Ausgestaltung von Sanierungskonzepten, dissertation, Wiesbaden 2008

Kleinschmidt, M. (2007): Venture Capital, Corporate Governance and Firm Value, dissertation, Wiesbaden 2007

Kley, K.-L. (2003): Informationsvermittlung durch Value Reporting?, in: Der Betrieb, 56th vol., 2003, No. 16, pp. 840–843

Klodt, T. (2000): Produktmärkte, Rent Sharing und Lohnhöhe - Eine ökonometrische Analyse mit Betriebspaneldaten, Frankfurt on the Main 2000

Knauer, T., Silge, L., Sommer, F. (2018): The shareholder value effects of using value-based performance measures: Evidence from acquisitions and divestments, in: Management Accounting Research, 2018

Knorren, N. (1998): Wertorientierte Gestaltung der Unternehmensführung 1998

Koch, J. (2005): Rechnungswesenbasierte Verfahren der Aktienbewertung - Theoretische und empirische Untersuchung des Residualgewinnmodels, dissertation, Wiesbaden 2005

Koelen, P. (2009): Investitionstheoretische Bewertungskalküle in der IFRS-Rechnungslegung - Möglichkeiten und Grenzen einer unternehmenswertorientierten Berichterstattung, dissertation, Cologne 2009

Köhler, K. (2015): Investor Relations in Deutschland - Institutionalisierung - Professionalisierung - Kapitalmarktentwicklung - Perspektiven, dissertation, Wiesbaden 2015

Kohn, W., Öztürk, R. (2017): Statistik für Ökonomen - Datenanalyse mit R und SPSS, 3rd edition, Wiesbaden 2017

Koller, T., Goedhart, M., Wessels, D. (2010): Valuation - Measuring and Managing the Value of Companies, 5th edition, Hoboken 2010

Komlos, J., Süssmuth, B. (2010): Empirische Ökonomie - Eine Einführung in Methoden und Anwendung, Berlin, Heidelberg 2010

Königsgruber, R., Palan, S. (2013): Earnings management and participation in accounting standard-setting, in: Central European Journal of Operations Research, 21st vol., 2013, published online, pp. 1–22

Konté, M. A. (2010): Behavioral Finance and Efficient Markets: Is the Joint Hypothesis Really the Problem?, in: Journal of Behavioral Finance, 7th vol., 2010, No. 1&2, pp. 19–29

Körnert, J., Wolf, C. (2007): Systemtheorie, Shareholder Value-Konzept und Stakeholder-Konzept als theretisch konzeptionelle Bezugsrahmen der Balanced Scorecard, in: Zeitschrift für Controlling & Management, 51st vol., 2007, No. 2, pp. 130–140

Köster, C. (2015): Bestellmengenentscheidungen bei asymmetrisch verteilter Nachfrage - Experimentelle Evidenz im Newsvendor-Problem, dissertation, Wiesbaden 2015

Kothari, S. P. (1992): Price-earnings regressions in the presence of prices leading earnings, in: Journal of Accounting and Economics, 15th vol., 1992, No. 2-3, pp. 173–202

Kothari, S. P. (2001): Capital markets research in accounting, in: Journal of Accounting and Economics, 31st vol., 2001, No. 1-3, pp. 105–231

Kothari, S. P., Shu, S., Wysocki, P. D. (2009): Do Managers Withhold Bad News?, in: Journal of Accounting Research, 47th vol., 2009, No. 1, pp. 241–276

Kothari, S. P., Zimmerman, J. L. (1995): Price and return models, in: Journal of Accounting and Economics, 20th vol., 1995, No. 2, pp. 155–192

Kousenidis, D. V., Ladas, A. C., Negakis, C. I. (2013): The effects of the European debt crisis on earnings quality, in: International Review of Financial Analysis, 30th vol., 2013, pp. 351–362

Kräkel, M. (2015): Organisation und Management, 6th edition, Tübingen 2015

Kraus, K., Strömsten, T. (2012): Going public : the role of accounting and shareholder value in making sense of an IPO, in: Management Accounting Research, 23rd vol., 2012, No. 3, pp. 186–201

Kraus, P. (2011): Die Auswirkungen von Corporate Governance und Nachhaltigkeit auf den Unternehmenserfolg - Eine Betrachtung im Kontext der wertorientierten Unternehmensführung, Cologne 2011

Krause, H.-U., Arora, D. (2010): Controlling Kennzahlen - Key Performance Indicators, 2nd edition, Munich 2010

Krebs, D. M. (1988): In Honor of Sandy Grossman, Winner of the John Bates Clark Medal, in: Journal of Economic Perspectives, 2nd vol., 1988, No. 2, pp. 111–135
Kremer, P. (2008): Konzerncontrolling - Ein unternehmenswertorientierter und beteiligungsspezifischer Ansatz, dissertation, Berlin 2008
Kreyer, F. (2009): Strategieorientierte Restwertbestimmung in der Unternehmensbewertung - Eine Untersuchung des langfristigen Rentabilitätsverlaufs europäischer Unternehmen, dissertation, Wiesbaden 2009
Krol, F. (2009): Wertorientierte Unternehmensführung im Mittelstand - eine empirische Analyse von Einfluss- und Wirkungsfaktoren, dissertation, Hamburg 2009
Krotsch, S. (2006): Industrialisierung in der Abwicklungs- und Transformationsfunktion von Banken - Ein stochastisches Modell, dissertation, Wiesbaden 2006
Kruschwitz, L., Löffler, A. (2006): Discounted Cash Flow - A Theory of the Valuation of Firms, Hoboken, San Francisco, Weinheim 2006
Kugler, P. L. (2006): Information Mirages an experimentellen Wertpapiermärkten, dissertation, Wiesbaden 2006
Kühnberger, M. (2014): Fair-Value Accounting, Bilanzpolitik und die Qualität von IFRS-Abschlüssen. Ein Überblick über ausgewählte Aspekte der Fair Value-Bewertung, in: Zeitschrift für betriebswirtschaftliche Forschung (zfbf), 66th vol., 2014, No. 5, pp. 428–450
Kuhne, D. (2015): Multiple Regression als Konzept zur Absatzprognose, in: Gansser, O., Krol, B. (editors), Markt- und Absatzprognosen - Modelle - Methoden - Anwendung, Wiesbaden 2015, pp. 3–26
Küting, K., Weber, C.-P. (2015): Die Bilanzanalyse - Beurteilung von Abschlüssen nach HGB und IFRS, 11th edition, Stuttgart 2015
Kyriazis, D., Anastassis, C. (2007): The Validity of the Economic Value Added Approach, in: European Financial Management, 13th vol., 2007, No. 1, pp. 71–100
La Porta, R., Lopez-de-Silanes, F., Shleifer, A., Vishny, R. (2000): Investor protection and corporate governance, in: Journal of Financial Economics, 58th vol., 2000, No. 1-2, pp. 3–27
Labbé, M., Schädlich, F. (2008): Risikomanagement und Controlling als Lösungsbeitrag für bestehende Corporate Governance Probleme in der Unternehmenspraxis, in: Brauweiler, H.-C. (editor), Unternehmensführung heute, Munich 2008, pp. 321–345
Labhart, P. (1999): Value Reporting - Informationsbedürfnisse des Kapitalmarktes und Wertsteigerung duch Reporting, dissertation, Zürich 1999
Labhart, P., Volkart, R. (2001): Value Reporting, in: Coenenberg, A. G., Pohle, K. (editors), Internationale Rechnungslegung - Konsequenzen für Unternehmensführung, Rechnungswesen, Standardsetting, Prüfung und Kapitalmarkt, Stuttgart 2001, pp. 115–142
Labhart, P., Volkart, R. (2009): IR als Wertsteigerungsmanagement, in: Kirchhoff, K. R., Piwinger, M. (editors), Praxishandbuch Investor Relations - das Standardwerk der Finanzkommunikation, 2nd edition, Wiesbaden 2009, pp. 201–220
Lachnit, L., Müller, S. (2012): Unternehmenscontrolling - Managementunterstützung bei Erfolgs-, Finanz-, Risiko- und Erfolgspotenzialsteuerung, 2nd edition, Wiesbaden 2012
Laier, R. (2011): Value Reporting - Analyse von Relevanz und Qualität der wertorientierten Berichterstattung von DAX-30 Unternehmen, dissertation, Wiesbaden 2011
Lambert, R. A., Larcker, D. F., Weigelt, K. (1993): The structure of organizational incentives, in: Administrative Science Quarterly, 38th vol., 1993, No. 3, pp. 438–461
Lambert, R. A., Leuz, C., Verrecchia, R. E. (2007): Accounting Information, Disclosure, and the Cost of Capital, in: Journal of Accounting Research, 45th vol., 2007, No. 2, pp. 385–420
Lambert, R. A., Leuz, C., Verrecchia, R. E. (2011): Information Asymmetry, Information Precision, and the Cost of Capital, in: Review of Finance, 16th vol., 2011, No. 1, pp. 1–29
Lambert, R. A., Verrecchia, R. E. (2015): Information, Illiquidity and the Cost of Capital, in: Contemporary Accounting Research, 32nd vol., 2015, No. 2, pp. 438–454
Lammert, J. (2010): Kommunikationsformen freiwilliger unternehmenseigener Transparenz und fundamentale Kapitalmarkteffekte - Voluntary Disclosure, Accounting Quality und Personal Communication, dissertation, Wiesbaden 2010

Landsman, W. R., Magliolo, J. (1988): Cross-Sectional Capital Market Research and Model Specification, in: The Accounting Review, 63rd vol., 1988, No. 4, pp. 586–604

Landsman, W. R., Maydew, E. L. (2002): Has the Information Content of Quarterly Earnings Announcements Declinded in the Past Three Decades?, in: Journal of Accounting Research, 40th vol., 2002, No. 3, pp. 797–808

Landsman, W. R., Shapiro, A. C. (1995): Tobin's q and the Relation between Accounting ROI and Economic Return, in: Journal of Accounting, Auditing & Finance, 10th vol., 1995, No. 1, pp. 103–118

Landsmann, C. (1999): Finanzplanorientiertes Konzerncontrolling - Konzeption eines wertorientierten Steuerungsinstrumentes, dissertation, Wiesbaden 1999

Lang, M., Raedy, J. S., Yetman, M. H. (2003): How Representative Are Firms That Are Cross-Listed in the United States? An Analysis of Accounting Quality, in: Journal of Accounting Research, 41st vol., 2003, No. 2, pp. 363–386

Lang, M., Smith Raedy, J., Wilson, W. (2006): Earnings management and cross listing: Are reconciled earnings comparable to US earnings?, in: Journal of Accounting and Economics, 42nd vol., 2006, No. 1-2, pp. 255–283

Lange, T. A. (2005): Kapitalmarktbasierte Preismodelle für Firmenkundenkredite als Beitrag zur wertorientierten Steuerung in Banken, in: Lange, T. A., Schulze, H. (editors), Wertmanagement in Banken, Wiesbaden 2005, pp. 113–134

Langguth, H. (2008): Kapitalmarktorientiertes Wertmanagement - Unternehmensbewertung, Unternehmenssteuerung und Berichterstattung, Munich 2008

Lattwein, J. (2002): Wertorientierte strategische Steuerung - Ganzheitlich-integrativer Ansatz zur Implementierung, dissertation, Wiesbaden 2002

Laux, C., Leuz, C. (2009): The crisis of fair-value accounting: Making sense of the recent debate, in: Accounting, Organizations and Society, 34th vol., 2009, No. 6-7, pp. 826–834

Laux, H. (2006a): Unternehmensrechnung, Anreiz und Kontrolle - Die Messung, Zurechnung und Steuerung des Erfolges als Grundprobleme der Betriebswirtschaftslehre, 3rd edition, Berlin, Heidelberg 2006

Laux, H. (2006b): Wertorientierte Unternehmenssteuerung und Kapitalmarkt - Fundierung finanzwirtschaftlicher Entscheidungskriterien und Anreize für deren Umsetzung, 2nd edition, Berlin, Heidelberg 2006

Laux, H., Schabel, M. M. (2009): Subjektive Investitionsbewertung, Marktbewertung und Risikoteilung - Grenzpeise aus Sicht börsennotierter Unternehmen und individueller Investoren im Vergleich, Berlin, Heidelberg 2009

Lawrence, H. (1986): A Transaction Data Study Of Weekly And Intradaily Patterns In Stock Returns, in: Journal of Financial Economics, 14th vol., 1986, No. 1, pp. 99–117

Lazar, C. (2007): Managementvergütung, Corporate Governance und Unternehmensperformance - eine modelltheoretische und empirische Untersuchung, dissertation, Wiesbaden 2007

Le Roy, S. F. (1976): Efficient Capital Markets: Comment, in: Journal of Finance, 31st vol., 1976, No. 1, pp. 139–141

Le Roy, S. F., Porter, R. D. (1981): The Present Value Relation: Tests Based on Implied Variance Bounds, in: Econometrica, 49th vol., 1981, No. 3, pp. 555–574

Lee, C. M. (2001): Market efficiency and accounting research: a discussion of "capital market research in accounting" by S. P. Kothari, in: Journal of Accounting and Economics, 31st vol., 2001, No. 1, pp. 233–253

Lee, K.-W., Yeo, G. Hian-Heng (2016): The association between integrated reporting and firm valuation, in: Review of Quantitative Finance and Accounting, 47th vol., 2016, No. 4, pp. 1221–1250

Lehmann, G. (2012): Wertorientiertes Management mittelständischer Unternehmen - Potenziale der Ermittlung von Eigenkapitalkosten sowie Herleitung von Konzeptanforderungen im Rahmen eines Delphi-Verfahrens, Munich 2012

Leuz, C., Verrecchia, R. E. (2000): The Economic Consequences of Increased Disclosure, in: Journal of Accounting Research, 38th vol., 2000, Supplement: Studies on Accounting Information and the Economics of the Firm, pp. 91–124

Leuz, C., Wysocki, P. D. (2016): The Economics of Disclosure and Financial Reporting Regulation: Evidence and Suggestions for Future Research, in: Journal of Accounting Research, 54th vol., 2016, No. 2, pp. 525–622

Lev, B. (1989): On the Usefulness of Earnings and Earnings Research: Lessons and Directions from Two Decades of Empirical Research, in: Journal of Accounting Research, 27th vol., 1989, pp. 153–192

Leven, F.-J. (1998): Investor Relations und Shareholder Value, in: Müller, M., Leven, F.-J. (editors), Shareholder Value Reporting, Wien, Frankfurt 1998, pp. 45–62

Lewis, T. G., Lehmann, S. (1992): Überlegene Investitionsentscheidungen durch CFROI, in: Betriebswirtschaftliche Forschung und Praxis, 1992, No. 1, pp. 1–13

Lewis, T. G., Stelter, D. M. (1993): Mehrwert schaffen mit finanziellen Ressouorcen, in: Harvard Business Manager, 1st vol., 1993, No. 4, pp. 107–114

Lewis, T. G., Stelter, D. M., Casata, T., Reiter, M. (1995): Steigerung des Unternehmenswertes - Total Value Management, 2nd edition, Landsberg / Lech 1995

Lindemann, J. (2004): Rechnungslegung und Kapitalmarkt - eine theoretische und empirische Analyse, dissertation, Cologne 2004

Lindemann, J. (2006): Kapitalmarktrelevanz der Rechnungslegung - Konzepte, Methodik und Ergebnisse empirischer Forschung, in: Journal of Business Economics, 76th vol., 2006, No. 10, pp. 967–1003

Lintner, J. (1965): The Valuation of Risk Assets and the Selection of Risky Investments in Stock Portfolios and Capital Budgets, in: The Review of Economics and Statistics, 47th vol., 1965, No. 1, pp. 13–37

Lippe, Peter von (2011): Ein Beispiel für die Anwendung von Methoden für Panel-Daten - Working Paper, URL: http://www.von-der-lippe.org/dokumente/Taupool.pdf, last accessed: 11th August 2017

Liu, W., Strong, N. (2003): Post-earnings -announcement Drift in the UK, in: European Financial Management, 9th vol., 2003, No. 1, pp. 89–116

Lo, A. W., Mamaysky, H., Wang, J. (2000): Foundations of Technical Analysis: Computational Algorithms, Statistical Inference, and Empirical Implementation, in: Journal of Finance, 55th vol., 2000, No. 4, pp. 1705–1770

Lo, K., Lys, T. Z. (2000): The Ohlson Model: Contribution to Valuation Theory, Limitations and Empirical Applications, in: Journal of Accounting, Auditing & Finance, 15th vol., 2000, No. 3, pp. 337–367

Lo, K.; Lys, T. Z. (2001): Bridging the Gap Between Value Relevance and Information Content, Working Paper

Loderer, C., Roth, L., Waelchli, U., Joerg, P. (2010): Shareholder Value: Principles, Declarations and Actions, in: Financial Management, 39th vol., 2010, No. 1, pp. 5–33

Loose, T. (2009): Tax Management der kapitalmarktorientierten internationalen Unternehmung, dissertation, Cologne 2009

Lopatta, K., Kaspereit, T. (2014): The World Capital Markets' Perception of Sustainability and the Impact of the Financial Crisis, in: Journal of Business Ethics, 122nd vol., 2014, No. 3, pp. 475–500

Lorenz, M. (2009): Unternehmensbewertungsverfahren - Theoretische Verbesserungen, empirische Evidenz und Strategieimplikationen, dissertation, Wiesbaden 2009

Lorson, P. (1999): Shareholder Value Ansätze: Zweck, Konzepte, Entwicklungstendenzen, in: Der Betrieb, 52nd vol., 1999, No. 26/27, pp. 1329–1339

Lorson, P. (2004): Auswirkungen von Shareholder-Value-Konzepten auf die Bewertung und Steuerung ganzer Unternehmen, Herne, Berlin 2004

Losbichler, H. (2012): Das Nachhaltigkeits-Paradoxon des Shareholder Value, in: ZfCM - Zeitschrift für Controlling & Management, 56th vol., 2012, No. 4, pp. 266–270

Lovata, L. M., Costigan, M. L. (2002): Empirical analysis of adopters of economic value added, in: Management Accounting Research, 13th vol., 2002, No. 2, pp. 215–228

Lücke, W. (1955): Investitionsrechnung auf Grundlage von Ausgaben oder Kosten?, in: Zeitschrift für handelswissenschaftliche Forschung, 7th vol., 1955, pp. 310–324

Lüdenbach, N., Hoffmann, W.-D., Freiberg, J. (2015): Haufe IFRS-Kommentar, 13th edition, Freiburg, Munich 2015

Lueg, R., Schäffer, U. (2010): Assessing empirical research on value-based management: guidelines for improved hypothesis testing, in: Journal für Betriebswirtschaft, 60th vol., 2010, No. 1, pp. 1–48

Lugo, S., Croce, A., Faff, R. (2015): Herding Behavior and Rating Convergence among Credit Rating Agencies: Evidence from the Subprime Crisis, in: Review of Finance, 19th vol., 2015, No. 4, pp. 1703–1731

Lukas, A. (2004): Unternehmensbewertung und intellektuelles Kapital - Preisfindung im Merger & Acquisitions-Prozess, Berlin 2004

Lumby, S., Jones, C. (2003): Corporate Finance - Theory and Practice, 7th edition, London 2003

Lummert, S., Schumacher, M. (2009): Bilanz- und Kennzahlenanalyse von Unternehmen, in: Schacht, U., Fackler, M. (editors), Praxishandbuch Unternehmensbewertung - Grundlagen, Methoden, Fallbeispiele, 2nd edition, Wiesbaden 2009, pp. 51–80

Lundholm, R. J. (1995): A Tutorial on the Ohlson and Feltham/Ohlson Models: Answers to Some Frequently Asked Questions, in: Contemporary Accounting Research, 11th vol., 1995, No. 2, pp. 749–761

Lütkeschürmer, G. (2012): Die Berücksichtigung von Finanzierungsrisiken bei der Ermittlung von Eigenkapitalkosten bei der Unternehmensbewertung, dissertation, Cologne 2012

Macharzina, K., Wolf, J. (2012): Unternehmensführung - das internationale Managementwissen, Konzepte - Methoden - Praxis, 8th edition, Wiesbaden 2012

Machuga, S. M., Pfeiffer, R. J., Verma, K. (2002): Economic Value Added, Future Accounting Earnings and Financial Analysts' Earnings Per Share Forecasts, in: Review of Quantitative Finance and Accounting, 18th vol., 2002, No. 1, pp. 59–73

Maditinos, D. I., Sevic, Z., Theriou, N. G. (2007): Investors' behaviour in the Athens Stock Exchange (ASE), in: Studies in Economics and Finance, 24th vol., 2007, No. 1, pp. 32–50

Maditinos, D. I., Sevic, Z., Theriou, N. G. (2009): Modelling traditional accounting and modern value-based performance measures to explain stock market returns in the Athens Stock Exchange (ASE), in: Journal of Modelling in Management, 4th vol., 2009, No. 3, pp. 182–201

Malkiel, B. G. (1991): Efficient Market Hypothesis, in: Eatwell, J.; Milgate, M.; Newman, P. (editors), The World of Economics, London, Basingstoke 1991, pp. 211–218

Malkiel, B. G. (1995): Returns from Investing in Equity Mutual Funds 1971 to 1991, in: Journal of Finance, 50th vol., 1995, No. 2, pp. 549–572

Malkiel, B. G. (2005): Reflections on the Efficient Market Hypothesis: 30 Years Later, in: The Financial Review, 40th vol., 2005, No. 1, pp. 1–9

Mallin, C. (2012): Institutional investors: the vote as a tool of governance, in: Journal of Management & Governance, 16th vol., 2012, No. 2, pp. 177–196

Malmi, S., Ikäheimo, S. (2003): Value Based Management practices - some evidence from the field, in: Management Accounting Research, 14th vol., 2003, No. 3, pp. 235–254

Malmström, B. (2006): Wertorientiertes Management bei der Stinnes AG, in: Schweickart, N., Töpfer, A. (editors), Wertorientiertes Management - Werterhaltung - Wertsteuerung - Wertsteigerung ganzheitlich gestalten, Berlin, Heidelberg 2006, pp. 637–647

Maniora, J. (2017): Is Integrated Reporting Really the Superior Mechanism for the Integration of Ethics into the Core Business Model? An Empirical Analysis, in: Journal of Business Ethics, 140th vol., 2017, No. 4, pp. 755-786

Mankiw, N. G., Taylor, M. P. (2012): Grundzüge der Volkswirtschaftslehre, 5th edition, Stuttgart 2012

Markowitz, H. (1952): Portfolio Selection, in: The Journal of Finance, 7th vol., 1952, No. 1, pp. 77–91

Marsh, T. A., Merton, R. C. (1986): Dividend Variability and Variance Bounds Tests for the Rationality of Stock Market Prices, in: American Economic Review, 76th vol., 1986, No. 3, pp. 483–498

Matschke, M. J., Brösel, G. (2013): Unternehmensbewertung - Funktionen - Methoden - Grundsätze, 4th edition, Wiesbaden 2013

Mayr, S. (2010): Stakeholdermanagement in der Unternehmenskrise - eine unternehmensethische Betrachtung, dissertation, Wiesbaden 2010

McLemore, P., Woodward, G., Zwirlein, T. (2015): Back-tests of the Dividend Discount Model Using Time-varying Cost of Equity, in: Journal of Applied Finance, 25th vol., 2015, No. 2, pp. 75-94

Melnyk, S. A., Bititci, U., Platts, K., Tobias, J., Andersen, B. (2014): Is performance measurement and management fit for the future?, in: Management Accounting Research, 25th vol., 2014, No. 2, pp. 173–186

Mensch, G. (2008): Finanz-Controlling, 2nd edition, Munich 2008

Merton, R. C. (1987): A Simple Model of Capital Market Equilibrium with Incomplete Information, in: Journal of Finance, 42nd vol., 1987, No. 3, pp. 483–510

Metten, M. (2010): Corporate Governance, dissertation, Wiesbaden 2010

Metze, T. (2010): Supply Chain Finance - die wertorientierte Analyse und Optimierung des Working Capitals in Supply Chains, dissertation, Lohmar, Cologne 2010

Meyer, C. A. (2007): Working Capital und der Unternehmenswert - eine Anlayse zum Management der Forderungen und Verbindlichkeiten aus Lieferungen und Leistungen, dissertation, Wiesbaden 2007

Meyer, M. (2005): Unternehmenswertorientierte Berichterstattung auf Basis der IAS/IFRS - eine bilanztheoretische und bilanzpolitische Betrachtung aus deutscher Sicht, dissertation, Wiesbaden 2005

Middelmann, U. (2001): Neuere Entwicklungen des wertorientierten Controlling - Potenziale und Realisierungen in der Praxis - dargestellt am Beispiel ThyssenKrupp, in: Die Betriebswirtschaft (DBW), 61st vol., 2001, No. 4, pp. 493–508

Mikołajek-Gocejna, M. (2014): Investor Expectations in Value Based Management, Cham, Heidelberg, New York, Dordrecht, London 2014

Milgrom, P., Stokey, N. (1982): Information, Trade and Common Knowledge, in: Journal of Economic Theory, 26th vol., 1982, No. 1, pp. 17–27

Mills, T. C., Jordanov, J. V. (2003): The size effect and the random walk hypothesis: evidence from the London Stock Exchange using Markov Chains, in: Applied Financial Economics, 13th vol., 2003, No. 11, pp. 807–815

Milne, M. J. (2002): Positive accounting theory, political costs and social disclosure analyses: a critical look, in: Critical Perspectives on Accounting, 13th vol., 2002, No. 3, pp. 369–395

Mir, A. E., Seboui, S. (2006): Corporate governance and earnings management and the relationship between economic value added and created shareholder value, in: Journal of Asset Management, 7th vol., 2006, No. 3/4, pp. 242–254

Modello, E. (2015): Aktienbewertung - Theorie und Anwendungsbeispiele, Wiesbaden 2015

Mohnen, A. (2002): Performancemessung und Steuerung von Investitionsentscheidungen, dissertation, Wiesbaden 2002

Mohnen, A., Bareket, M. (2007): Performance measurement for investment decisions under capital constraints, in: Review of Accounting Studies, 12th vol., 2007, No. 1, pp. 1–22

Moir, L., Kennerley, M., Ferguson, D. (2007): Measuring the business case: linking stakeholder and shareholder value, in: Corporate Governance: The international journal of business in society, 7th vol., 2007, No. 4, pp. 388–400

Möller, H. P., Hüfner, B. (2001): Empirische Kapitalmarktforschung, in: Gerke, W., Steiner, M. (editors), Handwörterbuch des Bank- und Finanzwesens, 3rd edition, Stuttgart 2001, pp. 1276–1293

Möller, H. P., Hüfner, B. (2002): Zur Bedeutung der Rechnungslegung für den deutschen Aktienmarkt - Begründung, Messprobleme und Erkenntnisse empirischer Forschung, in: Seicht, G. (editor), Jahrbuch für Controlling und Rechnungswesen, Vienna 2002, pp. 405–463

Mölls, S. H., Strauß, M. (2007): Bewertungsrelevanz der Rechnungslegung - Stand und Implikationen der empirischen Forschung für Aktionäre und Regulierer, in: Journal of Business Economics, 77th vol., 2007, No. 9, pp. 955–995

Mondello, E. (2015): Aktienbewertung - Theorie und Anwendungsbeispiele, Wiesbaden 2015

Morich, S. (2007): Steuerung der Effektivität kapitalmarktorientierter Unternehmenspublizität - Eine kennzahlengestützte Konzeption am Beispiel des Geschäftsberichts, dissertation, Wiesbaden 2007

Moro, B. (2014): Lessons from the European economic and financial great crisis: A survey, in: European Journal of Political Economy, 34th vol., 2014, pp. S9–S24

Mossin, J. (1966): Equilibrium in a Capital Asset Market, in: Econometrica, 34th vol., 1966, No. 4, pp. 768–783

Mueller, F. (2011): Sales Management - control strategies in banking - strategic fit and performance impact, dissertation, Wiesbaden 2011

Müller, M. (1998): Shareholder Value Reporting - ein Konzept wertorientierter Kapitalmarktinformation, in: Müller, M., Leven, F.-J. (editors), Shareholder Value Reporting, Wien, Frankfurt 1998, pp. 123–144

Müller, M. (2006): Harmonisierung des externen und internen Rechnungswesens - eine empirsiche Untersuchung, dissertation, Wiesbaden 2006

Müller, S. (2007): IFRS: Grundlagen und Erstanwendung - Gestaltung und Auswirkungen der Umstellung, Berlin 2007

Myers, J. N. (1999): Implementing Residual Income Valuation with Linear Information Dynamics, in: The Accounting Review, 74th vol., 1999, No. 1, pp. 1–28

Myers, R. (1996): Metric Wars, in: CFO, 12th vol., 1996, No. 10, pp. 41–50

National Grid (2012): Annual Report

Neely, A., Gregory, M., Platts, K. (1995): Performance measurement system design, in: International Journal of Operations & Production Management, 15th vol., 1995, No. 4, pp. 80–116

Neely, C. J., Weller, P. A., Ulrich, J. M. (2009): The Adaptive Markets Hypothesis: Evidence from the foreign exchange market, in: Journal of Financial and Quantitative Analysis, 44th vol., 2009, No. 2, pp. 467–488

Nguyen, T., Romeike, F. (2013): Versicherungswirtschaftslehre - Grundlagen für Studium und Praxis, Wiesbaden 2013

Nichols, D. C., Wahlen, J. M. (2004): How do earnings numbers relate to stock returns? A review of classic accounting research with updated evidence, in: Accounting Horizons, 18th vol., 2004, No. 4, pp. 263–286

Nicolai, A., Seidl, D. (2010): That's Relevant! Different Forms of Practical Relevance in Management Science, in: Organization Studies, 31st vol., 2010, No. 9-10, pp. 1257–1285

Nowak, K. (2003): Marktorientierte Unternehmensbewertung - Discounted Cash Flow, Realoptionen, Economic Value Added und der Direct Comparison Approach, 2nd edition, Wiesbaden 2003

Nye, R. P. (2014): Understanding and Managing the Credit Rating Agencies - A Guide for Fixed Income Issuers, London 2014

Oberdörster, T. (2009): Finanzberichterstattung und Prognosefehler von Finanzanalysten, dissertation, Wiesbaden 2009

Obermeier, T., Gasper, R. (2008): Investitionsrechnung und Unternehmensbewertung, Munich 2008

Obst, H. (2009): Darstellung des Abschlusses, in: Buschhüter, M., Striegel, A. (editors), Internationale Rechnungslegung, Wiesbaden 2009, pp. 81–95

O'Byrne, S. F. (1997): EVA and Shareholder Return, in: Financial Practice & Education, 7th vol., 1997, pp. 50–57

O'Hanlon, J., Peasell, K. (2002): Residual Income and Value-Creation: The Missing Link, in: Review of Accounting Studies, 7th vol., 2002, No. 2-3, pp. 229–246

Ohliger, T. (2016): Berücksichtigung nichtlinearer Zusammenhänge bei der Insolvenzprognose - Eine empirische Untersuchung unter Verwendung generalisierter additiver Modelle, dissertation, Cologne 2016

Ohlson, J. A. (1995): Earnings, Book Values and Dividends in Equity Valuation, in: Contemporary Accounting Research, 11th vol., 1995, No. 2, pp. 661–687

Oliveira, L., Rodrigues, L. Lima, Craig, R. (2010): Intangible assets and value relevance: Evidence from the Portuguese stock exchange, in: The British Accounting Review, 42nd vol., 2010, No. 4, pp. 241–252

Ossadnik, W. (2009): Controlling, 4th edition, Munich 2009

Ossadnik, W., Barklage, D. (2003): Anspruch und Wirklichkeit der Wertorientierung von Unternehmen des Neuen Markts, in: Der Betrieb, 56th vol., 2003, No. 24, pp. 1285–1290

Ostrowski, O. (2007): Erfolg durch Desinvestition - eine theoretische und empirische Analyse, dissertation, Wiesbaden 2007

Padberg, T. (2015): Bankbilanzanalyse - Am Beispiel börsennotierter deutscher Banken, 3rd edition, Stuttgart 2015

Paetzmann, K. (2012): Corporate Governance - Strategische Marktrisiken, Controlling, Überwachung, 2nd edition, Wiesbaden 2012

Palli, M. C. (2004): Wertorientierte Unternehmensführung - Konzeption und empirische Untersuchung zur Ausrichtung der Unternehmung auf den Kapitalmarkt, dissertation, Wiesbaden 2004

Palupski, R. (2002): Management von Beschaffung, Produktion und Absatz - Leitfaden mit Praxisbeispielen, 2nd edition, Wiesbaden 2002

Pape, U. (2010): Wertorientierte Unternehmensführung, 4th edition, Sternenfels 2010

Pape, U. (2015): Grundlagen der Finanzierung und Investition, 3rd edition, Berlin, Munich, Boston 2015

Paul, J. (2014): Beteiligungscontrolling und Konzerncontrolling, Wiesbaden 2014

Paulitschek, P. (2009): Aufsicht über den Berufsstand der Wirtschaftsprüfer in Deutschland - eine agcenytheoretische Analyse, dissertation, Wiesbaden 2009

Paulo, S. (2002): Operating Income, Residual Income and EVA: which metric is more value relevant - a comment, in: Journal of Managerial Issues, 14th vol., 2002, No. 4, pp. 500–506

Payne, J. E., Sahu, A. P. (2004): Random Walks, Cointegration, And The Transmission Of Shocks Across Global Real Estate And Equity Markets, in: Journal Of Economics And Finance, 28th vol., 2004, No. 2, pp. 198–210

Pedersen, T., Thomsen, S. (2003): Ownership Structure and Value of the Largest European Firms: The Importance of Owner Identity, in: Journal of Management & Governance, 7th vol., 2003, No. 1, pp. 27–55

Peemöller, V. H., Hofmann, S. (2005): Bilanzskandale - Delikte und Gegenmaßnahmen, Berlin 2005

Peixoto, S. (2002): Economic Value Added - Application to Portuguese Public Companies, in: Working Paper, 2002, pp. 1–17

Pellens, B. (2001): Publizität, in: Gerke, W., Steiner, M. (editors), Handwörterbuch des Bank- und Finanzwesens, 3rd edition, Stuttgart 2001, pp. 1742–1754

Pellens, B., Fülbier, R. U., Gassen, J., Sellhorn, T. (2017): Internationale Rechnungslegung, 10th edition, Stuttgart 2017

Pellens, B., Hillebrandt, F., Tomaszewski, C. (2000): Value Reporting - Eine empirische Analyse der DAX-Unternehmen, in: Wagenhofer, A., Hrebicek, G. (editors), Wertorientiertes Management - Konzepte und Umsetzungen zur Unternehmenswertsteigerung, Stuttgart 2000, pp. 177–207

Pellens, B., Schmidt, A. (2014): Verhalten und Präferenzen deutscher Aktionäre - Eine Befragung von privaten und institutionellen Anlegern zum Informationsverhalten, zur Dividendenpräferenz und zur Wahrnehmung von Stimmrechten, in: Studien des Deutschen Aktieninstituts, Frankfurt on the Main 2014

Pellens, B., Tomaszewski, C. (1999): Kapitalmarktreaktionen auf den Rechnungslegungswechsel zu IAS bzw. US-GAAP, in: Zeitschrift für betriebswirtschaftliche Forschung (zfbf), 1999, Special issue 41, pp. 199–228

Penman, S. H. (2013): Financial Statement Analysis and Security Valuation, 5th edition, Singapore 2013

Penman, S. H., Richardson, S. A., Tuna, I. (2007): The Book-to-Price Effect in Stock Returns: Accounting for Leverage, in: Journal of Accounting Research, 45th vol., 2007, No. 2, pp. 427–467

Perridon, L., Steiner, M., Rathgeber, A. (2016): Finanzwirtschaft der Unternehmung, 17th edition, Munich 2016

Peters, H. (2009): Wirtschaftsmathematik, 3rd edition, Stuttgart 2009

Peters, S. (2009): Entscheidungsnützlichkeit der Leasingbilanzierung nach IFRS und US-GAAP - eine Analyse der aktuellen Reformbestrebungen, dissertation, Cologne 2009

Petersen, M. A. (2008): Estimating Standard Errors in Finance Panel Data Sets: Comparing Approaches, in: Review of Financial Studies, 22nd vol., 2008, No. 1, pp. 435–480

Pfaff, D., Bärtl, O. (1998): Externe Rechnungslegung, internes Rechnungswesen und Kapitalmarkt, in: Zeitschrift für betriebswirtschaftliche Forschung (Zfbf), 50th vol., 1998, No. 9, pp. 757–777

Pfaff, D., Stefani, U. (2003): Wertorientierte Unternehmensführung, Residualgewinne und Anreizprobleme, in: Zeitschrift für betriebswirtschaftliche Forschung (Zfbf), 2003, Sonderheft - Marktwertorientierte Unternehmensführung - Anreiz- und Kommunikationsaspekte, pp. 51–76

Pfeiffer, G. M., Shields, T. W. (2015): Performance-Based Compensation and Firm Value - Experimental Evidence, in: Accounting Horizons, 29th vol., 2015, No. 4, pp. 777–798

Picard, N., Behncke, N., Hoffmann, T. (2014): Integrated Reporting: Weiterentwicklung der klassischen Finanzberichterstattung, in: Zerfass, A., Piwinger, M. (editors), Handbuch Unternehmenskommunikation - Strategie, Management, Wertschöpfung, 2nd edition, Wiesbaden 2014, pp. 939–952

Picot, A., Dietl, H., Franck, E., Fiedler, M., Royer, S. (2012): Organisation - Theorie und Praxis aus ökonomischer Sicht, 6th edition, Stuttgart 2012

Piehler, M. (2007): Kontraktgestaltung bei M&A-Transaktionen - bedingte Zahlungsstrukturen zur Verbesserung des Einigungsbereichs, dissertation, Wiesbaden 2007

Piwinger, M. (2009): IR als Kommunikationsdisziplin, in: Kirchhoff, K. R., Piwinger, M. (editors), Praxishandbuch Investor Relations - das Standardwerk der Finanzkommunikation, 2nd edition, Wiesbaden 2009, pp. 13–33

Plaschke, F. J. (2003): Wertorientierte Management-Incentivesysteme auf Basis interner Wertkennzahlen, dissertation, Wiesbaden 2003

Pleier, N. (2008): Performance-Measurement-Systeme und der Faktor Mensch - Leistungssteuerung effektiver gestalten, dissertation, Wiesbaden 2008

Poeschl, H. (2013): Strategische Unternehmensführung zwischen Shareholder-Value und Stakeholder-Value, Wiesbaden 2013

Poodig, T., Dichtl, H., Petersmeier, K. (2008): Statistik, Ökonometrie, Optimierung - Methoden und ihre praktischen Anwendungen in Finanzanalyse und Portfoliomanagement, 4th edition, Bad Soden 2008

Poshakwale, S. (2002): The Random Walk Hypothesis in the Emerging Indian Stock Market, in: Journal of Business Finance & Accounting, 29th vol., 2002, No. 9 & 10, pp. 1275–1299

Prätsch, J., Schikorra, U., Ludwig, E. (2012): Finanzmanagement - Lehr- und Praxisbuch für Investition, Finanzierung und Finanzcontrolling, 4th edition, Berlin, Heidelberg 2012

Preinreich, G. (1938): Annual study of economic theory : the theory of depreciation, in: Econometrica, 6th vol., 1938, No. 3, pp. 219–241

Preißler, P. R. (2008): Betriebswirtschaftliche Kennzahlen, Munich 2008

Preißner, A. (2010): Praxiswissen Controlling - Grundlagen - Werkzeuge - Anwendungen, 6th edition, Munich 2010

Pricewaterhouse Coopers (PWC) (2017): Manual of Accounting - IFRS 2015, Volume 1, Haywards Heath 2017

Pro-Active Accounting Activities in Europe (PAAinE) (2009): The Needs Of Users Of Financial Information - A User Survey

PwC (2007): Measuring Assets and Liabilities - Investment Professionals' Views, URL: https://www.pwc.com/gx/en/ifrs-reporting/pdf/measuringassetssurvey.pdf, last accessed: 23rd October 2016

Quick, R. (2012): Kennzahlengestützte wertorientierte Berichterstattung in den Geschäftsberichten deutscher Indexunternehmen, in: Der Betrieb, 65th vol., 2012, No. 5, pp. 244–249

Ramana, D. V. (2005): Market Value Added and Economic Value Added: some empirical evidence, in: Working Paper, 2005

Ramezani, C. A., Soenen, L., Jung, A. (2002): Growth, Corporate Profitability and Value Creation, in: Financial Analysts Journal, 58th vol., 2002, No. 6, pp. 56–67

Rapp, M. S., Schellong, D., Schmidt, M., Wolff, M. (2011): Considering the shareholder perspective: value-based management systems and stock market performance, in: Review of managerial science, 5th vol., 2011, No. 2/3, pp. 171–194

Rappaport, A. (1983): Corporate performance standards and Shareholder Value, in: Journal of Business Strategy, 3rd vol., 1983, No. 4, pp. 28–38

Rappaport, A. (1986): Creating Shareholder Value - the new standard for business performance, New York, Toronto, Oxford 1986

Rappaport, A. (1987): Linking competitive strategy and Shareholder Value analysis, in: Journal of Business Strategy, 7th vol., 1987, No. 4, pp. 58–67

Rappaport, A. (2006): 10 ways to create Shareholder Value, in: Harvard business review, 84th vol., 2006, No. 9, pp. 66–77

Rau, R. (2010): Market Inefficiency, in: Baker, H. K., Nofsinger, J. R. (editors), Behavioral Finance - Investors, Corporations and Markets, Hoboken 2010

Rausch, B. (2008): Unternehmensbewertung mit zukunftsorientierten Eigenkapitalkostensätzen - Möglichkeiten und Grenzen der Schätzung von Eigenkapitalkostensätzen ohne Verwendung historischer Renditen, dissertation, Wiesbaden 2008

Rautiainen, A., Sippola, K., Mättö, T. (2017): Perspectives on relevance: The relevance test in the constructive research approach, in: Management Accounting Research, 34th vol., 2017, No. 1, pp. 19–29

Raynor, M. E. (2009): End shareholder value tyranny: put the corporation first, in: Strategy & Leadership, 37th vol., 2009, No. 1, pp. 4–11

Reichelstein, S. (2000): Providing managerial incentives: Cash Flow versus accrual accounting, in: Journal of Accounting Research, 38th vol., 2000, No. 2, pp. 243–269

Reichmann, T. (2011): Controlling mit Kennzahlen - die systemgestützte Controlling-Konzeption mit Analyse- und Reportinginstrumenten, 8th edition, Munich 2011

Reifschneider, C. (2007): Informationeller Anlegerschutz - Ökonomische Analyse der Konkretisierung und Durchsetzung sekundärmarktbezogener Informationspflichten in Deutschland und den USA, dissertation, Wiesbaden 2007

Reim, J. (2015): Erfolgsrechnung - Wertsteigerung durch Wertschöpfung - Grundlagen, Konzeptionen, Instrumente, Wiesbaden 2015

Reimsbach, D. (2014): Pro forma earnings disclosure: the effects of non-GAAP earnings and earnings-before on investors' information processing, in: Journal of Business Economics, 84th vol., 2014, No. 4, pp. 479–515

Reinganum, M. R. (1981): Misspecification Of Capital Asset Pricing - Empirical Anomalies Based on Earnings' Yields and Market Values, in: Journal of Financial Economics, 9th vol., 1981, No. 1, pp. 19–46

Reinganum, M. R. (1983): The Anomalous Stock Market Behavior of Small Firms in January, in: Journal of Financial Economics, 12th vol., 1983, No. 1, pp. 89–104

Reinke, J. (2010): Impairment Test nach IAS 36 – Grundlage, Durchführung, abschlusspolitisches Potenzial, dissertation, Berlin 2010

Reitwiesner, B. (2001): Integrierte Rendite-/Risikosteuerung in der Industrieunternehmung, dissertation, Wiesbaden 2001

Renwick, C. (2012): Does IFRS stand for information risk?: A Comment, in: Financial Analysts Journal, 68th vol., 2012, No. 6, pp. 12–13

Richartz, J. (2009): Anreizsysteme zur Steuerung der Hersteller-Händler-Beziehung in der Automobilindustrie, dissertation, Frankfurt on the Main 2009

Richter, F., Honold, D. (2000): Das Schöne, das Unattraktive und das Hässliche an EVA & Co., in: Finanz Betrieb, 2nd vol., 2000, No. 5, pp. 265–274

Richter, R., Furubotn, E. G. (2003): Neue Institutionenökonomik - eine Einführung und kritische Würdigung, 3rd edition, Tübingen 2003

Rickards, R. C. (2009): Leistungssteuerung kompakt, Munich 2009

Riedl, J. B. (2000): Unternehmenswertorientiertes Performance Measurement, dissertation, Wiesbaden 2000

Rieg, R. (2015): Dynamics of value-based management: does shareholder value cause short-termism?, in: Journal of Management Control, 26th vol., 2015, No. 2-3, pp. 193–224

Rosenberg, B., Reid, K., Lanstein, R. (1985): Persuasive evidence of market inefficiency, in: Journal of Portfolio Management, 11th vol., 1985, No. 3, pp. 9–16

Ross, S. A. (1973): The economic theory of agency: the principal's problem, in: American Economic Review, 63rd vol., 1973, No. 2, pp. 134–139

Ross, S. A. (1976): The Arbitrage Theory of Capital Asset Pricing, in: Journal of Economic Theory, 13th vol., 1976, No. 3, pp. 341–360

Ross, S. A. (2005): Neoclassical Finance, Princeton 2005

Rossignolo, A. F., Fethi, M. Duygun, Shaban, M. (2013): Market crises and Basel capital requirements: Could Basel III have been different? Evidence from Portugal, Ireland, Greece and Spain (PIGS), in: Journal of Banking & Finance, 37th vol., 2013, No. 5, pp. 1323–1339

Rubinstein, M. (2001): Rational Markets: Yes or No? The Affirmative Case, in: Financial Analysts Journal, 57th vol., 2001, pp. 15–29

Rudolph, B. (2005): Zur Neuausrichtung der Steuerung des Kreditrisikos der Banken, in: Gramlich, D., Hinz, H. (editors), Kapitalmarkt, Unternehmen und Information - Wertanalyse und Wertsteuerung von Unternehmen auf finanziellen Märkten, Wiesbaden 2005, pp. 39–62

Ruf, M. (2014): Systematische Finanzinformation und Kapitalmarktkommunikation – Modellarchitektur und Implementierungsansatz, dissertation, Wiesbaden 2014

Ruhnke, K., Simons, D. (2012): Rechnungslegung nach IFRS und HGB - Lehrbuch zur Theorie und Praxis der Unternehmenspublizität mit Beispielen und Übungen, 3rd edition, Stuttgart 2012

Ruhwedel, F., Schultze, W. (2002): Value Reporting: Theoretische Konzeption und Umsetzung bei den DAX 100-Unternehmen, in: Zeitschrift für betriebswirtschaftliche Forschung (Zfbf), 54th vol., 2002, No. 7, pp. 602–632

Ruhwedel, F., Thale, S. (2013): Pro-Forma-Ergebnisse - Augenwischerei oder Transparenzgewinn? Verwendung von Pro-Forma-Kennzahlen bei DAX- und MDAX-Unternehmen, in: Controlling, 25th vol., 2013, No. 7, pp. 386–393

Rutherford, B. A. (2002): Design and Implementation of Return on Capital Employed Performance Indicators Within a Trading Regime: The Case of Excecutive Agencies, in: Financial Accountability & Management, 18th vol., 2002, No. 1, pp. 73–101

Ryan, H. E., Trahan, E. A. (1999): The Utilization of Value-Based Management: An Empirical Analysis, in: Financial Practice & Education, 9th vol., 1999, No. 1, pp. 46–58

Ryan, H. E., Trahan, E. A. (2007): Corporate financial control mechanism and firm performance: the case of Value-Based Management systems, in: Journal of Business Finance & Accounting, 34th vol., 2007, No. 1 & 2, pp. 111–138

Salzer, E. (2004): Investor Relations - Management und IPO-Erfolg, dissertation, Wiesbaden 2004

Sawczyn, A. (2011): Unternehmerische Nachhaltigkeit und wertorientierte Unternehmensführung - Empirische Untersuchung der Unternehmen im HDAX, dissertation, Hamburg 2011

Schabel, M. M. (2004): Investitionssteuerung, Periodenerfolgsrechnung und Economic Value Added, dissertation, Wiesbaden 2004

Schacht, U., Fackler, M. (2009): Discounted-Cash-flow-Verfahren - Eine Einführung, in: Schacht, U., Fackler, M. (editors), Praxishandbuch Unternehmensbewertung - Grundlagen, Methoden, Fallbeispiele, 2nd edition, Wiesbaden 2009, pp. 205–232

Schachtner, D. (2002): Die Beziehung zwischen werbungtreibendem Unternehmen und Werbeagentur - theoretische Systematisierung und empirische Überprüfung eines Prinzipal-Agenten-Modells, dissertation, Wiesbaden 2002

Schaefer, C. (2004): Steuerung und Kontrolle von Investitionsprozessen - Theoretischer Ansatz und Konkretisierung für das öffentliche Beteiligungscontrolling, dissertation, Wiesbaden 2004

Schäffer, U., Botta, J. (2011): Lohnen sich wertorientierte Steuerung und wertorientierte Vergütung wirklich?, in: Zeitschrift für Controlling & Management (ZfCM), 55th vol., 2011, No. 5, pp. 316–317

Schäffer, U., Lewerenz, U. (2011): Die Entwicklung der wertorientierten Unternehmenssteuerung im DAX, in: Zeitschrift für Controlling & Management (ZfCM), 55th vol., 2011, No. 5, pp. 295–298

Schaier, S. (2007): Konvergenz von internem und externem Rechnungswesen - Bedarf für eine Neustrukturierung des Rechnungswesens?, dissertation, Wiesbaden 2007

Schaier, S. (2008): Erklärungsansätze für eine Konvergenz von internem und externem Rechnungswesen, in: Betriebswirtschaftliche Forschung und Praxis, 60th vol., 2008, No. 2, pp. 122–136

Scheer, L. (2008): Antezedenzen und Konsequenzen der Koordination von Unternehmensnetzwerken - eine Untersuchung am Beispiel von Franchise-Systemen und Verbundgruppen, dissertation, Wiesbaden 2008

Schenk, U. (2003): Konzernrechnungswesen und Verhaltenssteuerung, dissertation, Aachen 2003

Schier, S. (03.12.2014): Kurze Freude - Der DAX knackt die psychologisch wichtige Marke von 10.000 Punkten, kann sich aber nicht darüber halten, in: Handelsblatt, 03.12.2014, No. 233, pp. 26–27

Schierenbeck, H., Wöhle, C. B. (2012): Grundzüge der Betriebswirtschaftslehre, 18th edition, Munich 2012

Schloemer, M. (2003): Zur Veränderung der Bedeutung der Rechnungslegung deutscher Unternehmen im Zeitablauf, dissertation, Frankfurt on the Main 2003

Schmeisser, W. (2010): Corporate Finance und Risk Management, Munich 2010

Schmeisser, W., Clausen, L. (2009): Controlling und Berliner Balanced Scorecard Ansatz, Munich 2009

Schmeisser, W., Rönsch, M., Zilch, I. (2009): Shareholder Value Approach versus Corporate Social Responsibility - Eine unternehmensethische Einführung in zwei konträre Ansätze, Munich 2009

Schmeisser, W., Spree, J. (2008): Unternehmensbewertung in praktischer Anwendung, in: Schmeisser, W., Görlitz, B., Spree, J., Clausen, L., Schindler, F. (editors), Einführung in die Unternehmensbewertung, Munich, Mering 2008, pp. 93–169

Schmidlin, N. (2013): Unternehmensbewertung & Kennzahlenanalyse - Praxisnahe Einführung mit zahlreichen Fallbeispielen börsennotierter Unternehmen, 2nd edition, Munich 2013

Schmidt, M. (2005): Rechnungslegung von Finanzinstrumenten - Abbildungskonzeptionen aus Sicht der Bilanztheorie, der empirischen Kapitalmarktforschung und der Abschlussprüfung, dissertation, Wiesbaden 2005

Schmidt-Tank, S. (2005): Indexeffekte an europäischen Kapitalmärkten - eine Analyse aus der Perspektive börsennotierter Unternehmen, dissertation, Wiesbaden 2005

Schmolke, K. Ulrich (2007): Institutionelle Anleger und Corporate Governance – Traditionelle institutionelle Investoren vs. Hedgefonds, in: Zeitschrift für Unternehmens- und Gesellschaftsrecht, 36th vol., 2007, No. 5, pp. 701–744

Schmundt, W. (2008): Die Prognose von Ertragssteuern im Discounted Cash Flow-Verfahren, dissertation, Wiesbaden 2008

Schneck, O. (2006): Handbuch alternative Finanzierungsformen, Weinheim 2006

Schneider, D. (2001): Oh EVA, EVA, schlimmes Weib: Zur Fragwürdigkeit einer Zielvorgabe-Kennzahl nach Steuern im Konzerncontrolling, in: Der Betrieb, 54th vol., 2001, No. 48, pp. 2509–2514

Schneider, K. (2011): Modernes Sourcing in der Automobilindustrie, dissertation, Wiesbaden 2011

Schneider, N. C. (2007): Kundenwertbasierte Effizienzmessung - Der Beitrag von Marketingmaßnahmen zur Unternehmenswerterhöhung in der Automobilindustrie, dissertation, Wiesbaden 2007

Schneider, U. (2012): Abgestimmtes Verhalten durch institutionelle Anleger: Gute Corporate Governance oder rechtspolitische Herausforderung?, in: Zeitschrift für Unternehmens- und Gesellschaftsrecht, 41st vol., 2012, No. 4, pp. 518–534

Scholz, A. (2008): Kapitalerhaltung durch Solvenztests - eine ökonomische und experimentelle Analyse, dissertation, Wiesbaden 2008

Schönherr, M. (2016): Wertorientiertes Logistikmanagement - Modelle zur Bewertung logistischer Maßnahmen aus Sicht des Unternehmenswertes, dissertation, Wiesbaden 2016

Schredelseker, K. (2001): Is the Usefulness Approach Useful?, in: McLeay, S., Riccaboni, A. (editors), Contemporary Issues In Accounting Regulation, New York 2001, pp. 135–154

Schreiner, A. (2007): Equity Valuation Using Multiples - An Empirical Investigation, dissertation, Wiesbaden 2007

Schremper, R., Pälchen Oliver (2001): Wertrelevanz rechnungswesenbasierter Erfolgskennzahlen, in: Die Betriebswirtschaft (DBW), 61st vol., 2001, No. 5, pp. 542–559

Schröder, A. (2009): Prinzipien der Panelanalyse, in: Albers, S., Klapper, D., Konradt, U., Walter, A., Wolf, J. (editors), Methodik der empirischen Forschung, 3rd edition, Wiesbaden 2009, pp. 315–330

Schultze, W., Hirsch, C. (2005): Unternehmenswertsteigerung durch wertorientiertes Controlling - Goodwill-Bilanzierung in der Unternehmenssteuerung, Munich 2005

Schultze, W., List, T., Schabert, B., Dinh, T. (2018): Economic consequences of implementing and communicating value based management systems, in: Journal of Business Finance & Accounting, 45th vol., 2018, No. 5-6, pp. 511–543

Schultze, W., Steeger, L., Schabert, B. (2009): Wertorientierte Berichterstattung (Value Reporting): Konzeptioneller Rahmen und Anwendung bei deutschen börsennotierten Unternehmen, in: Controlling, 21st vol., 2009, No. 1, pp. 13–22

Schultze, W., Weiler, A. (2007): Performancemessung und Wertgenerierung: Entlohnung auf Basis des Residualen Ökonomischen Gewinns, in: Zeitschrift für Planung & Unternehmenssteuerung, 18th vol., 2007, No. 2, pp. 133–159

Schumann, J. (2005): Residualgewinn-orientierte Unternehmensbewertung im Halbeinkünfteverfahren: Äquivalenz- und Transparenzaspekte, in: Finanz Betrieb, 7th vol., 2005, No. 1, pp. 22–32

Schumann, J. (2008): Unternehmenswertorientierung in Konzernrechnungslegung und Controlling - Impairment of Assets (IAS 36) im Kontext bereichsbezogener Unternehmensbewertung und Performancemessung, dissertation, Wiesbaden 2008

Schwartz, R. A. (1970): Efficient Capital Markets: A Review of Theory and Empirical Work: Discussion, in: Journal of Finance, 25th vol., 1970, No. 2, pp. 421–423

Scott, W. R. (2012): Financial Accounting Theory, 6th edition 2012

Seidel, L. J. (1995): Review - Improving Business Reporting—A Customer Focus: Meeting the Information Needs Review - Improving Business Reporting - A Customer Focus: Meeting the Information Needs of Investors and Creditors; Comprehensive Report of the Special Committee on Financial Reporting, in: Accounting Horizons, 9th vol., 1995, No. 3, pp. 119–124

Seifert, U. (2006): Aktienrückkäufe in Deutschland - Renditeeffekte und tatsächliche Volumina, dissertation, Wiesbaden 2006

Serfing, K. (2008): Controlling, Rating und Kapitalmarkt, in: Weber, L., Lubk, C., Mayer, A. (editors), Gesellschaft im Wandel - Aktuelle ökonomische Herausforderungen, Wiesbaden 2008, pp. 169–190

Sharpe, W. F. (1964): Capital Asset Prices: A Theory of Market Equilibrium under Conditions of Risk, in: Journal of Finance, 19th vol., 1964, No. 3, pp. 425–442

Sharpe, W. F. (1970): Efficient Capital Markets: A Review of Theory and Empirical Work: Discussion, in: Journal of Finance, 25th vol., 1970, No. 2, pp. 418–420

Sharpe, W. F., Alexander, G. J., Bailey, J. V. (1999): Investments, 6th edition, Upper Saddle River 1999

Shavell, S. (1979): Risk sharing and incentives in the principal and agent relationship, in: The Bell Journal of Economics, 10th vol., 1979, No. 1, pp. 55–73

Shih, Y.-C., Chen, S.-S., Lee, C.-F., Chen, P.-J. (2014): The evolution of capital asset pricing models, in: Review of Quantitative Finance and Accounting, 42nd vol., 2014, No. 3, pp. 415–448

Shivdasani, A., Zenner, M. (2005): How to Choose a Capital Structure: Navigating the Debt-Equity Decision, in: Journal of Applied Corporate Finance, 17th vol., 2005, No. 1, pp. 26–35

Shleifer, A. (2000): Inefficient Markets - An Introduction to Behavioral Finance, Oxford, New York 2000

Shleifer, A., Summers, L. H. (1990): The Noise Trader Approach to Finance, in: Journal of Economic Perspectives, 4th vol., 1990, No. 2, pp. 19–33

Shu, T. (2013): Institutional Investor Participation and Stock Market Anomalies, in: Journal of Business Finance & Accounting, 40th vol., 2013, No. 5-6, pp. 695–718

Siebrecht, F., Heidorn, T., Klein, H.-D. (2001): Economic Value Added zur Erklärung der Bewertung europäischer Aktien, in: Finanz Betrieb, 3rd vol., 2001, No. 10, pp. 560–564

Siefke, M. (1999): Externes Rechnungswesen als Datenbasis der Unternehmenssteuerung - Vergleich mit der Kostenrechnung und Shareholder-Value-Ansätzen, dissertation, Wiesbaden 1999

Siepermann, M. (2008): Risikokostenrechnung - Erfolgreiche Informationsversorgung und Risikoprävention, Berlin 2008

Skrzipek, M. (2005): Shareholder Value versus Stakeholder Value, dissertation, Wiesbaden 2005

Söllner, A. (2008): Einführung in das internationale Management - eine institutionenökonomische Perspektive, Wiesbaden 2008

Sommer, U. (15.12.2014): Sturm auf Aktien?, in: Handelsblatt, 15.12.2014, No. 241, p.1

Sparling, D., Turvey, C. G. (2003): Further thoughts on the relationship between Economic Value Added and stock market performance, in: Agribusiness, 19th vol., 2003, No. 2, pp. 255–267

Spectris (2012): Annual Report

Spremann, K. (1989): Agent and Principal, in: Bamberg, G., Spremann, K. (editors), Agency theory, information, and incentives, Corrected reprint of the 1st edition edition, Berlin 1989, pp. 3–37

Spremann, K. (1990): Asymmetrische Information, in: Journal of Business Economics, 60th vol., 1990, No. 5, pp. 561–585

Spremann, K. (2008): Portfoliomanagement, 4th edition, Munich 2008

Spremann, K., Gantenbein, P. (2005): Kapitalmärkte, Stuttgart 2005

Stark, A. W., Thomas, H. M. (1998): On the empirical relationship between market value and residual income in the UK, in: Management Accounting Research, 9th vol., 1998, No. 4, pp. 445–460

Stauber, J. (2012): Finanzinstrumente im IFRS-Abschluss von Nicht-Banken - Ein konkreter Leitfaden zur Bilanzierung und Offenlegung, 2nd edition, Wiesbaden 2012

Steger, J. (2014): Kennzahlen und Kennzahlensysteme, Herne 2014

Steinhauer, L. (2007): Die Objektivierung des kapitalmarktorientierten Value Reporting - Möglichkeiten und Grenzen des Economic Value Added, dissertation, Cologne 2007

Stephan, J. (2006): Finanzielle Kennzahlen für Industrie- und Handelsunternehmen, dissertation, Wiesbaden 2006

Stewart, G. B. (1999): The quest for value: the EVA management guide, New York 1999

Stiefl, J., Westerholt, K. von (2008): Wertorientiertes Management - Wie der Unternehmenswert gesteigert werden kann, Munich 2008

Stier, C. (2017): Risikomanagement und wertorientierte Unternehmensführung - Effizienz und Monopoleffekte, Wiesbaden 2017

Stoetzer, M.-W. (2017): Regressionsanalyse in der empirischen Wirtschafts- und Sozialforschung, Berlin 2017

Stoney, C., Winstanley, D. (2001): Stakeholding: confusing or utopia? Mapping the conceptual terrain, in: Journal of Management Studies, 38th vol., 2001, No. 5, pp. 603–626

Stoxx (2015): Stoxx Index Methodology Guide (Portfolio based indices) - November 2015

Stromann, H. (2003): Wertrelevanz deutscher und US-amerikanischer Rechnungslegungsinformationen - Theoretische und empirische Analyse des Feltham-Ohlson-Modells, dissertation, Wiesbaden 2003

Stührenberg, L., Streich, D., Henke J. (2003): Wertorientierte Unternehmensführung - Theoretische Konzepte und empirische Befunde, Wiesbaden 2003

Stüker, D. (2008): Evaluierung und Steuerung von Kundenbeziehungen aus Sicht des wertorientierten Controllings, dissertation, Wiesbaden 2008

Sullivan, R., Timmermann, A., White, H. (1999): Data-Snooping, Technical Trading Rule Performance, and the Bootstrap, in: Journal of Finance, 54th vol., 1999, No. 5, pp. 1647–1690

Symrise (2012): Annual Report

Tabak, B. M. (2003): The random walk hypothesis and the behaviour of foreign capital portfolio flows: the Brazilian stock market case, in: Applied Financial Economics, 13th vol., 2003, No. 5, pp. 369–378

Tahat, Y. A., Alhadab, M. (2017): Have accounting numbers lost their value relevance during the recent financial credit crisis?, in: The Quarterly Review of Economics and Finance, 66th vol., 2017, pp. 182-191

Tantalo, C., Priem, R. L. (2016): Value creation through stakeholder synergy, in: Strategic Management Journal, 37th vol., 2016, No. 2, pp. 314–329

Tappe, R. (2009): Wertorientierte Unternehmensführung im Mittelstand - eine Überprüfung der Anwendbarkeit, Frankfurt on the Main 2009

Taylor, S. J. (1982): Tests of the Random Walk Hypothesis Against a Price-Trend Hypothesis, in: Journal of Financial and Quantitative Analysis, 17th vol., 1982, No. 1, pp. 37–61

Teall, J. L. (2007): Governance and the market for corporate control, Wolverhampton 2007

Telefonica (2013): Annual Report - Integrated Report 2013

TGS Nopec Geophysical (2013): Annual Report

Theis, J. C. (2014): Kommunikation zwischen Unternehmen und Kapitalmarkt - Eine theoretische und empirische Analyse von Informationsasymmetrien im Unternehmensumfeld, dissertation, Wiesbaden 2014

Thomsen, S., Pedersen, T. (2000): Ownership Structure And Economic Performance In The Largest European Companies, in: Strategic Management Journal, 21st vol., 2000, No. 6, pp. 689–705

Tietz-Weber, S. (2006): Interessengruppen und Rechnungslegungsregeln, dissertation, Wiesbaden 2006

Timmreck, C. (2006): Kapitalmarktorientierte Sicherheitsäquivalente - Konzeption und Anwendung bei der Unternehmensbewertung, dissertation, Wiesbaden 2006

Tinz, O. (2010): Die Abbildung von Wachstum in der Unternehmensbewertung - eine theoretische und empirische Analyse der Möglichkeiten und Grenzen einer objektivierten und transparenten Abbildung von Wachstum nach IDW S 1, dissertation, Cologne 2010

Tischer, S., Hildebrandt, L. (2014): Linking corporate reputation and shareholder value using the publication of reputation rankings, in: Journal of Business Research, 67th vol., 2014, No. 5, pp. 1007–1017

Töpfer, A. (2012): Erfolgreich Forschen - Ein Leitfaden für Bachelor-, Master-Studierende und Doktoranden, 3rd edition, Wiesbaden 2012

Töpfer, A., Duchmann, C. (2006): Ganzheitliches Konzept des wertorientierten Managements, in: Schweickart, N., Töpfer, A. (editors), Wertorientiertes Management - Werterhaltung – Wertsteuerung - Wertsteigerung ganzheitlich gestalten, Berlin, Heidelberg 2006, pp. 3–64

Torabian, F. (2010): Bilanzielle Bewertung von Finanzinstrumenten - Vergleich der Bewertungskonzeption nach HGB und IFRS hinsichtlich der Informationsfunktion der Rechnungslegung, dissertation, Wiesbaden 2010

Trautwein, A. (2007): Wertrelevanz von Patentinformationen im Kontext der Rechnungslegung - Eine empirische Betrachtung für börsennotierte Kapitalgesellschaften in Deutschland, Wiesbaden 2007

Truemann, B. (1986): Why do managers voluntarily release earnings forecasts?, in: Journal of Accounting and Economics, 8th vol., 1986, No. 1, pp. 53–71

Tsalavoutas, I., André, P., Evans, L. (2012): The transition to IFRS and the value relevance of financial statements in Greece, in: The British Accounting Review, 44th vol., 2012, No. 4, pp. 262–277

Tucker, B., Parker, L. (2014): In our ivory towers? The research-practice gap in management accounting, in: Accounting and Business Research, 44th vol., 2014, No. 2, pp. 104–143

Tversky, A., Kahneman, D. (1992): Advances in Prospect Theory: Cumulative Representation of Uncertainty, in: Journal of Risk and Uncertainty, 5th vol., 1992, No. 4, pp. 297–323

Urban, M. P. (2015): The influence of blockholders on agency costs and firm value - an empirical examination of blockholder characteristics and interrelationships for German listed firms, dissertation, Wiesbaden 2015

Varmaz, A. (2006): Rentabilität im Bankensektor - Identifizierung, Quantifizierung und Operationalisierung werttreibender Faktoren, dissertation, Wiesbaden 2006

Varnholt, N. T., Lebefromm, U., Hoberg, P. (2012): Controlling, 2nd edition, Munich 2012

Vater, H., Meckel, M., Hoffmann, C., Fieseler, C. (2008): Zur Bedeutung qualitativer Erfolgsfaktoren der Kapitalmarktkommunikation für die Unternehmensbewertung und deren Auswirkungen, in: Der Betrieb, 61st vol., 2008, No. 48, pp. 2605–2611

Velte, P., Stawinoga, M. (2016): Integrated reporting: The current state of empirical research, limitations and future research implications, in: Journal of Management Control, 2016

Velte, P., Stiglbauer, M., Sepetauz, K. (2011): Entwicklung der Risiko- und Prognoseberichterstattung am deutschen Kapitalmarkt, in: Journal für Betriebswirtschaft, 61st vol., 2011, No. 2-3, pp. 123–177

Velthuis, L. J., Wesner, P. (2005): Value Based Management - Bewertung, Performancemessung und Managemententlohnung mit ERIC, Stuttgart 2005

Vollmer, R. (2008): Rechnungslegung auf informationseffizienten Kapitalmärkten, dissertation, Wiesbaden 2008

Vorstius, S. (2004): Wertrelevanz von Jahresabschlussdaten - Eine theoretische und empirische Betrachtung von Wertrelevanz im Zeitverlauf in Deutschland, dissertation, Wiesbaden 2004

Wagenhofer, A. (2006): Zusammenwirken von Controlling und Rechnungslegung nach IFRS, in: Wagenhofer, A. (editor), Controlling und IFRS-Rechnungslegung - Konzepte, Schnittstellen, Umsetzung, Berlin 2006, pp. 1–20

Wagenhofer, A. (2013): Bilanzierung und Bilanzanalyse - Eine Einführung, 11th edition, Vienna 2013

Wagenhofer, A., Dücker, H. (2007): Die Messung von „Earnings"-Qualität, in: Journal für Betriebswirtschaft, 57th vol., 2007, No. 3-4, pp. 263–297

Wagenhofer, A., Ewert, R. (2015): Externe Unternehmensrechnung, 3rd edition, Wiesbaden 2015

Wahlen, J. M., Baginski, S. P., Bradshaw, M. T. (2015): Financial Reporting, Financial Statement Analysis, and Valuation - A Strategic Perspective, 8th edition, Boston 2015

Wall, F., Greiling, D. (2011): Accounting information for managerial decision-making in shareholder management versus stakeholder management, in: Review of managerial science, 5th vol., 2011, No. 2/3, pp. 91–135

Wang, C. (1997): Incentives, CEO compensation and Shareholder Wealth in a dynamic agency model, in: Journal of Economic Theory, 76th vol., 1997, No. 1, pp. 72–105

Wappenschmidt, C. (2009): Ratinganalyse durch internationale Ratingagenturen, dissertation, Frankfurt on the Main 2009

Wasley, C. E., Wu, J. S. (2006): Why do managers voluntarily issue Cash Flow forecasts?, in: Journal of Accounting Research, 44th vol., 2006, No. 2, pp. 389–429

Wassermann, H. (2011): Kapitalmarktorientierung in Accounting und Controlling, Wiesbaden 2011

Watson, D., Head, A. (2010): Corporate Finance - Principles & Practice, 5th edition, London 2010

Watts, R. L., Zimmerman, J. L. (1978): Towards a Positive Theory of the Determination of Accounting Standards, in: The Accounting Review, 53rd vol., 1978, No. 1, pp. 112–134

Watts, R. L., Zimmerman, J. L. (1979): The Demand for and Supply of Accounting Theories: The Market for Excuses, in: The Accounting Review, 54th vol., 1979, No. 2, pp. 273–305

Watts, R. L., Zimmerman, J. L. (1986): Positive Accounting Theory, London, Sydney, Toronto 1986

Watts, R. L., Zimmerman, J. L. (1990): Positive Accounting Theory: A Ten Year Perspective, in: The Accounting Review, 65th vol., 1990, No. 1, pp. 131–156

Weber, G. (2006): Eigenkapitalkosten ausgewählter Unternehmen auf Basis der modernen Kapitalmarkttheorie – eine empirische Anwendung des CAPM für die Holz verarbeitende Industrie, Druckmaschinen- und Papierindustrie, dissertation, Wiesbaden 2006

Weber, J. (2009): Erfahrungen mit wertorientierter Steuerung, in: Der Betrieb, 62nd vol., 2009, No. 7, pp. 297–303

Weber, J., Bramsemann, U., Heineke, C., Hirsch, B. (2017): Wertorientierte Unternehmenssteuerung - Konzepte - Implementierung - Praxisstatements, 2nd edition, Wiesbaden 2017

Weber, J., Schäffer, U. (1999): Balanced Scorecard & Controlling - Implementierung - Nutzen für Manager und Controller - Erfahrungen in deutschen Unternehmen, Wiesbaden 1999

Weber, J., Schäffer, U. (2016): Einführung in das Controlling, 15th edition, Stuttgart 2016

Weber, R. J. (2011): Die Entscheidung über die Auftragsannahme in der Wirtschaftsprüfung - Ein qualitätssicherendes Instrument im Rahmen der Jahresabschlussprüfung, dissertation, Wiesbaden 2011

Weber, S. (2008): Selektionskriterien beim Investment in aktive US-Aktienfonds, dissertation, Wiesbaden 2008

Wehrheim, M., Schmitz, T. (2009): Jahresabschlussanalyse - Instrumente, Bilanzpolitik, Kennzahlen, 3rd edition, Stuttgart 2009

Weiß, M. (2006): Wertorientiertes Kostenmanagement - Zur Integration von wertorientierter Unternehmensführung und strategischem Kostenmanagement, dissertation, Wiesbaden 2006

Weißenberger, B. E. (2003): Anreizkompatible Erfolgsrechnung im Konzern - Grundmuster und Gestaltungsalternativen, Wiesbaden 2003

Weißenberger, B. E. (2006): Ergebnisrechnung nach IFRS und interne Performancemessung, in: Wagenhofer, A. (editor), Controlling und IFRS-Rechnungslegung - Konzepte, Schnittstellen, Umsetzung, Berlin 2006, pp. 49–79

Weißenberger, B. E. (2007): IFRS für Controller - Alles, was Controller über IFRS wissen müssen, Munich 2007

Weißenberger, B. E. (2009): Shareholder Value und finanzielle Zielvorgaben im Unternehmen, in: Wall, F., Schröder, R. (editors), Controlling zwischen Shareholder Value und Stakeholder Value - Neue Anforderungen, Konzepte und Instrumente, Munich 2009, pp. 39–60

Weissmann, F. (2005): Unternehmen steuern mit Controlling - Leitfaden und Toolbox für die Praxis, Berlin, Heidelberg, New York 2005

Wellner, K.-U. (2001): Shareholder Value und seine Weiterentwicklung zum Market Adapted Shareholder Value Approach, dissertation, Marburg 2001

Wendt, S. (2011): Die Auswirkung von Corporate Governance auf die Fremdfinanzierungskosten von Unternehmen - eine empirische Analyse der Folgen von Aktientransaktionen durch Insider, dissertation, Wiesbaden 2011

Wenzel, A. (2006): Kapitalstrukturpolitik in Wachstumsunternehmen - Eine empirische Untersuchung deutscher Unternehmen auf Basis von Jahresabschlussinformationen, dissertation, Bad Soden 2006

Wenzel, J. (2005): Wertorientierte Berichterstattung (Value Reporting) aus theoretischer und empirischer Perspektive, dissertation, Frankfurt on the Main 2005

Wenzelburger, G., Jäckel, S., König, P. (2014): Weiterführende statistische Methoden für Politikwissenschaftler, Munich 2014

Werner, H. (2013): Supply Chain Management - Grundlagen, Strategien, Instrumente, Controlling, 5th edition, Wiesbaden 2013

Wichels, D. (2002): Gestaltung der Kapitalmarktkommunikation mit Finanzanalysten, dissertation, Wiesbaden 2002

Wiederhold, P. (2008): Segmentberichterstattung und Corporate Governance - Grenzen des Management Approaches, dissertation, Wiesbaden 2008

Wilson, T. C. (2015): Value and Capital Management - A Handbook for the Finance and Risk Functions of Financial Institutions, Chichester 2015

Wisniewski, T. P., Lightfoot, G., Lilley, S. (2012): Speculating on presidential success: exploring the link between the price–earnings ratio and approval ratings, in: Journal of Economics and Finance, 36th vol., 2012, No. 1, pp. 106–122

Wittich, G. (2001): Ad-hoc-Publizität und Insiderhandel, in: Gerke, W., Steiner, M. (editors), Handwörterbuch des Bank- und Finanzwesens, 3rd edition, Stuttgart 2001, pp. 15–23

Wohlgemuth, F. (2007): IFRS: Bilanzpolitik und Bilanzanalyse - Gestaltung und Vergleichbarkeit von Jahresabschlüssen, dissertation, Berlin 2007

Wolf, R. (2014): Measuring value-performance of listed stocks in China and Germany, in: Schmitz, E. (editor), German-Sino aspects of management - FOM Schriftenreihe Deutsch-chinesischer Wirtschaftsdialog, Essen 2014, pp. 1–33

Wolf, R. (2017): KGV oder KVV zur Performance-Messung der TOP-Unternehmen in Deutschland, Frankreich oder Italien, in: Kaluza, B., Braun, K. D., Beschorner, H., Rolfes, B. (editors), Betriebswirtschaftliche Fragen zu Steuern, Finanzierung, Banken und Management, Wiesbaden 2017, pp. 205–224

Wolf, R., Hoffmann, H. (2017): Eignung erfolgswirtschaftlicher Kennzahlen zur Performance Messung, in: PiR - Internationale Rechnungslegung, 2017, No. 12, pp. 380–384

Wollscheid, D. (2013): Gestaltung zielkonsistenter Anreizsysteme für riskante Investitionen, dissertation, Wiesbaden 2013

Wollschläger, D. (2017): Grundlage der Datenanalyse mit R - Eine anwendungsorientierte Einführung, 4th edition, Berlin 2017

Wöltje, J. (2011): Betriebswirtschaftliche Formelsammlung, 5th edition, Freiburg 2011

Wöltje, J. (2013): Investition und Finanzierung, Freiburg, Munich 2013

Wöltje, J. (2016a): Bilanzen lesen, verstehen und gestalten, Munich 2016

Wöltje, J. (2016b): Jahresabschluss - Schritt für Schritt, 2nd edition, Konstanz, Munich 2016

Wooldridge, J. M. (2013): Introductory Econometrics - A Modern Approach, 5th edition, Mason 2013

Worthington, A. C., West, T. (2004): Australian Evidence concerning the Information Content of Economic Value Added, in: Australian Journal of Management, 29th vol., 2004, No. 2, pp. 201–223

Wu, J. S., Zhang, I. X. (2014): The Adoption of Internationally Recognized Accounting Standards: Implications for the Credit Markets, in: Journal of Accounting, Auditing & Finance, 29th vol., 2014, No. 2, pp. 95–128

Wulf, I., Niemöller, J., Rentzsch, N. (2014): Development toward integrated reporting, and its impact on corporate governance: a two-dimensional approach to accounting with reference to the German two-tier system, in: Journal of Management Control, 25th vol., 2014, No. 2, pp. 135–164

Wuntsch, M. von, Bach, S. (2012): Wertorientierte Steuerplanung und Unternehmensführung in der globalen Wirtschaft, 2nd edition, Munich 2012

Yeh, T.-M. (2014): Large Shareholders, Shareholder Proposals, and Firm Performance : Evidence from Japan, in: Corporate Governance : An International Review, 22nd vol., 2014, No. 4, pp. 312–329

Zantow, R., Dinauer, J. (2011): Finanzwirtschaft des Unternehmens - Die Grundlagen des modernen Finanzmanagements, 3rd edition, Munich 2011

Zeileis, A. (2004): Econometric Computing with HC and HAC Covariance Matrix Estimators, in: Journal of Statistical Software, 11th vol., 2004, No. 10, pp. 1–17

Zell, M. (2008): Kosten- und Performance Management - Grundlagen - Instrumente - Fallstudien, Wiesbaden 2008

Zhang, G. (2001): Private Information Production, Public Disclosure and the Cost of Capital: Theory and Implications, in: Contemporary Accounting Research, 18th vol., 2001, No. 2, pp. 363–384

Zhang, G. (2014): Accounting Information and Equity Valuation - Theory, Evidence and Applications, New York, Heidelberg, Dordrecht 2014

Zimmermann, J., Werner, J. R., Hitz, J.-M. (2011): Buchführung und Bilanzierung nach IFRS - Mit praxisnahen Fallbeispielen, 2nd edition, Munich 2011

Zinkann, R. (2010): Nachhaltiges Unternehmertum statt Shareholder Value, in: Krüger, W.; Schubert, B. von; Wittberg, V. (editors), Die Zukunft gibt es nur einmal! - Plädoyer für mehr unternehmerische Nachhaltigkeit, Wiesbaden 2010

Zirkler, B. (2002): Der Economic Value Added (EVA) als Konzept für den Mittelstand, in: Kostenrechnungspraxis, 2002, Special issue No. 1, pp. 98–103

Zirkler, B., Nobach, K. (2008): Implikationen der IFRS für ein integriertes Management Reporting, in: Gleich, R., Horváth, P., Michel, U. (editors), Management Reporting - Grundlagen, Praxis und Perspektiven, Berlin 2008, pp. 367–387

Zülch, H., Benary, C.-E., Hottmann, J. (2016): Welche Informationsquellen sind für die Anlageentscheidung am relevantesten? - Eine Meta-Analyse der Informationsbeschaffung institutioneller und individueller Investoren, in: Der Betrieb, 2016, No. 26-27, pp. 1509–1515

Zwerenz, K. (2015): Statistik - Einführung in die computergestützte Datenanalyse, 6th edition, Berlin, Munich, Boston 2015

Zwirner, C. (2014): Kapitalisierungszinssätze in der Unternehmensbewertung - eine empirische Analyse inländischer IFRS-Konzernabschlüsse 2013, in: Corporate Finance, 5th vol., 2014, No. 9, pp. 381–386

The manufacturer's authorised representative in the EU is Springer
Nature Customer Service Centre GmbH, Europaplatz 3, 69115 Heidelberg,
Germany. If you have any concerns regarding our products, please
contact ProductSafety@springernature.com

Printed and bound by CPI Group (UK) Ltd, Croydon, CR0 4YY
30/09/2026
02225597-0007